D1519807

PERKINS SCHOOL OF THEOLOGY

ALSO BY JOSEPH L. ALLEN

Love and Conflict: A Covenantal Model of Christian Ethics
War: A Primer for Christians

Lois and Joe Perkins breaking ground for the Perkins quadrangle, February 8, 1949.

Perkins School of Theology
A CENTENNIAL HISTORY

Joseph L. Allen

Foreword by
Harold W. Attridge

SOUTHERN METHODIST UNIVERSITY PRESS
Dallas

Requests for permission to reproduce material from this work should be sent to:
  Rights and Permissions
  Southern Methodist University Press
  PO Box 750415
  Dallas, Texas 75275-0415

Cover photo: Perkins Chapel and the Bridwell Library, © SMU 2010.
Photo by Hillsman S. Jackson

Jacket and text design: Tom Dawson

Library of Congress Cataloging-in-Publication Data
Allen, Joseph L., 1928–
    Perkins School of Theology : a centennial history / Joseph L. Allen ; foreword by Harold
    W. Attridge. — 1st ed.
        p. cm.
    Includes bibliographical references and index.
    ISBN 978-0-87074-570-6 (alk. paper)
    1. Perkins School of Theology—History—20th century. 2. Perkins School of Theology—
History—21st century. 3. Methodist theological seminaries—Texas—Dallas—History—20th
century. 4. Methodist theological seminaries—Texas—Dallas—History—21st century.
5. Dallas (Tex.)—Church history—20th century. 6. Dallas (Tex.)—Church history—21st
century. I. Title.
    BV4070.P47A45 2011
    230.07'3767642812—dc22

                                                                                    2010051395

Printed in the United States of America on acid-free paper

10   9   8   7   6   5   4   3   2   1

To the members of the Perkins faculty,
past and present

Contents

A Centennial History of
Perkins School of Theology

A century, a fragment of an instant in cosmic, much less divine, time, is nonetheless for most of us mortals a considerable span of years. It is a delight to celebrate and to remember what a century of dedication and hard work has achieved in creating a major institution devoted to theological education, Perkins School of Theology at Southern Methodist University.

Like all the institutions to which so many of us have given our time, talent, and treasure, Perkins is a marvel of human ingenuity and perhaps divine Providence. The school was conceived in the hope of preparing pastoral leaders for the Methodist Church in the Southwest, and it has grown into an institution that does that and much more. The roots of Perkins are firmly planted in the Methodist annual conferences of the region, and it has constantly drawn nourishment from those roots as it has nurtured the church with its graduates. It has also been a witness to the ecumenical breadth of theological scholarship, both within the realm of American Protestantism and the broader world of Christian fellowship.

My own connection with Perkins benefited from that commitment to ecumenical diversity. When I joined the faculty in 1977, I believe I was the first Roman Catholic, and I arrived midway in the history of the "second Perkins" described in Joe Allen's masterful history. I was warmly embraced by an intellectually rigorous but thoroughly committed Christian community for the eight years that I participated in the life of the school. I shall always treasure the nurturing collegiality that I found there before hearing a call, first to the University of Notre Dame and eventually to Yale Divinity School. In these days I find myself connected to Perkins in several ways: through an honorary degree bestowed on me by the university in 2008 but even more through the personal connections, both with colleagues from days of yore, such as Vic Furnish, Charles Wood, Bill Babcock, and the author of this monograph, and through current Perkins faculty such as Jaime Clark-Soles, who passed through the hallowed halls of Yale on the way to her Ph.D. degree.

Reading through Joe's history of the school filled in many gaps in the recollection of the school that I had from my relatively brief time there. It recalled many familiar names, some known personally, some only by reputation. Joe's history reminded me of some of the battles that our predecessors fought, about desegregation and the inclusion of women at the heart of the life of the church, a battle still ongoing in my own Roman Catholic communion. This history also taught me about the struggles that took place after my departure, ostensibly about faculty appointments but perhaps more profoundly about the ways in which the school would be shaped for the next generation. All of us involved in theological education can tell analogous tales about the ways in which people of fundamentally shared conviction can have profound differences. That is the stuff of the history of the Christian church.

This history also tells a wonderfully inspiring tale of shared and growing vision that united clergy and dedicated lay benefactors in the creation of an extraordinary gift to the church. The story encompasses the relationship between leaders of the school and generous benefactors, such as the Perkins and Bridwell families, who gave so much of their own resources to enable the school to grow and develop. Joe's history focuses on details of the story that are crucial to the outcome. Bridwell Library is a treasure, not only for Perkins but for the whole region and for theological scholarship generally. Joe's account of how that treasure came to be, under the leadership of Decherd Turner, whom I well remember from my faculty days, is worth the whole book.

But Decherd was not alone. This book also tells the story of the other relatively unsung heroes, from the deans, such as Joe Quillian and Jim Kirby, under whom I served, and their recent successors, to the numerous faculty whose imagination and commitment shaped and reshaped the curriculum to the trustees and benefactors who fell in love with the idea of a nationally, if not internationally, respected school of theology. This story and more appears in the pages of Joe Allen's history of Perkins.

The tale encompasses both the ups and the downs of life at Perkins in its first century. Some points of tension seem now to be relics of the past, such as the efforts to desegregate the school in the 1950s. Joe documents well the increasing diversity of the faculty and student body in the decades since, and Perkins, like most theologi-cal schools, now takes for granted a racially and internationally diverse body of stu-dents. Some controversies that troubled the school in the more recent past still affect contemporary churches, including debates about homosexuality and ordination of homosexual clergy. Tensions within the faculty sometimes rose to a flash point, as they did in 1992, about the role of various criteria for making critical decisions about appointment and tenure. Joe explores the tensions, reveals the fault lines within the faculty, and catalogs the efforts that it took to bridge them. Many of our institutions have felt similar growing pains at some point in the last several decades as we have developed into more complex and encompassing communities of learning.

Another thread running through this history is the way in which the faculty has continually thought about the needs of the communities that its graduates aimed to serve. On numerous occasions faculty members asked themselves how best to shape a curriculum that will prepare men and women for roles of leadership in those com-munities. This is an issue with which all theological schools continually grapple. All divinity schools wrestle with striking the right balance between grounding in the traditional disciplines and practical engagement with contemporary practice in vari-ous professional roles and in complex social settings. Two major factors complicate the situation at Perkins. One that generally affects the world of theological educa-tion is the religious landscape into which graduates of our theological schools enter. Religious life in the United States has been changing dramatically in the last fifty years, with denominations, including The United Methodist Church, shifting gears and exploring new ways of raising pastoral leadership. New opportunities for ministry have presented themselves in varied settings—in congregations, hospitals, schools, social service agencies, and on the streets. Preparing graduates for such an array of professional opportunities is always a complex business. Perkins has been imaginative and entrepreneurial in meeting that challenge, particularly with its shifting array of degree and certificate programs, and in its experimentation, only partially successful, with off-site education. This shifting landscape has also affected enrollments, which have waxed and waned considerably during the last half-century, a process that this history meticulously tracks.

A second factor, common to all university-related divinity schools, is the tension between the professional education that the school provides, with all its complexity, and the role of the divinity school as a part of an institution devoted not simply to teaching but to fundamental research in a variety of intellectual fields. Perkins has managed to combine those two functions well, as the lengthy list of works by the faculty during the last hundred years attests. Joe's history also notes the important role of Perkins in the university's Graduate Program in Religious Studies, which has gradually improved its standing in the realm of doctoral education. Keeping in view both professional education and basic research in the theological disciplines can be a challenge, but it is essential for the life of both the church and the university that institutions such as Perkins make serious efforts to do so.

Another thread running through this history may be a bit mundane but nonetheless important for tracing the life of an institution such as Perkins. "Build it and they will come" might have been the motto of Dean Hawk in the early days of the current Perkins campus. What a wise decision it was to locate Perkins where it now resides and not where it originally was situated, on the site of the current SMU School of Law. And what a series of wise decisions followed: to expand the campus, to build and renovate a library, to refurbish the gracious Perkins chapel, and to create new academic and common spaces in the first decade of the twenty-first century that will serve the school well for years to come. The heart of a school of theology consists of its faculty and students, but they need a nurturing and inspiring place to gather for study, for formative collegiality, and for inspiring worship. The story of the attention to the bricks and mortar of Perkins is another testimony to the love of so many faculty, staff, and benefactors for this singular institution.

I was honored to participate, in however small a way, in the history that Joe Allen relates, and it has been an equal delight to relive it and learn more of it in Joe's lucid prose. Any of us concerned with the future of theological education in the United States, and in the world at large, can learn a great deal from the stories that Joe Allen's history of Perkins has to tell and the efforts of a hundred years dedicated to shaping a major institution of theological learning.

HAROLD W. ATTRIDGE

The Reverend Henry L. Slack Dean and Lillian Claus Professor of New Testament
Yale University Divinity School

Interpreting Perkins's History

S outhern Methodist University, including its School of Theology, was chartered in 1911 and opened for classes in 1915. Speaking at a Perkins faculty luncheon in March 1991, John Deschner took the occasion, before his
retirement that spring, to offer an interpretation of the history of Perkins School
of Theology. It can be divided, Deschner suggested, into three periods: from 1915
to 1951, when the school served its region and had modest academic aspirations;
from 1951 to sometime in the 1980s, a time of growing reputation and widened
influence; and, since then, a reconstitution of the school in ways yet to be realized—a "third Perkins."[1]

Deschner's interpretation is sufficiently apt that I have organized the history that
way. It is useful, though, only with qualification. History seldom admits of sharp
breaks between periods; more often the changes are gradual, and there are important
continuities, as is apparent in this case. Even so, his triad points to significant changes
in Perkins's history.

Part I is about the first Perkins, which was not named Perkins School of Theology until 1945 but was known as the School of Theology of Southern Methodist University. Chapter 1 discusses the prehistory of the university, actions that led
to its location and charter in 1911, the gathering of a faculty and a student body
for the first classes in 1915, and the early years of the school up to 1920, under
two deans and an acting dean. Chapter 2 is about the years of Paul B. Kern's
deanship—from 1920 to 1926—when the School of Theology, with a new vision
of its future, enlarged its faculty and worked to prepare students for missions
at home and abroad. Chapter 3 takes the school from the departure of Kern in

1926 to that of the long-time SMU president Charles C. Selecman in 1938. This period includes seven years when the School of Theology was led by an acting dean, James Kilgore, and the first five years under the next dean, Eugene Blake Hawk. This was a time of holding on, seeking not to lose ground in the face of financial hardship. Chapter 4 brings the school from the appointment of SMU's next president, Umphrey Lee, through the remainder of the years when Hawk was dean and describes the initial gifts to the School of Theology by Joe and Lois Perkins and J. S. Bridwell that led to the construction of a new theology quadrangle and the prospect of a much enlarged school—developments that made possible the emergence of the second Perkins.

The second Perkins is the subject of part II. It stretched from 1951 to perhaps the mid- or late 1980s. Chapters 5 and 6 recount the history of the school under the deanship of Merrimon Cuninggim, from 1951 to 1960: the "new curriculum"; the largely new, mostly young, and much enlarged faculty; the excitement of heightened theological dialog among them and with the students; and the 1952 racial desegregation of the Perkins student body, with subsequent actions that preserved that move in the face of serious opposition.

The other dean whose work falls entirely within the second Perkins was Joseph D. Quillian Jr. Chapters 7 and 8 are about the years of his deanship, from 1960 to 1981, when Perkins built on Cuninggim's initiatives, developed a required internship, initiated the Mexican American Program, took the first steps toward bringing about a faculty diverse in gender and ethnicity, and much else.

In 1951 the new theological library building was dedicated as Bridwell Library. As its life spans the entirety of the second and third periods of Perkins history, it seems appropriate to sketch its development in chapter 9—the last chapter in part II.

The early steps of faculty diversification in the 1970s provided a foretoken of the third Perkins, but it more fully emerged in the 1980s and early 1990s, as with greater diversity came increased tensions and a faculty characterized by a mixture of collegiality and conflict. Chapter 10 is about the period in which this transition took place—the years of James Kirby's deanship. This was a time of continuing to pursue the vision of the second Perkins while trying to cope with new realities that did not readily fit that vision.

Chapters 11 and 12, about the third Perkins in the years of the deanship of Robin W. Lovin and that of William B. Lawrence thus far, take us a decade into the twenty-first century.

Each period of Perkins's history has seen creativity, opportunities seized and opportunities missed, achievements but also shortcomings, matters in which to rejoice and matters of which to repent. In this, Perkins School of Theology is not unlike other institutions. Overall, its accomplishments as a theological school have been noteworthy. The afterword offers a brief reflection on this history and the challenges of the near future.

In his 1941 book, *The Meaning of Revelation*, H. Richard Niebuhr wrote, "The patterns and models we employ to understand the historical world may have had a heavenly origin, but as we know and use them they are, like ourselves, creatures of history and time; though we direct our thought to eternal and transcendent beings, it is not eternal and transcendent; though we regard the universal, the image of the universal in our mind is not a universal image."[2]

That is true not only when the subject is God's revelation but also when one seeks to portray human relationships. For forty-one years I was an active member of the Perkins faculty, from 1957 to 1998, and in retirement I have maintained connections with Perkins and its faculty. I certainly do not have an objective or universal view of Perkins's history. I was closely involved in many of the events described herein and was, and am, committed to what I have considered to be the school's well-being and its mission. I have worked alongside many others who have interpreted this history through different lenses and whose commitments have been somewhat like and somewhat different from mine. I make no claim that this is a picture of Perkins's history "as it really was," or that my commitments were simply right and any who differed with them were misguided. Though a participant in the history, I have striven to be evenhanded and accurate, relying not mainly on my memory but on the documents and voices that provide evidence of what happened and to read that evidence critically, even though that does not immunize me from misinterpretations.

The material available about Perkins's history is voluminous: hundreds of boxes of archives in Bridwell Library; scores of books by past and present faculty, administrators, former students, and outside observers; copious periodicals; and numerous active and retired faculty, alumni/ae, and others willing to share their experiences. Delving into this vast store has been invigorating and daunting. In the process I have discovered much of which I was ignorant at the time and for years thereafter and have had some of my preconceptions shattered. This has disposed me to refrain from painting an overly simple picture of how matters developed or what they signify.

JOE ALLEN
Dallas

---

1. James Kirby, "Mission in the Nineties," Faculty Conference, September 20–21, 1991, Kirby Papers, Bridwell Library, SMU; Daniel Cattau, *Dallas Morning News*, May 24, 1993. Kirby's report to the faculty that fall referred only to John Deschner's having spoken to the faculty about three periods of Perkins history. In a later article on Deschner and Schubert Ogden, Cattau briefly sketched what he had learned about the idea.
2. H. Richard Niebuhr, *The Meaning of Revelation* (New York: Macmillan, 1941), 10.

Acknowledgments

Many people have assisted me in this study. I especially want to thank Dean Bill Lawrence, who invited me to undertake it, provided a stipend, let me use his study room in Bridwell Library, allowed me to attend meetings of the faculty, and encouraged the project along the way. Former deans Jim Kirby and Robin Lovin were generous with their time and helped me understand facets of the history that were insufficiently illuminated by the written records. Ruben Habito and Richard Nelson, associate deans, facilitated the work in ways appropriate to their office. Sixty present and former members of the Perkins faculty and administration talked individually with me about Perkins's history, and some supplied documents otherwise difficult to find. Roberta Cox, Paul Escamilla, and Timothy McLemore made the resources of Perkins's Office of Public Affairs available in many ways. Janelle Hampton, registrar and director of academic services at Perkins, repeatedly gave me access to nonconfidential records in her office. Duane Harbin, assistant dean for informational technology and institutional research, provided computer equipment for the project.

Bridwell Library is a hospitable environment for research and writing. I am indebted to its director, Roberta Schaafsma, and its associate director, Jim McMillin, for making the library's resources available and offering wise counsel. Several other library staff members gave assistance, including Timothy Binkley, Jane Lenz Elder, Sally Hoover, Heather Oglevie, Elizabeth Perry, Clyde Putman, Dan Slive, Jon Speck, and Eric White. Before his retirement in 2007 Page Thomas, another member of the library's staff, shared his knowledge of the archives and Methodist resources, directing me to much material of which I would otherwise have been ignorant. Archives in

SMU's DeGolyer Library were made available to me through the assistance of Joan Gosnell, the university archivist, and microfilmed materials of the Fondren Library Center were repeatedly helpful.

My thanks go to S. Leon Bennett, former SMU vice president for legal affairs and government relations, and to Mary Anne Rogers of SMU's Office of Legal Affairs for permitting me to read the minutes of the SMU Board of Trustees, Executive Committee, and Board of Governors. Hillsman Jackson and Laura Graham gave me access to the university's photography files. I owe thanks to Ruth Morgan, former SMU provost and vice president for academic affairs, for her interest and insight in response to my inquiries. My appreciation also goes to Marshall Terry, SMU English professor, creative writer, administrator, and historian of the university, who shared some of his knowledge of that history as it bears upon Perkins.

Former Perkins students who provided information and insight about Perkins include Bishop Monk Bryan, Bishop John Wesley Hardt, Virgil M. Matthews, Mac McPherson, David Pailin, Gordon Roe, and John Thornburg. Katherine Kern Buckner of Chapel Hill, North Carolina, in replying to my inquiry about her father, Bishop Paul B. Kern, helped me understand an aspect of his time as dean of the School of Theology. Robert W. Goodloe Jr. gave of his time to respond to my questions about his father's years on the Perkins faculty.

The Perkins Faculty Symposium, chaired in 2006–2008 by Ruben Habito and in 2008–2010 by Hugo Magallanes, provided four occasions for groups of faculty and staff to discuss drafts of several chapters of the history. Faculty members' questions and comments offered new insights and saved me from a number of errors.

Charles Curran and Victor Furnish read the entire manuscript, made several valuable suggestions, and corrected a number of mistakes. Other active or retired Perkins faculty and staff members who read and responded to large or not-so-large portions of the manuscript include Billy Abraham, Tonya Burton, Pat Davis, Michael Hawn, John Holbert, Jim Kirby, Bill Lawrence, Robin Lovin, David Maldonado, Bill McElvaney, Alyce McKenzie, Jim McMillin, Schubert Ogden, Marjorie Procter-Smith, Roberta Schaafsma, Jeanne Stevenson-Moessner, Ed Sylvest, Page Thomas, Jeannie Treviño-Teddlie, Theo Walker, Jim Ward, and Charles Wood. They have corrected mistakes, called omissions to my attention, and suggested several improvements. I alone am responsible for the outcome, including all its errors of judgment and detail.

My wife, Mary David, who has shared my involvement in Perkins life, has followed this project with great interest, accepting without protest all the hours I have spent in Bridwell Library, listening to me talk about the history ad infinitum, and asking questions for which I often did not have good answers.

PERKINS SCHOOL OF THEOLOGY

PART I

The First Perkins

Beginnings, 1911–1920

S outhern Methodist University received its charter in 1911 and opened for classes on September 22, 1915. During that academic year 706 students enrolled for study in the College of Arts and Sciences, the School of Music, and (with a handful of graduate students) the School of Theology.[1] That it would begin at all, and in Dallas at that time, had seemed unlikely for years.

A century and more ago, Texas Methodists were ambivalent about education for ministers. On the one hand, Texas Methodists in the last half of the nineteenth century increasingly recognized the value of basic schooling as well as a college education, not only for doctors, lawyers, and teachers but also for preachers, who needed to be educated themselves if they were to lead their people.[2] Methodists, like other groups, had started several colleges in small Texas towns from the 1840s through the 1870s, but all but one closed, mainly for financial reasons. The Reverend Francis Asbury Mood, president of one of those colleges, Soule University at Chappell Hill, Texas, came to believe that his institution could not survive. In 1869 he began to plan for a central college that would be supported by all of Texas Methodism, and his efforts led to the opening of Southwestern University in Georgetown in 1873. Then in 1891 Methodists founded Polytechnic College in Fort Worth. At the turn of the century these were the two Methodist institutions in Texas that provided four years of college education.[3]

Even so, in the late nineteenth century Texas Methodists had serious questions about what kind of education preachers should have. Texas was still near the frontier, and many could remember the raids of Comanches and Kiowas. Most people lived on farms, had little contact with towns and cities, and struggled to survive. Heavily influenced by the revival movement, many Texas Methodists thought that the only book ministers needed was the Bible, that the way to learn to preach was to preach, and that too much education would create a gulf between ministers and the farmers plowing the fields.[4] Hiram Abiff Boaz later recalled that when he entered college in 1891, only a few members of his annual conference were college graduates, and some people thought too much education was a handicap. His former pastor, a leader in the conference, had not completed college and was sure Boaz was making a mistake by entering Southwestern University.[5]

Yet some early Texas preachers were well educated, and some Methodist leaders in Texas were strongly committed to improving education, including for ministers. Notable among them was Robert Stewart Hyer, a dedicated lay churchman and a professor of science at Southwestern University, who became its president in 1898. Hyer had a vision of Southwestern as a university in fact as well as in name, but he became convinced this could not happen so long as it was located in a small town far from cities that could provide students and financial support. For several years, beginning in 1906, he quietly pursued the idea of moving it to Dallas. During this time he entered into discussions with Boaz, then the president of Polytechnic in Fort Worth, who preferred that Southwestern move to his city instead. Talk of moving Southwestern became public in 1909, and the next year Hyer and Boaz exchanged letters expressing their differing opinions about where it should be located.[6] Their exchange was published in the *Texas Christian Advocate* in the spring of 1910.[7]

Dallas leaders strongly supported the idea of a move to their city. At the same time it aroused such opposition in Georgetown that Hyer and his supporters in North Texas gave up the idea of moving Southwestern and proposed instead to build a new Methodist university there. With this proposal in mind, and at the suggestion of Bishop James Atkins, members of the five Methodist annual conferences in Texas voted in the fall of 1910 to establish a commission on education, made up of four delegates from each of the five annual conferences, to consider the idea and take appropriate action.[8]

In January 1911 the commission voted to establish a new university. The competition between Dallas and Fort Worth was intense, verging on bitter. After visiting sites in both places and receiving bids from citizens of Fort Worth and Dallas, the commission voted in early February to locate the campus north of Dallas, in what eventually became the city of University Park. On April 13 it voted to name the school Texas Wesleyan University, but the very next day it reversed itself and chose the name Southern Methodist University. The commission designated Hyer as president, Boaz as vice president, and Frank Reedy (then the bursar of Southwestern University) as bursar. Southern Methodist University was chartered on April 16, 1911, and work began on building a campus, gathering a faculty, and recruiting students.[9]

From the start those who planned for a new university intended for it to include a theological school. A number of Texas Methodist leaders thought it a high priority to have a school of theology in the Southwest. In 1910 the nearest Methodist school of theology was at Vanderbilt, which not only was far away in Nashville but had recently sued to sever its ties to the Methodist Episcopal Church, South (MECS). These leaders saw that, regardless of how the Vanderbilt lawsuit was decided, having a Methodist seminary nearby would mean that more of their ministers would get seminary degrees. Accordingly, the plans for the new university included a graduate school of theology. In 1914, responding to the Vanderbilt issue, the General Conference of the Methodist Episcopal Church, South, recommended that SMU and Emory University in Georgia be designated as its institutions with schools of theology, and in this connection it expressed its pleasure at the establishment of SMU.[10]

A year earlier the Commission on Education had begun a campaign, spear-headed by Boaz, to raise $1 million for the new university, half to be used for buildings and half for endowment. As a part of this campaign the General Education Board, a private organization in New York City founded by John D. Rockefeller, made a donation of $200,000 to SMU. One condition was that the money could not be used for specifically theological instruction, because the board was non-sectarian and could never promote sectarianism. The board could and did donate money to be used for the College of Arts and Sciences of SMU, and it permitted the university to include a school of theology so long as no General Education Board money was used to support it.[11] Thus money for the theology school had to come from other sources. Hyer told the commission that Methodists in the region were demanding establishment of a theological department. He said the New Mexico and Oklahoma annual conferences were cooperating in founding the university mainly because it would have such a department, and he argued that at least $200,000 should be set aside for that purpose.[12]

Starting a new school of theology under any conditions is an ambitious project, even more so when it is part of a new university. In 1915 those who founded the SMU School of Theology mostly did not try to emulate the older university-related schools of theology, such as those at the University of Chicago, Union Theological Seminary in New York, and Yale, with their renowned faculties and their diversified programs with national and international appeal.[13] The SMU founders sought more modestly to train Methodists in the MECS west of the Mississippi who intended to become pastors of local churches. That was demanding enough under the circumstances.

THE CAMPUS AND THE STUDENTS

When SMU opened in 1915, one building, Dallas Hall, had been completed and was ready for use; another, a women's dormitory to be named Atkins Hall, was nearly finished; and three other dormitories were under construction. All were situated on high ground in an open field of Johnson grass far from any residences, just north of the town of Highland Park and six miles from downtown Dallas, population 92,104 in 1910. There were no sidewalks or paved streets nearby. Hillcrest Avenue, on the west side of the campus, was a graveled, dusty country road that ended at the north end of the campus.

For the first few years Dallas Hall housed all the work of the university, except lodging for students. Kenneth Pope, who entered SMU in 1920, later described the layout this way: In the basement were a bookstore, soda fountain, and barber's chair; science laboratories were on the west end. The first floor housed the administrative offices, including those of the president and the registrar. In the east wing of the first floor were some classrooms and the library. On the second floor were classrooms and professors' offices. The third floor of the east wing contained the School of Theology, "most of the music department," and a small auditorium for the use of both departments. In the west wing of that floor was the university auditorium, where the daily compulsory chapel service was held. At that time, Pope said, "SMU was little more than a fetus among educational institutions."[14]

In 1915 thirteen students with bachelor of arts degrees from "recognized colleges" were the first graduate students to enter the theology school as candidates for theological degrees.[15] They were mostly from small towns in north and northwest

Texas; only two were from outside the state. Eleven students were enrolled for bachelor of divinity degrees. Two, Umphrey Lee of Ferris, Texas, and Robert W. Goodloe from Olney, Texas, were seeking master's degrees as a step toward doctoral study.

Twelve students at the graduate level were candidates for certificates in theology. These students did not have bachelor's degrees from approved colleges. They could receive certificates upon completion of requirements similar to those for the bachelor of divinity degree.[16] In a third category of theological students were forty-seven undergraduates who took some courses at the theology school that would count toward their undergraduate degrees. Finally, eighteen pastors serving churches in or around Dallas (including A. Frank Smith, later a bishop and for twenty-two years chair of the SMU Board of Trustees) were taking "extension courses" at the School of Theology while they continued their ministerial work. Beginning in January 1916 the school offered four of these one-hour classes each Tuesday, to enable busy pastors to keep their minds stimulated and to become acquainted with life on campus.[17] (In later years this would be called "continuing education.") That brought the total to ninety theological students in the first year.

The number of graduate students in the school remained fairly constant in the first five years: twenty at the lowest point (1916–17), thirty-one at the highest (1917–18). However, there was a marked shift away from those without recognized undergraduate degrees. By 1919–20 no such students were enrolled, and thereafter the number never exceeded three at any time. The number enrolled for B.D. degrees gradually increased to twenty-six in 1919–20. In contrast to the graduate theological students, the number of undergraduate students taking courses at the school fluctuated considerably. Fifty-seven were enrolled in 1917–18, but that number fell to thirteen in 1918–19, reflecting the impact of World War I on college enrollment; the next year it jumped to sixty. The number of pastors taking theological extension courses fell to five in the school's second year and did not regain its initial number until the 1920s.[18]

All the SMU students were white, and almost all the graduate theological students were men. Two women were enrolled for a theological certificate in 1917–18 and two others in 1918–19, but none of the four was awarded a certificate, and only one man received a certificate before the 1920s. On the other hand, undergraduate women began to enroll in graduate theological courses in significant numbers beginning in 1919–20, when there were sixteen.

Throughout the 1910s the graduate theological students continued to be overwhelmingly from Texas—75 to 80 percent—most often from Dallas or small towns within a hundred-mile radius. Of those few not from Texas, most were from Arkansas. As for their college background, several who graduated between 1920 and 1923 had done their undergraduate work, or had at least completed it, at SMU; several at Southwestern University, and some at Hendrix College in Conway, Arkansas; Polytechnic College in Fort Worth; the University of Texas (in Austin); the University of Arkansas; Henderson-Brown College (as it was then named) in Arkadelphia, Arkansas; and various others.[19] Though the information is not available, these colleges were probably also well represented before 1920. The enrollment in the school in this period, like that in SMU's College of Arts and Sciences, was for the most part narrowly regional.

These students came with eager expectations. They were young, the university was young, and several faculty members—of the school and of the college—were youngish. Undergraduates, graduate theological students, and students in the music school all took classes in the same building—Dallas Hall—and graduate theological classes included many junior and senior undergraduates. Flora Lowrey from Hillsboro, Texas, who transferred to SMU in 1915 for her senior year, reflected years later on what it had been like for her: "There was a rapport between the first faculty and the first student body; our relationship was informal. There were no snack bars, no place to drink a cup of coffee together, but we walked together through paths (there were no walks), talked together in the parlor, discussed issues in the classrooms and offices. We all had the same goals. We were establishing a university, setting precedents, and laying a foundation. The spirit of endeavor was high, and we worked together in perfect accord."[20]

Highland Park Methodist Church, Lowrey remembered, was a brown frame church near its present site, and she, Umphrey Lee, and a few others organized its first Sunday school. Its first pastor was A. Frank Smith, then in his twenties. The students' spiritual life was nurtured by professors in the School of Theology. "By and large we were a fervent[ly] religious student body with a goal, and I suspect with a great deal of sanctimony."[21]

THE EARLY THEOLOGICAL FACULTY

Edwin D. Mouzon played a central role in choosing SMU's initial theological faculty. In 1908 Robert Hyer had brought Mouzon, then the pastor of Travis Park Methodist Church in San Antonio, to head Southwestern University's Department of Theology. Two years later Mouzon was elected a bishop. Even so, in 1914 Hyer asked Mouzon to move to Dallas, add the School of Theology deanship to his episcopal duties, and "begin organizing the faculty." Mouzon accepted and together with Hyer and other church leaders began that year to recruit a faculty.[22]

Hyer's determination to appoint one prize prospect suggests how the recruiting proceeded. When Hyer began looking for faculty, he asked a colleague in the Department of Hebrew at the University of Chicago to name the best student that department had ever had, and the answer was Ivan Lee Holt.[23] In spring 1915 Holt, then a Methodist pastor in Cape Girardeau, Missouri, had a visit from W. D. Bradfield of Dallas, then the editor of the *Texas Christian Advocate*. Bradfield asked Holt to join the faculty of SMU's School of Theology. Holt did not seem interested. So Hyer went to see Holt himself. When the younger man commented that he did not want to leave the preaching ministry, Hyer offered him the university chaplaincy, a professorship, and the post of chair of the School of Theology faculty. Not even that swayed Holt, who declined in writing a few days later. Then Mouzon sent Holt a telegram seeking a meeting in Nashville, Tennessee. At that meeting Mouzon asked Holt, "If you are so devoted to the pastorate, why not give a few years of your life to training other men for it?" Holt accepted.[24]

In June 1915 Frank Seay became the first School of Theology faculty member to arrive on campus. He had taught both New Testament and philosophy at Southwestern, so Hyer and Mouzon were well aware of his ability. Seay would become the star of the original School of Theology faculty. He found much to do that first summer. The university had no catalog, and Seay helped a new English professor, John H. McGinnis, put one together. As there was no library, President Hyer asked his secretary, Dorothy Amman, to assemble one, and Seay helped her obtain some of the books, theological and otherwise.[25] In an article published in the *Texas Christian Advocate* on July 1, Seay encouraged pastors to send books they were not using. He listed about forty books the library needed, most in biblical studies, a few in philosophy, and "any book written by a Southern Methodist." Two weeks later he published a second list, including several works on the Bible and some on church history. In a third article on July 15, he reported that he had received donations of ten books on the first list, as well as more than two hundred recent, usable titles, plus many no less valuable older works. "Drop us a card and we shall send postage," he promised the pastors.[26]

When SMU opened that September, the School of Theology faculty consisted of four full-time members: Holt in Hebrew and Old Testament interpretation, Seay in New Testament Greek and interpretation, Paul B. Kern in English Bible, and James Kilgore in pastoral theology and religious education. Each received an annual salary of $3,000.[27] Two others had been expected, but Fitzgerald S. Parker, general secretary of a Methodist agency in Nashville, who was to teach doctrine, decided not to come, and Gross Alexander, formerly on the Vanderbilt theological faculty and slated to teach church history, died.

Listing their primary fields does not tell the whole story. The faculty was so small that first year, Holt also taught courses in sociology (the term then in use by the theological faculty for an area that included social ethics) and church history, Seay in philosophy and ethics for advanced undergraduates, Kilgore in psychology and logic, and the bursar, Frank Reedy, in Sunday school pedagogy (religious education). In addition to his teaching duties, Holt filled the other posts Hyer had originally offered him. He chaired the faculty, presiding in the absence of the dean, and served as university chaplain, with responsibility for the compulsory daily chapel services and for many conferences with students.[28] As dean, Mouzon was of course a member of the faculty, but with his work as bishop he was able to attend only three of the fourteen faculty meetings that academic year, and at the end of the first year he resigned the deanship.[29] He became chair of the SMU Board of Trustees, a position he held for three years, until June 1919. In that post he continued to show great interest in the School of Theology and exerted considerable influence in its development.

Several others joined the faculty between 1916 and 1920. In fall 1916 Horace M. Whaling arrived to teach church history; that November, Hoyt Dobbs, previously pastor of several Methodist churches, assumed the deanship Mouzon had vacated. In January 1918 Jesse Lee Cuninggim (father of Merrimon Cuninggim, later dean of Perkins) became professor of Sunday school pedagogy, and the following fall Comer Woodward came to teach sociology, dividing his time between the School of Theology and the College of Arts and Sciences. Ivan Lee Holt departed in 1918 to become pastor of St. John's Methodist Church in St. Louis; he had hoped to become dean of the School of Theology in 1916, and his disappointment may have influenced his decision to leave.[30] Others, some drawn from the undergraduate faculty, taught at the school part time.

Several members of the early faculty were young. When they arrived, Holt was twenty-nine, and Kern, Seay, Whaling, and Dobbs were in their thirties. Of the older faculty, Mouzon was forty-six upon arrival at SMU; Kilgore, fifty; and Cuninggim, forty-eight. Holt was the only one with a Ph.D. (University of Chicago, 1909). Seay had done postgraduate work at Chicago, Harvard, the University of Berlin, and Oxford but declined to take a doctoral degree. Each of the others had either a B.D. or M.A., or both, except Mouzon, whose formal education stopped with a bachelor's degree. Several had studied at Vanderbilt and some at Chicago. Mouzon and Seay had been on the Southwestern faculty before coming to SMU, and Kern and Cuninggim had taught at Vanderbilt.[31] All were active church leaders. All had had experience as pastors before joining the School of Theology faculty, serving Methodist churches in a number of states across the South. All were originally from the South, and they shared a commitment to the theological education of southern pastors.

From the writings of the faculty during those years we can identify some features of their theological stances. They affirmed critical biblical scholarship and were anti-fundamentalist but not aggressively so. The lists of books Seay wanted for the library included several major works by critical biblical scholars of the time, including S. R. Driver's *An Introduction to the Literature of the Old Testament* and A. S. Peake's *The Bible: Its Origin, Its Significance, and Its Abiding Worth*.[32] In Seay's *An Outline for the Study of Old Testament History*, he listed in the bibliography some books he designated anticritical, some conservative, and some critical. He commented, "A genuine student should not read merely one side, but should endeavor to get as many viewpoints as possible."[33]

Ivan Lee Holt reflected a similar stance regarding the Bible. Years later he reported that when he was a member of the School of Theology faculty and was teaching a Bible class at the Dallas YMCA, he once told the class that some think of the Creation story in Genesis 1 as a literal and scientific account, others as occurring over a long period of time, and still others refuse to consider the story as scientific fact but point to its important emphasis on God as Creator. Some reporters played up what Holt said as unorthodox. Because some people thereafter canceled their pledges to SMU, Holt resigned so as not to embarrass the university. Hyer tore up the resignation, commenting, "I am sure that anyone who cancels a subscription over this is a person whose pledge was never more than ten dollars."[34] Hyer's support for academic freedom trumped Holt's caution.

Their writings also provide some indication of their conception of the Christian life. For Paul Kern, "To be a Christian is to be a friend of God as he is made known to us in the person of Jesus Christ." Friends of Christ would not be willing to live sinfully, as that would grieve him. They would share his purpose with all the world and be constantly active in serving him. Salvation, Kern said, is a gradual process of becoming spiritual people. The church's program is to Christianize all life, from the local community to the international order, and creating a Christian world order requires first creating a Christian fellowship in local churches.[35] Kern's conception of conversion was akin to that of the nineteenth-century theologian Horace Bushnell, and of social action suggestive of social gospel leaders like Walter Rauschenbusch.[36]

Jesse Cuninggim expressed a similar view of the Christian life. He wrote that Christians' purpose is to imbue society with the ideals of Christ. They do that by supporting high ideals in industry, commerce, education, and public life and by developing sound Christian character in each person. The Sunday school, he added, mainly aims at the latter.[37]

It would be fair to characterize the theological orientation of these early faculty members as a moderate, optimistic liberalism. They believed that the Bible is central to theological study, that Jesus is central to the Bible and is the ideal for the Christian life, and that they should seek to Christianize individuals and, through them, the wider society. They believed they could contribute to progressive improvement in the goodness of individuals and justice in the world.

Their receptiveness to theological currents of their time contrasts with the reaction of Hiram Abiff Boaz, who was not a member of the theological faculty but served as SMU's vice president from 1911 to 1913 and its president from 1920 to 1922. Boaz was a minister, but he lacked a seminary degree and went to study in 1914–15 at Columbia University and Union Theological Seminary. He later wrote that one of the seminary professors asked him whether he would make a commotion when he returned to Texas and preached the new things he had learned in New York. He answered that he would not make any commotion at all. He did not expect to preach the modernism he was hearing at Union because he did not believe it. The professor laughed and said, "We don't care whether you believe it or not. We may not believe it next year." Boaz replied that this was one reason why he did not accept Union Seminary's doctrines: "You are not all agreed. You seem to be on a floating island and drifting most anywhere. When you come to final conclusions, make a landing somewhere, and agree on your doctrines, and the preaching of those doctrines produces more and better fruit than the doctrines I have been preaching for years it will be time for me to come to your point of view and to begin preaching your doctrines."[38]

The School of Theology faculty was not merely an array of individuals whose offices were in the same building. It was for years a group of colleagues working closely together. This is apparent from the entries in the small notebook that contains the typed minutes of seventy-seven faculty meetings from the fall of 1915 to mid-1920. The minutes of the first meeting record that the School of Theology faculty "met informally on the banister railing at Mr. Kern's residence."[39] Usually, the faculty met in Hyer's office in Dallas Hall, though he did not attend a School of Theology faculty meeting until the fourth year. As chair of the faculty, Holt presided, except on the rare occasions when Mouzon could attend. Frank Seay was the secretary. In the first year there were usually four in attendance, including Kern and Kilgore, supplemented on a few occasions by C. S. Wright, the university vice president, and Frank Reedy, the bursar.

These few were responsible for deciding what had to be done to start a theological school and for seeing that it happened. They had no preexisting structure on which to rely, although other seminaries provided them with ideas. Undoubtedly, they were influenced by the pattern of theological studies that William Rainey Harper and his followers had introduced at the University of Chicago and by the experience several faculty members had had at the Vanderbilt School of Theology. What courses should they offer? Which courses should be required? Should there be a theology school catalog, who should put it out, and how often? What should the class schedule look like? What should be the grading system? Should there be a summer school? Temporary decisions had been made about some of these matters before the school opened, but now the faculty could set policies for the future.

At the meeting of March 31, 1916, the Committee on Curriculum (Seay and Holt) proposed a set of requirements for the bachelor of divinity degree. The four men discussed them in detail and postponed action until the next meeting.[40] On April 8 they adopted a report that required 150 term hours (the academic year included fall, winter, and spring terms) for the degree.

Required coursework:

FIELD	TERM HOURS
Old Testament	6
New Testament	6
Biblical languages	13 in Hebrew or New Testament Greek
Church history and missions	9
Psychology and philosophy of religion	12*
Religious efficiency	12**
Public speaking and voice training	6
Total term hours in required courses:	64

*Six term hours at the "advanced" (i.e., senior undergraduate) level, six hours at the graduate level.

**Religious efficiency included various aspects of the practice of ministry, such as preaching and church administration—later referred to as "the practical courses."

Candidates for a bachelor of divinity degree would be required to take thirty-nine additional term hours of graduate electives and forty-seven term hours of other electives that "may be from the *advanced* courses, though the student is advised, so far as possible, to choose *graduate* rather than *advanced* electives."

Within these electives, graduate and advanced, in the second year the student was to choose a major, with thirty term hours, fifteen of which had to be at the graduate level, and a minor, with fifteen term hours, nine of which had to be at the graduate level.[41]

If they took the equivalent of freshman and sophomore English, students without a degree from an approved undergraduate school would receive the certificate in theology but no degree, when they completed the same requirements as B.D. candidates, except that biblical languages would be elective.[42] The certificate in theology remained an option until 1950; the last one was awarded in August 1948.

At the end of the first year, the report of the School of Theology to the board of trustees identified several features that were deemed distinctive of the school: keeping the graduate theological students in close touch with the upper-level undergraduates, taking the work of the school to pastors in the field as well as those on campus, and providing training in religious efficiency.[43] All these features are reflected in the faculty's decisions about its work and the curriculum requirements.

The requirements for the B.D. degree allowed graduate theological students to take much of their work at the senior level—"advanced courses"—in the undergraduate college. This curriculum omitted some fields that later would be required. Whereas the initial temporary curriculum of 1915 required courses in doctrine, religious education, and sociology, these requirements were omitted from the 1916 curriculum, presumably because of the absence of faculty to teach them.[44] On the other hand, a student had to take thirteen term hours in a biblical language, a requirement eliminated in 1924. The requirement in religious efficiency was there from the first and remained a major part of the curriculum.

The 1916 curriculum was changed two years later. Beginning in 1918, the faculty added three requirements for the B.D.: three term hours in Christian doctrine, nine in religious education, and nine in sociology, additions reflecting the presence of new members of the faculty: Dobbs, Cuninggim, and Woodward.[45]

From the start the theology school faculty wished to educate not only enrolled students but also local ministers and the members of local Methodist churches. The number of students enrolling in the Tuesday extension courses varied from five to fifty-five for the first several years. In February 1916 the faculty compiled a list of books to recommend to preachers in the Southwest for general reading.[46] After Jesse Cuninggim joined the faculty in January 1918, he led the faculty in providing correspondence courses for pastors across the South, an activity in which he had previously been involved.[47] School of Theology faculty members also frequently taught and preached in local churches and often arranged for students to teach there as well. In September 1918 Horace Whaling was appointed to serve as acting pastor of Highland Park Methodist Church, in addition to his regular faculty responsibilities. He held that position until the annual conference in the fall of 1919, when Paul Kern became acting pastor.[48]

In June 1919 the executive committee of the board of trustees established the Fondren Lectureship of Christian Missions. W. W. Fondren of Houston, "being vitally interested in the cause of Christian Missions," agreed to pay SMU $10,000 in each of the next five years to establish a trust fund. The interest from that fund, the agreement stated, was "to be used annually or as often as practicable in procuring some competent person, or persons, to deliver lectures on Christian missions . . . under the auspices of Southern Methodist University." A committee composed of the bishop of the Texas Annual Conference, the chair of the SMU board, the president of SMU, and the theological faculty was to choose the lecturer.[49] The Fondren Lectures began in 1920. In 1936 they, along with other lectures, were organized into Ministers' Week, which became a major event in the life of the School of Theology for decades to come. In 1959 Dean Merrimon Cuninggim reported that Ella Fondren, widow of W. W. Fondren, had given two hundred shares of Standard Oil stock to supplement the Fondren Lectures' endowment.[50]

THE GREAT WAR AND THE SCHOOL OF THEOLOGY

The United States entered World War I—"the Great War"—on April 6, 1917. A week later the executive committee of the board gave Hyer authority to require the military training of male students, including seminarians.[51] Before long a military training unit was on the campus. Early in the fall the School of Theology faculty recommended exempting from military training any theological students who were serving churches, older than draft age, or working to pay their school expenses if military training would jeopardize their continuing in school.[52]

The war did not lead to a decrease in the school's enrollment, in contrast to that of undergraduate men, which fell by 30 percent between 1916–17 and 1917–18.[53] Some seminary men were called up, however, and on at least one occasion the faculty had to decide what to do about a student's credits if he had to leave school in the middle of a term.[54] In May 1918 the theology faculty scheduled a meeting to consider its relation to the war situation. After much discussion faculty members voted unanimously "that it is the highest patriotic and religious duty of the members of the Faculty to carry on the work of the School, during the war making such adjustments in the work of the Church in general as may be necessary." That fall Dobbs reported that fourteen former School of Theology students had been accepted as military chaplains and that the school needed to offer all its dormitory space to accommodate two hundred cadets who would soon be on campus. When the war ended, the theology school soon returned to normal; in January 1919 the dean reported increased enrollment for the winter term and anticipated an even larger enrollment in the spring term.[55]

CRISIS AFTER CRISIS

Several crises occurred during the academic year 1919–20. First, President Hyer called a meeting of the theology faculty for September 26 and announced that Dean Dobbs was ill. Hyer asked James Kilgore to take over organization of the theology school faculty during Dobbs's illness. Thereupon the faculty sent a resolution to Dobbs, noting that he had remained at his desk nearly all summer and that he needed a rest. Faculty members assured him they would carry on the work until he was sufficiently rested to resume his duties. At the next meeting they elected Kilgore chair of the faculty during Dobbs's absence.[56]

Another crisis was more difficult to manage—the university's growing debt and Hyer's inability to deal with it. The university had been in serious financial straits for some time, running a deficit every year since it opened, and by 1919 the debt had reached the huge sum of $358,697.[57] Hyer had never been good at raising money and had left that responsibility mainly to others. In the spring of 1919 a visiting committee of the Methodist Episcopal Church, South, expressed deep concern about the problem, which it described as "little short of desperate."[58]

In June, Hyer persuaded twenty Dallas businessmen to lend the university a total of $40,000 to get it past the immediate financial crisis, but this only increased the debt without resolving the problem. The trustees had by then become so dissatisfied with the situation that they considered asking Hyer to resign. The problem was to find another leader who could solve the problem. When their efforts became known, the college faculty, with support from the theology professors, issued a statement of strong support for Hyer, which calmed matters but left the financial problem as serious as before.[59]

A confrontation occurred at the June 1919 meeting of the board of trustees. Mouzon read a letter of resignation from a board member from North Texas, R. H. Shuttles, who declared, "Conditions exist at the University, which make it impossible for me to continue my service." Board members urged Shuttles to withdraw his resignation, and later he agreed to continue on the executive committee until the annual conferences met in the fall. Next, Mouzon himself resigned as chair of the board. When members tried to get him to reconsider, the minutes enigmatically record that he "stated some of the conditions which made it impossible for him to continue in his present relation to the Board, and further stated that his action had been carefully considered and must be accepted as final." Board members could do nothing but accept his resignation (though Mouzon, like Shuttles, continued on the executive committee). Hyer tried to put the best face on it, pointing in his report to the possibility of a small reduction in the next year's deficit, new loans that had been secured, and his estimate that more money would be forthcoming from the annual conferences. His report would not have reassured the troubled board members. But all they could bring themselves to do at that meeting was to express the wish that Hyer give up his teaching of physics so that he could give more time to university administration.[60] That did not happen, and it likely would not have resolved the problem, which was Hyer's lack of talent or drive for raising money.

Finances did not improve as the academic year wore on. By September it was clear the university would have another deficit in 1919–20. In November the executive committee granted Horace Whaling a leave of absence from teaching church history in the School of Theology so he could spend time fund-raising; soon thereafter the trustees named him vice president for the period when he would be in the field soliciting funds.[61]

Late that fall board members approached Hiram A. Boaz, who had been the university's vice president and chief fund-raiser from 1911 to 1913 and had now moved to a church administrative position in Louisville, Kentucky. They invited Boaz to come to Dallas, and he met with four members of the executive committee. As Boaz later told it, Shuttles said to him, "'Dr. Boaz, unless you accept the presidency of the University and help us get out of debt we will be compelled to close the doors of the institution next September.'" The new board chair, Judge Joseph E. Cockrell, put it more starkly: "I don't believe you, or any other man, can save the University. It is gone, hook and line. But I want to see you try it." Boaz asked him not to repeat that to anybody else; he thought the university could be saved and that he could do it. Boaz was reluctantly willing but only if several conditions were met, including that Hyer would agree to the change and that they begin immediately to raise $1 million for endowment.[62] Thereupon W. D. Bradfield, a member of the executive committee, went to Hyer and asked him to resign. Hyer was thunderstruck, but he agreed to step down.[63]

On February 11, 1920, the student newspaper, the *Daily Campus*, reported Hyer had resigned, but the process was not yet complete.[64] At the board meeting on February 20, 1920, Cockrell, the chair, reviewed the financial situation and explained that the executive committee had looked for a capable leader for the fund-raising campaign to save SMU and that subsequently Hyer had resigned. In his resignation statement Hyer explained that he had always directed his efforts toward planning the university and its buildings, selecting a faculty, and striving for high ideals in scholarship: "For a number of years there has been a growing feeling that a college president must be a diplomatist in politics or a promoter in finance; the president of a State Institution should be the former, the president of a private institution should be the latter; while the president of a church institution must be both."

Thus, with dignity and no resistance, he turned over the presidency to Hiram A. Boaz. The board accepted Hyer's resignation, named him president emeritus, and asked him to continue as professor of physics at the same salary he had received as president. The board then elected Boaz to be the second president of Southern Methodist University.[65] For all his shortcomings as a fund-raiser, Robert Stewart Hyer had been an academic leader of strength and insight. He knew what constituted quality education, and he put that ahead of all else in his years as president. It would be nearly two decades before SMU would have another president with comparable academic judgment.

In the midst of the turmoil triggered by Hyer's resignation, still another crisis struck the School of Theology. On February 14, 1920, Frank Seay died of influenza. He was thirty-eight, had been one of the original theology faculty members, and was highly esteemed by both his colleagues and the students. Less than a year earlier, in April 1919, the other theology faculty members had learned that Seay had decided to leave SMU to accept a position at the University of Texas. In dismay they had sent him a statement of deep appreciation for his character and work and called his attention to a communication from the board of its intention to increase salaries in 1920. That would enable him, his colleagues said, to remain at SMU with less sacrifice, and they seriously requested that he reconsider. He did; he wrote to thank them for their action and to say that matters had so developed that he could remain at SMU, "in a fellowship that has been so absolutely satisfactory as the one we have enjoyed in the last few years."[66] But now, suddenly, Seay was gone. Included in the School of Theology faculty minutes is a statement by Dobbs expressing the faculty's grief and shock and its appreciation for Seay's character, ability, influence, and work.[67]

The week after the change of presidents, Dobbs returned to resume his duties as dean and to pick up some of Seay's work. Yet on March 5, only a few days later, he submitted his resignation as dean, expressing his intention to remain as professor of Christian doctrine. He explained that on his return he had added much of Seay's work in New Testament to his usual responsibilities—as dean, in recruiting students, and in his own field of doctrine—and because he had been absent for so long, he thought it his duty to step aside, effective immediately.[68]

Boaz then named Paul Kern to serve as acting dean of the School of Theology until June 15. At the time Kern was professor of ministerial efficiency, acting pastor of Highland Park Methodist Church, and university chaplain. It was understood that he would resign as Highland Park pastor as soon as a replacement could be found.[69] As it turned out, Boaz subsequently asked Kern to continue as dean. Dobbs did not remain at SMU; the following November he became the pastor of the First Methodist Church in Anniston, Alabama. This series of crises and changes in leadership concluded the initial era in the life of the School of Theology.

---

1. Lewis Howard Grimes, *A History of Perkins School of Theology*, ed. Roger Loyd (Dallas: Southern Methodist University Press, 1993), 1; Walter N. Vernon, *Methodism Moves across North Texas* (Dallas: Historical Society, North Texas Conference, Methodist Church, 1967), 239; Hemphill Hosford, "Recollections," 1965, DeGolyer Library archives, Southern Methodist University.
2. Vernon, *Methodism Moves*, 68.

3. Ibid., 65–68, 174–75; Mary Martha Hosford Thomas, *Southern Methodist University: Founding and Early Years* (Dallas: Southern Methodist University Press, 1974), 11–12.
4. Thomas, *Southern Methodist University*, 11–12. See also H. Richard Niebuhr, Daniel Day Williams, and James M. Gustafson, *The Advancement of Theological Education* (New York: Harper and Brothers, 1957), 4–5.
5. Hiram Abiff Boaz, *Eighty-four Golden Years: An Autobiography of Bishop Hiram Abiff Boaz* (Nashville, Tenn.: Parthenon, 1951), 56.
6. Thomas, *Southern Methodist University*, 14–20.
7. *Texas Christian Advocate*, March 24, April 7, and April 21, 1910.
8. Thomas, *Southern Methodist University*, 23–27; Walter N. Vernon, Robert W. Sledge, Robert C. Monk, and Norman W. Spellmann, *The Methodist Excitement in Texas: A History* (Dallas: Texas United Methodist Historical Society, 1984), 258; "Report of the Educational Commission," manuscript, pp. 1–2, Bridwell Library archives.
9. Minutes of the Commission on Education, 1911–14, 25, 38–44, Bridwell Library archives; Thomas, *Southern Methodist University*, 32.
10. *Journal of the Seventeenth General Conference of the Methodist Episcopal Church, South*, May 6–23, 1914, 236.
11. *Texas Christian Advocate*, November 9 and 23, 1911.
12. Commission on Education, minutes, 127–28.
13. For an assessment of these and other seminaries in the early 1920s, see Robert L. Kelly, *Theological Education in America: A Study of One Hundred Sixty-one Theological Schools in the United States and Canada* (New York: George H. Doran, 1924).
14. W. Kenneth Pope, *A Pope at Roam: The Confessions of a Bishop* (Nashville, Tenn.: Parthenon, 1976), 37–38.
15. *Bulletin of Southern Methodist University*, June 1916, 125. The *Bulletin* was the university catalog and included the School of Theology's offerings.
16. Ibid., 77.
17. Ibid., 71–72, 125–27.
18. Registration for the previous year, in various categories, with the home town of each student, is listed in each *Bulletin* in the early years.
19. *Bulletins* began to list B.D. candidates' undergraduate colleges in 1920; commencement programs began to do so in 1921.
20. Flora Lowrey, "Recollections," eight-page typescript, 1964, DeGolyer Library archives.
21. Ibid.
22. *Bulletin*, June 1916, 69.
23. Ivan Lee Holt, "Early Years at S.M.U.: Recollections of Bishop Ivan Lee Holt," n.d., 1, Ivan Lee Holt Papers, DeGolyer Library archives.
24. Ibid., 1–2.
25. Dorothy Amman, "Southern Methodist University, 1913–1915," October 24, 1939, 4–5, DeGolyer Library archives.
26. *Texas Christian Advocate*, July 1 and 15, 1915.
27. SMU Board of Trustees minutes, June 3, 1915, Southern Methodist University Office of Legal Affairs.
28. Board of trustees minutes, June 8, 1916; *Bulletin*, December 1915, 28–33, and June 1916, 8, 68; Thomas, *Southern Methodist University*, 66. Kern was listed in the June 1915 *Bulletin*, 30–31, as scheduled to teach sociology in 1916–17, including courses called "The Social Message of Jesus" and "The Social Program of the Churches."
29. School of Theology faculty minutes (hereinafter "faculty minutes"), May 14, 1915–June 22, 1920, Bridwell Library archives.
30. Edwin D. Mouzon to Jas. H. McCoy, June 13, 1916; Mouzon to E. R. Hendrix, June 13, 1916, Edwin D. Mouzon Papers, Bridwell Library.
31. *Who's Who in American Methodism*, edited by Carl F. Price (New York: E. B. Treat, 1916); *Who's Who*

in Methodism, edited by Elmer T. Clark (Chicago: A. N. Marquis, 1952); *Who Was Who in America*, vols. 1 and 3 (Chicago: A. N. Marquis, 1943, 1960).

32. S. R. Driver, *An Introduction to the Literature of the Old Testament*, 11th ed. (New York: Charles Scribner's Sons, 1905); A. S. Peake, *The Bible: Its Origin, Its Significance, and Its Abiding Worth*, 5th ed. (London: Hodder and Stoughton, 1914).

33. Frank Seay, *An Outline for the Study of Old Testament History* (Nashville, Tenn.: Methodist Episcopal Church, South, 1917), 211–12.

34. Holt, "Early Years at S.M.U.," 8.

35. Paul B. Kern, "Building the Christian Fellowship," chap. 3 in Worth M. Tippy and Paul B. Kern, *A Methodist Church and Its Work* (Nashville, Tenn.: Lamar and Barton, 1919), 31–32, 35–36.

36. See Horace Bushnell, *Christian Nurture* (New York: Charles Scribner's Sons, 1888); Walter Rauschenbusch, *Christianizing the Social Order* (New York: Macmillan, 1912).

37. Jesse L. Cuningggim and Eric M. North, *The Organization and Administration of the Sunday School* (Nashville, Tenn.: Smith and Lamar, 1919), 15–16.

38. Boaz, *Eighty-four Golden Years*, 94–96.

39. Faculty minutes, October 22, 1915.

40. Ibid., March 31, 1916.

41. Ibid., April 8, 1916; *Bulletin*, June 1916, 75–77.

42. *Bulletin*, June 1916, 77.

43. Board of trustees minutes, June 8, 1916.

44. *Bulletin*, July 1915, 15.

45. Ibid., June 1918, 103, and June 1919, 105.

46. Faculty minutes, January 12 and February 24, 1916.

47. Faculty minutes, February 15, September 9, and October 3, 1918, and June 7, 1919.

48. Faculty minutes, September 9, 1918; *General Minutes of the Annual Conferences of the Methodist Episcopal Church, South, for the Year 1918*, p. 114, and 1919, 81. For many years the Methodist denominations have published a volume of the general minutes annually. Hereinafter they are designated simply *General Minutes* or *Minutes*, with the year and the name of the relevant denominational body.

49. Minutes of the Executive Committee of Southern Methodist University, June 1, 1919, SMU Office of Legal Affairs.

50. Merrimon Cuningggim's report to the Trustees' Committee on the School of Theology, January 7, 1959, Merrimon Cuningggim Papers, Bridwell Library.

51. Executive committee minutes, April 13, 1917; Thomas, *Southern Methodist University*, 62–63.

52. Faculty minutes, undated meeting, fall 1917.

53. *Bulletin*, June 1917, 145, and June 1918, 152.

54. Faculty minutes, February 18, 1918.

55. Faculty minutes, May 29 and 31 and September 9, 1918; January 13, 1919.

56. Faculty minutes, September 26 and October 10, 1919.

57. Board of trustees minutes, May 2, 1922.

58. Board of trustees minutes, June 9, 1919.

59. Thomas, *Southern Methodist University*, 73–74.

60. Board of trustees minutes, June 9, 1919; executive committee minutes, June 17, 1919.

61. Executive committee minutes, September 18, November 13, and December 1, 1919.

62. Boaz, *Eighty-four Golden Years*, 100–102.

63. Ibid., 102; Ray Hyer Brown, *Robert Stewart Hyer: The Man I Knew* (Salado, Texas: Anson Jones, 1957), 162.

64. SMU *Daily Campus*, February 11, 1920.

65. Board of trustees minutes, February 20, 1920.

66. Faculty minutes, April 8 and April 22, 1919.

67. Faculty minutes, undated entry following the minutes for March 12, 1920.

68. Executive committee minutes, March 5, 1920.

69. Ibid.; *Daily Campus*, March 10, 1920.

Reorganization, 1920–1926

When Hoyt Dobbs resigned as dean of the School of Theology in March 1920, SMU President Hiram A. Boaz appointed Paul Kern acting dean and later that spring asked him to continue as dean. With vision and energy during six years in that post, Kern strengthened the School of Theology in several ways. He reorganized and enlarged the faculty, initiated a creative revision of the curriculum, and oversaw the construction of a new building that provided more adequate quarters for the school.

Paul Bentley Kern was born in 1882 in Alexandria, Virginia, where his father, John A. Kern, was a Methodist pastor. After two years at Randolph-Macon College, Paul Kern completed his A.B. degree at Vanderbilt, was ordained a Methodist minister, and continued his studies at Vanderbilt, receiving his master's and B.D. degrees in 1905. At that time his father was professor of practical theology at Vanderbilt. The son taught for two years at Vanderbilt and then was pastor of churches in central Tennessee until 1915, when he became a member of the original faculty of the SMU School of Theology.[1]

HIRAM A. BOAZ'S PRESIDENCY

Kern began his deanship in 1920 under Hiram Boaz, whose presidency of SMU was quite different from Robert Stewart Hyer's. Hyer was a scholar and a teacher, dedicated to developing a university of high quality. He had insight and skill in relating to faculty members, and they respected and admired him for it, but he had neither time nor inclination to be a fund-raiser.

In contrast, during the two years Boaz was president, he dedicated himself primarily to saving the university from financial ruin. From February 20 to May 20,

1920, Boaz held two positions simultaneously: president of SMU and secretary of the Board of Church Extension of the Methodist Episcopal Church, South, headquartered in Louisville, Kentucky. As he recognized, "Under such conditions it was not possible for me to do satisfactory work at either place but I did the best I could." When he gave up the church extension position and moved to Dallas, he began a campaign to raise $1 million for the endowment and pay off the university's debts. He persuaded Wallace Buttrick, secretary of the General Education Board, the private New York organization founded by John D. Rockefeller, to support giving SMU a third of that million, provided that SMU would raise the other two-thirds, pay off its debts, restore to endowment and to building funds the money the university had taken to use for other purposes, and set up a proper system of accounting, which it lacked. By November 1920 Boaz had secured pledges for two-thirds of $1 million. He also had persuaded several Wichita Falls businessmen, including J. J. Perkins, to buy fifty lots that SMU owned north of the campus and thus to retire $100,000 of the university's debt. Boaz also began moving toward an adequate system of accounting, and he started the practice of preparing a budget for the coming year, which appears to have been an innovation for SMU.[2] Though he did not fully resolve the financial crisis, Boaz led people both inside and outside the university to believe these problems could be solved, and he made enough progress toward a solution that others were able to continue these efforts and make the financial situation less precarious. By June 1924, two years after Boaz left SMU, the university had paid off its debt, the endowment was worth more than $1.5 million, and the buildings were valued at $1.5 million.[3]

Boaz's presidency did less, however, to advance SMU's educational purpose. So that he might devote his time to the financial campaign, he left decisions about the internal life of the university largely to A. S. Pegues, dean of the college, and to Dean Kern of the School of Theology. Since Boaz was concerned about the spiritual atmosphere of the campus, he recommended holding a revival in the fall of 1920 and agreed to lead it himself. He judged it a great success: "The entire student body was greatly moved Godward." He was also eager for SMU to develop a winning football team, which it had not had, and in this he was encouraged by some Dallas business-men. In 1921 he brought about the resignation of the head coach and brought in to replace him Ray Morrison, under whom the team significantly improved and who remained SMU's head coach through the 1934 season. Boaz directed the vice president, Horace Whaling, to assist the coach "in any way he could," including offering "the usual inducements" to persuade good players to come to SMU. Faculty and students alike roundly criticized Boaz for spending the university's money on the sports program in a time of fiscal tightness, but he ascribed this criticism to their opposition on other, unrelated issues. In 1922, after Boaz had departed, football's Southwest Conference brought charges that SMU's recruiting methods had broken the conference's rules. This was a source of controversy on campus for several years.[4]

As president, Boaz was the mirror image of Hyer. Hyer was unable to handle the financial difficulties, whereas Boaz had considerable success in doing so. Hyer knew what constituted a strong university and strived mightily to create one; Boaz gave little evidence of any educational philosophy and left the academic life of the university to others.

When the General Conference of the Methodist Episcopal Church, South, met at Hot Springs, Arkansas, in May 1922, it elected five bishops. Boaz, who attended as a delegate from the Central Texas Conference, received strong support on ballot after ballot but not enough to be elected. Finally, on the eighth ballot he was the fifth bishop chosen. Hoyt Dobbs, who in 1920 had given up the deanship of the School of Theology, was elected fourth. The College of Bishops assigned Boaz to Japan, Korea, and Manchuria for four years, after which he was reassigned to the southwestern United States. Because he was not to leave for Asia until July 19, the board of trustees asked him to continue as SMU president until that time, and he agreed.[5]

THE PLAN TO REORGANIZE
THE SCHOOL OF THEOLOGY FACULTY

In March 1920, when Boaz named Paul Kern to be acting dean of the School of Theology, its small faculty had two vacancies that had to be filled. One was the position that Frank Seay had held. To teach Seay's courses for the remainder of the academic year, Kern obtained the services of B. Harvie Branscomb, who had come to the SMU philosophy department in the fall of 1919 after several years at Oxford University, where he was a Rhodes Scholar studying New Testament at Wadham College. At the June 12 meeting of the board of trustees, Kern nominated Branscomb to continue in the New Testament position, and he was so appointed.[6] Branscomb took a leave of absence in 1923–24 to complete his Ph.D. at Union Theological Seminary and Columbia University, then returned to SMU. In his absence Kern filled the New Testament position with another Rhodes Scholar, George F. Thomas, who stayed at SMU the following year as associate professor of philosophy of religion and then took a position at Princeton University.[7]

The other vacancy, in Old Testament, had not been filled since Ivan Lee Holt's departure in 1918. For that position Kern chose John A. Rice, then pastor of a Methodist church in Sumter, South Carolina. Rice, fifty-eight, had served several years as a pastor in South Carolina, followed by six years as president of Columbia College for Women in Columbia, South Carolina. He then had done doctoral study in Old Testament at the University of Chicago. From 1910 to 1914 he was pastor of First Methodist Church in Fort Worth and vice president of the Commission on Education that established SMU in 1911. He had also been pastor of prominent churches in Alabama, Louisiana, Missouri, and again in South Carolina. In nominating him to serve as professor of Old Testament, Kern described Rice as "one of the best qualified men in that field in our entire Church" and observed that his book on the Old Testament would be published that fall.[8]

In the six years Kern was dean (1920–26), the School of Theology saw an almost complete turnover in faculty. In the fall of 1920 the faculty consisted of seven professors. Kern was professor of ministerial efficiency; James Kilgore, philosophy of religion; Horace Whaling, church history, though he was on leave to raise money for the university; Comer Woodward, sociology; Jesse Cuninggim, religious education; Branscomb, New Testament; and Rice, Old Testament. When Kern left in 1926, only Kilgore remained.

Appointments during Kern's deanship reflected a plan for reorganizing the faculty that started to take shape in 1920. When Dean Dobbs had taken medical leave in the fall of 1919, Hyer had asked Kilgore to take over organization of the theology faculty during Dobbs's absence.[9] Hyer appears to have had in mind only the difficulties arising from Dobbs's leave. By the time the board of trustees met in February 1920, however, the theology faculty needed more extensive reorganization. At that meeting the board adopted a motion by Bishop Mouzon instructing its executive committee "to proceed in cooperating with the Dean of the School of Theology and the President of the University in the various matters necessary for the reorganization of the faculty of the School of Theology." At the same time it stipulated that Kern (not yet the acting dean, since the board expected Dobbs to return) was to be present at all meetings of the executive committee. It is not clear whether this was to oversee the faculty reorganization or for some other reason.[10] Kern may have already been thinking about reorganizing the faculty.

At the June 12 meeting of the board, Kern, who by then had been the acting dean for three months, outlined a reorganization plan for the theology faculty, describing it as an idea already being implemented.[11] The plan was this: First, the department of church history and missions would be divided into two departments, church history under Whaling (assuming he would return from his fund-raising duties), and missions, which would be handled by visiting professors.

Second, Dobbs's resignation, not only as dean but also from the faculty, raised the problem of how to continue the work of his department, Christian doctrine. Kern's plan was to merge the departments of Christian doctrine and philosophy of religion and for both to be taught by James Kilgore. Dobbs remained until his annual conference in Alabama met in the fall. J. F. Pierce, a minister in the North Texas Conference, briefly taught both Christian doctrine and church history but was unable to continue for health reasons. In February 1921 Kern asked Kilgore to teach the remainder of Dobbs's course in Christian doctrine.[12]

This change made possible a third: adding a new faculty position in practical theology. Kern would continue to teach homiletics in addition to his responsibilities as dean. He believed, though, that if the School of Theology was to provide education adequate for the work of the church, it would also need courses on ministering to the small town, rural, and city church. This new position was yet to be filled.

Carrying out the plan of reorganization might entail additional financial outlay, which led Kern to observe to the trustees that until 1920 the finances of the school had been "merged in the common budget of the University." Under that arrangement it was impossible to show the school's income and expenditures separately. Furthermore, Kern said, for the past two years some School of Theology funds had been used to cover general university expenses. Kern presented a tentative budget for the school with income and expenses of $36,200 each. The dean's salary would be $3,900. Each full-time faculty member would receive $3,300, with $1,650 in the School of Theology budget for Woodward, who taught only half his courses at the school and the other half at the college.[13]

Dean Kern soon encountered two difficulties in implementing the reorganization. One was finding someone to teach church history while Whaling was on leave from the School of Theology. In November 1920 Boaz notified the executive committee that he wished to keep Whaling on indefinitely as vice president and fund-raiser, stating that his work for the university was of great importance. The executive committee agreed. By June 1921 Whaling had resigned his church history position to be vice president, and the school now had that position to fill.[14]

The other difficulty was that Kern was unable to find someone to appoint for 1920–21 in ministerial efficiency (the position he now called pastoral administration). Because of the two vacancies, he brought in Robert Wesley Goodloe, a graduate of SMU (M.A., 1916) and Yale (B.D., 1918) who was serving as a pastor in Oklahoma, to teach both pastoral administration and church history for six months—the winter and spring terms of 1921—after which he would go to the University of Chicago to continue his doctoral studies.[15]

Kern was able to staff the missions position for a few years with visiting professors. For 1920–21 the Board of Missions of the Methodist Episcopal Church, South, sent as one-year appointments two men who had served as missionaries in East Asia, one in China and one in Japan. For 1921–22 it sent three more, one who had been in China, one in Korea, and one in Cuba (the latter was Benjamin O. Hill, who returned to the theology faculty in 1946). Then in 1922–23 the visiting professors came from missions in Japan and the Belgian Congo.[16]

By June 1921 Kern named a man for one of the regular faculty vacancies: J. Marvin Ormond, pastor of the First Methodist Church in Elizabeth City, North Carolina—the same pastorate from which Jesse Cuninggim had come to SMU in 1918. There was even more connection: Ormond, whose first name was Jesse, was named for Jesse Cuninggim, a kinsman. Ormond was forty-three and had served several rural and town charges in North Carolina; he already was widely recognized for his leadership in the field of the rural church. He was appointed professor of pastoral administration.[17]

THE JOHN A. RICE CONTROVERSY

As the new dean began reshaping the School of Theology faculty, a major controversy arose in 1921. In the fall of 1920 John A. Rice joined the theology faculty as planned, and the Macmillan Company published his book, *The Old Testament in the Life of Today*.[18] The work was drawn from lectures he had given around the country for twenty years, and Rice said it embodied his life's study and reflection.[19] One of his aims was to focus on people and books, rather than on texts and verses. Another was to help people disturbed about scientific biblical criticism. "The new knowledge," Rice said, "only makes faith easier."[20] His methods were those widely accepted by biblical scholars of the time. The book was a comprehensive, knowledgeable, and lucid presentation of the Old Testament, reflecting the work of some of the ablest scholars of the day.

In the January 1921 issue of the *Methodist Review*, a journal of the Methodist Episcopal Church, South, the reviewer declared that the volume was a long-needed masterpiece that would give the reader greater appreciation of the Old Testament and strengthen spiritual life.[21] In May a favorable, though less effusive, review appeared in the *Methodist Review* of the Methodist Episcopal Church, the northern Methodist branch. The reviewer observed that the book was not conservative but went further than the northern Methodists who wrote on the Old Testament. He surmised the author was more a preacher than a teacher or scholar and concluded, "There's a place for this book, and may good fortune attend it."[22]

Adverse Methodist reaction soon appeared. In April a retired Methodist minister from Louisiana wrote in an article in the *Texas Christian Advocate*, "I have read [Rice's book] from cover to cover. . . . It will sustain and enhance the author's reputation as a scholar and interpreter of the spiritual meaning of the Old Testament, and . . . it will cause many a believer to mourn. . . . Dr. Rice has brought us squarely up to the subject of the Chicago type of Biblical science. . . . I am in favor of a fight to a finish on the issue, and have no doubt of the outcome."[23]

That was a sign of things to come. Until October the *Advocate* was flooded with articles and letters on both sides of the issue. Its editor, A. J. Weeks, suggested that his readers not become overly excited by the matter. The university's board, administration, and faculty, he said, will safeguard the university's best interests. Weeks published a paper signed by all the students in Rice's classes stating "unreservedly that Dr. Rice has made the Bible a living book to us and that our ideas of its divine inspiration and value have been greatly strengthened."[24]

But Weeks failed to placate his readers. The *Advocate* received so many letters and articles on the issue that he declared it impossible to publish them all in a reasonable time.[25] Most of them strongly, often bitterly, opposed the book, some lamenting that SMU still employed its author.[26] Others defended Rice and objected to the way the discussion was being conducted or at least saw some merit in what he had written.[27] In July the *Advocate* published an article by Mouzon, citing Rice's strengths as the basis for SMU's decision to appoint him and highlighting what Mouzon saw as valuable parts of the book. At the same time he commented that he thought some of Rice's words were unnecessary to the book's purpose and should not have been expressed that way to immature students. Mouzon added, "It should not be overlooked that this attack on Dr. Rice and Southern Methodist University began with certain well known Baptists whose chief interest just now is looking after other people's business. We should let them know that we are well able to attend to our own affairs. We Methodists are not in the habit of trying to manage the affairs of the Baptist Church."[28]

Mouzon had a specific Baptist in mind—J. Frank Norris, pastor of the First Baptist Church of Fort Worth since 1909. Because Rice had been pastor of First Methodist Church in Fort Worth for several years, he would have been well acquainted with Norris's outlook, and Norris with his. Norris was a fundamentalist who, through spectacular preaching and attacks on opponents, had split his congregation and brought in thousands of new members to replace those who left. In the early 1920s he rebelled against the Baptist General Convention of Texas, claiming it had usurped the rights of local congregations, and he verbally attacked the president of Baylor University for tolerating a professor who, Norris claimed, taught evolution. Like other fundamentalists of the time, Norris linked the theory of evolution and higher biblical criticism to so-called German rationalistic heresies, which he thought threatened Protestantism and indeed civilization itself.[29] Although Rice's defenders did not name Norris in their articles, Paul Kern identified him in a letter as someone who stimulated the attacks, and years later Hiram A. Boaz wrote of Norris's violent criticisms of Rice.[30]

Rice wrote to the *Advocate* in his own defense. In a letter published in September 1921 he tried to answer "the long-drawn-out campaign of misrepresentation." He was charged, he said, with being a German rationalist and a Darwinian evolutionist, with seeing the Old Testament as a collection of myths and fairy tales, with making Moses into a magician, with denying the authority of the Bible, with undermining the faith of the tradition. All those charges, he declared, were absolutely false, and he challenged his critics to prove the book contained even one word of heresy. "From the first word of Genesis to the last of Revelation, rightly interpreted, [the Bible] is the Word of God." He reminded readers that the SMU Board of Trustees had "without dissent" called him to his faculty position and said he would neither abandon his principles nor desert his assigned post.[31]

Yet pressure from the church was too great for him. On October 3 he told the executive committee of the board he was going to resign. How much Boaz and members of the board pressed Rice to do so is not known. Boaz later portrayed the action as Rice's decision, but the sequence of events suggests that influential board members must have wanted Rice to resign. Rice attached four conditions to his resignation, and the executive committee accepted all four: It agreed to issue a statement commending his work as a professor both within and outside the university, repudiating the charges made against him; to see that he received a pastoral appointment equal to what he had held for many years; to assume any financial loss he might suffer; and to explain why it had accepted his resignation.[32]

The next day Judge Cockrell, who chaired both the board and its executive committee, read a statement he had written (and Kern had endorsed) that addressed the first and fourth conditions. It said Rice's students had all testified to his religious convictions, that his work had been highly satisfactory, and that there should be no blot on his good name because of the events leading to his resignation. After reviewing the mixed reception to Rice's book, the statement spoke of Rice's faith in the basics of Methodist belief and the truths of the Bible and noted many in the church regarded him with favor. "Yet," it concluded, "it is considered expedient that the resignation be accepted to take effect as soon as proper adjustment for his work can be made."[33]

President Boaz said that this statement would be sent to the School of Theology faculty soon after the executive committee meeting and that he would receive Rice's statement of resignation as soon as the theology faculty had approved the paper.[34] Cockrell's statement apparently was not released to the press.

Expedient it was, and Boaz later wrote that Rice's resignation led to much faculty unrest and that some of Rice's friends became hostile toward Boaz. Boaz had been popular with the faculty and students during his first year as president, but he said that there were difficulties now in his relationship to both groups.[35] Several members of the theological faculty met informally during October to discuss their position on the questions about Rice and his relationship to the school. Branscomb's account of their views was that while they did not agree with everything Rice said or wrote, his work in the School of Theology had been satisfactory and his relationships with the rest of the faculty harmonious. The faculty members "condemned the unfair criticism which had been made of him, and felt that Dr. Rice should not be allowed to leave our ranks without every effort being made through the press and on the [annual] conference floors to show that he had been misrepresented." At their last informal meeting Kern and professors Branscomb, Kilgore, Woodward, and two newly appointed professors, James Seehorn Seneker and Mims Thornburgh Workman, identified three fundamental principles they thought must be maintained and subsequently presented them to Boaz and to Mouzon:

> That we do not accept the judgment of Dr. Rice revealed in the articles of his critics in recent issues of the *Texas Christian Advocate*, and that we insist that in view of Dr. Rice's statement of faith and conformity with Methodist beliefs it is not proper for us to pass judgment upon his orthodoxy as a Methodist preacher and teacher.
>
> We insist that the administration shall say very frankly to our constituency that the University is conducting a theological seminary upon the recognized principles of the modern historical method of biblical interpretation, always in conformity with Methodist and Christian fundamentals.
>
> We further suggest as the best course of action that the President shall state to the annual conferences that in view of our inability after long and prayerful consideration to reach a solution which seems to be the Christian one and best to conserve the interests of the church and the University, and in view of the fact that the consequences involved in a wrong and hasty solution are of such dire-

ful character, that the President frankly ask the annual conferences to give the University further time to study and work on this matter and submit all the facts in the case to the meeting of the Board of Trustees in June [1922] and await their final action.

Branscomb read the group's statement of support for Rice at a later meeting of the theology school faculty, and the faculty included it in its minutes.[36]

One might ask why Boaz did not stand up for Rice, a man whom he considered a close friend and whose preaching he appreciated. Instead Boaz's reaction contrasted sharply with that of Hyer to Ivan Lee Holt's attempted resignation a few years earlier over a similar issue. Holt had submitted his resignation to avoid embarrassing the university, but Hyer tore it up, and that was the end of it. Hyer understood the importance of academic freedom; Boaz appears not to have realized what was at stake. The pressures in the case of Rice were far greater, but forthright leadership by Boaz would have shown faithfulness toward Rice, the faculty, and the students and might have strengthened the university's position in the face of later controversies.

By October 6 Rice had presented a long statement of resignation to the president, as promised. He closed with an expression of regret, for he was not sure his resignation would ultimately be for the good of SMU. If resigning meant compromising his convictions, he would instead stay on and endure the storm. But that was not the case, so he was presenting his resignation to avoid any harm that might accrue to the university.[37]

Shortly after Rice decided to resign, the Texas annual conferences began their previously scheduled fall meetings. On October 6 Boaz spoke in defense of Rice at the session of the Northwest Texas Conference in Amarillo. The SMU president began by announcing Rice's resignation—apparently the first the public had heard of it, for the next day the *Dallas Morning News* described it as "an unexpected turn."[38] Boaz said that Rice had been largely misunderstood and that he had heard some of Rice's lectures before they appeared in the book and found nothing objectionable in them. When he read the book, however, he found some things in it with which he could not agree.[39]

Boaz's defense, such as it was, failed to mollify Rice's opponents in the Northwest Texas Conference. That conference adopted the report of its board of education, which condemned ideas it supposed him to represent. It decried what it called propaganda that, "under the guise of modern scholarship assails much of the historical and miraculous elements of the Bible"; it declared the Bible to be both inspired and infallible and called upon the church's educational institutions not to use teachers whose words "attack or bring in question the verity of the Scriptures in their entirety." Two weeks later the West Texas Conference, meeting in San Antonio, adopted a similar, though more restrained, report.[40]

In the last week of October the North Texas Conference, meeting in Dallas, gave long and heated attention to the issue. The members of the conference's board of education included Kern and former president Hyer, both sympathetic to Rice. When the board's report came to the floor of the conference, W. L. Tittle, a minister strongly opposed to Rice and his book, offered an amendment that included some of the wording of the report adopted by the Northwest Texas Conference but was more specific. It congratulated the church and SMU upon the announcement of Rice's resignation, expressed gratification that the board of trustees had accepted the resignation, and urged "the proper authorities" to eliminate books like Rice's from all required courses at Methodist schools. A motion to amend the amendment and strike the reference to Rice from the report was defeated after long discussion, and the conference adopted Tittle's amendment by a vote of 138–51. Even then the matter was not over. The next day a minister protested the action of the majority and asked permission to include his protest in the conference minutes, but the conference did not support his request.[41] These actions of the North Texas Conference, meeting three miles from SMU, made clear that a large majority of the conference had little understanding of or tolerance for higher biblical criticism.

The remaining annual conferences in Texas were more restrained. The Central Texas Conference, to which Rice had belonged in 1910–14, met in Cisco in early November and adopted without debate resolutions affirming its faith in the inspiration and authority of the Bible. Then, in late November, the Texas Conference, meeting in Houston, made no mention at all of the incident as it adopted the report of its board of education.[42] This may have been in part because the chair of that board was the deeply respected James Kilgore of the SMU School of Theology.

In contrast to the Texas annual conferences, the action of the Louisiana

Conference in early November explicitly affirmed Rice. He had joined that annual conference when he came to SMU in 1920. Rice attended the conference of 1921, and it adopted a report taking satisfaction at the improved "religious spirit" at SMU "under the preaching of Dr. John A. Rice" and others.[43] Soon thereafter Mouzon, presiding over the East Oklahoma Conference, appointed Rice to be pastor of First Methodist Church in Okmulgee, Oklahoma, a church comparable in size and prestige to those where he had previously been pastor.[44] A year later Bishop John M. Moore gave Rice a more prestigious appointment—to Boston Avenue Methodist Church in Tulsa, where he remained for several years. At that same annual conference Kern transferred his own conference membership from North Texas to East Oklahoma, probably reflecting his frustration at the actions of the North Texas Conference the previous year.[45]

The outcome of the controversy left Rice in relatively good condition, appointed to positions in which he continued to make a contribution to the church for the remainder of his life—he was sixty-seven when he died in 1930. On the other hand, SMU missed an opportunity to affirm biblical scholarship and defend academic freedom and instead succumbed to the protests of vocal, unfriendly, and ill-informed critics. The university's administration found itself at odds with its faculty and its student body, a problem that would reappear before long. In the Methodist conferences and churches of the region, fundamentalist voices would become less prominent in the next few years, reflecting the reduced strength of that movement and the increase in seminary-educated ministers.[46]

THE FACULTY REORGANIZATION CONTINUES

Meanwhile other changes were taking place within the faculty of the School of Theology (see appendix A). In September 1921 Jesse Cuninggim resigned to become president of Scarritt College, then located in Kansas City, Missouri (it moved to Nashville in 1924). Kern then nominated James Seehorn Seneker as professor of religious education; he was appointed and began his work at the School of Theology during that fall. Born in 1885, Seneker received his undergraduate degree from the University of Missouri in 1910 and his B.D. from Vanderbilt in 1912. After some time as a pastor, he did graduate work at Union Theological Seminary and Columbia

University, where he was influenced by the religious educator George Albert Coe. Seneker received his master's from Columbia in 1919 and taught at the School of Theology until his retirement in 1956.[47]

Also in the fall of 1921 Kern added a young man, Mims Thornburgh Workman, as an instructor in Hebrew and Greek, a position he held for two years. He was also an instructor in Bible at the college. Workman, born in Little Rock in 1895, had completed a master's in New Testament Greek at Emory University and was now a student in the B.D. program. After he completed his B.D. studies in 1922, he was promoted to the rank of associate professor of biblical history and literature at the college.[48]

After his part-year at the School of Theology early in 1921, Robert W. Goodloe spent a year at the University of Chicago, working on his doctoral degree in church history. In the fall of 1922 Kern brought him back to the School of Theology as associate professor of church history. Goodloe was born in 1888 in Burleson, Texas, and graduated from Polytechnic College in Fort Worth in 1912. When SMU opened in 1915, he entered the master's program in religion (not the bachelor of divinity program) and received his master's in 1916; he was president of the first graduating class. In 1918 he graduated from Yale Divinity School with a B.D., served briefly as an army chaplain in France during the war, and worked for two years as a schoolteacher and Methodist minister in southwest Oklahoma. After joining the theology faculty, he received his Ph.D. degree from the University of Chicago in 1929. Goodloe remained at the School of Theology until his retirement, officially in 1957, though effectively in 1956, when he went to teach in the Philippines for three years. Afterward he taught at Wesley Theological Seminary in Washington, D.C., Hendrix College in Arkansas, and Centenary College in Shreveport, Louisiana. He died in 1966.[49]

After Rice resigned in the fall of 1921, Kern hired E. W. Alderson, pastor of the Methodist church in Plano, to teach Old Testament part time for the remainder of the 1921–22 academic year.[50] Kern then chose John H. Hicks to be associate professor of Old Testament, beginning in the fall of 1922. Born in 1887 in Stephenville, Texas, Hicks received his bachelor's degree from Southwestern University, his B.D. from Vanderbilt, and was awarded his Ph.D. degree by the University of Chicago in 1933. In 1915 he returned from his studies in Chicago to the Northwest Texas

Conference, where he served pastoral appointments until 1922. Hicks was another Chicago-educated Old Testament professor; and, like Rice, he came to be highly appreciated by his students. Unlike Rice, Hicks's writings did not meet with external attacks. He continued on the faculty until his retirement in 1957 and thereafter taught at McMurry College in Abilene, Texas, until his death in 1963.[51]

The 1920 reorganization plan had called for James Kilgore to add Hoyt Dobbs's courses in Christian doctrine to his own specialty in the philosophy of religion. In 1921–22, however, Kern asked W. D. Bradfield, pastor of Grace Methodist Church in Dallas since 1918, to teach a course each term—Christian doctrine in the fall and winter, and the history of Methodism in the spring. He then nominated Bradfield as professor of Christian doctrine, beginning in the fall of 1922, and Bradfield was appointed. Born in Daingerfield, Texas, in 1866, Bradfield received his B.D. degree from Vanderbilt in 1892 and was pastor of several churches, some prestigious, in central Texas, Galveston, Austin, San Antonio, Dallas, and St. Louis. From 1915 to 1918 he was editor of the *Texas Christian Advocate*. While on the theology faculty, he completed his master's degree at the University of Chicago in 1928. Bradfield has been described as a man of robust and tenacious opinions who emphasized essentials in doctrine; he was also an ardent opponent of alcoholic beverages and race-track betting. Like Kilgore, he served on the SMU Board of Trustees, from 1914 to 1932, and during ten of those years he was also a member of the faculty. He retired in 1936 and died in 1947.[52]

In 1922 Kern began to develop a new aspect of the plan for faculty reorganization. Since 1920 the Board of Missions of the Methodist Episcopal Church, South, had paid the salaries of visiting professors of missions at the School of Theology. In early 1923 that board and the Woman's Missionary Council together agreed to appropriate $9,550 annually to the School of Theology so that it could enlarge its program of foreign and home missionary education.[53] That spring Kern announced that this expansion had begun in 1922 and that he had budgeted a $10,000 increase in salaries for 1923–24, for a total of $36,000. The plan initially was to have one faculty position in Oriental missions, another in Latin American and European missions, a third in the Department of Rural Work, and a fourth in the city church and evangelism. "This enlargement of our missionary program," Kern declared, "will give the School of Theology one of the best equipments for missionary training to be found anywhere in this country. It will enhance very greatly the appeal of the School to its constituency in the Church."[54]

In March 1923, however, J. Marvin Ormond resigned to return to North Carolina to teach rural sociology at Duke, where he remained until his retirement in 1948.[55] Since 1918 Comer Woodward had been splitting his appointment in sociology between the School of Theology and the college, and Kern recommended to the board that Woodward be appointed professor of rural work in the school's expanded missionary training program. The board did not act on this recommendation, and Woodward, who was originally from Georgia, left SMU in 1924 to take an administrative position at Emory University in Atlanta.[56] No one taught rural church work in 1923–24.

In the spring of 1924 Kern chose Ora Miner to be professor of town and country church beginning the following fall. Miner, a minister in the Methodist Episcopal Church, had held a small-town appointment in western Pennsylvania from 1912 to 1918, when he joined the faculty of Iliff School of Theology in Denver. In 1923–24, after a controversy arose between modernists and fundamentalists involving teachings at Iliff, two professors resigned from the seminary, one of whom was Miner. That led Kern to bring Miner to SMU. Kern arranged for Miner, whom he described as "a forceful and magnetic speaker," to present his subject at various annual conferences of Texas. Miner continued on the theology faculty until 1933. Thereafter the school had no faculty position in town and country church for several years; instead professors in related fields offered courses in that field.[57]

Also in 1924 Kern appointed J. Richard Spann to fill the other home missions vacancy as professor of city church. Spann received his master's degree from SMU in 1917 and his B.D. from the Theological School of Drew University in Madison, New Jersey, in 1918; that year he also married Mouzon's daughter, Julia. During the final months of World War I, Spann served as a navy chaplain, then did postgraduate work at Union Theological Seminary and Columbia University, and afterward held pastorates in Texas and Missouri. At the School of Theology, in addition to his teaching in the field of the city church, he was in charge of the students' field work and assisted the dean with promotion and extension work. In anticipation of his School of Theology duties, Spann spent three months in the summer of 1924 studying supervised field work in other seminaries and studying the church's programs in large cities. Like Ormond, he did not remain long at SMU, however. Spann left in 1927 and thereafter served various pastoral appointments, including seven years at First Methodist Church, Baton Rouge, and five at Laurel Heights, San Antonio. In his later years he was secretary of the Commission on Ministerial Training of The Methodist Church, with offices in Nashville. He retired in 1961 and died in 1976.[58]

Although the Board of Missions of the Methodist Episcopal Church, South, had filled the School of Theology's position in foreign missions since 1920 with various visiting personnel with experience overseas, it apparently did not send anyone to that position in 1923–24. For 1924–25 Kern arranged for the appointment of Henry G. Barnett, who had missionary experience in China, Japan, Calcutta, and Syria. Thereafter Barnett left to continue graduate study. Kern negotiated with the Board of Missions again for 1925–26 and obtained the services of J. T. Meyers, who had been a missionary in Japan for twenty-five years. After that year Meyers returned to Japan.[59]

Kern must have considered this year-to-year arrangement unsatisfactory, for he next appointed Alfred W. Wasson, who was willing to stay longer. Wasson came to the School of Theology in the fall of 1926 as professor of missions and also taught history of religions; he remained until 1934. Born in 1880, he received his B.D. from Vanderbilt in 1905 (he was a classmate of Kern's) and his master of sacred theology degree from Union Theological Seminary in New York in 1921. From 1905 until 1926 he was president of Union Methodist Theological Seminary in Seoul, Korea, and was held in high regard for his work in that post. In 1931, while at SMU, he earned his Ph.D. degree from the University of Chicago. In 1934 Wasson moved to a position with the Board of Missions of the Methodist Episcopal Church, South, and after the union of three Methodist branches in 1939 he continued in a similar position with the Board of Missions and Church Extension of The Methodist Church. After retiring from the board in 1950, he returned for several years as a visiting professor to what was by then named Perkins School of Theology.[60]

One other faculty appointment was made toward the end of Kern's deanship. In 1925 Harvie Branscomb resigned his position as professor of New Testament and joined the Duke University faculty. The SMU vacancy was filled by Charles McTyeire Bishop, a nephew of Horace Bishop, a Texas minister who had been instrumental in SMU's founding and for whom Bishop Boulevard on the SMU campus was named.

Charles Bishop was born in 1862 and educated at Emory and Henry College in Virginia. For more than twenty years he served as a pastor in North Carolina, Missouri, and Texas. From 1911 to 1922 he was president of Southwestern University, following Robert S. Hyer in that position. Bishop then served two brief pastorates in Houston and Oklahoma before coming to the theology faculty, where he remained until his retirement in 1934.[61]

Between 1920 and 1926 Paul Kern oversaw the almost complete restaffing of the School of Theology faculty. In doing so, he followed the reorganization plan worked out in 1920 and revised in light of later events. In the fall of 1926, after Kern's departure, the faculty numbered nine: Kilgore (acting dean), Bishop, Bradfield, Goodloe, Hicks, Miner, Seneker, Spann, and Wasson. This compared with seven in 1920, one of whom was on leave. With the help of the Board of Missions, Kern had increased the size of the faculty, though the increase was to prove temporary when funding from that source ceased. Kern's appointments resulted in a faculty that remained relatively stable for the next several years. Of the nine listed, only one soon left (Spann, in 1927); five stayed into the early- to mid-1930s (Bishop, Bradfield, Kilgore, Miner, and Wasson); and three remained until the mid-1950s (Goodloe, Hicks, and Seneker).

CHANGES IN THE CURRICULUM

When Kern became dean in 1920, the curriculum in force was the one adopted in 1916, with the added requirements and other minor modifications of 1918 and 1919. The 1920 plan for reorganization of the faculty brought a change in how the required courses were listed in the *Bulletin*, as the catalog was then called. For the first time the school listed nine departments: Christian doctrine, church history, ministerial efficiency, missions, New Testament, Old Testament, philosophy of religion, religious education, and sociology. Each department encompassed a field in which the school had a professor or for which there was a perceived need of an appointment. The next year, however, the *Bulletin* listed only eight departments: Christian doctrine and philosophy of religion had merged, as Kern had proposed in 1920.

More significant was that, beginning in 1920, the school had added two requirements for the B.D. degree. Each student now had to "prepare a dissertation upon an approved subject in his major department," the subject to be approved by that department at least one term before graduation. Furthermore, each student was to submit to an oral examination that would cover at least forty-five term hours of coursework. These requirements continued through the 1923–24 academic year.[62]

The reorganization of the faculty, with its program of foreign and home missionary education, meant that the B.D. curriculum needed to reflect these changes. During 1923–24 the faculty undertook a major revision that applied to students entering in the fall of 1924 and afterward. The goals of the new curriculum were twofold, intended to meet the needs of the church in a new day. The first was to ensure that students entering all forms of ministry received "instruction in certain fundamental subjects," so that they had "an introduction to the entire theological field." Of the ninety semester hours required for graduation (the whole university was now moving from the term to the semester system), all B.D. students were required to take fifty-seven hours of basic courses:

COURSE	SEMESTER HOURS
Old Testament	6
New Testament	6
Church history	6
Religious education	6
Christian doctrine	6
Philosophy of religion	6
Ministerial efficiency	6
Missions	6
Public speaking	3
Sociology	6

Some explanation is needed. The requirement in missions included two, three–semester-hour courses, "The History of Religions" and "The Science of Missions." The six semester hours in sociology included "Church and Society," a course that dealt with the church as a social organization and with Christian social teachings, and "The Church and Modern Social Problems." The requirement of a biblical language was eliminated.

The second goal of this curriculum was to provide "training for diversified and specialized forms of ministerial service." Beyond the basic requirements, students could specialize in any one of five forms of ministry:

> General pastorate
> Town and country church
> Social service and city work
> Foreign missions
> Religious education

Whatever form of ministry they chose, students had to complete fifty-seven semester hours of courses from that group; they also had to take three semester hours in public speaking, a two-semester-hour course in church music (both were taught by professors from other departments of the university), and in the last four groups, "supervised group courses to be selected" with the approval of the faculty head of that group. In the general pastorate group, the additional courses included six semester hours in Bible, three semester hours in Christian doctrine, three semester hours in homiletics (years later these would be called "distribution requirements"), three semester hours of supervised fieldwork, and thirteen semester hours of unrestricted electives. Beyond this pattern of courses, the new curriculum, as in 1920, required all B.D. students to write a dissertation and take an oral examination.[63]

The new emphasis of the School of Theology on foreign and home missionary education was reflected in three of the five groups. Alternatively, a student could opt for the general pastorate or specialize in religious education. For the first time, then, the B.D. curriculum of the school combined general theological education with specialization in one of several diverse forms of ministry.

In the fall of 1925 the School of Theology initiated a master's degree in church administration (M.C.A.). Spann, who had joined the faculty in 1924, gave special attention in his courses to church administration as well as to the city church, and he was probably the moving spirit behind the introduction of this program. Its purpose, as stated in the catalog, was "to prepare young men and young women for positions of executive leadership in local churches"—positions of director of religious education, director of young people's work, church secretary, church financial secretary, and church business manager. Like the B.D., it required a bachelor of arts degree from an approved college. The M.C.A. as adopted was to be a two-year degree, requiring thirty semester hours of work in the basic fields of theological study, followed by thirty additional semester hours, mostly in the city church and religious education, plus a thesis.[64]

When a committee brought the M.C.A. proposal before the theology faculty in April 1925, Kilgore proposed that the degree be given by the School of Theology, not by the graduate school, and the faculty accepted that proposal. Branscomb then urged that, along with special education in church administration, the school should provide graduate studies for workers in religious education. However, Seneker, professor of religious education, opposed offering a new degree, arguing that all special preparation should be provided through intensive study in the existing master of arts program. The consensus of the faculty differed with Seneker on this, maintaining that the intention of the M.C.A. was not intensive study but "a more general preparation, designed to meet the need of workers in the wide field of general administration of Church affairs." That interpretation prevailed in the faculty vote; Seneker voted against the proposal and "requested that the minutes record his vigorous protest."[65]

The School of Theology awarded its first M.C.A. degree on September 1, 1927, to Martha Miller Christopher—the first woman to receive a degree from the SMU School of Theology. From then through 1930 eleven students—ten women and one man—received the degree. After that the school awarded only one more M.C.A. degree, in 1938, though the *Bulletin* continued to list the degree through 1939–40.[66] The decline in students electing the program probably reflects Spann's departure in 1927 and a lesser interest in the degree by his eventual replacement.

For all the faculty's rationale and concern for diverse forms of ministry, in fall 1926 it abandoned its 1924 B.D. curriculum, dropping all the talk of preparation for diversified ministries, save for the M.C.A., which it retained. The 1926 B.D. required thirty "majors" for graduation; ten majors constituted an academic year's full load. Of these, sixteen majors and six "minors" were prescribed courses. Apparently, a minor met half as many hours per week and carried half the credit of a major. These requirements were distributed unevenly across the various theological fields; for example, four majors were required in New Testament, three in Old Testament, and one in church history. This distribution seems to have been intuitive, though the study committee reported as among its general principles that "there should be more courses required in Bible," and "there should be more freedom in elective courses." The

1926 curriculum retained the dissertation and oral examination requirements, and it reinstated the requirement of a biblical language for students majoring in Old or New Testament. "Majoring" appears to have meant taking six "majors" in one field.[67]

STUDENTS IN THE KERN YEARS

The 1920s saw an increase in the number of students enrolled in the School of Theology.[68] Until 1920 the number of graduate theological students each year had ranged from twenty to thirty-one, and the number of undergraduates taking School of Theology courses toward their undergraduate degree had ranged from thirteen to sixty. In the years of Kern's deanship these figures ranged from thirty-two to sixty-nine graduate theological students each year and from sixty to eighty undergraduates in School of Theology courses. The number of students receiving bachelor of divinity degrees increased correspondingly: between one and nine each year through 1919 and then between seven and sixteen in each of the Kern years. The number of pastors in the area taking extension courses rose sharply from the single digits in some years before 1920 to between twenty-nine and sixty in the early Kern years. After 1924 they fell again into the teens. Beginning in 1919 few students enrolled for a certificate in theology—often none and seldom more than one in any given year until 1950, when the school eliminated that option.

As the number of students increased, women became more numerous in School of Theology courses. Beginning in 1923, three to five women were enrolled for the B.D. degree each year, though none completed the program until after Kern's departure in 1926. Among undergraduates, significant numbers of women continued to take School of Theology courses in each of Kern's years as dean.

The School of Theology, like SMU generally, continued to recruit its students overwhelmingly from the region west of the Mississippi River and south of Kansas. Throughout the Kern years students from Texas made up a majority of those enrolled in the school, sometimes as much as 64 percent. Even so, that was not as high a proportion as before 1920. Several students also regularly enrolled from Arkansas and Missouri. In the twenties the school began to attract a few students each year from Mississippi and Tennessee and occasionally one or two from the Rocky Mountain and West Coast states.

A large proportion of the graduate theological students had received their undergraduate degrees from either SMU or Southwestern University. Each year from 1920 to 1926 graduates of these two institutions made up 40 to 50 percent of the School of Theology graduate student body; SMU grads outnumbered those from Southwestern almost two to one. Other colleges contributing significant numbers to School of Theology enrollment were Hendrix, the University of Texas, Henderson-Brown, Centenary, and Central in Missouri. As the Kern years wore on, the school increasingly drew students from a greater number of colleges both within and outside the region.

Beginning in 1921 a small number of international students came to constitute a new ingredient in the School of Theology's enrollment. In 1921 a U.S. citizen who had lived and worked for several years in Cuba, Benjamin O. Hill, who held a B.A. from Southwestern University, enrolled for the B.D. while he was a visiting professor in foreign missions at the school. Then, in 1922, Heiji Ito enrolled; his undergraduate degree was from Kwansei Gakuin University in Japan. He continued in 1923–24, and at the end of that academic year he received his B.D. degree and became the first international student to graduate from the SMU School of Theology. The academic year of 1923–24 also saw the enrollment of two students from Korea. One, Joon Ok Kim, received a certificate in theology in 1924. In the fall of 1924 another Japanese student enrolled. The next academic year saw a rise to seven internationals, one from Brazil and two each from China, Japan, and Korea. Perhaps some Asian students were attracted by theology faculty who had worked for years in East Asia and elsewhere. The School of Theology continued to be a regional school but not as narrowly so as before 1920.

Throughout this period Kern was constantly reminding the board of trustees of the need for better housing and more financial assistance for School of Theology students. In 1921 he told the board that of sixty-eight graduate and advanced (senior undergraduate) theological students, twenty-six were married. He reported that the school had purchased a building with apartments for eight couples, but "the need for another building is imperative." Forty-three students, he said, were either student pastors or pastors' assistants the previous year, and he asserted, "We could double our student body if we could give employment to those needing assistance." These problems continued throughout Kern's tenure as dean, and he pressed the board about them all that time.[69] In 1926 Moore, who then chaired the trustees' School of Theology committee, commented, "The students are not cared for as in other theological schools," with a dorm of their own and large scholarship funds.[70] Money was a constant problem both for the school and for its students. Deciding to go to seminary was financially risky.

THE APPOINTMENT OF CHARLES C. SELECMAN AS SMU PRESIDENT

In the midst of Kern's recruitment of a new School of Theology faculty, the General Conference of 1922 elected SMU's Hiram A. Boaz a bishop, and the College of Bishops assigned him to the Far East. On May 23 Judge Cockrell, the chair of the SMU board and its executive committee, appointed a committee of five to consider a list of those available for the position and to report to the board at the appropriate time. The committee consisted of Cockrell as chair, Bishop John M. Moore, Sam B. Perkins of Dallas (a businessman and the older brother of J. J. Perkins), R. Hall Shuttles of Dallas (a wholesale jeweler and a member of Highland Park Methodist Church), and Cullom Booth (presiding elder—the earlier title for a district superintendent—of the Methodists' Waco District).[71]

When Boaz left on July 19, the committee still had not agreed on a nominee to succeed him. Several names had come to the committee's attention, including that of Charles C. Selecman, the forceful and popular pastor of First Methodist Church, Dallas. Born in 1874, Selecman had attended but not graduated from Central College in Missouri, had done social service work in St. Louis, served in England and France with the YMCA in 1918, and been pastor of a church in Los Angeles before coming to the Dallas church in 1920.[72] During the summer of 1922 some Dallas pastors sent to a hundred or more Texas clergy a letter supporting the election of Selecman. At the urging of these Dallas pastors, four members of the committee met (Moore was out of the country) but were deadlocked 2–2—Shuttles and Perkins for Selecman, and Cockrell and Booth not ready to act. So they did not call a meeting of the board. Booth later explained, "To my mind, the fact that Dr. Selecman never finished his college course and holds no academic degree would be a very serious handicap to him. My judgment is that at this juncture we need a school man of proven ability. Then, too, I much prefer a layman, one who would make the building of a great university the supreme task of his life with no episcopal ambitions to divert his mind."[73]

On October 11 the board met and, after some vacillation, unanimously elected John Wynne Barton to be president of SMU. Barton, twenty-nine, had been a member of the original SMU faculty in 1915 in history and economics and later taught business administration. He also served as general manager of Shuttles's wholesale jewelry business. In May 1922 Barton was elected publishing agent of the Methodist Episcopal Church, South, and had recently moved to Nashville to assume that position.[74] The board asked Barton to take office no later than June 1923. To lead the university in the interim they chose James Kilgore as acting president.[75]

In 1915 James Kilgore had been an original member of the School of Theology faculty, teaching the psychology and philosophy of religion. Before that he had been a pastor in the Texas Conference, presiding elder of the Houston District, and a member of the Commission on Education that established SMU in 1911. He held bachelor's and master's degrees from Southwestern University and a master's degree from the University of Chicago. When Dean Dobbs was ill from late 1919 to early 1920, Kilgore had chaired the theology faculty until the dean was able to return. Later, from 1926 to 1933, Kilgore was acting dean of the School of Theology, and he was a member of the SMU Board of Trustees from 1911 until his death in 1950. Why he was chosen as acting president is suggested by what Selecman wrote about Kilgore after his death: "He was a man whose sturdy moral integrity, solid judgment and breadth of spirit eminently fitted him for distinguished usefulness in guiding and giving shape to a new institution, struggling with financial difficulties and educational problems. Recently the writer has been told that the younger professors in the institution looked to him for guidance and leaned upon his sane judgment and loyal friendship."[76] Here was someone who, though not chosen to shape the university in the long term, could provide steady leadership in the interim.

Meanwhile the board awaited word from John Wynne Barton. The board, however, had not consulted Barton before selecting him. He replied to its telegram, "I can hardly see how I can accept. I shall write you more fully when the letter referred to in your telegram is received." He did not write until December, and when he did, he declined the office, not a surprising response under the circumstances. After failing to attract Barton to the position, Cockrell wrote Ivan Lee Holt, then a pastor in St. Louis, to offer him the position, but Holt also declined.[77]

The board took no official action until the spring of 1923, and James Kilgore continued to carry out the duties of the presidency. The executive committee called a meeting of the board for March 21 and that morning unanimously elected Charles C. Selecman president on the first ballot, despite his limited formal education and his lack of experience in university administration. That afternoon Selecman accepted the position. Mary M. H. Thomas, in her history of the early SMU years, observes, "The faculty probably viewed his election with skepticism."[78] He was president from April 2, 1923, to September 1, 1938, far longer than either of his predecessors. In May 1938 Selecman was elected a bishop at the last general conference of the Methodist Episcopal Church, South.

Among its other actions on the day Kilgore stepped down, the SMU board formally received a letter from forty-eight faculty of the university expressing confidence in the way James Kilgore had handled university problems as acting president.[79]

KIRBY HALL

A few days after the election of Selecman as president of SMU, R. Harper Kirby and his wife, Annie, residents of Austin, paid a quiet visit to the SMU campus. On Monday, March 26, 1923, they made a gift of $100,000 to SMU, to be used to erect a building for the School of Theology. Since SMU opened, the School of Theology had had its quarters in the east wing of the third floor of Dallas Hall, along with most of the School of Music. That arrangement meant that adding someone to either faculty was a mixed blessing, for that only made things more cramped. Now the School of Theology would have a building that would, in Kern's words, "give material evidence of the dignity and importance of ministerial education."[80]

Years earlier Kirby had given up the practice of law and other fields for which he had studied and had gone into business—farming, ranching, timber, and oil. In all these he had been successful. For years he and Annie had been giving their money to support hundreds of churches in Texas. In each of the previous two years they had given the School of Theology $5,000 to be used as a loan fund for its students. Why were they giving this far larger sum to SMU now? W. D. Bradfield had been the Kirbys' pastor and close friend in Austin, and he and Harper Kirby had worked together for prohibition of alcoholic beverages and also sought to outlaw gambling and horse racing in Texas. The Kirbys were pleased that Bradfield was now a member of the theology faculty and that Selecman was the new president. They wanted their money "permanently invested in the cause of humanity and the Church," and they had high hopes for the future of the university.[81]

In May, Selecman appointed a building committee, and in June the executive committee approved a site for the new building—Harper and Annie Kirby Hall (the building that in the 1950s became Florence Hall in the Law School Quadrangle)—to the west of Dallas Hall. At the same time the executive committee limited the total cost of the building and its furnishings to $150,000. Construction began early in 1924, and the School of Theology moved into its new quarters that fall. Kirby Hall housed the School of Theology administration, faculty offices, classrooms, a small chapel, and—of great importance—the theological library. For the first time the theological holdings of the library were separated from the general university library in Dallas Hall. Kate Warnick, who had worked as assistant to the university librarian, Dorothy Amman, since 1918, now became the first librarian of the School of Theology. Moving the books was not easy. In December Warnick sent a three-by-five card to Kern with this message: "It seems that things are at a stand-still about bringing over the Theological books, until you can meet with the Library Committee to arrange some things."[82] Kern acted, and the books were moved.

The Kirbys' donation was by far the largest single gift to the School of Theology to that time. In addition to providing greatly enlarged quarters, the gift boosted the morale of everyone affiliated with the school. Yet even before the completion of Kirby Hall, Dean Kern presented the board with a list of "outstanding needs": a dormitory for the graduate ministerial students at a cost he estimated at $150,000; a chapel and library building ($100,000); an endowment for a fellowship for the best senior student each year ($10,000); twenty or more endowed scholarships ($2,500 each); and a substantial increase in loan funds.[83] His wish list accurately reflected the school's needs, although the prospects were dim. Two decades later Kirby Hall continued to house the entire School of Theology.

THE WORKMAN-BRANSCOMB INCIDENT

Soon after Selecman became president of SMU, a conflict about an SMU Bible professor developed that eventually had repercussions for the School of Theology faculty.

In 1922, after Mims Thornburgh Workman completed his B.D. degree, he became an associate professor of biblical history and literature in the college and no longer taught language in the School of Theology.[84] In May 1923 J. Frank Norris, the fundamentalist pastor of First Baptist Church, Fort Worth, who had ignited the controversy that had driven Rice off, hosted a meeting of the World Christian Fundamentals Association. The meeting featured attacks on SMU, as well as on Southwestern University and Texas Women's College, by some students from these institutions. A student of Workman's in the SMU College, Margaret Pilley, the daughter of missionaries to China, protested that Workman had called the first eleven chapters of Genesis myths and had questioned Christ's bodily resurrection. She dropped the course, fearing her faith would be shaken.[85] To the surprise of many, as reported by some SMU faculty and students who were present, an attorney rose to challenge the proceedings, saying, "If I were to attempt to convict a man for heresy, I would get testimony from his finished product, not from a little foreign born freshman who had sat in only two classes." At that, many of those present broke into applause. The attacks at that meeting subsided.[86]

Back at SMU, others, including an editorial writer for the *Daily Campus*, Charles W. Ferguson, defended Workman and SMU.[87] When the charges came to the attention of members of the SMU board, however, it asked Bishop Moore and Selecman to confer with Workman and advise him. The board then left the matter of his appointment to the president and the executive committee, and no action was taken at that time.[88]

In the spring of 1925, however, Workman again became the focus of outside criticisms. In early May, Selecman received complaints about comments Workman had made a month earlier at a meeting of Methodist ministers and workers at Grace Methodist Church. Selecman referred the matter to Dean Jennings of the college, who reported that he talked with Workman and advised him confidentially to take a leave of absence until the criticisms died down. Workman then made the mistake of telling his students the content of the dean's confidential discussion, and the students protested vigorously to the administration on his behalf. That was enough to seal his fate. Selecman referred the matter to the board of trustees, which terminated Workman's employment, not, they said, because of outside criticisms of him but because he had criticized the university administration in class and had said things that led to further such criticism from the student body. That, the trustees' statement said, was reprehensible.[89]

Nor was this all. On May 29 the university faculty unanimously adopted a resolution stating, "We as a faculty express our confidence in the administration this year."[90] The *Dallas Morning News* reported that action as expressing complete approval of the administration's policies. Thereafter Harvie Branscomb, of the theology faculty, sent a statement to the *News* in which he said the resolution should have been interpreted as expressing appreciation for "the happy and successful year under his administration" and "our confidence in Dr. Selecman personally." Branscomb went on to say that while he personally had voted for the resolution and would do so again, "I certainly did not mean by such a vote an indorsement [*sic*] of every policy that the administration might pursue, and particularly of its policy in the case of Mr. Workman." Branscomb said he opposed any effort to dismiss Workman, and added: "If faculty members of good training, acknowledged orthodoxy and wholesome influence are to be discharged because of the no doubt sincere objections of those outside the university who misunderstand them, I see little hope of building here in S.M.U. the spirit necessary to a great university. . . . But this difference of viewpoint, if it be a difference, does not mean that I do not appreciate the great work of Dr. Selecman along many lines during the last year. Nor, on the contrary, does that appreciation, expressed by formal vote of the faculty, mean approval of every administrative policy."[91]

The next morning, when Selecman read this statement in the paper, he telephoned Branscomb and, Branscomb said, told him, "'I have just read your gratuitous letter in the *Morning News* and want to say to you that the sooner you leave this campus the better.'"[92] The following day Branscomb resigned his faculty position, saying that he had been offered a professorship at Duke University.[93] He subsequently joined the faculty of the Duke University Divinity School.

When one considers both Workman's actions and Branscomb's carefully worded mixture of appreciation for Selecman and refusal to give his policies an unqualified endorsement, it is difficult not to conclude that Selecman was allergic to criticism of any kind. And he deeply disliked controversy.[94]

In July 1925 Selecman presented to the executive committee of the board the name of Charles McTyeire Bishop for the faculty position in New Testament that Branscomb had vacated, and Bishop was appointed.[95]

KERN'S DEPARTURE

For six years Paul Kern carried a heavy load as dean of the School of Theology. He was both "internal" and "external" dean, as the terms were sometimes used years later. Internally, he recruited virtually an entire new faculty, oversaw their work, traveled widely to recruit students, dealt with individual student cases, drew up and administered the School of Theology budget, supervised the curriculum and its workings, and saw to the physical facilities, both in Dallas Hall and afterward in Kirby Hall. Externally, he represented the school to the board of trustees, to the General Conference, often to the annual conferences of the Methodist Episcopal Church, South, and to various church agencies. He was the person most responsible for raising money for the school, and he was its chief public relations officer in the churches, the City of Dallas, and around the region.

That he found this load burdensome is suggested by a portion of his report to the board in June 1925 that he prepared but did not include in his presentation. There is need, he wrote, for a dean of students, to remove from the dean's work "such details as registration, courses of study, candidacy for degrees, individual academic problems of students, et cetera."[96] No dean of students was appointed, but beginning in 1925 the School of Theology had its own registrar, who undoubtedly relieved Kern of some of these details. In May 1926 the administration of the school consisted of Kern, Warnick as librarian, Nell Anders as registrar (she served in that post from 1926 to 1960), and two secretaries.[97]

Kern did his work with energy, initiative, and commitment to ministerial education. He kept before the students the vision of an effective, educated ministry. Kenneth Pope reports that once as a student in the School of Theology he

> went to Dean Paul B. Kern . . . and expressed a desire to quit school in order to get to the firing line at once. The Dean said a word or two about the need for an adequate foundation for the ministry and then told me of a student who, like myself, wanted to quit school and start preaching. His advisor said that if the

student would tell him where he, the student, would be preaching on Sunday, he, the advisor, would go out and preach for him if he would stay in school. The Lord gave me sense enough to take Dean Kern's advice.[98]

Kern was the moving force behind the reorganization of the theology faculty and in particular the creation of the program of missionary training. During his deanship the faculty adopted the creative new curriculum of 1924, even though it abandoned it two years later. In his reports to the board he constantly extolled the work of the faculty and sought better conditions for the students. While he was dean, the school received a major improvement in its physical facilities and in its morale in the gift of Kirby Hall. On his watch the annual income of the school increased by about 50 percent, from $36,200 in 1920–21 to $54,345 projected for 1926–27.[99] The School of Theology in 1926 was in far stronger condition than when he became dean in 1920.

In addition to the usual burdens of his administrative work, Kern in his last year as dean was under considerable stress. This may well have reflected both Selecman's recent dismissal of Harvie Branscomb and the inquiry of a West Texas Annual Conference committee in 1925–26 into whether the beliefs of theology faculty members were in accordance with Methodist doctrine. The committee's eventual report was supportive of the faculty, but Kern knew that he and the faculty were much more liberal theologically than many others in Texas Methodism.[100]

Kern called a meeting of the School of Theology faculty for June 30, 1926, and announced his intention to resign as dean and return to the pastorate. Two weeks later he presented his resignation to the executive committee of the board, effective September 1. Upon Kern's resignation Selecman designated James Kilgore as the acting dean. In October, Kern was appointed pastor of Travis Park Methodist Church in San Antonio, which that fall reported 3,062 members and a pastoral salary of $7,500. (Kern's most recent salary as dean had been $4,200.) After four years at Travis Park he was elected a bishop by the General Conference of 1930 and assigned to Asia for four years, the usual practice at the time. Afterward he returned to oversee annual conferences in the Carolinas and then from 1938 to 1952 the conferences in Tennessee. He was seventy-one when he died in 1953.[101]

1. *Who Was Who in America* (Chicago: A. N. Marquis, 1960), 3:472–73; *Who Was Who in America* (Chicago: A. N. Marquis, 1943), 1:670.
2. Hiram Abiff Boaz, *Eighty-four Golden Years: An Autobiography of Bishop Hiram Abiff Boaz* (Nashville, Tenn.: Parthenon, 1951), 103–107; Mary Martha Hosford Thomas, *Southern Methodist University: Founding and Early Years* (Dallas: Southern Methodist University Press, 1974), 77–79.
3. Board of trustees minutes, June 9, 1924, as cited in Thomas, *Southern Methodist University*, 80.
4. Boaz, *Eighty-four Golden Years*, 106–12; *Daily Campus*, April 20, 1922; Thomas, *Southern Methodist University*, 85–91.
5. Boaz, *Eighty-four Golden Years*, 113–14.
6. Board of trustees minutes, June 12, 1920.
7. Ibid., June 9, 1924.
8. *Minutes of the Annual Conferences of the Methodist Episcopal Church, South*, 1930, 194–95; board of trustees minutes, June 12, 1920.
9. Faculty minutes, September 26, 1919; see chap. 1.
10. Board of trustees minutes, February 21, 1920.
11. Ibid., June 12, 1920.
12. Faculty minutes, October 1 and 14, 1920, November 26, 1920, and February 8, 1921.
13. Board of trustees minutes, June 12, 1920.
14. Executive committee minutes, November 2, 1920; Board of trustees minutes, June 13, 1921.
15. Board of trustees minutes, June 13, 1921.
16. Ibid. and June 12, 1923; SMU *Bulletin*, 1922–23, 123, and 1923–24, 135.
17. Board of trustees minutes, June 13, 1921; *Duke Divinity School Bulletin* 19, no. 3 (November 1954): 62–64.
18. John A. Rice, *The Old Testament in the Life of Today* (New York: Macmillan, 1920).
19. *Campus*, December 8, 1920.
20. Rice, *Old Testament*, vii–viii.
21. J. L. Neill, review of John A. Rice's *The Old Testament in the Life of Today* in *Methodist [MECS] Review* 70, no. 1 (January, 1921): 170–72.
22. Robert W. Rogers, review of John A. Rice's *The Old Testament in the Life of Today*, *Methodist [MEC] Review* 94 (May 1921): 472–74.
23. S. A. Steel, "From the Pelican Pines," *Texas Christian Advocate*, April 14, 1921, 7.
24. A. J. Weeks, "The Methodist Church Can Look after Its Own Business," *Texas Christian Advocate*, June 9, 1921, 8.
25. "Criticism of Dr. Rice's Book," *Texas Christian Advocate*, Oct. 6, 1921, p. 8.
26. *Texas Christian Advocate*, July 7, 3; July 14, 3; August 4, 3; August 4, 8; September 8, 2; September 15, 2–3; October 6, 1921, 12–13.
27. *Texas Christian Advocate*, August 11, 2–3; August 18, 3; September 1, 12; October 6, 1921, 12.
28. Edwin D. Mouzon, "John A. Rice and His Book, 'The Old Testament in the Life of Today,'" *Texas Christian Advocate*, July 28, 1921, 8.
29. See Barry Hankins, *God's Rascal: J. Frank Norris and the Beginnings of Southern Fundamentalism* (Lexington: University of Kentucky Press, 1996), chaps. 1 and 2.
30. Robert Sledge, *Hands on the Ark: The Struggle for Change in the Methodist Episcopal Church, South, 1914–1939* (Lake Junaluska, N.C.: Commission on Archives and History, The United Methodist Church, 1975), 145n56, cites Paul B. Kern to Warren A. Candler, letter, June 1, 1921, in the Candler Collection, Main Library, Emory University. See also Boaz, *Eighty-four Golden Years*, 110.
31. "Dr. Rice and the Bible," *Texas Christian Advocate*, Sept. 22, 1921, p. 8.
32. Boaz, *Eighty-four Golden Years*, p. 111; Executive Committee minutes, October 3, 1921.
33. Executive committee minutes, October 4, 1921.
34. Ibid.
35. Boaz, *Eighty-four Golden Years*, 111.
36. Faculty minutes, January 13, 1922.
37. Executive committee minutes, October 11, 1921.

38. *Dallas Morning News*, October 7, 1921, 2.
39. Ibid.
40. *Texas Christian Advocate*, October 20, 1921, 13; *Texas Christian Advocate*, October 27, 1921, 5.
41. *Minutes of the Fifty-fifth Annual Session of the North Texas Annual Conference of the Methodist Episcopal Church, South*, edited and published by R. G. Mood and C. W. Dennis (no place, no date), October 26–31, 1921, 33–34, 58–59. Hereinafter citations to annual conference minutes, annuals, and journals will include the name of the annual conference, the denomination, the year, and the pages. Journals cited that were published from 1939 to 1967 are of annual conferences of The Methodist Church, and those published in 1968 and after are of annual conferences of The United Methodist Church, unless otherwise specified.
42. *Texas Christian Advocate*, November 17, 4, and November 24, 1921, 1, 4.
43. *Annual of the Louisiana Conference of the Methodist Episcopal Church, South, Seventy-sixth Session*, November 9–13, 1921, 32–33.
44. *Daily Campus*, November 16, 1921, 1; *Texas Christian Advocate*, November 17, 1921, 8.
45. *Minutes of the Annual Conferences of the Methodist Episcopal Church, South, for the Year 1922*, 270, 274.
46. See Norman F. Furniss, *The Fundamentalist Controversy, 1918–1931* (New Haven, Conn.: Yale University Press, 1954).
47. J. L. Cuninggim to Paul B. Kern, September 9, 1921, in the faculty minutes for that date; executive committee minutes, September 19, 1921; Lewis Howard Grimes, *A History of Perkins School of Theology*, edited by Roger Loyd (Dallas: Southern Methodist University Press, 1993), 68.
48. *Who's Who in Methodism* (Chicago: A. N. Marquis, 1952), 764; Walter N. Vernon, *Methodism Moves across North Texas* (Dallas: Historical Society, North Texas Conference, The Methodist Church, 1967), 283; SMU *Bulletin*, 1921, 20, 117; 1922, 18, 123; 1923, 18; 1924, 19.
49. Executive committee minutes, April 14, 1922; William H. Dickinson Jr., obituary of Robert W. Goodloe, *Journal of the Central Texas Conference of The Methodist Church*, 1967, 207–208; SMU *Bulletin*, 1921, 117, and 1922, 123; Robert W. Goodloe Jr., interview by author, March 28, 2007, Dallas.
50. Board of trustees minutes, May 2, 1922.
51. *Journal of the Northwest Texas Annual Conference of The Methodist Church*, 1964, 148.
52. Board of trustees minutes, June 13, 1921; faculty minutes, February 17 and September 19, 1922; executive committee minutes, September 30, 1922; board of trustees minutes, June 1–2, 1936; John M. Moore, obituary of W. D. Bradfield, *Journal of the North Texas Conference of The Methodist Church*, 1948, 86–87.
53. Public records vary as to the amount these organizations agreed to contribute: one said $10,000 a year (*Daily Campus*, May 9, 1923), another $9,550 (board of trustees minutes, June 12, 1923); a later board resolution spoke of $8,700 (board of trustees minutes, February 26, 1929). The actual amount contributed also varied (see board of trustees minutes, June 9, 1924, June 1–2, 1925, and June 4, 1926).
54. Faculty minutes, January 3 and February 28, 1923; board of trustees minutes, June 12, 1923.
55. *Duke Divinity School Bulletin* 19, no. 3 (November 1954): 59–64.
56. Board of trustees minutes, June 12, 1923.
57. Executive committee minutes, February 11, 1924; *Fall Minutes of the Annual Conferences of the Methodist Episcopal Church* (New York: Methodist Book Concern, 1912–24); SMU *Bulletins*, 1924–33; *Dallas Morning News*, May 21, 1924, 14; Paul Kern to D. E. Hawk and E. R. Barcus, October 11, 1924; Paul Kern to P. R. Knickerbocker and E. L. Egger, October 11, 1924, Paul Kern Papers, Bridwell Library.
58. Board of trustees minutes, June 9, 1924; *Encyclopedia of World Methodism*, edited by Nolan B. Harmon (Nashville, Tenn.: United Methodist Publishing House, 1974), 2:2222; SMU *Bulletins*, 1924–26.
59. Board of trustees minutes, June 9, 1924; June 1-2, 1925; and June 4, 1926.
60. *Who's Who in Methodism*, 1952, 722; SMU *Bulletins*, 1926–33, 1950–53.

61. *Dallas Morning News*, July 24, 1925; Charles Bishop, obituary, *Central Texas Conference Journal*, 1950, 124–25.
62. SMU *Bulletin*, June, 1920, 112–13; April, 1921, 130–43; and 1923, 145–46.
63. Ibid., 1924, 155–57.
64. Ibid., 1925, 161; attachment to the faculty minutes, April 30, 1925; *Bulletin*, 1926, 169.
65. Faculty minutes, April 30, 1925.
66. SMU commencement programs, September 1, 1927, and afterward (Registrar's Office, Perkins School of Theology).
67. SMU *Bulletin*, 1926, 168–69; faculty minutes, March 3 and 5, 1926.
68. Enrollment data are drawn from the annual catalogs (variously named) of the School of Theology, supplemented by reports of the dean recorded in the board minutes for each spring meeting, although these reports for different years are not always comparable and not always presented in terms consistent with data from the annual catalogs. Graduation data come from the annual commencement programs, frequently corrected in ink by Nell Anders, the School of Theology registrar for thirty-four years and a stickler for accuracy.
69. Board of trustees minutes, June 12, 1920; June 13, 1921; May 5, 1922; June 9, 1924; June 4, 1926.
70. Ibid., June 4, 1926.
71. Executive committee minutes, May 23, 1922.
72. *Who Was Who in America*, 3:772.
73. Cullom H. Booth to Edwin D. Mouzon, September 6, 1922, Edwin D. Mouzon Papers, Bridwell Library.
74. Board of trustees minutes, October 11, 1922; *Texas Christian Advocate*, May 18 and October 19, 1922; SMU *Bulletin*, 1916, 9, and 1922, 15; *Daily Campus*, October 14, 1922.
75. Board of trustees minutes, October 11, 1922.
76. *Texas Annual Conference Journal*, 1951, 114.
77. *Daily Campus*, October 20, 1922; board of trustees minutes, December 19, 1922; "Early Years at S.M.U.: Recollections of Bishop Ivan Lee Holt," n.d., 9, Ivan Lee Holt Papers, DeGolyer Library archives, SMU.
78. Executive committee minutes, March 10, 1923; board of trustees minutes, March 21, 1923; Thomas, *Southern Methodist University*, 85.
79. Board of trustees minutes, March 21, 1923.
80. Ibid., May 2, 1922, and June 12, 1923.
81. *Texas Christian Advocate*, March 29, 1933, 4–5; board of trustees minutes, June 12, 1923.
82. Faculty minutes, March 29, November 12, and December 3, 1923; executive committee minutes, May 8, 1923; June 2, 1923; board of trustees minutes, June 9, 1924; Grimes, *A History of Perkins School of Theology*, 31, 33; Kate Warnick to Kern, December 13, 1924, Kern Papers.
83. Board of trustees minutes, June 9, 1924.
84. Vernon, *Methodism Moves across North Texas*, 283; SMU *Bulletin*, 1921, 20, 117; 1922, 18, 123; 1923, 18; 1924, 19.
85. Furniss, *Fundamentalist Controversy*, 52–53; Vernon, *Methodism Moves*, 281–83; *Daily Campus*, May 5 and November 28, 1923.
86. Forest E. Dudley to Walter N. Vernon, July 18, 1966, cited in Vernon, *Methodism Moves*, 283. Vernon reports that in 1922–23 Dudley was a student assistant to Workman.
87. *Daily Campus*, May 5, 1923.
88. *Dallas Times Herald*, May 7, 1925, as cited in Thomas, *Southern Methodist University*, pp. 100, 202n121; Board of Trustees minutes, June 12, 1923.
89. *Dallas Morning News*, May 6, May 7, and June 3, 1925; board of trustees minutes, June 2, 1925.
90. Thomas, *Southern Methodist University*, 102, citing minutes of the general faculty, May 29, 1925, and *Dallas Morning News*, May 30, 1925.
91. *Dallas Morning News*, June 1, 1925.
92. Thomas, *Southern Methodist University*, 202n140, citing a letter to her from Harvie Branscomb, April 7, 1971.

93. *Dallas Morning News*, June 3, 1925.

94. Later occasions reflected a similar reaction to criticism and controversy. See, for example, board of trustees minutes, June 7, 1927 (against criticisms made in a student publication); and June 4, 1928 ("There has been a noticeable and commendable absence of radical student leaders on our Campus this year").

95. Executive committee minutes, July 14, 1925.

96. Board of trustees minutes, June 1, 1925. A typed line was later added at this point in the minutes: "Two preceding paragraphs deleted before reading—not official."

97. SMU *Bulletin*, May, 1926, 157.

98. W. Kenneth Pope, *A Pope at Roam: The Confessions of a Bishop* (Nashville, Tenn.: Parthenon, 1976), 46.

99. Board of trustees minutes, June 12, 1920, and June 4, 1926.

100. Katherine Kern Buckner (Kern's daughter), letter to author, August 13, 2008. She thought that her father's departure was connected with both the Branscomb incident and conservatism in the church.

101. Faculty minutes, June 30, 1926; executive committee minutes, July 15, 1926; *Minutes, Annual Conferences of the Methodist Episcopal Church, South*, 1926, edited by C. B. Haley (Nashville, Tenn.: Methodist Episcopal Church, n.d.), 214; board of trustees minutes, June 1, 1925; *Who Was Who in America*, 3:472–73.

Years of Struggle, 1926–1938

For the SMU School of Theology the years from 1926 to 1938 were a time of trying to hold on to past achievements. The difficulties included delay in naming a dean, questions about the administration of President Selecman, and finances. The selection of a dean was not accomplished until the appointment of Dr. Eugene B. Hawk in 1933, but the difficulties of the Selecman presidency remained until he was elected a bishop in 1938. From 1930 the School of Theology and the whole university suffered along with the rest of the country from the economic hardships of the Great Depression.

In the early 1930s the faculty positions in town and country church and urban church were eliminated to save money. Even so, Hawk made some enduring faculty appointments, oversaw a curriculum revision, and initiated Ministers' Week. After a decline in enrollment in the depths of the Depression, the size of the student body rebounded. But mostly this was a time of struggle to maintain the status quo. In 1938 the School of Theology was not much different from what it had been in 1926: it had a small faculty, a primarily regional appeal, modest sources of income, crowded quarters in Kirby Hall, and the likelihood that these conditions would continue.

SEEKING A REPLACEMENT FOR PAUL KERN

Paul Kern's departure in 1926 created two vacancies: the deanship and a faculty position in religious efficiency—more specifically, homiletics. Kern had resigned effective September 1, and the university did not attempt to fill either vacancy until the following summer. On July 1, 1927, James Kilgore, the acting dean, wrote to William C. Martin, pastor of the First Methodist Church of Port Arthur, Texas: "Dear Bro. Martin: I want to see you and talk over some matters with you—of importance to this institution and may affect you personally. Please let me know when I could find you at home, and I will run down and spend a day or two with you. An immediate answer will be appreciated."[1]

Martin had been Kilgore's student in philosophy of religion when Martin was studying at the School of Theology for his B.D. degree, which he received in 1921. Martin had then served four years as pastor of Grace Methodist Church in Houston and was now in his second year in Port Arthur. He had an outstanding record in seminary, and his work as a young pastor at both churches had been impressive.[2] Kilgore knew him well and expected a great future for him.

In the summer of 1927 J. Richard Spann, professor of church administration and city church, also left the School of Theology, creating another faculty vacancy. This gave Kilgore more leeway to offer Martin a faculty post in fields in which Kern and Spann had taught—homiletics and church administration. A few days later Martin wrote Kilgore a backhanded acceptance, saying that he had "not been able to find sufficient grounds for refusing to accept," and giving him permission to present his name to the board of trustees for appointment.[3]

Martin, though, soon had second thoughts. On August 10 he wrote Kilgore to say he had been too hasty in accepting his offer and to ask for more time to think about it. Surprised, Kilgore tried to reassure Martin and urged him to stick with his decision.[4] As Martin thought about it further, he wrote various people for advice, including Paul Kern, his former dean and now colleague in the pastorate. Kern replied confidentially that though he had no doubt Martin could ably fill the position and would be well received, he should weigh other considerations. The deanship remained unfilled, and the dean would want to teach. Which courses? Probably homiletics or church administration, and that would put Martin in an uncomfortable position. Kern advised Martin to teach Christian doctrine, the field in which he had done his best work anyway. Kern also warned him that much that was happening in the university administration was almost heartbreaking. This was, Kern said, a large part of why he left and the main reason Spann left. The School of Theology did not have these problems, but he despaired at the atmosphere in the rest of the university.[5]

A few days later Martin wrote Kilgore his "final reply" to the offer. The more he considered it, Martin explained, the more certain he became that accepting was not best for him or best for the school. He was not a scholar, he added, and his experience was too limited for the position offered. That reply angered Kilgore; he upbraided Martin and proposed to go to Port Arthur to talk with him further.[6] More correspondence followed, but Martin remained convinced that he belonged in the pastorate, not the academic world, at least for now.

This was only the first in a series of efforts by the university over several years to hire Will Martin. The question arose again in 1928, when he was offered not simply a position on the faculty but the deanship. Could he come as associate dean until he learned the work and could assume the deanship? Alternatively, or additionally, could he teach ministerial efficiency?[7] Both Selecman and Kilgore, sometimes in concert and sometimes at cross-purposes, kept coming back to Martin, and Martin kept wavering but ultimately sticking to his contention that the pastorate was his calling. He would come in 1929, he said, but in the fall of 1928 he was offered the pastorate of First Church, Little Rock, and he went there. In early 1929 Martin learned that SMU had offered the deanship to Forney Hutchinson, long-time pastor of St. Luke Methodist Church in Oklahoma City, but Hutchinson had declined. In May 1929 Bishop John M. Moore formally offered Martin the deanship on SMU's behalf. Martin asked that the appointment be delayed until after annual conference in November, but by then his bishop (Boaz) wanted him to stay until after General Conference in May 1930. And so it went. Martin finally left Little Rock in November 1931, but he went to the pastorate of First Methodist Church, Dallas, not to SMU.

As a result of these futile discussions, Kilgore remained acting dean with no idea from year to year how long the university would need his services in that post.

When Selecman looked for a dean for the School of Theology, he considered able pastors, preferably of prestigious pulpits in the Southwest. Martin had early shown his ministerial ability and was moving up rapidly. Hutchinson had been pastor at St. Luke for ten years when he was approached. One of Selecman's close friends among Texas pastors was Eugene Blake Hawk, a member of the Central Texas Conference. Born in 1881, Hawk received his bachelor's degree from Emory and Henry College in Virginia and his B.D. from Vanderbilt. After several pastorates in the Central Texas Conference and three years as a presiding elder, in 1925 he was appointed to First Methodist Church, Fort Worth, where he remained until 1931. While Hawk was at First Church, SMU conferred on him the honorary degree of doctor of divinity. Hawk next was appointed to the pastorate of a large church in Louisville, Kentucky, where he was serving when Selecman nominated him in June 1933 to be dean of the School of Theology. The board of trustees duly elected Hawk, and he assumed the office that September.[8] Hawk also came as professor of homiletics, thus filling both the deanship and Kern's teaching specialty.

THE SELECMAN PRESIDENCY IN THE KILGORE YEARS

The SMU president supervises the administrative structure within which the School of Theology carries on its work. The president nominates deans and new faculty to the board, proposes reappointments and promotions, oversees the university budget (including that of the School of Theology) and its fund-raising, is the chief face of the university to the wider public, and voices the purposes and standards of the university. The School of Theology operated within the opportunities and limits provided by the administration of the university president.

In Selecman's case the university faculty had initially been skeptical of a president who did not have a college degree. Skepticism deepened into opposition on the part of many after Selecman's treatment of M. T. Workman in 1925 and the summary dismissal of Harvie Branscomb for stating publicly a nuanced and discriminating stance toward the president's policies.

Selecman's hypersensitivity to criticism erupted again in 1927 in an incident that involved the SMU yearbook, *The Rotunda*. That year the editors dedicated the yearbook to Selecman, writing what they intended as humorous needling: "President Chas. Selecman and Dr. Geiser of the Biology Department have both made a determined race this year for Saddle Burr dedication by their infamous actions around the campus. We are familiar with the high-handed methods of Prexy in running the school and all its occupants by his big stick policy. We have all heard and seen him enter Chapel (ha! ha! ha! etc.) in that MODEST and SELF-RETIRING way, tell how good he is and that he is still in charge of the University."[9]

The attempted humor was lost on Selecman, who was offended and demanded an apology. The two students behind the spoof apologized in a letter to Selecman and then went around locating copies of the yearbook and tearing out the dedication page. Only with difficulty did SMU administrators and faculty persuade Selecman to forgo punishment of the students. The faculty adviser to *The Rotunda* staff, Joseph D. Doty, a history professor, suffered a more serious penalty. He had previously been granted a leave for 1927–28 to work on his doctoral degree with the expectation that afterward he would return to SMU. After the yearbook appeared, the board, at Selecman's behest, called Doty to appear before the trustees, reprimanded him, and granted him his leave of absence but then left "his future relation to the University . . . in the hands of the President with power to act." Doty did not return to SMU after his leave.[10] The president's handling of the Workman, Branscomb, and Doty incidents must have had a chilling effect on the faculty's willingness to exercise freedom of expression.

During the first Workman difficulty, in 1923, one of his student supporters, Charles W. Ferguson, had been an editorial writer for the *Daily Campus.* In 1929 Ferguson published a novel, *Pigskin,* a thinly disguised satire on Selecman, various other university personnel, and SMU generally. Among Ferguson's characters were Horace Ethelmore Dickey, "a cross between the Apostle Paul and Benito Mussolini" who served a chancellor of the fictitious Martha Sumner University; and the dean of the School of Religion, Reginald Keith, defiant beneath a surface agreeableness.[11] By then Ferguson was beyond the reach of university administrators.

Selecman had his strengths, however. He made major contributions to the financial and physical development of SMU. In 1923 and afterward he continued the efforts of his predecessor to put the university on a firm financial footing. By the spring of 1924 SMU was out of debt and had an endowment of $1.5 million and buildings worth an equal sum.[12] Thereafter he oversaw the establishment of the School of Law and the School of Engineering, both in 1925. During his administration the university added several buildings, including Kirby Hall (dedicated in 1924); McFarlin Auditorium (1926); the first floor of what later became the Perkins Administration Building (that part was dedicated in 1926); Ownby Stadium (1926); Hyer Hall for the physical sciences, named in honor of the president emeritus (1927); two dormitories for women (1927); and Patterson Hall (1928). Also during Selecman's presidency W. W. and Ella Fondren provided Humble Oil stock valued at $400,000 for a library building, though construction was not completed until 1940, after Selecman's departure.[13]

When the search committee had been looking for a president in 1922, one of its members, Cullom Booth, had wanted to have a lay president, "with no episcopal ambitions to divert his mind."[14] Selecman indeed had episcopal ambitions. In May

1930 the General Conference of the Methodist Episcopal Church, South, met in Dallas, and Selecman led the clergy delegates from the North Texas Conference, as he had in 1922 and 1926. Three bishops were to be elected in 1930, and Selecman's name was prominent among the possibilities. On the first ballot Selecman placed fourth, with 98 votes; he needed 266 for election on that ballot. That was his high point in the voting. On the third ballot he placed seventh with 66 votes, while Arthur J. Moore was elected with 233, and Paul Kern—Selecman's former subordinate as dean of the School of Theology—was elected with 227. Selecman did even worse thereafter, falling to 11 votes on the ninth and last ballot, on which A. Frank Smith became the third electee that year.[15]

Selecman's friends tried to console him. Several faculty members and administrators gave a banquet in his honor later that month. Then, at their June 2 meeting, the trustees raised his salary by 25 percent. A few days later Eugene B. Hawk, still a pastor in Fort Worth, wrote Selecman, "Just a line to tell you that I often think of you and am proud of the record you are making. . . . If you ever have a Sunday off, I want you to spend it in Fort Worth and preach for me here at First Church. You always have an open door this way."[16]

One result of the building program was a return to major indebtedness. Through 1931 the debt on the building program amounted to $439,754, and the interest paid on that debt since 1924 had created a cumulative deficit in the operating budget of $113,628, as contrasted with the absence of debt in 1924. Yet since Selecman had become president, the value of plant and endowment together, less indebtedness, had increased to $2.9 million, nearly double its value in 1924. This indebtedness, anathema to local business leaders, plus a controversy about dismissal of the business manager of the athletic department for drunkenness, led R. H. Shuttles, then chair of the university's board, to try to fire Selecman in 1931. W. D. Bradfield, the School of Theology professor, wrote a lengthy, well-documented rebuttal in support of the president. Bradfield showed that Shuttles and other members of the board had approved each step of Selecman's building program and argued that not to have fired the athletic department business manager would have done serious damage to the university. Shuttles's effort failed, and thereafter he resigned as chair, to be replaced in 1932 by Bishop John M. Moore.[17]

In the middle of this controversy, the university faculty circulated a petition, signed by forty-one of ninety-five faculty members who held the rank of assistant professor or higher, asking to appear before the board: "Realizing that the genuine cooperation and mutual confidence between administration and faculty which is essential to the sound development of any university does not and cannot exist at Southern Methodist University under the present President, we, the undersigned members of the faculty, agree that, if the Board of Trustees cares to consider our opinion, we stand ready to confer with the said Board at its annual meeting in June, 1931."[18] Despite Selecman's past responses to internal controversy and criticism, the signatories included three deans and eight department chairs. Those who chose not to sign included Kilgore, acting dean of the School of Theology, and nearly all the theology faculty.[19] The board did not respond to the petitioners' request and affirmed its confidence in the president.

A further result of the controversy was the departure from the university of its vice president, Horace M. Whaling Jr., who had come to SMU as professor of church history and missions and then in 1920 had moved to the vice presidency in order to raise money for Boaz. It appears that Whaling might have been considered a candidate to succeed Selecman and was becoming critical of the administration. Aware of this, Selecman informed the board of his displeasure, and in the fall of 1931 Whaling left the university to become pastor of Oak Lawn Methodist Church in Dallas.[20]

SCHOOL OF THEOLOGY FINANCES, 1926–1938

The late 1920s began a period of seriously restricted financial resources for the School of Theology. One reason was the failure of the Board of Missions of the Methodist Episcopal Church, South, to maintain the sizable contributions it had made to the school since 1924. That failing became part of a more serious problem—the onset of the Great Depression.

In the late 1920s the denomination's Board of Missions ended the generous annual support for the School of Theology's program of foreign and home missionary education that in 1923 it had agreed to provide. In response the SMU board resolved in 1929 that "a committee from the Board of Trustees be appointed to urge the Board of Missions to arrange to carry out its agreement with us to furnish $8700.00 per year to maintain a department of missions in S.M.U. We have added three men to our faculty to take care of the work outlined by the Board of Missions, and we have been embarrassed by their failure to make provision for carrying out their agreement."[21]

The failure of the Board of Missions to honor its commitment left a huge hole in the school's budget—about one-sixth of its anticipated income. In 1930 Selecman reported to the SMU board that "after consulting with officials of the Board of Missions, we are assured that at least 65% of this amount may be depended upon. These funds will come in in March, April, and May of next year."[22] "Next year," though, was 1931, by which time the Great Depression was creating serious financial problems for everyone, including SMU, the Board of Missions, and the whole denomination.

The budgets presented by Kilgore and Hawk reflect the School of Theology's opportunities and difficulties in the late 1920s and early 1930s. A comparison of their budgets and Kern's makes clear the significance of the problem. In 1922 Kern budgeted both income and expenses for the school for the fiscal year 1922–23 at $37,700. The 1923–24 budget, embodying Kern's plan to expand the missionary training program, predicted income of $52,400 and expenses of $52,790. The income and expense budgets stayed close to that level for the next three years, through 1926–27, and after Kern's departure fell back to between $44,400 and $48,300 for each year from 1927–28 through 1934–35.[23] In the late 1920s much of this reduction probably reflects the failure of the Board of Missions to honor its commitment.

By 1930 the Great Depression had begun, and it deepened from year to year. In June 1930 Selecman's report to the board of trustees characterized the fiscal year as "very difficult financially" because of the Depression. He recommended few increases in salaries, and those modest, and he announced SMU had postponed its financial campaign indefinitely because of economic conditions.[24] The following year he presented a sharply reduced university expense budget and nonetheless expected a deficit for the year. Again the university undertook no financial campaign. In light of the Depression and a drought, Selecman thought it unwise to seek donations from people sorely beset financially themselves.[25]

By June 1932, even with an income of $678,200 anticipated for 1932–33, the board foresaw a deficit in the university's operating budget of more than $53,000. To help cope with the emergency, the board reduced all salaries and wages for 1932–33 by 20 percent. That meant a professor with a base salary of $3,600 suddenly was to be paid $2,880 that year. That practice continued for years. In 1937 the board raised salaries to 84 percent of base and later to 90 percent; only in January 1943 did salaries go back to 100 percent of base.[26] In 1933 the executive committee set "the maximum regular salary" (before calculating the 20 percent reduction) in all schools of the university at $4,000, but few professors had a base salary that high. In another move to reduce costs the executive committee recommended to the board that faculty members in all schools teach at least twelve hours a week, except in the law school, which required its professors to perform special work outside class. The board, however, amended that recommendation to take into consideration special outside work, such as continuing education for pastors, required of the School of Theology faculty.[27]

By 1935–36 the School of Theology budget had recovered from the worst years of the Depression. Hawk reported income for that year of $55,170, the largest portion from the denominational and annual conference offices, and expenditures of $48,473. In 1936–37 income rose to $58,539 and expenditures to $55,681, modestly higher than the peak budgets of the mid-1920s. School of Theology budgets remained in that range through the 1938–39 fiscal year.[28] Resources remained tight but no longer desperate.

THE FACULTY UNDER KILGORE AND IN HAWK'S EARLY YEARS

Compared with the almost complete turnover of the School of Theology faculty during the Kern deanship, the full-time faculty under Kilgore was relatively stable (see appendix A). In the fall of 1926 it consisted of nine professors: Kilgore, philosophy of religion; Bishop, New Testament; Bradfield, Christian doctrine; Goodloe, church history; Hicks, Old Testament; Miner, town and country church; Seneker, religious education; Spann, church administration and city church; and Wasson, missions.

The most immediate faculty need was to fill the position in homiletics. In 1927 Kilgore brought in Umphrey Lee, pastor of Highland Park Methodist Church next door, to teach homiletics, presumably until Kilgore could land William C. Martin for the position. Lee had received his bachelor's degree in 1914 from Trinity College (near Ennis, Texas), and his master's from SMU in 1916. He had done work toward his Ph.D. degree at Union Theological Seminary and Columbia University (he received the degree in 1931). After a year as pastor in Ennis, he had been appointed to Highland Park in 1923, just in time to oversee construction of its new late Gothic-style building, the last details of which were being completed in 1927. Lee was well received at Highland Park, and in his first four years there the congregation's membership had nearly doubled, from 750 to 1,398. Along with his pastorate, Lee taught homiletics at the School of Theology until 1932, with a year of leave in 1928–29 for study and travel.[29] In 1932–33 Will Martin, by then the pastor of First Church, Dallas, taught homiletics, and thereafter it was taught by the new dean, Eugene B. Hawk.

A pressing need was more money to pay the professors. In 1926 Emma Lehman, a charter member of Grace Methodist Church in Dallas, left $100,000 to SMU, which in turn designated $85,000 of that amount for the School of Theology. After some discussion about how the money should be used, the decision was made to endow a chair in the School of Theology to be known as the Lehman Chair of Christian Doctrine. In 1931 W. D. Bradfield, who had been pastor of Grace Church from 1918 to 1922, was named the Lehman Professor; he held that title until his retirement in 1936. Thereafter no one was named to that chair until decades later.[30]

While Kilgore was acting dean, two of the nine regular faculty members departed—Spann in 1927 and Miner in 1933. Kern had written Martin in 1927 that certain aspects of the SMU administration were the main reason for Spann's departure. One opinion offered later by a knowledgeable observer is that Spann became exasperated in his dealings with Selecman while serving on a committee to investigate the SMU athletic program.[31]

To replace Spann, in the fall of 1928 Kilgore brought Harold G. Cooke to the faculty as professor of city church. Cooke had received a B.A. from Southwestern University and B.D. from SMU and then served several pastorates across the Southwest. In 1927, when he was thirty-seven, he became pastor of Grace Methodist Church in Dallas, which then had 1,885 members; this was his primary work while he was on the School of Theology faculty. As his first year with the school coincided with Umphrey Lee's year of leave, Cooke taught homiletics in addition to courses on the city church and on church administration. In the fall of 1930 the bishop appointed him to First Methodist Church in Paris, Texas, and that put an end to his teaching at SMU. He continued in the pastorate, then was for several years a presiding elder, and in 1943 became president of McMurry College in Abilene, where he remained until his death in 1958.[32] The School of Theology did not make another appointment to the city church position for several years after his departure.

In June 1933 Ora Miner's position as professor of the town and country church became a casualty of the university's belt-tightening moves during the Depression. Despite their appreciation for his work and many requests for his retention, the trustees voted to merge town and country work with that done by other professors in the School of Theology.[33] With the departures of Cooke and Miner, the home missions dimension of Kern's missionary education program—city church and town and country church—disappeared.

When Hawk became dean in the fall of 1933, Kilgore retired as acting dean but continued on the faculty for two more years—to age seventy—as professor of the philosophy of religion. Thus in the fall of 1933 the School of Theology faculty numbered eight: Hawk, Bishop, Bradfield, Goodloe, Hicks, Kilgore, Seneker, and Wasson.

Unlike Kilgore, Hawk oversaw several faculty appointments in his early years as dean. The primary reason was retirements. Charles McTyeire Bishop, seventy-two, retired in 1934; Kilgore, seventy, retired in 1935; and Bradfield, also seventy, retired the next year. All these retirements reflected the trustees' decision in January 1934 to mandate faculty retirement "on the first day of September nearest the attained age of seventy years."[34] In addition, in 1934 Wasson accepted a position with the Board of Missions of the Methodist Episcopal Church, South.

One of Hawk's first faculty appointments was to the New Testament position. Wesley Davis, born in 1893, had done his seminary studies at Emory University, had been a pastor in Missouri for twelve years, and had been studying toward his Ph.D. degree at Yale intermittently since 1920. In 1934 Hawk nominated him as associate professor of New Testament, to begin the position January 1, 1935. The understanding was that once Davis received his Ph.D., he would be promoted to full professor. That did not happen until 1943. Davis was revered as a patient and kind professor by his faculty colleagues, seminary students, and the people in the large adult class at Highland Park Methodist Church whom he taught for twenty-three years. He remained on the theology faculty until his retirement in 1959 and then taught three more years on a part-time basis. He died in 1975.[35]

Because Kilgore and Bradfield would be retiring in successive years, it was decided to combine the work in their fields, philosophy of religion and Christian doctrine, when Kilgore retired. Bradfield would head that department in 1935–36, and one new professor would be added in 1934 and become a full professor upon Bradfield's retirement. The new appointee in 1934 was Nenien C. McPherson, who had studied at Emory University and at Garrett Biblical Institute in Evanston, Illinois, had a Ph.D. degree from Northwestern University, and was completing three years as a professor at Garrett. He served as associate professor of philosophy of religion and ethics at the School of Theology. McPherson, however, left in 1936 to take a position with the denomination's Board of Christian Education in Nashville. At that point the theology school abandoned the idea of combining the two fields.[36]

When Bradfield retired in 1936, Hawk brought James T. Carlyon in to teach Christian doctrine. Born in Canada in 1884, Carlyon had degrees from Missouri Wesleyan, Boston University, and Harvard; he had received his Ph.D. degree from Chicago in 1925. Along the way he had been a pastor for several years in Missouri and then a professor of New Testament in Denver. Because Davis was not scheduled to arrive until January 1935, Hawk appointed Carlyon as visiting professor of New Testament for the fall of 1934. His students appreciated him as a patient interpreter of Christian doctrine and a kind counselor. For more than seven years he was a daily radio preacher at station WFAA in Dallas. After his retirement in 1954 he served as an associate pastor at Lovers Lane Methodist Church in Dallas until 1963; he died in 1970.[37]

Finding a replacement in philosophy of religion proved more difficult. In the summer of 1936 Hawk was unable to persuade John Keith Benton of Drew University to take this position.[38] Thereafter a visiting professor, W. H. Bernhardt, spent two years at the school, followed by another visiting professor for two years, Adrian M. Screx, who arrived in the fall of 1938.

The School of Theology had had no professor of sociology since the departure of Ora Miner in 1933. In 1935 Hawk nominated Paul A. Root for this position, the title of which changed over time but eventually became sociology of religion and ethics. Root, born in 1903, was twenty-seven when he completed his undergraduate degree at Asbury College in Wilmore, Kentucky, then did his B.D. at Duke and completed his Ph.D. degree there in 1935, just before coming to the School of Theology. Fred Gealy later observed of Root that after twenty-seven years in conservative religious patterns, he made a radical shift in orientation and moved into the "more turbulent waters of contemporary religious thought." Root proved to be a clear-headed and stimulating colleague, academically versatile, and on occasion an able interim pastor, as he was at First Methodist Church, Dallas, in the summer of 1944.[39]

The field of missions proved to be another difficult appointment to make. After Wasson left in 1934, Guy W. Sarvis came from Vanderbilt as visiting professor of missions and sociology for one year. Along with a course on world missions, he taught sociology courses in that year before Root's appointment. In his first two years Root taught courses on the history of religions and on missions in addition to those in his own field of sociology. The following year, 1937–38, another visiting professor, J. Paul Reed, taught missions and history of religion.[40] When Selecman resigned in 1938, the missions position still had not been filled on a permanent basis.

With these changes the faculty in the fall of 1938 included only three members who preceded Hawk's arrival: Goodloe, Hicks, and Seneker, all of whom remained into the mid-1950s. In his first five years as dean, Hawk appointed three professors who continued beyond 1938: Carlyon, Davis, and Root. During the previous fifteen years, though, the size of the permanent faculty had shrunk. Before he resigned, Kern had brought the faculty to ten with the appointment of Wasson; in Kilgore's early years as acting dean it varied between nine and ten; after Cooke left in 1930 and Miner in 1933, the number dropped to eight; and in 1938 there were seven, plus Serex as visiting professor of philosophy of religion. Of the seven permanent faculty members, four had Ph.D. degrees, and Davis would complete his in 1943. This constituted a higher proportion of earned doctorates than at any previous point. These professors were well prepared in their fields, and on the whole they provided a competent seminary education in the fields they covered, even though none was well known on the national theological scene. Hawk, who had not been an educator previous to his appointment as dean, was upgrading the faculty.

Along with their teaching—in the School of Theology, correspondence courses, and continuing education—five of the nine theology faculty members earned advanced degrees between 1928 and 1933: Bradfield, Goodloe, Hicks, Lee, and Wasson. While he was on the theology faculty, Umphrey Lee was its most productive author (see appendix C), with several books, the best known of which was *The Lord's*

Horseman, a well-researched and eminently readable biography of John Wesley. Lee completed the book in 1928 after a labor of eight years.[41]

MINISTERS' WEEK

In its early years the School of Theology faculty provided "extension courses" for pastors in the area, correspondence courses after 1918 for pastors at a distance, and, from 1919 to 1922, a training school of two weeks in June for pastors and others without a seminary degree.[42] Then, after W. W. Fondren established a trust fund in 1919, the school offered the Fondren Lectures on Christian missions each year beginning in 1920.[43]

In January 1936 Hawk initiated Ministers' Week, apparently taking the idea from a similar venture begun the year before at Emory University's Candler School of Theology.[44] To the Fondren Lectures, given that year by Charles R. Brown, dean of Yale Divinity School, Hawk added another set of lectures by Edwin Lewis, a professor at Drew Theological Seminary. The sessions, held in McFarlin Auditorium over five days, were intended primarily for Methodist pastors though open to those of other denominations and to other interested church workers. Nearly four hundred ministers from twenty-three annual conferences in eleven states registered, and Selecman called the occasion "a pronounced success."[45] In 1937 the Fondren Lecturer was Albert C. Knudson, dean of the Boston University School of Religion; other lecturers that year were William Adams Brown, a professor at Union Theological Seminary, R. H. Edwards of Cornell University (a specialist in personal counseling), and Hicks of the School of Theology faculty. Attendance grew over the years, and the mid-1940s saw the addition of two more endowed lectureships to the program. Ministers' Week was a significant expansion of the school's continuing education program.

THE CURRICULUM, 1926–38

While Kilgore was acting dean, the B.D. curriculum did not change. The arrival of Hawk as dean in 1933, however, presaged a curriculum revision. From 1935 to 1937 the faculty made several changes. First was a reduction in the number of "majors" required for graduation, from thirty to twenty-seven—nine each academic year, to align the School of Theology more closely with requirements in leading seminaries.[46] In this connection, in 1936-37 the school was admitted to membership in the American Association of Theological Schools.[47]

A second change, in 1935, was in the organization of the fields of study. Whereas the previous curriculum had simply listed the several fields, now the faculty organized them into three groups. Group I, "Fields Dealing with the Historical Development of Religion," included fields I, Old Testament; II, New Testament; and III, church history. Group II, "Fields Dealing with the Interpretation of the Christian Religion," included fields IV, theology and philosophy of religion, and V, Christian ethics and social problems. Group III, "Fields Dealing with the Work of the Church at Home and Abroad," included fields VI, religious education; VII, missions, psychology of religion, and history of religion; and VIII, homiletics and pastoral theology (which also included public speaking and church music). The reason for the groupings, the faculty explained, was not to change the content of the courses, nor to affect a student's field of concentration, but to help readers of the catalog see each specialized area as part of the faculty's total work, rather than as a group of unrelated departments.[48] In the title of Field IV what had been called Christian doctrine now was named theology. In the 1936–37 *Bulletin*, though, it was once again called Christian doctrine. The bulletins included no explanation of either term nor of any distinction between them.

A third change was in the distribution of the required courses. The faculty now reduced the number of required "majors" in Bible from seven to five (except for students electing a biblical language) and instituted small increases in some other fields—church history, Christian doctrine, religious education, and history of religions. These changes reflect the familiar and endless discussions that occur within seminary faculties about which fields have what degree of importance for ministerial education. The theology faculty held meeting after meeting, some specially called, to thrash out this issue, often with little apparent progress. The minutes for the faculty meeting of December 17, 1934, for example, read (in full): "This meeting was a continuation of the discussion, interest centering on what subjects should be required. No conclusion was reached."[49]

A fourth change was that the oral examination required until 1937 was replaced that year by a written comprehensive examination covering the basic courses in the curriculum, for which the faculty would prepare a syllabus to guide students' preparation.[50] This requirement led to repeated requests to faculty members to hand in material for the syllabus, especially because this was a new requirement and the students had not known about it when they took the courses, some as much as three years earlier. The level of student anxiety is easily imaginable. Failures might occur, and in fact did, after which the student might take a second comprehensive examination within three to twelve months.[51]

A fifth and last change was that a thesis, which had previously been required, now became optional with the approval of the student's advising professor. The professor could also recommend that an approved thesis be substituted for the section of the comprehensive examination related to the field of the thesis.[52]

Considering all these changes, the B.D. curriculum now was more demanding, at least on paper. The curriculum continued to be highly structured, requiring specific courses that comprised more than two-thirds of the work needed for graduation. In this respect it did not differ from the curricula of many other seminaries of that time and for years afterward. This curriculum, with minor adjustments, remained in effect into the mid-1940s.[53] As for the degree of master of church administration, the catalog last listed it in 1939–40. Almost no students had enrolled in it for years, and dropping it simply recognized this reality.

THE STUDENT BODY

During Kern's deanship the number of graduate students enrolled at the School of Theology had increased from thirty-two in his first year (1920–21) to a high point of sixty-nine (1923–24). Under Kilgore it continued to grow; during each academic year between 1928 and 1932 the school counted more than ninety graduate students, not including undergraduates in the seminary courses or seminary students in the summer school. In 1932–1936, however, the Depression took its toll, and the numbers in each of those academic years ranged between sixty-six and seventy-four. The regular terms in 1936–37 saw a sharp recovery in enrollment, to ninety-seven, the highest in the history of the school to date.[54]

While Kern was dean, sixty to eighty undergraduates enrolled for School of Theology courses each year. After 1928 that figure dropped sharply. From 1928 to 1933 seventeen to twenty-two undergraduates took courses at the School of Theology in a given year, and after 1933 the figure did not exceed nine and was never more than 10 percent of the school's graduate student enrollment. The decline continued until 1944–45, when this information was no longer reported. By then School of Theology courses taught only graduate-professional students, with few exceptions.

After 1923 women regularly enrolled for the B.D. degree. The first woman to receive that degree at SMU was Catherine O'Dell, who came to the School of Theology with an undergraduate degree from Southwestern University and completed her B.D. studies in June 1928. In 1931 two women graduated with the B.D.: Elna Lucy Martin, with a thesis on China missions, and Jewell Posey, whose thesis was on rural social work; both reflected the school's program in missions. Thereafter no woman graduated with a B.D. until 1937 (Jean Lanace LaGrone), and then none until the mid-1940s.[55] The total enrollment of women peaked at ten in 1928–29 and eleven in 1929–30; thereafter it declined and was never more than six in any year until the late 1940s.

The first Hispanic to receive a B.D. from SMU graduated in September 1927: Oscar Machado da Silva, who had enrolled after receiving his B.A. from Birmingham-Southern College in Alabama. He was followed by Antonio Pedro Rolim, who received his B.D. in 1928, and Alfredo Nañez, who graduated in 1932. Felix Segovia, who came to the School of Theology from Nuevo Leon, Mexico, without an undergraduate degree, received a certificate in theology in 1933. After that, Hispanics disappeared from among the graduates, to reappear only in the mid-1940s and after.[56]

After the first three international students, all from East Asia, received B.D. degrees or certificates in the mid-1920s, no more did so until Wataru Isaac Nagamachi, from Kwansei Gakuin University in Japan, graduated in August 1930. On June 7, 1932, Sante Uberto Barbieri, from Brazil, received his undergraduate, master's, and divinity degrees—all from SMU and all on the same day. He later became a bishop in the Methodist Church in Brazil. Young Bin Im from Korea, with his undergraduate degree from SMU, also received his divinity degree in 1932. From then through August 1941 seven international students, from China, Korea, and Japan, received divinity degrees. After Pearl Harbor no international students graduated until 1948.[57]

Compared with the previous period, little change occurred between 1926 and 1938 in which states or colleges and universities sent students to the School of Theology. The school's student body continued, as in the early twenties, to be overwhelmingly from the Southwest, though with significant exceptions, and overwhelmingly male and of northern European ancestry, though again with significant exceptions.

THE CONCLUSION OF THE SELECMAN PRESIDENCY

Although President Selecman had failed to be elected a bishop in 1930, he still held episcopal ambitions. Again in the General Conference of 1934 he failed to realize them. The conflict on the board of trustees in 1931 between Selecman and its chair, R. H. Shuttles, had spilled over into the North Texas Annual Conference of 1932 and had left marked antagonism toward Selecman which was still present a year later. In the fall of 1933, as James Kirby explains, "the anti-Selecman forces . . . had made careful advance preparation and elected their delegates" to the 1934 General Conference.[58] In the preceding three General Conferences Selecman had headed the North Texas clerical delegation. This time he managed only to be elected first alternate delegate, which ensured that he would have little visibility.

By the time of the General Conference in Birmingham, Alabama, in the spring of 1938, antagonism to Selecman was still present, though not as extensive. At the North Texas Annual Conference in the fall of 1937, Selecman was elected as the fourth clerical delegate out of seven. William C. Martin, about to begin his seventh year as pastor of First Methodist Church, Dallas, became the seventh delegate. That gave hope to some of Selecman's enemies, who thought if Martin were elected a bishop, that would block Selecman, for surely the General Conference would not choose two bishops from the same annual conference. It turned out otherwise. After much disagreement the General Conference voted to elect seven bishops. On May 3 Ivan Lee Holt, of the original School of Theology faculty in 1915 and long a pastor in St. Louis, was elected first. On the next ballot, taken the same day, the fourth bishop to be elected was Selecman. The sixth elected, on the same ballot, was Martin, to his great surprise.[59]

At the June 7, 1938, meeting of the SMU Board of Trustees, Selecman resigned the presidency of SMU, "to become effective at the earliest date convenient to the Board of Trustees." At the same time the board elected Bishop A. Frank Smith as its new chair, to replace John M. Moore, who was retiring as an active bishop. For decades Moore had been a leading figure in the negotiations toward union of three branches of American Methodism, and with the agreement of the three bodies on a plan of union, he would be giving major attention in the next year to preparation for the Uniting Conference of The Methodist Church.[60] As the new board chair, Smith appointed a committee, chaired by Holt, to determine how long Selecman would continue in office and to bring nominations for president to the board in November.[61]

Selecman must have anticipated how to handle the situation if he were elected a bishop, causing SMU to be temporarily without a president. At the board meeting in January 1938, he had nominated Hawk to be vice president of the university, explaining that one vice president was ill and another had just resigned. The board then made its intention more explicit: it elected Hawk as vice president "to act in administrative capacity in the absence of the President."[62] Thus, when Holt's Committee on Nominations made its first report on June 7, it recommended that Selecman continue as president until August and that Hawk, the vice president, "then take up the duties of Acting President and serve until a President is named, provided this President has not been selected at that time."[63]

President Selecman's resignation closed an era in both the university and its School of Theology, though the ramifications of the change in presidents were far from evident at the time. Selecman had done much for the university. He had helped to rescue it from financial crisis in the early 1920s, had overseen construction of several new buildings, and had seen it through the depths of the Depression. Yet his lack of a college degree had met with early faculty skepticism, and his highhandedness and intolerance of criticism eventually evoked widespread faculty hostility and bitterness. His critics accused him of being more interested in vocational courses than in the liberal arts and more interested in success for the football team than in the well-being of faculty members.[64] At the School of Theology, where his support had been stronger, the opportunity to choose a new president was a time of mixed hope and trepidation.

1. James Kilgore, letter to William C. Martin, July 1, 1927, William C. Martin Papers, Bridwell Library, Southern Methodist University.
2. See James E. Kirby, *Brother Will: A Biography of William C. Martin* (Nashville, Tenn.: Abingdon, 2000), chap. 3.
3. Martin to Kilgore, August 1, 1927, Martin Papers.
4. Ibid., August 10, 1927; Kilgore to Martin, August 13, 1929, Martin Papers.
5. Paul B. Kern to William C. Martin, August 19, 1927, Martin Papers.
6. Martin to Kilgore, August 22, 1927; Kilgore to Martin, September 3, 1927, Martin Papers.
7. Kirby has described these conversations in detail in *Brother Will*, chaps. 3 and 4.

8. Board of trustees minutes, June 6, 1933, and June 4, 1934; *Who's Who in Methodism* (Chicago: A. N. Marquis, 1952), 311.

9. *The Rotunda* (Dallas: Southern Methodist University Press, 1927), 309.

10. Mary Martha Hosford Thomas, *Southern Methodist University: Founding and Early Years* (Dallas: Southern Methodist University Press, 1974), 147, citing letters from the students and from three administrators; board of trustees minutes, June 7, 1927.

11. Charles W. Ferguson, *Pigskin* (New York: Doubleday, Doran, 1929), 34, 57.

12. Board of trustees minutes, June 9, 1924.

13. A brief description of every building up to 1965 is to be found in James F. White, *Architecture at SMU: 50 Years and Buildings* (Dallas: Southern Methodist University Press, 1966).

14. Cullom H. Booth to Edwin D. Mouzon, September 6, 1922, Edwin D. Mouzon Papers, Bridwell Library.

15. *Dallas Morning News*, May 7 and 11, 1930; *Journal of the Twenty-first General Conference of the Methodist Episcopal Church, South*, 1930, edited by Curtis B. Haley (Nashville, Tenn.: Methodist Episcopal Church, South, n.d.), 206, 211, 228.

16. Board of trustees minutes, June 2, 1930; Eugene B. Hawk to Charles C. Selecman, June 9, 1930, Charles C. Selecman Papers, Bridwell Library.

17. W. D. Bradfield, "A Reply to Mr. R. H. Shuttles' Attack upon the President of Southern Methodist University," an address to the bishops and members of the North Texas Annual Conference, in Session at Gainesville, Texas, October 27, 1932, 10–18, 20–21 (no place, no publisher, no date of publication), James Kilgore Papers, Bridwell Library; board of trustees minutes, June 1–2, 1931, June 7, 1932.

18. Quoted in Thomas, *Southern Methodist University*, 152, from a copy in the personal files of Professor Herbert Gambrell.

19. Thomas, *Southern Methodist University*, 152–53.

20. Board of trustees minutes, June 7, 1932; Thomas, *Southern Methodist University*, 152, citing W. D. Bradfield, "An Interior View of Our Troubles at Southern Methodist University," Office of the President, SMU, 1931, 28.

21. Board of trustees minutes, February 26, 1929.

22. Ibid., June 2, 1930.

23. Ibid., May 2, 1922; June 12, 1923; June 9, 1924; June 1–2, 1925; June 4, 1926; June 7, 1927; June 4, 1928; February 26, 1929; June 2, 1930; June 7, 1932; June 3, 1933; June 4–5, 1934.

24. Ibid., June 2, 1930.

25. Ibid., June 1–2, 1931.

26. Ibid., June 7, 1932, February 5, 1942, and January 26, 1943; executive committee minutes, February 26, 1943.

27. Executive committee minutes, March 31, 1933; board of trustees minutes, June 6, 1933.

28. Board of trustees minutes, June 1–2, 1937, June 7, 1938, June 6, 1939, and June 4, 1940.

29. Winifred Weiss and Charles S. Proctor, *Umphrey Lee: A Biography* (Nashville, Tenn.: Abingdon, 1971), 58–59; *General Minutes*, Methodist Episcopal Church, South, 1923, 63, and 1927, 135.

30. Walter N. Vernon, *Methodism Moves across North Texas* (Dallas: Historical Society, North Texas Conference, The Methodist Church, 1967), 249; SMU *Bulletin*, October 1930, 173; faculty minutes, February 3, 1927; board of trustees minutes, June 3, 1929. The board minutes give the amount designated for the School of Theology as $75,000; the School of Theology *Bulletins* from 1930 and thereafter record it as $85,000.

31. Douglas Jackson, retired Perkins School of Theology professor, interview by author, June 19, 2007, Dallas.

32. *Who's Who in Methodism*, edited by Elmer T. Clark (Chicago: A. N. Marquis, 1952), 150; *General Minutes*, The Methodist Church, 1958, 61.

33. Board of trustees minutes, June 6, 1933.

34. Ibid., January 31, 1934.

35. Ibid., June 4, 1934; Fred D. Gealy, obituary for Wesley Davis, *North Texas Conference Journal*, 1976, 162–63.

36. Board of trustees minutes, June 4–5, 1934; *Bulletin*, October 1935, 141, and October 1936, 147, 168 (registrar's corrections in her copy in the Bridwell archives); Eugene B. Hawk to John Keith Benton, July 4, 1936, Eugene B. Hawk Papers, Bridwell Library.

37. Board of trustees minutes, June 5, 1934; *Bulletin*, October 1937, 17, 153, 172; obituary for James T. Carlyon, *North Texas Conference Journal*, 1971, 172; Hawk to Benton, June 26 and July 4, 1936, Hawk Papers.

38. Hawk correspondence with Benton, 1936, Hawk Papers.

39. Fred D. Gealy, "Paul Adelbert Root—In Memoriam," *Perkins School of Theology Journal*, fall 1947, 11–13; board of trustees minutes, June 4, 1935.

40. Board of trustees minutes, June 4, 1935; *Bulletin*, October 1934, 159, 168 (with registrar's correction in ink), and October 1937, corrections and additions on p. 178.

41. Umphrey Lee, *The Lord's Horseman* (New York: Century, 1928), republished as *The Lord's Horseman: John Wesley the Man* (New York: Abingdon, 1954).

42. *Bulletins* for each year from 1918; faculty minutes, October 3, 1918, and January 3 and 13, 1919, and others; Western Training School booklets for 1920, 1921, and 1922; and *Service*, published three to six times a year by the School of Theology from 1920 to 1926. All are available in the Bridwell Archives.

43. Executive committee minutes, June 1, 1919.

44. Program, First Annual Ministers' Week at the Candler School of Theology, January 21–25, 1935 (Bridwell Archives).

45. *Bulletin*, October 1936, 150, and October, 1937, 156; board of trustees minutes, June 1, 1936.

46. Executive committee minutes, February 25, 1938.

47. Board of trustees minutes, January 18, 1937.

48. *Bulletin*, October 1935, 148; faculty minutes, February 6, 1935.

49. *Bulletin*, October 1934, 149, and October 1937, 164; faculty minutes, December 17, 1934.

50. *Bulletin*, October 1937, 165.

51. Faculty minutes, January 5 and February 3, 1938.

52. *Bulletin*, October 1937, 165.

53. See, e.g., *Bulletin* for 1945–46, pt. 7, pp. 18–19.

54. Board of trustees minutes, January 18, 1937; enrollment data are drawn from the *Bulletins* of the School of Theology.

55. SMU commencement programs, June 5, 1928, and afterward, Registrar's Office, Perkins School of Theology.

56. Ibid.

57. Ibid. Some international students attended the School of Theology but did not graduate; the *Bulletins* in these years list the names of students and where they were from.

58. Kirby, *Brother Will*, 209.

59. Ibid., 234–35; *Journal of the Twenty-Third General Conference of the Methodist Episcopal Church, South*, 1934, 71, 97–100.

60. See John M. Moore, *The Long Road to Methodist Union* (New York: Abingdon-Cokesbury, 1943). The respective church bodies named the denomination resulting from the 1939 union The Methodist Church; the denomination resulting from the 1968 union became The United Methodist Church, capitalizing *The* in each instance.

61. Board of trustees minutes, June 7 and November 7, 1938.

62. Ibid., January 18, 1938.

63. Ibid., June 7, 1938.

64. See Thomas, *Southern Methodist University*, 85, 98–102, 145–55; Marshall Terry, *"From High on the Hilltop . . .": A Brief History of SMU* (Dallas: Southern Methodist University, 2001), 25–29.

Laying New Foundations, 1938–1951

C hanges that occurred between 1939 and 1960 proved to be decisive for the subsequent history of the Perkins School of Theology. Together they transformed the school from a relatively small, financially struggling, regionally oriented seminary into a larger, financially more secure, widely respected, and internationally oriented institution—into what John Deschner would later call "the second Perkins." The most important changes between 1939 and 1951 were the selection of Umphrey Lee as president of Southern Methodist University in 1939; the gifts of large sums of money from Joe and Lois Perkins during and after 1944 to the School of Theology, which was then named for them; the initial enlargement of the Perkins faculty; gifts of J. S. Bridwell and his daughter, Margaret Bridwell Bowdle, for a theology library building; and the siting of the Perkins Quadrangle on a large tract at the southwest corner of the university. Together these events made possible the further transformation of Perkins that began in 1951.

THE NEW PRESIDENT

From the start of the search for a university president in 1938, the name of Umphrey Lee was prominent. Lee, who was born in 1893, was a member of the first SMU class of graduate students in 1915, served as the first president of the student body, and graduated in 1916 with a master's degree. Beginning that fall he studied for and, in 1931 received, a Ph.D. degree from Columbia University, with special attention to philosophy, the Hellenistic period, and, in his dissertation, the background of Methodism. During breaks from his Ph.D. studies he was pastor at Cisco, Texas; director of the Wesley Bible Chair at the University of Texas; and later a pastor at Ennis, Texas. Then, from 1923 to 1936, he was pastor of Highland Park Methodist

Church, adjacent to the SMU campus. When Lee went to Highland Park, its membership was 750 and it had no parsonage. During his years there the membership tripled in size, and he oversaw the construction of a new church building. For five years he taught a course in homiletics at the School of Theology. He was well known and well liked, not only at the School of Theology but also by many others at the university and a wide array of Dallas business leaders. Along the way he published several books, with special attention to Methodism and John Wesley, about whom he became a widely recognized scholar. In 1936 he accepted the deanship of Vanderbilt University Divinity School and was there when the SMU trustees began considering who should become the university's next president.[1]

Bishop Charles C. Selecman gave up his work as SMU president in August 1938. Between his departure and the arrival of the new president, Dean Hawk served as acting president while continuing as dean of the School of Theology. That necessitated having someone else teach his classes, and James Carlyon and Paul Root each offered to teach a course in pastoral theology.[2]

The trustees' nominating committee considered about thirty candidates, narrowed the list to six, and interviewed all, including Lee, either as a committee or through individual board members.[3] Lee declined to come to Dallas for an interview, for which he could have had several good reasons, such as that the board members already knew him well enough, or to keep his interest in the position quiet.[4]

When the trustees met on the morning of November 7, Bishop Holt submitted six names for consideration, including Umphrey Lee's, followed by a presentation of information about each. In the afternoon session the board, meeting in executive session, reduced the six names to four, then to two, and then arrived at a motion to elect Lee as president of SMU. The motion was carried unanimously. Lee accepted and assumed his duties on March 2, 1939.[5] When he arrived, the whole campus was filled with rejoicing and expectation, faculty and students alike. Well they might have rejoiced. Now they had a president who had solid academic credentials, who knew what constituted a great university, and from the start pointed SMU in that direction. Lee was the second SMU president who was a professional educator (the other was its first president, Robert Stewart Hyer). Lee was its first president to hold an earned doctoral degree and the first with wide personal knowledge of the Western intellectual world. His taking the university presidency was the first of several steps that made possible the transformation of what before long was renamed Perkins School of Theology.

Umphrey Lee's report to the board on June 6, 1939, showed he was a president of a different stripe. He began with his conception of the goal of SMU, which, he said, should not try to imitate the large state universities. Rather it should provide instruction and guidance not available at large institutions or at those prohibited from pursuing religious aims. SMU should not be "just another good university." He saw in it the potential to play a leadership role in the Southwest comparable to the roles of Vanderbilt and Duke in the Southeast or that of Oberlin in the Midwest.[6]

A further indication of Lee's expectations came in the same report when he listed the faculty publications of the preceding twelve months—a clear signal to the faculty. The total list included only five books from a faculty of 129 that academic year. One was Paul Root's *The Nature and Social Significance of Tradition*. Among articles and chapters in edited books, Lee listed four by School of Theology faculty—one by James T. Carlyon and three by Fred D. Gealy, who had arrived only in January as visiting professor of missions.[7]

This was a president the faculty could admire and attempt to emulate, one who recognized and valued quality academic work, one who understood their calling and shared their hopes. At the same time he had won the respect and support of a board made up largely of clergy and increasingly inclusive of businessmen. His was an unusual combination of strengths.

ONGOING FINANCIAL DIFFICULTIES
FOR THE SCHOOL OF THEOLOGY

The beginning of Umphrey Lee's presidency was a time of continued financial stringency for the School of Theology. In 1940 Hawk described the situation in a letter to A. Frank Smith, the bishop who chaired the board of trustees. The School of Theology, Hawk explained, did not share in the university's general endowment, nor had it in recent years received contributions from the annual conferences in the region, for Selecman had asked that those gifts go to the university. Furthermore, the School of Theology was the only SMU school charged overhead—$4,000 annually—even though it had provided its own building. Hawk feared that this situation was likely to be permanent.[8]

In his report to the SMU administration for the year 1939–40, Hawk compared the budget for 1940–41 with those of several other Methodist theological schools. He reported the budget for the seminary at Drew University was $250,000; Boston, $175,000; Duke, $150,000; and Emory, $75,000 to $100,000. "The budget of our school," he wrote, "will be less than $60,000." If this situation was not remedied, he foresaw serious adverse consequences. Already, scholarship funds were insufficient to allow the student body of the School of Theology to grow beyond its 222 students that year. Also the school needed a modern apartment dormitory, and Hawk expected that prospective students would go north and east to seminary instead of to SMU. The School of Theology's expected income actually shrank by about 9 percent in the next three years, from $57,850 in 1940–41 to $52,550 in 1943–44. Relatively little of the school's income came from endowment. Budgeted income for the 1941–42 fiscal year was $55,973, of which $14,700 was expected from endowment—a little more than 26 percent of total income.[9] Physical facilities were as limited as the budget. Since 1924, when Harper and Annie Kirby Hall was completed, it had housed the entire School of Theology—administration, faculty offices, classrooms, chapel, and library. This was adequate for a small faculty and student body but had no room for growth.

Lee took office shortly before the Uniting Conference of The Methodist Church, held in Kansas City, Missouri, from April 26 to May 10, 1939. It brought together in one body the Methodist Episcopal Church, the Methodist Episcopal Church, South, and the Methodist Protestant Church. The prospects were that Methodist union would make matters worse financially for the School of Theology. Although Lee, Hawk, and the School of Theology faculty strongly favored union, it presented a serious financial challenge. The School of Theology had in recent years been receiving from $38,000 to $40,000 a year from the Methodist Episcopal Church, South. The proposal by those planning for denominational finances after union was for the church to give several of the nine Methodist theological schools equal amounts, which would result in a reduction of about $15,000 a year from what the School of Theology had been receiving. Hawk, who became deeply involved in the denomination's discussions of this issue, insisted that for the next quadrennium, 1940–44, each seminary should receive what it had received during the previous quadrennium. Representatives of Candler School of Theology at Emory, in a similar circumstance, worked alongside Hawk to try to maintain the previous level of support. As it turned out, the church substantially reduced the money the School of Theology received after union, money that came from the Commission on World Service and Finance, the agency that supervised denominational funds. In 1940–41 the School of Theology's actual receipts from the commission were about $26,000, approximately $13,000 less than the School of Theology had budgeted. The following year the receipts from the denomination were about $7,500 less than under the policy that predated union. Because most of the School of Theology's budget went for salaries and scholarships, the school could not reduce the budget without severely crippling its work.[10]

Hawk tried to replace the World Service funds by appealing to the various annual conferences in the region to provide scholarships. He reported to the trustees that nearly all the conferences had provided scholarships, and this partially offset the reduction in funds from World Service and Finance. By 1943 the nine theological schools had worked out a formula for what percentage of their share of the World Service funds would go to each school, a tolerable arrangement for the time being.[11] Even so, the School of Theology continued to operate within severe financial limits.

Meanwhile its student body had been growing. Through the 1937–38 academic year it had reached ninety-seven, not including those attending the summer term, the handful of undergraduates, or those taking correspondence courses. In the following six years it grew almost every year, from 122 in 1938–39 to 174 (plus three enrolled for certificates) in 1943–44.[12] The exception was 1939–40, when the School of Theology had to reduce its enrollment to 115. The school dropped some students who were not doing well and refused admission to some who would otherwise have been accepted.[13] The decision was undoubtedly based on finances, and scholarship money from the annual conferences in subsequent years eased the pressure to hold down enrollment. Even so, given the size of classrooms in Kirby Hall, the limited housing for seminary students, and the small faculty, a growing student body was a mixed blessing.

Despite the financial situation, in the spring of 1938 Hawk established the Circulating Library of the School of Theology, from which ministers could borrow books to assist in their continuing education. At Hawk's recommendation the trustees' executive committee authorized using $1,500 from a special fund to purchase books for this purpose. At the same time he proposed that the School of Theology begin a quarterly publication to be sent to graduates, other ministers, and friends of the school. Although the executive committee approved the proposal, publication of the *Perkins School of Theology Journal* did not begin until 1947. On January 1, 1939, though, the circulating library opened under the direction of Paul Root, with the assistance of Howard Grimes, a seminary student. The next year Hawk reported to the board the response "has been beyond all expectation," and new books were being purchased as funds permitted.[14]

CHANGES IN THE FACULTY, 1938–1944

The budget was tight, but theological education had to continue. During these years Hawk was able to add one full-time faculty member and one part-timer (see appendix A). Still casting about for a visiting professor for the missions position, Hawk brought to the faculty Fred D. Gealy, whose versatility commended him under the circumstances. After twelve years as a professor at Aoyama Gakuin Methodist College in Tokyo, Gealy was returning to the United States because of his wife's poor health and the markedly unfriendly political climate in Japan. Hawk had identified Gealy as a person to teach missions because of his years in Japan. Besides, Gealy's academic field was New Testament, and as Wesley Davis was to be on leave in the spring term of 1939 to continue work on his dissertation, Gealy could fill in during Davis's absence. Gealy, who originally was from Pennsylvania, received his bachelor's degree at Allegheny College there, obtained his bachelor of sacred theology and Ph.D. degrees from Boston University, and took a master's in sacred theology at Union Theological Seminary in New York, with further study at Basel, Berlin, and Chicago. He was also an organist and choir director, having organized the Oratorical Society of Tokyo and directed it for fourteen years. In January 1939 Gealy began at SMU as visiting professor of missions; in 1940 he became professor of New Testament Greek, missions, and church music. Soon after his arrival Gealy founded the Seminary Singers at Perkins. In 1947 he had it listed in the catalog as a credit course, and he directed it until his retirement in 1959.[15] In 1959–60 Gealy taught part time at Perkins and then left to become one of the original faculty members of the new Methodist Theological School in Delaware, Ohio. After several years he returned to Dallas, where he died in 1976.

In 1941 Hawk made a part-time appointment that foreshadowed the future

Perkins field of pastoral care. Russell L. Dicks was one of the early ministers to perceive the importance of clinical ministerial education as part of one's preparation to provide pastoral care. He received clinical training at Massachusetts General Hospital in the 1930s and served as a chaplain there and an instructor at several seminaries in the Boston area. After three years of similar work in Chicago, in September 1941 he came to Highland Park Methodist Church in Dallas as an associate pastor. Hawk worked out an agreement with Highland Park whereby the School of Theology would pay a fourth of Dicks's salary, in return for which he would teach two courses each year: "Pastoral Work" in the fall, including "clinical requirement of pastoral calls under supervision," and "Personality Problems" in the spring. In the spring of 1943 Dicks asked for a six-month leave from the School of Theology and Highland Park. The Army-Navy YMCA and the Federal Council of Churches' Commission on Religion and Health had asked him to work with them to conduct seminars in counseling in military defense areas. The following fall he resigned his Dallas positions to work with the Federal Council of Churches.[16] Thereafter the School of Theology had no faculty member in pastoral care until Robert Elliott arrived in 1955.

In the spring of 1944 the School of Theology had eight full-time faculty members and received half-time assistance from the university's professor of speech, Mary McCord. The school had a budget of $52,550 and a regular-term graduate-professional student body of 174, with all its work conducted in the crowded Kirby Hall.

THE PERKINSES' INITIAL LARGE GIFT
TO THE SCHOOL OF THEOLOGY

Joe and Lois Craddock Perkins had moved from modest beginnings, financially and socially, to a position of great wealth and influence. Joe Perkins was born in Lamar County, Texas, in 1874, the son of a cattle drover. As a young man Joe went west in Texas and eventually settled in Decatur, where in 1907 he opened a store. Before long he had organized a chain of stores in nine cities. In 1909 he moved to Wichita Falls. In the next several years he expanded and diversified his business interests to include oil drilling, leasing, and refining, as well as coal mining, ranching, real estate, and banking, in addition to his mercantile interests. He became enormously wealthy. He was, as Walter Vernon expressed it, "hard-working, wise, talented—and fortunate." In 1911 Perkins joined the First Methodist Church in Wichita Falls, where he soon moved into positions of leadership.[17]

Lois Craddock was born in 1887 to a family of modest means (her father was a blacksmith) in China Springs, Texas, a village north of Waco. When she was three, the family moved west to sparsely populated Coke County. Lois was the sixth child and the fourth daughter, much to her parents' disappointment, for they wanted a boy. She described herself as a quick learner with a good memory, a lover of books, someone who made friends easily, and a spitfire who argued readily with her domineering father. When she finished high school, she told her father she was going to college. Because she had no money, she decided to go to Southwestern University and borrow the money from the school. Although she did not graduate, she did earn a teacher's certificate, and for two years she taught in the small town of Robert Lee, not far from where she had grown up. In 1913 she took a position, almost by accident, in Wichita Falls (she was waiting there for the next train out and used the time to interview with the school superintendent). Before long she met Joe Perkins, and in 1918 they were married. She was a devout Christian and a wise counselor, and during the forty-two years of their marriage she was a shaping influence in his decisions. Bishop A. Frank Smith later said, "Lois directed his thinking. He always says that he doesn't do anything without her approval."[18]

The Perkinses' close relation to Southern Methodist University began in the 1920s. Joe Perkins's older brother, Sam B. Perkins, was an SMU trustee beginning in 1922, and in 1928 Joe Perkins became a board member. In 1939 Joe was elected to membership on the board's executive committee and the budget committee; both positions meant he was closely involved in decisions about the university's finances. He also became a close friend of Hawk's. When Umphrey Lee became president in 1939, Hawk continued to head the School of Theology, but he stepped down as acting president of the university to become its administrative vice president, a position he held for several years. In that post he regularly met with the trustees and its executive committee, and he worked closely with its members, including Joe Perkins. Hawk and Perkins corresponded in those years, and Hawk assiduously cultivated the relationship.[19]

Another SMU connection with the Perkinses developed through Smith. He had been a student at Southwestern University while Lois Craddock was there. Later, as a bishop, Smith was on the SMU board for several years before he became its chair in 1938, a position he held until 1960. During all that time he worked with Joe Perkins on board business. They corresponded often and became close friends.[20] A further close connection with SMU existed between the Perkinses and Paul E. Martin, the Methodist presiding elder of the Wichita Falls District from 1935 to 1938 and the Perkinses' pastor from 1938 to 1944. In 1944 Martin was elected a bishop, and during this period he was a member of the SMU board and its Committee on the School of Theology.

Joe and Lois Perkins had made sizable gifts to Southern Methodist University before 1944—in particular, money for the Perkins Hall of Administration (between 1930 and 1939) and the Joe Perkins Gymnasium (completed in 1942). Two incidents moved them to decide to give large amounts of money to the SMU School of Theology. Today we do not know the order in which these incidents occurred. One began at a meeting of the SMU trustees in February 1944, when President Umphrey Lee challenged the board to remedy the university's poor financial situation. Comparing SMU with five other private institutions, especially Methodist-affiliated Duke, he pointed out that SMU was spending 10 to 24 percent more of its educational expenses than those other institutions for instruction, that is, primarily for professors' salaries. That was not because SMU was paying its faculty higher salaries; to the contrary, its maximum faculty salary was well below average for the more prestigious universities. Nor was SMU overstaffed; in comparison with other similar institutions, it was understaffed, and its administrative officers were overloaded. Far from spending too much on libraries, SMU was at the bottom of the library expenditure list. Then why did so much of SMU's budget go for instruction? "The answer is very simple," Lee told the board. "We are trying to operate a university on an inadequate budget. We do not have enough money to carry on the type of work which we have undertaken to do." In that context he proposed that the board raise tuition and continue its annual fund-raising campaign in Dallas. Then came the centerpiece. He recommended that the board approve a campaign that year to raise $5 million for SMU's endowment, including $1.5 million and possibly as much as $2 million for the School of Theology. "This is," Lee concluded, "a crucial hour in the history of SMU."[21]

The board readily raised tuition except in the School of Theology, which at that time did not charge tuition. As for raising $5 million for endowment, Smith later recalled that "Mr. Perkins got up and said: 'Well, I will give $50,000 and that is all.'" Nobody else volunteered to make a donation, the meeting adjourned for lunch, and Lee told Smith, "Our campaign is dead." Smith recounted that as he walked over to lunch with Joe Perkins, Perkins said, "I am going to make a million dollars, and I don't know what to do with it." Smith replied, "You ought to give that million dollars here to establish a school of theology." After further conversation Perkins went home and then called Smith to say, "Lois is interested in that. Write me some letters and tell me what you have in mind."[22]

The other incident instrumental in the Perkinses' decision also occurred early in 1944. Paul Martin, in his sixth year as their pastor, visited their home and put before them a vision of how the School of Theology could provide theological education for future clergy in the region. The Perkinses knew Martin well, respected him deeply, and would have taken his counsel with great seriousness. It was probably after both these incidents that the Perkinses visited SMU and met with Hawk, who reinforced what Smith and Martin had said.[23]

Thus began a process that culminated in the largest single benefaction to an American seminary up to that time. Getting there was not simple. Bishop Smith apprised Lee of his conversation with Perkins, and Smith and Lee decided to ask a prominent Dallas architect, Mark Lemmon, to design a larger school of theology complex, with the original Kirby Hall as its center. Meanwhile Smith continued writing to Joe Perkins and suggested that the School of Theology should be named for the Perkinses. Joe Perkins resisted that idea, but Smith persisted. At the General Conference in Kansas City in late April and early May 1944 they talked further. Smith recorded in his journal that Joe Perkins "said that he would give [SMU] $350,000 of Tidewater Oil Stock," but Lois Perkins told Smith, "Don't you let him do that. It is not enough." The conversations progressed rapidly, and the Perkinses mentioned that they were considering a larger gift—$3 million to start and "probably two or three millions later." Sometime that spring Smith and Lee went ahead and asked Lemmon to draw up a sketch of three buildings (two dormitories and a chapel) that might be added to the existing Kirby Hall. Smith decided to show the Perkinses the sketch when the Methodists' South Central Jurisdictional Conference met in Tulsa in June.[24]

At the jurisdictional conference, on June 13, 1944, during a meeting with Umphrey Lee, Paul and Mildred Martin, and A. Frank Smith, Joe and Lois Perkins made a commitment to the school. Joe Perkins said, "Lois and I have talked it over and have decided to give a million dollars to the School of Theology." Martin, who later that week was elected a bishop, afterward wrote, "This was the time in which the project definitely came into being, although the [public] announcement was not made until several months later."[25]

In the second half of 1944 and in early 1945, the Perkinses remained in communication with Smith, Hawk, and others while working out the details of the gift. The couple developed a variety of ideas; for example, Joe Perkins wrote Lee in September 1944 that he was going to give the School of Theology the returns from the sale of three hundred calves on a ranch in Oklahoma, the amount to be added to the endowment fund.[26] The high point came on December 27, when the Perkinses conveyed major oil properties to SMU as part of the newly created Perkins Endowment Fund. The proceeds from these properties for the corpus of the endowment would eventually be worth about $1.35 million.[27]

SMU announced the Perkinses' actions during the School of Theology's Ministers' Week on February 6, 1945, at a meeting of the trustees and in the presence of a number of guests. In a document made public at that time, the Perkinses declared:

Actuated by the belief that the future Peace of the World is dependent upon the work and influence of all the Churches of all Peoples and of all Nations, and knowing that there is not now an adequate number of Ministers in any of the Churches, and desiring to do all we can toward relieving this crisis, we, J. J. Perkins and wife, Lois Perkins, are creating the Perkins Endowment Fund for the purpose of developing and enlarging the School of Theology of Southern Methodist University at Dallas, Texas in the hope that it will become one of the really great Theological Schools of our Nation.[28]

The intention of the Perkinses and of university officials was that the School of Theology would have three more buildings—two dormitories and a chapel, and that no more than $550,000 of the endowment could be used for that purpose. The remainder of the gift was to remain as a permanent endowment fund, so that only the income could be used for the support of the School of Theology.[29]

Immediately after the announcement, Lee read a resolution delegating management of the endowment fund to the board's executive committee, expressing appreciation to the Perkinses, and changing the name of the school to Perkins School of Theology. The board adopted the resolution.[30] From that point on, SMU's School of Theology was a different entity. That day marked a giant step toward the transformation of the school, even though the size of the gift would grow considerably during the next few years.

DEVELOPMENTS IN PERSONNEL AND PROGRAM, 1944–1951

With the large gifts from the Perkinses in 1944 and after, Perkins School of Theology underwent a number of changes. One was a sharp increase in the number of students. Whereas the School of Theology's graduate professional enrollment in the regular terms in 1943–44 had reached 174, it grew to 210 in 1947–48, 302 in 1949–50, and 369 in 1950–51.[31] These students continued to meet for classes in the old Kirby Hall, which had been built for a much smaller school.

With a larger prospective budget Hawk quickly set about enlarging the Perkins faculty. In the fall of 1944 the eight full-time faculty were Hawk in homiletics and pastoral theology, and, in order of seniority, James Seehorn Seneker in religious education, Robert W. Goodloe in church history, John Hicks in Old Testament, Wesley Davis in New Testament, Paul Root in sociology of religion and ethics, James Carlyon in Christian doctrine, and Fred Gealy in history of religions, New Testament Greek, and church music. In addition, the SMU professor of speech, Mary McCord, divided her time between the College of Arts and Sciences and the theology school. By 1950–51 Hawk had enlarged the faculty to fourteen full-time equivalents.[32]

As he began adding faculty members, Hawk had the local church and the field of religious education uppermost in his mind. Since the early 1940s students and alums had made many requests that the department of religious education be strengthened. Many complained that Seneker's courses dealt mainly with the philosophy of religious education and neglected the practical. As a result a subcommittee of the trustees' Committee on the School of Theology conferred with Seneker in 1943. The problem continued, and in 1944 the committee recommended to the trustees that the school establish a new "department of the local church," which would offer courses not only for church administrators but also for educational directors. The committee also recommended that Seneker "be retained in his present position, though some courses must be transferred to the new Department."[33]

The first new appointment to the faculty was that of A. W. Martin, previously a district superintendent in the North Arkansas Conference, to head the new Department of the Local Church, beginning in the fall of 1945. Martin had a special interest in the rural church, as well as in the education of supply pastors—ministers without a seminary degree—and from 1951 until his retirement in 1957 he directed Perkins's field work program. When Martin began planning for his courses, though, Seneker objected to Martin's proposal to teach a course on the organization and administration of the local church, a subject similar to that in one of Seneker's courses. That fall Martin wrote to Hawk, "I have tried to deal firmly, yet sympathetically and fairly with Dr. Seneker in this matter, and I believe that in time we can work out a good many of the difficulties." The faculty approved this and other of Martin's courses, and the new department came into being.[34]

The next addition came in January 1946, when Hawk hired Earl Marlatt as professor of philosophy of religion and homiletics. Born in 1892, Marlatt had received his seminary and Ph.D. degrees from Boston University and had done graduate study at Berlin and Oxford. In late 1945 he had resigned after several difficult years as the dean of the Boston University School of Theology. Hawk, who had worked with him in their capacities as Methodist seminary deans, sympathized with Marlatt in regard to his unpopularity with the BU administration and theology faculty. After Merrimon Cuninggim became the Perkins dean in 1951, Marlatt's title changed to professor of philosophy of religion and religious literature, which it remained until he retired in 1957. Howard Grimes, who was a colleague during Marlatt's last eight active years, observed that he became "increasingly eccentric" as the years went on.[35]

In 1946 Mary McCord, who had taught speech at SMU since 1919, retired. In the fall of 1946 Thomas Marsh joined the faculty as associate professor of speech, teaching three-fifths of his courseload at Perkins and two-fifths at the college. Marsh held a seminary degree from Chicago Theological Seminary and a Ph.D. in speech from Northwestern University; he had seven years of experience as a pastor in the

Chicago area.[36] He continued at SMU until his unexpected death from a heart attack at age sixty-one in 1963.

The other new arrival in 1946 was Benjamin O. Hill, who was visiting professor of missions and counselor to Latin American students. Hill had been a pastor in Cuba with the Methodist Board of Missions from 1907 to 1929, with a year in 1921–22 as visiting professor of missions at the School of Theology, and from 1929 to 1946 he had taught at Lydia Patterson Institute in El Paso. He remained at Perkins until 1952.[37]

Paul Root, who since 1935 had taught sociology and, before Gealy's arrival, missions, had proved to be a strong member of the faculty both academically and in carrying out special responsibilities, such as directing the Circulating Library, but he became restless. In 1944 Hawk wrote Lee that Root thought he could teach two courses in the School of Theology and still do his work as interim pastor of First Methodist Church in Dallas. Hawk feared Root would not be happy on the theology faculty, since he thought of himself as an unusually able preacher who would never reach his potential as an School of Theology professor. Root remained on the Perkins faculty, but in the spring of 1947 he was offered the deanship of the Duke University Divinity School, where he had been held in high esteem since his student years there. Root accepted and was making plans to leave SMU when on May 9 he had a heart attack and three days later died. He was forty-four.[38]

In the fall of 1948 Hawk brought in William Warren Sweet, a widely known professor of American church history who had just retired after twenty years at the University of Chicago, to be professor of church history, providing Perkins with greater depth in that field.[39] Sweet also served as chair of the faculty at Perkins until 1951. He retired in 1952, taught a year at Pomona College in California, and died in 1959.

L. Howard Grimes had received his B.D. degree from the School of Theology in 1940 and then his master of sacred theology degree from Union Theological Seminary in 1941, with a thesis on the sociology of conversion that reflected Paul Root's influence. After serving as an associate pastor at First Methodist Church in Houston, then as an army chaplain during the Second World War, and returning to his earlier position in Houston, Grimes completed his Ph.D. at Columbia in 1949. When Hawk brought him to Perkins that fall, it was in a dual capacity—to teach both sociology of religion and religious education. After Merrimon Cuninggim became dean in 1951, Grimes moved entirely into religious education. He remained on the Perkins faculty until his retirement in 1982 and died in 1989.[40]

The next faculty appointment, in the fall of 1950, was William A. Irwin as professor of Old Testament. A Canadian, Irwin had taught at the University of Toronto from 1919 to 1929 and then at the University of Chicago (where he had earned his Ph.D.) until he retired in 1950. He taught at Perkins as visiting professor in the fall of 1949 and then from 1950 until his second retirement in 1955.[41] Like Sweet, Irwin provided greater depth in a basic field in response to the enlarged student body. He proved to be a stimulating teacher and colleague, both before and after his Perkins retirement.

Also in 1950 Hawk appointed George C. Baker Jr., formerly a pastor in San Antonio and the SMU chaplain since 1949, to be a part-time professor of homiletics. Baker continued in this dual capacity until 1955, when he became the first occupant of the McCreless Chair of Evangelism at Perkins, a position he held until his retirement in 1970.[42] He died in 1974.

By the 1950–51 academic year, then, the ongoing faculty, not including short-term visiting professors, adjuncts, and lecturers, had nearly doubled since 1945. In later years some thought that the enlargement of the Perkins faculty occurred during the years of Merrimon Cuninggim's deanship, from 1951 to 1960, and indeed Perkins did experience most of its growth then. But Hawk took the initial steps, enlarging the 1944 faculty by about 65 percent. The early stages of the Perkins gift made this possible, and the rapid growth of the student body made it imperative.

Another change made possible by the improvement in the financial situation was publishing the *Perkins School of Theology Journal*, finally implementing Hawk's 1938 proposal to the board. The first issue appeared in the fall of 1947 under the editorship of Tom Marsh. In a short introductory article Hawk explained that the *Journal*'s purpose was to maintain contact with friends and graduates who had done so much for the seminary.[43] Thereafter the *Journal* appeared at least twice a year. In its early years it usually had a "Dean's Page," articles by Perkins faculty members, and book reviews under the editorship of Fred Gealy.

In the mid-1940s came gifts to establish two more Ministers' Week lectureships. In 1944 Mrs. George L. Peyton of Mexia, Texas, established a lectureship on preaching in memory of her late husband through a gift of $10,000. The following year Ben D. Jackson and several of his brothers and sisters gave $10,000 to establish a lectureship on the Bible in memory of their parents, Robert Malone Jackson and Ella Jemison Jackson, long-time members of Methodist churches at Tennessee Colony and Palestine, Texas. Of these gifts Lee observed, "This provides for Ministers' Week three endowed lectureships and completes the program that can be conveniently handled for that event."[44]

THE NEW PERKINS QUADRANGLE

The most visible result of the Perkins gifts was the construction of a new theology quadrangle. On July 20, 1945, the executive committee of the SMU board appointed a building committee for Perkins School of Theology; the committee consisted of S. B. Perkins, chair; Hawk; and Eugene McElvaney, Dallas banker and SMU trustee, with Umphrey Lee and Frank McNeny, the executive committee chair, as ex officio members. The building committee employed Mark Lemmon as architect for the Perkins Quadrangle, as it came to be called, and Lemmon drew up plans and discussed them with the committee members.[45] Lemmon's plans located the theology school in a cluster of buildings at the northwest corner of the university (where the law school stands today). That the Perkins Quadrangle came to be situated elsewhere was an important step in the transformation of the school.

While planning was slowly proceeding, Bishop John M. Moore, now retired, wrote to Joe Perkins in May 1947 to propose that the quadrangle be located not at the northwest corner of the campus but on a large empty tract that the university owned north of Highland Park Methodist Church. Perkins replied, "I find myself unable to agree with you on your suggestion. The location now is a very outstanding location and I would certainly hate to give it up for some other location on the campus."[46] For many people that would have ended the matter, but not for Bishop Moore. Although he was now eighty and suffering from sciatica and other ailments, he drew up a six-page, single-spaced letter that he mailed on August 25 to Joe Perkins, Lee, Hawk, and A. Frank Smith.[47] In it Moore set out several reasons why the quadrangle should be located on the site he had suggested—he thought it was twenty acres or more—between the women's dormitories and Highland Park Church, and between Bishop Boulevard and Hillcrest Avenue.[48]

First, Moore said, "it is the most prominent and attractive unoccupied spot on University Hill." Second, it had enough space for all the buildings the school would ever desire or need: for educational work, residential buildings, a chapel, a library, attractive landscaping, near to what was still referred to as "the University Church" (Highland Park Church). That space, he said, "has what a great Theological School like Perkins should have."

Furthermore, the School of Theology, he wrote, was not simply another department but was entitled to a major place on the campus. The Lemmon plan had the quadrangle on only four acres, which would accommodate only part of Perkins; other parts would have to be located elsewhere. The Lemmon plan offered no space for expansion or for beautification. Moore went on to mention what other theological schools had done and were doing—in particular, Southern Baptist and Presbyterian seminaries and Vanderbilt.

Moore thought the Perkins buildings would have to be much more extensive than the building committee envisioned: a larger Kirby Hall, an ample library building, an impressive chapel, a gymnasium, social center, and refectory, and three dormitories for single men, married couples, and families with children. He wanted to make Perkins as good as the best seminaries in the country in its faculty, in the education provided, and in its facilities and location. Competition for the best students would especially come, he thought, from Union in New York, Yale, Drew, Garrett, and Boston. Moore was convinced that the larger location would serve those purposes best.

A week later Joe Perkins responded. He and Lois had discussed the matter with "various interested parties," he wrote, and "I am not at all sure but that you are correct in the suggestion which you have made." He went on to say that they needed to talk the matter out further, but he expected a final decision about location in late September, when he and several SMU leaders would be attending the Seventh Ecumenical Methodist Conference in Springfield, Massachusetts.[49]

Not all were so readily convinced by Moore's argument. Hawk wrote to Smith, "I hate very much to think of us getting out of our commanding location on the campus." The site at the northwest corner of the university would be larger than that of Union, Garrett, and Duke. But moving to the tract near Highland Park Church would remove Perkins from the academic center of the university. Hawk thought it might be better if the dormitories for married students with children were off campus. In mid-September, however, when he realized that both Joe and Lois Perkins favored the larger site, Hawk gave his attention to the implications of that move. The plans being developed for the smaller location added a chapel and two dormitories to the existing Kirby Hall. In the larger location three buildings would look inconsequential. It would be important for the new buildings to command respect, which would require spending $1 million to $1.5 million on the buildings and grounds. Joe Perkins would need to move some of the money he had planned for endowment to go toward the physical plant.[50]

On September 26, 1947, at the conference in Massachusetts, Lee, Hawk, and Smith discussed with the Perkinses the idea of building on the larger site, at a cost of $2 million. The Perkinses agreed with enthusiasm, and the question of location was settled. On October 10 the Trustees Committee on the School of Theology recommended the larger location to the board, and on October 31 the board approved this recommendation, setting aside about fourteen acres in the southwest part of the campus near Highland Park Church for the use of Perkins School of Theology.[51]

With the location settled, the building committee moved quickly to work out a plan for the new buildings. In the winter 1947–48 issue of the *Perkins Journal*, Hawk described the new plan: next to Bishop Boulevard would be a library, classroom-administration building, and a chapel; behind them, near Hillcrest Avenue, would be two apartment buildings for married students and a dormitory for single men—a significantly larger complex than in the earlier plan, along with space for further expansion.[52]

J. S. BRIDWELL AND THE LIBRARY

Hawk had been working for some time to interest Joseph S. Bridwell of Wichita Falls in supporting a new library building for Perkins. Bridwell was born in Missouri in 1885, lived in Oklahoma for a short while, and in 1909 moved to Wichita Falls. Although he first went into real estate, almost half his transactions as early as 1913 involved oil leases. In 1921 he leased land near Nocona, Texas, which proved to be a major oil field. Soon he established the Bridwell Oil Company, and by the 1940s and 1950s he was the largest independent oil operator in Texas. In addition, he accumulated more than 160,000 acres of ranchland in Archer and Clay counties and had more than six thousand head of livestock. Like Joe Perkins, Bridwell became a member of First Methodist Church in Wichita Falls. Before long he was also a member of the boards of SMU and the Methodist Orphanage in Waco.[53]

By the summer of 1945 conversations between Hawk and Bridwell had reached the stage at which Bridwell wrote, "Wish you would give me an idea of what you think that program [the library] would cost, and it is possible I might be able to find somebody that has that loose 'change' they could put in it." Hawk replied that a new library would cost $150,000, that this library would be known throughout the country, and that he hoped Bridwell's name would in some way be associated with the School of Theology. The conversations continued, and by the fall of 1948 Bridwell had decided to build the library. He wrote to Hawk, "You were instrumental in having me change my idea [from building a women's dormitory] to the library, you and Joe Perkins." Bridwell signed papers to provide for the library should he die before completion of the project. That fall Bridwell and his daughter, Margaret Bridwell Bowdle, gave their initial gift of $250,000 for the building—significantly more than Hawk had earlier sought. Other substantial Bridwell gifts to the library followed, including a 1962 gift for the purchase of more than two hundred fifteenth-century books; money for enlarging the building; and additional large gifts made through the Bridwell Foundation after Bridwell's death in 1966.[54]

Notable among other gifts to the library during this period was one in 1947 from Annie Hughey of Charlotte, Texas, of oil property valued at $250,000, the income from which was to go toward "the purchase of books, carrying on of research, and the necessary expenditures for the library, apart from the salaries of the librarian and staff." Hawk said he hoped the income from that endowment would make Bridwell Library one of the best theological libraries in the region.[55]

Among Hawk's actions in the later years of his deanship was the appointment of a new librarian. Kate Warnick had been the librarian for the School of Theology since November 1918, caring for the collection that from 1924 was located in Kirby Hall. After Fred Gealy joined the faculty in 1939, he had often chaired the faculty committee on the library, and in 1947 Hawk appointed him part-time library director in addition to his regular faculty responsibilities. Then, in 1950, Hawk chose Decherd H. Turner as the first full-time director of Bridwell Library. Warnick continued on the library staff for many years as research librarian. Turner had received his undergraduate degree from the University of Missouri and his B.D. from Vanderbilt, and he had done graduate work at the library school of Peabody College in Nashville. From 1948 to 1950 he was the librarian of the religion section of the Joint University Libraries at Vanderbilt University. He assumed his Bridwell Library duties on September 1. That fall Hawk wrote to Bishop Smith, "We have been very fortunate in having Decherd Turner as our Librarian. He is really a wonder. I have never had greater satisfaction in the employment of any man on the staff here since I came to the University."[56]

CONSTRUCTING AND DEDICATING THE QUADRANGLE

With these major gifts assured, the groundbreaking for the new quadrangle was scheduled for February 8, 1949. As Hawk explained, the event should occur during Ministers' Week, which "brings together some 1,000 to 1,200 preachers, and it is the psychological time to have a program such as we have in mind."[57] On that happy occasion Joe and Lois Perkins joined in turning spadefuls of dirt, and Joe Perkins announced the names of the buildings. In the center of the quadrangle would be the Lois Perkins Chapel, reflecting, it is said, Joe Perkins's appreciation for the Georgian chapel at the Yale Divinity School. On Bishop Boulevard and south of the chapel would be the new Harper and Annie Kirby Hall (retaining the name of the original Kirby Hall up campus, which was renamed Florence Hall). Opposite Kirby Hall would be the library, to be named Bridwell Library. Behind these buildings along Hillcrest Avenue would be two dormitories for single men, Smith Hall, named in honor of A. Frank Smith; Perkins Hall, for Sam B. Perkins, Joe Perkins's older brother; and two dormitories for married students, Martin Hall, for Bishop Paul Martin, former pastor of First Methodist Church in Wichita Falls; and Hawk Hall, for Eugene B. Hawk.

Construction proceeded apace, and in the fall of 1950 the process of moving into the new buildings began. The move was completed by the end of January 1951, in time for the dedication of the quadrangle on February 8, during Ministers' Week. The daylong ceremonies included an address by Ernest C. Colwell, president of the University of Chicago, to an estimated thirty-five hundred people gathered in McFarlin Auditorium; the introduction of the visibly happy principal donors, Joe and Lois Perkins, Joe Bridwell, and his daughter, Margaret Bridwell Bowdle; and the formal dedication of each building in turn. Joe Perkins ventured the opinion, "As far as I know it is the only theology school ever completed as a unit." Lois Perkins added, "Now that this school is finished, its faculty has a big job to do. These new buildings just represent a physical plant. It's a good job well done . . . but the big spiritual job is up to the faculty."[58]

The *Dallas Morning News* estimated that as of the dedication the Perkinses had donated $5 million to the School of Theology, including buildings and endowment. To that, Lois Perkins commented, "The size of a donation never excited Jesus."[59]

Actually, the construction of the quadrangle was not yet complete. In the fall of 1951, only six weeks after Merrimon Cuninggim had assumed the deanship, he wrote Lee that Perkins needed another building. Even with the new Kirby Hall, he said, the school was already short of space. The faculty had to offer fewer courses and seriously limit registration for some of them in order to fit the classes into the available classrooms. Besides, the professors desperately needed more office space, and the school had no small seminar rooms for upper-level courses. "For all these reasons I recommend the construction of a new classroom and office building, if the funds are available." The funds proved to be available. The Perkinses agreed to donate the additional money for the new building, expected to cost $450,000, and later they gave another $35,000 for furnishings. The new building was located just south of the new Kirby Hall, completed in the 1953–54 academic year, dedicated during Ministers' Week of 1954, and named for the former SMU president and now bishop Charles C. Selecman. It included an auditorium that, at the request of the dean and the Perkins faculty, was named the Lois Perkins Auditorium. Another building was opened in 1959—a dormitory for married students, appropriately named for Bishop John M. Moore.[60]

With the dedication of the new Perkins quadrangle in 1951, Eugene B. Hawk attained the pinnacle of his achievements as dean. He had taken office in 1933, in the depths of the Depression, when the financial situation of the School of Theology was precarious and the faculty and the student body were small and regionally oriented. He had had strong support on which he could draw: faculty members deeply committed to their work, widespread support in southwestern Methodism for the school, and the strong and supportive leadership of the SMU trustees, whose chairs during his deanship were two bishops, Moore, from 1932 to 1938, and Smith, from 1938 on.

It was fitting that soon after the dedication of the quadrangle Lois Perkins wrote

Hawk, "It was really your day, Feb. 8, 1951, and if anyone has a monument to them, it is you. As I said, we gave a little money, then sat back and watched others work. We realize what a gigantic task the erection of this great school has been. But you have not failed in any way."[61]

Yet the transformation of the Perkins School of Theology was still in process. In the midst of his preparations for the dedication, Hawk learned that he was about to be replaced as dean.

---

1. Winifred T. Weiss and Charles S. Proctor, *Umphrey Lee: A Biography* (Nashville, Tenn.: Abingdon, 1971), 34–40, 55–56, 58–70, 79–81, 93; *General Minutes*, Methodist Episcopal Church, South, 1923, p. 63; *Who's Who in Methodism*, edited by Elmer T. Clark (Chicago: A. N. Marquis, 1952), 413; Mary Martha Hosford Thomas, *Southern Methodist University: Founding and Early Years* (Dallas: Southern Methodist University Press, 1974), 166.

2. Executive committee minutes, September 30, 1938.

3. Board of trustees minutes, November 7, 1938. Thomas says the list had eight names (*Southern Methodist University*, 166); Weiss and Proctor (*Umphrey Lee*, 92–93) cite six names as prominently mentioned. The board of trustees' minutes report that the committee presented six names; some are on Weiss and Proctor's list and some are not.

4. The board of trustees' minutes for November 7, 1938, record that Frank L. McNeny, vice chair of the board, traveled east and interviewed Lee, among others. Thomas (*Southern Methodist University*, 166) and Weiss and Proctor (*Umphrey Lee*, 93) report that Lee did not have an interview with the full nominating committee, and the board minutes confirm this.

5. Board of trustees minutes, November 7, 1938; Weiss and Proctor, *Umphrey Lee*, 96.

6. Board of trustees minutes, June 6, 1939.

7. Ibid. The publications cited by Lee were Paul A. Root, *The Nature and Social Significance of Tradition* (Dallas: Mathis, Van Nort, 1938); J. T. Carlyon, "The Impact of Gnosticism on Early Christianity," in John Thomas McNeill, Matthew Spinka, and Harold R. Willoughby, eds., *Environmental Factors in Christian History* (Chicago: University of Chicago Press, 1939); Fred D. Gealy, "Jesus the Layman," *Crozer Quarterly* 15 (July 1938): 176–86; Gealy, "Problems Faced by Christians in Japan," *45th Foreign Missions Conference* (no further information provided in the minutes); and Gealy, "Japanese Christians and the Sino-Japanese Conflict," *Christian World Facts*, no. 19 (autumn 1938): 10–13.

8. Eugene B. Hawk to A. Frank Smith, September 30, 1940, Eugene B. Hawk Papers, Bridwell Library.

9. "Reports of Administrative Officers of Southern Methodist University" for the academic year 1939–40, p. 20, Hawk Papers; board of trustees minutes, June 3, 1941.

10. Board of trustees minutes, statement by the president, February 6, 1940; see also the minutes of June 3, 1941, and June 8, 1942.

11. Board of trustees minutes, June 3, 1941; "Distribution of Theological Schools' Share in Distribution of World Service Funds for Month of August, 1943," and "Annual Report to the General Commission on World Service and Finance of The Methodist Church by the Nine Methodist Schools of Theology to Which an Appropriation for the Quadrennium Was Made by the General Conference of 1944, Meeting in Kansas City," June 1, 1945, Hawk Papers.

12. These figures are derived from the tables provided by the School of Theology registrar, Nell Anders, in each annual *Bulletin*. They include only graduate theological students in the fall, winter, and spring terms and exclude undergraduates, special students, auditors, and the summer session. This produces smaller figures each year than those cited in the trustees' minutes but allows for comparison over the years.

13. Hawk to Paul Neff Garber, November 7, 1939, Hawk Papers.
14. Executive committee minutes, February 17, 1938; board of trustees minutes, February 7, 1939; Lewis Howard Grimes, *A History of Perkins School of Theology*, edited by Roger Loyd (Dallas: Southern Methodist University Press, 1993), 69; *Perkins Perspective* 16, no. 3 (March–June 1977).
15. Executive committee minutes, July 6, 1938; board of trustees minutes, June 6, 1939; *Bulletin*, October 1938, additions on pp. 181, 189; note by Kate Warnick on Ministers' Week Program for 1939, Bridwell archives; SMU *Bulletin*, October 1940, 162; Grimes, *A History of Perkins School of Theology*, 76; *Bulletin*, 1947–48, 39.
16. *Who's Who in Methodism*, 1952, p. 190; Hawk to Russell Dicks, January 23, 1941, Hawk Papers; executive committee minutes, October 29, 1943; Grimes, *A History of Perkins School of Theology*, 71, 226n52; *Bulletin*, 1942–43, pt. 7:28–29; Dicks to Hawk, April 22, 1943, Hawk Papers; board of trustees minutes, May 31, 1943; executive committee minutes, October 29, 1943.
17. Walter N. Vernon, *Methodism Moves across North Texas* (Dallas: Historical Society, North Texas Conference, The Methodist Church, 1967), 242. See also *The New Handbook of Texas* (Austin: Texas State Historical Association, 1996), 5:152; and Norman W. Spellmann and Betty B. Spellmann, *History of First Methodist Church Wichita Falls, Texas: A Century of Faith, 1881–1981* (Dallas: Southern Methodist University Printing Department, 1981), 39.
18. Lois Craddock Perkins, *The History of My Life. Mrs. J. J. (Lois) Perkins. February 1932* (privately printed; copyright by Elizabeth Perkins Prothro, 1993); Spellmann and Spellmann, *History of First Methodist Church*, 51; *New Handbook of Texas*, 5:153; Vernon, *Methodism Moves*, 242; Norman W. Spellmann, *Growing a Soul: The Story of A. Frank Smith* (Dallas: Southern Methodist University Press, 1979), 322, citing A. Frank Smith, interview by Charles S. Braden, January 23, 1962, in the Charles S. Braden Papers, Bridwell Library.
19. *Bulletin*, 1922, 22–23; 1928, 15; 1939, 11. The Hawk-Perkins correspondence is in the Hawk Papers.
20. Spellmann, *Growing a Soul*, 319, 322–28, 330.
21. Board of trustees minutes, February 8, 1944.
22. Spellmann, *Growing a Soul*, 320–21 (Spellmann cites the interview by Braden).
23. Todd Rasberry, interview by author, August 26, 2009, Dallas; *Perspective*, winter 2009, 18. Rasberry, director of development at Perkins, attributes the account of Martin's visit to descendants of Joe and Lois Perkins who had heard family members tell the story.
24. Spellmann, *Growing a Soul*, 322, citing Smith's daily journal for May 2, 1944; Grimes, *A History of Perkins School of Theology*, 85.
25. Spellmann, *Growing a Soul*, 323; Walter N. Vernon, *Forever Building: The Life and Ministry of Paul E. Martin* (Dallas: Southern Methodist University Press, 1973), 117.
26. Hawk to Smith, September 30, 1944, Hawk Papers.
27. "Establishing the Perkins Endowment Fund for the Support of the School of Theology at Southern Methodist University at Dallas, Texas," Hawk Papers; Spellmann, *Growing a Soul*, 324; board of trustees minutes, June 25, 1945.
28. "Establishing the Perkins Endowment Fund."
29. Ibid.
30. Board of trustees minutes, February 6, 1945.
31. See *School of Theology Catalogs* for those years. Unless otherwise noted, all references to the catalog are to the School of Theology's catalog.
32. Catalogs, 1945–51.
33. Board of trustees minutes, June 26, 1944.
34. Paul Martin to Hawk, June 5, 1945; A. W. Martin to Hawk, October 8, 1945, Hawk Papers.
35. Grimes, *A History of Perkins School of Theology*, 70.
36. Board of trustees minutes, June 24, 1946.
37. *Perkins School of Theology Journal*, fall 1948, 12.
38. Hawk to Lee, August 10, 1944, Hawk Papers; Fred D. Gealy, "Paul Adelbert Root—in Memoriam," *Perkins Journal*, fall 1947, 11–13; H. Neill McFarland, conversation with author, May 24, 2007.

39. *Perkins Journal*, fall 1948, 13.
40. William Richey Hogg, introduction to Grimes, *A History of Perkins School of Theology*, xi–xx; *Bulletin*, 1949–50, pt. 7:4.
41. Edward C. Hobbs, foreword to *A Stubborn Faith: Papers on Old Testament and Related Subjects Presented to Honor William Andrew Irwin* (Dallas: Southern Methodist University Press, 1956), v–ix.
42. Catalog, 1950–51, 4, and 1956–57, 12.
43. *Perkins Journal*, fall 1947, 3.
44. Board of trustees minutes, February 5, 1946; catalog, 1946–47, 18–19.
45. Building committee minutes, Southern Methodist University, July 20, 1945, Hawk Papers.
46. J. J. Perkins to John M. Moore, June 3, 1947, John M. Moore Papers, Bridwell Library.
47. From a paper by Bruce C. Galloway, citing Moore letters from 1946 to 1948, for a course taught by Professor Tom Marsh, Moore Papers.
48. Moore to Perkins, Lee, Hawk, and Smith, August 25, 1947, Moore Papers.
49. Perkins to Moore, September 4, 1947, Moore Papers; Spellmann, *Growing a Soul*, 326.
50. Hawk to Smith, August 29, 1947, Hawk Papers; Spellmann, *Growing a Soul*, 326; Hawk to Smith, September 15, 1947, Smith Papers, cited in Spellmann, *Growing a Soul*, 488.
51. Spellmann, *Growing a Soul*, 327 (citing Smith's daily journal entry for Saturday, September 27, 1947); Eugene B. Hawk, "The New Quadrangle," *Perkins Journal*, winter 1947, insert; board of trustees minutes, October 31, 1947.
52. Hawk, "New Quadrangle."
53. Jack O. Loftin, "Bridwell, Joseph Sterling," *The New Handbook of Texas* (Austin: Texas State Historical Association, 1996), 1:732; Mary Basham Loggie, "Joseph Sterling Bridwell," a thesis, Department of History, Midwestern University, August 1967, 26, Bridwell Library Papers.
54. J. S. Bridwell to E. B. Hawk, June 30, 1945; Hawk to Bridwell, July 5, 1945; Hawk to Charles C. Selecman, July 13, 1945; Bridwell to Hawk, November 16, 1948, quoted in a letter from Hawk to Smith, November 29, 1948; Bridwell to Hawk, November 16, 1948, all in Hawk Papers; "Bridwell Giving to Perkins," Bridwell Library Papers; *Bridwell at Fifty: Books, Benefactors, and Bibliophiles, An Exhibition at Bridwell Library, Perkins School of Theology, Southern Methodist University, 8 February–2 June, 2001*, curated by Valerie R. Hotchkiss (Dallas: Bridwell Library, 2001).
55. Decherd Turner to Hawk, August 8, 1951; Hawk to Turner, August 8, 1951, Hawk Papers.
56. Board of trustees minutes, May 18, 1990; Hawk to Smith, December 22, 1950, Hawk Papers. In 1953 Turner was also appointed assistant professor of bibliography at Perkins (Board of Trustees minutes, May 5, 1953).
57. Hawk to Smith, November 16, 1948, Hawk Papers.
58. *Dallas Times Herald*, February 8, 1951.
59. Ibid., February 9, 1951, and April 9, 1952.
60. Merrimon Cuninggim to Umphrey Lee, October 10, 1951, Merrimon Cuninggim Papers, Bridwell Library; *Dallas Morning News*, April 9, 1952; executive committee minutes, September 11, 1953; board of trustees minutes, May 6, 1954.
61. Stuart M. Doss, "Theology Thrives under SMU Dean," *Dallas Morning News*, February 25, 1951.

PART II

The Second Perkins

Reenvisioning the Future, 1951–1954

T he arrival of Merrimon Cuninggim as dean in the fall of 1951 marks the beginning of the second Perkins. Cuninggim was a remarkable person: he had a magnetic personality yet was not one who sought the spotlight. His quick intelligence and avid desire to learn were accompanied by a strong drive to win any contest of intellect or skill, yet he never put down those he had bested. His commitment to social justice was deep, and he displayed courage in pursuing it. He was keenly discerning of ability in others, and his own inner sense of security allowed him to choose able people to work with. As a leader his strength lay not in dominating the scene but in challenging and assisting those around him to maximize their potential. He may have lacked sufficient understanding of the fears and insecurities of those who disagreed with him, and he could have worked more patiently and steadily in cultivating outside supporters. Yet he did not take opposition personally, and he offered charitable interpretations of what he considered to be mistaken positions. His strengths far outweighed his weaknesses.

Cuninggim was born May 12, 1911, in Nashville, Tennessee. His father, Jesse Lee Cuninggim, was professor of Sunday school pedagogy (religious education) at the SMU School of Theology from 1918 to 1921 and thereafter was for twenty-two years the president of Scarritt College in Kansas City and then Nashville. Merrimon was educated at Vanderbilt (A.B., 1931), Duke (M.A., 1933), Oxford (A.B., 1935, as a Rhodes Scholar; diploma in 1936), and Yale (B.D., 1939, Ph.D., 1941). While at Oxford he was the British intercollegiate tennis champion and contended at Wimbledon. After completion of his studies he held faculty posts at Emory and Henry College and at Denison University. In 1944 he was ordained an elder in The Methodist Church and received into full connection in the Holston Annual

Conference in the southern Appalachians. From 1944 to 1946 he was a chaplain on the battleship *Tennessee*. After the war he served as professor of religion and chair of the department at Pomona College until 1951. His wife, Whitty, was a person of comparable ability and strength of character who joined actively in the life of the academy and the wider community. They had three daughters.[1]

When Umphrey Lee was dean of Vanderbilt Divinity School, he would have had occasion to work with Jesse Cuninggim as president of Scarritt and would have come to know Merrimon then, if not earlier. In 1943–44 and again in 1946 Lee, in his capacity as SMU president, contacted Merrimon Cuninggim about coming to SMU as director of religious life on the campus. In 1946 Cuninggim considered the idea seriously but decided "it is not the kind of thing that I ought to try to do at the moment." Instead he took the job at Pomona.[2] In November 1950 Lee approached Cuninggim again, this time about the deanship of Perkins. Cuninggim came to Dallas for a private visit on November 30, after which he wrote to thank Lee and his wife for their hospitality and for "such a frank and challenging picture of the situation in the Perkins School."[3] Matters moved rapidly, and on December 19 Cuninggim met quietly off campus with Lee, the School of Theology Committee of the Board of Trustees, and both Joe and Lois Perkins. The result was an invitation to become the dean of Perkins at the start of the 1951–52 academic year, which Cuninggim accepted.[4]

Such transactions often have complicating features. After the December 19 meeting, Lee wrote Cuninggim, "One of our friends" wants to be sure that the man coming "is not a crank on labor matters." He suggested that Cuninggim write him, Lee, about it, and he would pass the letter on. Cuninggim then enclosed a letter to Lee in which he briefly set forth a balanced statement, appreciating labor's right to organize but recognizing problems with both labor and management. Lee presumably gave it to a conservative trustee, and that seems to have taken care of the question.[5]

A more serious complication was that Lee had not discussed the deanship with Dean Hawk, who was not expecting to retire until 1952. Hawk learned about Cuninggim's appointment on December 9, 1950, from his friend Jack Benton, the dean of Vanderbilt Divinity School.[6] In his history of Perkins, Howard Grimes (at this point relying, as he says, upon his memory) records the story that Hawk had an unnamed friend in mind to be his successor and had even talked with him about the position. When Hawk saw the friend on a train, to his surprise the friend told him Cuninggim would be appointed.[7] Assuming this story is reliable, the person Hawk had in mind to succeed him as dean was Jack Benton. After Lee gave Hawk official word of the appointment in early January, Lee wrote Cuninggim that he felt Hawk was offended that Lee had not said anything about it earlier. By February Lee thought Hawk approved of the decision.[8] Although Hawk wrote to congratulate Cuninggim warmly on the appointment, and they continued to work together on the transition, Hawk apparently resented how the appointment had been handled.[9] This affected events after Cuninggim arrived.

In Cuninggim's January 1 letter of acceptance to Lee, he added, "If it meets with your approval I want to do a little confidential exploring with [Professor Albert C.] Outler [of the Yale Divinity School faculty]. I'll wait on this until I hear from you." Lee telegraphed Cuninggim to get in touch with Outler immediately. The next day Lee wrote Cuninggim to explain further: "I wired you yesterday about Outler because Doctor Hawk had made an engagement for us to have dinner with Doctor Outler Tuesday, the 9th, in Atlantic City." That dinner turned out well; Lee judged that Outler was "definitely interested in coming to Dallas," though he had not yet decided and planned to talk it over with Cuninggim. That Cuninggim was going to be dean strongly appealed to Outler. (It was later reported that Lee had approached Outler for the deanship and that Outler had urged Lee to recruit Cuninggim instead.[10] Outler and Cuninggim had been at Yale together when Outler was doing his doctoral studies and Cuninggim his seminary degree.) Salary they could work out. Outler wrote to Hawk of his "unabashed admiration for the job you have done in building the foundations and opening the way for a significant job of work there in the Southwest." A complication, though, was that Outler was scheduled for a sabbatical leave in 1951–52 and did not want to give it up. As it turned out, he was not able to work out a leave for that year from Yale Divinity School, and in April 1951 Lee and Cuninggim encouraged him to come to Perkins, which he did.[11]

Albert C. Outler was born November 17, 1908, to a south Georgia Methodist minister and his wife. After receiving an undergraduate degree at Wofford College in Spartanburg, South Carolina, in 1928, Albert Outler taught English and was a pastor for two years. He received his seminary degree at Emory University (B.D., 1933). In 1931 he and Carlotta Smith were married; they had two children, a daughter and a son. After several years as pastor and associate pastor in Georgia, he did his doctoral study at Yale (Ph.D., 1938). He then joined the Duke University Divinity School faculty in historical theology, where he remained until 1945. At that point he moved to the Yale Divinity School faculty and in 1948 was designated Timothy Dwight Professor of Theology.[12]

John Deschner has written that Outler's move to Perkins—"leaving a histori-cally distinguished chair for a professorship in a denominational Southern seminary of middle rank"—astonished his friends and acquaintances.[13] It also astonished many who respected him from a distance. I recall my own reaction as I was completing my first year of seminary study at Yale: "Why does he want to do that?" I would have been in his course in systematic theology the following year, and instead he was going off to some place in Texas. Little did I know about either Outler or that place in Texas. Only much later did I realize that Outler had reason to hope he could help bring Perkins into the top tier of theological schools in America.

Lee was hoping to keep the new dean's appointment quiet, since he did not want to upstage Hawk and the dedication ceremonies for the new quadrangle, which were scheduled for February 8, 1951. So instead of asking the trustees to meet on February 9 to confirm Cuninggim's appointment, he arranged for the confirmation to take place in May. Cuninggim agreed and did not attend the dedication, though he thought there was no chance of keeping the appointment quiet. Already the news was out around Yale (much to Outler's annoyance, as he had wanted to break the story himself at a later time).[14] The Perkins faculty knew before the February 8 dedi-cation. Lee had met to discuss the matter with Goodloe, Hicks, and Carlyon, and Lee reported to Cuninggim, "I think you are coming in with the full support of the faculty." When Hawk and William Warren Sweet, the chair of the faculty, wrote Cuninggim about plans for the teaching staff for 1951–52, he replied that he was "in no position to take part in the planning." He appreciated their letting him know what they were doing, but, as he told Lee, "other than for my interview with Outler, . . . I have no desire to horn in on the show until the time has come."[15]

In January Hawk was assuming Cuninggim would take over the responsibilities of dean at the end of the fiscal year, June 30. As the time drew nearer, though, he decided he preferred to retire on September 1, which would be exactly eighteen years after he had become dean. The date was satisfactory to both Lee and Cuninggim.[16]

Hawk, however, was still unhappy about how the change in deans had been handled. He wrote Joe Perkins on April 23, "I do not know that there is any need for going into details in this matter. However, some time if you would like to know my side of this picture I will be very glad to give it to you. There are just some things that should not be done."[17]

When the trustees met on May 11, they elected Cuninggim to be dean of Perkins. Hawk had been administrative vice president of SMU since 1939 in addition to his responsibilities as dean. The board retained him as vice president and assigned him "larger responsibilities as second in command at the university." He would be acting president in Lee's absence and would chair SMU's administrative board.[18] The next day the Perkins faculty gave a dinner in the dining room of Perkins Hall in honor of the Hawks.

MOVING INTO THE DEANSHIP

With the arrival of Merrimon Cuninggim and Albert Outler and the retirement of Hawk, the Perkins faculty consisted of fourteen full-time members and two part time (see appendix A). There were four regular faculty in Bible (John Hicks and William A. Irwin in Old Testament; Wesley Davis and Fred Gealy in New Testament), three in the history of Christianity (Robert W. Goodloe, Albert Outler, and William Warren Sweet), and one in missions (Benjamin O. Hill, visiting professor from 1946 to 1952). Gealy taught part time in the history of religions, and five faculty members taught Christian thought and life (James Carlyon, Earl Marlatt, Outler, Howard Grimes in social ethics, and, to the extent that he would be teaching, Cuninggim in social ethics). Two taught religious education (Grimes and James Seehorn Seneker), one taught the local church (A. W. Martin), one church music (Gealy), and one taught speech part time (Thomas Marsh). In addition, George Baker Jr., the university chaplain, taught part time in homiletics. Several professors were adjuncts or in a visiting capacity in philosophy of religion, homiletics, contemporary Judaism, social ethics, church history, and church administration.[19]

There was a large gap in ages between the majority of older and minority of younger faculty. By the fall of 1951 eight were sixty or older. At seventy Sweet was the oldest, followed by Hill, Carlyon, Irwin, Seneker, Hicks, Goodloe, and Martin. Marlatt was fifty-nine, and Davis and Gealy were fifty-seven. Of the younger ones,

Marsh was fifty; Baker, forty-seven; Outler, forty-two; Cuninggim, forty; and Grimes, thirty-six. The median age was fifty-nine and a half. As SMU had a mandatory retirement age of sixty-five, eleven of the sixteen might have been expected to retire during the next eight years.

The arrival of a new dean heralds a time of change. Add to that the approaching retirements, the new quadrangle, the Perkins endowment money, the larger student body, and high expectations. Appropriately, Cuninggim soon initiated a series of faculty seminars to discuss the needs and plans of the school, both to give direction to the changes and to enhance the faculty's sense of collegiality.[20] The faculty members were to meet roughly every two weeks for supper, followed by the presentation of a paper by one of them and informal discussion. Goodloe led off the first session on October 24 with a paper on Perkins's primary task. The discussion was wide-ranging, including questions of standards, difficulty of the curriculum, number of students to be admitted, and whether Perkins should have a graduate program beyond the B.D. (Outler was for it, Grimes was against).[21] Cuninggim's memo a week later was upbeat. He identified several matters of common agreement, in particular that the primary task was to prepare parish ministers, and that a second would be to institute graduate study beyond the B.D. He acknowledged that the faculty had differences about means and timing, but he found the agreements to be more significant than the differences: "A good groundwork for the discussions ahead."[22]

To initiate the November 7 seminar, Sweet presented a paper on fields in which more staff was needed. Cuninggim's assessment of that session's discussion was negative: no consensus, confused thinking, little constructive outcome, emerging differences of opinion; disappointing session.[23]

At the next seminar they discussed names of potential new colleagues. Cuninggim reported on a recent trip to the Northeast. "Best meeting yet," he noted. Then came a session called "The Task of the Minister" (a paper by Cuninggim). In the discussion Irwin cautioned, "Begin by asking, 'What do students need to know?' rather than what to teach." On February 15 A. W. Martin introduced the topic of field work. The group wrestled with how field work might integrate the various in-class and off-campus experiences, the need for careful supervision, and how faculty should be involved in supervision. On March 7 Irwin initiated the discussion with three- and four-year curriculum plans. Future ministers need both content and practical considerations, he argued; the Bible is the heart of the curriculum, but church history is "scarcely secondary" to the Bible; and the minister must be a scholar. Some courses are essential and must be required of all, but the time is short, and we must recognize individual differences. Students need a chance to study the biblical languages. They need many electives. With Irwin's contributions, that session was provocative. It was followed by one on March 21 in which Davis, Grimes, and Outler responded to Irwin, and Irwin gave a rebuttal in which he proposed a pattern of core courses. "See the thing as a whole," he urged, "and set up the courses on the basis of it."[24] Two more sessions, one introduced by Marlatt, the other by Carlyon, concluded the series.[25]

In his report to Lee on the 1951–52 academic year, Cuninggim summarized what he thought the seminars had achieved. He judged that they had led to a gain in faculty morale. In these sessions the members communicated with each other and in the process discovered they did not differ as much as some had thought. They examined the present state of the school, the minister's task, the kind of school they needed in order to educate for that task, and what type of program Perkins should offer.[26]

The seminars also set the stage for a major endeavor the following academic year, when Cuninggim appointed a committee on curricular revision that he charged with writing a proposal for faculty action.

The year 1951–52 saw two other important moves to strengthen the faculty's work. One, discussed earlier, was to plan for another building that would provide more classrooms and more and larger offices for faculty. Construction of Selecman Hall soon began. Including the small auditorium named for Lois Perkins, its total cost was $517,785, plus $35,000 for furnishings, all paid for by Joe and Lois Perkins. The building was completed in the winter of 1953–54.[27]

The other move was to hire three new faculty members for the fall of 1952. On March 5 Joseph W. Mathews accepted an invitation to become the first full-time teacher in Christian ethics at Perkins since the death of Paul Root in 1947. Mathews had studied at Asbury College, Drew, and Yale and was teaching at Colgate University. His Ph.D. dissertation was still incomplete.

Also on March 5 Edward C. Hobbs, a graduate student at the University of Chicago, was invited to join the faculty in New Testament. Because Hobbs was an

Episcopalian, his appointment involved more than a routine process. If he accepted, he would be the first non-Methodist full member of the Perkins faculty. Cuninggim argued, in correspondence with Bishop Smith (and, one presumes, in discussion with the faculty), that having non-Methodist faculty members should not be a problem so long as most of the faculty were Methodists and so long as professors were Methodist if they were in fields where being a Methodist was especially important.[28] The faculty minutes merely noted, "This possible objection was carefully examined, and in the light of all factors involved, decision was made to proceed with the invitation."[29]

The third new faculty appointment for the academic year was Marvin T. Judy as assistant to A. W. Martin, director of field work, and part-time teacher of church administration. After seminary Judy had done graduate study in rural sociology at Iowa State University. Following faculty discussion at its April 16 meeting, Cuninggim invited Judy, and he accepted.[30]

One change in 1951–52 was the tightening of admissions standards. Before 1951 the dean had, in effect, been the admissions officer, and any applicant with an undergraduate degree (sometimes a degree from a nonaccredited college) was admitted. Cuninggim changed this policy. First, he appointed a faculty admissions committee of five, chaired initially by Albert Outler. The committee, rather than the dean, would decide whom to admit.[31] Second, the committee recommended standards that were then approved by the faculty. The requirements were not rigorous; among others, the applicant had to have an undergraduate degree from an accredited college with a grade point average of C+ or better, although extenuating circumstances would be considered, and had to be perceived as having the "gifts and graces" for ordained ministry. The faculty also operated with a limit of four hundred on total enrollment.[32] The result was that some applicants were rejected. Cuninggim reported to Lee that even though the Committee on Admissions had accepted "the largest class in the School's history" for the fall of 1952, "they were still called upon to turn down approximately one in every three who applied for entrance sometime during the year, almost one in two who applied for September." This created a new experience for clergy around the region, who might sponsor someone who felt called to preach but then did not get accepted. The surprise, Cuninggim said, was not that some clergy objected but that "the objections are no more numerous or no more serious than they are." As time passed, the school rejected fewer applicants, perhaps because fewer of those with weak records applied. From his experience as chair of the admissions committee from 1954 to 1959, Grimes writes that only ten were turned down in 1955, though twenty-five were rejected in 1959.[33]

DESEGREGATING THE PERKINS STUDENT BODY

The Perkins student body had begun to grow soon after the announcement in 1945 of the initial major gift from the Perkinses and with the end of World War II. The total graduate-professional enrollment for the regular terms in 1940–41 was 137. Growth was moderate during the war years, but it accelerated thereafter. The total stood at 182 in 1945–46, 224 in 1947–48, and 394 in 1950–51.[34] While he was dean, Hawk proposed to Lee an enrollment of five hundred in the fall of 1951, but Lee replied that for various reasons this could not be done, especially given the school's limited resources.[35] The larger student body of this period was more diverse in that it included some veterans returning from the war, but it continued to be lily white with limited exceptions. It also continued to be composed almost entirely of men.

Early in Merrimon Cuninggim's conversations with Umphrey Lee about coming to Perkins, he asked Lee how soon the school would admit Negroes (the accepted terminology of the time) as regular students at Perkins. "With great pride Lee responded, 'The way is open now. You can start working on it the day you come.'"[36] As Cuninggim reported it, Lee had sounded out some friends on the board of trustees about the idea, and the response was sufficiently positive that he had raised the question at the November 1950 meeting of the board. In turn, the board "committed the matter of admission of negroes to the School of Theology to the administration with approval of the principle and with the direction that the administration be given power to act, if, as and when, it seems to be timely and proper." This action set no restrictions on the activities of any black students who might be enrolled; it simply did not deal explicitly with that kind of question.[37]

A few blacks had attended Perkins several years earlier, though not as regularly enrolled students. In 1946 Dwight Culver was working on a Ph.D. thesis at Yale titled "The Negro in the Methodist Church." He wrote Hawk that someone had told him that Perkins now admitted Negro students. That would be an unusual step for a southern school. Would Hawk clarify the school's policy? Hawk replied that Perkins had two classes for Negro students, one in church history and the other in New Testament. They met in the afternoon, not in morning classes with the regular seminary students, but they were receiving the same kind of work as in the regular classes.[38]

By 1949 black students were apparently taking classes with whites, though still not enrolled. That spring, in answer to an inquiry from Waldo Beach, a professor at Duke University Divinity School, Hawk wrote that Perkins had had Negro students for four or five years. They were not enrolled but attended classes and received grades. The professor certified the grades to any institution the student might indicate. None of the regular Perkins students had complained about the blacks' presence; rather students and faculty had welcomed them. Their presence had never been mentioned to the trustees, although the president and individual trustees knew about it.[39]

After the board gave its permission in the fall of 1950, Hawk enrolled two black students for the winter quarter, and the Perkins faculty passed a resolution expressing its delight at this development.[40] When Cuninggim became dean in September 1951, he found that the two black students had not made adequate grades and had had to be dismissed. He then wrote letters to a number of educators at black colleges and visited several black colleges across the South. He wanted to make sure that this time desegregation succeeded, and therefore he wanted only their ablest students, and he wanted more than a token one or two.[41] As a result Perkins admitted five black students, all of whom arrived on campus for the fall semester of 1952. They were John W. Elliott of Edenton, North Carolina (with a degree from Shaw University), James A. Hawkins of Jackson, Tennessee (Lane College), James V. Lyles of Texarkana, Arkansas (Philander Smith College), Negail R. Riley of Oklahoma City, Oklahoma (Howard University), and Albert Cecil Williams of Austin, Texas (Samuel Huston College—later to be named Huston-Tillotson College). They attended classes and chapel with other Perkins students, were enthusiastically accepted by the other students, used the library, ate in the Perkins cafeteria, and lived in the Perkins Dormitory for single men (four of the five did; the fifth, Elliott, was married and lived in town). Cuninggim noted that this was nearly two years before the Supreme Court's decision in *Brown v. Board of Education* and more than three years before the Montgomery bus boycott led by Martin Luther King Jr. Perkins made no public announcement of the desegregation.[42]

Many years later Cecil Williams wrote of his reaction as a college senior to being accepted by Perkins. In a conversation he had with a white friend, Bob Breihan, a recent Perkins graduate, Breihan asked Williams if he realized the historical significance of the blacks' being admitted to Perkins. "I said I sure did. . . . Finally, after so many years, it was happening," Williams later recalled. "The color line was being crossed, and acceptance could be ours. Bob became excited and animated, swept up in the proposition. He began telling me about Perkins; how it looked, how the accommodations were, what instructors to seek and avoid. Except I wasn't listening. Perkins was a *white* seminary. That's all I needed to know."[43]

Williams also told of his ambivalent feelings as a first-year Perkins student: anxious but pretending otherwise; always smiling but inwardly hostile; resentful that students and faculty could reject him, although they did not. Married students invited him to dinner in their homes. Nobody treated him as an inferior. "So," he asked himself, "why wasn't I satisfied?"[44]

In Cuninggim's determination to see this "Perkins Experiment" (as he called it) succeed, he and the five students agreed from the start of the fall semester on a process of mutual consultation for dealing with problems as they arose and, where possible, before they arose. The students and the dean would meet and share questions or problems. Cuninggim would give them advice, but they would be free to make their own decisions. On that basis the students made several decisions early on: to eat in the Perkins cafeteria but not in the SMU Student Union, to attend SMU home football games at the Cotton Bowl and sit in the SMU student section (which was in violation of Texas's Jim Crow laws at the time, so their attendance had to be carefully worked out with the SMU Athletic Department), and to participate in SMU intramural athletics—basketball and baseball but not football, which was more violent.[45]

Several black students commented on these discussions later in letters to Cuninggim. James Lyles wrote, "The method of consultation proved to be of great value. It gave the persons involved an opportunity to sense, understand, and share the nature of the problems and their solution. At no time do I recall a direct order being given. If it had, I would not have honored it."[46] To James Hawkins the consultations "proved to be one of the important steps that we took last year. It was by our looking at problems realistically that enabled us to approach them with a saneness that otherwise we might not have had. It also gave us a chance to feel free to discuss with one who was interested in us and our problems."[47] For Negail Riley their discussions were "very rich and rewarding, for here we met, not necessarily concerned about ourselves, but about the precedents that our actions would set, about the long range effects of our deliberations."[48]

Not everything went smoothly that fall. The Perkins cafeteria was not open on Sundays. A couple of months into the fall semester, one black student was on campus on a Sunday, and a white student invited him to go with him to the dining hall in the student union. They happened to sit at a table with an undergraduate woman, who thereafter wrote her mother what a wonderful experience it had been. Her mother did not think it was wonderful. She and other mothers of SMU women students from the same town contacted President Lee, which led to an earnest conversation between Lee and Cuninggim. Cuninggim did not challenge Lee's right to decide where the black students could eat but said that he himself could not do so. Cuninggim described in detail their method of mutual consultation. Lee already knew about it generally, wanted specific examples, and agreed that the method was right. Thereafter the black students decided they would not again eat in any university dining hall except at Perkins, at least until they were more fully accepted in the wider university.[49]

As the spring semester approached, a white student went to Howard Grimes, director of men's housing for Perkins, and said he would like to room with a black student. Grimes looked into it, and the result was that all four single black students had white roommates in the spring of 1953.[50] In March or April a few trustees became concerned about the situation and shared their worries. Cuninggim was not sure what was bothering them, but he concluded that they intended to bring up the matter at the May meeting of the board, with the intention of getting the board to impose some restrictions.[51] Cuninggim thought questions about Perkins should come first to the board's Committee on the School of Theology, and so he wrote Paul Martin, its chair, to request that the bishop call a meeting of the committee, perhaps for the afternoon or evening before the board's May 5 meeting.[52]

The committee met on the evening of May 4. As Cuninggim reported the discussion, previous policy and decisions were discussed at length, and the committee took no action. Yet, he wrote, committee members agreed that it would be best not to bring up the question at the next day's board meeting, that committee members should assure those with questions that they should trust the committee, which was looking into the matter, and that the consultations between the black students and the dean would continue. Accordingly, nothing was said about the matter at the board meeting.[53] Years later Cuninggim described as tense both the meeting of the committee and that of the board, the first because of opposing points of view within the committee, and the second because nothing was said about the question. He later explained that the consensus emerged not so much in the committee meeting as in a breakfast he had the next morning with Bishop A. Frank Smith, who in the committee meeting had tried hard to get Cuninggim to compromise and impose restrictions on the black students. "Everyone present but myself was in favor of some such restriction [i.e., on the black students' rooming with white students], and at one time in the meeting I remember that the whole group was standing around my chair in which I was still seated!"[54]

Cuninggim concluded that the focus of the problem, though not the only issue, was that some Negro students had white roommates. Because of the policy of mutual consultation, he felt obligated to write the four single black students in July and explain the problem. He assured them he was not giving the SMU housing office any directions on the matter but was leaving it to the students themselves to decide. He made clear that he hoped they would be alert to people's sensitivities and advised them to room only with each other instead.[55] On August 7, after a three-and-a-half-hour conference with the dean, the four students responded to him in writing. They said they had decided to room with each other, but they had written the university housing officer to say that they regarded this decision as a retreat and an unwarranted compromise. Rather, they said, all of SMU should rejoice in what had been done earlier in 1952–53.[56]

Meanwhile the issue intensified. On Friday, August 14, Joe and Lois Perkins came to Dallas to look at how construction of Selecman Hall was progressing. Joe Perkins, in a conference with Cuninggim, asked what had been done about the Negro students' rooming with whites and explained that Hawk had written him, saying that he would be visiting W. R. Nicholson, a wealthy rancher and member of the board who was concerned about the issue. Hawk went on to say, according to Joe Perkins, that if the matter had been settled, Nicholson was ready to help the university in a handsome way, but if not, the consequences would be serious. Joe Perkins showed Cuninggim a copy of Hawk's letter. Though Joe Perkins did not tell Cuninggim what he planned to do, later that day Perkins called Hemphill Hosford, the university provost, and said, "I want the Negroes out of the dormitory."[57]

Then, on August 17, Joe Perkins wrote William C. Martin, the resident bishop of the Dallas–Fort Worth area, the following letter:

Dear Bishop Martin:

I was in Dallas Friday and Saturday of last week and I found the negro situation as affecting SMU had never been worked out.

To my way of thinking this is a matter of extreme importance and it should not be delayed any longer. I hope you will get in behind this actively and help work it out. I rather think the time may come when the Universities of our Nation may find it necessary and desirable to permit negroes to attend but we are a long way from that situation now. My interest and zeal in SMU would suffer a very severe "heart attack" if this is not straightened up in the very near future.

I hope you will actively interest yourself in this and work it out in a way that will be pleasing to all of us.

Your friend,

J. J. Perkins[58]

Perkins sent copies of this letter to other bishops, board members, SMU administrators, and Merrimon Cuninggim. On August 19 Cuninggim wrote Joe Perkins a long and cordial letter. He thanked him for sending copies of Hawk's letter, of his reply, and of his letter to Martin; it was "exceedingly thoughtful." He assured Perkins that he shared his concern that the problem work out happily. Then he reported progress, in that he had continued to follow the procedure of mutual consultation with the Negro students and that they had decided to room only with each other. But, he added, if what he had heard of Hawk's attitude was true, Hawk might not share the committee's feelings. Cuninggim gathered that Hawk wanted the school to impose far more restrictions on blacks' participation in school life and that Hawk wanted to do this "by some authoritarian decision, a technique which, though much easier than consultation, I try not to use." Cuninggim told Joe Perkins he was sure that Hawk would not want to do anything that would harm the school's reputation but that what Hawk appeared to want would inevitably harm it, locally as well as nationally. He encouraged Perkins to share his letter with Hawk and to encourage Hawk to talk with Cuninggim about the problem.[59]

In fact, little could be done at that time to address Joe Perkins's concern. Lee had had a heart attack during the spring and had taken a leave of absence to recuperate. Paul Martin, who chaired the School of Theology committee, was on an extended episcopal trip overseas. Smith's wife had had a serious heart attack, so the bishop had to stay close by in Houston.

On August 24 W. C. Martin responded to Perkins's letter, thanked him again for his continuing generosity toward the school, and tried to calm him down. He expressed regret that Paul Martin was out of the country but said that if it seemed wise for the School of Theology committee to meet before the November board meeting, he would try to be available. He added, "I have a feeling that if Dr. Hawk . . . would cease agitating the issue, it would be easier to find a satisfactory solution."[60]

As days passed and nothing changed, Perkins wrote Cuninggim again. He reiterated his unhappiness: "I think you now know the Board of Trustees never at any time approved or authorized the action which was taken. . . . I presume we are obligated to take care of these four Negroes if they show up, . . . but under no conditions do we want to take on any others and we want to get rid of these four just as soon as we can."[61] Cuninggim, as he had long planned, was in Carlisle, Pennsylvania, attending a meeting of the National Council on Religion in Higher Education. Upon receiving Perkins's letter, he called the school to make clear that the black students were not to be removed from the dormitory and no other changes were to be made.[62]

Cuninggim then took a step that proved to be of great importance in responding to the disaffection, as he later called it. While in Carlisle, he wrote a seven-page paper, "Memorandum on the Negro Problem," which he intended to share with members of the School of Theology committee, the board, and others who would be interested.[63] In it he set forth a brief history of Negroes as Perkins students and how he had proceeded. He described his recruiting of Negro applicants, the acceptance of the five, and the decision for the four single men to stay in the dormitory ("the normal and proper course to enable them to become regular students"). He noted that the board had acted in November 1950 to approve the admission of Negroes and that this action had set no restrictions that would prohibit their assignment to the dormitories. He explained his method of mutual consultation with the five students, whereby they would discuss problems, he would advise, but they would decide what they would do or not do. He spoke of his own caution and theirs and how successfully this method had worked during the 1952–53 academic year. The students, he said, had made some "self-restricting decisions." "In moments of great trial they have been loyal to the method which we have been pursuing; and I will be loyal to them."[64]

Then he moved to the concerns a few board members had raised the previous spring, summarized the committee meeting of May 4 and the board's not mentioning the matter on May 5, and explained the process by which the four single Negro students had decided not to room with whites that fall. Yet, he continued, some people were still disturbed. Joe Perkins had "generously shared with me a copy of the letter he had received on the matter" (Cuninggim did not identify the writer of the letter). Cuninggim observed that those who were disturbed would be satisfied only by abandoning the method of consultation and imposing authoritarian regulations—moving the black students out of the dormitories and perhaps imposing other restrictions. But that, he said, would represent a shift in the philosophy underlying the whole process. The consequences of such a move would be disastrous—loss of support from some of the university's best friends, disaffection of students and faculty, resentment and condemnation by the regional as well as the national Methodist Church, and disappointment by Perkins alumni, other seminaries, other educational institutions, and the American public. The school would sense their contempt, because it would reflect "their and our awareness that Christian principles had been at stake and we had proved faithless to them." This would be the spiritual consequence; outward results would be that the school would not be able to recruit a single first-rate person for the faculty and that dishonor would come to the Perkins name.[65]

Then he identified several arguments against the existing policy toward black students:

> Why take the Negroes out of the dormitory? Or do anything else that would be authoritarian and regulatory?
>
> Because their being in the dormitory has aroused the opposition of those in contact with them? No.

Because they themselves have misused the privileges they have possessed? No. Because the University has received unfavorable publicity about it? No. Because the University officials were not aware of what was going on and the thing was done in secret? No. Because it was never intended to consider them as regular students and somehow advantage has been taken of the Board's original action? No; that would have to be the honest answer for all except for those few who once imagined it might actually be possible to limit their activity solely to classroom attendance. Because we are moving too far ahead of the general procession, and our constituency would not support us? No, as all current samplings of opinion and experience indicate. Because the policy of mutual consultation between them and me, on the basis of which they have guided their actions, has failed? No. Because either the things done or the methods followed are out of harmony with the basic character and purpose of the University or of the Church? No. None of those reasons is available for our defense, for none of them is sound.

Then why?

There is no reasonable explanation at all; and the explanations based on personal taste will not be sufficient to save us from disaster.[66]

He concluded that he was convinced the trustees, fully informed, would not take such a step. A constructive response to the situation could be accomplished. It would be the honorable way, the way of love and of firmness, and the way to heal the wounds.[67]

When Cuninggim returned from Pennsylvania, he met with various university officials. Those conversations, he said, followed a certain pattern: their arguments about why the school should submit to the pressures, his rejoinder that the committee had agreed to stick with the policy, their retort that the matter was far more serious now, his question whether both sides were to be heard, their assurance that they should be. "Thereupon I pulled out and read my memorandum. This nearly always changed the nature of the discussion." When he read it to Hemphill Hosford, the provost, and Willis Tate, the university vice president, who were acting on Lee's behalf during his recuperation, "They both said, 'Well, we are with you.'"[68]

On September 3 Joe Perkins wrote Cuninggim that he had discussed the matter with Bishop Smith and that both had concluded they should leave things as they were until Paul Martin returned in the late fall. Cuninggim responded that after receiving Perkins's letter, he had conferred with Smith on September 12. They concluded that the appropriate place for further discussion of the matter was in the School of Theology committee after Paul Martin's return and that meanwhile the school would follow the consensus reached by the committee at its spring meeting. He informed Joe Perkins that two new Negro students, Marshall Hodge and Bernie P. Perry, had been admitted but that one would live in town and the other by himself in the dormitory, consistent with the decision of the four returning single Negro students.[69] And there the matter stood until Paul Martin's return.

At the Faculty Pre-School Conference on September 15, Cuninggim read the faculty his memorandum. He later reported:

> The reaction was electric. If there was any one occasion more important than another in shaping the faculty morale during the time I was at Perkins, it was that particular moment, for from that time on we were a genuine group with a deeply-based sense of common cause. To be sure, there were two or three, as I was later to learn, who thought that, if philanthropic persons or elder statesmen on the Board were unhappy, the School should change its ways in order to make them happy. But in the days that followed, as I met with various members of the University administration and the Board of Trustees, I never once doubted that I had the almost solid backing of the faculty and student body.[70]

Howard Grimes remembered that the situation at the faculty conference was tense. "Cuninggim said unequivocally that if the Board required him to take the black students out of the dormitory he would resign."[71]

In the midst of the furor Cuninggim tried to puzzle through why the disturbance had arisen as it did. Much later he wrote that his predecessor, Hawk, appeared to have been largely, though not entirely, the source of the disturbance and that Hawk had gathered allies among conservative businessmen and perhaps a minister or two on the board. Cuninggim thought Hawk's target was not Cuninggim but Lee. Cuninggim gathered from some that Hawk saw Lee as an enemy who had chosen Cuninggim as dean without informing Hawk and had removed Hawk a year early. As Cuninggim interpreted it, Hawk thought he had found a way to embarrass Lee.[72]

It also appears that, in addition to whatever other motives Hawk might have had, he genuinely believed it was wrong for the black students to be living in the dorms and eating in the dining rooms, let alone rooming with white students. In April 1953, writing to Paul Martin, Hawk said that when he had learned of the black and white students' rooming together, he was "unprepared to believe it," that he had never even suggested that black students would be on the campus for anything more than their classes, and that he believed the trustees had acted only to allow the black students to register in order to receive credit for their studies.[73]

By late November Paul Martin had returned from abroad, and on November 25 Cuninggim went to Little Rock and spent seven hours with him discussing the problem. Cuninggim read Martin the memorandum, and they went over the problem together in great detail. They agreed that compromise was not possible. Martin said he would go to Wichita Falls the next week to see Joe Perkins and try to convince him that they could not go back. In discussing how Joe Perkins might react, they agreed that he would need some ground that he could express publicly for changing his position. Cuninggim's notes on their conference show that he suggested he take the blame, perhaps for not having consulted as much as he should have. Not that Cuninggim believed he was to blame, but Perkins would need an "out," and they did not want the blame to rest on Lee, for then Hawk would have won. Cuninggim made clear to Martin how seriously he viewed the situation and how far he was willing to go, so far as his own career was concerned, to get the issue settled properly. What they needed was some statement from the School of Theology committee in case any further problems arose.[74]

Paul Martin's visit with Joe Perkins helped to smooth the way for the upcoming meeting of the School of Theology committee. Martin wrote of that visit: "One evening, Mr. Perkins in the direct fashion that always characterized him asked me, 'Do you believe if this matter is not settled in an amicable manner, it will hurt the University?' I replied in the affirmative. Then he simply but sincerely said, 'This is the only consideration. The University must rise above any hurt feelings that can develop. The School of Theology is our first love.'"[75]

By the time the committee met on January 25, 1954, the issue had already been settled. After discussing other matters, the dean presented the issue of the school's policy toward its Negro students. Those present were asked to express their thinking, and Perkins said he had been unhappy. The dean then described the working of the successful policy in as restrained a way as possible.[76] William C. Martin moved that the committee express its belief that the present policy should be continued, and the motion was approved.[77] Then, to the surprise of those present, Lois Perkins, who had been invited to attend, said, "I don't agree with my husband on this particular matter. And if he had shared with me the letter from Dr. Hawk last summer, we never would have had any trouble."[78] Cuninggim later wrote that throughout all those days he knew of only one person in or close to the university administration who never tried to change or weaken the policy at Perkins: William C. Martin.[79] So was the issue settled as to the desegregation of the Perkins School of Theology student body.

Three weeks after the meeting of the School of Theology committee, Joe Perkins wrote Hawk, "The negro question did not work out as I would like for it to have done but I guess what has happened can not be undone and it could work out as the correct thing to have done."[80]

At his graduation Cecil Williams was interviewed by the *Star Post*, a Dallas newspaper with an African American readership. He said that the five black seminary students had hoped to be treated as regular students with all the accompanying privileges and that during his three years at Perkins all he had hoped for, and more, had come about.[81]

In October 1955, after the five had graduated, Cuninggim wrote each man to ask for reflections on the group's experience at SMU. In his response Negail Riley identified two characteristics that underlay the adjustments of those three years: honesty and discretion. The five, he said, had been frank with one another, recognizing their new situation and their own inadequacies. Some in the community had hatred toward blacks but recognized that for Jesus the "neighbor was all-inclusive." For them, the five blacks' being honest broke down barriers to others' being honest. The professors also related to the black students honestly. The five had inadequate educational backgrounds, he said, but had to be responsible for their work just like every other student. The five understood the need for discretion. For example, their decision not to take part in a community swimming party resulted from a discreet consideration of the situation. As the larger community was not altogether benign, it was not ready for that step. Yet Riley expressed regret that what happened at Perkins did not encourage a public statement by SMU that what was done was right. "Could not the school have stood with Paul and said, 'I am not ashamed . . .'?"[82]

THE NEW CURRICULUM

Concurrent with the process of desegregation, Perkins undertook a major study and revision of the curriculum for its primary program, the bachelor of divinity degree. The rationale for the previous curriculum was not clear. It required twenty-seven "majors" for graduation, nine majors a year (on the quarter system) for three years. The School of Theology had begun to label courses "majors" and "minors" in 1926. A major equaled one-third of a quarter's work, and a minor counted for one-half of a major.[83] Twelve majors were specifically required, of which three were in Division A, the historical development of Christianity (Bible and church history); three in Division B, the interpretation of religion (philosophy of religion, Christian doctrine, sociology of religion, including ethics, and history of religions); and six in Division C, the work of the church at home and abroad (various "practical" fields). Students were required to take ten additional majors distributed among the divisions. The remaining five majors were electives. Each professor taught a required course; Cuninggim observed that some thought this was the faculty members' underlying concern.[84]

The series of faculty seminars in 1951–52 had given much attention to determining Perkins's primary task, what students need to know, and how the curriculum might be structured. These seminars, involving extended discussion among the members, enhanced faculty morale and identified a large area of common outlook as well as some differences of opinion. That set the stage for the next move. At its first meeting in the fall of 1952, the faculty approved Irwin's motion to establish a committee of up to five members to study how the curriculum should be revised and bring proposals to the faculty as soon as possible. At the October 8 meeting Cuninggim announced the makeup of the Committee on Curricular Revision: Davis as chair, with Grimes, Irwin, Mathews, and Cuninggim.[85] The intention was to put the new curriculum into effect in the fall of 1953.[86]

The committee's membership was an indication of change to come. Wesley Davis was the only member who had joined the faculty before 1949 (he had arrived in 1935). Because he had chaired the faculty curriculum committee (the Course of

Study Committee) for the preceding six years, he brought close acquaintance with the existing curriculum. The other four members had arrived in successive years: Grimes in 1949, Irwin in 1950, Cuninggim in 1951, and Mathews that fall of 1952. One might expect them to be more open to curricular change than those of greater seniority. In the faculty seminars of the previous year, Irwin had urged his colleagues to ask fundamental questions as they made curricular decisions, in particular, what do students need to know? He would want an explicit philosophy for the committee's recommendations. Given Davis's irenic spirit and conscientious work ethic, these five would likely work well as a team.

In November their first report to the faculty identified six points of agreement:

The program of study would cover six semesters, or three years (the faculty had voted the preceding spring to return to the semester system).

A minimum of ninety semester hours would be required for graduation.

Approximately a third of the ninety hours would be in electives.

The other two-thirds would be required work, with at least twelve semester hours in Bible.

Satisfactory knowledge of the contents of the English Bible would be required for graduation.

New students would be admitted only in the fall, except when that would create a hardship for applicants, in which case the decision would be left to the Admissions Committee.

After discussion, the faculty approved the first four points, referred the fifth (knowledge of the English Bible) to the committee for a more specific recommendation, and amended the sixth to say that "the normal time for entrance is September and that students be encouraged to begin their seminary work at that time."[87]

As the process continued, some discontent emerged in the faculty. In February A. W. Martin sent a memo to the committee in which he proposed not putting the curriculum revision into effect in the fall of 1953. "This faculty simply is not ready for the change," he said. "There are basic differences of opinion as to the nature of the seminary's task." The differences he saw were not between old and new faculty but instead were fundamental differences in their views about theological education.

Furthermore, the school did not have adequate faculty to carry out what was being contemplated, and there was not enough time to gain the cooperation of church leaders.[88] Whatever the validity of Martin's claims, a week before his memo Goodloe had moved in a faculty meeting to accept the committee's basic outline of the curriculum, and the faculty had adopted his motion.[89]

In the spring 1953 issue of the *Perkins Journal*, Davis provided an account of "the new curriculum" and its underlying philosophy, of which, he said, the details were being worked out. The primary task of the school is to train students to lead the church's activities so that it can reach its goal. Yet in the midst of rapid social change the church's objectives must periodically be redefined. In this light the committee asked what the minister ought to know and be able to do and how best to bring about this knowing and doing.[90]

What, Davis asked, is the minimum a minister should know? The curriculum must enable a student to understand thoroughly "(a) the faith of the Christian community as it is embodied in the scriptures and in the tradition of the church; (b) the world in which the Christian community has developed and now exists; and (c) the organization and program of the world-wide and local church, and the essential techniques for the effective execution of the tasks of the pastor." That answer led to the proposal of a four-division structure:

A. To prepare the minister for his task, which is that of understanding and fostering the program of the church. Thus Division I is *The Life and Work of the Church*.

B. To show that the church exists within, not outside of, its society, and that, though it is moulded by that society, it must nevertheless challenge its unchrist-like character. Division II is therefore entitled *Christianity and Culture*.

C. To show that the church cannot accomplish its task unless it knows clearly whereof it speaks. Thus, Division III is *The Christian Heritage*.

D. To show that the heart of the heritage is the Bible, and the revelation of God in Christ which it contains. Division IV therefore is *Biblical Studies*.[91]

Each division would offer a required "core" course in four segments, stretching through a student's first two years of study. It would be necessary for all the professors in a division to work together to construct it, and in teaching in a segment of it, each would need to keep in mind what was going on in the other segments. As Cuninggim pointed out in a later article, gone was the old structure of many departments within which each professor could plan and teach a required course as he pleased.[92]

Through the spring and into the summer and fall, the members of each division worked to shape their division's core. What emerged was this: Division I included a semester each on local church administration and church education, plus two semesters that included worship, sacred music, and preaching. Division II included a semester each of the courses entitled "Christian Thought and Western Philosophy," "Christian Mission and Other Religions," "Christian Action and Contemporary Society," and "Christian Insight and Personal Counseling." Division III provided two semesters in the first year devoted to the history of the church (in the first semester, "The Expansion of the Christian Church"; in the second, "The Development of the Christian Message"). In the second year would come "The Content of the Christian Faith" and "The Principles of the Christian Life." Division IV assigned two semesters to Old Testament and two to New Testament (one of each in each of the first two years). Each testament included a semester's study of the literature and a semester on the message of that testament. In addition to these core requirements, each Methodist student was required to complete a four-hour course in Methodist history, polity, and doctrine.[93] Beyond the core courses, close to a third of the curriculum was reserved for electives, to be taken in the third year.

One aim of the Committee on Curricular Revision was to integrate field work into the total educational experience. As Cuninggim had said, field work is not primarily to aid the student financially, nor to provide immediate service to the local church, but to educate the student. To that end Division I courses for the first year included the "Field Work Laboratory," in which a student served under supervision in a local church or social service agency. Each faculty member would participate in this supervision at least one Sunday a month.[94]

A central aim of the curriculum was to integrate all the fields. The emphasis was on the minister's task as a whole, so that the various subjects were "not marbles in a jar but slices off the same loaf." It sought to break down the line between content and practical courses and, within each division, to overcome the separation of the various fields.[95]

Some observations are in order about the new curriculum's significance. First, this curriculum was in line with a wider effort by seminaries at the time to find greater order and unity in theological study. Perkins pursued that goal by identifying a required core of theological study foundational to all the rest, after which students were free to elect various advanced courses. The Perkins curriculum, like the core curriculum developed in the same period by the Federated Theological Faculty of the University of Chicago, sought unity and order through a conviction about what was essential in Christian faith.[96]

Second, the new curriculum was a sharp departure from what preceded it: in its philosophy of ministerial education (indeed, in *having* an explicit philosophy), in seeking to derive what is required from what the minister needs to know and do, in the faculty's sense of involvement in a cooperative endeavor (and not only a sense of it but the necessity of working together to design and teach the required courses), and in the emphasis upon the integration of the student's total seminary educational experience.

Third, Division II was a new creature. Traditionally theological education has been divided into Bible, history of Christianity, theology and ethics, and practical theology, usually organized in three or four divisions. Division II did not fit that scheme. Instead it was an effort to take seriously the society and culture within which the church exists and the necessity to "challenge [the] unchristlike character" of that society. Each segment of the division's core involved a dialog between Christian faith and one or more secular disciplines or historical processes: philosophy, social and psychological studies, the contexts of Christian mission, and other religions. Dialog with other disciplines had already been present in such courses as the philosophy of religion and the sociology of religion. The new curriculum embodied the principle of interdisciplinary dialog in one-fourth of the core curriculum.

Fourth, the fundamental pattern that emerged in the 1952–53 revision endured, with variations, for decades. There were repeated curriculum revisions after 1953—in 1956–57, 1959–60, 1962–63, 1965, 1966, 1968–69, 1981–82, and 1989–90; and in all these variations there endured the effort to integrate the student's total seminary study, the requirement of approximately two-thirds core and one-third electives, the cooperative endeavor of the faculty in each division in planning its core, and the conviction that field work (later renamed field education) must be integrated into the total educational experience and adequately supervised. Many details also endured, though many saw revision. What might appear to be a departure from this pattern was a short-lived requirement in the mid-1960s of a set of comprehensive examinations instead of a body of core courses. But the departure was more apparent than real; the required examinations were to cover roughly the same fields as those that had been required in the core courses, and nearly all the students, frightened out of their wits by the specter of comprehensive exams, prepared for the exams by taking almost every course that had previously been required. Another apparent departure—the internship that was required beginning in 1970—was again an embodiment rather than a rejection of convictions expressed in the new curriculum of 1953.

Fifth, some difficulties were readily evident in the pattern of core courses adopted in 1953. The division of the two semesters of church history into institutional history and the history of Christian thought was artificial and misleading. Eventually, it was revised. Similarly, the distinction within the study of each testament between the literature and studying its message would not hold up. Before long it too was revised. The effort to cover both the Christian mission and other religions in a single-semester course was unsatisfactory, and by 1957 each of the two subjects had its own one-semester segment of the core—though that led to an expansion in the total core requirement. Also, it was difficult to deal adequately with the several aspects of ministry in the Division I core; the faculty made various attempts to solve this problem over the years.

In its basic shape and in many of its details, the new curriculum was judged to be a success. Its durability attested to the validity of that judgment. Its existence gave a new sense of direction to the students' education and enhanced the esprit and collegiality of the faculty. These were among the notable qualities for which this period of the history of Perkins was remembered.

A NEW PRESIDENT FOR SOUTHERN METHODIST UNIVERSITY

After Umphrey Lee suffered the mild heart attack in April 1953 and took leave through the summer to recuperate, Willis Tate, the vice president, was given "general executive responsibilities."[97] Lee continued to take responsibility for major university decisions, however, and as his health improved he returned to an office on the campus. He presented his report to the November 5 meeting of the trustees and resumed his duties, though with much time for rest. Still, his doctor thought he should not return to his full schedule of activities, and on March 11, 1954, Lee submitted his resignation as president to A. Frank Smith, board chair.[98]

The trustees straightaway established the office of chancellor of the university and named Lee to that position with a salary, without administrative responsibilities, and with membership on the executive committee of the board. The board also appointed a special nominating committee, chaired by Paul Martin, to search for a new president. That committee in turn asked the board to set up several other committees (of students, alumni, and Dallas citizens) to make recommendations about a successor to Lee.[99] At the regular spring meeting of the board on May 6, Paul Martin reported for the committee. He presented a list of "basic requirements for the job ahead" and then the committee's nomination: Willis M. Tate, the university's vice president. The board then elected him by secret ballot.[100]

Tate, born in 1911, received his bachelor's degree from SMU in 1932 and stayed to complete a master's degree in sociology. After several years of teaching school in San Antonio, in 1942 he became assistant to the pastor of First Methodist Church in Houston. In 1945 he came to SMU as assistant dean of students, and he became dean of students in 1948. In the late 1940s, along with his administrative duties, he worked toward a Ph.D. degree in sociology at the University of Texas. In 1950 he was made vice president in charge of development and public relations at SMU. During Lee's medical leave in 1953, Tate, along with Hosford, the provost, handled the administrative responsibilities of the university, which included major attention to the issue of black Perkins students in the dormitories. Tate was to be SMU president longer than anyone to date. In the 1950s he proved to be strongly supportive of Merrimon Cuninggim on the issue of racial desegregation and much else.[101]

1. *Who's Who in Methodism* (Chicago: A. N. Marquis, 1952), 168; F. Thomas Trotter, foreword to Merrimon Cuninggim, *Uneasy Partners: The College and the Church* (Nashville, Tenn.: Abingdon, 1994), 9–15; Lewis Howard Grimes, *A History of Perkins School of Theology*, edited by Roger Loyd (Dallas: Southern Methodist University Press, 1993), 92; *Dallas Morning News*, November 5, 1995.
2. Correspondence between Umphrey Lee and Merrimon Cuninggim, May 7–22, 1946, Cuninggim Papers, Bridwell Library.

3. Cuninggim to Lee, December 3, 1950, Cuninggim Papers.

4. Lee to Cuninggim, December 3, December 12, and December 20, 1950; Cuninggim to Lee, December 25, 1950, and January 1, 1951, Cuninggim Papers.

5. Lee to Cuninggim, December 21, 1950; Cuninggim to Lee, December 25, 1950, Cuninggim Papers.

6. Eugene B. Hawk to Cuninggim, January 19, 1951, Hawk Papers, Bridwell Library; Cuninggim to Lee, January 29, 1951, Cuninggim Papers.

7. Grimes, *A History of Perkins School of Theology*, 93.

8. Lee to Cuninggim, February 3, 1951, Cuninggim Papers.

9. Hawk to Cuninggim, January 19, 1951; Cuninggim to Lee, January 29, 1951 and April 25, 1951, Cuninggim Papers.

10. See, for example, John Deschner, "Merrimon Cuninggim: A Remembrance," *Perkins Perspective*, summer 1996, 9.

11. Cuninggim to Lee, January 1, 1951; Lee to Cuninggim, January 3, 1951; Lee to Cuninggim, January 4, 1951; Lee to Cuninggim, January 11, 1951, Cuninggim Papers; Outler to Hawk, January 9, 1951, Hawk Papers; Cuninggim to Lee, January 29, 1951; Lee to Cuninggim, February 3, 1951; Cuninggim to Lee, April 16, 1951, Cuninggim Papers.

12. *Who's Who in Methodism*, 1952, 513; John Deschner, "Albert Cook Outler: A Biographical Memoir," *Our Common History as Christians: Essays in Honor of Albert C. Outler*, edited by John Deschner, Leroy T. Howe, and Klaus Penzel (New York: Oxford University Press, 1975), ix–xxi.

13. Deschner, "Albert Cook Outler," xiii.

14. Lee to Cuninggim, January 23, 1951; Cuninggim to Lee, January 29, 1951, Cuninggim Papers.

15. Lee to Cuninggim, February 3, 1951; Cuninggim to Lee, January 29, 1951, Cuninggim Papers.

16. Lee to Cuninggim, April 19, 1951, Cuninggim Papers.

17. Hawk to J. J. Perkins, April 23, 1951, Hawk Papers.

18. Board of trustees minutes, May 11, 1951.

19. *Perkins School of Theology Catalog*, 1951–52, pp. 4-5.

20. Faculty minutes, October 17, 1951, Cuninggim Papers.

21. Cuninggim, memo to faculty, October 24, 1951, "Faculty Seminars" file, Cuninggim Papers.

22. Ibid.

23. Cuninggim's notes on the November 7, 1951, seminar, Cuninggim Papers.

24. Cuninggim's notes, "Faculty Seminars" file, Cuninggim Papers.

25. Cuninggim memo, April 7,1952, in faculty minutes, 1951–52, Cuninggim Papers.

26. Merrimon Cuninggim, "Report to President Umphrey Lee on 1951–52," Cuninggim Papers.

27. Board of trustees minutes, November 2, 1952, and November 5, 1953; executive committee minutes, September 11, 1953.

28. Cuninggim to Bishop A. Frank Smith, February 4, 1952, Cuninggim Papers.

29. Faculty minutes, March 5, 1952, Cuninggim Papers.

30. Faculty minutes, April 16 and May 7, 1952, Cuninggim Papers.

31. Grimes, *A History of Perkins School of Theology*, 105; faculty minutes, September 22, 1951, Cuninggim Papers.

32. Faculty minutes, March 5, 1952, Cuninggim Papers.

33. Merrimon Cuninggim, "Report for 1951–52, Perkins School of Theology, S.M.U., June, 1952," 1–2, Cuninggim Papers; Grimes, *A History of Perkins School of Theology*, 105.

34. Catalog, 1946–47, 35; 1948–49, 43; 1951–52, 50.

35. Hawk to Lee, March 10, 1951; Lee to Hawk, March 12, 1951, Hawk Papers.

36. Merrimon Cuninggim, *Perkins Led the Way: The Story of Desegregation at Southern Methodist University* (Dallas: Perkins School of Theology, Southern Methodist University, 1994), 9.

37. Board of trustees minutes, November 10, 1950; Cuninggim, *Perkins Led the Way*, 8; Merrimon Cuninggim, "Memorandum on the Negro Problem, Perkins School of Theology, S.M.U., September 1, 1953," 2, Cuninggim Papers.

38. Dwight W. Culver to Hawk, December 1, 1946; Hawk to Culver, December 9, 1946, Hawk Papers.

39. Hawk to Waldo Beach, April 30, 1949; see also Hawk to Murray O. Johnson, February 17, 1947, and Hawk to Mrs. M. C. Van Gundy, January 17, 1950, Hawk Papers.
40. Hawk to Paul Lanier, January 24, 1951, Hawk Papers; faculty minutes, January 3, 1951; Grimes, *A History of Perkins School of Theology*, 77.
41. Merrimon Cuninggim, "Integration in Professional Education: The Story of Perkins, Southern Methodist University," *Annals of the American Academy of Political and Social Science* 304 (March 1956): 109; Cuninggim, "Memorandum," 2; Cuninggim, *Perkins Led the Way*, 10.
42. Cuninggim, *Perkins Led the Way*, 10; Cuninggim, "Memorandum," 1.
43. Cecil Williams, *I'm Alive! An Autobiography* (San Francisco: Harper and Row, 1980), 57.
44. Ibid., 59.
45. Cuninggim, "Memorandum," 11–18.
46. James Lyles to Cuninggim, October 20, 1955, in *Black Seminarians at Perkins: Then and Now* (Dallas: Bridwell Library, 1994), n.p.
47. James A. Hawkins to Cuninggim, August 6, 1953, in *Black Seminarians at Perkins*, n.p.
48. Negail R. Riley to Merrimon Cuninggim, October 14, 1955, in *Black Seminarians at Perkins*, n.p.
49. Cuninggim to Charles Braden, August 7, 1964, pp. 2–3, Cuninggim Papers.
50. Grimes, writing in *A History of Perkins School of Theology* in the 1980s, speaks of two black students with white roommates (112); Cuninggim writes in 1994 in *Perkins Led the Way* that four black students had white roommates (19). Cuninggim's letter to four of the five black students—to Hawkins, Lyles, Riley, and Williams, July 24, 1953 (Cuninggim Papers)—indicates that the correct number was four. See also Grimes to Cuninggim, August 17, 1953, Cuninggim Papers. Eugene B. Hawk, in a letter to Paul Martin (April 3, 1953, Hawk Papers), writes that he had learned that "five white students were rooming with five negroes"; however, he was apparently misinformed, in that one black student was married and lived in town.
51. Cuninggim, "Memorandum," 3.
52. Cuninggim to Paul Martin, April 20, 1953, Cuninggim Papers.
53. Cuninggim, "Memorandum," 4.
54. Cuninggim to Braden, 6–7.
55. Cuninggim to Hawkins, Lyles, Riley, and Williams, July 24, 1953; Cuninggim, "Memorandum," 4–5.
56. Cuninggim to Smith, August 17, 1953; Hawkins, Lyles, Riley, and Williams to Cuninggim, August 25, 1953; Cuninggim to Hawkins, Lyles, Riley, and Williams, September 1, 1953; Cuninggim to Braden, 7–8, all in Cuninggim Papers.
57. Cuninggim to Smith, August 17, 1953; Hemphill Hosford to J. J. Perkins, August 17, 1953, both in Cuninggim Papers; Cuninggim, "Memorandum," 5.
58. J. J. Perkins to Bishop William C. Martin, August 17, 1953, Cuninggim Papers.
59. Cuninggim to Perkins, August 19, 1953, Cuninggim Papers.
60. William C. Martin to Perkins, August 24, 1953, Cuninggim Papers.
61. Perkins to Cuninggim, August 27, 1953, Cuninggim Papers.
62. Cuninggim to Braden, 9.
63. Cuninggim, "Memorandum."
64. Ibid., 2, 3.
65. Ibid., 5, 6.
66. Ibid., 7.
67. Ibid.
68. Cuninggim to Braden, 10.
69. Perkins to Cuninggim, September 3, 1953, Cuninggim Papers; Cuninggim to Perkins, September 12, 1953, Cuninggim Papers.
70. Cuninggim to Braden, 11.
71. Grimes, *A History of Perkins School of Theology*, 114.
72. Cuninggim to Braden, 5; Cuninggim to Smith, August 17, 1953, Cuninggim Papers.
73. Hawk to Bishop Paul E. Martin, April 3, 1953, Hawk Papers.

74. Cuninggim, "Notes on Conference with Bishop Paul Martin, November 25, 1953," Cuninggim Papers; Cuninggim to Braden, 11–12.

75. Grimes, *A History of Perkins School of Theology*, 115.

76. Cuninggim to Braden, 11; Cuninggim, *Perkins Led the Way*, 25.

77. Perkins School of Theology Committee minutes, January 25, 1954, Cuninggim Papers.

78. Cuninggim to Braden, 11.

79. Ibid., 10.

80. Perkins to Hawk, February 13, 1954, Hawk Papers.

81. Cuninggim, "Integration in Professional Education," 112, citing the *Dallas Star Post*, May 28, 1955.

82. Riley to Cuninggim, October 14, 1955, in *Black Seminarians at Perkins*, n.p.

83. Grimes, *A History of Perkins School of Theology*, p. 31.

84. Catalog, 1950–51, 29–56; Merrimon Cuninggim, "The New Curriculum at Perkins," *Christian Century* 71 (April 28, 1954): 514–15.

85. Faculty minutes, September 24 and October 8, 1952.

86. Cuninggim, "The Dean's Page," *Perkins Journal*, fall 1952, 4.

87. Faculty minutes, November 21, 1952.

88. A. W. Martin memo, February 19, 1953, Cuninggim Papers.

89. Faculty minutes, February 13, 1953.

90. Wesley Davis, "The New Curriculum," *Perkins Journal*, spring 1953, 10–16.

91. Ibid., 11-12.

92. Cuninggim, "New Curriculum at Perkins," 514.

93. Catalog, 1953–54, 43–48.

94. Merrimon Cuninggim, "The State of the School," *Perkins Journal*, spring 1952, 4; catalog, 1954–55, 48, 51.

95. Catalog, 1954–55, 45; Cuninggim, "New Curriculum at Perkins," 514, 515. See also the catalog for 1953–54, 45–46.

96. H. Richard Niebuhr, Daniel Day Williams, and James M. Gustafson, *The Advancement of Theological Education* (New York: Harper and Brothers, 1957), 84–86.

97. Executive committee minutes, June 4, 1953.

98. Winifred T. Weiss and Charles S. Proctor, *Umphrey Lee: A Biography* (Nashville, Tenn.: Abingdon, 1971), 172, 186; board of trustees minutes, November 5, 1953.

99. Board of trustees minutes, March 30 and April 8, 1954.

100. Ibid., May 6, 1954.

101. *Who's Who in Methodism*, 1952, p. 671; Walter Vernon, "Tate, Willis McDonald," *The New Handbook of Texas* (Austin: The Texas State Historical Association, 1996), 6:210.

Dallas Hall in the 1920s.
(Courtesy of SMU digital collections)

Bishop Edwin D. Mouzon.
(Courtesy of Calvert Bros., Nashville, Tenn.)

SMU Presidents, c. 1956. From left: Charles C. Selecman (1923–38), Hiram Abiff Boaz (1920–22), bust of Robert S. Hyer (1911–20), Umphrey Lee (1939–54), Willis Tate (1954–72, 1974–75).

Dean Paul B. Kern, c. 1920.

Old Kirby Hall (now Florence Hall).

The School of Theology faculty, c. 1937. Front row, from left: James T. Carlyon,
Dean Eugene B. Hawk, James Seehorn Seneker. Back row: John H. Hicks, Paul A. Root,
Robert W. Goodloe, Wesley C. Davis.

From left: President Umphrey Lee, Joe and Lois Perkins, Bishop A. Frank Smith, c. 1945.
(Courtesy of L. B. Haskins, *Dallas Morning News*)

Dean Merrimon Cuninggim, 1960.

The Perkins faculty, fall 1954. Front row, from left: William A. Irwin, President Willis Tate, A. Lamar Cooper, A. W. Martin, Joseph W. Mathews, L. Howard Grimes, Edward C. Hobbs, Thomas H. Marsh, Marvin T. Judy. Back row: Dean Merrimon Cuninggim, Robert G. McCutchan (visiting professor), Decherd Turner, Benjamin O. Hill, Joseph D. Quillian, James Seehorn Seneker, John H. Hicks, Robert W. Goodloe, H. Neill McFarland, Douglas E. Jackson, Wesley C. Davis, Albert C. Outler, Charles H. "Joe" Johnson, Fred D. Gealy, C. Herndon Wagers, George C. Baker.

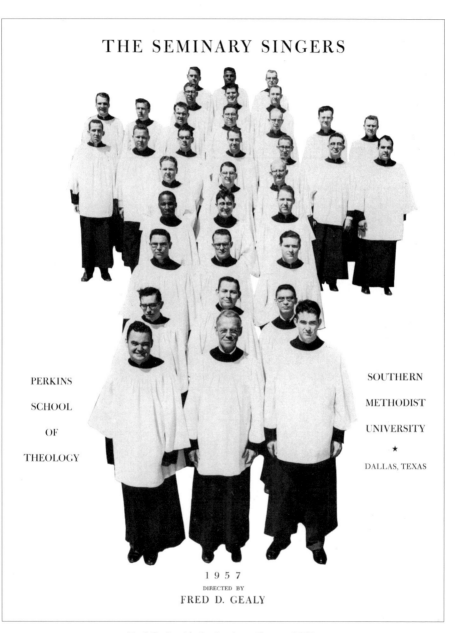

THE SEMINARY SINGERS

PERKINS
SCHOOL
OF
THEOLOGY

SOUTHERN
METHODIST
UNIVERSITY
★
DALLAS, TEXAS

1957
DIRECTED BY
FRED D. GEALY

Fred Gealy with the Seminary Singers, 1957.

Dean Joseph D. Quillian at his desk, fall 1960.
(Courtesy of Messina Studios)

Dean Joseph D. Quillian and Joseph S. Bridwell, early 1960s.
(Courtesy of Messina Studios)

Decherd Turner with an incunable, 1979.
(Courtesy of R. E. "Bob" Tenney & Associates)

Master of Sacred Music faculty, fall 2002. From left: Lloyd Pfautsch, director, 1959–64; Kenneth Hart, director, 1987–2005; Jane Marshall, faculty, 1979–86; Carlton R. Young, director, 1964–75.
(©SMU 2002, photo by Tres Smith)

Roger Deschner, director of the Master of Sacred Music Program, 1975–91.

James M. Ward, 1988.

Continuing Transformation, 1953–1960

I n the summer of 1952 Dean Cuninggim reported to President Lee, "The most serious faculty problem is the smallness of the staff." In the fall of 1951, he explained, "the student-faculty ratio was a disastrous 29–1."[1] The Perkins student body had been growing rapidly (see table 1 in appendix B), from 182 in 1945–46 to 440 in 1951–52. This growth reflected the end of World War II, publicity about the Perkinses' gifts, and, after 1950, the new physical plant of the school. Between 1952 and 1960 the figures ranged between 364 and 421.

Until January 1951, when the new quadrangle opened, the increased student body strained the physical facility—the old Kirby Hall. Even after 1951, although the new buildings eased the student housing situation, classroom space in the new Kirby Hall was inadequate. In the fall of 1951 Cuninggim asked the trustees for another classroom and office building, explaining that the school was managing only by offering fewer courses and by limiting enrollment in some of them so that the students could be accommodated in the existing classrooms. Joe and Lois Perkins generously provided the money for what became Selecman Hall, which opened in time for the spring semester of 1954. But the small size of the faculty continued to pose a difficulty. In Cuninggim's opinion faculty members were both underpaid and overworked, and he set out to remedy both problems.[2]

The size of the student body made faculty additions essential, and increases in the school's income over several years made them possible. The financial increases came from three sources. First, the Perkinses, in their gifts to the school's endowment, had stipulated that income each year from certain designated properties would go to increase the endowment, and as the endowment grew so did the income from the endowment. Budgeted income from the endowment thus rose from $18,000 in the

1949–50 fiscal year to $36,100 in 1952–53, to $107,000 in 1956–57, and then to $185,000 in 1959–60, the last year of Cuninggim's deanship. Second, actions taken by the General Conference of 1952 led to an annual increase of about $50,000 in contributions from World Service funds of The Methodist Church. When added to gifts from other sources, the gift line in the income budget rose from $60,000 for 1951–52 to $141,000 for 1952–53, and held steady at $160,000 or more in each of the remaining years of Cuninggim's tenure. Third, budgeted income from tuition, fees, and rents grew from $45,000 in 1949–50 to $165,000 in 1957–58 and continued at that level or higher. Perkins charged nominal fees but no tuition until 1952, when it established a tuition charge of $120 per quarter and provided scholarship aid based on the student's financial situation. Tuition remained at that rate, adjusted to the semester system, until 1959–60, when it rose to $250 per semester, or $500 for the regular academic year.[3]

Total budgeted income for Perkins rose from $154,000 in 1951–52 to $283,000 in 1956–57 and then to $523,750 in 1959–60, the last year of Cuninggim's deanship (see table 2 of appendix B). Although actual income was sometimes smaller, sometimes larger, than what was budgeted, and expenses sometimes exceeded income and sometimes did not, these figures illustrate the sharp increase in available financial resources in these years.

ENLARGING THE FACULTY

As financial resources grew, Cuninggim rapidly added faculty throughout the 1950s. Three new faculty members had arrived in the fall of 1952 (Joe Mathews in Christian ethics, Edward Hobbs in New Testament, and Marvin Judy in church administration and field work). With the help of adjunct professors, it became possible to make two realignments in teaching responsibility. Fred Gealy could now give most of his time to his field of New Testament, although he would still teach church music, and Howard Grimes, who had been teaching social ethics as well as religious education, could now concentrate on the latter. But many more additions were needed.

From 1953 to the fall of 1960, thirty-one new people joined the Perkins faculty, some with administrative as well as teaching responsibilities (see appendix A). This meant throughout his deanship Cuninggim spent much of his time making faculty appointments: developing lists, gathering information about the prospects, interviewing them himself (often several for one position), hosting quiet or public visits, and moving those he nominated through the process, often to a successful conclusion but sometimes not. The number of faculty added varied widely from year to year: one in 1953 but five in the fall of 1954, plus one more the following January. In the fall of 1955 three more full-time faculty joined the school, along with two who divided their time between Perkins and elsewhere in the university. Three new Perkins faculty arrived in 1956, five more in 1957, four in 1958, three in 1959, and four in 1960.

Several new faculty members were replacements for those who departed. From 1954 to 1959 nine faculty members retired (in order of retirement: Carlyon, Irwin, Seneker, Goodloe, Hicks, Marlatt, Martin, Davis, and Gealy). By 1960 the only active faculty members who had come to Perkins before Cuninggim were Tom Marsh (1946), Howard Grimes (1949), George Baker (1949), and Decherd Turner (1950). Six of those hired while Cuninggim was dean left by or before 1960. Joe Mathews, who had not completed his dissertation, resigned in 1956 to go to the Ecumenical Institute in Austin, Texas, and later to an organization of the same name in Chicago. Charles "Joe" Johnson left for the faculty of the Garrett Biblical Institute in 1957 but returned to the Perkins faculty in 1958. In 1958 Edward Hobbs accepted a position at the Church Divinity School of the Pacific. Richard Bush took an appointment with the Methodist Board of Missions as of January 1960. David Shipley departed in 1960 to join the faculty of the new Methodist Theological School in Ohio. Emmanuel Gitlin took a medical leave in 1959 and left the faculty in 1960.

With the appointments that Cuninggim made, the faculty grew from sixteen (two part time at Perkins) in the spring of 1951 to thirty-three in the fall of 1960. This figure does not include visiting professors and lecturers, of whom there usually were twenty to twenty-five each year—mostly teachers in the Perkins summer school or the summer Approved Supply Pastors' School, or Ministers' Week lecturers, plus a few who offered one course a year in the fall or spring. Of the thirty-three, six (Joe Quillian, Wayne Banks, Lamar Cooper, Floyd Curl, J. B. Holt, and Sterling Wheeler) held administrative positions in the fall of 1960, with classroom responsibilities of half time or less. One newcomer held a joint appointment at Perkins and the School of Music (Lloyd Pfautsch), and James B. "Barney" McGrath taught part time at Perkins and part time in SMU's Speech Department.

The enlarged faculty brought other changes. By the fall of 1956 the student-faculty ratio had already been cut roughly in half since 1951, and the faculty was developing depth in several fields.[4] By 1960 Perkins had moved from one or two faculty members in each field to three in Old Testament (in the order in which they joined the faculty: Kermit Schoonover, W. J. A. Power, James Ward), three in New Testament (William R. Farmer, Victor Furnish, William C. Robinson Jr.), three in the history of Christianity (Albert Outler, Richey Hogg, Frank Littell), five in theology and philosophy (Outler, Herndon Wagers, John Deschner, Schubert Ogden, Van Harvey), four in ethics (Cooper, Douglas Jackson, myself, Fred Carney), four in homiletics (Baker, Quillian, Wheeler, Grady Hardin), two in church administration (Judy, Curl), and three in Christian education (Grimes, Johnson, Banks). Some taught part time and held administrative responsibilities. The reason for the additions was to deal with the large student body, but the presence of colleagues in one's field was a valuable by-product.

Other appointments—Neill McFarland in history of religions, Robert Elliott in pastoral care, and Hogg in missions—ensured coverage for fields that had been without specialists for some time. Lloyd Pfautsch's arrival solidified Perkins's offerings in church music and heralded the introduction of the master of sacred music degree. Roger Ortmayer became the first full-time specialist in the arts in the school's history, although a university art professor had taught part time in the School of Theology in its early years.

As it grew, the Perkins faculty also became diverse denominationally. When Edward Hobbs, an Episcopalian, was considered in 1952, Cuninggim had found it necessary to argue that so long as most of the faculty members were Methodist, having some non-Methodists would not be a problem. When he proposed Herndon Wagers's appointment for 1954, one faculty member (Marlatt) voted against him on the ground that he was not a Methodist (his membership was with the Disciples of Christ).[5] Thereafter a prospect's denomination occasioned little comment. Kermit Schoonover was a member of the Society of Friends; Van Harvey, a Presbyterian; and Lloyd Pfautsch, a member of the United Church of Christ. Cuninggim, though, continued to propose mainly Methodists for the faculty, and they remained a large majority.

Beginning in 1950 Rabbi David Lefkowitz of Dallas's Temple Emanu-El taught a course in contemporary Judaism as a visiting professor. In the same capacity Rabbi

Levi Olan taught that course from 1952 until 1978; Temple Emanu-El gave him time off to do this, in effect paying his stipend. When Perkins gave him an honorarium, Olan refused to accept it, and from that time he was listed as a contributor to the Scholarship Fund. Olan, Cuninggim said, "sometimes called us to our senses [in faculty meetings] with the word of challenge, 'In this situation, gentlemen, we've simply got to figure out what is the Christian thing for us to do.'" Olan received an honorary doctor of humane letters degree from SMU in 1968.[6]

The new arrivals sharply lowered the age of the faculty. When Cuninggim became dean in the fall of 1951, the median age was fifty-nine and a half. In the fall of 1960, just after his departure, it was forty-one. Of the thirty-three faculty members in the fall of 1960, only one (Curl) was in his sixties, and five (Baker, Marsh, Outler, Schoonover, and Wagers) were in their fifties. Twenty-five were in their thirties or forties, nearly evenly divided between the two, and two (Furnish and Power) were not yet thirty. Cuninggim shaped the Perkins faculty for decades to come. Of thirty-four faculty appointed while he was dean, nineteen remained at Perkins until they reached retirement, and eight of the thirty-four did not retire until 1991–2001—three to four decades after his departure.

The faculty members of the fifties had much in common: most were relatively young; most were Methodist; many had done their graduate study at Chicago, Union, or Yale; most were ordained ministers; and several had had pastoral or military chaplaincy experience, or both. All this helped them work well with one another. Yet the key to their collegiality was Cuninggim's vision of the kind of faculty they could become and the way he exemplified that vision in his deanship.

THE FACULTY'S WORK TOGETHER

Dean Cuninggim's report to the faculty at its preschool conference in September 1956 set forth his interpretation of the recent changes at Perkins and his vision for the faculty. He observed that more than half the full-time faculty had arrived since 1952, and he spoke of the quality of its individual members. About the new curriculum he declared that the real changes were less in content than "in the broad and intangible area of human relationships . . . in the atmosphere created by the new program." Discussion went on among students, among faculty, and between the two groups far more than previously, bringing their fields and concerns to bear on ultimate questions of life. If the faculty was too close to the process to be aware of this change, visitors recognized it and spoke about it. Cuninggim saw in this interchange the emergence of a faculty, a collegium.[7]

In contrast to "the two extremes of authoritarianism and irresponsibility," Cuninggim said he coveted "a system of shared responsibility in which each of us has his defined task and all of us have a voice in establishing the definition of that task." If Perkins was to achieve a different atmosphere in its intellectual life and interpersonal relations, if it was to work as a sort of democracy, it must achieve this in the area of faculty business and not only in scholarly reflection and teaching. Cuninggim's philosophy of administration, he said, was one of "group responsibility and individual leadership," avoiding the dual temptations to dominate or to leave decisions to others. The ideal, he said, was for each member to recognize the authority of the faculty as a whole and the derivative authority of the various committees and individuals as matters were delegated to them, so that each person would be responsible in the conduct of faculty business. "The ideal is clear, but the performance is not easy."[8]

Cuninggim's way of working with the faculty did much to achieve this vision. He conducted meetings in ways that involved the faculty in deliberation and action about what the policies should be. Toward that end, in the fall of 1952 he initiated the annual Faculty Pre-School Conference. The first was an all-day session in Dallas a week before classes began. Subsequent preschool conferences met at the Lakeview Methodist assembly ground near Palestine, Texas, during a weekend, until 1959, when there was a one-day conference in Dallas. These conferences combined business and recreation, provided an opportunity for the dean to report on the state of the school and for faculty response and discussion, and allowed for discussion of topics of importance other than the business of regular faculty meetings (among them, the relationship of the seminary to the university and the church, Perkins worship life, and graduate studies in religion at SMU). The preschool conferences introduced new faculty members to their colleagues and oriented them to the faculty's work. The conferences strengthened the faculty as a community.

A major way Cuninggim shared responsibility with the faculty was through the process of appointing new faculty. His predecessors would receive faculty members' suggestions, but the decision to nominate someone to the president and trustees for appointment was entirely the dean's, without formal faculty discussion. Cuninggim changed that process. In the winter and spring of 1952, while he was considering the appointments of Mathews and Hobbs, he raised the question of a procedure by which faculty could voice their opinions before someone was invited to join the faculty. The dean suggested and the faculty voted that "in the appointment of any full-time member of the staff, adequate opportunity, represented usually by at least a three-day waiting period between the visit of the prospect and the making of the offer, be allowed for all to express their opinions about the matter."[9] On the face of it this action left some ambiguity about whether faculty opinions would be expressed in a faculty meeting or individually to the dean. However, in several cases during the 1952–53 academic year the dean in a meeting of the faculty proposed or nominated someone for appointment, followed by faculty discussion and a secret ballot on whether to move ahead toward issuing an invitation.[10] That procedure became standard, and it has continued ever since, though with considerable elaboration of the process. By 1953–54 it had become the practice, whenever feasible, for the person under consideration to visit the campus, providing an opportunity to meet the faculty before it took formal action.[11] When I went through the process in January 1957, I met individually with every faculty member who could fit into the schedule and with small groups of those in the two divisions of which I would be a member, as well as with larger faculty gatherings. It was not yet the policy to have the visitor present a formal paper; that step developed some years later.

The best test of the significance of a faculty vote on an appointment would come when the vote was negative. Understandably that was rare. If the dean proposed a name, obviously he favored the appointment, and he would ordinarily have had opportunity beforehand to sound out the opinions of a number of faculty members. On one occasion in the latter half of the 1950s, however, the faculty vote was 15–12 against going ahead with an invitation. The dean had proceeded in the usual way with the person he saw as the leading prospect for one position, that person had visited the campus and met with faculty, and strong reservations as well as strong support for the appointment had surfaced before discussion in a faculty meeting. The minutes of that meeting record that the dean's recommendation of the person "was discussed at length." After the negative vote the dean did not proceed with the nomination. My impression at the time was that although Cuninggim did not agree with the arguments against extending an invitation, he thought it unwise to proceed in that case, given the extent of faculty opposition. He would have been within his authority as dean if he had recommended the appointment to the provost. This instance illustrates both the seriousness with which Cuninggim intended for the faculty to participate in the major decisions of the school and the ardor with which the faculty seized the opportunity to do so.

In the faculty discussion on that occasion and in other faculty meetings, the untenured faculty on tenure track—from five to eight people in each year from 1954–55 to 1959–60—participated in the same way as did tenured faculty.

The most important limit on faculty participation in policy was on decisions about the school's budget. These were matters between the dean and the appropriate university officers. On occasion Cuninggim would share detailed information about the categories of the budget with the faculty, followed by discussion.[12] Administrative control of the budget was standard policy, and faculty members did not think it inappropriate.

More questionably, during Cuninggim's deanship the school had no stated faculty rank and tenure policy. He had his own policies, apparently, but faculty members did not know what they were and had no role in discussing them. One practice was that those who came to the faculty without their doctoral degrees usually were appointed as instructors. When they had received their doctoral degrees, they were promoted to the rank of assistant professor, although that practice was not always followed. Charles Johnson was hired as an assistant professor even though he was still working on his dissertation; upon its completion he was promoted to associate professor. Cuninggim may have been influenced in this case by Johnson's age—at the time of his initial appointment Johnson was older than most of his instructor colleagues—but this is to seek a rationale where none was publicly known. That the absence of a stated rank and tenure policy was perceived to be a problem is supported by what happened right after Joseph D. Quillian Jr. was named as Cuninggim's successor in February 1960: three untenured faculty (Ogden, Harvey, and I) went together to ask Quillian to institute a formal rank and tenure policy after he became dean. Quillian agreed a stated policy was needed.

Much of the faculty's participation in policy was through committee work. In a given year a faculty member without an administrative position was a member of two to five of the sixteen or so Perkins faculty committees. On the one hand this allowed much opportunity for faculty initiative and input about policy. On the other, it was, and continued to be, a heavy burden on faculty time. The cost of policy participation was a reduction in the time for teaching and publishing. Often, nonadministrative faculty had administrative responsibilities of a time-consuming nature, such as carrying out the admissions process, directing orientation, supervising the registration of students each semester, dealing with the many details necessary for Ministers' Week, or directing the summer session. Faculty members varied considerably in the time they devoted to committee and administrative responsibilities, but some of this burden fell upon all. The employment of more administrators would have helped remedy the problem. In 1956 Cuninggim appointed Richard Bush as director of school-church relations, followed in 1959 by J. B. Holt, providing relief to faculty in the admissions process and in other ways. Further expansion in the number of administrators did not occur until after Quillian became dean.

THE INTELLECTUAL LIFE OF THE PERKINS COMMUNITY

Along with faculty members' participation in policy making, their academic interchange increased as the Cuninggim years progressed. Cuninggim placed a high value on interdisciplinary dialog. Victor Furnish remembers that when Cuninggim first contacted him about joining the Perkins faculty, the dean emphasized that faculty members needed to look beyond their own special fields and develop an interest in the work of their colleagues.[13] A notable occasion for interdisciplinary discussion came with the introduction of the new curriculum in 1953. Because the core course in each division was conceived as a single course with several segments, the faculty members in each division had to work together to organize, and often to teach, each segment. This kind of dialog did not cease with the initial organization of the core. It was necessary to bring each new faculty member into the discussion, and sometimes the new member became the stimulus to reorganize a division's core. For example, Richey Hogg and Neill McFarland both arrived after the new curriculum was in place. When they undertook together in 1955–56 to teach the segment of Division II devoted to the Christian mission and other religions, they concluded that it was impossible to deal adequately with both subjects in one semester. Their experience led the faculty to change the curriculum in 1957 to require a one-semester course on world Christianity and another on other religions.

New faculty also initiated changes in the Division III core. Originally, its third segment had been called "The Content of the Christian Faith," and the fourth, "The Principles of the Christian Life." After Joe Mathews left in 1956, and John Deschner and Schubert Ogden arrived that fall, they judged this separation to be theologically untenable. The result, beginning in the fall of 1958, was the combination of the two into a single team-taught, two-semester course entitled "The Interpretation of the Christian Message in Thought and Action" and later, simply, "The Interpretation of the Christian Message." That course, with its major written assignment, the Credo, was a central part of the curriculum for decades. It became the occasion for a long-running, mutually productive dialog between Deschner and Ogden, as well as others who from time to time joined in team-teaching the course: Outler, Harvey, me, and eventually other, later faculty.

That did not complete the reorganization of that part of the Division III core. Fred Carney and I, both ethicists, agreed that reflection on the content of Christian faith and reflection on Christian action were theologically inseparable, but we nevertheless held that the latter would unavoidably receive short shrift in a course organized primarily around the former. Thus 1961 saw the inclusion of a fifth Division III core segment, initially entitled "Christian Ethics" and, later, "Moral Theology." The shape of the new curriculum, even after it was no longer new, continued to be an occasion for faculty dialog.

Cuninggim observed that informal discussion was far more extensive among both faculty and students than it had been previously. The morning class schedule made some room for this to happen. Classes met from 8:00 to 8:50 a.m. and from 9:00 to 9:50, followed by chapel from 10:00 to 10:30. Between chapel and eleven o'clock classes came "coffee hour" in the Selecman Hall parlor. For a half hour faculty and students crowded into this modest-sized room for refreshments and discussion, so many people there was scarcely room to move. Small groups would gather, some around this professor or that, pursuing such issues as Bultmann's demythologizing, or what difference being a Christian should make in one's life, or strategies for racial desegregation, until time came for the next class. Discussion continued in the hallways, in faculty offices, in the dormitories, and in student carpools between campus and home. James E. Kirby Jr., who entered Perkins as a student in 1954, observed that in those years he first experienced being "a junior member of the academic community," participating in intellectual inquiry.[14] Bob Darrell, president of the Perkins Student Council in 1958–59, described Perkins as the locus of several continually changing theological viewpoints, with vigorous conversation among students and faculty. "The Perkins community," he wrote, "is asking questions; it is actually engaged in seeking answers. . . . Yes, it is exciting to be at Perkins these days!"[15]

Along with the vigor of conversation came a significant increase in the volume of faculty publications. Among the books published in the 1950s were works by Merrimon Cuninggim, John Deschner, Fred Gealy, Robert W. Goodloe, Howard Grimes, Richey Hogg, William A. Irwin, and Marvin Judy (see appendix C). In addition, eight faculty members completed their doctoral dissertations and received their degrees, either immediately before coming to Perkins or soon thereafter.

The writings of two other Perkins authors in this decade attracted sufficient attention at Perkins and in the wider theological world that more extended mention is warranted. Soon after Albert Outler came to Perkins, he gave a series of lectures at several universities that led to his writing *Psychotherapy and the Christian Message*.[16] He presented the two as both allies and rivals—allies in their common concern for human health and well-being but rivals because of their different perspectives. The book explores this dual relation in their approach to four issues: the human self and its freedom, the human quandary, the human possibility, and ethics.

In the 1950s Outler also published two major works in the history of Christianity, both of which reflect his continuing theological reflection. The first was volume 7 of the Library of Christian Classics, his translation and editing of *Augustine: Confessions and Enchiridion*. Outler characterized these two works, the one early and the other late in Augustine's ministry, as "the nearest equivalent to summation in the whole of the Augustinian corpus." He then followed in 1957 with *The Christian Tradition and the Unity We Seek*, which he had given as lectures at the University of Virginia and again in the Washington, D.C., area. In it he argued that the sense of community in Jesus Christ is primary to the ecumenical movement, whereas defining terms and explaining doctrines is derivative and explicative—a thesis he developed with numerous insights.[17]

Schubert Ogden completed his University of Chicago doctoral work in 1958 with his dissertation, "Christ without Myth: A Study in Constructive Theology Based on a Critical Analysis of the Work of Rudolf Bultmann," which received an award for the best dissertation that year at the University of Chicago in education, sociology, or theology. The dissertation became the basis of his book *Christ without Myth: A Study Based on the Theology of Rudolf Bultmann*. The theological problem, as Ogden saw it, was how to work in obedience to the New Testament proclamation and the theological tradition, yet embrace the criticism of that tradition arising from "modern man's picture of himself and his world." Examining Bultmann's proposed solution, the demythologizing and existential interpretation of the New Testament, Ogden found it to be structurally inconsistent in maintaining that authentic existence can be realized only through the historical event Jesus of Nazareth. Instead, Ogden argued, authentic existence is always a possibility because of God's unconditional love, yet the decisive manifestation of this love is "the event Jesus of Nazareth."[18] This book, as much as that of any other faculty member, became a stimulus to theological discussion within Perkins for a number of years.

While preparing *Christ without Myth* for publication, Ogden also brought out his own translation of twenty of Bultmann's shorter writings. In his introduction he sought to explain the unity and structure of Bultmann's thought, thus providing an understanding of his work as a prerequisite for any criticism.[19]

Faculty members publishing in this period were scattered across the four divisions, and they included many of the newer faculty along with some whose arrival predated Cuninggim's. The prospect was good for continued extensive publication in the future.

WORSHIP AT PERKINS IN THE FIFTIES

After the dedication of Perkins Chapel in 1951, weekday services were held there, usually from 10:00 to 10:30 a.m. By 1959 the pattern had developed that chapel services were held on Tuesdays, Wednesdays, and Fridays, whereas on Thursdays came a convocation in Lois Perkins Auditorium to present various topics of interest to the Perkins community. No classes or formal school occasions were scheduled on Mondays until late afternoon. A joint committee of students and faculty planned the worship services, and in 1956 the faculty formalized this arrangement with its own three-member worship committee that would work with the student committee. Attendance was voluntary but was expected for all members of the seminary community.[20]

In the fall of 1957 J. Claude Evans of South Carolina became the university chaplain, and on September 21, 1958, he began Sunday morning worship services in the chapel for the campus community. On that first occasion about 550 students attended, and approximately 150 others were turned away for lack of room. Perkins students and their families were welcome at Sunday services as their field education responsibilities permitted.[21] Some Perkins faculty and their families also participated.

On the evening of December 17, 1959, Perkins held the first service in what became a tradition, a Christmas worship service in Perkins Chapel, preceded by a Christmas dinner in McElvaney Hall. At the worship service Lloyd Pfautsch directed the Seminary Singers, and Konnie Konecki led the university choir in singing Christmas music. H. Grady Hardin was the liturgist, and Claude Evans read a classic Christmas sermon.[22] A forerunner to this tradition was held in 1948 with a program of Christmas music led by Fred Gealy and the Seminary Singers during the last chapel service of the fall semester. The 1959 change arose from a recommendation by Richey Hogg, then the chair of the faculty's Community Affairs Committee, that Perkins adopt a pattern followed at Yale Divinity School.[23]

OTHER ACADEMIC PROGRAMS

Between 1951 and 1960 several changes occurred in academic programs other than the bachelor of divinity. The 1952–53 Perkins catalog listed three degrees in addition to the B.D.: master of arts, a one-year program in the graduate school in any of several fields of religious studies, with courses taught primarily by Perkins professors; bachelor of arts in religious education, a one-year program primarily at Perkins, with an undergraduate degree as a prerequisite; and master of religious education, a slightly longer program in the graduate school, again requiring an undergraduate degree.[24]

The School of Theology faculty had included a professor of religious education during almost all its early history—first Jesse Cuninggim, then James Seehorn Seneker—and the subject had been required for the bachelor of divinity degree since 1918.[25] The school offered no degree in this field, however, until 1945, when it announced the bachelor of arts in religious education, an undergraduate program that required twelve hours of advanced courses in religion at the college and nine courses in religious education at the School of Theology. The program, which began in 1947, had only three candidates the first year and none after that, and in the spring of 1952 the faculty terminated it.[26]

In the fall of 1954 Perkins introduced a master of religious education degree that conformed to the recommendations of the American Association of Schools of Religious Education. At that time the faculty in the field included Seneker, who would retire in 1956; Howard Grimes, who had joined the faculty in 1949; and the newly appointed Charles "Joe" Johnson. The new program required sixty, and later sixty-four, semester hours, half in Division I, The Life and Work of the Local Church (and designated courses in Division II), largely in courses related to church education, plus a project.[27] Enrollment in this program grew to fifteen in 1960–61, mostly women, in a period when almost no women were enrolled for the B.D. degree.[28]

Since 1920 the School of Theology had required its bachelor of divinity students to take a course in church music. From then until 1939 the course, taught by faculty from the School of Music, usually emphasized voice training, congregational singing, and *The Methodist Hymnal.* Soon after Fred Gealy's arrival in 1939, the required course in church music became a regular part of his course offerings, and he founded the Seminary Singers. In 1940 he added an elective on the church choir, and in 1947 the Seminary Singers became a credit course.[29] The new curriculum in 1953 incorporated the requirement in church music into the team-taught Division I core segment initially entitled "Worship and Sacred Music," and later "Public Worship." Gealy continued to offer a church music elective and to direct the Seminary Singers.

Cuninggim had larger ambitions for church music at Perkins. In the spring semesters of 1954 and 1955 he brought in as a visiting professor in church music Robert Guy McCutchan, who had edited *The Methodist Hymnal* of 1935. In the spring of 1955 Cuninggim, in consultation with President Tate; Orville Borchers, dean of the SMU School of Music; and others, worked out a plan for a faculty position in sacred music, a dual appointment to the Perkins and the School of Music faculties. The first occupant of the position would help to develop a program for training ministers of music but would not necessarily become the director of the program. In June of that year Cuninggim proposed someone for the position and the Perkins faculty approved, but that effort did not meet with success.[30]

On November 28–29, 1955, at Cuninggim's initiative, Perkins and the School of Music hosted the "Consultation on Church Music" to explore the idea of a program to train ministers of music. Among the twenty-nine people attending were four from the Perkins faculty (Cuninggim, Baker, Gealy, and Quillian); three from the School of Music faculty, including Borchers; and a number of national and regional figures in church music, including John Finley Williamson, president of Westminster Choir College; Hugh Porter, director of Union Theological Seminary's School of Sacred Music; Ruth Krehbiel Jacobs, executive director of the Choristers' Guild; and several organists and ministers of music of large churches. The three sessions dealt with the role of music in the church, the religious and musical responsibilities of the minister of music, and the shape of a training program for ministers of music.[31] It was, Cuninggim noted, "a most stimulating meeting," with the result that Perkins would look for an outstanding person to direct the program. The plan was that in the first year this person would spend a third of her or his time at Perkins, a third at the School of Music, and a third planning for the degree program for ministers of music, which, it was hoped, would begin the following year. The major administrative responsibility for the program would lie with Perkins. There would be an administrative committee composed of the deans of the two schools and the provost, and after a director had been chosen, a curriculum committee would be established that would include faculty members from both Perkins and the School of Music.[32]

Finding the right person to direct the program was more difficult than anticipated. Several promising possibilities in 1956 and 1957 did not materialize. Then in May 1958 Cuninggim announced the appointment of Lloyd Pfautsch, a specialist in choral conducting with both bachelor of divinity and master of sacred music degrees from Union Theological Seminary, as associate professor of sacred music at Perkins and the School of Music. Upon his arrival that fall Pfautsch chaired a committee to plan the degree program; its members were deans Cuninggim and Borchers (both ex officio), Gealy and Wagers from Perkins, and Eugene Ellsworth and Farrold Stephens from the School of Music faculty.[33] In the spring semester of 1959 both faculties approved the committee's proposal, and the master of sacred music degree program was inaugurated the following fall.

As amended slightly in 1960, the program required sixty semester hours of graduate-level courses in music and theology—thus two years of study. Requirements included a minimum of twenty semester hours at the School of Theology, with courses in church education, worship, hymnology, Christianity and the arts, New

Testament, and the history of Christianity.[34] Pfautsch observed that this was a higher percentage of work in theology than anywhere else and that some schools offering a sacred music degree required no theological study at all.[35] By the fall of 1960 the M.S.M. program had enrolled four students, and by the following fall, twelve—eight men and four women.[36]

Perkins introduced the master of sacred theology program in the fall of 1956 as graduate professional education for the pastoral and related ministries, distinct from graduate research education for teaching in the academy. The requirement for admission was a B.D. degree from an accredited seminary with grades or standardized tests indicating above-average seminary work. The program required at least two semesters of study, to include twenty-four semester hours of coursework and six semester hours for a project. Students were to major—take 50 percent of their coursework—in one of the divisions. At first there was no language requirement, but beginning in 1959 those majoring in Division IV, the Bible, were required to take a minimum of two semesters of work in either Hebrew or Greek. The project was to be on a topic of major practical concern to the student, and it was to be followed by an oral examination on the project in relation to the student's professional competence as a whole.[37] Enrollment in the master of sacred theology program grew from one the first year to twenty-five two years later.

At its preschool conference in the fall of 1957, the faculty gave special attention to the question of what Perkins's program of graduate studies should be. Reporting later that fall to the School of Theology committee of the board of trustees about that discussion, Cuninggim observed that along with the new master of sacred theology graduate-professional degree, there should be another program emphasizing graduate-level research, one that would prepare college and university teachers. Such a program would express the aim of the graduate school to inaugurate the Ph.D. degree in fields in which the university could excel. Although a Ph.D. program in religion would be under the jurisdiction of the graduate school, the Perkins faculty would be closely related to it. The faculty's discussion helped to clarify its principles and lay a foundation for later planning for graduate study.[38]

Informal conversations soon began between members of the Perkins faculty and Claude Albritton, dean of the SMU Graduate School, who in June 1958 appointed a planning committee for the doctoral program in religion, consisting of ten SMU faculty, with Albert Outler as chair and Stuart Henry of the Department of Religious Studies as executive secretary. Uppermost in their minds was the question of whether SMU would have the resources for a doctoral program comparable to the best programs offered elsewhere in the country. After careful consideration, including visits to the campus of every university in the United States that offered a Ph.D. degree in religion, the planning committee on January 28, 1959, decided "that S.M.U. can and should undertake a doctoral program in religion."[39] The following fall the trustees determined that the next field to offer the Ph.D. degree (after economics) would be religion but recognized a problem: finding the money to underwrite it.[40] Sufficient funds were not available until the 1960s. In the meanwhile the Perkins faculty participated in planning the curriculum and library acquisition lists.

In this period Perkins moved beyond joint academic programs within SMU and formed cooperative relationships with other theological schools in the Southwest. During the 1955–56 academic year the Institute of Religion, a program providing clinical pastoral training for theological students, was established at the Texas Medical Center in Houston. Its original sponsors, besides Perkins, were Austin Presbyterian Theological Seminary, Brite College of the Bible at Texas Christian University, Episcopal Theological Seminary of the Southwest, Southwestern Baptist Theological Seminary, the Board of Administration of the Texas Medical Center, and, soon thereafter, the Graduate Seminary of Phillips University in Oklahoma. The Institute of Religion provided clinical pastoral training under professional supervision both at the seminary and graduate levels. For B.D. students it offered a twelve-week summer term, and for those working on the master of sacred theology and other master's degrees, two semesters of training in the regular academic year. Its original faculty consisted of Dawson C. Bryan as director and Samuel Southard and LeRoy Kerney as professors of pastoral care.[41] Robert Elliott, who had recently arrived to teach pastoral care at Perkins, kept the Perkins faculty informed and involved in its developments. By 1958 the institute's faculty members were recognized as members of the Perkins faculty and of the faculties of the other seminaries.[42]

The representatives of the participating institutions had met in November 1954, for the Conference on Theological Education in the Southwest, as a part of a study, "Theological Education in America," by H. Richard Niebuhr and his associates. Thereafter leaders from these seminaries began working to bring about a vehicle for their continuing cooperation. By 1958 they had drawn up a constitution and had chartered the Council of Southwestern Theological Schools, Inc., as a nonprofit corporation in Texas. Its purposes were to advance theological education in the Southwest, to pursue activities of common interest, and to consider any problems in their relationships.[43]

CONTROVERSIES ABOUT ACADEMIC FREEDOM

While Perkins in the 1950s was developing new programs and new relationships with other institutions, it also twice faced challenges to academic freedom within SMU. In January 1954 John Beaty, a tenured professor and former chair of the SMU English Department, wrote and mailed to various friends and patrons of SMU an eight-page pamphlet entitled, "How to Capture a University."[44] In it he declared that an influential non-Christian group was trying to dominate Southern Methodist University. He especially objected to an article in SMU's literary journal, *Southwest Review,* for fall 1953, which criticized his earlier book, *Iron Curtain over America,* and accused him of being anti-Semitic, a charge he denied.[45] The source of the charges in the *Southwest Review* was, he claimed, the Anti-Defamation League of B'nai B'rith, which he called a propaganda organization, a "Jewish Gestapo." He went on to say that B'nai B'rith had bought influence in Perkins School of Theology for seventy-five dollars. This was a reference to the two annual prizes in social ethics, totaling seventy-five dollars, for seniors at Perkins that were established in 1953 by the George Levy Lodge of B'nai B'rith, the oldest Jewish service organization.[46] Beaty further claimed that SMU allowed communists to spread propaganda in its halls. This had happened, he judged, without the SMU administration's being aware of the aim or substance of the so-called infiltration. But he was sure that the administration would welcome suggestions from "patriotic Christians" who imitated the communists' methods.

Beaty's pamphlet appeared while Umphrey Lee, after his heart attack, was considering whether to continue as president. In February Lee issued a statement that said, in part: "I desire publicly and gladly to take full responsibility for the cordial relations now existing between the University, Temple Emanu-El, B'nai B'rith, as well as with other religious groups in the city. I accept full responsibility for the cooperation of the University with Catholic, Protestant and Jewish leaders in the National Conference of Christians and Jews."[47] At the March 30, 1954, meeting of the SMU

Board of Trustees to receive and accept Lee's letter of resignation because of his continuing ill health, the board also made an initial response to Beaty's pamphlet, establishing a committee of eight trustees to investigate his allegations and sending a letter to friends and patrons of the university assuring them it was conducting an inquiry and would consider the issue further at its May meeting.[48]

At the May 6 meeting, in addition to electing Willis Tate as the new president, the board reported on its inquiry into Beaty's allegations. The committee had called before it Beaty and a number of other witnesses. On the basis of the committee's report, the board concluded that the facts did not bear out Beaty's allegations and deplored Beaty's failure to present his charges to the university's administrators or to request permission from the *Southwest Review* to answer its criticisms in its pages. Instead he had circulated his allegations to students, patrons of the university, and the press. The board declared its loyalty to the democratic ideals underlying American life and to the "high Christian ideals on which it was founded."[49]

The board could have dismissed Beaty from the university but did not. In 1932 Beaty had brought charges against a fellow member of the English Department, and when they were not sustained by the university, he had written a letter to all Methodist ministers in Texas and Oklahoma, urging them to write board members and ask for an investigation. Because of his actions the board had in 1933 amended the university's by-laws to read, "If any member of the faculty or employee of the University shall present any grievance or statement to others than the President of the University or the Trustees of the University, such act shall be sufficient grounds for dismissal from the faculty or the employ of the University as the case may be."[50] The combination of firmness and restraint in the university's 1954 response apparently reflected the efforts of both Umphrey Lee and Willis Tate, who had been exercising executive responsibilities during Lee's illness. The university did not want to be seen as suppressing the academic freedom of the faculty, even when it was misused. Marshall Terry, long-time member of the English Department and administrator, observed that Tate's actions in the Beaty matter set the tone for his years as SMU president.[51]

After Beaty's pamphlet appeared, Albert Outler composed a letter that he proposed the Perkins faculty send to Temple Emanu-El and to the George Levy Lodge of B'nai B'rith, lamenting Beaty's unjust attack and reaffirming the long cooperation between Perkins and the Dallas Jewish community. The faculty unanimously accepted the letter, it was sent, and in reply several people associated with B'nai B'rith and Temple Emanu-El wrote back to express their appreciation for Perkins's stance.[52]

Another incident threatening academic freedom arose in the spring of 1958. The undergraduate Student Forum Committee, desiring to have an academic discussion of the menace of communism, invited John Gates, a former communist and former editor of the communist *Daily Worker*, to speak on campus on the afternoon of April 23. In those years right-wing groups had been agitating and accusing people of being communist sympathizers. The atmosphere in Dallas was such that some people did not even want books on communism in the library, let alone have a former communist speak on campus. That Gates was no longer a communist was irrelevant to them. President Tate learned about the invitation through an article in the *Daily Campus*, and he was soon the recipient of much criticism. He was determined, however, to support the students' action. He thought they should have the right to invite whomever they wished to hear, and he believed that in the free exchange of ideas, the truth would win and fallacies would be exposed.[53]

Sterling Wheeler, vice president for development and public relations, took charge of plans for the program. The students had also invited Herbert A. Philbrick, a former FBI counterspy, to respond to Gates. Wheeler arranged for a three-person panel to ask Gates questions after his address: Lloyd M. Wells, a government professor; Douglas Jackson from Perkins; and Claude Evans, the university chaplain. Forty-five hundred people, mostly students, turned out for the occasion—many more than McFarlin Auditorium could hold. The overflow went to the Student Center to listen to a broadcast of the proceedings.[54] Everything went calmly, and, with the support of the board and many Dallas citizens, the administration rode out the abuse. Tate said he was proud of the faculty members who pinned Gates down on his assumptions and ambiguities, and Tate noted that many felt SMU had matured in the eyes of the wider academy and that in the future the students would have enough guidance to calculate the repercussions in advance.[55]

These two events in Willis Tate's presidency illustrate his commitment to academic freedom. In this context the SMU faculty, including those at Perkins, could be confident of administration support in the face of attacks that might arise in the wider community. A few years later the SMU chapter of the American Association of University Professors nominated Tate for the national AAUP's prestigious Alexander

Meiklejohn Award "for significant action in support of academic freedom," and in 1965 he received the award.[56]

MERRIMON CUNINGGIM'S DEPARTURE AS DEAN

On January 16, 1960, the Perkins faculty came together in a meeting called by President Tate to announce the resignation of Merrimon Cuninggim as dean. Cuninggim had accepted the position of director of the Danforth Foundation as of April 1, 1961, and from July 1, 1960, he would be engaged in study and travel to prepare for his new work. The Danforth Foundation, with offices in St. Louis, was a prestigious foundation concerned with religion and higher education, and, as Tate later explained, its director would have great influence on education throughout the country and beyond.[57]

Tate had already set in motion a process for the selection of a new dean. He first convened the Board of Trustees Committee on the School of Theology, chaired by Paul Martin and composed of four bishops, four other ministers, and two laity. As Tate later reported, the committee advised him to gather names of qualified people, on the Perkins faculty, on other faculties, and among the pastors of churches.[58] In his January meeting with the faculty, he asked Herndon Wagers to be the faculty's representative for consultation with him about the appointment, and Tate encouraged all the faculty members to express their ideas about it to Wagers. After consultation with the trustees' committee, Tate identified these qualities for the candidate they were seeking: "A commitment to the needs and the program of The Methodist Church, especially in our Jurisdiction, along with a basic concern for the Methodist ministry, proven educational and administrative ability, academic competence, and a sense of priority for this particular task. We agreed that we wanted a person who would be sensitive to the needs and the hopes of the Church and a person who could be counted on to work faithfully for good relationships between the seminary and the local churches."[59]

On February 26, 1960, in a letter to the Methodist ministers in the South Central Jurisdiction, Tate described the procedure he had used and announced that Joseph D. Quillian Jr., a Perkins professor, would become dean on July 1, 1960. Tate explained that his survey had resulted in a list of forty-five candidates, including administrators, professors, and pastors. In meetings with the trustees' committee, the list was narrowed to five—three members of the Perkins faculty, including Quillian, and two from outside the faculty. It became his conviction, Tate said, that the "most logically indicated" choice was Quillian.[60]

Before Cuninggim left Perkins, he responded to a problem that had been disturbing him for some time. Lynn Landrum, a columnist for the *Dallas Morning News*, had written a number of articles insinuating that this or that person or group might be a communist. He had, Cuninggim said in April, written at least ten columns in the previous six weeks attacking the National Council of Churches. Finally, Cuninggim asked the *News* for space to reply, and the *News* granted it. From April 6 to 10, 1960, the paper published five of his articles on its editorial page. He went on the offensive from the start:

> With a pose of weighing his "evidence" objectively, he [Landrum] stacks his cards so that the truth is lost in the shuffle. He repeats charges that have been shown to be unfounded smears. He accepts the testimony of discredited witnesses. . . . These are Communist-style tactics. They are not those of decency and fair play.

And again:

> Notice how Landrum does it: "This column does not assert or believe that the National Council . . . is 100 per cent Communist." (Feb. 23) . . . This may once have been effective strategy in high-school debating, but it is not designed to get at the truth. It fosters suspicion safely and cheaply. . . . The point is, the National Council is the co-operative arm of each of the churches that has chosen to participate. . . . If somebody attacks the National Council of Churches he is attacking my church, and me, just as much as if he were vilifying my pastor or Sunday school teacher. . . . Where does that leave Mr. Landrum? The funny thing is, he is a member of the National Council! He is a member of the same denomination I am. . . . But don't misunderstand. I don't think Mr. Landrum is thereby 100% Communist![61]

When justice was at stake, Cuninggim was a fighter, and he went on fighting to the end of his years in Dallas.

1. Merrimon Cuninggim, "Report for 1951–52, Perkins School of Theology, S.M.U., June, 1952" Cuninggim Papers, Bridwell Library, p. 6.
2. Ibid., 6–7.
3. Board of trustees minutes for 1949 to 1960; Cuninggim, "Report for 1951–52," 8–9, Cuninggim Papers; catalog, 1951–52, 13; 1952–53, 16; and 1959–60, 19–20.
4. Cuninggim, "Report to the Faculty," Faculty Pre-School Conference for 1956, 2, Cuninggim Papers.
5. Faculty minutes, December 21, 1953; Earl Marlatt to Cuninggim, December 21, 1953; Cuninggim to Marlatt, January 1, 1954, Cuninggim Papers.
6. Cuninggim, unpublished manuscript, 1990, Cuninggim Papers.
7. Cuninggim, "Report to the Faculty," 1956, 4–5.
8. Ibid., 5–6.
9. Faculty minutes, March 19, 1952.
10. Faculty minutes, September 24, 1952, February 11, 1953, and April 23, 1953.
11. Faculty minutes, December 21, 1953, and March 19, 1954.
12. This is reflected in the faculty minutes for November 21, 1952, and the "Statement on Expense Budgets" prepared for that meeting (Cuninggim Papers).
13. Victor Furnish to Joe Allen, July 23, 2008, in the author's personal files.
14. Cuninggim, "Report to the Faculty, 1956," 4, Cuninggim Papers; James E. Kirby Jr., interview by author, August 23, 2007, Dallas.
15. C. Bob Darrell, "A View of the Theological Horizon at Perkins," *Log* [Perkins student newspaper], February 5, 1959, 2.
16. Albert C. Outler, *Psychotherapy and the Christian Message* (New York: Harper and Row, 1954).
17. Albert C. Outler, ed., *Augustine: Confessions and Enchiridion* (Philadelphia: Westminster, 1955), 16; Albert C. Outler, *The Christian Tradition and the Unity We Seek* (New York: Oxford University Press, 1957), xi, 65–66.
18. *Log*, September 17, 1959, 3; Schubert M. Ogden, *Christ without Myth: A Study Based on the Theology of Rudolf Bultmann* (New York: Harper ad Brothers, 1961), 153.
19. Rudolf Bultmann, *Existence and Faith: Shorter Writings of Rudolf Bultmann*, selected, translated, and introduced by Schubert M. Ogden (New York: Meridian, 1960), 13, 21.
20. Catalog, 1952–53, 27; 1956–57, 9; 1959–60, 38–39.
21. Ibid., 1959–60, 38–39; board of trustees minutes, November 6, 1958.
22. *Log*, December 15, 1959, 1.
23. Michael Hawn, "Master of Sacred Music Reunion Celebrates Fifty Years of Vision: A Presentation for the Master of Sacred Music Alumni/ae Reunion," September 19, 2005, 2, Joseph Allen Papers, Bridwell Library.
24. Catalog, 1952–53, 32–33.
25. *Bulletin*, June 1918, 103.
26. Catalog, 1945–46, 20; 1948–49, 29–30; faculty minutes, April 16, 1952. From 1947 the name of the program became bachelor of religious education.
27. Faculty minutes, April 2, 1954; Catalog, 1955–56, 44, and 1956–57, 42.
28. See Catalog, 1961–62, 86, for 1960–61 enrollment figures.
29. Catalog, 1940–41, 185.
30. Merrimon Cuninggim to Robert Guy McCutchan, June 9 and June 17, 1955, Cuninggim Papers; faculty minutes, June 14, 1955.
31. "Report on the Consultation on Church Music," Cuninggim Papers.
32. Merrimon Cuninggim, Report to the Trustees' Committee on the School of Theology, April 1, 1957, Cuninggim Papers; "Proposal for Organization of a Graduate-level Program for Training Ministers of Music at S. M. U.," Cuninggim Papers.
33. Lloyd Pfautsch, "A New Response to an Ageless Commission," *Perkins Journal*, spring 1959, 19.
34. Catalog, 1959–60, 51, and 1960–61, 51.
35. Pfautsch, "A New Response," 19.

36. Catalog, 1961–62, 86, and 1962–63, 87.
37. Ibid., 1957–58, 45–46, and 1959–60, 49–51.
38. Merrimon Cuninggim, "Report to the Trustees' Committee on the School of Theology," October 14, 1957, Cuninggim Papers.
39. Board of trustees minutes, November 6, 1958, and May 7, 1959; "The Planning Committee on a Doctoral Program in Religion at SMU to the Dean, the Prudential Committee and the Faculty of the Graduate School of Southern Methodist University," April 28, 1959, Graduate Program in Religious Studies files.
40. Board of trustees minutes, November 5, 1959.
41. Catalog, 1956–57, 8, 36–37.
42. Ibid., 1958–59, 41.
43. Program for the Conference on Theological Education in the Southwest, November 26–27, 1954, Cuninggim Papers; catalog, 1959–60, 43; charter, Council of Southwestern Theological Schools, Inc., Cuninggim Papers.
44. John Beaty, "How to Capture a University," January 20, 1954, Cuninggim Papers; board of trustees minutes, March 30, 1954.
45. John Beaty, *Iron Curtain over America* (Dallas: Wilkinson, 1951).
46. Catalog, 1953–54, 26–27.
47. Public letter from Umphrey Lee, president, February 13, 1954, Cuninggim Papers.
48. Board of trustees minutes, March 30, 1954.
49. Ibid., May 6, 1954.
50. Board of trustees minutes, January 24–25, 1933; Mary Martha Hosford Thomas, *Southern Methodist University: Founding and Early Years* (Dallas: Southern Methodist University Press, 1974), 138–42.
51. Marshall Terry, *"From High on the Hilltop . . .": A Brief History of SMU* (Dallas: Southern Methodist University, 2001), 38.
52. Faculty minutes, February 19, 1954; Merrimon Cuninggim and Wesley Davis to the George Levy Lodge of B'nai B'rith, February 22, 1954; Levi A. Olan, rabbi, Temple Emanu-El, to Merrimon Cuninggim, March 2, 1954; Herman I. Kantor to Cuninggim, Feb. 25, 1954; Carl B. Flaxman to Cuninggim, March 11, 1954; Stanley M. Kaufman, for the George A. Levy Lodge of B'nai B'rith, to Cuninggim, March 12, 1954; Lewis B. Lefkowitz, president, Temple Emanu-El, to Cuninggim, March 15, 1954, all in Cuninggim Papers.
53. Terry, *"From High on the Hilltop,"* 39–40. At the time Terry was a staff member in the university's public relations office under Sterling Wheeler, the vice president.
54. SMU *Campus*, April 18, April 23, April 25, 1958.
55. Executive committee minutes, May 2, 1958; board of trustees minutes, May 8, 1958.
56. Terry, *"From High on the Hilltop,"* 46–47.
57. Faculty minutes, January 16, 1960; Willis Tate, "To Ministers of the Methodist Church in the South Central Jurisdiction," February 26, 1960 (attachment to the faculty minutes).
58. Tate, "To Ministers of the Methodist Church."
59. Ibid.
60. Ibid.
61. Merrimon Cuninggim, "Straighten that Slice!" *Dallas Morning News*, April 6, 1960; Merrimon Cuninggim, "Church Council, Its Membership," *Dallas Morning News*, April 8, 1960.

Sustaining the Process, 1960–1969

In 1960 an external observer could readily have seen Perkins's new and enlarged physical plant, a sizable endowment, a younger and far larger faculty drawn from other regions as well as the South and from other denominations as well as Methodism, and a larger and more diverse student body. Changes in attitude and outlook were no less important: the faculty's sense of having an ecumenical and international mission, the spirit of dialog and inquiry among faculty members and students alike, and the faculty's collegial manner of conducting the school's business and of teaching within the "new curriculum."

Faculty, staff, and students might wonder whether the momentum of the second Perkins could be sustained after the departure of Merrimon Cuninggim, who had mobilized and spearheaded the changes of the fifties. Would young faculty members stay and mature at Perkins or would they scatter to accept attractive offers from other schools? Would the excitement of theological inquiry endure or might it subside into business as usual in preparing students for routine church leadership? Would faculty collegiality continue, or would it be eroded by partisan conflicts and pursuit of individual goals? Much would depend on the new dean and on his interaction with faculty, students, the university, and the church.

JOE QUILLIAN'S UNDERSTANDING OF HIS DEANSHIP

Joseph Dillard Quillian Jr. began his service as dean on July 1, 1960. He was born in Buford, Georgia, northeast of Atlanta, in 1917. Several of his immediate family went into law: his father became a justice of the Supreme Court of Georgia, and two brothers became lawyers. Several others entered the church's special ministry. Joe Quillian experienced pulls in both directions. He had been planning to study law but felt a call to the ministry instead. After graduating from nearby Piedmont College in 1938, he received his bachelor of divinity degree from Vanderbilt Divinity School in 1941, having been a student pastor all three of his seminary years. The following year he was appointed as assistant pastor of West End Methodist Church in Nashville. With the onset of World War II, he became a chaplain in the U.S. Navy in 1942, eventually serving in the Aleutian Islands and then at two hospitals in New York. After the war ended, he left the navy in 1946 and from then until 1950 studied in Yale University's department of religion for his Ph.D. degree while serving as a Methodist pastor. He received the degree in 1951 with a dissertation in the field of moral philosophy. In 1950 he took an appointment in the Tennessee Conference of The Methodist Church as president of Martin College, a small unaccredited church-supported school. During four years as president he was able to bring the school accreditation, increase faculty salaries, and put matters in a better financial condition. When in 1954 Quillian joined the Perkins faculty, he began as a full professor, unlike most of the new faculty members, teaching worship and preaching. From 1956 to 1960 he chaired the Committee on Course of Study, which oversaw the new curriculum, and in that position he worked closely with the dean. His wife, Elizabeth, better known as Betty, had grown up in Spokane, Washington; they had five children.[1]

Quillian knew how high his predecessor had set the bar, but he did not intend to keep things as they were. Thus the introduction to his report to the 1960 fall faculty conference: "Making a better school out of a good one is the job that is proximately before us. Making Perkins one of the best seminaries in the world is the job that is ultimately before us."[2] That was his objective from the start. Given the many assets of Perkins—faculty, university administration, trustees and benefactors, The Methodist Church in the Southwest, students, alums, and physical facilities—he was optimistic that both the proximate and ultimate jobs could be accomplished in the next fifteen years.[3]

Joe Quillian's conception of his role vis-á-vis the faculty benefited greatly from his six years of observing Merrimon Cuninggim and the Perkins faculty in action. Quillian expressed his idea this way:

> The nature of the deanship is determined by the nature of the faculty, in that he is the dean *of* the faculty and not dean *over* the faculty—hence, representative of,

for, and to the faculty. With the consultative process being the way of working to which we are committed, it is the dean's business to represent in a sustained way the faculty's best self and wisdom as he consultatively learns it, both to the faculty and to others. In this function, he acts both of and for the faculty. As a member of the faculty and as a churchman, I found this a prime asset under my predecessor. Now as dean, I find, if different at all, that it is an even more valued asset. What it adds to the responsibility of the dean, it more than relieves in the tension of the dean.[4]

Later he observed that the dean is "the representative colleague" with the responsibilities of keeping the faculty members fully aware of their best selves and gaining proper faculty consideration of all appropriate matters.[5]

Leading consultatively may not have been Joe Quillian's natural bent. He was a strong-willed and decisive person who might have been comfortable setting the policies of the school on his own and then implementing them. Yet he had experienced six years of dialogic, consultative Perkins faculty interaction. He saw that this process could work for this faculty, that it enhanced faculty morale, that it provided wisdom the dean needed, and that the faculty expected him to be that kind of dean, so that not to have led by consultation would have called down the wrath of the faculty upon his head. All this was behind his assertion that "the nature of the deanship is determined by the nature of the faculty." He believed that being dean of the Perkins faculty, at least in that period, necessitated being a consultative leader.

This, then, was largely how he proceeded as dean within the school. He was characteristically willing to have his opinions challenged and was open to modifying his position in the face of counterarguments, and yet his strong opinions continually drove him to press toward what he thought was good for the school. After a few years on the job he told Willis Tate, "I really have never felt especially unequal to the job of serving as dean, but I do feel more nearly on top of my job now than at any time heretofore. I have had to learn quite a bit about the dynamics of 'consultative administration,' including patience."[6]

Joe Quillian was wedded to his work. Schubert Ogden later observed that Quillian "was the hardest working, day in day out, nose-to-the-grindstone academic administrator that I have ever known. . . . He simply worked all the time."[7] His desk was legendary—so covered with papers that one could scarcely see the desk. Once when Merrimon Cuninggim returned for a visit, he walked into the dean's office to wait for Quillian. "Look at that desk!" he exclaimed, and he picked up a denominational magazine and threw it in the wastebasket, muttering, "What's he keeping that for?" Just then Quillian arrived or Cuninggim might have cleaned off his desk.

In faculty meetings, after his opening comments and during discussion of committee reports, Quillian would pull out a sketch pad and begin, not to doodle, but to draw a mandala—an elaborate concentric figure, which he colored. He did this without a straight edge, always drawing the same large pattern but with innumerable variations. Over the years he drew countless mandalas and gave many away. He would simultaneously draw and follow the discussion, interjecting questions and comments as appropriate. His drawing did not seem to interfere with his chairing.

Much of Joe Quillian's outside work was with other bodies in the academy. He constantly worked with the SMU administration, not only concerning Perkins business, such as the budget and faculty appointments, but also as a strong university leader respected by those in the administration and the other schools. Beyond SMU he was for two years president of the Association of Theological Schools, the organization of theological schools in the United States and Canada. He played a major role for many years in the work of the Association of United Methodist Theological Schools. However, it was his work with the churches to which I shall give special attention.

For all Merrimon Cuninggim's accomplishments as an "inside dean," he was less successful in relating to the church people of the region. After he resigned as dean, several clergy wrote to Tate, begging him to appoint a dean who would give greater attention to the churches. One declared, "The resignation may be Providential for our Methodism." Another, in a telegram, wanted "someone who is basically loyal to evangelical traditions and the heritage of Methodism and is not ashamed of them."[8] Although that was not a fair characterization of Cuninggim, it nevertheless reflected feelings widespread in the churches.

Joe Quillian was well aware of the need to repair relations with Methodist clergy, and he quickly set out to do so. Years later he recalled, "I worked pretty much on a crusade basis to restore the seminary to an effective working relationship with the Church, we being in something of a semi-estranged situation in 1960."[9] His first public statement after the announcement of his appointment as dean reflects his approach: "I enter into the work of my predecessors with esteem and appreciation for them and what they have done. I enter into the work of my present colleagues—the Perkins and university faculties, the Perkins alumni, and the preachers, administrators, and laymen of The Methodist Church in the South Central Jurisdiction—with enthusiasm and confidence for what we may do together."[10] He did not intend to play Dean Cuninggim off against his predecessor Dean Hawk or the School of Theology against Methodists in the region; he appreciated them all. They were all his colleagues, and he intended to work with them.

After Hawk's retirement he and Cuninggim had had little communication. The day Quillian was designated as the new dean, however, Hawk telephoned him to offer his full support. Quillian later reported, "We got together after that, and he filled me in on the history of the School and gave me good advice when I asked for it." In January 1963, with President Tate's approval, Quillian asked Hawk to serve as consultant to the dean, specifically, about the development program, endowed funds, prospective patrons with whom Hawk had close connections, and making accessible Hawk's papers relevant to the history of Perkins. They would meet twice a week, and Hawk would receive a stipend and have an office in Kirby Hall. Hawk said it would be his pleasure to do this. The consulting began that February and continued until Hawk's death the following October.[11]

One critic of Perkins was Lynn Landrum, the *Dallas Morning News* columnist who had insinuated that liberal church leaders were communists. That September Joe Quillian arranged to have lunch with Landrum and afterward wrote Cuninggim that they "had a good solid, headbutting time of it." Landrum, he said, tried "to indicate a considerable difference between me and my predecessor, but found quite immediately that he had no future in that direction. I was neither currying his favor nor asking any immunity in my interview with him, and was perfectly willing to be wide open and on the record. I do not know what will come of it in the long run, but he at least knows with some clarity the signals by which I am playing."[12] James Brooks, the geology professor who later became university provost, noted that "there was never a deleterious column afterward."[13]

From his early years as dean, Quillian frequently spent time with church administrators, ministers, and laity in his effort to improve relationships. One Sunday in

November 1961, for example, he preached in Paris, Texas, and that afternoon met with about sixty people "to discuss theological education and Perkins School of Theology. We had a very pleasant time together, covering all sorts of things, including communism and *Christ without Myth*" (Ogden's book, which some people in the churches found disturbing).[14] Quillian was adept at discussing controversial subjects so as to have "a very pleasant time together."

In February 1962 he spent four hours with the Oklahoma Annual Conference bishop, W. Angie Smith, and his district superintendents. Quillian gave a fifteen- to twenty-minute statement about the seminary's purpose and what it was doing and then responded to questions. It was, he said, "a real good meeting from stem to stern." He wrote Tate that Bishop Smith and his cabinet members were greatly supportive and that there was good progress in overcoming any difficulties in the relationship. He expected to have similar sessions in all the annual conferences when he could arrange them.[15]

In 1964 Quillian learned that Joe Bridwell occasionally expressed criticisms of the school. Lois Perkins, herself steadfastly supportive, apparently was the source of that information; she said she wished Bridwell would stop doing this. One day that April, Quillian went to Wichita Falls and talked with Bridwell about his criticisms. Quillian reported to Tate that Bridwell seemed happy and reassured and was "very much with us."[16]

For Quillian, having good relations with the church was as important as improving the internal quality of Perkins. In a statement a few years later, he expressed his understanding of the relation of his inside and outside work: "Perkins School of Theology is committed to being a first-rate seminary that is in close and effective relationship with the Church. Such a seminary is more rare than should be the case. Two extremes most often prevail: a good theological school academically but at a distance from or in antagonism with the Church, or: a denominational trade-school close to the Church but timid and ineffectual academically."[17]

INITIATING THE GRADUATE PROGRAM IN RELIGION

Even though the Perkins faculty had grown from sixteen in 1951 to thirty-three in the fall of 1960, Quillian intended to enlarge it further. Late in 1960 he listed for Tate the appointments he needed to make: two in preaching and worship (one as his own replacement, the other to replace W. B. J. Martin, visiting professor of homiletics since 1959); a new appointment in Old Testament, another in New Testament (for a total of four teaching each testament), and one in American church history.[18] Before long he was expressing more expansive ideas. In the spring of 1964, having by then made appointments in worship, American church history, and pastoral care, Quillian wrote Tate about the idea of adding another eight to ten faculty members as finances allowed. By then, he ventured, SMU might well have the largest and strongest group of theological scholars and teachers in the world.[19]

Enlarging the faculty was not an end in itself; a major purpose was to staff a graduate program granting the Ph.D. degree in religion. In the fifties Merrimon Cuninggim had told the young faculty members he was recruiting, as one way of attracting them, that the plan was to develop a doctoral program in religion. In 1958 Dean Claude Albritton of the SMU Graduate School had appointed a planning committee chaired by Albert Outler that, after thorough research and reflection, recommended that SMU establish a doctoral program in religion. In November 1959 the trustees approved the proposal with the understanding that the program would be part of the graduate school but would use Perkins resources. Wesley Davis and Fred Gealy, who had just retired, would work on planning for the program.[20] This is where matters stood with the Graduate Program in Religion when Joe Quillian became dean. The problem now was to find the money to support it.

What was at stake, as Quillian saw it, was not only staffing the program but also retaining Perkins's already well-known faculty. In the sixties other schools continually tried to hire one or another faculty member away from Perkins. A principal consideration in holding "some of our first-rate associates . . . and assistant professors," he explained, "is the matter of the Graduate Program in Religion."[21] The period from 1961 to 1964, when the program was not yet in operation, was especially difficult. In the spring of 1962 Quillian reported that Schubert Ogden had had "six bona fide offers in the run of this year," though Quillian thought only one, from the University of Chicago, was strongly appealing. Ogden remained at Perkins in the face of repeated approaches until 1969, when he accepted an offer from Chicago. In the fall of 1962 Vanderbilt made a vigorous effort to recruit Van Harvey, but he declined. During the same year Herndon Wagers's seminary alma mater, the College of the Bible in

Lexington, Kentucky, invited him to become its dean. At first he intended to accept, then decided to remain at Perkins. In 1963 Union Theological Seminary approached John Deschner about succeeding Henry Pitney Van Dusen as president of Union and Richey Hogg about becoming director of its Missionary Research Library. Both declined.[22] In the spring of 1963 Quillian wrote Tate, "We have remained intact," but continuing to do so "will depend considerably on our being able to move into the Graduate Program in Religion within the next year or two, and our being able to make reasonable advances in salaries."[23] A year later Quillian exulted, "We are not losing a single faculty member this year."[24]

It was under these circumstances that Quillian tried to raise money for the GPR. In the summer of 1963 Quillian entered into discussions with C. L. Lloyd, a Dallas oilman, whose son, Charles Lloyd Jr., had entered Perkins's new independent study program for a bachelor of divinity degree in the fall of 1960. When the elder Lloyd became interested in the Graduate Program in Religion, Quillian initially mentioned to him the idea of providing "seed money" to enable it to get started.[25] Lloyd agreed and committed $25,000 a year for three years. More important, he added at the end of one letter that "at some later date it might develop that I would be interested in sponsoring a program such as you mentioned in your letter."[26] As Quillian commented to Willis Tate, what was most important was not the exact amount of the seed money but that additional comment. "What this really could mean eventually," Quillian observed, "is an endowment of $5,000,000.00."[27] At the same time Quillian informed Lloyd that it was necessary to delay the opening of the Graduate Program in Religion from the fall of 1964 to the fall of 1965, because in the fall of 1964 Albert Outler would be in Rome as an observer at the Vatican Council.[28]

Quillian remained in communication with Lloyd and on July 3, 1965, wrote him with several aims in mind. First, he brought him up to date on progress toward the graduate program, for which the faculty was setting up the course of study and deciding how many and which students to admit. Then Quillian acknowledged receipt of $25,000 from Lloyd and informed him that he had also secured a grant for $25,000 from The Methodist Church's General Board of Education, in addition to which he might "get as much as $20,000 more," so as to be in good financial condition for the 1965–66 year. Then he moved to his principal subject. After the program's third year its costs would rise sharply, and he would need to discuss the idea of Lloyd's arranging to endow the program. What Quillian had in mind, he said, was to ask Lloyd to set aside $5 million in his will for that purpose and to transfer any part of that amount that he could now. "As you know, I do not like to try to come up on a person's 'blind side,' so am laying clearly before you what I will be asking you to consider when we can get together." That way, he said, Lloyd would have time to think about it and perhaps discuss it with his son Charles.[29]

The Graduate Program in Religion admitted its first students and opened in the fall of 1965 with Quillian as chair and Van Harvey as director. Although Lloyd remained positive about the program, he kept his own counsel, and when he died in April 1968, Quillian still did not know whether he had provided for it in his will.[30] As it turned out, he had—sufficiently to allow the program to operate for years to come.

PERKINS AND THE SMU MASTER PLAN

Planning for the Graduate Program in Religion was part of a larger SMU program of self-examination and change. In the fall of 1961 Tate reported to the trustees that the time had come for SMU to rethink its purposes and role as a university. It was undergoing a transition from an undergraduate college with several professional schools to a university emphasizing research as well as teaching and aiming to provide academic as well as professional leadership for the region.[31] This report marked the beginning of the process that led to the creation of the SMU Master Plan.

In 1962 the SMU administration established an office with three full-time staff members to conduct its self-study: Jesse Hobson, an educational specialist; Johnnie Marie Grimes, a long-time assistant to Tate; and Marshall Terry, a member of the English Department. In addition, it appointed three outside academic consultants, a faculty planning committee of six, a ten-member student committee, and a large committee of laity from around the country.

Albert Outler of Perkins chaired the faculty committee and exercised major influence on the plan's development.[32] As Terry remembered it, Outler was the one who conceived of the central idea in the master plan—the University College.[33] It would be the vehicle for providing all SMU undergraduates with basic education—"the usually acknowledged marks of academic competence and of self-motivated interest in the life of inquiry." These marks would include

> articulate speech (oral and written) in one's mother tongue; the ability to read and interpret both informative and imaginative literature; familiarity with both scientific methodology (in at least one specific science) and the import of science for modern society; an appreciation of the arts and letters of our western modern society; an understanding of *another* language than English (e.g., Italian or higher mathematics); the beginnings of an exploration into the great humane questions of truth, value and faith as these have been proved and illuminated in the Judeo-Christian tradition and the philosophical dialogue with that tradition in the history of the European and American civilizations.[34]

All undergraduates would take courses simultaneously in the University College and in one of the other undergraduate schools: the reorganized College of Humanities and Sciences, the School of Business, School of Engineering, or the newly created School of the Arts, the degree-granting undergraduate schools of the university. The University College would draw its faculty from all the schools of the university— undergraduate and graduate—to teach new courses, such as "The Nature of Man" and "Discourse and Literature." The University College thus was a way of unifying SMU's undergraduate studies—all the schools that offered undergraduate degrees. It was at the same time a way of involving the faculty, undergraduate and graduate-professional, in basic university education. Its aim was twofold: to produce well-educated people and a more unified university.

In November 1962 Outler reported to the trustees on behalf of the Faculty Planning Committee. The following May the trustees voted unanimously to adopt the master plan.[35] Though the structure changed over time, the master plan's idea of basic education continued to influence undergraduate education at SMU for decades to come.

Once the master plan was adopted, faculty from the several schools did the work of developing and teaching the new University College courses. Among Perkins faculty, Douglas Jackson came to be deeply involved in this work, chairing the team-taught interdisciplinary course "The Nature of Man" for several years. After 1970

Edwin Sylvest of Perkins taught the same course for a number of years. (In 1976 "The Nature of Man" was revised and renamed "Self and Society.") In the 1964 Perkins Honors Day address John Deschner conveyed the spirit of the master plan: "Our school has wisely and rightly been made an integral part of a growing, increasingly serious university, a university which is dedicating itself more resolutely every month to being the cultural memory, the intellectual conscience, and the embodiment of man's inquiry after true and useful knowledge in the modern Southwest."[36]

The master plan was one way in which Perkins faculty members played a major part in the life of the wider university in the sixties. To mention only a few of the other important roles of Perkins faculty members, Albert Outler chaired the SMU Faculty Senate in 1961–62 and Douglas Jackson in 1965–66, and Neill McFarland was university vice president and provost from 1966 to 1972.

THE FACULTY IN THE SIXTIES

When Joe Quillian assumed the deanship, he faced a twofold challenge regarding the faculty. Most important was to maintain the morale of the fifties and to retain the faculty. If he could do that, then he could pursue the second task—to expand its size in the ways he thought were needed.

Morale remained high. The faculty soon realized that Perkins under its new dean would continue to strive toward the excellence it had envisioned under Merrimon Cuninggim. Soon after the Faculty Conference in September 1960, Quillian wrote his predecessor, "We really had a royally good conference. I believe that each member of the faculty felt with considerable seriousness his own responsibility as we consulted together under a new administration."[37] Plans to initiate a stated rank and tenure policy, the prospect of a graduate program, improvements in the salary scale, and the continuation of the open and vigorous discussions of previous years—these were among the ingredients that contributed to a conviction among faculty members that Perkins was an excellent place to work over the long term. That conviction helped retain faculty members who had received attractive offers, and in turn their staying further enhanced morale.

In a memo written in 1963 Quillian tried to identify the elements in the school's morale. One contributing condition he listed was the absence of any "senatorial courtesy" in faculty discussions but instead the expectation that each professor could give an account to colleagues for judgments made in his own field and for proposals for the conduct of his courses. Another was the lack of any quotas for professorial ranks. Theoretically, he thought, the faculty could be made up entirely of full professors. That removed the potential problems of jealousy and maneuvering about promotions.[38]

From 1961 to the fall of 1969, eighteen new people, not including visiting professors and adjuncts, joined the Perkins faculty (see appendix A), and thirteen departed. The new arrivals provided greater depth in some fields, especially pastoral care, with the additions of Thompson Shannon (later replaced by Harville Hendrix) and David Switzer. In church history Franklin Littell left after only two years at Perkins, to be replaced by Klaus Penzel, and five years later William Babcock arrived as a specialist in early church history. Dick Murray's arrival strengthened the work in Christian education, and Frederick Streng's did likewise in the history of religions. In worship and preaching James White filled the vacancy created by Joe Quillian's moving to the deanship, and soon thereafter Ronald Sleeth added strength in homiletics. Joe R. Jones's appointment in 1965 constituted an addition in the field of theology, but when Van Harvey left in 1968 and then Schubert Ogden in 1969, another appointment—of Leroy T. Howe in 1969—was necessary simply to maintain the same number in that field as earlier. The 1966 appointment of David Robertson, a 1962 Perkins B.D. graduate, created a fourth position in Old Testament, but after Robertson decided to change his academic field and left Perkins in 1969, that fourth position was not filled. In 1969 William M. Longsworth, another Perkins B.D. graduate (1965), took a nontenure-track position in Christian ethics, adding further depth there. These additions and attempted additions reflected Joe Quillian's intention to build a larger faculty that could better serve the Graduate Program in Religion and other new endeavors. There had been thirty-three faculty in the fall of 1960; by the fall of 1969 it had experienced a net increase of five, for a total of thirty-eight, including faculty with part- or full-time administrative responsibilities.

One arrival in 1960, as a member of the School of Music faculty, was the organist Robert T. Anderson, who for thirty-six years played for services in Perkins Chapel, taught organ students, and attracted many of those students to the Master of Sacred Music Program. As an undergraduate he had been a student of Lloyd Pfautsch's at Illinois Wesleyan University, and Pfautsch's word about the new M.S.M. program is what initially attracted Anderson to SMU. He became internationally known as a concert and recording artist, teacher of organ workshops and master classes, and consultant for organ design and installation in the United States.

In 1964 Quillian appointed Bishop William C. Martin, who had just retired from the active episcopacy, to a new position initially titled "consultant in conference relations and lecturer in church administration." When Bishop Will Martin retired from Perkins in 1968, Quillian appointed Bishop Paul E. Martin to that position. In 1972 the title became "bishop in residence," and since then a succession of retired bishops has occupied the position for four or eight or twelve years each.

Other new arrivals in the sixties filled vacancies created by departures. In 1964 Carlton R. Young took the position in church music when Lloyd Pfautsch became full time in SMU's School of Music. Alsie Carleton arrived in 1964 to take the position in field education and church administration that Floyd Curl had vacated in 1962. Upon Carleton's election to the episcopacy in 1968, Quillian appointed Claus Rohlfs, who spearheaded the development of the intern program. In addition to their administrative responsibilities for field education, Curl, Carleton, and Rohlfs also directed the summer program of courses for pastors without seminary degrees. In Curl's time at Perkins this was called the School for Approved Supply Pastors; under Carleton, Rohlfs, and their successors, it was named the Courses of Study School.

Of the thirteen faculty members who departed from Perkins in the sixties, five went to other academic positions (Harvey, Littell, Ogden, Pfautsch, and Shannon). Two others (Carleton and Roger Ortmayer) took church administrative positions, two went to appointments in the Southwest Texas Conference (Floyd Curl and Sterling Wheeler), one retired (Bishop William C. Martin), one (Charles "Joe" Johnson) left academic life without taking a church appointment, one changed fields (David Robertson), and one died (Tom Marsh, in 1962). The appointment in Christianity and the arts was not continued after Ortmayer left, and after Marsh died, Barney McGrath, who by then was teaching primarily in the university's Speech Department, took up his Perkins work in the field of speech on a part-time basis. Ogden's position was filled only when he returned three years later.

A major contribution to the faculty's morale and confidence about the school's future was the institution in 1961 of a stated rank and tenure policy. Strange as it may seem, no explicit faculty-approved rank and tenure policy had previously existed, either at Perkins or the rest of the university. In December 1960 Quillian announced to the faculty the appointment of an ad hoc committee to recommend to the Perkins faculty policies on rank and tenure. The committee was composed of six full professors and two assistant professors, representing all four divisions, and was chaired by Franklin Littell, who had just joined the faculty as professor of church history.[39]

With dispatch the committee reported to the faculty the following February, proposing a permanent committee on rank and tenure "to serve in an advisory capacity to the Dean with regard to rank and tenure." It was to consist of six members, all with the rank of professor, two elected each year by the teaching faculty for three-year terms, plus the dean ex officio. The committee was to function "by the sense of the meeting," not by unanimity and not by ballot on individuals.

The report identified five standards for "normal progression" in rank and tenure, though it made no attempt to rank these standards in importance: teaching ability; scholarly research and writing; contributions to the academic world, in general and at SMU; contributions to the church; and being "an edifying member of the community." The report described normal procedures for review, with instructors subject to annual review; assistant professors initially appointed for three years, renewable for three years, with right to annual review; and associate professors having tenure "unless specifically excepted," with right of annual review after five years. Though there were, as the committee observed, further matters to be decided, it recommended this plan as a beginning.[40] After much discussion and some changes in wording, the faculty adopted the report. It elected six professors to an interim rank and tenure committee to serve until the following fall.[41] This action initiated a policy in which the faculty had a voice in rank and tenure decisions; amendments were made over the years in light of actual practice.

In the 1960s the Perkins faculty continued to publish at the increased rate seen in the Cuninggim years (see appendix C). In Bible studies William R. Farmer's work revolved around the question of which of the synoptic gospels was the earliest; his answer was Matthew. Victor Furnish continued his focus on Paul's theology and ethics, foreshadowing his later attention to Paul's ethics. James Ward's primary research interest was the eighth-century prophets' discourse about God and the world.

Fred Carney continued to work on the early seventeenth-century Dutch political theorist Johannes Althusius, the subject of Carney's dissertation at the University of

Chicago. In the early sixties Howard Grimes concentrated on movements among the laity that he saw as signs of the renewal of the church. In 1963–64 Neill McFarland spent a second year of field research in Japan (he had done research there in 1956–57), studying the new religious movements of Japan, which led to his later book on that subject. James F. White, who joined the faculty in 1961, published extensively on the relation of church architecture to worship, as well as on the emerging renewal of Christian worship.

Albert Outler's scholarship in the 1960s had two foci: ecumenical activities and Wesley studies. He first become involved in ecumenical matters at the Third World Conference on Faith and Order at Lund, Sweden, in 1952; later chaired the World Council of Churches' Theology Study Commission on Tradition and Traditions; and remained active in the commission through its 1963 meeting in Montreal.[42] A new direction for Outler's ecumenical activities suddenly arose in 1962. That summer the World Methodist Council invited him to be one of its three official observers at the Roman Catholic Church's Second Vatican Council, which was to convene in September. He attended all four sessions of the council—each fall from 1962 to 1965. Far more than an observer, he was active behind the scenes in discussions with the Catholic bishops and their *periti* (experts in theology), and more publicly in addresses to gatherings of Catholics and of non-Roman observers. As he said, "Some of us got pretty deeply involved in the drafting processes and the review processes of the successive stages of the documents of the council."[43] From 1962 to 1966 he wrote a number of articles and papers about the council, fifteen of which were subsequently published in 1967 under the title *Methodist Observer at Vatican II*.[44] During those years he moved from skepticism and "no little alarm" in 1962 about the prospects of the council to amazement at what it had accomplished and cautious optimism about the Roman church's future relations with the "separated brethren" in other churches. Its impact, he predicted, would depend largely on what Catholic leaders, and especially the pope, did to follow it up.[45]

Along with his ecumenical activity, Outler worked at recovering his own denomination's tradition. In 1964 his edited volume, *John Wesley*, became the first volume in the series A Library of Protestant Thought.[46] Outler selected from writings that showed various dimensions of Wesley's theological work: as a leader of a religious revival, as a theological teacher in the Anglican church, and as a participant in the doctrinal controversies of his time. He introduced the volume with an interpretation of Wesley's theology as interwoven with his life and work.

In this connection, under the leadership of Robert E. Cushman, dean of Duke Divinity School, a board of directors was formed in 1960 to initiate plans for the Wesley Works Editorial Project. Outler and Dean Merrimon Cuninggim had been involved in early discussions about this project. From 1961 to 1970 Joe Quillian, as chair of the Wesley Works Editorial Committee and a member of its board of directors, participated in laying the foundations for this multivolume project.

A fundamental methodological problem to which Schubert Ogden gave attention in the sixties, as well as earlier, was how to be faithful to the New Testament proclamation and the theological tradition while also taking seriously the criticism of that tradition arising from the modern picture of human existence. This was the problem he explored in *Christ without Myth* (1961), an examination of Bultmann's project of demythologizing the New Testament and existentialist interpretation of it, and again in *The Reality of God and Other Essays* (1966).[47] In the latter he argued that secularity (different from secularism) presupposes God as the ground of human significance, and he developed his "dipolar" conception of God as "at once supremely relative and supremely absolute."[48]

The year 1966 also saw the publication of Van A. Harvey's *The Historian and the Believer: The Morality of Historical Knowledge and Christian Belief.*[49] The problem of the book arose from the application of the methods of critical historical study to the New Testament and, in particular, to the life of Jesus. While historical biblical criticism leads to judgments with more or less probability, faith, Harvey argued, must have a certitude that is not subject to erosion by the next archeological discovery. Harvey presented this as a moral problem—"the historian's morality of knowledge, or ethic of assent." His response to the problem gave special attention to what he called a "perspectival image of Jesus."[50]

During their ten years together at Perkins, Harvey and Ogden were in continual and vigorous dialog, and in their books each took special note of this. Harvey, Ogden said, "has so carefully reacted to all of the essays that he deserves much of the credit for whatever of worth they may contain," and Harvey declared that Ogden "was always selflessly available for conversation and help, without which this book scarcely would have taken its present shape."[51] With the intellectual ferment this dialog produced, one can readily imagine the dismay on the part of the dean, faculty, and students at Harvey's and Ogden's leaving Perkins, in 1968 and 1969, respectively.

During this decade The Methodist Church brought out its first revision of *The Methodist Hymnal* since the 1930s.[52] The General Conference of 1960 authorized the appointment of a committee to prepare the new hymnal. Under the editorship of Carlton Young, the committee presented its report to the General Conference of 1964, and the new hymnal appeared in 1966. Joe Quillian was a member of the Hymnal Committee, and Fred Gealy was a consultant.

THE OFFICE OF ASSOCIATE DEAN

In the early years of his deanship, Joe Quillian judged he would need to give a large portion of his time to development. If so, he would need to free himself from many of the details of being an inside dean. His solution was to appoint an associate dean to oversee many of the academic aspects of Perkins's life. Even so, Quillian continued to be closely involved, especially in chairing faculty meetings, guiding the process of recruiting new faculty, and participating in the work of some of the faculty committees.

At the faculty meeting of January 10, 1964, Quillian announced that Herndon Wagers had agreed to become associate dean, beginning two weeks later with the start of the spring semester.[53] Wagers had come to the Perkins faculty in 1954 as professor of philosophy of religion. He had gained the esteem of his colleagues as a person of wisdom and discretion, which was reflected in Tate's choosing Wagers in the winter of 1960 to be the faculty's representative in consultations with the president about the choice of a new dean. As associate dean, Wagers continued as a classroom teacher, though on a much reduced scale—one seminar in the fall semester instead of the normal load of two courses each semester. That April, Quillian wrote to Willis Tate, "Herndon has turned out to be a tremendous help serving part-time as Associate Dean with regard to academic matters. He has the full confidence of Faculty and students, and could not be working more perceptively and loyally with me."[54]

Wagers was associate dean for two and a half years. As Van Harvey looked toward a leave in 1966–67, he indicated that upon his return he did not want to continue in his position as chair of the Graduate Program in Religion. Wagers then expressed a preference to follow Harvey as chair rather than continue as associate dean, and Quillian agreed to that change.[55]

Quillian appointed Neill McFarland to succeed Wagers as associate dean. Like Wagers, McFarland had joined the faculty in 1954; by 1966 he was professor of the history of religions. McFarland had, like Wagers, shown administrative ability in handling various faculty committee responsibilities. He assumed the position of associate dean in July 1966 and immediately set about its work in an effective way. In September, Tate began looking for someone to appoint quickly as acting provost of the university. When Quillian mentioned to Tate that he needed to find someone like McFarland, who was doing such an excellent job as associate dean, Tate took the comment more seriously than Quillian had expected. He asked McFarland to serve as acting provost for the remainder of the 1966–67 academic year, McFarland accepted, and suddenly Quillian was, as he said, "bereft of a superb associate dean."[56] McFarland met with similar appreciation from Tate, who the following January reported to the trustees, "The things that have happened to this job since he took over are absolutely miraculous. He has moved some tremendous problems off this desk and attacked the fundamentals. . . . Every dean, without exception, has expressed his approval and thinks he is great."[57] The board forthwith elected McFarland to continue as provost, a position he held until the end of 1972.

After giving some thought to choosing the next associate dean from within the faculty, this time Quillian brought in someone from outside. In April 1967 he placed before the faculty the name of David Switzer as academic associate dean and, for a three-year term, assistant professor of pastoral theology. Following the usual procedure, the faculty discussed the proposal and recommended that the dean nominate Switzer for the appointment.[58] Because Thompson Shannon had left his pastoral care position in 1967, Switzer's arrival served a dual purpose. He continued as associate dean for two years. Even though the occupants of the office changed frequently in its early years, Quillian had established the academic associate deanship as a fixture in the Perkins administrative structure.

CHANGES IN THE BACHELOR OF DIVINITY
CURRICULUM IN THE SIXTIES

For decades the "new curriculum" inaugurated in 1953 remained the basic template for the B.D. degree, though with many modifications. As initially conceived and in most subsequent revisions, it required the equivalent of three full-time academic years of study, of which approximately two-thirds was in required "core" studies and one-third in electives, plus a field education requirement. The chief difficulty the faculty faced with this curriculum, and the reason for many of the changes, was that faculty members kept thinking of other subjects they believed should be included in the core or of courses they thought should have more required hours. The result was a continual urge to enlarge the core, encroaching on the time left for elective and advanced work. Faculty members were similarly committed to students' having significant elective work, with opportunities to delve more deeply into areas of their special interest. To a large extent the changes in the B.D. curriculum from 1960 to 1965 were efforts to resolve this tension between core and electives.

The revision that took effect in 1960 made room for students to take more courses in a single semester and in the total degree program. For several years before 1960, ninety-six semester hours and field education had been required for the B.D. degree, with sixty-seven hours of core and twenty-nine of electives. Most courses, core and elective, carried four semester hours of credit, though a few had one or two hours of credit each. The normal courseload per semester was sixteen hours. The 1960 curriculum changed this so that most courses carried *three* hours of credit, with ninety hours required for graduation plus field education, and a normal full load of five courses—fifteen or sixteen hours. Now core courses met three hours a week instead of four. The previous configuration had left room for twenty-four, four-semester-hour courses, but the revision allowed for thirty, three-semester-hour courses. The faculty seized the opportunity to add several three-hour required courses: "Christianity and the Arts," "Christian Ethics," and (for those not taking a biblical language), exegesis of a book in the English Bible. The resulting core totaled sixty-three semester hours. That left room for nine electives, whereas previously there had been room for only seven.[59]

Whatever its merits, this arrangement put the faculty as well as the students in a bind. A faculty member had to teach in three hours what had been taught in four, and most saw that as short-changing important aspects of their courses. Most faculty members, whatever they did with the class hours, were inclined to require about the same volume of papers as before and to expect a similar level of knowledge on examinations. That put the students under greater pressure, for now if they were taking a full load, they had five courses instead of four; this resulted in less mastery of each subject. If they reduced their load, they either had to go to summer school or extend their time in seminary, perhaps by as much as a year.

In 1960 the faculty introduced what it initially called the Honors B.D. program and in 1962 renamed the Independent Study Program. Its aims were to encourage students to pursue the various fields of theological study in greater depth and to develop greater independence and responsibility for their learning. To achieve this the program removed nearly all the specific core course requirements and replaced them with a group of comprehensive examinations to be taken during the first two years. Students were required to take only thirty hours of coursework, all in electives except for a course in worship and preaching. They also had to meet the field education requirement. The minimum grade-point average for admission to the program was 3.5 on a 4-point scale.[60]

In the first year one student was admitted to the Honors B.D. program—Charles L. Lloyd Jr. Three more entered it in 1961, six in 1962, and small numbers in subsequent years. A special faculty committee was appointed to oversee the program and to prepare and grade the examinations. The program continued until 1980, when it was dropped, since few students had expressed interest in it since 1970.[61]

The curriculum instituted in 1963 was a radically different effort to solve the tension between required courses and electives. Students entering that fall and afterward were no longer required to take the many core courses. Instead, in the spring semester of their senior year they were to take five 4-hour comprehensive examinations: one each in Bible, history of Christianity, theology and ethics, Christianity and culture, and the ministry. To prepare for the examinations they could fulfill the required eighty-eight hours of coursework in whatever way they chose, with the restriction that Methodist students had to take six hours of Methodist studies and a course in pastoral responsibility. The core principle was retained; it was simply transferred from courses to examinations. The aims of this curriculum were to increase students' responsibility for their own learning (like the Independent Study Program) and facilitate greater integration of the various theological fields.[62] In the spring of 1964 Quillian commented, in a letter to Tate, "I believe that we now have a curriculum with which we can live for at least a decade."[63] Less than a year and a half later the faculty voted to terminate this curriculum.

The system of comprehensive examinations required that the faculty provide entering students with materials to help them understand what would be expected: syllabi and bibliographies in the various fields, and a sample set of published examinations. That required long hours of work by the faculty to prepare the materials. Faculty members had anticipated that the system of examinations would free the students to take more electives. In that they were greatly disappointed. Most students were so worried about the exams that they took nearly all the courses that had previously been required.

A small number of students who had entered before the requirement of the comprehensives nevertheless elected to take them in the spring of 1965. James Ward was appointed examination director for that occasion. Under his supervision the faculty prepared the examinations, the students took them the week of May 10–14, and the faculty graded them that same week. Between the students' fear about taking them and the faculty's distaste for preparing and reading them, almost nobody looked on this curriculum with favor.

The fallout came at the faculty fall conference in October 1965. When the curriculum came up for discussion, there was, as understated in the minutes, "considerable discussion." After a while Van Harvey moved that the comprehensives no longer be required, and the faculty approved the motion by something close to unanimity.[64] This was the shortest—and most impulsive—curriculum review in Perkins's history.

The discussion at the fall conference indicated that any comprehensive feature in the curriculum should aim not at examination but at integration of the various fields. Someone ventured that a senior paper written in conjunction with a senior colloquy might help students to integrate their seminary studies.[65] Pursuing this idea later that fall, the Course of Study Committee proposed a senior colloquy in the fall of 1966 on the subject of the Second Vatican Council. The faculty approved this, upcoming senior students gladly opted for the colloquy requirement rather than comprehensives, and Richey Hogg was appointed chair of a committee to plan the colloquy, with Albert Outler, recently returned from the concluding session of the Vatican Council, as a member of the committee.[66]

The curriculum for which the senior colloquy was to be the integrating element included these requirements: Of a required ninety-six semester hours, each student had to complete at least sixteen hours in each of the four divisions—the Church and Its Ministry, Christianity and Culture, the Christian Heritage, and the Bible. In addition, students were to pass an oral preaching examination, fulfill their field education requirement, participate in the senior colloquy, and, if they were candidates for the Methodist ministry, complete two semester hours of study each in Methodist history, doctrine, and polity.[67]

Here, then, was a move from a curriculum full of specific requirements, by means of core courses or examinations, to one that gave students considerable freedom. In Division II, Christianity and Culture, for example, instead of being accountable for basic study in six different fields, one could now pick any four courses in the division (most courses were again offered for four semester hours), as long as one met the prerequisites for taking advanced courses. John Holbert, who graduated under the colloquy curriculum, declared that this was the best curriculum of all for him, because he had the freedom to take whatever he wanted. Some faculty were less enthusiastic, in that a student preparing for pastoral ministry might graduate without a course deemed important, perhaps in one of the testaments or ethics or pastoral care. The faculty advisory system tried to encourage students to make reflective choices, but the decisions were theirs. Furthermore, the faculty dropped the required oral preaching examination in 1967, before it was ever given.[68] A student preparing to enter the pastoral ministry might then graduate without ever having taken a course or any other assistance in preaching. Few did, but I remember one advisee who adamantly refused to take a preaching course, even though he had never preached. Every curriculum has its strengths and weaknesses.

The senior colloquy on Vatican II proved to be valuable for the whole community. Lectures by Outler, several other Perkins faculty, and distinguished visitors (Father Walter Burghardt, Professor Friedrich Gogarten, Monsignor George G. Higgins, and others) introduced the large class to the council, its background, and several of its documents. Weekly preceptorial sessions helped students to digest the readings.

Faculty from across the curriculum served as advisers to students in the preparation of the project paper, on one of the major documents of the council and its pastoral application in a local church.[69]

The colloquy curriculum continued for two more years. In the fall of 1967 the topic was the church and social revolution, and I was the colloquy chair. The topic for fall 1968 was the Bible and the modern church, with Victor Furnish as the chair. By the spring of 1968, however, plans were underway for a major self-study of all aspects of Perkins life. As a result, the 1968 colloquy was reduced in scope and the 1969 colloquy, projected to be on the future shape of the ministry, was suspended.[70]

THE SIZE AND COMPOSITION OF THE PERKINS STUDENT BODY

The period from 1960 to 1969 was a time of smaller enrollment in Perkins's bachelor of divinity program (see appendix B, table 3). The numbers of B.D. students declined each year from 1960 through 1966, then recovered the next three years, only to decline again in 1970. However, with the new Graduate Program in Religion and because of a large increase in the number of nondegree students in 1968 and 1969, the total number in all programs was virtually the same in 1969 as in 1960.

For Quillian the decline in B.D. students was deeply disturbing. "It is imperative," he said, "that we do a very thorough job of recruiting all over the country, supported by an adequate scholarship program."[71] He viewed recruitment for ministry as a problem for many seminaries, not only for Perkins. In a 1962 memo he detailed what he saw as fourteen causes of the difficulty; several were aspects of what we can characterize as a cultural shift: the declining opinion of the church and its ministry in the eyes of the public, increasing competition for the services of able young people, reduced home influence and diminished spiritual depth in the home, and the absence of a clear image of the ministry, in contrast to earlier periods.[72] In the same period Quillian reported that the quality of the students was improving: more than 50 percent of those admitted for the fall of 1964 had college grade-point averages of 3.0 or better.[73]

Some other Methodist seminaries also experienced enrollment declines in the sixties, especially Garrett Biblical Institute in Illinois and the Theological School of Drew University in New Jersey, both of which experienced declines of more than 30 percent between 1960 and 1970. In the same years, however, some other Methodist seminaries realized increases, including Candler, Claremont in California, Duke, Iliff, Interdenominational Theological Center in Atlanta, and Wesley in Washington, D.C.[74] These variations suggest that widespread sociocultural changes are not a sufficient explanation. In addition, individual seminaries experience distinctive conditions that can lead to enrollment declines or increases, such as an internal crisis, the introduction of a new and attractive degree program, or a merger with another seminary. In the cases of Perkins and Garrett, one such condition was the opening in 1962 of a new Methodist seminary in the region—St. Paul School of Theology in Kansas City, Missouri; probably other circumstances were also at work.

Along with the decline in numbers, the internal makeup of the student body was beginning to change. Whereas previously most of the women students at Perkins had been in the master of religious education program, in the latter part of the sixties a few more women were seeking bachelor of divinity degrees. Between 1954 and 1965, only two women had graduated with the B.D. degree, but in 1966 two women received their B.D.; in 1967, four; in 1968, one; and in 1969, four.[75] This was the period in which the shift in gender enrollment began that in later years led to a markedly different distribution.

During the sixties African Americans and Hispanics sustained rather than increased their numbers. The years following the graduation from Perkins of the first five blacks in 1955 saw an average of only one black B.D. graduate each year through 1969—small numbers but a constant presence. Hispanics had been among the seminary's students since the late 1920s, though few enrolled until after World War II. The years from 1945 to 1969 saw a modest increase to an average of one Hispanic B.D. graduate per year through 1969.

Enrollment of international students was a different matter. After World War II, during which Perkins had virtually no international students, the school graduated an average of one a year through 1957, most from the Far East (China, Japan, the Philippines, South Korea), and a few from Latin America (especially Brazil and Cuba). Their numbers sharply increased after 1956, largely because of the introduction that year of the master of sacred theology (S.T.M.) degree. From 1958 through 1969 forty-four international students received Perkins degrees, twenty-three of them earning the S.T.M., twelve the B.D., eight the master of religious education, and one the master of sacred music. While most still came from the Far East, several were from India and a few from Australia, New Zealand, Europe, and Canada. Of these forty-four, only four were women.

PERKINS ACTIVISM IN THE SIXTIES

The sixties were a time of student unrest nationally, and this affected SMU and Perkins as well as universities throughout the country. Following the Supreme Court's 1954 ruling that segregated schools were unconstitutional, and Martin Luther King Jr.'s successful campaign in Montgomery, Alabama, in 1955–56 to desegregate the buses, students in the early sixties became active across the South for civil rights. The first lunch-counter sit-in to receive widespread attention occurred on February 1, 1960, at a Woolworth's department store in Greensboro, North Carolina, and the idea was soon copied. In Nashville a Vanderbilt School of Religion student, Jim Lawson, was arrested in February of that year and subsequently expelled from Vanderbilt because he would not promise not to participate in further sit-ins.

That spring the Perkins Student Council unanimously adopted a carefully con-structed statement occasioned by the sit-ins. It declared that while civil law has a claim upon the Christian that is derived from God's law, civil law may be put to a bad use. In such a case, a Christian's only recourse may be to appeal to God's law as a judg-ment on the unjust situation. When they disobey unjust racial laws, Christians must bear witness to the authority of civil laws, accept the consequences of disobedience, and hope that nonviolent resistance may be an expression of God's law.[76]

Perkins students did not confine their response to statements. In October 1960 Bob Webber, president of the Perkins Student Council, asked Quillian if Perkins stu-dents could take part in a small demonstration. The dean told Webber not to tell him what he had in mind, because he did not want "to sanction a demonstration ahead of time, which, among other things, would remove the authenticity from the demon-stration to begin with," or "to get in the position of blocking a demonstration that was a matter of conscience and principle with any of the students."[77] Soon thereafter several Perkins students joined members of the Dallas black community in picketing the H. L. Green department store in downtown Dallas. The pickets chose Green's because, they said, the store manager had made insulting remarks to a black youth who had attempted to eat at the store's all-white lunch counter. The demonstrators' aim was to encourage blacks and whites to trade elsewhere and thus bring economic pressure on the store.[78]

At that time all four restaurants on Hillcrest Avenue across from the university refused to serve blacks. On January 9, 1961, a group of sixty to seventy Perkins and other SMU students, including one black student, entered University Drug at Hillcrest Avenue and McFarlin Drive and quietly occupied all the seats at the lunch counter and in the booths. The students made clear that they were acting as individuals in protest against the store's refusal to serve a black fellow student who had previously received service in another department of the store. As police watched and a crowd gathered, the store's staff tried without success to persuade the students to leave. Then, at 11:00 a.m., an extermination firm hired by the store's owner entered and filled the air with roach spray. The students continued to sit quietly. The owner then had the spray turned directly on the students, and still they sat. Frank Littell, a professor at Perkins, happened by the store, saw what was happening, and went in to support the students. After an hour and a half the owner simply closed the store and the protesters left. Later that day about twenty students returned carrying placards and picketed the store. Charles Merrill, the Perkins student who was the group's publicity chair and who wrote an article about the event for the Perkins student publication, the *Log*, noted that this "step was taken in probably the most conservative municipality in the state by students of one of the state's most conservative schools."[79]

About three weeks earlier another Hillcrest establishment that served food, Henry's, had, after several months of negotiations with the students, agreed to serve customers without regard to race. Students also sat-in at a third, the Toddle House, but the manager said he would not serve Negroes "until directed to do so by the Toddle House chain."[80] Then, around the middle of February, about fifty students, including two blacks, held a "stand-in" protest at the Majestic Theatre in downtown Dallas.[81] Such actions were characteristic of Perkins students' concern and reflected their careful planning.

The SMU administration responded to these actions with restraint. Sterling Wheeler, vice president for public relations and development (and a Perkins professor), said the university expected the group to abide by the laws and the university's regulations, and so far they had done so. He would not comment on the effect the demonstrations might have on the university's annual sustentation drive. His department issued a press release that said SMU did not "encourage or condone" the sit-ins but "will not deny complete civic freedom to her students," who "do not represent the University" and "act only as individual citizens."[82]

The assassination of President John F. Kennedy in Dallas on November 22, 1963, became an occasion for further Perkins involvement in community controversy. On the Sunday after the assassination, the Reverend William A. Holmes preached a sermon at Northaven Methodist Church, parts of which were later repeated on television, in which he said, "The spirit of assassination has been with us [in Dallas] for some time," and then recalled several incidents in Dallas history expressing hate and extremism. Immediately after the television broadcast, the Holmes family began receiving threatening telephone calls, and as a result, they were placed under police protection and moved to a friend's home.[83] The following Friday, at a specially called meeting, the Perkins faculty unanimously voted to endorse and support Holmes's stand. In a statement he later made public, Dean Quillian said, "The issue basically is one of the freedom of the pulpit and the right of a person to say what he believes without being subjected to threat and attempted intimidation."[84]

Many in the top business leadership of Dallas, organized as the Dallas Citizens Council, were angered by the criticism from various sources that followed the assassination. One chief executive officer, Dan Williams of Southland Life Insurance Co., responded specifically to Perkins's participation in that criticism: "That group out at the Perkins School of Theology . . . is just a bunch of liberals trying to stir up things where there wasn't really anything to get stirred up about. They never said anything before. Why should they come out now when they were sure to get national attention?"[85] Critics from Perkins, like Professor Douglas Jackson, made clear, though, that they saw much to be "stirred up about." "Under the present business leadership," Jackson told a reporter from *Fortune Magazine*,

smaller groups [than the Dallas Citizens Council] concerned with a variety of Dallas community interests are deprived of the feeling of representation or participation in the decision-making process. They are deprived of means to make their problems known and make them count. The leadership is a paternalistic structure which makes it difficult if not impossible for the individual to be represented and take part in decisions that concern him. Small groups have no means for being listened to or heard. These small groups cannot bring their problems to the attention of the decision makers with any force or support and they cannot take any part in the decisions because the leadership is an informal and unofficial body.[86]

In 1965 Perkins students and faculty participated in Martin Luther King Jr.'s campaign for voting rights for blacks. Early that March several Perkins students, led by Jack Singleton and Carl Evans, went to Selma, Alabama, to join King's supporters in publicizing recent police brutality there and the lack of voter registration. Their aim, Evans said, was to support civil rights legislation about voter registration in Texas by calling attention to the problem in Alabama. Later that month a busload and several carloads of Perkins students and faculty went to Alabama to participate in the movement's march from Selma to Montgomery. Fred Carney took an active role in helping to organize that trip; he and two other professors, William C. Robinson and James Ward, were among those on the bus.[87]

From the mid- to the late-1960s student activism nationally took on a largely different shape. Sit-ins, picketing, and marches in the early sixties had been nonviolent, a cooperative endeavor between blacks and whites, and respectful of governmental and university authority even when protesting laws deemed unjust. In the fall of 1964 came the Free Speech Movement at the University of California, Berkeley, when approximately a thousand people were arrested for occupying a building in defiance of university authority. In 1966 Stokely Carmichael expelled whites from the Student Nonviolent Coordinating Committee (SNCC), in which blacks and whites had previously worked together. Then, in the spring of 1968, Columbia University students, largely mobilized by Students for a Democratic Society (SDS), confronted the university administration. During that conflict students occupied the university president's office, rifled his files, burned a professor's notes, and were eventually removed by force. On April 11, 1968, Martin Luther King Jr. was assassinated, and a wave of violence and protests erupted around the country. On college campuses student protests continued: at San Francisco State College in 1968, at Cornell University in 1969, and many others. The street violence in Chicago by students and others outside the 1968 Democratic National Convention attracted widespread attention. The unrest reached its apex, though not its end, when the Ohio National Guard killed four students at Kent State University in May 1970, followed a few days later by state and local security officers' killing of two black students at Jackson State College in Mississippi.[88]

In the early sixties the prevailing issue for the protesters had been civil rights. From 1965 on, the dominant issue became the war in Vietnam, though civil rights continued to receive attention. By the late sixties an attitude of defiance toward the national government and other forms of authority had often replaced the students' earlier respect. On many campuses, as at Berkeley and Columbia, students protested what they saw as unjust restrictions on free speech and other campus activities by university administrations. Students not only saw certain policies as unjust; often they rejected "the system," including university governance, and in the name of participatory democracy demanded a voice in university decisions.

In this context protests by some SMU and Perkins students became more assertive, though to a milder degree than in the cases mentioned earlier. The years from 1967 to 1969 saw two series of events in which student groups challenged the university administration. The first began in April 1967, when an SDS group attempted to set up a table in the Umphrey Lee Student Center and, upon being denied permission because the group had no charter as an SMU organization, petitioned for a charter. The faculty-student committee for student organizations granted a temporary charter, and things went along quietly for several months. The following October the local group disbanded because of conflict with what its chapter president saw to be the views of SDS leaders from out of town. A small number of members decided to continue and asked the university's permission to be reorganized under the leadership of a student named J. D. Arnold. Then came a series of events the administration considered disruptive. The core issue was the group's distribution of a publication, *Notes from the Underground*, under a new editor and with different content. Because of its content, including its use of what university leaders deemed "obscenity for obscenity's sake," President Tate banned its distribution on campus. When Arnold continued its distribution in defiance of the president's ban, the university's Faculty Discipline Committee suspended him. He appealed the suspension, but eventually he agreed to leave the campus for good.[89]

During the summer of 1968, following the destructive conflict at Columbia University, SMU officials drew up what they entitled a "Plan of Action in Case of Disruptive Tactics on Campus by Students" and circulated it to top university administrators. The plan set forth in detail what was to be done in case of a demonstration, who was to be notified, and what steps they were to take. It stipulated that all the university's actions were to be "calm, firm, and fair," and that while the university must not overreact, it must make clear that disruptive actions "will not be tolerated."[90]

A second challenge to the university administration came in the spring of 1969 from a campus organization named the Black League of Afro-American and African College Students of SMU, or BLAACS. At that time about forty black undergraduate and twenty-one black graduate students were enrolled at SMU, including nine at Perkins. About thirty of the undergraduates organized BLAACS, and after working on the project for a considerable period, with several occasions for public discussion, these students formulated a series of demands that several brought to Tate's office on Friday, April 25, though he was not present at the time. The following Monday he met with the students to discuss their document, which covered six areas of concern, all centering on making the educational experience relevant to black men and women.[91]

On Friday, May 2, with the assistance of several university groups, including administrators, faculty, and students, Tate provided a lengthy written response. He explained that he had approached his meeting with the students "in mutual seriousness and in basic trust" and that the university's intention in its response was to realize the students' "personal growth and development." He then set forth several ways the university would respond: by revising the governing board of the Student Union to make it more representative of students; employing two black students to assist in recruitment of black students, along with an enlarged advisory and tutorial program and increased financial assistance for black students; revising the liberal studies courses, including "The Nature of Man," to reflect black history and to increase relevance to the black experience; instituting better pay and working conditions for black wage-earning employees; developing a proposal for an Afro-American Program; establishing a human relations board with representatives from various ethnic groups; and making an effort to find a house for business and social affairs for black students. Tate further clarified the statement to say that by the fall of 1969 the university would accept two hundred admissible black students if they were available, would try to have at least five black faculty members in liberal studies, and would begin a black studies program with a black coordinator. That same day the university announced it had hired Keith Worrell, a black student from Barbados who was graduating from Perkins that year, to help teach "The Nature of Man."[92] Then, on June 12, Tate announced that Irving Baker would join the university on June 15 as an assistant to the president and director of the Afro-American Studies Program.[93]

The response to Tate—by black students, the faculty, and the trustees—was overwhelmingly positive and appreciative. As Tate explained, the university had dealt with the matter on a rational basis and had avoided mistakes some other institutions had made. The "Plan of Action" drawn up the previous summer had prepared for a crisis. Yet the manner in which BLAACS conducted its challenge and the way the administration responded created not a crisis but an opportunity to improve both education and the relations between the various groups on campus.

Protests at Perkins took two forms in 1968–69. One was a challenge to propriety and responsibility in journalism. In the spring of 1967 the Perkins Student Council authorized a student newsletter that would deal with matters of mutual concern of an extracurricular nature. The *Perkins Newsletter* first appeared on March 16 on a biweekly basis, with brief items of news and opinion. In the fall of 1968, however, along with news items and unobjectionable opinion, the newsletter frequently included matters that others deemed offensive: profanity thrown in here and there, a short "poem" notable for its crudity, and a student's so-called Notes from My Diary, which featured insensitive comments and off-color allusions intended to be humorous. When student letters to the editor expressed indignation, the editor (a third-year B.D. student) explained his "editorial policy": "As editor, I will not impose any standard upon the content of the material. . . . I personally feel uncomfortable when I try to judge what is profane and what isn't." At that point Quillian wrote the president of the Perkins Student Council to request a meeting with the council to discuss its responsibilities regarding the newsletter, commenting that its material "may be interpreted as libelous as well as being flagrantly irresponsible to the community." After he met with the council and raised a number of questions, the *PN*'s pages were somewhat more restrained.[94]

Of greater substance that academic year was a student challenge to the system of governance of Perkins School of Theology. Students asked why they should not have a greater voice in setting the policies of the school and, if they were to be effective, an actual voting presence in the school's policy-making bodies. That question became part of the agenda of the major self-study Perkins undertook during the 1968–69 academic year.

1. Willis M. Tate to Ministers of the Methodist Church in the South Central Jurisdiction, February 26, 1960, Joseph Allen Papers, Bridwell Library; "Quillian Elected Dean of Perkins Starting July 1," *Texas Christian Advocate*, March 4, 1960, 1; "Quillian Appointed New Perkins Dean," [SMU] *Mustang*, May–June, 1960, 5; Perkins catalogs, 1955–60.
2. Joseph D. Quillian Jr., "Report of the Dean to the Faculty, Lakeview, September 23, 1960," 1, Quillian Papers, Bridwell Library.
3. Ibid.
4. Ibid., 2–3.
5. Joseph D. Quillian Jr., "The Esprit de Corps of the Perkins Faculty—What and Why?" February 16, 1963, Quillian Papers.
6. Joseph D. Quillian Jr. to Willis M. Tate, April 19, 1965, Quillian Papers.
7. Schubert M. Ogden, interview by James Brooks, April 28, 2004, Southern Methodist University Archive Series.
8. The letters are in the Quillian Papers. Lewis Howard Grimes quoted them without names in *History of the Perkins School of Theology*, edited by Roger Loyd (Dallas: Southern Methodist University Press, 1993), 126.
9. Joseph D. Quillian Jr., "Basic Information and Proposals Concerning Perkins Finances and the Future of the School," a Report to the Trustee Committee for Perkins School of Theology, December 7, 1978," 5, Quillian Papers.
10. *Texas Christian Advocate*, March 4, 1960, p. 1.
11. Joseph D. Quillian Jr., to Eugene B. Hawk, January 2, 1963; Hawk to Quillian, January 7, 1963; Quillian to Hawk, January 10, 1963; Quillian to Jay Osborne, February 18, 1963; Joseph D. Quillian Jr., "Eugene B. Hawk, the Building Dean," all in Quillian Papers.
12. Joseph D. Quillian Jr., to Merrimon Cuninggim, September 28, 1960, Quillian Papers.
13. Ogden interview.
14. Quillian to Tate, November 27, 1961, Quillian Papers.
15. Ibid., February 19, 1962, Quillian Papers.
16. Ibid., April 24, 1964, Quillian Papers.
17. Joseph D. Quillian Jr., "Anticipated Budgetary Needs for Perkins School of Theology," 1965–66, Quillian Papers.
18. Quillian, to Tate, December 5, 1960, Quillian Papers.
19. Ibid., April 24, 1964.
20. Board of trustees minutes, November 5, 1959.
21. Quillian to Tate, May 24, 1962. See also Quillian to Cuninggim, September 17, 1963, Quillian Papers.
22. Quillian to Tate, May 24, 1962; Quillian to Tate, November 30, 1962; Quillian to Cuninggim, September 17, 1963; Quillian to Cuninggim, October 1, 1963; Quillian to Joseph L. Allen, November 11, 1963, Quillian Papers.
23. Quillian to Tate, April 22, 1963, Quillian Papers.
24. Ibid., April 24, 1964, Quillian Papers.

25. Quillian Jr., to C. L. Lloyd, August 9, 1963, Quillian Papers.
26. Lloyd to Quillian, December 2, 1963, Quillian Papers.
27. Quillian to Tate, February 10, 1964, Quillian Papers.
28. Quillian to Lloyd, February 10, 1964, Quillian Papers.
29. Ibid., July 3, 1965, Quillian Papers.
30. Quillian to Howard Grimes, April 17, 1968, Quillian Papers.
31. Board of trustees minutes, November 3, 1961.
32. Minutes of the Executive Committee of the Board of Trustees, October 19, 1962; Marshall Terry, *"From High on the Hilltop. . .": A Brief History of SMU* (Dallas: Southern Methodist University, 2001), 43.
33. Marshall Terry, interview by author, November 14, 2007, Dallas.
34. Albert C. Outler, "The Idea of a University College" (typescript, no date, with an accompanying memo indicating that it was sent to Quillian by Johnnie Marie Grimes on February 25, 1963), 5, Quillian Papers.
35. Board of trustees minutes, November 11, 1962, and May 10, 1963.
36. John W. Deschner, "The Task of a Theological School in the Church and University," address on Honors Day at Perkins School of Theology, April 23, 1964 (typescript), Quillian Papers.
37. Quillian to Cuninggim, September 28, 1960, Quillian Papers.
38. Quillian, "Esprit de Corps."
39. Faculty minutes, December 16, 1960.
40. "Report of the ad hoc committee on rank and tenure," February 24, 1961, Quillian Papers.
41. Faculty minutes, February 24, 1961.
42. "Oral Memoirs of Albert Cook Outler," Religion and Culture Project, Program for Oral History, Baylor University, 1974.
43. Ibid.
44. Albert C. Outler, *Methodist Observer at Vatican II* (Westminster: Newman Press, 1967).
45. Ibid., chaps. 1 and 15.
46. *John Wesley*, edited by Albert C. Outler (New York: Oxford University Press, 1964).
47. Schubert M. Ogden, *Christ without Myth: A Study Based on the Theology of Rudolf Bultmann* (New York: Harper and Brothers, 1961), and *The Reality of God and Other Essays* (New York: Harper and Row, 1966).
48. See especially Ogden, *Reality of God*, 2, 6, 44, 48.
49. Van A. Harvey, *The Historian and the Believer* (New York: Macmillan, 1966).
50. See especially Harvey, *Historian and the Believer*, chaps. 1 and 8.
51. Ogden, *Reality of God*, xi; Harvey, *Historian and the Believer*, xiv–xv.
52. *The Methodist Hymnal* (Nashville, Tenn.: Methodist Publishing, 1966).
53. Faculty minutes, January 10, 1964.
54. Quillian to Tate, April 24, 1964, Quillian Papers.
55. Quillian to Outler, October 25, 1965, Quillian Papers.
56. Quillian to several Perkins faculty members on leave (Fred Carney, Van Harvey, Dick Murray, William C. Robinson, James Ward), September 22, 1966, Quillian Papers.
57. Board of trustees minutes, January 5, 1967.
58. Faculty minutes, April 7, 1967.
59. Catalog, 1960–61, 60–62.
60. Ibid., 1961–62, 60, and 1962–63, 60–61.
61. Perkins Senate minutes, May 9, 1980; Curriculum Committee report to the Perkins Senate, May 7, 1980, Allen Papers.
62. Catalog, 1963–64, 33–35.
63. Quillian to Tate, April 24, 1964, Quillian Papers.
64. Grimes, *History of the Perkins School of Theology*, 133; faculty minutes, October 9, 1965. My memory coincides with Grimes's account of the discussion.
65. Faculty minutes, October 9, 1965.

66. Ibid., December 10, 1965, and January 14, 1966.
67. Catalog, 1966–67, 35–36.
68. Faculty minutes, February 10, 1967.
69. "Syllabus for the Senior Colloquy: Studies in Vatican II, Fall Semester, 1966," Quillian Papers.
70. "Recommendations concerning Senior Colloquy," memo to the faculty from the Enlarged Committee on Course of Study, March 28, 1968; faculty minutes, April 4 and September 27, 1968, Quillian Papers.
71. Quillian to Tate, November 27, 1961, Quillian Papers.
72. Ibid., April 28, 1962, Quillian Papers.
73. Ibid., April 24, 1964, Quillian Papers.
74. *Fact Book on Theological Education, 1971–72*, edited by Marvin J. Taylor (Dayton, Ohio: American Association of Theological Schools in the United States and Canada), 37–41.
75. Graduation data are from SMU commencement programs (Perkins registrar's office).
76. *Dallas Times Herald*, April 5, 1960.
77. Quillian to Cuninggim, October 7, 1960, Quillian Papers.
78. Carroll Brown, "Perkins Students and Picketing," *Log*, October 27, 1960.
79. J. Charles Merrill, "Perkins Students Aid in Conducting Off-Campus 'Sit-In,'" *Log*, February 2, 1961, 1, 4; Mike Engleman, "Stronger Sit-ins Will Continue," *Daily Campus*, February 1, 1961.
80. *Daily Campus*, February 10, 1961.
81. Ibid., February 15, 1961.
82. Ibid., February 1 and 8, 1961.
83. Ibid., December 11, 1963.
84. Faculty minutes, November 27, 1963.
85. Richard Austin Smith, "How Business Failed Dallas," *Fortune Magazine*, July 1964, 158.
86. Ibid., 159.
87. *Daily Campus*, March 10, 12, and 24, 1965; James M. Ward to Joe Allen, December 30, 2008, in the author's personal files. Victor Furnish also helped in the planning but was unable to go on the march.
88. For accounts of student protests in this period, see *The Report of the President's Commission on Campus Unrest* (Washington, D.C.: U.S. Government Printing Office, 1970); Ronald Fraser et al., *1968: A Student Generation in Revolt* (London: Chatto and Windus, 1988); and Alexander W. Astin, *The Power of Protest: A National Study of Student and Faculty Disruptions with Implications for the Future* (San Francisco: Jossey-Bass, 1975).
89. *Daily Campus*, April 14, 19, and 26, October 26, November 10 and 22, and December 5, 1967, and January 19, 1968; board of trustees minutes, November 10, 1967; board of governors minutes, December 7, 1967. (The board of governors replaced the executive committee of the board of trustees from 1963 to 1987. See chap. 8.)
90. "Plan of Action in Case of Disruptive Tactics on Campus by Students," with cover letter to administrators, dated August 26, 1968, Quillian Papers.
91. Board of trustees minutes, May 9, 1969; "No Time for Committees," *Daily Campus*, May 1, 1969.
92. "BLAACS Gain Reply in Tate's Statement," *Daily Campus*, May 2, 1969, 1; "BLAACS Get Reply," *Daily Campus*, May 2, 1969, 2, 5, and 12; board of trustees minutes, May 9, 1969.
93. Board of governors minutes, June 12, 1969.
94. *Perkins Newsletter*, March 16, 1967, and October 21, November 4, 11, and 18, and December 2 and 9, 1968; Quillian to John Bengel, November 6, 1968; minutes of the Perkins Student Council, November 11, 1968; Joseph D. Quillian Jr., "The Perkins Newsletter and Some Questions It Raises," Quillian Papers.

CHAPTER 8

Self-study and After, 1968–1981

A
t the faculty meeting in December 1967, Dean Quillian read a paper stating that it was time for Perkins to undertake a major self-study. It was reason enough, he explained, that SMU was conducting a self-study in connection with the Southern Association of Colleges and Schools and was requiring each school to conduct its own self-study. But there were numerous other reasons, among them, that the American Association of Theological Schools would soon be reviewing Perkins, that Perkins needed to clarify its relation to the Graduate Program in Religion, and that Perkins needed to examine the idea of a professional doctoral program, its efforts in field education and internship, and its continuing education program. Furthermore, in the face of a cultural crisis of faith and the lack of clarity about the vocation of ordained ministry, Perkins needed to consider how it could best serve the church in a time of rapid change. Quillian suggested that an adequate self-study would occupy most of a calendar year, so that the faculty would need to start planning for it right away.[1] As he later observed, Perkins "has not had a real self-study since 'coming of age' in her present era," that is, since the self-study of 1952–53.[2]

Thus began a process that proved to be in some respects a turning point in the life of the school. Throughout the next semester and summer the dean, the faculty, and student leaders set up the structures through which to conduct the self-study, which became a major endeavor during the 1968–69 academic year.

Quillian set the tone for the self-study. He faced it, he said, with concern but with confidence, because the faculty and the student body were committed and competent, and "we will come out of it with more strength than we have yet had." Nobody, he said, should come to premature opinions but should be open to whatever changes needed to be made, some of which no one had yet thought of. The questions he raised about Perkins's programs and procedures reflected his own openness to change: should the faculty have four divisions or fewer or more? What should be the length of the basic professional degree? What should it be called? Should the curriculum return to the senior colloquy or to comprehensive examinations? Should the school have "an intern dimension"? What programs should Perkins have in urban ministry?[3]

From March to September 1968 a committee structure emerged for the conduct of the self-study. The dean appointed three committees to examine different aspects of the life of the school. The Committee on Curriculum consisted of eight faculty members and eight students and was chaired by Fred Carney. The Committee on Academic Life, with seven faculty and five students, was initially to be headed by Albert Outler, but Ronald Sleeth replaced him as chair early in its work. The Committee on Organization and Administration was made up of four faculty and four students; John Deschner was its chair. Overseeing the process was the Steering Committee, led by the dean; other members were Wayne Banks as secretary; the chairs of the other three committees; Bishop W. Kenneth Pope, who had recently become chair of the Board of Trustees Committee for the School of Theology; and two students, John Bengel, in his second seminary year and president of the student council, and Dugald Stewart, a senior.[4]

The committee work during the 1968–69 academic year was strenuous. The curriculum committee met twenty times for two hours between September and April, and along the way various members prepared long reports, some of them thirty to forty typed pages, for committee consideration. Individual committee members spent many hours consulting nonmembers, both faculty and students, to help formulate proposals that would be workable and widely accepted. Their aim was to obtain consensus about some creative proposals. All the committees spent two weekends, one in late January and the other at the end of February, at self-study retreats in Waxahachie, Texas, to try to complete their recommendations.[5]

A marked departure from previous self-studies was the extent of student participation. The stimulus for a strong student role was twofold. One, as I described earlier, was that Perkins students shared in the widespread spirit of protest against institutional authority in the late sixties. Although Perkins students were far more moderate than those at Berkeley or Columbia, some were suspicious of Perkins administrators and faculty, and they wanted a voice in decisions about school policy. As John Holbert, a Perkins student at the time, later observed, the students then were actively engaged in the wider society. Seventy, he said, were members of Perkins's Social Action Committee. Some were in seminary to avoid being drafted into the armed services and sent to Vietnam. "The ethos was different," he said, from that of earlier and later years.[6]

Second, Quillian and faculty members recognized the need to involve students, not only to avoid destructive confrontation but also because they believed it was the right thing to do. One way to involve students was to put several on each self-study committee. For another, the dean held seven open hearings for the wider Perkins community, one in September and the rest between the middle of March and the first of May 1969. The early one was to give students and faculty the opportunity to discuss the purposes and problems of Perkins before the committees began their work. The early spring hearings were to inform the community about the directions the proposals were taking and to invite feedback. The last two spring hearings brought the recommendations from all three committees to audiences of sixty and fifty-five students, for their questions, suggestions, and vote on the proposals.[7]

On May 9, 1969, the faculty adopted, with some amendments, a major document from the Self-Study Committee on Organization and Administration, approved the resolutions of the Self-Study Committee on Curriculum, and referred several documents from the three committees to the appropriate bodies so that their recommendations could be implemented in the fall of 1969.[8]

The chief change coming out of the work of the Committee on Organization and Administration was the creation of the Perkins Senate as the primary governing body of the school. Initially, the senate's membership consisted of all Perkins faculty members, twelve Perkins students elected by students, and the chair of the Board of Trustees Committee on the School of Theology, ex officio.[9] Two alumni/ae were added as members beginning in the fall of 1971, and eventually student membership was increased to fifteen.

Beginning in mid-May 1969 the senate replaced the faculty as the body to "consider, act or advise on all matters of concern to the community of the Perkins School of Theology." To be consistent with university policy, however, certain matters were reserved for action only by the faculty, including admission of students to degree candidacy and granting of degrees, application of academic policy and rules to individual students, and election of members to the faculty Rank and Tenure Committee. After that spring the faculty met to conduct business only when it was necessary to act on matters like these. It continued to meet "as guild," that is, to discuss matters pertaining to teaching and the profession, but it no longer met as a body to deliberate on school policy. When the senate came into existence, students also became members of its standing committees: faculty, curriculum, academic procedures, recruitment and admissions, community life, school relations, and long-range planning.[10] The number of student members on each committee varied from two on some to eventually as many as nine on community life.

These changes provided formal procedures for a continual student voice in school policy—a widely appreciated result. Over time, however, some faculty members came to believe that something desirable had been lost through the creation of the senate. In 1968 the regular faculty and administrators numbered about forty; the senate in 1970–71 had fifty-six members, and thereafter it became even larger. When groups increase significantly in size, they tend to become more formal, and some important policy issues are for all practical purposes decided before they are formally approved. Furthermore, with the almost complete turnover of student members each year, it was difficult for student senators to develop any continuity in their senate participation. Because it no longer gathered to consider policy, the faculty lost the continual interchange that would have helped to bind its members together as a working group. The senate was a creative response to the times, though not without its costs.[11]

In addition to proposing the senate, the Self-Study Committee on Organization and Administration reported on several administrative subjects. In a paper on financial policy it recognized that seminary operating costs were rising rapidly and that Perkins was in an increasingly competitive market for both faculty and students. It recommended that the Senate Committee on Faculty provide a policy advisory to the dean, that Perkins plan its finances five years in advance, that it set targets for faculty compensation (salary plus benefits) that would compare favorably with the salary scale of the American Association of University Professors, and that it give greater attention to endowment gifts from individuals.[12] Another paper surveyed Perkins's administrative structure, listed strengths and weaknesses, and made several proposals.[13] Still another reported briefly on the current state of Perkins's buildings and the need to improve office conditions for faculty and administrators.[14] Finally, a short paper listed twelve ways in which communications at Perkins could be improved.[15] These four papers, taken together, provided the most comprehensive examination of the Perkins organizational structure in the school's history. The faculty referred all four to the senate for consideration the following fall.[16]

The Self-Study Committee on Curriculum considered not only the B.D. program but the whole array of programs, degree and nondegree, offered by the Perkins faculty. The committee presented these programs in tabular form (see table 8.1). It differentiated the several programs into those offering preparation for leadership in the church and those offering preparation for leadership in the academy. Within each track it differentiated basic from advanced degree programs, and within each degree program it distinguished between the study of what it called "the theological sciences" and the operational competence appropriate to a particular program.

Table 8.1. Four Degree Programs for Perkins

CHURCH LEADERSHIP			ACADEMY LEADERSHIP		
Basic degree (B.D.)	Shared historical, systematic, and practical sciences of theology	Basic operational competency appropriate to ministry	Basic degree (M.A.)	Shared historical, systematic, and practical sciences of theology	Basic operational competency appropriate to teaching and research
	Specialiazation as <u>focus</u> in a function or role of ministry			Specialization as a <u>field</u> of teaching and research	
Advanced degree (D.Min.)	Shared historical, systematic, and practical sciences of theology	Advanced operational competency appropriate to ministry	Advanced degree (Ph.D.)	Shared historical, systematic, and practical sciences of theology	Advanced operational competency appropriate to teaching and research
	Specialization as a <u>focus</u> in a function of ministry			Specialization as a <u>field</u> of teaching and research	

Source: "Self-Study Report on Curriculum and Degrees," March 1969, Joseph D. Quillian Jr. Papers, Bridwell Library, Southern Methodist University. Until 1970 Perkins offered the bachelor of divinity (B.D.) degree, which that year was renamed the master of theology (M.Th.). In 1981 Perkins adopted the designation for this degree, generally accepted elsewhere, master of divinity (M.Div.). To avoid confusion, this table refers to the doctor of ministry (D.Min.) degree, although it went by another name during the self-study.

A fundamental judgment of the committee, approved by the faculty, was that Perkins's primary curricular responsibility was to provide basic education for church leadership. A corollary of this judgment was that in planning the curriculum and allocating its resources, the faculty should give major emphasis to that program.[17]

In the midst of the social unrest of the late 1960s, several other seminaries were experimenting with radical departures from traditional curricula, such as reducing or eliminating required courses and moving to pass/fail grading. Members of the Perkins committee to review the curriculum might then have felt outside pressure to do something radical. Instead, as one member, Victor Furnish, later observed, "We kept looking beyond the present pressures to ask what ought to go into ministerial education."[18] The 1969 revision of the B.D. curriculum was simultaneously a return to one resembling that of the 1950s and early 1960s and a creative reshaping of that program. The colloquy curriculum of 1966 had required in each division simply sixteen semester hours without specifying required courses, plus the senior colloquy. In contrast, the 1969 revision returned to a required core plus electives. In the theological sciences it required two semesters in Old Testament, two in New Testament (with variations for those taking biblical languages), two in the history of Christianity, one in the history of religions, and a four-course sequence in Division III: faith and philosophy, moral theology, and two semesters of systematic theology.

This curriculum provided some flexibility within the requirements in the theological sciences. As before, students could fulfill the core requirements in biblical studies by taking either the English-language or the biblical language route. They could place out of core courses in all the theological sciences by examination and would receive academic credit for doing so. There was also an effort to offer smaller classes, either by having discussion sessions within the large lecture courses or by providing options for meeting a particular core requirement, as was done in the history of religions with a required course in Hinduism, Buddhism, or Islam.[19]

The self-study introduced two innovations to help students gain basic operational competence for ministry. One was to bring together work in the various aspects of ministry in two 2-semester courses, "Church and World" and "The Ministry of the Church." "Church and World," to be taken in the first seminary year, would interpret the social environment of the church, drawing especially upon the social and psychological sciences. In the second year "The Ministry of the Church" would presuppose this social environment and analyze critically the various operations of ministry. The two courses were to include general lectures for the entire class, small groups for discussion, and involvement in both the community and the church. Both would make use of case study methods, and both would be team-taught by perhaps three faculty members each semester. A fifth semester course, "Practical Theology," was to provide a historical and theological study of the church.[20]

These innovative ideas proved difficult to implement. "Church and World" was offered for only two years, 1970–72; "The Ministry of the Church" and "Practical Theology," for only one, 1971–72. Thereafter they were replaced by individual one-semester courses on various so-called functions of ministry, such as preaching, worship, pastoral care, church education, and the like. The yearlong ministry courses were difficult to organize and teach, especially because faculty members in this area were all specialists in particular functions of ministry rather than in their unity and interrelations. The professors much preferred to teach in their own more restricted fields. Furthermore, the more inclusive courses were not popular with the students. Thus this first innovative plan for "operational competence" soon disappeared.[21] In sharp contrast, the second innovation for operations, the internship, was well received and continues to this day.

Although the curriculum committee gave most of its attention to the basic program for church leadership, it also examined several other programs and referred its reflections to the appropriate bodies within Perkins and the university.[22] As for programs for leadership in the academy (M.A., Ph.D.), it made a number of suggestions that were available for later consideration at Perkins and the Graduate School.

The committee gave considerable attention to whether there should be a pastoral doctoral degree program, working especially with a model of a such a degree program that added two years and one summer to the first two years of the B.D. program. In the end the committee deferred decision on this question and on the future of the existing master of sacred theology (S.T.M.) program to later Perkins bodies.[23] In 1973 Perkins announced a doctor of ministry degree (D.Min.), and it accepted no more new S.T.M. students after the fall of 1975.[24] As introduced in 1973, the doctor of ministry degree provided a choice between two tracks. In the first, students admitted before completing the master of theology (as the B.D. was renamed in 1970) were required to have previously completed sixty semester hours of seminary, including the general requirements and the internship, and to demonstrate ability to work exegetically in either Hebrew or Greek. They then would take forty-two additional hours, including a specialization in an area of ministerial practice and another specialization in either Bible, history of Christianity, systematics, or moral theology. The other track was open to students who had already completed the master of theology plus at least two years of full-time ministerial experience. This track required twenty-four semester hours, including a twelve-semester-hour concentration in an area of ministry; nine semester hours total in the biblical, historical, systematic, and moral fields; and a project. To these twenty-four semester hours was added in 1975 the required three-semester-hour "Seminar on Practical Theology."[25]

The question arose early in the self-study year whether the master of religious education and master of sacred music programs should be discontinued. Some committee members argued that these two programs did not adequately educate students for ministry in those areas and that it would be better for students to concentrate on church education or church music as a part of the B.D. program. Others held that in the absence of the master of religious education, those wanting to be directors of Christian education would simply go into that work without a theological degree, and that without the master of sacred music, those wanting to be ministers of music would take a master of music degree and still become ministers of church music.[26] The future of both was referred to the senate for later examination. As it turned out, the master of sacred music was retained, but the master of religious education was discontinued, with no more recipients of the degree after 1971—until 1979, when it was reinstated.

The Graduate Program in Religion had admitted its first students in the fall of 1965, and the first two students were granted their Ph.D. degrees in 1970. When Van Harvey, who was director of the program, resigned in 1966 for a year's research leave, Herndon Wagers became the director and continued in that office until 1974. Although the 1968–69 Perkins curriculum self-study took the graduate program into consideration, its work did not affect this program directly. Instead, the Steering Committee of the Graduate Program in Religion, with Schubert Ogden as its director beginning in 1974, undertook a review of the program in 1975–76. A major result of this review was the reconception and renaming of the program as the Graduate Program in Religious Studies, a title "appropriate to the goals of advanced teaching and scholarship in religious studies, as distinct from Christian theology." This became the official title in 1977. A second result was to combine what had previously been two programs for the master's and Ph.D. degrees into one. These and other changes expressed the commitment of the graduate program faculty, both those from the SMU Department of Religion and those from Perkins, to the continuation of the program.[27]

The Self-study Committee on Academic Life and Work had a broad and amorphous charge: to "study the functioning of the Perkins community with primary reference to its academic purpose," including attention to the faculty, students, library, and Perkins's relation to other schools of the university.[28] This charge led to considerable duplication of the work of the other two committees, especially in the attention Academic Life and Work gave to the B.D. curriculum.

A number of resolutions resulted from this committee's work. Most resolutions about the curriculum took the form of goals to be achieved rather than ways of achieving them: "that the student be a full partner in the academic enterprise at Perkins," that the curriculum "enhance the student's powers of verbal expression, of critical thought and of independent study," and that the curriculum be more flexible. In addition, it recommended a Perkins monograph series and a plan for evaluation of teaching. Among its proposals for the life of the community were a Perkins commons room, weekly common meals at noon in Selecman Auditorium, an orientation retreat to include wives and children as well as new students, and a more effective program of testing for new students—all of which were referred to the new senate's Community Life Committee. Academic Life and Work commended the community's worship life and recommended that the existing pattern of services be continued.[29]

CREATING THE PERKINS INTERN PROGRAM

When in 1969 the Self-Study Committee on Curriculum recommended an intern program, it proposed that it replace Perkins's existing program of field education. Between 1945 and 1968 a series of administratively able and church-savvy directors of field work/field education—A. W. Martin, R. F. Curl, Marvin Judy, and Alsie Carleton—had studied what was done at other seminaries, labored to devise an adequate program, and attempted to place students in situations in which they would gain desirable kinds of experience. Cuninggim had asserted early in his tenure as dean that seminary education must include "guided experience" as well as serious study and that this guided experience, field work, must exist for the education of the student—an indispensable part of every student's educational experience—not primarily as financial aid or immediate service to the church.[30]

Yet it was never clear what kind of program it should be. In the mid-1950s it consisted of two parts: a requirement that first-year students participate in the life of a local church or service agency and small-group discussions of this experience within the required courses in the life and work of the church. In this plan all faculty members were to assist in guiding students in the first-year experience, though levels of faculty interest and fitness for this assistance varied widely.[31] For a short while in the late 1950s, the requirement included participation in "Parish Week," when, for a week in the fall, groups of students would go with a faculty member to a district in the region, where they would participate in the life of the churches and meet to discuss their activities.[32] In 1958 that program was replaced by a system of parish visitation with written reports by the students.[33] That too was short-lived.

Of longer duration—from 1958 to 1970—was the catalog requirement that each B.D. student must accumulate six (after 1966, five) units of field work during the three years of study. A unit was earned by one semester's significant involvement in a local church or service agency. Reflecting the faculty's desire for this involvement to be primarily educational, in 1959 the name of the activity was changed to field education.[34] The Field Education Office oversaw students' placements, received their reports, and granted units of credit. Yet problems persisted, as they did in other seminaries, and the change in the program's name did not solve them. It was seldom clear what a placement was supposed to accomplish (beyond students' being involved) or how to accomplish it, and at no point was there a plan to ensure adequate supervision either by the school or by the local church or service agency.

Into this situation came the self-study of 1968–69. Quillian's earliest memo about the need for a self-study noted "the present concern about the field education and internship dimensions."[35] In a March 1968 memo, his list of questions to be considered included, "Should we establish an intern dimension in our requirements?" and "How can we devise effective supervisory procedures for field education or possible internship?"[36] What he had in mind by the term *internship* is not clear. Sometimes Perkins students had voluntarily taken a year off from classes to work in a local church or elsewhere, then returned to school. For years Lutheran seminaries, as well as some other Protestant and many Roman Catholic seminaries, had required a full-time internship, often for a year, for the master of divinity or similar degrees. These internships varied considerably as to what the seminary expected, the kind of supervision provided, and the remuneration to the student.[37]

In the process of its deliberations, the Self-Study Curriculum Committee judged that Perkins's program of basic education for church leadership should combine "superior instruction and learning in theological science with first-rate training for operational competency." In the past, two barriers to achieving operational competency had been the absence of a substantial block of time for students to concentrate on the practice of ministry uninterrupted by the classroom schedule and assignments, and the lack of adequately trained supervisors. What the committee proposed was an internship of ten weeks or more, ordinarily during the summer between the second and third seminary years, in which the student would carry out ministerial acts directed by a trained supervisor and would examine these acts critically with the supervisor.[38] In May 1969 the faculty approved the proposal for an internship under trained supervisors to replace the existing field education program.[39]

In the summer of 1968 the director of field education, Alsie Carleton, was elected a bishop of The United Methodist Church and assigned to the Albuquerque, New Mexico, area. Quillian quickly appointed a replacement, Claus H. Rohlfs Sr., of San Antonio. Born in Germany in 1921, Rohlfs had emigrated with his family to the United States in 1931. After service in the Pacific Theater in World War II, he completed his college degree at Temple University in 1949 and his bachelor of divinity degree at Perkins in 1952. Thereafter he served several pastorates in the Southwest Texas Conference and in 1967 was appointed to the San Antonio District.[40] Rohlfs attended the faculty conference in late September 1968, but his responsibilities as district superintendent prevented him from moving to Dallas until January 1969.

As soon as the faculty approved a required internship, Rohlfs energetically set about developing a model for the program as well as support for the idea in the churches of the region. He had ample time to do so: students entering in the fall of 1970 and after were subject to the internship requirement, but they would not actually intern until the summer of 1972. In the summer of 1969 Rohlfs held a series of twelve meetings at Perkins, inviting to each a few carefully chosen pastors and some of their leading lay members to hear the program explained and to make suggestions. Their response was enthusiastic. In July 1969 people trained in clinical pastoral education met with faculty members to discuss intern supervision, which Rohlfs saw as a key to the success of the internship. The following November brought a consultation on internship models from various other fields: hospital chaplaincy, medical education, pastoral counseling, and the experiences of a few pastors who had supervised internship students. Over this time Rohlfs drew upon expertise from a wide array of sources: Dr. Glenn Lembke of the Aerospace Medical Center in San Antonio, who for a few years was a part-time consultant to the Perkins program; Kenneth Pepper of the Pastoral Counseling Center of Dallas; the Reverend Ronald Sunderland, who had written his master of sacred theology thesis at Perkins on supervision in clinical pastoral education. Rohlfs also explored the required internship program for Lutheran seminary students and one for social workers in San Antonio and elsewhere. As the model was developing, in the fall of 1970 Rohlfs and Lembke held meetings with the bishops, their cabinets, and other leaders in eight episcopal areas of the region. They presented the model they were working on and invited questions, thereby clarifying the internship both for themselves and for the church leaders.[41]

The main features of the model that initially emerged from this process were that

The student would be placed in a congregation or agency to engage in the practice of ministry under supervision.

The placement would be negotiated by the school, the congregation/agency, and the student.

The congregation's decision to have an intern would require a vote by the administrative board.

The pastor or agency professional would be called a "field instructor"; the congregation would be a "teaching congregation"; the intern student would be a "minister-in-training."

The congregation/agency would provide a cash stipend to the intern plus other benefits.

All placements would be in relation to a field unit of three to six interns who would meet together for mutual support and guidance.

A psychological consultant would be affiliated with each field unit to lead growth groups of interns and spouses and to supervise the field instructors.

Field instructors would be required to go through a five-day training program.

Each field unit would meet for several seminar sessions during the internship, most to be led by Perkins faculty and one by the resident bishop.

The intern requirement could be fulfilled by a ten-week, eighteen-week (one semester), a nine-month, or twelve-month placement.

As the model developed, it became clear that a ten-week summer internship would be inadequate. The pastor would be on vacation part of that time, the church would not be in its regular pattern of activity, and the time was too short. In May 1972, then, the Perkins Senate eliminated the ten-week option for students entering in the fall of 1972 and thereafter, except for some who were permitted to take clinical pastoral education as an alternative. Another change was to give credit hours for the internship—initially, six semester hours, eventually increased to twelve.[42]

By the time of the first internships in 1972, the planners, led by Claus Rohlfs, had carefully constructed the program. Numerous church leaders in the region had participated in its development and were strongly supportive. Supervision—the key ingredient—had become tripartite: a field instructor, psychological consultant, and Perkins intern staff member. As the time approached for the first internships, the Perkins staff had to grow to carry out the plans and join in the supervision. In June 1971 James Gwaltney, formerly pastor of West Shore United Methodist Church in Richardson, Texas, became the associate director of the intern program. Then, in 1972, Craig Emerick, previously associate pastor at West Shore, became the assistant director. This was the beginning of what became a pioneering and esteemed venture in ministerial education.

NONDEGREE PROGRAMS FOR MINISTERS AND LAITY

Before 1965 George Baker Jr. had directed a program called Perkins Outreach, which offered various series of one-day lectures and discussions by faculty for districts, smaller ministerial groups, or local churches. When Dick Murray joined the faculty in 1965, it was with the understanding that along with teaching Christian education he would further develop the Perkins program of continuing education. In his first year Murray initiated several new study possibilities for ministers and laity that he enlarged after a year of study, 1966–67, at Union Theological Seminary in New York.

He began with a guided reading program. A faculty member would develop a three- to four-page reading guide focusing on a particular topic and providing an introduction and suggestions for six to ten reading selections. Individuals, or preferably a group of ten or more, could register for a nominal fee and either buy the books or have them mailed on loan from Perkins. Groups were encouraged to meet every two weeks to discuss a reading selection, and at the conclusion Perkins would arrange for a faculty member to spend a day with the group discussing the subject. By the fall of 1967 fourteen reading guides were available, including Albert Outler's "The Vatican Council and Protestants," Victor Furnish's "Some Current Trends in New Testament Interpretation," and Robert Elliott's "On Grief and Death." By 1975 Perkins was offering forty-one reading guides. In 1976 Murray reported that this program had in ten years included 753 groups in forty states, enrolling eight hundred to twelve hundred people each year.[43]

A second option was to travel to Perkins for a residential seminar of three, five, or nine days, either in the summer or the academic year. The first two seminars were held in the spring of 1966, when twenty people enrolled in a seminar on preaching and fifteen in another on art and architecture. By the mid-1970s about a thousand people were enrolling in these seminars each year.[44] A third option was to arrange through the registrar's office to audit most of the basic courses. All these programs were informed by one of Murray's convictions about education—that "each person needs to be part of a learning group" and enter into dialog with others "as they are confronted by printed resources, the changing nature of the world, and the depth of the Gospel."[45]

Two other summer continuing education programs began in the mid-1960s. The Christian Educators' Seminar, conducted in cooperation with the Methodist Board of Education, began in 1965 and continued for many years. The Church Music Seminar began around that time, initially under the leadership of Carlton Young, and continues today.

To strengthen relations with its alumni/ae, Perkins in 1971–72 organized the Perkins Alumni Council to serve in an advisory role to the school. With two members from each annual conference in the jurisdiction plus nine at-large members, its first president was the Reverend Ray Branton of New Orleans, followed the next year by Charles Lutrick of Lubbock. In its early years the council studied such subjects as continuing education, models for ministry, financial aid, the internship, and planning for Ministers' Week and made recommendations to Perkins.[46]

The 1973–74 academic year saw the founding of a parallel group of laity, the Perkins Lay Advisory Council. Initially under the leadership of Leo Baker of Dallas, the council consisted of laity from the various annual conferences of the region. Its chief aims were to improve communication between the church and the seminary so that United Methodist laity would become better acquainted with Perkins and its faculty and vice versa, and to provide active lay support for the school. By the following year the Lay Advisory Council included 131 United Methodist men and women. As the result of a suggestion by Judge Woodrow Seals of Houston, a member of the council, Perkins held its first Laity Week in May 1974, to give laity the opportunity to come to Perkins for serious study, with classes, seminars, public lectures, and worship services.[47] Since 2004 it has been known as the Perkins Theological School for the Laity and has been held in early March each year.

ENROLLMENT AND ADMISSIONS IN THE SEVENTIES

The 1960s were a time of decline in enrollment in Perkins's bachelor of divinity program, although the total Perkins enrollment, plus the new Ph.D. program, was roughly the same in 1969 as in 1960. From 1970 to 1972 enrollment for the master of theology (M.Th., as the B.D. was renamed) remained similar to that of the previous four years (see appendix B, table 3). From 1973 to 1976, however, the number of new master of theology students increased significantly, so that total enrollment moved up to 461. After 1976 the size of entering M.Th. classes fell back to earlier levels. Three programs contributed to an increase in total enrollment by the late 1970s. First, most M.Th. students now had to complete three and a half to four academic years of credit (instead of three, as previously) because of the internship requirement. This meant that the same number of entering M.Th. students would during their seminary careers tend to produce an increase of as much as one-third in M.Th. enrollment. Second, beginning in 1973 enrollment for the master of sacred music increased to two to three times the average of the previous decade. Third, the numbers of new doctor of ministry students more than made up for the termination of the master of sacred theology degree.

In the 1970s the number of women in the master of theology program rapidly increased, from ten in the fall of 1970 to forty-six in 1975 and seventy-nine in 1980. In 1970 women had constituted 3.9 percent of students seeking the M.Th. degree; by 1980 they were 23.9 percent. In the same period the number of men in that program increased from 246 in 1970 to 301 in 1975, then fell back to 251 in 1980. Without the increase of women entering the program leading to ordination, the total number of M.Th. students would have been much lower.

From the late 1960s through 1973–74, only seven to nine African American students enrolled in all Perkins programs each year. The fall of 1974, though, saw the start of an upward trend: twelve blacks enrolled that fall, followed by twenty-one in 1976, twenty-two in 1978, and twenty-seven in 1980.[48]

The number of Hispanics was modestly larger in the 1970s than previously, increasing to nine in the fall of 1976, seven in 1978, and nine in 1980. In the late 1970s one native American was enrolled in the master of theology program. International students were present in large numbers in the seventies: seventeen to twenty-five each year of the decade. Most numerous were those from South Korea and from sub-Saharan Africa. Usually, 15 to 25 percent of the international students were enrolled for the master of sacred theology and later the doctor of ministry degree.[49]

The 1972 General Conference of the UMC adopted a new social principles statement which, in a section on "the nurturing community," included a passage affirming that "homosexuals no less than heterosexuals are persons of sacred worth, who need the ministry and guidance of the church." In debate on the floor of the conference this passage was amended to add the words, "though we do not condone the practice of homosexuality and consider this practice incompatible with Christian doctrine."[50] With this General Conference action as background, in 1975 Dean Quillian, at David Switzer's recommendation, appointed an ad hoc committee, chaired by Switzer, to discuss issues related to openly homosexual students who might enroll at Perkins. In the spring of 1976 that committee of twelve, including faculty, intern staff, and students, suggested guidelines for the Committee on Academic Procedures in dealing with individual cases. Its guidelines did not come to the Perkins Senate for discussion or action but were intended simply for informal discussion.[51]

In the spring of 1980 the Perkins Committee on Recruitment and Admissions admitted an openly homosexual applicant, a member of the Metropolitan Community Church, to the master of theology program and notified the student. Quillian learned of this action after the fact. Soon a second application arrived from a member of the Metropolitan Community Church, and then a third. Quillian allowed the first admission to stand but asked the committee to hold the other two applications without action until he could consult the appropriate university officials. He also wanted to see what action the UMC General Conference would take regarding homosexuals and ministry at its quadrennial meeting, April 15–25.

At the May 9 meeting of the Perkins Senate the dean read a statement that the school was instituting an interim policy of no admission of openly homosexual students (aside from the one already admitted), arguing that the UMC prohibited the use of church funds for homosexuals, that the master of theology degree "is in order to ordination," and (erroneously at that time) that the UMC prohibited the ordination of homosexuals. The discussion in that meeting and in a senate meeting called for May 13 showed considerable disagreement about the relation of the M.Th. degree to ordination, and Quillian conceded that Perkins admitted people to the master of theology program who were not planning to seek ordination. Nevertheless, since it was impossible to work out a formal policy so late in the semester with full consultation of the Senate, the SMU administration, and the Trustee Committee for Perkins, the dean decided that his directive of no admission would be in effect until it was deliberately changed through established procedures.[52]

The dean called a senate meeting in November 1980 to discuss policy concerning admission of "openly acknowledged" homosexuals to Perkins. After two hours of discussion, the senate requested that the Committee on Recruitment and Admissions study the question and report to the Senate soon.[53] Preparing a report likely to be adopted by the senate involved much consultation, especially between the committee chair, Charles Wood, and the dean, but also between committee members and numerous other faculty members and students, and between Wood and the dean-designate, James Kirby.

On March 20, 1981, the committee brought a two-part report to the senate. In the first part it reported an interpretation of existing admissions policy as it related to the question of admitting homosexuals to Perkins degree programs. This part made clear that intending or being qualified for ordination was not a requirement for admission to any Perkins degree program and that the United Methodist Book of Discipline did not require the school to certify that Perkins students met the church's requirements for ordination. The report explained how the committee dealt with applications, how that process differed from the church's process of certification for ministry, and the need to bring the dean into the committee's deliberations when admitting a particular student "seems likely to have an extraordinary impact on the school." The question of financial aid, it concluded, was a matter distinct from that of admission.[54]

In the second part the committee judged that the existing admissions policy adopted by the senate was generally adequate for dealing with applications from homosexuals. It further declared that "there are no grounds to suppose that homosexuality per se is a disqualification for admission to any Perkins degree program," though in specific situations it might be, and that it was advisable not to try to identify all the specific kinds of situations but rather to deal with each case individually. The committee also judged it best not to adopt a policy of admitting people "without regard to sexual orientation," as there might be some sexual orientations that would be barriers to admission, and it noted that the term *sexual orientation* was itself ambiguous. The committee therefore recommended that the senate "reaffirm its official statement of policy on admissions, as revised in 1977, as the policy of the school, and that it direct the Committee on Recruitment and Admissions to act in accordance with this policy as of this date." After discussion the senate approved this recommendation without a dissenting vote.[55]

Quillian disagreed with the senate's action, but he did not vote because he presided over the meeting. He would have preferred that the matter not be decided until after the new dean took office that summer, and he said he could not conscientiously support admitting homosexuals to seminary "unless I am ready to defend homosexuality as a morally acceptable practice." Yet he was willing for the senate to override his judgment, in which case he hoped the matter would be kept quiet so that he did not have to make a public statement.[56] No record has come to light that he made any public statement about the matter.

THE FACULTY AND ITS WORK

Between 1970 and 1981 the turnover in the faculty was greater than in the 1960s. In these years Quillian made twenty-four appointments to the faculty plus nine to the intern staff (see appendix A). (Intern associate directors were not designated as faculty until 1984.)[57] In the same period twenty-three left the faculty, and three left the intern staff.

The twenty-four faculty appointments included administrators and library staff with courtesy faculty rank. Of these, twelve were in Division I (The Church and Its Ministry). Two in succession were in evangelism (George Hunter and David Watson), two in church music (Roger Deschner and, as a continuing adjunct professor, Jane Marshall), one in pastoral care (Ruth Barnhouse), and three in succession as bishops-in-residence (W. Kenneth Pope in 1972, O. Eugene Slater in 1976, and W. McFerrin Stowe in 1980). Two carried special responsibilities in black studies (Nathaniel Lacy in 1970 and Zan W. Holmes Jr. in 1974), and two had special responsibilities for the Mexican American Program (Alfredo Nañez in 1970 and Roy Barton in 1974).

The one appointment with primary membership in Division II (Christianity and Culture) was Charles B. Thomas in the field of sociology of religion, who joined the faculty in 1978 after Marvin Judy's retirement. In Division III (the Christian Heritage) Quillian made two appointments in church history (Edwin E. Sylvest Jr., with a specialization in Hispanic Christianity, and Richard Heitzenrater in the history of Methodism) and two in systematic theology (Schubert Ogden, who returned in 1972 to the Perkins position he had left three years previously, and Charles M. Wood, who arrived in 1976). During Ogden's mandatory public visit to Perkins before his reappointment, he was heard to remark, "*All* my memories of this place are good!" Five appointments were of faculty in Division IV (Bible): two in Old Testament (Phyllis Bird in 1972 and John Holbert in 1979) and three in New Testament (William W. Mount Jr. in 1970, Virgil P. Howard in 1975, and Harold W. Attridge in 1977).

In 1980 two Bridwell Library staff members were appointed with courtesy faculty rank: Jerry Campbell as director and Roger Loyd as associate director. The new intern program required two to five associate and assistant directors at any one time, including replacements of any who had departed. The nine intern appointments, in order of their arrivals, were James A. Gwaltney, Craig L. Emerick, Zan W. Holmes Jr. (who at first carried both classroom and internship responsibilities), Emma Justes, Rosalie Lawson, Marvest Lawson, Martha Gilmore, Richard E. Stewart, and K. Dale Hensarling.

The departures consisted largely of retirements: thirteen faculty, in contrast to only one in the sixties. The Perkins faculty was no longer so young. Among the retirees was Albert Outler after twenty-eight years at Perkins, during the last five of which he had held a specially designed position as research professor of theology, teaching half time. Other retirees who had begun their Perkins teaching during Merrimon Cuninggim's deanship or earlier were George Baker, Lamar Cooper, Grady Hardin, Marvin Judy, Levi Olan, Kermit Schoonover, Herndon Wagers, and, in 1981, Joe Quillian. Three bishops-in-residence retired in succession—Paul Martin, Kenneth Pope, and Eugene Slater, and in 1973 Alfredo Nañez retired after initiating the Mexican American Program.

More faculty than in previous periods—seven—moved to academic positions elsewhere. In order of their departures they were William C. Robinson, Ronald Sleeth, Carlton Young, Joe Jones, William Mount, William Longsworth, and, in 1980, the librarian Decherd Turner. In three decades as director of Bridwell Library, Turner had overseen a remarkable change in the size and stature of the library collections. One faculty member left to attend graduate school (Nathaniel Lacy), two went into private counseling practice (Robert Elliott and Harville Hendrix), and one moved to a Methodist board position (George Hunter). One member of the intern staff (Emma Justes) went to the faculty of another seminary, and two took positions outside the academy (Rosalie Lawson and Marvest Lawson).

Some departures reflected rank and tenure policy and procedures. This did not always involve a formal negative recommendation by the dean. When Quillian had good reason to believe that a formal rank and tenure review would result in tenure's not being granted, he would talk with the person well ahead of the time of review and encourage him or her to seek another position. By 1970 the criteria for promotion and election to tenure had become more precise, and the faculty had raised its expectations. The initial rank and tenure policy adopted in 1961 had listed several criteria but had not prioritized them. That changed with the policy revision adopted by the senate in 1970.[58] It stated that "the Rank and Tenure Committee's evaluative counsel to the Dean shall weigh teaching and scholarly productivity as the paramount concerns" on the list of seven criteria. (The other five were service to Perkins, SMU, the church, the academy, and the civil and cultural community.) It added that if someone is superior in both paramount criteria and "other factors are reasonably supportive," that person may be promoted. If the person is "merely acceptable" in one of those two, "he or she should evidence unusual strength" in the other to warrant promotion.

During this time the job descriptions of three Perkins faculty members changed. In 1977 Virgil Howard, who had arrived in 1975 as visiting assistant professor of New Testament, became assistant professor of preaching, a position that had been vacated by Ronald Sleeth's departure the previous year. In 1978 Leroy Howe, who was concluding six years as associate academic dean, resumed full-time teaching. The departure that year of Harville Hendrix, who taught pastoral care, had led Howe to reassess his interests, responding to a suggestion from Quillian, with the result that in 1979 Howe became professor of theology and pastoral care.[59] Then, in 1979, Zan Holmes's responsibilities changed, as I shall explain later in this chapter.

In the 1970s faculty members continued to publish extensively, as they had in previous years (see appendix C). In 1972 Fred Carney took the lead in organizing a new outlet for faculty scholarship and dialog: the Faculty Symposium. In its early years the symposium met four to six times each academic year to discuss topics of academic interest to the members. All Perkins faculty members were invited, and attendance varied widely, from a dozen to twenty-five or more. In the 1970s the members gathered in the evening at the Umphrey Lee Student Center for dinner, after which one professor would respond to a paper circulated previously by a colleague. For the first several years papers focused on an agreed-upon theme. In 1972–73 it was "The normative in Christian theology," chaired by Carney; the next year, "The humanum," with John Deschner chairing; then "The Bible in theology and church," led by Victor Furnish. In later years members would present topics of current individual research, or there might again be a common theme—perhaps an important recent book, such as Hans Küng's *On Being a Christian*, which was the theme for 1978–79.[60] The symposium has continued to provide a structured opportunity for intrafaculty dialog.

Several new arrivals in the 1970s reflected the move to ethnic and gender diversity in both the Perkins faculty and intern staff. Although there was ethnic and gender diversity in the Perkins student body well before 1969, the faculty still consisted entirely of men of northern European descent. Faculty members had been concerned about this for some time, but the usual procedures for making new appointments had not changed the situation. If ethnic and gender diversity were to be achieved, it would require actions specifically directed toward doing so.

Procedures for selecting new Perkins faculty had become more explicit and elaborate during the first decade of Quillian's deanship. In the early 1960s there was no formal job description for each position, nor was there a task force for each. When an appointment was needed, the dean held discussions with the faculty of the pertinent division and proceeded from there. By the fall of 1965 a formal statement had emerged, "Procedure for Securing New Faculty Members."[61] After initial discussion between the dean and the faculty of the division that had the vacancy, the division would provide a job description, which would then need to be approved by the faculty, dean, and provost. The division would then develop a list of names, secure information about each, and with the dean establish a ranking of them. There was no task force to carry out this process. The dean would contact the top name on the list and, if matters appeared positive, would invite this person for a formal visit to the campus. After the visit the dean would talk with individual faculty members to assess the response. If it seemed indicated, the dean would place the prospect's name before the faculty for discussion and an advisory vote. With a favorable vote the dean would recommend the appointment to the provost. As the faculty vote was only advisory to the dean, there was no clear number of negative votes that would disqualify the prospect. Instead, the dean was guided by both the tenor of the discussion and the reasons faculty members gave for their votes, as well as by the number of negatives. This 1965 statement had the virtue of clarifying the faculty's formal role in the process, in a context in which faculty members sometimes feared that the dean might be tempted to proceed without adequate faculty consultation.[62]

When the Perkins Senate came into being as a result of the 1968–69 self-study, its by-laws stipulated that one mandate of the Committee on Faculty was to "propose and supervise the process by which the Senate offers its advisory to the Dean in the selection of new faculty members." Pursuing that charge, the Committee on Faculty developed a new statement in the fall of 1969, "Procedure for Selecting and Obtaining New Faculty," which the senate subsequently adopted. Changes from the previous statement included highlighting the requirement of adequate consultation with the appropriate division of the faculty and appointing a task force to draw up a job description and develop a list of names. After the prospect's visit the dean would talk with individual senate members and confer with the task force in deciding whether to place the name before the senate. The new statement also recognized that some circumstances might call for faster action than these time-consuming procedures allowed. It provided that "in unusual circumstances and with the prior approval of the Committee on Faculty," the dean could proceed "more quickly than usual."[63]

Nowhere in either of these two statements is there mention of ethnic or gender diversity as a consideration in the process of faculty selection. This does not mean that faculty members were not concerned about inclusiveness. They and the dean wanted a more inclusive faculty, but up to the fall of 1969 they proceeded on the assumption that this would come about through the usual procedures. This assumption was about to change.

In the latter part of the 1968–69 self-study, Richey Hogg circulated a brief paper, "A Proposal in Three Parts," for use in a self-study open hearing, in which he proposed that Perkins provide and list in its catalog "certain black-oriented studies," as well as "courses related to the interests of those preparing to serve [Perkins's] Latin American constituency." He suggested a number of courses in each category and pointedly observed that these proposals implicitly implied Perkins's adding African American and Latin American members to its faculty. In the same paper he proposed the long-range goal of developing a relationship with the (Catholic) University of Dallas and "the emerging Dallas Catholic seminary."[64]

Quillian and other faculty members kept Hogg's proposal in mind as they moved in the fall of 1969 to implement self-study decisions. In its December meeting, in response to Quillian's report on faculty and staff additions for 1970, the Perkins Senate unanimously approved a motion "that the Committee on Faculty proceed with the investigation of possibilities for the appointment of a Black faculty/staff person and a Mexican-American faculty/staff person, and that the committee move with dispatch but not without concern for our general procedures in such matters."[65]

In January 1970 the Perkins Senate appointed the Task Force for a Black Faculty Member, consisting of four Perkins faculty and Clifton Bullock, a black master of theology student, with Irving Baker, director of the SMU African American Studies Program, as consultant. The task force was so designated because of Perkins's need "to make a special effort to obtain a black faculty member." In the job description the task force identified two main purposes of the appointment: "To assist black students to become effective leaders in the church," and to present to all Perkins students and faculty, white as well as black, "the experience of the black community and especially of the black churches." The appointment might be in any of several specialized fields, provided the person was "gifted primarily in the knowledge and interpretation of the black churches."[66]

In April the dean, following the recommendation of the task force, proposed the Reverend Nathaniel Lacy as assistant professor of practical theology and coordinator of black studies, and the Senate unanimously advised Quillian to proceed with the appointment.[67] Lacy, originally from Louisiana, held a bachelor's degree from Tufts University and had received his B.D. from Perkins in 1960 with honors. For the next decade he had been a pastor and program director in the Southern California–Arizona Annual Conference, where he was well known as a talented teacher, able to translate theology into the experience of the black community. He joined the faculty in the fall of 1970. During the next four years he taught various courses on church and community and the black church, was adviser to the Black Seminarians, the African American student organization at Perkins, on occasion taught SMU undergraduate courses, and was active in the wider Dallas community. In 1974 Lacy left the faculty to pursue doctoral study.

In the summer of 1974 Zan W. Holmes Jr. joined the Perkins faculty. He had received his undergraduate degree from Huston-Tillotson College and his B.D. and master of sacred theology degrees from Perkins. For ten years he had been pastor of Hamilton Park Methodist Church in Dallas and then a district superintendent in the West Texas and North Texas Annual Conferences. A well-known Dallas leader, he had served two terms as a state representative in the Texas legislature from Dallas County. Holmes came to the Perkins faculty and staff in several capacities: as an associate director of the intern program (half time), associate professor of practical theology (to teach one course in preaching each year, not on tenure track), and, succeeding Nathaniel Lacy, as coordinator of black concerns and adviser to the Black Seminarians. At the same time he became pastor of St. Luke "Community" United Methodist Church in East Dallas, then a congregation of 128 members. During his twenty-eight-year pastorate it grew to a membership of more than five thousand.[68] In 1979 Holmes ended his part-time position in the intern program and became associate professor of preaching on a three-fourths time basis while continuing as pastor of St. Luke. At the General Conference of 1992 he was elected a member of The United Methodist Church's nine-member Judicial Council.

In 1979 Richard E. Stewart came to the intern program as an associate director. With a bachelor's from Wiley College in Marshall, Texas, and a B.D. from Perkins in 1960, Stewart had served as a chaplain in the U.S. Army, attaining the rank of lieutenant colonel. Along the way he had received a master of science degree from Long Island University and had given special attention to the field of pastoral care, including consulting and lecturing on alcohol and drug abuse and on racism.[69] Stewart remained with the intern program until 1982.

Also in 1979 Charles B. Thomas Jr. joined the Perkins faculty as assistant professor of the sociology of religion. He had received his bachelor's with honors from Cornell University and his master's and Ph.D. degrees from Harvard, with a dissertation on the clergy and the Boston school desegregation case.[70] Thomas remained on the Perkins faculty until 1985, when he went to the faculty of a northeastern university.

When Quillian retired in 1981, then, the Perkins faculty and intern staff included three African Americans: Holmes, Stewart, and Thomas.

During the same period Perkins added Mexican Americans to the ranks of its faculty and intern staff. In June 1969 the Reverend Leo D. Nieto, of the Austin, Texas, field staff of the United Methodist Board of Missions, sent a letter to Richey Hogg with a copy to Quillian. Nieto said he had read Hogg's "Proposal in Three Parts," from the previous April, as well as SMU Alumni Association reports, and that he did not detect in them the same "seriousness of intent" about the Mexican American population of the Southwest as about the black population. Nieto proposed that Perkins hold a consultation attended by Mexican American alumni, current Mexican American students, Rio Grande Annual Conference representatives, and other resource people to study and plan for a Mexican American/Latin American studies program at Perkins.[71] In response Quillian expressed appreciation for his letter and added "we are indeed serious about an effective program in Mexican-American studies at Perkins, and the idea of a consultation this fall is something that we definitely will pursue."[72]

On December 19, 1969, the Mexican American Consultation took place at Perkins. Forty-six people participated: pastors, district superintendents, and other leaders of the Rio Grande Conference, Bishop O. Eugene Slater (presiding bishop of that conference), Bishop Kenneth Pope (chair of the Theology Committee of the SMU Board of Trustees), laity involved in Hispanic American work in Texas, three students, and eighteen Perkins faculty members. The central question of the consultation was what should be done in the Perkins curriculum "to prepare Mexican-American and Anglo-American ministers more adequately for service in the contemporary church?" How should it be done, and with what leadership?[73] Responses from leaders in the Rio Grande Conference were positive and even more so about what followed.

In April 1970 Quillian announced the appointment of Alfredo Nañez as professor of practical theology and lecturer in Mexican American studies.[74] As a youth, Nañez had intended to study medicine in Mexico City, but the Mexican Revolution intervened. He emigrated to Texas, became a Methodist, enrolled in an academy in San Antonio, learned English, and became a pastor. In 1930 he received his bachelor's degree from Southwestern University, and in 1932 he became the third Hispanic to receive a B.D. degree from the SMU School of Theology. After appointments as a pastor and as a district superintendent, he was for twenty years executive secretary of the Board of Education of the Rio Grande Conference. From 1966 to 1970 he was president of the Lydia Patterson Institute in El Paso, and from there he came to the Perkins faculty. His work at Perkins included teaching one course each semester, continuing his project of writing a history of the Rio Grande Conference, completing a second edition of a Spanish-language hymnal, and helping to plan Hispanic American studies at Perkins.[75] He retired from Perkins in 1973.

Another 1970 appointment had a major long-term impact on the Mexican American Program at Perkins. In the spring of 1970 the Louisiana native Edwin E. Sylvest, of Anglo ancestry, who had taken his B.D. at Perkins in 1962, completed his Ph.D. dissertation at SMU on Franciscan mission theory in New Spain in the sixteenth century.[76] That fall he was appointed assistant professor of church history at Perkins. Although for several years his teaching was primarily in SMU's University College, he was at the same time deeply involved in the planning and development of the Mexican American Program and as an adviser to the Chicano Seminarians, the Mexican American student organization at Perkins. During the 1970s he improved his fluency in Spanish, joined the Rio Grande Conference of the UMC, spent the 1973–74 academic year as a visiting professor at Union Seminary in Mexico City (lecturing in Spanish), learned to read the Aztec language, Nahuatl, and was promoted to associate professor with tenure in 1976. He was Perkins's specialist in the history of Hispanic Christianity.

Following Alfredo Nañez's retirement, Roy D. Barton came to Perkins in January 1974 as director of the Mexican American Program and associate professor of practical theology. Barton, educated at Texas Western University, Trinity University in San Antonio, and Perkins (B.D., 1957), had been a pastor in the Rio Grande Conference, then executive secretary of its board of education, and since 1968 the director of the Conference Council on Ministries.[77] He participated in the initial December 1969 consultation that led to establishment of the program and was strongly committed to its continued development. Barton continued as director of the Mexican American Program until his retirement in 1995.

Between 1972 and 1980 six women joined the Perkins faculty and intern staff. In response to an inquiry in September 1971 from SMU's Ad Hoc Committee on the Status of Women, Quillian explained Perkins's practice in seeking candidates for faculty positions. He observed that Perkins had not given priority to seeking women, but he saw no resistance by Perkins faculty or administrators to appointing women faculty on the same basis as men. He added that he thought Perkins needed to consider women for any faculty appointments in order to break the male monopoly. "This is something that I will discuss with the Perkins Senate," he added.[78]

That November the Perkins Senate approved a job description for a faculty position in Old Testament, since an OT professor would be on leave two of the next three years and Kermit Schoonover would be retiring in 1975. The job description was standard except for the inclusion of an item under "desirable": "Age—preferably a person under 40." And at the end of the list of characteristics, the task force added that it "would like to note its interest in making a special effort to tap all sources of information concerning women, ethnic minority, and Roman Catholic candidates."[79]

In March 1972 Phyllis Bird, who that month received her doctor of theology degree from Harvard Divinity School, made a formal public visit to Perkins, followed soon thereafter by an affirmative senate vote as advisory to the dean. She arrived that fall as assistant professor of Old Testament—the first woman member of the Perkins faculty. Phyllis Bird was a United Methodist with an undergraduate degree in sociology from the University of California and a B.D. from Union Theological Seminary in New York. In addition to her doctoral study at Harvard, she had studied at the University of Heidelberg.[80] Her curriculum vitae at the time of her visit listed various levels of knowledge of twelve languages, including German, Spanish, and Japanese, in addition to an array of ancient Near Eastern languages. When one faculty member did not find French on the list, he asked her about it. "Oh," she said, "I forgot to list French." Bird was promoted to associate professor with tenure in 1978 and remained at Perkins until 1985, when she went to a position at Garrett-Evangelical Theological Seminary.

At the April 1, 1974, meeting of the senate, Quillian announced that Jim Gwaltney had resigned as associate director of the intern program, effective July 1, to become executive director of Growth Seminars, Inc. In the brief discussion that ensued, Phyllis Bird "urged that high priority be given to consideration of a woman for the position."[81]

Before the senate meeting of April 19, when discussion of this position would be on the agenda, two master of theology graduates of the class of 1973, Janice Riggle Huie and Mimi Raper, sent a letter to the Perkins Senate by way of Quillian. They voiced appreciation for their three years at Perkins and briefly retold their serious commitment to ministry in local churches. They expressed the hope that Perkins was willing to affirm and support its women students as well as its women graduates and added that a highly significant expression of that support would be to consider a woman for the post of associate director of the intern program.[82]

The day of the senate meeting another letter arrived, this one from Phyllis Bird. She prefaced her concern with this explanation: "I had no intention on coming to Perkins of being or becoming an advocate or interpreter for women's concerns; I was little educated in the history and psychology of women in the ministry and person-ally ill disposed to the role of advocate or interpreter. However, I find myself forced into this position because I hear no other spokesmen."[83] Then she came to the issue at hand. The crucial area in the Perkins curriculum for women students, she said, is the internship—even more crucial than for men. Unlike in the classroom, where women have shown they can excel, in ministry women find almost no models, do not have other women's previous pastorates from which to learn, and face congrega-tions and supervising pastors with no previous experience with women as pastors.

Women interns often have no opportunities to share their experiences, and none of the supervisors or counselors has had the same sorts of experiences. In this situation, she declared, "the single most important contribution . . . that Perkins can make to its women ministerial candidates is to provide at least one woman on the field education staff with professional training and experience that would enable her to serve both as a model and as an interpreter to women in transition to full time ministry."[84]

Introducing the senate discussion that Friday afternoon, Dean Quillian observed that although an intern staff position was one that technically he could simply recommend to the provost, he welcomed senate contributions to the subject. An hour's discussion followed, at the end of which the dean scheduled another meeting to continue the discussion the following Monday morning.[85] On Monday the senate discussed the issue for nearly two hours, much of it emphasizing the importance of having a woman intern staff member and, on the other hand, pointing to the necessity of acting quickly so as to have a replacement for Jim Gwaltney by July 1. Before adjournment there was consensus on the need to appoint a task force to deal with the opening—a departure from previous procedure concerning intern staff.[86]

On May 10, at the next senate meeting, Quillian proposed for this position the name of a man on the faculty of the Institute of Religion in Houston; he subsequently declined the position. The dean then arranged for William Longsworth, instructor in Christian ethics, to serve as acting associate director in the intern program during 1974–75 and made plans to find a full-time person in the fall, "with careful attention to meeting the particular needs of both competence and quality for Perkins."[87]

The next week John Deschner, acting on behalf of the Committee on Faculty, appointed a new task force to consider a new intern staff appointment. It consisted of three professors, James Ward (chair), Phyllis Bird, and William Longsworth, and Barbara Ruth, the student council president. Deschner told them the main need was to strengthen the intern program's counseling resources, and he encouraged them to take Bird's memorandum seriously.[88] In the fall the task force presented a job description stating that the position "is meant to be filled by a woman," who would be an assistant or associate director in the intern program and might teach part time. On November 8 the senate approved the job description without a dissenting vote.[89]

In April 1975 Quillian placed before the senate the name of the Reverend Emma Justes as associate director of the intern program and counselor to students, and after discussion the senate advised him to proceed with the invitation. Emma Justes had received her B.D. degree from Colgate Rochester Divinity School in Rochester, New York, was an ordained Baptist minister, and was pursuing studies at Princeton Theological Seminary for her Ph.D. degree, which she completed after coming to Perkins.[90] She served on the intern staff from 1975 to 1979, when she left for a position on the faculty of Garrett-Evangelical Theological School.

In 1977 Rosalie Lawson and her husband, the Reverend Marvest Lawson, were both appointed associate directors of the intern program. Rosalie Lawson served in that capacity for two years and Marvest Lawson for one. She had previously been a professor of sociology and before that a missionary in Brazil; he had been a pastor and later a chaplain in the U.S. Navy.[91]

Upon Rosalie Lawson's departure in 1979, the Reverend Martha Gilmore became an associate director. A staff member in the intern program from 1977 to 1979, she had received her master of theology degree from Perkins in 1978. She was the first woman in Dallas County to be ordained as a minister in the Southern Baptist Convention.[92] Gilmore continued as an associate director until 1987 and returned to the staff in an adjunct capacity in the 1990s.

In 1979 Jane Marshall, a composer and conductor of church music who held master of sacred music (M.S.M.) and master of music degrees from SMU, became adjunct professor of church music conducting. She continued as adjunct professor until 1986, teaching in the M.S.M. program and in the summer church music seminar.

After Harville Hendrix left the Perkins faculty in 1978, and with Robert Elliott planning to leave in 1980, it was decided that rather than having two faculty positions in pastoral care plus a counseling chaplain, there would be three faculty pastoral care positions, with the responsibility of counseling chaplain rotating among the three.[93] Leroy Howe filled one of those positions beginning in 1979, as professor of theology and pastoral care.

As the task force for the other two pastoral care positions proceeded, the Perkins student senators brought a resolution to the senate that said, "We are convinced that there are compelling practical and theological reasons for increasing the presence of women in faculty positions at Perkins. . . . Resolved: That a woman be appointed to one or more of the faculty positions now open in Pastoral Care and Counseling." The senate approved the resolution by a large majority. Later in the same meeting, the dean placed the name of David Switzer, then the counseling chaplain, before the senate for an advisory as to whether he should be named associate professor of pastoral care, with tenure. The advisory vote was overwhelmingly favorable, thus filling the second pastoral care position.[94]

In October 1979 Dr. Ruth Tiffany Barnhouse made a stated visit to the campus in regard to the third pastoral care post, was thereafter invited to join the faculty, and arrived in the fall of 1980 as professor of psychiatry and pastoral care. With her bachelor's degree from Barnard College and medical degree from Columbia University, Ruth Barnhouse had been an attending staff psychiatrist at McLean Hospital in the Boston area and clinical assistant in psychiatry at Harvard University. Some years later she received the master of theology degree from Weston College School of Theology in Massachusetts. She then became an adjunct professor in pastoral theology at Virginia Theological Seminary and in 1978 was ordained in the National Cathedral (Episcopal) in Washington, D.C. She continued as a member of the Perkins faculty until her retirement in 1989.[95]

In the spring of 1981, then, the Perkins faculty and intern staff included four women: Barnhouse, Bird, Gilmore, and Marshall. Perkins's appointment of women to the faculty in the 1970s was part of a wider trend. In 1971 women constituted only 3.2 percent of the full-time faculty members of seminaries that were members of the Association of Theological Schools in the United States and Canada. By 1980 the figure had more than doubled, to 7.9 percent and continued to rise thereafter.[96]

While Perkins was bringing greater diversity to the faculty, the school developed policies requiring continuing attention to concerns of minorities and women. In the spring of 1974 the curriculum committee created the Task Force on Minority Curriculum Concerns, chaired by Professor Lamar Cooper, with Barton, Bird, Furnish, Lacy, and Murray as members. During the spring this group conducted four hearings in which it invited students to offer suggestions about curriculum needs related to minorities. The task force was reconstituted that summer with the departure of Lacy and the arrival of Holmes. Now Bird chaired it, with Barton, Hendrix, Holmes, Barbara Ruth, Sylvest, and me as members (I was there ex officio, as chair of the curriculum committee). With the assistance of the task force, the curriculum committee in February 1975 issued a report concerning blacks and Mexican Americans. The objectives of the report were "better education of minority students for ministry," "better education of minority students concerning their own cultures and traditions," and "better education of *all* students (minority and majority) in the appreciation and understanding of the cultures, concerns, and circumstances of all these minorities and of the majority group, in relation to the life of the church." Toward those ends the report offered several proposals about required courses, electives, and the internship. The Perkins Senate approved the proposals without a dissenting vote and encouraged the curriculum committee to continue to implement the principles and proposals of the report.[97]

In May 1975 came a second minority concerns report from the curriculum committee, this time on matters related especially to women. This report took the same form as the earlier one about blacks and Mexican Americans, with parallel objectives and with similar proposals for courses and the internship. Regarding the internship, for example, it proposed that women planning internships hold briefing sessions with women returned from internship, that the training of field instructors include matters relating to women in ministry, and that the program avoid having only one woman in any intern growth group. Again the senate approved without a dissenting vote.[98]

In the meantime, in March 1975, Zan Holmes and I formulated a proposal that the Perkins Senate create a task force on minority concerns with a five-year life, to be reviewed by the senate at the end of that time. The task force would be responsible for considering the needs and interests of Perkins minority groups and refer matters to standing committees as needed, to keep the senate informed about minority concerns "of over-arching community interest," to hear individual cases, to be available for consultation and dialog, to encourage appropriate activity that would educate the Perkins community about minority concerns, and to make an annual report to the senate. In April the senate approved this report without a dissenting vote.[99]

The first annual report of the Minority Concerns Task Force came up for senate consideration in November 1976. The discussion lasted two hours and focused on one sentence of the report: the proposal that "appropriate steps be taken to develop a positive plan for the desegregation of the Perkins faculty." Several suggestions emerged that the senate referred to the Committee on Faculty, chaired by Klaus Penzel, with the request for a report by its February 1977 meeting.[100] The February discussion of the committee's report was so lengthy that it was continued at a called meeting on March 11. This time the senate discussed the report for more than an hour, amended it at several points, and approved it without dissenting vote.[101]

The report as adopted, "Guidelines for Enlarging Minority and Woman Membership in the Perkins Faculty and Intern Staff," began by stating considerations fundamental to the subject: "S.M.U., including Perkins School of Theology, is an Affirmative Action/Equal Opportunity Employer. It is not enough to abide simply by the letter of the civil law in this regard. Our own concern and intentions as a community are such that we desire to obtain, as rapidly as is responsibly possible, increased minority and woman membership on the Perkins faculty and intern staff which will enhance the quality of the faculty and intern staff."[102]

Several guidelines followed. The first was to develop a name bank of "promising minority and woman scholar/teachers in the various theological disciplines and the intern program." Second, where an especially strong name emerged, the dean and Committee on Faculty should consider creating or reshaping a faculty position for that person. Third, where no qualified minority member or woman was found at the time, each task force should consider making an interim appointment while continuing the search—depending on several variable circumstances. Fourth, the task force was to place names in several rough categories: for example, "excellent," "considerably more than qualified," and "qualified." Within the top group the task force should give "priority consideration" to any minority members or women. If no minority members or women were in that top group, however, the task force should not move to a lower grouping, which could lead to a compromise of quality and might constitute reverse discrimination. Fifth and finally, faculty and students should identify and encourage qualified minority and women students to pursue graduate study in religion. The report described these guidelines as part of a process that should be reviewed annually.

The 1970s, then, were a time of continual attention to issues of diversity in the Perkins faculty, intern staff, and curriculum.

THE GROWTH OF THE PERKINS ADMINISTRATION

When Joe Quillian became dean in 1960, Perkins, not including Bridwell Library, had four administrators: the dean, the director of school church relations (J. B. Holt), the director of field education (Floyd Curl), and the director of academic procedures

(Wayne Banks). In addition, it had ten full- or part-time secretaries and several part-time student assistants. During Quillian's deanship Perkins added several full-time administrators: the director of continuing education (Dick Murray), several associate directors of the intern program, and a series of bishops-in-residence (William C. Martin, Paul E. Martin, W. Kenneth Pope, O. Eugene Slater, and W. McFerrin Stowe). Also added were directors or coordinators of the Mexican American Program (Alfredo Nañez and then Roy Barton) and of the black studies program (Nathaniel Lacy and then Zan Holmes).

The first academic associate dean was Herndon Wagers in 1964, followed by Neill McFarland in 1966 and David Switzer in 1967. In 1969 Switzer gave up this office and became Perkins's counseling chaplain until 1979, except for 1972–74, when the office was held by Pat Bujard, a counseling psychologist. From 1969 to 1972 James Ward was the academic associate dean, and the practice began of three-year terms in that office, with the possibility of reappointment for a further term or terms. Ward was followed in 1972 by Leroy Howe, who served until 1978, when Ward returned to the office and served four terms, until 1990. Ward also served as acting dean in 1972–73, when Quillian took the only leave he ever had until he retired as dean in 1981. At Quillian's retirement he said of James Ward, "I probably would not have undertaken the past three years as dean without his close colleague-ship. He and I have never had a minor variance, much less a disagreement," adding that Ward "has enabled me to get on with what I could do with a sense of confident balance." Of Leroy Howe as associate dean, Quillian observed that he "could keep more balls in the air at the same time without bumping or dropping any of them than anyone I have known." His "unfailing competence and considerateness were major contributions to my making it through."[103]

Before 1965 the downtown Dallas Cokesbury Book Store had provided books for Perkins courses. In January 1965 the Perkins Book Store opened for the first time as an auxiliary enterprise of the seminary.[104] Located in the basement of Perkins Hall, it was first managed by Margaret Harvey and then for several years beginning in 1966 by Rowena Hardin.

In 1967 J. B. Holt's title was changed to associate dean for college and church relations. Then in 1972 his position was redefined and he became associate dean of admissions and scholarships, and Robert Bell, a member of the Texas Conference, came as Perkins's director of public relations. William Matthews followed in that office in 1979.

In 1969 Quillian brought in a financial officer, Orlando "Lanny" Folsom, previously in SMU's financial office. Folsom provided invaluable service in that capacity until 1976, when his increasing disability led to redefinition of his responsibilities and then to his retirement in 1977. He was succeeded in 1976 as financial officer by Ken Black, who also had previously served in the SMU financial office. Black continued in this capacity until retirement in 1993. In 1973 Quillian appointed the first Perkins director of development, Brooks Jones.

In 1972 the office of director of community life was created. The first director, for two years, was Elaine Smith, who received a master of theology degree from Perkins in 1972. From 1974 to 1976 the codirectors were Mike Harper and Barbara Harper; he had received his master of theology degree in 1972. Then from 1976 to 1982 the director was Barbara Ruth, a 1978 Perkins graduate with a master of theology degree.

Thus from four administrators in 1960, the Perkins administration had grown to fourteen, not including the associate directors of the intern staff, when Quillian retired. The increase was necessary to handle the growing complexity of the school's needs, to prevent the dean's work from becoming impossible, and to remove administrative burdens from full-time teaching faculty.

Among the actions by the Self-Study Committee on Organization and Administration in 1969 was the proposal that each Perkins administrator submit an annual written report of his or her work to a senate standing committee, after which the committee would provide an appraisal of the administrator's work. Underlying this proposal was the principle that each Perkins administrator was responsible, not only in the university's administrative line of authority but also to "the appropriate deliberative bodies of the Perkins Community."[105] Thereafter each administrator reported to the appropriate committee each spring. Quillian gave his report to the Committee on Faculty, and the committee offered a response.

In the spring of 1970 the Committee on Faculty, with Richey Hogg chairing, introduced in the senate a suggested form for faculty annual reports. These reports were to be available only to the dean and the Rank and Tenure Committee, and it was understood that reporting in this way was for that year only and would be discussed further the following year. The senate accepted the idea and stipulated that reports were to be filed by June 1.[106] In February 1971 the senate revisited the idea, and as all the comments received by then had been favorable, it voted without dissent to continue the practice. Several reasons were offered: the reports would aid accountability, would be a useful resumé and opportunity for reflection for the faculty member, and would be the best way for the dean to know what each was doing.[107]

JOE QUILLIAN AND PERKINS FINANCES

Joe Quillian faced a considerable budget challenge throughout his deanship. In Merrimon Cuninggim's first year as dean, the Perkins expense budget had totaled $183,488.75. Nine years later, in Quillian's first year, it came to $528,250.[108] Prospects were for a continued increase at a similarly rapid rate, given Quillian's plans to enlarge the faculty. In that first year faculty salaries amounted to nearly 55 percent of total expenses, and he knew he needed to increase individual salaries to keep his faculty. There were also increases needed in other areas, such as the Bridwell Library budget, student scholarships, and an enlarged program of continuing education.

One source of increasing income was the original Perkins Endowment Fund. The arrangement was that income from certain Perkins properties would be added to the endowment each year, ensuring continual growth. Another source was the World Service budget of The Methodist Church. In the quadrennium ending in 1960, Perkins had received $116,250 each year from World Service; the figure for the next quadrennium was set at $125,000 per year.[109] It would likely continue to increase, although more slowly than expenses. Another major source was C. L. Lloyd, who endowed the Graduate Program in Religion.

Each year, though, Quillian faced the prospect of a deficit. Joe Perkins had died in 1960, but in the next few years Lois Perkins repeatedly came to Quillian's rescue. In January 1962 she gave $35,000 toward that year's budget. The following May she agreed to give $1 million to the Perkins Endowment Fund on a matching basis. In January 1963 she sent another check for $35,000. In January 1964 another check arrived for $20,000. That same month the Perkins Foundation contributed $200,000 toward the $1 million matching fund.[110] Later that year came another $25,000 to start the Perkins School of Theology Book Store, and in the next three years $34,000 more for building maintenance.[111] Quillian told Willis Tate that one day Lois Perkins had said "she did not have any interest at all in leaving any of her money to her children because 'you can ruin them that way.'" "In an earlier conversation," Quillian reported, "she had said that one thing she wanted to do before she died was to be sure Perkins School of Theology was adequately provided for."[112] Later Quillian wrote Tate, "What a wonderful benefactor she is in every way!"[113]

The other repeated source of gift money in the 1960s was J. S. Bridwell, his daughter, Margaret Bridwell Bowdle, and the Bridwell Foundation. Quillian estimated that from 1962 to 1971 they gave approximately $300,000 for special book purchases, including the Bridwell-DeBellis Collection of Fifteenth-Century Printing, and committed $1.75 million to build the Bridwell Library Annex.[114]

In 1961 Joe Quillian learned that the Southeastern Jurisdiction of The Methodist Church had adopted a program in 1960 for the support of Candler School of Theology and Duke Divinity School that apportioned to each local church, that is, as a required annual contribution, 1 percent of its total budget (aside from capital expenditures). One-fourth of this apportionment would go to annual conference boards of ministry for scholarships for seminary students. The other three-fourths would go to Candler and Duke.[115]

When Quillian learned of this plan, he initiated discussions in the South Central Jurisdiction about creating something similar for Perkins. Other leaders in the jurisdiction joined in the effort, which led to the adoption in the summer of 1964 of the South Central Jurisdiction Ministerial Education Fund. Each local church would contribute 1 percent of its budget, conference boards of ministerial training would receive 25 percent of the money in the fund, and the remainder would be divided between Perkins School of Theology and Saint Paul School of Theology in Kansas City, Missouri, with Perkins to receive 60 percent of that amount and St. Paul 40 percent.[116] Although the plan would take effect only as each annual conference implemented it, Bishop W. Kenneth Pope quickly called special sessions of his two conferences (North Texas and Central Texas) in the fall of 1964 and launched the program. Other annual conferences soon joined in.

Because Quillian was convinced that the seminaries would not receive adequate support from the denomination's Council on World Service and Finance, he began work to create a fund for ministerial education at the denominational level. In his role as president of what was then named the Association of Methodist Theological Schools, he took the lead in developing a plan to present to the 1968 General Conference. He explained, "The consultations were numerous and complex . . . involving many persons from all over the country."[117] The plan that came to the floor of the 1968 Uniting Conference was for the fund to begin in 1970, with an apportionment to each local church of 2 percent of its total budget, excluding various items. As in the two southern jurisdictions, 25 percent would go to the annual conferences for ministerial education. Of the remaining 75 percent, two-thirds would go to the seminaries according to a formula to be worked out.[118]

For all the careful preparations, widespread consultation, and judicious presentation by Quillian on the floor of the Uniting Conference of 1968, the proponents had to overcome strong resistance. Some delegates wanted to amend the plan to give priority to support of non-Methodist theological schools in their areas; this was defeated. Others wanted to change it from an apportionment, which had to be paid, to an "asking," which was voluntary; that too was defeated. Still others wanted to reduce the 2 percent figure to 1.5 percent; that was defeated, and then the conference approved the plan as proposed.[119]

The Ministerial Education Fund made a considerable difference to Perkins finances even in its early years. World Service in 1969–70 was giving $160,000, the South Central Jurisdiction was raising $60,000 to $180,000 for ministerial education at Perkins each year from 1965 to 1969, and the denominational fund in its first fiscal year (1970–71) gave Perkins $281,000. The funds from World Service were gradually decreased as the Ministerial Education Fund was phased in.[120] In 1978 Quillian reported that it was providing Perkins with more than $700,000 a year.[121]

In one of its reports the 1968-69 Perkins Self-Study Committee on Organization and Administration spoke briefly of Perkins's development strategy, which the committee had undoubtedly discussed at length with the dean. Written a year after the Uniting Conference, the report predicted that the Ministerial Education Fund would bring about $250,000 a year to Perkins, far less than it soon actually produced. The report went on to emphasize the importance to Perkins of individual gifts and observed, "The Dean has calculated that if costs double in ten years, 17 million of new endowment will be needed." The report concluded that it would be crucial to free about half the dean's time for development in coming years and to provide him with competent development assistance.[122]

Late in 1969 Quillian was suddenly thrust into the midst of university development, not just that of Perkins. On November 8 Jack Wilkes, the SMU vice president in charge of development, died unexpectedly. With a sense of crisis President Tate asked Quillian to accept an appointment as interim vice president for development and university relations, and Quillian accepted. Tate (speaking of himself in the third person) explained to the trustees that Quillian "could not find it in his heart to say no to him in this kind of request." Quillian made clear, though, as Tate reported it, that he was not interested in remaining permanently in that position, as his primary commitment was as a minister and thus to Perkins.[123] When the university found a replacement in development six months later, Quillian was elated.

Quillian did not appoint a Perkins development officer until 1973: Brooks Jones, who had for the previous three years been the vice president for development at Scarritt College. With the approval of Tate and the SMU Office of Development, Quillian wrote Jones, "Your principal duties will be to organize, coordinate and substantially operate the development program for Perkins. You will work in close relationship with me and also with the Development office of the University."[124] Jones continued in that office until he retired in 1978; he was followed that fall by Charles R. Allen.

A few weeks after his choice of Brooks Jones, Quillian wrote a paper, "Financial Development at Perkins: Past—Present—Future," in which he reviewed the development achievements of deans Hawk and Cuninggim, as well as his own up to that point.[125] He calculated that commitments made during Hawk's tenure totaled $13.3 million, 87 percent of which was from Joe and Lois Perkins. Of Cuninggim's tenure, Quillian wrote, "This was a period of major academic development of the school and modest financial development." He listed financial commitments during the Cuninggim years as the James Seehorn Seneker will, the amount of which Quillian did not provide but was later estimated at $1 million; a commitment from Sollie McCreless of San Antonio of $10,000 each year toward the McCreless Chair of Evangelism; and $793,941 in other funds. Quillian should also have listed for the Cuninggim years the Perkinses' gifts for the construction and furnishing of Selecman

Hall, which together totaled $552,785. Quillian had mistakenly included Selecman Hall as a commitment during the Hawk years.

Quillian's list of commitments during the years of his own deanship up to 1973 totaled $11.35 million, not including gifts from the jurisdictional and denominational Ministerial Education Funds. Nearly half this amount was in two Lloyd Trusts—$5.3 million—the first established in 1968 and the second through renegotiation with Mrs. Lloyd in 1972. Most of the remainder had come either from Lois Perkins or from the Bridwells. The School of Theology's financial condition as of February 28, 1973, as Quillian calculated it, included a total endowment of $13.7 million plus other assets, for a total of $14.88 million. Even so, he projected that Perkins needed to raise $10 million more in the next six or seven years to endow the intern program, the Mexican American Program, continuing education, more scholarships, and five chairs.

Among the major gifts that came to Perkins in 1974 was one from the estate of Mrs. Nell Ayres LeVan (she had made the initial commitment in 1968), estimated at $450,000. The widow of a Humble Oil executive, Nell LeVan directed that the bequest was to endow a chair in worship and preaching, and H. Grady Hardin became its first occupant.[126] Quillian had had notable success in development before hiring a Perkins development officer, and he continued to give major time to it thereafter.

THE APPOINTMENT AND RESIGNATION
OF PRESIDENT PAUL HARDIN

In the fall of 1971 the SMU Board of Governors proposed to create the office of chancellor of SMU.[127] The chancellor would be the university's chief executive officer, and the president would be the chief operations officer. In this arrangement Willis Tate would for the time being be both chancellor and president. This would, as the Board of Governors put it, "begin an orderly transition" to Tate's retirement five years hence.[128] The trustees subsequently adopted this proposal and instituted a search for a new president, while Tate prepared to become chancellor when the new president arrived. In May 1972 the trustees elected Paul Hardin III, then the president of Wofford College in Spartanburg, South Carolina, to succeed Tate as president. Hardin, with undergraduate and law degrees from Duke, had served on the faculty of the Duke Law School. He had been a lay delegate to the 1968 Uniting Conference and was currently president of the National Association of Schools and Colleges of The United Methodist Church. With Hardin's arrival Tate ceased to be president but continued as chancellor.

In his first meeting with the Board of Governors, President Hardin declared, "This is the finest Board I have ever belonged to. I appreciate the chance to work with you. I don't see any way that we can be stopped. I think we can keep working together. I am delighted to be here." Not long afterward he told the board of governors that he wanted "a world-class university, right up in the top," and that his goal was for SMU "to have a $150-million endowment by the end of this decade." His first priority, he said, was endowment. Tate reported that he and Hardin were very similar, even though they would have to do things differently, and that they had "a personal warmth and affection."[129]

From his early days in office Hardin exercised a close watch over SMU's athletic program. In December 1972 he dismissed the popular and successful football coach, Hayden Fry, and subsequently reported to the National Collegiate Athletic Association (NCAA) what he had learned about SMU's infractions of NCAA rules. As he told the board of governors, the NCAA "did have a dossier on SMU before we turned ourselves in, but we are getting full credit for having turned ourselves in. They do seem appreciative of the fact that we took charge and cleaned our own house."[130] Eventually, after its investigation, the NCAA imposed on SMU a two-year probation for football violations and a one-year probation for basketball, with no postseason competition and no appearance on any NCAA-controlled television series for either team while it was on probation. Chancellor Tate later observed that Hardin's "strong initiative was a mitigating factor in our punishment."[131]

In the midst of the NCAA investigation, in June 1974, Hardin resigned his office, effective that June 30, under circumstances that were not given adequate public explanation. Years later, in 1987, when another SMU athletics and governance crisis erupted, the *Fort Worth Star-Telegram* reported that Hardin, by then the president of Drew University, said he was fired by SMU more than a decade earlier. According to the *Star-Telegram*, Hardin said that he heard about the payments to athletes from the parent of a player. "I called Dave Smith [the athletic director] . . .

and he admitted it was going on. . . . I cut his contract from three years to one year, placed him on probation and reported the violation to the Southwest Conference. One month later I was asked to resign."[132]

In July 1974, not long after Hardin's resignation, 243 members of the SMU faculty, including thirty-six Perkins School of Theology faculty, signed and sent a statement to Chancellor Tate. It declared that the action of the board of governors requesting Hardin's resignation had been "improper and ill-timed" and had severely damaged the university's reputation. It further requested that the trustees meet no later than that September to review what had been done, to seek ways of rectifying the damage, and to make sure such actions would not happen again.[133]

The board of trustees held a called meeting in September. Early in a long, tense session, Edwin L. Cox, chair of the board of governors, offered his explanation of the resignation.

When it was indicated that the relationship of the President to the Board of Governors, acting as the Executive Committee to the Board of Trustees with each School Committee represented on it, had eroded so that a change was probably in order, the best course seemed to be to so inform the President and ask him to resign. We are sorry if this action was felt to invade anyone's prerogative, or if lack of due process occurred. . . . The action of asking for Paul Hardin's resignation was not precipitated by any single incident but by numerous events that seemed to be building into an increasingly difficult situation, to the point where a satisfactory relationship between the President and the Board of Governors had not evolved during his two years in office and it did not appear that it could evolve from that point forward.[134]

Cox's statement did not mention Hardin's actions regarding the university's athletic program. Cox declared that the board of governors had no desire "to become involved in the administration of the university."[135]

That meeting of the trustees also received a resolution from the SMU Faculty Senate that, among other things, asked the board to clarify the relationship between it and the board of governors and the president, so that the trustees would maintain their authority over the board of governors and safeguard the powers of the president from interference by the board of governors or by its individual members. A statement also came from the College of Bishops of the South Central Jurisdiction of The United Methodist Church, expressing "grave concern over the manner in which the recent president departed his post as president of the University." As trustees, the bishops, who were not members of the board of governors, pledged themselves "to a more faithful interest in and concern for Southern Methodist University."[136]

Whatever the hopes of faculty and church leaders, there was no public clarification of the relations of the two boards and no evident change in the way in which the board of governors conducted its work. The board of trustees continued to be a large body ill suited to hold the board of governors adequately to account.

When Hardin resigned, the board of governors asked Willis Tate to resume the office of president, and he loyally agreed to do so until a new president could be appointed. That appointment did not come until September 1975, with the election of James H. Zumberge as SMU's next president. At that point Tate retired, both as president and as chancellor, having initially become president in 1954. After his time as president of Drew, in 1989 Hardin became chancellor of the University of North Carolina at Chapel Hill.

During the crisis Perkins faculty members reacted strongly against Hardin's forced resignation and shared in the dismay at the damage to the university's procedures and reputation. Even so, Perkins carried on its educational endeavors much as before, with little, if any, noticeable loss of strength. University governance was a necessary context within which faculty and students worked, but Southern Methodist University, including Perkins, was a stronger educational institution than these university governance failures suggested.

QUILLIAN'S PREPARATIONS FOR RETIREMENT AND A NEW DEAN

Toward the end of his report to the Committee on Faculty in May 1974, Quillian wrote, "Assuming that I will continue to be of adequate usefulness as dean until I am due for mandatory retirement in 1982, I am beginning to think about priorities and procedures for the next eight years." He would, he said, ask the university administration to start the search process for his successor in the early fall of 1980, anticipating the new dean's taking office on June 1, 1981. In his final year Quillian would, he said, take care of his files, be available for advisory help to his successor, and transfer his contacts with major benefactors to the new dean.[137]

In 1976, though, the idea arose of his being elected a Methodist bishop that summer. He was approached about this possibility by friends in the Southwest Texas and Rio Grande conferences, and he agreed to serve if elected, whereupon those two conferences endorsed him for the office. Four bishops were to be elected, and for several ballots he was in contention, with a high-water mark of one hundred votes. After he failed to be elected, he confessed to being somewhat disappointed, mainly because he did not like to lose at anything, even a game of gin rummy. He knew, however, that he could work with these two annual conferences as dean, and he was "too accustomed to openness of colleagueship, substantive decisions consultatively arrived at, and steady mutual supportiveness to be able to adjust to a 'new style' of doing church business." So, he said, he went back "quite happily to the work where I know who I am and what I am doing."[138]

As the time of his retirement drew nearer, Quillian continued to be troubled that the future of Perkins might not be financially secure. In a long memo in the fall of 1978 to the Trustee Committee for the School of Theology, he tried to make sure that the Trustee Committee understood Perkins's financial situation and its future prospects. In 1977–78, he wrote, Perkins had had a deficit of $396,134, of which $370,967 consisted of charges by the university for services to the seminary and a charge for plant. He thought the plant charges reasonable but questioned the charge for services. The university's policy was to absorb Perkins's deficit into the university's deficit. Even so, he believed strongly that Perkins should "carry her own full weight financially," which would have required at least $275,000 more income than it had. His conclusion was that either Perkins must receive considerably more endowment and current gift support or the university would insist that the seminary cut its expenditures.[139]

The financial picture led him to a second concern, about the office of Perkins dean. He explained that he had tried to do too much by himself. He had worked "seven day weeks, ten hour days" but without the vision or effectiveness that a better work schedule would have allowed. It was important, he said, for his successor not to make the mistakes he had made. The office of dean of Perkins should be redesigned to free the dean from numerous day-to-day details, which should be left to an associate dean, operating as "executive dean." The Trustee Committee also needed to be redesigned, he continued, so that it exercised trust responsibilities for the seminary's policies.[140] Looking back, one wonders how much of the problem was the result of organizational structure and how much was owed to Quillian's own ways of working. Even so, his work had greatly strengthened Perkins's financial and other resources.

Well before the conclusion of his deanship, in January 1979 Quillian prepared an eleven-page document, "Concerning the Office of Dean of Perkins School of Theology," for the use of the provost and others who would have a role in choosing the next dean.[141] He explained that no retiring dean should try to influence who would be his or her successor. He felt, however, that he had a duty to offer comments about the office of dean of Perkins and its essential duties. There followed pertinent history of the three most recent deans (Hawk, Cuninggim, Quillian), Quillian's ideas about how the office should be reconceived (similar to the account in his earlier letter to the Trustee Committee), a long list of duties of the office, and desirable characteristics of a dean and associate dean.

Late that February, Quillian wrote James Brooks, the provost, asking to be relieved of his duties as dean on June 1, 1981, and asking for a year of terminal leave thereafter, when he could be available for consultation with his successor and winding up various important matters. He said he thought it desirable to act then so that the provost could move ahead with the process of choosing his successor.[142]

The following August the provost announced the ten-member Advisory Decanal Selection Committee for the Perkins School of Theology. Its chair was Alan Coleman, dean of the Cox School of Business (by then it was customary to have decanal search committees chaired by another dean). The vice chair was Professor Schubert Ogden, and the committee included two other Perkins professors (John Deschner and myself), one SMU professor from outside Perkins (Lloyd Pfautsch), one student (Mary Lou Santillán Baert), one representative of the alumni/ae (Lynn Mims), one representative of the active Methodist pastorate (Jack Heacock), Elizabeth Perkins Prothro (daughter of Joe and Lois Perkins) representing the board of trustees, and resident bishop W. McFerrin Stowe.[143] The committee drew up a description of the position that succinctly listed the essential duties of the office. It included a phrase recognizing but not mandating Quillian's idea of dividing its responsibilities: "Overseeing all administration of the School, . . . [and] appropriately dividing the several other responsibilities of the Dean's office with an Associate (or Executive) Dean."[144] The committee gathered a long list of names from which it identified a few people to be seriously considered. In the fall of 1980 James E. Kirby Jr., dean of the Theological School of Drew University, came to Dallas for a quiet visit with the selection committee, followed in early November by a public visit, and then on November 6 by an announcement to the Perkins Senate and the general public of his appointment as dean. Kirby would take office the following summer.[145]

Joe Quillian retired in 1981 after twenty-one years as dean and took a year of leave, most of it in the State of Washington, where he devoted much of his time to fishing. On the foundation laid by deans Hawk and Cuninggim, Quillian had left Perkins with a stronger and more diversified program of theological education.

1. Faculty minutes, December 8, 1967; Joe Quillian, "A Preliminary Comment Concerning a Perkins Self-study," December 8, 1967, Joseph D. Quillian Jr. Papers, Bridwell Library.
2. Quillian, "Preliminary Comments Concerning a Self-Study of Perkins School of Theology," March 6, 1968, Quillian Papers.
3. Ibid.
4. Ibid.; "Perkins School of Theology Self-Study 1968–69, Structure of Committees," April 22, 1968; Quillian to Self-Study Steering Committee, September 5, 1968; "The Committees," later undated document, all in Quillian Papers.
5. Minutes of the Self-Study Committee on Curriculum, November 15, 1968–January 22, 1969; Frederick S. Carney, "Toward the Renewal of Perkins: A Preliminary Document on Academic Programming Employing a Macro-Model," undated but distributed in the Perkins community by early September 1968; "Curriculum Committee of the Self-Study: Syllabus of Questions," November 13, 1968; Joseph L. Allen, "A Progress Report for the Curriculum Self-Study Committee," January 23, 1969; Victor P. Furnish, "Draft Projection of a Possible Advanced Degree Program in Pastoral Studies," February 20, 1969, all in Quillian Papers; and appointment books for 1968 and 1969, in the author's personal files.
6. John Holbert, in discussion at the Perkins Faculty Symposium, February 9, 2009.
7. Joe Quillian to the Perkins Faculty, September 24, 1968; minutes, Community Convocations, April 29 and May 1, 1969, Quillian Papers; and my personal appointment books for 1968 and 1969.
8. Faculty minutes, May 9, 1969.
9. "Proposed Articles of Operation and By-Laws for the Senate of the Perkins School of Theology, Southern Methodist University," April 28, 1969, 2, Quillian Papers.
10. Ibid., 1, 4, 7.
11. For further appraisal of the senate, see James M. Ward, "Dean Quillian as Dean of the Perkins Faculty," *Perkins Journal* 34 (spring 1981): 8–14; and Joseph L. Allen, "The Policy Process at Perkins in the Quillian Years," *Perkins Journal* 34 (spring 1981): 15–23.
12. "A Reconnaissance Report on the Financial Policy Questions Facing the Perkins School of Theology," April 28,1969, Quillian Papers.
13. "A Brief Survey and Recommendations Concerning Administration," April 28, 1969, Quillian Papers.
14. "Report on Buildings and Grounds," no author, no date, Quillian Papers.
15. "Communications," no author, no date, Quillian Papers.
16. Faculty minutes, May 9, 1969.

17. "Self-Study Report on Curriculum and Degrees," March 1969, 1, Quillian Papers.
18. Victor Furnish, in discussion at the Perkins Faculty Symposium, February 9, 2009.
19. "Self-Study Report on Curriculum and Degrees," 10–13, 14–16.
20. Ibid., 17; Perkins catalog, 1970–71, 60.
21. Class schedules for 1970–72, Perkins Registrar's Office; Lewis Howard Grimes, *A History of the Perkins School of Theology*, edited by Roger Loyd (Dallas: Southern Methodist University Press, 1993), 144–45.
22. "Part Two of the Self-Study Report on Curriculum and Degrees, Sections III through VII"; "Self-Study Report on Curriculum and Degrees," both in Quillian Papers.
23. "Part Two of the Self-Study Report on Curriculum and Degrees," 1–11; "Self-Study Resolutions on Curriculum and Degrees," April 23, 1969, 5, Quillian Papers.
24. Catalog, 1973–74, 52–56, and 1974–75, 49.
25. Ibid., 1973–74, 52–56, and 1975–76, 54.
26. For discussion of these arguments see Carney, "Toward the Renewal of Perkins," 5, 18; and Allen, "A Progress Report," 26–28.
27. "Subcommittee on the Future of the GPR to the Steering Committee of the Graduate Program in Religion," January 20, 1976, Graduate Program in Religious Studies Papers, Office of the Graduate Program in Religious Studies; *Bulletin of the School of Humanities and Sciences*, 1977–78, 148–50.
28. Quillian to Self-Study Steering Committee, September 5, 1968, 11–12.
29. Memo to the Perkins Community from the Committee on Academic Life and Work, March 19, 1969; "Self-Study Resolutions on Academic Life and Work," April 23, 1969, both in Quillian Papers.
30. Merrimon Cuninggim, "The State of the School," *Perkins Journal*, spring 1952, 4.
31. Catalog, 1957–58, 53.
32. Ibid., 33.
33. Faculty minutes, October 24, 1958.
34. Ibid., April 3, 1959.
35. Quillian, "A Preliminary Comment Concerning a Perkins Self-study."
36. Quillian, "Preliminary Comments Concerning a Self-Study of Perkins."
37. H. Richard Niebuhr, Daniel Day Williams, and James M. Gustafson, *The Advancement of Theological Education* (New York: Harper and Brothers, 1957), 118–21; Louis W. Bloede, "The Intern Year," in *Theological Field Education: A Collection of Key Resources*, edited by Donald F. Beisswenger, Tjaard G. Hommes, and Doran McCarty III (Mill Valley, Calif.: Association for Theological Field Education, 1981), 3:239.
38. "Self-Study Report on Curriculum and Degrees," 2–3, 17–18.
39. Faculty minutes, May 9, 1969; "Self-Study Resolutions on Curriculum and Degrees."
40. "Claus Herman Rohlfs, Sr.," *Southwest Texas Conference Journal*, 2004, 290–91.
41. Claus H. Rohlfs, "A History of the Development of the Perkins Intern Program," *Perkins Journal*, winter 1978, 1–12.
42. Ibid., 12–14.
43. "Program of Continuing Education, Perkins School of Theology, Southern Methodist University, 1976," 3, Quillian Papers.
44. Faculty minutes, May 16, 1966; "Program of Continuing Education."
45. Perkins Continuing Education Office, "Continuing Education at the Perkins School of Theology," 1967 brochure, Quillian Papers.
46. Catalog, 1972–73, 23; 1973–74, 23–24.
47. Ibid., 1973–74, 24–25, and 1974–75, 26–27, 125.
48. *Black Seminarians at Perkins: Then and Now* (Dallas: Bridwell Library, 1994), n.p.
49. From records in the Perkins registrar's office; Perkins School of Theology directories.
50. *Journal of the General Conference of The United Methodist Church*, 1972, 461; *The Book of Discipline of The United Methodist Church, 1972*, 86, paragraph 72.
51. David Switzer to Quillian, September 10, 1975; Wayne Banks and James Ward to members of the Switzer Ad Hoc Committee, March 10, 1976, both in Quillian Papers.

52. Joseph D. Quillian Jr., "Current Reference and Procedure Concerning Applications for Admission to P.S.T. by Homosexuals," May 9, 1980; Joseph D. Quillian Jr., "Concerning Admission of Homosexuals to Perkins School of Theology," May 13, 1980; Joseph D. Quillian Jr., "Present Policy Concerning Application to Perkins by Homosexual Persons," May 19, 1980, all in Quillian Papers; Perkins School of Theology Senate minutes, May 9, 1980. The 1976 *Book of Discipline of The United Methodist Church* prohibited giving church money to any gay group or "to promote the acceptance of homosexuality" (paragraph 906.13). Contrary to Quillian's arguments to the Perkins Senate in May, the 1980 General Conference on April 21 had actually voted down an amendment that would have prohibited the ordination or appointment in the UMC of any "self-avowed, practicing homosexual." That General Conference left the decision to the discretion of each annual conference (*Journal of the 1980 General Conference of The United Methodist Church*, 316–18).
53. Senate minutes, November 10, 1980.
54. Charles M. Wood, for the Committee on Recruitment and Admissions, to the Perkins Senate, "The Admission of Homosexuals to Perkins," March 16, 1981, Quillian Papers.
55. The Committee on Recruitment and Admissions to the Perkins Senate, "Report and Recommendation," March 16, 1981; Senate minutes, March 20, 1981.
56. Quillian to Charles M. Wood, March 2, 1981, Quillian Papers.
57. Senate minutes, May 4, 1984.
58. "Rank and Tenure Policy and Procedures," adopted by the Perkins Senate, May 8, 1970, Quillian Papers.
59. Leroy Howe, interview by Neill McFarland, 2000, SMU Archive Series.
60. I am relying on my memory and a personal file in regard to the early years of the symposium.
61. "Procedure for Securing New Faculty Members," attached to faculty minutes for October 10, 1965, Joseph Allen Papers, Bridwell Library.
62. This account is drawn from the statement itself, supplemented by my memory of how the process actually worked.
63. "Proposed Articles of Operation and By-Laws for the Senate"; catalog, 1971–72, 132; W. R. Hogg, chair of Committee on Faculty, memo to the Perkins Senate, December 10, 1969, with attachments, "Procedure for Selecting and Obtaining New Faculty," and the earlier "Procedure for Securing New Faculty Members," Quillian Papers; senate minutes, January 23, 1970.
64. W. Richey Hogg, "A Proposal in Three Parts," April 28, 1969, Quillian Papers.
65. Senate minutes, December 12, 1969.
66. "Task Force Statement Concerning a Black Faculty Member," report to the Perkins Senate, February 11, 1970, Allen Papers.
67. Senate minutes, April 10, 1970.
68. *Perkins Perspective* 14, no. 1 (September–October–November 1974): 7; board of trustees minutes, May 10, 1974; conference statistician's report, *Journal of the North Texas Conference* 2 (1974); *North Texas Conference Journal*, 2002, 358.
69. *Perkins Perspective* 19, no. 1 (fall 1979): 6.
70. Ibid., 2.
71. Leo D. Nieto to W. Richey Hogg, June 25, 1969, Quillian Papers.
72. Quillian to Nieto, July 1, 1969, Quillian Papers.
73. Papers on the Perkins Consultation on Mexican-American Studies, December 18, 1969, Quillian Papers.
74. Senate minutes, April 10, 1970.
75. Alfredo Nañez, "Biography of Alfredo Nañez," *History of the Rio Grande Conference of The United Methodist Church* (Dallas: Bridwell Library, 1980), v; Walter N. Vernon, "Nañez, Alfredo," in Roy R. Barkley, ed., *The New Handbook of Texas* (Austin, Texas: Texas State Historical Association, 1996), 4:935–36; *Perkins Perspective* 25, no. 2 (winter 1985–86); James M. Ward to participants in the Consultation on Mexican-American Studies (no date), Quillian Papers.
76. Edwin E. Sylvest Jr., *Motifs of Franciscan Mission Theory in Sixteenth-Century New Spain Province of the Holy Gospel* (Washington, D.C.: Academy of American Franciscan History, 1975).

77. *Perkins Perspective* 13, no. 2 (December 1973–January 1974–February 1974).
78. James Early, associate dean of faculties of humanities and sciences, to Quillian, September 24, 1971; Quillian to Early, September 28, 1971, Quillian Papers.
79. Attachment to Senate minutes, November 11, 1971.
80. *Perkins Perspective* 11, no. 4 (June–July 1972).
81. Senate minutes, April 1, 1974.
82. Janice Riggle Huie and Mimi Raper to Perkins Senate c/o Dean Joseph D. Quillian Jr., April 18, 1974, Quillian Papers.
83. Phyllis Bird to Perkins Senate, April 19, 1974, Quillian Papers.
84. Ibid.
85. Senate minutes, April 19, 1974.
86. Ibid., April 22, 1974.
87. Quillian to Huie and Raper, May 17, 1974; Quillian to the Perkins Senate, May 21, 1974, Quillian Papers.
88. John Deschner to James Ward, Phyllis Bird, Barbara Ruth, and William Longsworth, May 17, 1974, Quillian Papers.
89. Committee on Faculty to the Perkins Senate, "Job Description for a Staff/Faculty Position in Field Education," October 1, 1974; senate minutes, November 8, 1974.
90. Senate minutes, April 18, 1975; *Perkins Perspective* 15, no. 1 (September–October–November 1975): 5.
91. *Perkins Perspective* 17, no. 1 (fall 1977): 1, 3.
92. Ibid., 3.
93. Senate minutes, October 13, 1978.
94. Ibid., January 26, 1979.
95. Ibid., October 5 and November 9, 1979; *Perkins Perspective* 19, no. 3 (spring 1980): 1; board of trustees minutes, May 7, 1999.
96. William L. Baumgartner, ed., *Fact Book on Theological Education for the Academic Year 1987–1988* (Vandalia, Ohio: Association of Theological Schools in the United States and Canada, n.d.), 25.
97. Curriculum Committee to the Perkins Senate, "Minority Curriculum Concerns: Objectives and Curriculum Proposals Related Especially to Blacks and Mexican-Americans," February 10, 1975 (attachment to the senate minutes); senate minutes, February 14, 1975.
98. Curriculum Committee to the Perkins Senate, "Second report on Minority Curriculum Concerns: Objectives and Curriculum Proposals Related Especially to Women," May 2, 1975 (attachment to the senate minutes, May 9, 1975); senate minutes, May 9, 1975.
99. Zan Holmes and Joe Allen to the Task Force on Minority Curriculum Concerns, March 3, 1975 (attachment to the senate minutes); senate minutes, April 18, 1975.
100. "Annual Report of the Minority Concerns Task Force to the Perkins Senate," April 23, 1976 (attachment to the senate minutes of November 12, 1976); senate minutes, November 12, 1976.
101. Senate minutes, February 18 and March 11, 1977.
102. "Guidelines for Enlarging Minority and Woman Membership in the Perkins Faculty and Intern Staff," March 14, 1977 (attachment to the Senate minutes of March 11).
103. "Dean's Report to the Committee on Faculty, 1980–81," April 23, 1981 (senate minutes, May 8, 1981).
104. Faculty minutes, January 8, 1965.
105. "A Brief Survey and Recommendations Concerning Administration," 6, 8.
106. Senate minutes, May 8, 1970.
107. Ibid., February 12, 1971.
108. Board of trustees minutes, May 11, 1951; "Expense Budget, 1960–61," Quillian Papers.
109. Projected annual budgets in the Quillian Papers.
110. Faculty minutes, January 12, 1962, January 18, 1963, January 10, 1964; executive committee minutes, May 31, 1962.
111. Joseph D. Quillian Jr., "Financial Development at Perkins: Past, Present, Future" (no date, but internal evidence indicates that it was written no earlier than February 28, 1973), 3, Quillian Papers.

112. Quillian to Willis Tate, April 24, 1964, Quillian Papers.
113. Quillian to Tate, December 1, 1966, Quillian Papers.
114. Quillian, "Financial Development at Perkins," 3.
115. Joseph D. Quillian Jr., "Outline of the Ministerial Education Fund," May 9, 1979, 1, Quillian Papers.
116. *Daily Christian Advocate, South Central Jurisdiction* 7 (June 29, 1964): 8, and (July 2, 1964): 2.
117. "Outline of the Ministerial Education Fund," p. 2.
118. *Daily Christian Advocate: Proceedings of the Uniting Conference of The Methodist Church and the Evangelical United Brethren Church, 1968*, Dallas, April 26, 1968, 225.
119. Ibid., April 30, 1968, 365–70, 377—87.
120. The figures are from Perkins budget estimates in the Quillian Papers.
121. Joseph D. Quillian Jr., "Basic Information and Proposals Concerning Perkins Finances and the Future of the School," a report to the Trustee Committee for Perkins School of Theology, December 7, 1978, 6, Quillian Papers.
122. "A Reconnaissance Report," 7–8, 12.
123. Board of trustees minutes, November 14, 1969.
124. Quillian to Brooks Jones, February 5, 1973, Quillian Papers.
125. Quillian, "Financial Development at Perkins."
126. Senate minutes, September 13, 1974; Quillian, "Financial Development at Perkins," 3, Quillian Papers.
127. In 1963 the Executive Committee of the SMU Board of Trustees was reorganized to become the Board of Governors. Thereafter, most of its nineteen members were businessmen (and, in a few instances, women) from the Dallas area. It met frequently to make decisions about the university, subject to approval by the large and unwieldy board of trustees at its next meeting, which approval was routinely given.
128. Board of governors minutes, September 2, 1971.
129. Ibid., October 5, 1972, November 17, 1972, January 4, 1973.
130. Ibid., March 7, 1974.
131. Ibid., September 5, 1974.
132. Reported in the SMU *Daily Campus*, March 11, 1987, citing the *Fort Worth Star Telegram* of the previous day.
133. Attachment to the board of trustees minutes, September 27, 1974.
134. Board of trustees minutes, September 27, 1974.
135. Ibid.
136. Ibid.
137. Joseph D. Quillian Jr., "Dean's Report to the Committee on Faculty, 1973–74," 8–9 (senate minutes).
138. Joseph D. Quillian Jr., "Reflections on Not Being Elected a Bishop," July 15, 1976, Quillian Papers.
139. Joseph D. Quillian Jr., "Basic Information and Proposals Concerning Perkins Finances and the Future of the School," December 7, 1978, 1–2, 4–5.
140. Ibid., 6–7.
141. Joseph D. Quillian Jr., "Concerning the Office of Dean of Perkins School of Theology," January 30, 1979, Quillian Papers.
142. Quillian to James E. Brooks, February 26, 1979, Quillian Papers.
143. Board of governors minutes, September 6, 1979.
144. "Southern Methodist University, Perkins School of Theology, Administrative Position of Dean," no date (but approved by the decanal search committee in fall 1979), in the author's personal files.
145. Schubert M. Ogden to the Senate of Perkins School of Theology, November 6, 1980, in the author's personal files.

Bridwell Library

Bridwell Library came into existence as a part of the new Perkins quadrangle, dedicated in February 1951 while Eugene Blake Hawk was dean. Hawk had taken two steps that were especially important for Bridwell's early history. The first (with Joe Perkins's help) was persuading Joseph S. Bridwell and his daughter, Margaret Bridwell Bowdle, of Wichita Falls, Texas, to give the money—a quarter of a million dollars—for construction of the new library building. The second was appointing Decherd H. Turner as its first librarian.

DECHERD TURNER AND BRIDWELL LIBRARY, 1950–1980

With a bachelor of divinity degree from Vanderbilt Divinity School and graduate work in library science at George Peabody College in Nashville, Decherd Turner came to Bridwell Library from the post of librarian of the religion section of the Joint University Libraries at Vanderbilt University. Up to that time Kate Warnick had been the librarian of the School of Theology library, much appreciated by students and faculty alike. From the late fall of 1918 she had looked after the theology books as an assistant to the university librarian. Then, after construction of the original Kirby Hall in 1924, she became the School of Theology librarian, in which capacity she oversaw the extraction of about four thousand theological books from the general university collection in Dallas Hall and their move to new quarters. From then to 1950 she enlarged the theology school's library collection to thirty-five thousand volumes.[1] After Turner's appointment she remained on the library staff as reference librarian.

Turner arrived on his twenty-eighth birthday, September 1, 1950, during construction of the new building. That December he supervised the library's move from the old Kirby Hall to its new quarters. He and Warnick had two hundred boxes constructed, each to hold books from one shelf. She oversaw the packing of the boxes at the old Kirby Hall, and he supervised their unloading at the new building.[2] The new library opened on December 18, and the new quadrangle, including the library, was dedicated on February 8, 1951.[3]

When asked why he had left his position at Vanderbilt to come to Dallas, Turner replied that he was more interested in building a collection than in maintaining one.[4] Building it became his crusade. He devoted his acquisition efforts during the 1950s mainly to enlarging what he later described as "a useful collection of Nineteenth- and Twentieth-Century works." By the spring of 1961 Bridwell Library holdings had more than doubled to 76,035 volumes, with an expenditure for books, periodicals, and bindings since the library opened of $161,724.10.[5] That was a huge amount for the library budget at that time, but Turner found it insufficient. At the end of his first year, for example, the library budget was $1,300 in debt. After conferring with Dean Cuninggim, who found it difficult to absorb this amount, Turner called Joe Bridwell in Wichita Falls, who sent him the money the next day. In addition to Bridwell's contributions, Perkins had in 1947 received a large gift from Annie Hughey of Charlotte, Texas. In 1949 she requested that the income from her gift be used for Bridwell Library. Originally established with oil property valued at $250,000, the Annie Hughey Fund continued to grow after her death in 1969. In later years income from the fund went toward acquiring books for the general theological collection.[6]

Page Thomas, a long-time library staff member, remembered that Turner was good at obtaining what he wanted for the library and its collections; he managed to buy most sixteenth- to nineteenth-century English titles by persuading the faculty this material was background for Wesley studies. Since Albert Outler agreed, this argument was difficult to challenge. Later, when faculty members questioned Turner's purchase of fifteenth-century titles, he argued they were important for understanding Augustine and the influence of the early church fathers.[7]

From the time he came to Bridwell Library, Decherd Turner worked at cultivating the Bridwells' interest in books and in the library, as well as that of Elizabeth Perkins Prothro and her husband, Charles. Turner corresponded with them and frequently went to Wichita Falls, sometimes to attend the Perkins Lectures at First Methodist

Church there, sometimes to visit Bridwell when he was ill, sometimes to deliver a Christmas gift—characteristically, a book. On one occasion he sent Joe Bridwell letters from some Perkins students saying what the library meant to them. Elizabeth Perkins Prothro, whom Turner encouraged to develop what became a major Bible collection, later spoke of how he had increased people's knowledge of books and of libraries. Through his efforts the friends of Bridwell Library became interested both in books and in Turner himself. Bridwell later wrote a fellow book lover, "I am sure when you get to see Decherd in operation at Dallas you will really find what a dynamo he is and that he is a continuous performer."[8]

During Turner's first decade he was able to bring several special collections to the library, including the Sadie and David Lefkowitz Collection of Judaica, which the Sisterhood and Brotherhood of Temple Emanu-El in Dallas established in 1951 to honor the rabbi and his wife. This collection has since grown to more than three thousand volumes on Jewish history and culture. The next year saw Turner's acquisition of the Steindorff Collection of books on Egyptology, including seventeen hundred books and many offprints, pamphlets, photographs, clippings, and letters. In 1956 Turner accepted from Dan Ferguson and his wife a large collection of books on American history, especially of the Southwest and Texas. That occasioned dismay on the part of the director of SMU Libraries, Robert M. Trent, who thought that collection was worthless for scholars, especially those in the School of Theology.[9] Bridwell Library, though, was independent of the SMU librarian's authority, and Turner could have whatever gifts he chose to accept.

A noteworthy acquisition was the Methodist Historical Library, collected for many years by Bishop Frederick D. Leete. With the encouragement of Bishop William C. Martin, Leete gave the collection to SMU in 1956. When it was housed in Bridwell Library and dedicated on February 6, 1957, it included more than three thousand books, many of them first editions of works by John and Charles Wesley. The Leete collection was a major supplement to the larger Methodism collection already in Bridwell. Also in the Leete collection were more than ninety manuscript letters of John Wesley, a few letters of Charles Wesley, more than four hundred Methodist Disciplines, and other valuable items. Kate Warnick was appointed the collection's curator and continued in that capacity until 1979.[10] During Turner's years Bridwell also received the papers and libraries of bishops John M. Moore, Edwin Mouzon, Hiram A. Boaz, A. Frank Smith, William C. Martin, and other church leaders.

Foremost among the library's treasures is the Bridwell-DeBellis collection. In December 1961 Joe Zeppa of Tyler, Texas, called Eugene McElvaney, who at that time chaired the SMU Board of Trustees, and told him about a collection of 206 items of fifteenth-century printing—incunabula (from a Latin term referring to a cradle)—owned by a California friend of his. Frank V. DeBellis, Zeppa said, wanted to sell it for $100,000—a bargain price—but wanted it to be kept intact and to remain in the United States. When McElvaney relayed this information to Decherd Turner, he thought it too good to be true, but he agreed to look at the list of books. Turner did so on December 27 and pronounced it "amazing, or else the most skilled con job I've ever seen."[11]

The Executive Committee of the SMU board advised McElvaney to ask DeBellis to delay any decision so that SMU could determine whether the library could purchase the collection. Both Turner and Quillian contacted Bridwell, who hesitated, asking which was more important, enlarging the library building or acquiring this collection. Nonetheless, in mid-February Turner flew to San Francisco, where DeBellis met his plane. Turner took two nights and into a third day to look through the collection. Examples of its treasures were three early printings of the Bible (1475, 1478, and 1479), four editions of Augustine's *City of God* (1467 to 1483), and the first printing of Euclid's *Elements of Geometry* (1482). After examining only a fraction of the books, Turner wrote Quillian, "I'm three-fourths convinced we must bend every effort to get it. If forced to choose between bricks and books, let's take the books. . . . P.S.: In many ways I feel like the N.T. character who, after seeing the fruition of all his hopes, said, 'Lord, let thy servant depart in peace.'"[12] After Turner returned to Dallas, Bridwell wrote him, "[I] wish I could buy a little of your enthusiasm, but I am sure it is well founded."[13]

Quillian and McElvaney invited Turner; Bridwell; Hawk; Willis Tate, SMU president; Sterling Wheeler, SMU vice president; and Earl Hoggard, a pastor who was a friend of Bridwell's, to a meeting on February 21. As Quillian recounted it years later, McElvaney explained the situation, said they needed $100,000, and reported that Turner was willing to give $3,000 of his meager salary. At that point Quillian broke in and said, "I think we ought to give Mr. Bridwell the privilege of giving $100,000 for what will be the Bridwell-DeBellis Collection." Bridwell rose to the occasion and urged, "Let's call [DeBellis] now. He might drop dead of a heart attack." When Turner was asked how he was going to move the books, he replied that they should not move them all together but divide them up, so as not to "risk these foundation stones of Western civilization." Quillian thought Turner was being facetious, but he was dead serious. Turner would not let the movers pack the books. Instead, he went to California, wrapped each item, and packed them all in boxes. He wanted to ride back with them on one of the moving vans, but the movers would not allow it, so he flew back to Dallas and waited nervously for several days. The books arrived in good condition in mid-April.[14]

On September 27, 1962, Perkins School of Theology celebrated the opening of the Bridwell-DeBellis Collection with an academic festival in Perkins Chapel, followed by an exhibit of the collection in Bridwell Library. DeBellis, who came to the campus for the occasion, said that he decided SMU should have the books because he had found people there who were seriously interested, and because this part of the country had previously not had much fifteenth-century printing. Curt Buhler, an authority on fifteenth-century printing at the Pierpont Morgan Library in New York City, addressed the gathering, explaining the significance of the collection.[15]

After DeBellis's death in 1968, Decherd Turner, in gratitude for DeBellis's life and work, arranged for an exhibit of books and manuscripts to be held at the John Howell Book Store in San Francisco on February 11–14, 1969. On the evening of Monday, February 10, Turner; Quillian; Serena DeBellis, Frank's widow; and members of the Bridwell Foundation board gathered with others for a preview of the exhibit, and Quillian spoke of his memories of DeBellis. Serena DeBellis later wrote to Turner, "There is simply no way to say thank you to you, to Dean Quillian, to your assistants and to the Bridwell Foundation members. Last Monday evening was an evening to be cherished forever."[16]

Even before the Bridwell-DeBellis Collection came to the library, Decherd Turner knew the library building was too small and had been from the start.[17] By the late 1950s he had already had to add stacks in an unused space in the basement, and year by year the holdings increased. In early 1962, when Joe Quillian first talked with

Bridwell about acquiring the incunabula, the dean said he hoped Bridwell would also consider two other needs: an addition to the library building and an endowment for the library.[18]

Soon after the exhibition of the Bridwell-DeBellis collection that fall, Quillian wrote Bridwell again, not asking for an immediate reply but encouraging him to discuss these needs with his daughter, Margaret, Turner, and any others he wished to consult, and then, when he was ready, to give the dean a considered answer. Quillian estimated that the addition to the building might cost as much as $500,000. The library had already nearly run out of space for books, and the Graduate Program in Religion, which the dean hoped would begin the next year, would compound the problem. Furthermore, with the Bridwell-DeBellis Collection and other rare books, the library needed a vault with controlled temperature and humidity, to protect against pollutants as well as thieves and vandals. As for the library endowment, Quillian estimated a need for $1 million, the interest from which, conservatively invested, would bring in $40,000 a year. "We have the best theological librarian in this country in Decherd Turner," he said, as well as "the best theological faculty," which the dean judged would together make Bridwell Library the leading theological library. Quillian encouraged Bridwell to discuss all this with him when he was ready. "If it takes a year for you to decide, fine and well enough."[19]

It took Bridwell far longer than a year. In early December 1962 he was in the hospital with cancer and remained there until January. After that he was unable to return to work for several weeks and went to the hospital every few days for treatment. In June he began receiving cobalt treatments; he assured Turner these were helping him. On several occasions Turner visited Bridwell in Wichita Falls, which he much appreciated.[20]

Quillian continued to ask Bridwell for major contributions. In August 1963 he wrote detailing his hopes. He wanted Bridwell and his daughter, Margaret, to give the go-ahead for plans for the library addition, agree to cover its cost up to $500,000, and provide a $1 million endowment by July 1964. If that was not feasible, then Quillian hoped they would tell him to proceed with the library addition and that they would provide $40,000 a year until they could establish the endowment. He added, "I think by now that you know that I play directly and openly with you, and I am not at all trying to take up a position from which to bargain. I am asking you for precisely the support that I hope you will give us."[21]

In the spring of 1964 Bridwell pledged $100,000 for the library expansion. At that point Quillian wrote Willis Tate that Bridwell "really is very much with us" and that he had indicated his intention to finance the library enlargement.[22] Bridwell agreed that the annex would be "a very important addition to this building that should be just as practical and useable as is possible." Even so, he remained cautious, not wanting to spend anything on the project that was not necessary and proper—the way he had always proceeded in his own business affairs. He was, for example, suspicious of architects, and Quillian had to assure him that the architects' fees were standard.[23]

Bridwell continued to be strongly supportive of the library. On several occasions in 1964 he sent Turner large checks for book acquisitions.[24] Yet in the spring of 1965 he was not willing to approve Quillian's request to use part of the gift money for the architects' initial consultations and plans.[25] When Bridwell wrote Quillian at the end of 1965, still unconvinced of the need to work with an architect, he nevertheless enclosed a check for Bridwell Library.[26]

At some point in 1964 or 1965 Bridwell came to Dallas for a conference in the library with Turner, Quillian, and Lois Perkins. Bridwell asked Turner and Quillian about the size of the annex: "What did you have in mind?" When they told him, he said, "You boys are thinking too small!" He took them outside and stepped off what he thought should be the dimensions—much larger than they had envisioned. (Quillian later said, "That's really how it ended up being.") Bridwell then asked them, "Where are you boys going to get the money?" Lois Perkins replied, "We were hoping you would give it," to which Bridwell responded, "Ask Margaret. She's got a rich daddy." Getting a commitment from Bridwell was a long and slow process. As Quillian said, "Mr. Bridwell did not give money away in a hasty and unconsidered fashion."[27]

As the months went on, Bridwell's health continued to decline. In early April 1966 he was again having cobalt treatments, and in a telephone conversation he told Quillian he was not feeling well. Quillian told Willis Tate they should not wait any longer to push Bridwell about the annex. Quillian thought neither Turner nor

Charles Prothro, Lois Perkins's son-in-law, was optimistic that Bridwell would make a commitment to finance the annex before he died, but Quillian continued to be hopeful.[28] On April 23 Quillian wrote Bridwell, "Dear Partner: Richey [Hogg], Decherd and I enjoyed our visit with you very much. . . . You must know how deeply grateful I am for your indicating your plan to build the Bridwell Annex at an anticipated cost of approximately $800,000. I will await further word from you at your convenience. . . . I have called you 'Partner' for several years with a feeling of more affection and appreciation than you might have realized. The fact of your personal relationship always will be an ingredient of inspiration and strength to me."[29]

Joe Bridwell died on Monday, May 9, 1966, at the age of eighty-one. A busload of Perkins faculty, students, and administrative staff attended the service in Wichita Falls that Wednesday.[30] Only later did Quillian learn that before his death Bridwell had arranged for the establishment of the J. S. Bridwell Foundation. Its board consisted of Herbert B. "Herb" Story, president; Clifford G. Tinsley; A. T. Junk (all three from Wichita Falls and long-time officials in Bridwell's enterprises); and Ralph Bridwell, a nephew, of Abilene, Texas. Although Margaret Bridwell Bowdle was not a member of the foundation board, Quillian was confident her wishes would have a bearing on the board's actions. Charles Prothro told Quillian that Story, one of his closest friends, thought, as Quillian put it, "the clear first thing that the Bridwell Foundation ought to do is to do something really substantial for Bridwell Library as something of a memorial to Mr. Bridwell." After Prothro advised Quillian that $800,000 was much too low a figure for the annex, Quillian decided they would request about $2.5 million from the Bridwell Foundation.[31]

Construction on the annex was much delayed for two reasons. One was that the Bridwell Foundation could not make a large grant until Bridwell's estate was finally settled with the Internal Revenue Service. That did not happen until 1969. The foundation's trustees, however, fully supported building the annex and were able to send Quillian money in October 1967 to proceed with the plans.[32] Then in September 1969 Herb Story brought Willis Tate a check for a large part of the cost of constructing the annex.[33]

The other reason for delay was Decherd Turner's uncertainties about the plans. In 1967 Quillian had engaged the architectural firm of Collins and Dryden to draw up the design. When in the spring of 1968 they could not agree on a plan, Quillian,

Turner, and Horace Dryden, the architect, went together to Switzerland, Denmark, Sweden, and England from May 6 to 23 to inspect libraries. Turner later commented that the trip was not his idea. "I went with dragging feet—but am tremendously glad that it was scheduled—for there have been some stunning developments in European library construction and installation in the past three or four years. . . . We found ways of saving thousands of dollars on installations alone."[34]

Even so, the pace did not pick up. That summer Turner explained that he was far more interested in the book collection than in the building, though he knew they had to enlarge it. He wanted to make the building mistakes on paper, before incorporating them in steel and concrete, and he acknowledged he was to blame if things went too slowly. "The Dean and the Architects are about worn to a thread with me, but it all just has to be just right!"[35]

The plans were not completed until November 1969. On November 17 letters went out to eight companies inviting bids, and on December 11 the architects, Turner, Quillian, and other SMU officials met in Bridwell Library to open them. Then came the shock. The total of the low bid and other costs of the project was nearly $2.8 million. Quillian had hoped for a bid of not much more than $2.2 million.[36] Yet they were determined to move ahead. Rejecting the ideas of cutting the expansion in half or postponing it, they went over the plans in detail and were able to reduce the costs substantially. They proceeded with construction, and, in the end, with the benefit of their cuts and a favorable turn in the economy, total costs came to $1.435 million.[37] The Bridwell Library Annex was dedicated on September 27, 1973. September 27 had become virtually a sacred day for Turner, since it was the date on which the Bridwell-DeBellis Collection had first been exhibited.

On the day of the dedication representatives of the Bridwell Foundation signed an agreement establishing the Decherd Turner Book Acquisition Fund. To initiate the fund the foundation made an endowment gift to the university, the income from which would be used "to enhance the Rare Book Collection of the Bridwell Library."[38]

Turner was also manager of the library staff, though he directed less attention to that than to acquisitions. Before 1980 Bridwell Library never had more than seven staff members at a time, and before 1960 there were usually only three: Decherd Turner, Kate Warnick, and a circulation librarian. In the summer of 1959, when the position of circulation librarian became vacant, Turner appointed Jimmy Ed Clark, an African American who had just received his B.D. degree from Perkins. As a student, Clark had assisted in the library for three years, and that summer he was taking courses in library science, hoping to become a librarian. To give him the opportunity to develop his library experience, Turner planned to keep Clark on at Bridwell as long as possible. However, although the Perkins student body had been desegregated in 1952, that had not yet happened with SMU staff positions. To get around that problem, Turner resorted to the subterfuge of listing Clark in the records as a "student assistant." That was all right with Cuninggim and later with Quillian, and Clark remained on the library staff until 1963, with a leave in 1961–62 for further study in library science. In 1974 Turner appointed another African American, John Hooper, as circulation librarian, a position he held until his retirement in 1986.[39]

Page Thomas joined the staff in 1961 on a one-year arrangement as circulation librarian while Clark was on leave. He had had no previous experience in library work, but, he said, "Mrs. Warnick took me under her wing and gently guided me through the circulation procedures." Upon Clark's return in 1962, Turner put Thomas to cataloging books (with no previous experience). Thomas stayed on, holding first one responsibility and then another, and finally retired in 2007 as one of the more knowledgeable staff members about what was in Bridwell and where it was. Quillian once asked Thomas how he had survived working with Turner so many years. Thomas replied, "I learned a long time ago to stay out of his way and do what I was asked to do immediately." As Thomas recalled it, Turner "demanded your time and energy during work hours, and many times beyond." "We had," he said, "a very close working relationship, but it was always 'Mr. Thomas' and 'Mr. Turner.' I only remember one time that he called me Page but immediately corrected it."[40]

In 1961 Turner for the first time appointed an assistant librarian—Elizabeth Twitchell—though the position was soon retitled associate librarian. She remained until 1964, when she moved to the staff of the SMU science library. At that point Page Thomas became associate librarian for a brief time. Travis Jordan and then Jerene Simmons also served as associate librarians during the Turner years. Another position added in the 1960s was that of periodicals librarian, first staffed in 1962 by Leora Kemp, then from 1968 to 1978 by Mac McPherson, who came to the Bridwell staff a year after completing his B.D. degree at Perkins. Turner told McPherson to purchase any book or journal that was needed for theological education, and Turner would find the money.[41] Still another new position was that of administrative assistant to the director, staffed from 1973 into the 1980s by Ruth Smith, who had worked part time at Bridwell since 1967.

Even with these additions, demands on the library staff were heavy, especially after Kate Warnick fully retired. She had retired from her full-time library responsibilities in 1961, but as she knew more about the Methodist Historical Collection than anyone else the library could have hired, she continued on a part-time basis as librarian of that collection. When she retired again in 1979, she had served the libraries of the university and the School of Theology for sixty years and six months, under every SMU president up to that time.[42]

In 1980 Decherd Turner declared, "Had the Bridwell-DeBellis Collection not come, our whole history would have been entirely different."[43] Indeed, it would have: once it was secured, Turner set out in earnest to build up the library's rare book collection, and the presence of the Bridwell-DeBellis Collection so enhanced Bridwell Library's and Decherd Turner's reputations that it greatly increased his prospects for acquiring the kinds of books he wanted.

Between 1962 and 1980 Bridwell Library acquired several valuable collections. For years Rabbi Levi A. Olan of Temple Emanu-El in Dallas taught the course "Contemporary Judaism" at Perkins. In 1963 friends of Rabbi Olan honored him on his sixtieth birthday by establishing the Levi A. Olan Collection of Fine Books with a gift of fifty-five volumes. The collection, which has since grown much larger, reflects Olan's interest in the relation of art and biblical text.[44]

In 1954 Turner had learned of a noteworthy Bible collection belonging to Thomas J. Harrison of Pryor, Oklahoma. The collection contained, for example, a fifteenth-century Bible printed in three volumes; an Erasmus Bible printed in 1519; and the Second Erasmus Greek New Testament, which, legend has it, Martin Luther used when working on his German New Testament in 1522. Turner thought no other collection in the country was as complete in sixteenth- and early seventeenth-century Bibles and that Bridwell Library could not possibly afford to buy it. Although Turner visited Harrison and established a continuing friendship, when Harrison died in 1963, he had not decided on a permanent home for the collection. His brother,

Welch Harrison, offered it to Bridwell Library for its care and use for $16,000, the amount a court accepted as its value. The Harrison Bible Collection thus came to Bridwell Library in March 1964 for a fraction of its worth. It was dedicated on October 14, 1964, in a special service of thanksgiving in Perkins Chapel.[45]

In the early 1960s Turner analyzed Bridwell Library's holdings of sixteenth- and seventeenth-century books, with the aim of "developing a representative collection for these periods." He checked what Bridwell held against Yale Divinity School librarian Raymond Morris's *A Theological Book List* and found that of the 5,472 items in Morris's bibliography, Bridwell lacked 1,145 titles.[46] More than half those works were out of print, but Turner gave priority in 1962–63 to acquiring the in-print items.[47]

During the next several years Turner pursued acquisitions from three periods: the fifteenth century—incunabula; English printing from 1475 to 1640, that is, works listed in A. W. Pollard and G. R. Redgrave's *A Short-Title Catalogue of Books Printed in England, Scotland, & Ireland and of English Books Printed Abroad, 1475–1640* and known as the *STC*; and English works from 1641 to 1700, that is, those listed in Donald Goddard Wing's *Short-Title Catalogue of Books Printed in England, Scotland, Ireland, Wales and British America, and of English Books Printed in Other Countries, 1641–1700*, known as *Wing*. By the spring of 1965 Bridwell's incunabula collection had increased to 275 and continued to grow. The *STC* items increased from twenty-four in 1962 to 125 in 1965 and 400 in 1970. The *Wing* collection grew from fifty-nine in 1962 to 671 in 1965 and about 1,800 in 1970.[48] Along with these three periods, a fourth—the eighteenth century, with the Wesley and early Methodist materials—continued to be of major importance.

Building the collection from these periods involved overseas trips by several Perkins figures. In December 1963 Albert Outler, on the way home from the second session of the Vatican Council, spent a week in London searching through bookshops for books Wesley had recommended for his preachers; Outler acquired for the library about three hundred volumes published in 1600 and after.[49] In September 1965 Mr. and Mrs. Frederick D. Leete Jr. sent Kate Warnick to London, where she was able to obtain a collection of letters by John Wesley and his contemporaries.[50]

The chief traveler was Decherd Turner. In the spring of 1965 Joe Quillian obtained Joe Bridwell's consent to use some of his gift money so that Turner could spend two and a half or three months in England, Scotland, France, and Italy, looking for old books. He went that fall, had considerable success, and in the process became acquainted with the European book market.[51] Then, in early June 1966, Turner learned that on June 14 Sotheby's of London was going to auction a fine copy of the Lübeck Bible of 1494, which Turner considered to be the finest illustrated fifteenth-century Bible. But Bridwell had died, Margaret was critically ill, and the Bridwell Foundation was not yet in a position to help with the purchase. On June 12 Arthur Haddaway of Fort Worth, a book collector and friend of Bridwell Library's, agreed to pay Turner's airfare to London and lend him $18,000 to $25,000 to see what he could do at the auction. On the day of the auction Turner bought the Lübeck Bible for £7000, or $19,582.50. The loan was subsequently repaid.[52]

Seven months later, on January 30, 1967, Turner received a portfolio about incunabula that were being offered by a Mr. Chiasi of Milan, Italy. Turner spent all night analyzing it, and the next day he wrote Margaret Bridwell Bowdle and the Bridwell Foundation officers that "it is the largest single Collection of Fifteenth Century items to be put up since the Bridwell-DeBellis Collection. It is completely worthy to stand along side its temporal peers." The collection included sixty-seven items from the fifteenth century and Martin Luther's *De Captivitate Babylonica Ecclesiae*, printed in Wittenberg in 1520. With the support of Margaret, Herb Story, and Joe Quillian, Turner called Chiasi on February 6 and three days later boarded a plane for Milan. There he spent two days and the intervening night going through the collection and was able to purchase the forty items he wanted for just under $60,000. Back in Dallas, he wrote Margaret and the foundation officers to report on his trip. We should announce the acquisition, he said, on September 27, 1967, "exactly five years to the day from the first great announcement from this institution. . . . In the meantime, my thanks to you are beyond words."[53]

Turner's next big acquisition came three years later, when Bridwell Library was able to acquire a set of thirty-one leaves of the Gutenberg Bible, printed before 1456, containing the complete books of Jeremiah and Lamentations and one leaf of Baruch. This had been part of the Trier Fragment of the Gutenberg, discovered in a farmhouse near Trier in 1828. After more than a century in the Trier Stadtbibliothek, it came to be privately owned. When in 1970 John M. Crawford Jr. of New York, the owner since 1953, offered it to Bridwell Library, a number of friends of the library, led by Mr. and Mrs. Carr P. Collins Jr., gave $82,500 to make the purchase possible. This action placed Bridwell Library fiftieth among the world's libraries in the possession of entire copies or fragments of the Gutenberg Bible, the first large book printed with movable type. Bridwell Library celebrated the occasion on November 16, 1971.[54]

In early 1971 Lone Mountain College in California decided to sell its rare book collection. Turner was aghast. "The very idea of a school's selling their Rare Book Collection is just about the most awful thing I can think of," he said, then added, "when a school decides to sell its soul, then I owe it to my own school to profit as much as possible from the other's decision." He flew to San Francisco, looked at the collection, and after a few weeks of uncertainty that he would be able to make the acquisition, was able to obtain thirty-five lots of fifteenth-century printing. To mark the occasion, Bridwell Library on September 27, 1971, formally held an exhibition and a ceremony honoring Margaret Bridwell Bowdle, who had made this acquisition possible. Her gift brought the number of Bridwell's incunabula past five hundred. Joe Quillian wrote Margaret of his delight at her decision. "It also means much to me in that your personal support has contributed in a key fashion to our being able to keep Decherd Turner as librarian of Bridwell Library."[55]

In 1976 several events marked the growing strength and reputation of the Bridwell Library special collections. The Grolier Club of New York City, among whose 125 members are some of the most respected book collectors in the world, is the oldest book club in the United States. That year its nine members from Texas included Everett DeGolyer, Stanley Marcus, Charles Prothro, and Decherd Turner. In October 1975 the Grolier Club president, Herman W. Liebert, librarian emeritus of Yale's Beinecke Rare Book Library, wrote Turner to seek his advice about a large group of the club's members' making a trip to see various book collections in Texas and to ask Turner to chair the planning committee if the trip took place. Turner replied, "The prospect of a visit by the Grolier Club is the best sounding activity that I have yet encountered for 1976. Of course, you are most welcome." He would be honored, he said, to help plan and execute the trip, which he did. As he later observed, the Grolier Club's "coming to a young library is its ultimate public baptism and acceptance."[56]

On May 1, 1976, about forty Grolier Club members, many from the New York area, several from elsewhere in the country, and a few from England and Switzerland, arrived in Dallas to begin their Texas tour. That evening the group visited Bridwell Library, where members viewed several displays, including one hundred books from the library's collection and a selection of sixteen from the private collection of Charles and Elizabeth Prothro.[57] After visits to SMU's DeGolyer Library and to collections in several other Texas cities, Liebert wrote Turner, "The Grolier Club has been received by kings, cardinals, and dukes on its travels, but never has it been received so royally as on the trip that you made possible for us. It was flawless, and we all know that was because you were its architect. And what books! I have not yet recovered from seeing, as the beginning of the Bridwell exhibition, nine books printed before 1471. After that, I kind of glazed over."[58]

That year Bridwell Library made major additions to its collection of fine printing, which had been one of Decherd Turner's interests, following his interest in collecting incunabula. Stanley Marcus, while a student at Harvard, had taken a course taught by Bruce Rogers, a distinguished book designer of the early twentieth century. Thereafter Marcus tried to collect everything Rogers designed, and on May 1, during the Grolier Club's visit, Marcus presented eighty-five Rogers items to Bridwell Library.[59]

Later in 1976 Turner completed the acquisition for Bridwell Library of what he liked to call "the Triple Crown of Modern Typography," attained by no other library thus far. The three works making up the Triple Crown are the Kelmscott *Chaucer*, printed in 1896 (of which there exist thirteen copies on vellum), the Ashendene *Dante*, 1909 (seven copies on vellum), and the Doves Press Bible, 1903–1905 (only two copies on vellum). With the acquisition of the last of these, Bridwell Library, on January 16, 1977, held what Turner described as "a modest public ceremony" and the SMU Board of Trustees called "a spectacular" to mark the occasion. After a ceremony in Perkins Chapel and high tea in Bridwell Library, the three books were displayed, and Colin Franklin, literary scholar of Oxford, addressed the guests. The event was dedicated to the memory of Margaret Bridwell Bowdle, who had died only months earlier, on November 9, 1976.[60]

The general theological collection continued to grow, along with the considerable attention to special collections. In 1961 Bridwell Library housed 76,035 volumes; by May 1979, the total had reached 180,000. In the academic year 1960–61 the library's expenditures for books, periodicals, and binding came to $15,226—

roughly the average spent in each year since 1951. From 1961–62 to 1972–73, how-ever, the smallest amount for those line items was $64,947 and the largest, $153,504. Then in 1973–74 expenditures for those items jumped to $184,489. From 1974–75 to 1978–79, the annual amount ranged from $404,521 to $535,167.[61] This rapid increase was a sign of inflation in the cost of books—not only rare books but also ordinary theological works assigned in classes. It reflected both Turner's determina-tion to bring Bridwell Library into the top rank of theological libraries in the country and the greatly increased financial resources on which he could draw.

Since its dedication in 1951, Bridwell Library had operated under the direction of the Perkins deans—Cuninggim and then Quillian—and independently of the other SMU libraries. In 1978 Claude Albritton retired as SMU's dean of libraries, and John Hall retired as director of central university libraries (which included Fondren Library and several others but neither Bridwell Library nor the Underwood Law Library). The provost, James Brooks, took that occasion to ask Victor Furnish of Perkins, chair of the SMU Faculty Senate Library Committee, to head up a special study of the relations of the various university libraries. Should they all work under one system with a dean of libraries to oversee them all? Although the provost's office was initially inclined strongly toward such a system, Joe Quillian as dean of Perkins and Charles Galvin as dean of the School of Law were strongly opposed. In the spring of 1978 the faculty committee recommended that Bridwell and Underwood libraries, having distinctive responsibilities and constituencies from the other libraries, remain inde-pendent of the central university libraries, whereas the other university libraries would be under one director. The provost was persuaded to approve this. As Furnish later observed, "Had their original idea prevailed, I think the story of Bridwell might be rather different than it is."[62]

At the November 2, 1979, meeting of the SMU Board of Trustees, Elizabeth Perkins Prothro reported for the Committee on University Libraries that Decherd Turner had resigned as director of Bridwell Library. In June 1980 he would leave Bridwell to become director of the Humanities Research Center at the University of Texas in Austin. She declared that Turner had made Bridwell Library "the gemstone of the Southern Methodist University libraries" and, for many, had "enlarged our horizons of book knowledge and of libraries." "We are proud," she said, "of what Decherd Turner has accomplished while he has been here at SMU." Provost Brooks added, "His replacement will not be easily found for there really is only one Decherd Turner."[63] A decade earlier Quillian had told Herb Story, "When Decherd rounds out his work at Perkins School of Theology as librarian of Bridwell Library, it will have been the single most notable career in the entire field of theological libraries in this country."[64] Nothing that had happened by 1980 would have caused Quillian to revise that judgment. Turner directed the Humanities Research Center from 1980 until he retired in 1988, having made noteworthy acquisitions there, as he had at Bridwell Library. He died July 7, 2002, at age seventy-nine.[65]

1980–1985: JERRY CAMPBELL AS BRIDWELL LIBRARY DIRECTOR

The search committee for the new director, chaired by James Ward, included faculty from both Perkins and elsewhere in the university; students as well as faculty; the director of central libraries (Robert W. Oram); Herb Story of the Bridwell Foundation; and, ex officio, the provost and the dean of Perkins. Moving with dispatch, it presented a job description that was adopted by the Perkins Senate on November 9, 1979. In late January Jerry Campbell, librarian at Iliff School of Theology in Denver, visited the campus in connection with the position. At the February 15 meeting of the senate, Quillian presented Campbell's name for senate discussion, the senate advisory was positive, and Campbell was invited to take the position.[66]

Jerry Dean Campbell, from the town of Kress in northwest Texas, received his undergraduate degree from McMurry College and his master of divinity from Duke University Divinity School. He also received a master's degree in library science at the University of North Carolina, Chapel Hill, and in 1972 he joined the staff of the Ira J. Taylor Library of Iliff. In 1976 he became library director, the position he held when he agreed to become director of Bridwell Library.

In his first report to the Bridwell Foundation after his arrival in the summer of 1980, Campbell declared Bridwell Library "to be a truly magnificent and extraordinary working theology library," both as a graduate theological library and in its special collections.[67] Although that was true in many respects, the library also had some serious weaknesses. When an Association of Theological Schools team conducted the regular ten-year review of Perkins in the fall of 1980, it identified, along with the library's notable strengths, several problems that needed attention. These included the absence of any policy statement for collection development, a collection of current periodicals that was too small (three hundred), the lack of basic Hispanic material for Perkins's Mexican American Program, an inadequate number of staff, the need to change from the Dewey to the Library of Congress classification system, the need to catalog and restore the rare book collection, and the need to reactivate the faculty library committee and improve communication between the faculty and the library. "Mr. Turner," the review observed, "created a work of art and Perkins can be proud to own it. . . . Some changes are unavoidable and Mr. Campbell will need all the help and support from the Perkins community."[68]

In the late summer of 1980, although he had just arrived, Campbell was able, with Bridwell Foundation funds, to obtain a collection of works—more than twelve hundred titles—from the fifteenth to the twentieth centuries that were by and about the fifteenth-century reformer and martyr Girolamo Savonarola. The acquisition was accomplished, Campbell said, "against considerable competition." The collector was an elderly Italian, Mario Ferrara, who had devoted his career to studying Savonarola. Campbell saw this acquisition as "the kind of collection that continues to lift Bridwell toward a place of excellence among American libraries."[69]

Another acquisition during Campbell's first year was the purchase, in November 1980, of the Walter Kaufmann Library of German Philosophy. Kaufmann, a Princeton University philosopher, had collected the works of the major German philosophers from 1600 to 1914. Campbell considered this to be a superior collection crucial to Bridwell Library's needs. He circulated the fifteen-page list of titles to several faculty members, including Schubert Ogden, who advised him, "Beyond any question in my mind, this is an outstanding library that we would do well to acquire if we can."[70]

Campbell took seriously the accreditation team's list of the library's problems. He set out immediately to enlarge the Bridwell staff. In the fall of 1980 he brought Roger Loyd, a long-time friend and a 1971 Perkins M.Th. graduate, from his position as director of the Wesley Foundation at Texas Tech to be associate librarian, a position he held until 1992. During his five years as director, Campbell brought the size of the professional staff up to eleven, including new staff for cataloging and acquisitions. In his first year he changed the outdated Dewey classification system. Books already classified according to the Dewey system were left that way, but from 1981 acquisitions were classified in the Library of Congress system, each system having its own section of the stacks. He remedied another problem not mentioned in the accreditation report by installing a security system to provide protection both for rare books and stack books against the dangers of fire and theft.[71]

As a further response to the accreditation team's report, Campbell formulated an acquisitions policy that put a higher priority on the general theological collection. Soon after he arrived, he explained matters this way to Charles and Elizabeth Prothro: "The future collecting may turn slightly more toward books that serve the dual causes of scholarship and rare books. This is a focus we need for the immediate future to bring us some added academic strength and to make our dollars go further."[72] By November 1982 the Perkins report to the SMU Board of Trustees stated that one of its goals for the next five years was "to enhance the quality of the Bridwell Library so that it is the foremost theological research library in the Southwest." Pursuing that goal would involve continuing to fill gaps by careful acquisitions, increasing the number of periodicals, and adding materials in Spanish. These actions would strengthen Bridwell as a doctoral research library, enable the faculty to publish more, and provide fine support for Perkins's educational programs.[73] During Campbell's five years as director, the collection increased from 183,000 to 215,000 volumes.[74]

The Bridwell Foundation continued to make major gifts to the library during these years. In 1973 it had established the Decherd Turner Book Acquisition Fund. While Jerry Campbell was library director, the foundation made several additional large contributions to this fund and established the J. S. Bridwell Endowed Librarian Fund.[75]

In the spring of 1985 Jerry Campbell resigned as director of Bridwell Library to become director of the Duke University Libraries. Before his departure he wrote the Bridwell Foundation trustees to thank them for their continued generosity: "For the library, Bridwell Foundation has been the difference between average and outstanding. With the support from the Foundation, Bridwell Library is nationally recognized for the strength of its holdings and has, in addition, clearly become the theological library with the brightest future." He hoped the relationship between the foundation and the library would endure. It would be "a key factor in the effectiveness and confidence of the first Bridwell Endowed Librarian soon to be chosen." In the same letter he suggested several things that still needed to be done at Bridwell Library: remodeling of the building (which "might reach $500,000"), replacement of the original furnishings, provision for full-time maintenance, increasing the book fund endowment to $1 million, and special book purchases that from time to time might be made but for which the earnings of the Book Fund would be insufficient.[76]

In April 1985 the Perkins faculty established a task force, with Leroy Howe as its chair, to draw up the job description for the position of director of Bridwell Library. The next fall the task force became the search committee, and in February 1986 it brought Robert Maloy, director of libraries at the Smithsonian Institution, for a public visit.[77] That spring Maloy was appointed as the first J. S. Bridwell Foundation Endowed Librarian and professor of church history, with the understanding that he would take up his responsibilities at Bridwell in August 1987. In the meanwhile Roger Loyd served as interim director.

Bridwell Library made several advances in the two years after Campbell's departure. During this period SMU's libraries were continuing the process of automating their records. In the late 1970s they had introduced the Online Computer Library Center (OCLC), which made accessible a national database of more than seventeen million bibliographic records. Turner brought the first OCLC terminal to Bridwell Library so that its staff members would not have to go to Fondren Library to catalog the books. Then, in the early 1980s, funds were raised to convert catalog records to a machine-readable form. In 1985 the Pew Charitable Trust gave SMU a grant of $500,000 to complete this process, so that by the end of 1987 the university would have a computerized library catalog. Roger Loyd oversaw the early stages of this process for Bridwell Library, and Robert Maloy, after his arrival, carried it further. Loyd also began looking into the possibility of introducing compact shelving to conserve stack space.[78]

Under Loyd's leadership Bridwell's professional staff grew to sixteen by 1986–87. Among the additions, Richard Heitzenrater, since 1985 the first Albert C. Outler Professor of Wesley Studies, that year also became the director of the Bridwell Library Center for Methodist Studies. Wanda Smith, who had for years assisted Outler in his Wesley research and then was assistant to Jerry Campbell, became Heitzenrater's assistant. Also for the first time Bridwell employed a full-time reference librarian, Mimi Davis, to guide the library's users into the various collections.[79]

The Bridwell Foundation continued its generous support with a large gift in

December 1985 and another the following December. These gifts enabled the continued growth of the two endowed library funds—the Turner Book Acquisition Fund and the Endowed Librarian Fund. By the fall of 1986 the library's total collections had grown to approximately 245,000 volumes and its periodical subscriptions to about 750, an increase of more than four hundred since 1980.

ROBERT MALOY'S DIRECTORSHIP, 1987–1992

Robert Maloy had received his bachelor's degree from the University of Dayton (Ohio), his master's in library science from the University of Chicago, and his doctor of sacred theology degree in church history from the University of Fribourg, Switzerland. A priest in the Marianist Order of Dayton, he had been, before coming to Bridwell Library, director of the libraries of the School of Theology in Claremont, California (1972–75), of Union Theological Seminary in New York (1975–79), and of the Smithsonian Institution (1979–87).

Maloy had been planning for Bridwell Library's renovation for almost a year before he arrived in August 1987. At the request of the dean, James Kirby, he had visited Perkins on October 10, 1986, for a consultation about the renovation, after which he provided Kirby with several typed pages of recommendations as to the design of each room and area. When he arrived as director on August 10, 1987, he was ready to move quickly to initiate the renovation.

Although the addition of the annex in 1973 had greatly enlarged Bridwell Library, the design and use of its space presented serious problems. In October 1987 SMU engaged the architectural firm of Helmuth, Obata, Kassabaum for the project. That fall, under the leadership of Kirby and Maloy and in consultation with the faculty, four goals of the renovation were identified: to improve the research environment by improving design, space, and comfort for readers and providing access to the disabled; to establish a book exhibition gallery that would make Bridwell's collections available to the university and the wider public; to preserve the collections by stabilizing temperature and humidity, controlling harmful light, improving air filtration, providing adequate security, and establishing a conservation laboratory; and to improve economy of operations, save energy, simplify maintenance, conserve space for future collection growth, and organize staff areas for more effective work patterns. Preserving the collections was especially important. Maloy had new heating, air-conditioning, and ventilation systems installed that would help to preserve the books, and he had all the library's windows replaced with glass that would keep out destructive solar radiation. He also oversaw the installation of compact shelving in the stacks. These changes were well worth the great cost they entailed.[80]

Initial projections in February 1988 for the cost of the renovation came to $6.9 million, a figure that did not include architects' fees or other related costs. With urging from Kirby, in March the cost estimates were reduced to $5.4 million. Thereafter the Bridwell Foundation agreed to cover most of the cost of the renovation, which it did between March 1988 and October 1989.[81]

The process of renovation, carried out by the Dal-Mac Company, unavoidably disrupted library activities for more than a year. Between May 15 and June 15, 1988, Bridwell Library staff members moved essential activities elsewhere, transferring reference and loan services to the basement of Perkins Dormitory, next door to Bridwell. Acquisitions and cataloging work went to the Central University Library. Graduate students' carrels were relocated to a room in Selecman Hall. When readers needed a book or a periodical, they would submit a request at the circulation desk in Perkins Dormitory, and once a day runners would go into the library and bring out the requested items to the circulation desk. Special collections, including archives and rare books, were simply not available. The renovation was sufficiently far along that on October 19, 1989, Perkins rededicated the library with a service of worship in Perkins Chapel, followed by a procession of the faculty and guests from the chapel to the library for further ceremonies, lunch, and a tour of the building. Full services of the library were restored in November with the completion of the basement stacks.[82] Under Maloy's close supervision the renovation improved the interior of the library functionally and rendered it aesthetically elegant.

One purpose of the renovation was to provide a book exhibition gallery. A generous gift from Charles Prothro made possible a four-thousand-square-foot area on the first floor that was named the Elizabeth Perkins Prothro Galleries in honor of his wife, on the occasion of their wedding anniversary. The gallery space, with four connected rooms and an alcove, was furnished with special exhibition cases designed to protect old books and manuscripts from damage from air, light, and heat. Its dedication took place with an inaugural exhibition from January 17 to early June 1990: a selection of one hundred Bible manuscripts and printings that Elizabeth Perkins

Prothro had collected for more than twenty-five years.[83] With far better care for the books, and with the galleries and an increased staff, Maloy enabled Bridwell Library to function as a rare book library, not only a great collection.

Maloy was acutely aware of the library's need for a more secure financial base. After completion of the renovation, therefore, he asked the Bridwell Foundation to establish an endowment that would be much larger than the previous ones and would support library acquisitions as well as other expenses. Herb Story, president of the foundation, agreed that this would be done.

Maloy also further enlarged the staff. He began staff reorganization in early 1988 while planning for the renovation, assigning Roger Loyd to be chief of reader services in addition to his responsibilities as associate librarian. Loyd was now to supervise and assist in planning for what was now called the Loans Department (circulation), with Lillie Jenkins-Carter as its head. Maloy also asked Loyd to work closely with Laura Randall, newly appointed head of the Reference Department, to upgrade the reference collection.[84]

In 1989, following the renovation, Maloy brought Isaac Gewirtz from the rare book room of the New York Public Library to be the Bridwell rare book and manuscript librarian, and Jon Speck, from Atlanta's High Museum, to be the exhibits designer. By 1990 Page Thomas held various responsibilities, including cataloging special collections; Linda Umoh headed cataloging for the general collection; and Ellen Lethcoe Frost was in charge of acquisitions. Early in 1991 Maloy brought Jan Sobota, internationally renowned in bookbinding, restoration, and conservation, as the first director of the library's Book Conservation Laboratory. Other staff additions were Jim Powell as interlibrary loan librarian and Roberta Cox as administrative assistant.[85] Maloy developed explicit job descriptions, clarified who reported to whom, and reduced the number of staff members reporting directly to him.

For some years the faculty's Curriculum Committee had had a library subcommittee. In April 1988, on the recommendation of the Curriculum Committee, the faculty voted to reestablish a standing committee on the library. Part of the committee's responsibility was "to make recommendations to the faculty about those policies concerning the library which properly fall under the faculty areas of responsibility."[86] Victor Furnish was appointed to chair the new committee.

During the next few years Dean Kirby and the library committee together helped the library to respond to various library users. After communications from students, alumni/ae, and others, the library modified its policies about access to the stacks and about charges for checking out books.

In June 1992 Robert Maloy resigned as director of Bridwell Library.[87] The preceding January, Roger Loyd, the associate librarian, had accepted an invitation to become the librarian of the Duke University Divinity School Library, effective July 1, 1992. After receiving Maloy's resignation, Kirby asked Richard Heitzenrater to be the interim director of Bridwell Library during the 1992–93 academic year, which he did. Heitzenrater recognized Maloy's contributions in getting the library building renovated and operating and said that he hoped to continue building the collection and serving its users. "We won't be making any major changes this year, but there are some fine adjustments that we'll initiate that will help make Bridwell Library more user friendly."[88] With faculty approval in October of a job description for the position of director of Bridwell Library, a committee chaired by Victor Furnish began the search for a new director.

VALERIE HOTCHKISS AS BRIDWELL LIBRARY DIRECTOR, 1993–2005

In the spring of 1993 Valerie R. Hotchkiss was appointed the J. S. Bridwell Foundation Endowed Librarian, director of Bridwell Library, and associate professor of medieval studies. She assumed her new responsibilities in July. Hotchkiss received her bachelor's degree in classical languages and literature from the University of Cincinnati, her master's in library science from Southern Connecticut State University, and her Ph.D. in medieval studies from Yale University, where her dissertation adviser was Jaroslav Pelikan. Before coming to Bridwell, she headed the circulation department at the Yale Divinity School Library and from 1989 to 1993 was director of the library of Austin Presbyterian Theological Seminary.[89]

In her first report to the Bridwell Foundation, Hotchkiss offered an analysis of the library that both appreciated its strengths and recognized present difficulties. It combined, she said, a large theological library with its remarkable rare book library. Its general collection was one of the strongest west of the Mississippi, and its special collections rivaled or surpassed those of the East Coast theological libraries. "This is the library built by Decherd Turner, one of the greatest librarians of this century. . . . He deserves most of the credit for forming the collections," she said.[90]

But Bridwell Library, she perceived, was in some ways two libraries: a theological collection supporting the education of ministers and a special collections research library. These two libraries had at times become unbalanced, so that Perkins students were not encouraged to use the remarkable special collections. In the past several years the library's mission had become blurred, and faculty, students, and staff were concerned about the future. The staff was talented and sufficiently large, though the library needed an archivist to organize the backlog of accumulated papers and manuscripts. Most staff members, she said, saw their work as service-oriented.[91]

She found the state of the Bridwell budget distressing. In the recent past less money had been available for acquisitions, because of both the expanded staff and the costs of maintaining the automated catalog. To redirect some funds to acquisitions, she had decided not to fill the vacant position of associate librarian; because that adversely affected her work, she would consider reinstating the position if funds could be found. If Bridwell was to claim its place as one of the country's best theological libraries, it needed to expand the general acquisitions fund by 50 percent and double the special collections budget.[92]

It was crucial that the library have a unified vision. She envisioned Bridwell Library's primary purpose, already expressed in its mission statement, as "support[ing] the curriculum of the Perkins School of Theology and the Religious Studies program at Southern Methodist University." The library, she said, needs to "refocus on this mission." This vision would bring the two components of the collection "into balance and harmony," so that while the library encouraged theological students to use its resources, it also welcomed scholars and graduate students to do original research.[93]

She explained that since her arrival four months earlier, she had already taken steps to welcome alumni/ae and local religious leaders to the library and had offered free borrowing privileges for one year. Staff members were providing bibliographic instruction sessions for faculty and students. She had had the entryway redesigned, with a display of recent faculty publications, and had allowed free access to the stacks, not only for faculty and students but for all alumni/ae, area religious leaders, and interested laity. She looked forward to a holiday party in December and hoped that the library could be a center of community life. In conversation with the faculty library committee and the curator of special collections, she was drafting guidelines for development of the collections. In addition, she had spent much of the past several months reestablishing contacts with donors. She expressed special appreciation for the generosity of the Bridwell Foundation.[94]

Among her several goals for the coming year were continuing the changes she had already initiated, enhancing the acquisitions budget, introducing a visiting scholars and ministers program with short-term fellowships for research in the library, increasing the available computer databases and training students and faculty in their use, reconfiguring one of the reading rooms into a Methodist studies room, developing a comprehensive preservation and conservation program, and working constructively with the other SMU libraries. These were ambitious goals, she recognized, and they would require both more funding and much hard work. But they were important if Bridwell was to become "the best theological library in the United States."[95]

In the summer of 1994 the Bridwell Foundation provided the library with the large endowment Robert Maloy had earlier requested, donating $10 million to Bridwell Library, and thereby established the J. S. Bridwell Foundation Endowed Library Fund. This brought the total of gifts up to that time from J. S. Bridwell, Margaret Bridwell Bowdle, and the Bridwell Foundation to $24 million. This latest gift, together with benefactions from various sources from time to time, meant that in 1995 for the first time all funding for acquisitions for both the general and special collections came from endowment income.[96]

Income from the new endowment soon grew to have a major impact on the work of the library. By 1996 the library had almost recovered from the decrease in the acquisitions budget between 1990 and 1994, and the library could expect continued increases in income for this purpose. The endowment fund supported several other library needs as well, including the Visiting Ministers' Program (initiated in 1994–95), the Visiting Scholars' Program (from 1995–96), the Judaica Lecture Series (first given in 1994), library exhibitions, and the library's preservation program. It also made possible further enlargement of the library staff.[97]

In the next several years the Bridwell Library endowments continued to grow, though not without interruption. During the national economic downturn in 2000–02, the various funds declined in their market value, with the Bridwell Foundation Endowed Library Fund shrinking by about 11 percent. By 2004, however, it and the other endowments, the Bridwell-Turner Acquisitions Endowment and the Endowed Librarian Fund, had recovered most of the lost ground. February 2001 saw the establishment of a fourth endowed fund. To celebrate the library's fiftieth anniversary, the Bridwell Foundation, under the leadership of Mac Cannedy since 2000, pledged to match 2-for-1 what the library raised from other sources. The library met the challenge, and the foundation's gift made possible the establishment of the Bridwell Associates Endowed Fund, the proceeds from which went to support the library's publications program.[98]

Hotchkiss's arrival as director brought about a change in the staff's work together, as well as in its size and personnel. To encourage two-way communication with the staff, she initiated regular meetings: weekly with department heads and monthly with the whole staff. To reshape the perception of the library to one of access and service, she changed the name of the Loans Department, making it once more the Circulation Department, redefined the position, and hired Jorge Cruz as the new circulation manager.[99]

After the J. S. Bridwell Foundation Endowed Library Fund was established in 1994, it became financially possible to make some needed changes in the library staff. In October 1995 Hotchkiss reestablished the position of associate librarian with the appointment of Duane Harbin, who came with fifteen years of theological library experience at Yale University.[100] In 1996 Page Thomas added to his long experience at Bridwell Library the position of director of the Center for Methodist Studies. Other changes included the addition of Eric White in 1997 as curator of special collections, Jane Lenz Elder in January 2002 as reference librarian (following Laura Randall's retirement), and, in 2005, Elizabeth Haluska-Rausch as a second curator of special collections. Hotchkiss perceived a need for an archivist, but none was appointed during her tenure. Duane Harbin left the Bridwell staff in 2001 to become Perkins's assistant dean for information technology and institutional research. In January 2002 James McMillin, with a Ph.D. degree in history from Duke and a specialization in the American South, arrived as the new associate director of Bridwell.

A prominent part of the library's activities has been its program of exhibits. Two major exhibits before the 1988–89 renovation were "The Bridwell-DeBellis Collection of Fifteenth-Century Printing," curated by Decherd Turner and held on August 25, 1962, to celebrate that collection; and "One Hundred Books from the Special Collections of Bridwell Library," also curated by Decherd Turner, and held on May 1, 1976, on the occasion of the Grolier Club visit. There were few other exhibits before 1989, the number limited by the size of the staff and lack of an adequate exhibition gallery.[101]

Since the library renovation the number of Bridwell exhibitions, curated by various people and designed by Jon Speck, has been extensive. The larger and more prominent exhibitions have been in the Elizabeth Perkins Prothro Galleries, beginning in 1990 with "The Bible: 100 Landmarks from the Elizabeth Perkins Prothro Collection," curated by Robert Maloy. From that point to the conclusion of Valerie Hotchkiss's tenure as director of Bridwell Library, the galleries hosted forty-seven exhibitions, an average of more than three each year. To accompany these exhibits, Bridwell provided catalogs, brochures, and other publicity materials, some of which won awards from the American Library Association.

From 1997, when the library began counting the exhibition visitors, to Hotchkiss's departure in 2005, visitors per exhibit ranged from 613 to 3,775. Among many noteworthy exhibits was "*Ex Libris* Decherd Turner," curated by Eric White, September 6 to December 13, 1997, with 1,051 visitors, when Turner, in recognition of his seventy-fifth birthday, donated more than 120 fine and rare books to Bridwell, each in honor of a friend. Another was "Bridwell at Fifty: Books, Benefactors, & Bibliophiles," February 8 to June 2, 2001, curated by Valerie Hotchkiss, with 3,088 visitors.[102]

Smaller exhibits have usually been displayed in the library's entry hall, without a catalog but with explanatory descriptions. From 1989 to the summer of 2005 there were 107 such exhibits, spanning a wide range of topics and most often curated by a library staff member. The exhibits, large and small, publicize the library's holdings, increase its visibility in north Texas and beyond, and contribute to the education of the wider community. They promote one of the library's goals—"to be not only a great research library, but also a cultural and intellectual center."[103]

Bridwell acquisitions continued apace, supported by the endowed funds despite the ups and downs of the market. Valerie Hotchkiss continued the practice, initiated by Decherd Turner, of building the collections from two directions; that is, acquiring the latest books in theology and religious studies while at the same time building the collection retrospectively—filling in gaps in past periods. This was necessary for a young library like Bridwell, she said. "It is time-consuming and expensive, but the only way to build a great library."[104]

As part of $7 million in gifts to Perkins, in 1996 Charles and Elizabeth Prothro donated the Elizabeth Perkins Prothro Bible Collection, valued at more than $1.5 million, to Bridwell Library. The collection, extending from medieval manuscripts to recent fine printings, had previously been on loan to the library for exhibitions and research. Now it became part of the library's permanent collection. Valerie Hotchkiss described it as "probably the finest Bible collection in the country."[105]

Bridwell continued to enlarge its collection of incunabula. Eric White reported that in 1996–97 the library acquired its 750th incunabulum: the first complete edition of the *Summa Theologica* of Saint Antoninus, an early fifteenth-century archbishop of Florence, published in five volumes in 1477–79 and 1486. On November 23, 2004, the collection reached the magic number of one thousand, and the library celebrated the occasion with an exhibit the following spring.[106]

Despite the addition of the library annex in 1973 and the 1989 renovation, space continued to be a problem. More room was needed to accommodate the growth of the collections, to improve service to the public through the library's many cultural programs, and to make new technologies accessible to the public. In 2001–02 Hotchkiss estimated that the library had less than five years of growth space remaining. Another problem was that in the renovation the Turner Rare Book Reading Room had been located to the second floor behind the Cataloging Department. Hotchkiss wanted to move it to a more easily accessible location. The library could be expanded by adding a third floor to the existing structure, though that would be a major expense. For the time being other, smaller measures were preferable, such as adding several more rows of stacks in what had been a small public reading area.

In the summer of 2005, after twelve years as the J. S. Bridwell Endowed Librarian and director of Bridwell Library, Valerie Hotchkiss accepted the position of rare book librarian at the University of Illinois in Urbana. Dean Bill Lawrence set up a search committee chaired by former dean Jim Kirby. In the meantime James McMillin, the associate library director, served as Bridwell's interim director.

ROBERTA SCHAAFSMA AS DIRECTOR OF BRIDWELL LIBRARY

On April 1, 2007, Roberta A. Schaafsma became the J. S. Bridwell Endowed Librarian and the fifth director of Bridwell Library. Since 1993 she had been the associate director of the Duke Divinity School Library, where among her responsibilities were supervision of reference services and collection development. She received her bachelor's degree from Central Michigan University, her master's in library science from the University of Michigan, Ann Arbor, and her master of arts in theology from Chicago Theological Seminary. Since 2004 she had been a member of the board of directors of the American Theological Library Association and was currently the board's secretary.[107]

In a report to the Bridwell Foundation at the end of 2007, Schaafsma reviewed the library's work and identified its challenges and opportunities. She noted that for the past few years much of the staff's time and energy had been devoted to the special collections—acquiring and exhibiting them and related programs. She pointed out that Bridwell Library's mission is to support the needs of the Perkins faculty and students, and that in some ways the library had allowed this mission to lag behind what other theological libraries provide: the library had been slow to provide a full complement of databases, and the lecture series had been directed mainly to the interests of outside groups rather than Perkins students and faculty.[108]

Hotchkiss had said earlier that Bridwell Library was in some ways two libraries. Schaafsma noted that this had become increasingly so—"theological library and special collections library—with seemingly divergent missions located in one building." During the next year she would attempt to bring all the library's areas into a balance that serves Perkins, "its primary user community." The goal of library services would call for public programs directed toward the seminary community and for technology to improve the public and staff access to databases. She planned to appoint a head of special collections to whom the several staff members related to special collections would report, as well as an electronic services librarian to provide the staff with greater expertise in that area. Regarding space, she observed that the renovation of 1989 created a building designed to exhibit the rare books and manuscripts and to encourage individual research. Current students, though, wanted group study rooms as well as quiet study spaces. Like her predecessor she recognized the problematic location of the Decherd Turner Reading Room and the pressing need for more stack space. These problems called for a long-term vision for the library building.

Changes during 2008 included extending the library's hours on Friday and Saturday evenings, upgrading staff and public scanners and computers, and adding access to several new databases in religion and theology. After Page Thomas retired in

2007, Daniel Slive joined the library staff as head of special collections and Christine Willard as reference and digital services librarian in 2008. In 2009 Timothy Binkley became the Bridwell Library archivist. By 2008 collections had grown to 304,123 books and 46,084 periodical volumes, plus comparably large bodies of microforms, audiovisuals, and archives. In 1952–53 Bridwell Library had spent a modest total of $27,050 for all purposes, and by 2009 it received the income from four large Bridwell Foundation endowed funds, in addition to the Annie Hughey Fund and numerous smaller gifts.[109] As had occurred in the Hotchkiss years, the library in 2007–08, in order to cope with the need for stack space, withdrew titles beyond the scope of the library's responsibility and transferred many volumes to other libraries on the SMU campus. Like other SMU libraries, Bridwell was looking to off-site storage for low-use items. In 2009 Schaafsma and her team were working on increasing library space and relocating the Decherd Turner Reading Room.[110]

In the spring of 2009 Bridwell Library updated its mission statement for the first time since 1994, with two aims: to emphasize the library's connection to Perkins School of Theology and to restate the library's goals and the variety of forms of its service and work. The new statement begins: "The mission of Bridwell Library is to provide services and scholarly resources to support Perkins School of Theology and its twin tasks of theological education and theological reflection."[111] In the six decades since its dedication, Bridwell Library has become an impressive part of the work of Perkins School of Theology.

---

1. Decherd Turner, "Bridwell Library," in Olin W. Nail, ed., *History of Texas Methodism 1900–1960* (Austin, Texas: Capital Printing, 1961), 485.
2. Fay Walston, "The History of Bridwell Library" (unpublished term paper, Texas Women's University, Denton, May 1970), 6, citing Walston's interview of Kate Warnick, April 12, 1970, Bridwell Library Papers.
3. Decherd Turner, "The Bible and the Bridwell Library," in *The Bible: 100 Landmarks from the Elizabeth Perkins Prothro Collection* (Dallas: Bridwell Library, 1990), xi.
4. Walston, "History of Bridwell Library," 8, citing her interview of Decherd Turner, February 10, 1970.
5. Turner, "Bible and the Bridwell Library," xi; "Bridwell Library: Statistical Profile from Its First Day of Public Service, December 18, 1950," in "Bridwell Library: A Report of Activities," May 1979, Bridwell Library Papers.
6. Decherd Turner, interview by Joseph D. Quillian Jr., May 28, 1980, SMU Archive Series.
7. Page Thomas to Joe Allen, January 11, 2009, in the author's personal files.
8. J. S. Bridwell to Decherd Turner, January 18, 1962; Bridwell to F. V. DeBellis, September 13, 1962. J. S. Bridwell Letters, 1956–66, Bridwell Library Papers; board of trustees minutes, November 2, 1979.

9. *Special Collections in the Libraries at Southern Methodist University* (Dallas: SMU Printing Department, 1973), 19–21, 25–26; 1989 edition (Dallas: SMU Publications, 1989), 16; Robert M. Trent to Merrimon Cuninggim, March 2, 1956, Cuninggim Papers, Bridwell Library.

10. Mrs. John H. Warnick, "The Romance of Methodism: The Methodist Historical Library, Inc.," *Perkins School of Theology Journal* 10, no. 1 (fall 1956): 17–21; *Special Collections*, 1989, 14; board of trustees minutes, May 11, 1979.

11. Minutes of the Executive Committee of the Board of Trustees, January 12 and October 19, 1962; Joseph D. Quillian Jr., interview by Howard Grimes, May 19, 1981, SMU Archive Series; Turner to Margaret Bridwell Bowdle et al., January 31, 1967, Bridwell Foundation Correspondence, 1965–69, Bridwell Library Papers.

12. Bridwell to Quillian, February 12, 1962; Turner to Quillian, February 15, 1962, both in Quillian Papers; Turner interview.

13. Bridwell to Turner, February 19, 1962, Bridwell Letters, 1956–66.

14. Quillian interview; Bridwell to Turner, April 19, 1962, Bridwell Letters; Turner interview; Thomas to Allen, February 2, 2009, in the author's personal files.

15. *Dallas Morning News*, September 28, 1962.

16. Turner to Quillian, November 11, 1968; Turner to Quillian, January 31, 1969; Serena DeBellis to Turner, February 17, 1969, all in Quillian Papers.

17. Faculty minutes, October 4, 1950; Turner interview.

18. Quillian to Willis Tate, February 2, 1962, Quillian Papers.

19. Quillian to Bridwell, October 6, 1962, Bridwell Letters.

20. Bridwell to Turner, December 5 and 26, 1962, and January 28, March 5, March 7, March 9, May 4, June 3, and June 25, 1963, all in Bridwell Letters.

21. Quillian to Bridwell, August 26, 1963, Bridwell Letters.

22. Board of governors minutes, April 3, 1964; Quillian to Tate, April 24, 1964, Quillian Papers.

23. Bridwell to Quillian, October 21 and November 16, 1964; Quillian to Bridwell, November 18, 1964, all in Bridwell Letters.

24. Bridwell to Turner, February 4, April 7, July 22, and December 4, 1964, all in Bridwell Letters.

25. Quillian to Bridwell, May 11, 1965; Bridwell to Quillian, May 18, 1965; Quillian to Turner, May 16, 1966, all in Bridwell Letters.

26. Bridwell to Quillian, December 31, 1965, Bridwell Letters.

27. Quillian interview.

28. Quillian to Tate, April 11, 1966, Quillian Papers.

29. Quillian to Bridwell, April 23, 1966, Bridwell Letters.

30. Quillian to the Perkins community, May 9, 1966, Quillian Papers.

31. Quillian to Tate, June 3, 1966, Quillian Papers.

32. Ibid., November 8, 1966, Quillian Papers; Herbert B. Story to Turner, October 10, 1967, Bridwell Foundation Correspondence, Bridwell Library Papers.

33. Quillian to Story, September 9, 1969, Bridwell Foundation Correspondence.

34. Quillian to J. Osborne, business manager, SMU, April 15, 1968, Quillian Papers; Turner to Clifford D. Tinsley, June 15, 1968, Bridwell Foundation Correspondence.

35. Turner to Tinsley, June 15, 1968; Turner to Margaret Bridwell Bowdle, Clifford Tinsley, A. T. Junk, Herbert Story, and Ralph Bridwell, July 17, 1968; Turner to Bowdle et al., August 1, 1968, all in Bridwell Foundation Correspondence.

36. Joseph D. Quillian to Mrs. J. J. [Lois] Perkins, December 12, 1969; Joseph D. Quillian Jr., "Report on Opening the Bids for Bridwell Library Annex" (attachment to the letter to Perkins); Quillian to Tinsley, December 23, 1969, all in Bridwell Foundation Correspondence.

37. Financial statement, Bridwell Library Extension, February 24, 1974; Quillian to Story, March 4, 1974, both in Quillian Papers.

38. "The Decherd Turner Book Acquisition Endowment Fund: Agreement, September 27, 1973, between the J. S. Bridwell Foundation and Southern Methodist University," Quillian Papers.

39. Turner to Cuninggim, June 8 and June 22, 1959; Cuninggim to Tate, June 30, 1959, both in Merrimon Cuninggim Papers, Bridwell Library.

40. Thomas to Allen, January 11, 2009.
41. Mac McPherson to Joe Allen, February 21, 2009, in the author's personal files.
42. Robert M. Trent, director of libraries, to Provost Hemphill Hosford, November 18, 1960, Quillian Papers; board of trustees minutes, May 11, 1979.
43. Turner interview.
44. Turner, "Bible and the Bridwell Library," xiii.
45. Walston, "History of Bridwell Library," 25–27; Turner, "Bible and the Bridwell Library," xiii–xiv.
46. Raymond P. Morris, *A Theological Book List*, produced by the Theological Education Fund of the International Missionary Council (Naperville, Ill.: Allenson's, 1960).
47. Southern Methodist University Libraries Annual Report, 1961–62, April 15, 1962, 1, Bridwell Library Papers.
48. A. W. Pollard and G. R. Redgrave, comps., *A Short-Title Catalogue of Books Printed in England, Scotland, & Ireland and of English Books Printed Abroad, 1475–1640* (London: Bibliographical Society, 1926); Donald Goddard Wing, comp., *Short-Title Catalogue of Books Printed in England, Scotland, Ireland, Wales and British America, and of English Books Printed in Other Countries, 1641–1700* (New York: Index Society, 1945–51); Reference Department, Indiana University Libraries, www.indiana.edu/~librcsd/cdrom/Detailed/60.html; Southern Methodist University Libraries Annual Report 1964–65, April 15, 1965, 4; Turner to Bowdle et al., November 10, 1969, Bridwell Foundation Correspondence; Walston, "History of Bridwell Library," 11.
49. Southern Methodist University Libraries Annual Report, 1963–64, April 15, 1964.
50. Ibid., 1965–66, April 20, 1966.
51. Quillian to Bridwell, May 11, 1965; Bridwell to Quillian, May 18, 1965; Quillian to Bridwell, May 24, 1965, all in Bridwell Letters; Quillian to Albert C. Outler, October 25, 1965, Quillian Papers.
52. Turner, "Bible and the Bridwell Library," xv–xvi; Turner to Bowdle et al., November 2, 1966, Bridwell Foundation Correspondence.
53. Turner to Bowdle et al., January 31 and February 14, 1967; Quillian to Story, January 31 and February 9, 1967, all in Quillian Papers.
54. Turner, "Bible and the Bridwell Library," xvii–xviii; Quillian to William B. Heroy Jr., June 3, 1970, Quillian Papers.
55. Turner to Quillian, March 5, 1971; Turner to Bowdle et al., March 9 and April 8, 1971; Turner to Bowdle, April 28, 1971; Quillian to Bowdle, May 5, 1971, all in Quillian Papers; *Perkins Perspective* 11, no. 1 (November 1971); Turner, "Bible and the Bridwell Library," xvi–xvii.
56. Herman W. Liebert to Turner, undated; Turner to Liebert, October 6, 1975, Bridwell Library Papers; Turner interview.
57. Turner, "Bible and The Bridwell Library," xviii–xix.
58. Liebert to Turner, May 14, 1976, Bridwell Library Papers.
59. *Special Collections*, 1989, 13; Turner interview; Turner, "Bible and the Bridwell Library," xix.
60. Turner to Quillian, September 20, 1976, Quillian Papers; board of trustees minutes, May 13, 1977; *Bridwell at Fifty: Books, Benefactors, and Bibliophiles, An Exhibition at Bridwell Library, Perkins School of Theology, Southern Methodist University, 8 February–2 June, 2001*, curated by Valerie R. Hotchkiss (Dallas: Bridwell Library, 2001), 23, 26, 27; Turner, "Bible and the Bridwell Library," xix–xx; *Perkins Perspective* 16, no. 2 (December 1976–January–February 1977); *Perkins Perspective* 16, no. 3 (March–June 1977).
61. "Bridwell Library: Statistical Profile."
62. Board of trustees minutes, May 12, 1978; Victor Furnish to Joe Allen, March 22, 2009, in the author's personal files.
63. Board of trustees minutes, November 2, 1979.
64. Quillian to Story, April 23, 1969, Bridwell Foundation Correspondence.
65. *Perspective*, fall 2002, 24.
66. Ibid.; senate minutes, January 25 and February 15, 1980.
67. Bridwell Library, Perkins School of Theology, "Report of Activities, November 1980," reports to the Bridwell Foundation, Bridwell Library Papers.

68. "Report of the Association of Theological Schools Visiting Team Concerning Its Visit, October 26–29," 1980, 11–15, James E. Kirby Jr. Papers, Bridwell Library.

69. Bridwell Library, "Report of Activities, November 1980," 3–4; *Special Collections*, 1989, 14.

70. Bridwell Library, "Report of Activities, November 1980," 4; "Prospectus on a Recommended Acquisition for Bridwell Library, Submitted to the Bridwell Foundation, November 21, 1980, by the Director of Bridwell Library, Jerry D. Campbell," Bridwell Foundation Correspondence, 1971 and after, Bridwell Library Papers.

71. James E. Kirby to Provost Hans Hillerbrand, May 13, 1983, Kirby Papers; Jane Wolfe, "Chapters and Verse," *D Magazine* 12, no. 4 (April 1985): 78.

72. Jerry Campbell to Mr. and Mrs. Charles Prothro, November 21, 1980, Bridwell Foundation Correspondence.

73. Board of trustees minutes, November 5, 1982.

74. "Report of the Association of Theological Schools Visiting Team," 2; Wolfe, "Chapters and Verse," 80.

75. Campbell to Story, October 2, 1981; Kirby to Story, December 15, 1981; Story to Edwin L. Cox, December 6, 1982; Campbell to Story, January 19, 1984, all in Bridwell Foundation Correspondence; Roger Loyd to Story, March 2, 1987, attachment, "Bridwell Giving to Perkins," 1948–1986, Bridwell Library Papers.

76. Campbell to Story, Tinsley, and Bridwell, July 25, 1985, Quillian Papers.

77. Faculty minutes, April 12 and May 3, 1985, and January 30, 1986.

78. "The Library Automation Program for the Libraries at Southern Methodist University," no date, Kirby Papers, Bridwell Library; Roger Loyd to Kirby, August 14, 1985, and June 11, 1986, Kirby Papers; Thomas to Allen, January 11, 2009.

79. Roger Loyd, "For the Good of the Order: Bridwell Library Issues," address to the Perkins faculty luncheon, September 25, 1986, Kirby Papers.

80. "Renovation of the Bridwell Library," November 16, 1987, Kirby Papers; *Renovation Newsletter*, no. 1 (April 15, 1988), Kirby Papers; James Kirby, interview by author, November 12, 2008, Dallas.

81. "SMU-Bridwell Library Project Costs, February 1, 1988"; Kirby to Robert Maloy and Roger Loyd, "Some Thoughts on Remodeling," February 4, 1988; Ed Williams to Kirby, Maloy, Ken Black, H. R. Patterson Jr., March 16, 1988, all in Kirby Papers; Story to A. Kenneth Pye, March 25 and October 18, 1989, Bridwell Foundation Correspondence.

82. *Renovation Newsletter*, no. 1 (April 15, 1988); Maloy to Members of the Faculty, August 25, 1988; Roger Loyd, "Bridwell Library Move," July 10, 1989; Order of Service, October 19, 1989, all in Kirby Papers; *Perspective*, winter 1990, 5.

83. *The Bible: 100 Landmarks from the Elizabeth Perkins Prothro Collection: A Guide to the Inaugural Exhibition in the Elizabeth Perkins Prothro Galleries Prepared by the J. S. Bridwell Foundation Librarian* (Dallas: Bridwell Library, 1990), ii, vii–viii; *Perspective*, fall 1992, 3.

84. Maloy to Loyd, January 13, 1988; "Bridwell Organization," spring 1988, both in Kirby Papers.

85. *Perspective*, winter 1990, 2, 3, 5; spring 1991, 12.

86. Faculty minutes, April 8, 1988.

87. Kirby, interview by author, November 12, 2008.

88. *Perspective*, fall 1992, 19.

89. Ibid., summer 1993, 28; fall 1993, 21.

90. Valerie R. Hotchkiss, "Report to the J. S. Bridwell Foundation, November 1993," submitted to Herbert B. Story, president of the board of trustees, Bridwell Library Papers.

91. Ibid., 1–6.

92. Ibid., 5–7.

93. Ibid., 8–9.

94. Ibid., 9–11, 13.

95. Ibid., 15–18.

96. *Perspective*, summer 1994, 11; *Bridwell at Fifty*, 36.

97. Valerie R. Hotchkiss, "Report to the Board of Trustees of the J. S. Bridwell Foundation for the Period from June 1, 1995 to May 31, 1996," November 1996, Bridwell Library Papers.

98. Hotchkiss, reports to the Bridwell Foundation, for June 1, 2001, to May 31, 2002, and June 1, 2003, to May 31, 2004, Bridwell Library Papers.
99. Hotchkiss, "Report to the J. S. Bridwell Foundation, November 1993," 12–13.
100. Hotchkiss, "Report to the Bridwell Foundation for June 1, 1995 to May 31, 1996."
101. "Bridwell Library Exhibits," compiled by Jon Speck; Hotchkiss, "Report to the Bridwell Foundation for June 1, 1997 to May 31, 1998," November 1998, Bridwell Library Papers.
102. "Bridwell Library Exhibits"; Hotchkiss, reports to the Bridwell Foundation for June 1, 2000, to May 31, 2001, January 2002; and for June 1, 2001, to May 31, 2002, February 2003, Bridwell Library Papers.
103. Ibid.; "Bridwell Library Exhibits."
104. Hotchkiss, "Report to the Bridwell Foundation for 1997–98," and update through February 2003.
105. *Perspective*, spring 1997, 6, 17; faculty minutes, December 6, 1996.
106. Eric White, reports on special collections, in Hotchkiss, reports to the Bridwell Foundation, 1996–97 and 2003–04; "Bridwell Library Exhibits."
107. *Perspective*, fall 2007, 13.
108. Roberta A. Schaafsma, "Report to the J. S. Bridwell Foundation … for the period from June 1, 2006 to May 31, 2007," December 2007, Bridwell Library Papers.
109. "Bridwell Library: Statistical Profile."
110. Roberta A. Schaafsma, "Report to the J. S. Bridwell Foundation for June 1, 2007 to May 31, 2008," November 2008, Bridwell Library Papers; Roberta Schaafsma, interview by author, November 21, 2008, Dallas.
111. "New Bridwell Library Mission Statement," Bridwell Library Papers; Roberta Schaafsma to Joe Allen, September 19, 2009, in the author's personal files.

PART III

The Third Perkins

A Time of Transition, 1981–1994

J ames Edmund Kirby Jr. was the first Perkins graduate to serve as dean of the school. A native of northwest Texas, born in 1933, he had grown up in a number of Methodist parsonages of churches where his father, also a graduate of Perkins, had served as pastor. After Kirby and his fiancée, Patty Boothe, graduated from McMurry College in 1954, they both entered Perkins that fall, he to study for his bachelor of divinity and she for her master's in religious education. They were married in the summer of 1955. After completing their degrees, they spent the academic year 1957–58 in England, where as the recipient of the John M. Moore Fellowship from Perkins, he did research at Cambridge University on early British Methodist history. Upon their return in 1958 he served for two years as pastor of the First Methodist Church in Roby, Texas, meanwhile completing work for his master's in sacred theology in 1959. In 1960 he entered the doctoral program in religion at Drew University in the field of church history, serving in 1960–61 as pastor of the Methodist church in Milford, Pennsylvania. He received his Ph.D. degree in 1963 with a dissertation on Bishop Matthew Simpson of the Methodist Episcopal Church. For the next four years Kirby was assistant professor of religion at Sweet Briar College in Virginia. In 1967 he became professor of religion at Oklahoma State University, where he established and chaired the Department of Religion and then was director of the School of Humanistic Studies. In 1976 he returned to Drew as dean of its theological school, the post he held until coming to Perkins as dean in 1981.[1]

Early in Kirby's time as dean, on November 20, 1983, Lois Perkins died at the age of ninety-five. She had been a strong voice for the School of Theology since 1944, when she encouraged her husband, Joe Perkins, to give far more money to the school than he had initially intended. In the controversy in 1953–54 about desegregating the Perkins student body, though her husband wavered, she firmly supported desegregation. After her husband died in September 1960 (Joe Quillian had succeeded Merrimon Cuninggim as dean that July), Lois Perkins became a member of the SMU Board of Trustees and of the board's Committee on the School of Theology and remained so until 1976. Not long after Quillian became dean, she wrote him, "Perkins School and SMU are the two greatest interests of our lives. . . . I want to assure you that in spite of our interest in Perkins, we will never interfere in the least. Just our prayers and best wishes will be with you." She read the faculty's books and wrote the deans supportive letters. Quillian said of her, "Mrs. Perkins is certainly one of the brightest spots in my life."[2]

On November 22 a busload of Perkins faculty and students attended her memorial service in Wichita Falls, and Joe Quillian delivered the eulogy. On January 19, 1984, Perkins held another memorial service for her in the chapel, with Dean Kirby preaching the sermon.[3] Lois Perkins was matchless in the history of Perkins School of Theology.

RESHAPING THE SEMINARY ADMINISTRATION

In 1978, as Dean Joe Quillian was anticipating his retirement, he recommended that the office of dean of Perkins be redesigned, so that an "executive dean" would attend to the internal details of managing the school. The Advisory Decanal Selection Committee recognized Quillian's idea but left this decision to the incoming dean. Jim Kirby, reporting to the Committee on Faculty toward the end of his first year as dean, took note of Quillian's recommendation about the office and commented, "It is more than full-time but I feel confident that with your continued help and support it can be managed and with style."[4]

The key administrative position at Perkins after the dean is that of associate dean for academic affairs. James M. Ward had been associate dean in Quillian's last three years, and he continued as such for Kirby's first nine years: a long and effective tenure in an increasingly demanding position. Ward's experience and judgment were such that he might have been chosen as dean in 1981. His loyal assistance to Kirby over the years is thus all the more impressive. After Ward returned to full-time teaching in 1990, Charles Wood served as associate dean until 1993. David Maldonado succeeded him and continued as associate dean during Robin Lovin's early years as dean.

Several of Kirby's early administrative appointments resulted from retirements. J. B. Holt, who had been the admissions officer since 1959, had postponed his retirement for one year—to 1982—so that the new dean could make that appointment. In Holt's place Kirby appointed Linn Caraway Richardson (M.Div., Perkins, 1981) as director of admissions and recruitment.[5] She remained in that post until 1994, when she was followed by Harry S. Wright Jr. (M.Div., Perkins, 1989), who stepped up after serving as assistant director of admissions from 1991 to 1994; he held the position until 1996.

In 1982 Wayne Banks, director of academic procedures since 1960, took a disability retirement. His replacement was Guy D. Garrett (B.D., Perkins, 1959; Ph.D., Boston University), with twenty years of service in Asia.[6] To Garrett's duties as director of academic procedures was added responsibility for student financial aid. He served in this office until 1992 and was succeeded by Janice A. Virtue (M.B.A., Indiana University; M.Div., Perkins, 1991).

Claus H. Rohlfs Sr., who from 1969 had been director of the intern program and of the Courses of Study School, retired in 1983 and returned to an administrative position in the Southwest Texas Conference. Bert Affleck (B.D., Perkins, 1958; Ph.D., Drew University), the new director of the intern program and the Course of Study School, as the latter now was known, came with wide experience in interethnic and cross-cultural programs, most recently as a pastor in El Paso. He was already well acquainted with the intern program, having served for five years as a field instructor.[7]

Along with personnel changes, Kirby made a number of changes in the structure of Perkins administration. One position proved difficult to define and to fill on a long-term basis. With Barbara Ruth leaving as director of community life in May 1982, Kirby reorganized that office to combine various responsibilities: orientation, convocations, the chapel, and liaison with students and student organizations.[8] Patty Evans, who had been assisting in the master of sacred music program, served as acting director of community life for 1982–83. Then, in the fall of 1983, David Watson, who was completing six years as assistant professor of evangelism, became associate dean for community life, but he left the next year for a position with the United Methodist Board of Discipleship in Nashville. Watson was followed by Beverly Sawyer (M.Div., Perkins, 1979), who was associate dean for four years and in August 1988 resigned for personal reasons. That September Kirby appointed Susanne Johnson, who had completed six years as assistant professor of Christian education, to succeed Sawyer. After three years in that post Johnson returned to the faculty in 1991 as associate professor of Christian education. Kirby then merged the office of admissions with the community life office, and Linn Caraway became associate dean for admission and community life. In 1993 the office was renamed associate dean of students, and Caraway served in that post until 1999, when she took a local church appointment in Plano, Texas.

Another structural change in the early 1980s involved combining two offices. In 1981 Dick Murray, who had directed Perkins's continuing education since 1965, was promoted to the rank of professor and moved to full-time teaching. John Holbert, who had for two years been visiting professor of Old Testament, then became associate director of continuing education and the doctor of ministry program (D.Min.). In 1982, upon the retirement of Howard Grimes, who had been directing the D.Min. program, Holbert became director of both. William Matthews, who had come to Perkins in 1979 as director of Perkins relations (public relations), shared responsibilities as associate director of continuing education.

Kirby had further ideas in mind for the directorship of continuing education and the D.Min. program. As of January 1, 1985, he brought in Stanley J. Menking from the Theological School at Drew University to direct both programs. Holbert moved to full-time teaching in the field of preaching. When Kirby had been dean at Drew, he had had ample opportunity to appreciate Menking's administrative ability as his associate dean. In 1987 Menking's title at Perkins became associate dean for external affairs, adding oversight of the office of Perkins relations to his earlier responsibilities. He continued as associate dean until his retirement in 1997. Marilyn Alexander (M.Div., Perkins, 1990) succeeded Matthews in Perkins relations in 1990, with the new title of director of alumni/ae relations and the alumni/ae Loyalty Fund, the annual campaign for contributions from Perkins alumni/ae; she held that position until 1996.

Kirby also appointed two directors of Bridwell Library: Robert Maloy in 1987 and Valerie Hotchkiss in 1993.

Perkins has had a financial officer since 1969. Following Lanny Folsom, Ken Black held that office from 1976 until his retirement in 1993. Although his office was located at Perkins, he reported directly to SMU's financial office. As Kirby later explained, the dean would work with the provost to draw up the budget, and the financial officer would oversee the budget's operation and supply information on a vast array of details, such as the large number of scholarship funds. "Ken was a meticulous record-keeper," Kirby recalled, "an indispensable part of the whole enterprise."[9] Succeeding him as financial officer in 1993 was Linda Hervey, who previously had been manager of tax and special projects for Mobil Oil Corporation.[10]

When Kirby agreed to come to Perkins as dean, he insisted that the school have its own full-time development officer, appointed as a staff member of the university's development office. The university made a commitment to do this.[11] In January 1982 Joan Ronck, regional campaign director at Vanderbilt University, became Perkins's development officer.[12] Although she stayed only until December 1983, in that short time donations to the Loyalty Fund increased from $29,000 to more than $70,000, and when she left, Perkins was ready to launch its campaign to establish an endowment for the intern program. Kirby observed in 1983, "Two years ago we had nothing which could be described as an organized program in development."[13]

In March 1984 James Lewis, previously a staff member in the SMU Development Office, succeeded Ronck as the Perkins development officer. In August 1985 Kirby told the faculty that "with the strong leadership of two excellent Directors of Development, in four years we have raised a total of $10,400,000. I suspect that in no comparable period have we done as much."[14] In Lewis's three years at Perkins the school raised much of the money for three endowed chairs (the Outler Chair, the Perkins Chair in Homiletics, and the Bridwell Library director), made good progress in the university's Decade Ahead campaign for $12 million, and, in Kirby's words, was "well along toward achieving our goal of $5.5 million for the Intern Program endowment."[15] Lewis left in July 1987 to become director of development at Millsaps College in Mississippi.

Debra Hulse-Bowles, who had been director of alumni relations at McMurry College, was the Perkins development officer from September 1987 to June 1991. In April 1988, Kirby reported, "This year we have received major capital gifts and commitments in the amount of $7,000,000."[16] Priscilla Neaves (M.Div., Perkins, 1985), director of development from 1991, completed the funding of the W. J. A. Power Chair of Biblical Hebrew Language and Old Testament Interpretation.[17] After her resignation in 1993, Kirby left the position unfilled in 1993–94 so that his successor could make the appointment.

With the help of these development officers and the directors of the Loyalty Fund, Perkins's fund-raising efforts had considerable success during the Kirby years. In 1981 the Perkins annual Loyalty Fund drive raised barely $29,000; in 1993 it reached $122,000. When Kirby became dean in 1981, the book value of Perkins's total endowment was $17.3 million. In May 1994 its book value was $41.5 million and its market value, $66.3 million.[18]

The size of the Perkins administrative structure, not including the Bridwell Library staff (which grew considerably), remained stable during Kirby's deanship. In Quillian's last year as dean (1980–81), Perkins had eight full-time administrators, five part-time administrators, and a support staff of fifteen. In Kirby's last year there were nine full-time administrative positions (one temporarily vacant), two part-time administrators, and sixteen support staff.

Kirby worked to improve the administrators' lines of communication. In his first year he reorganized the Administrators' Consultation (program and budget heads), arranged for them to have regular meetings, and instituted the practice of having each suggest a budget for the following year and project a budget for the next five years. Thereafter he reduced the number of administrators reporting directly to the dean, so that some reported through the academic, external affairs, and community life associate deans. Unlike his predecessor, Kirby maintained a fairly clean desk and kept track of how he distributed his time among various responsibilities (he noted that in 1981–82 he spent 20 percent of his time on activities related to development).[19] He had the skills of an effective administrator.

THE PERKINS FACULTY IN THE KIRBY YEARS

As dean, Jim Kirby made twenty-nine new appointments to the Perkins faculty—classroom and intern faculty and administrators with faculty rank (see appendix A)—so that in the fall of 1994 the faculty totaled thirty-nine. On the face of it, this was a reduction of six from its size when he arrived in 1981, but the actual long-term reduction was three: two intern and one classroom faculty members. As for the other three, two administrators who left had had courtesy faculty rank in 1981, whereas their successors in 1994 did not; and Kirby left the appointment of an associate director of the library to the next dean.

Kirby's twenty-one classroom faculty appointments included three in Division I (Bible, in the renumbered divisional order): Danna Nolan Fewell in Old Testament and Jouette Bassler and C. Clifton Black in New Testament. The two in Division II (the Christian heritage in its religious and cultural context) were Ruben L. F. Habito in the history of religions and Edward W. Poitras in world Christianity. Five were in Division III (the interpretation of the Christian witness): Ellen T. Charry, Millicent C. Feske, Luis G. Pedraja, and Joerg Rieger in systematic theology, and Theodore D. Walker Jr. in ethics and society. The largest number of appointments came in Division IV (the church and its ministry): John Wesley Hardt as bishop-in-residence, Susanne Johnson and Deidre Palmer in Christian education, Marjorie Procter-Smith in Christian worship, David Maldonado in church and society, Kenneth W. Hart and C. Michael Hawn in church music, William J. Abraham in evangelism, Patricia Howery Davis in pastoral care, James Wharton in preaching, and William K. McElvaney in preaching and worship.

Two of those listed occupied new positions: Wharton in 1985 was named to the newly endowed Lois Craddock Perkins Professorship in Homiletics, and Hart in 1987 became the director of the master of sacred music program. Hart's appointment meant that for the first time Perkins had two full-time professors in church music.

Another appointment involved a first in Perkins history. In the history of religions, after Neill McFarland retired in 1988, a swap was arranged in 1989 between Perkins and the SMU Department of Religious Studies. Ruben Habito, a specialist in Zen Buddhism, came to Perkins from the religious studies department in exchange for Frederick Streng, who had taught history of religions at Perkins since 1966 and now transferred to religious studies. Streng was still an active member of that department when he died in 1993.

Richey Hogg's retirement in 1987 led to a redefinition of the field of world Christianity. Rather than fill that vacancy right away, Perkins brought in two visiting professors in succession: M. M. Thomas, director of the Christian Institute for the Study of Religion and Society in Bangalore, India, and a leader in the World Council of Churches, who taught at Perkins in 1987–88; and Bishop Yap Kim Hao of The Methodist Church in Malaysia and Singapore, former general secretary of the Christian Conference of Asia, who taught at Perkins from 1988 to 1990. After the field was redefined as "the contemporary Christian community in a global setting," Edward Poitras, for twenty-five years a missionary and teacher in South Korea, joined the faculty in January 1990.[20]

Another visiting professor in that period was retired bishop James S. Thomas of the North Central Jurisdiction, who from 1988 to 1992 was Distinguished Visiting Professor of Practical Theology. During his time at Perkins he completed a history of the Central Jurisdiction of The Methodist Church.[21]

Several developments at the University in the 1980s had a special bearing on the Perkins faculty. In the spring of 1983 the university appointed seven faculty from the various schools as University Distinguished Professors, including Victor Furnish and Schubert Ogden from Perkins and Robert T. Anderson from the Meadows School of the Arts, who as chapel organist had long been closely involved in the master of sacred music program. At the same time it was announced that John Deschner would be appointed to the reinstituted Lehman Professorship in Christian Doctrine, which had been vacant since William D. Bradfield's retirement in 1936.[22] These four and the other University Distinguished Professors were included in the Collegium, a group of SMU endowed chair–holders that Provost Hans J. Hillerbrand had organized the preceding fall for interdisciplinary discussion of scholarly topics.

In addition to John Deschner, three professors already at Perkins were appointed to endowed chairs during Kirby's deanship. In 1985 Richard Heitzenrater became the first Albert Cook Outler Professor of Wesley Studies. The first W. J. A. Power Professor of Hebrew Language and Old Testament, in 1991, was the man in whose honor it was named, Bill Power. After John Deschner retired, Charles Wood was named the next Lehman Professor of Christian Doctrine in 1993. When William McElvaney joined the faculty in 1985, he was the LeVan Professor of Preaching and Worship, the position earlier held by H. Grady Hardin, and William Abraham arrived the same year as McCreless Associate Professor of Evangelism.

In the 1980s SMU established two new university professorships that significantly supplemented Perkins's faculty resources. In 1983–84 the Committee on Ethics in the University Curricula, an advisory group initiated by Hillerbrand, recommended an increase in the level of ethics education at SMU.[23] The year 1985 saw the endowment of two university chairs in ethics and human values. One was the Cary M. Maguire University Professorship of Ethics, held by William F. May, who joined the faculty in the fall of 1985. May had founded the Department of Religious Studies at the University of Indiana and subsequently had moved to Georgetown University's Kennedy Institute of Ethics, where he worked in medical ethics. The other endowed chair was the Elizabeth Scurlock University Professorship of Human Values, to which was appointed David Martin, formerly a sociologist of religion at the London School of Economics. The occupants of both chairs were available to teach in all the schools of the university, and both May and Martin taught from time to time at Perkins and in the Graduate Program in Religious Studies. After Martin returned to a position in England in 1989, the university in 1991 appointed to the Scurlock Chair Charles E. Curran, a Catholic moral theologian who for most of his career had been a faculty member at Catholic University in Washington, D.C. In 1993, with Fred Carney's retirement in mind, Division III arranged for May and Curran each to teach one Perkins course every academic year. Given that agreement, Kirby did not make an appointment to replace Carney.

In the intern program, in addition to naming Bert Affleck to succeed Claus Rohlfs as director, Kirby appointed five associate directors between 1982 and 1988: Lynn Mims, Virgil Howard (who in 1984 moved to the intern program from teaching preaching), Mary Lou Santillán Baert, Marilyn Spurrell, and Thomas W. Spann. Intern associate directors were designated as faculty beginning in 1984.[24]

Thirty-five members left the Perkins faculty during Kirby's deanship, including library directors and administrators with courtesy faculty rank. In thirteen years this was a large turnover. Eighteen retired, sixteen went elsewhere, and one, Roger Deschner, died in the fall of 1991 after a long illness. Howard Grimes, the last remaining member of Dean Eugene B. Hawk's faculty, retired in 1982. Nine of Dean Merrimon Cuninggim's appointments retired: in the order of their initial appointments they were Douglas Jackson, Neill McFarland, Richey Hogg, John Deschner, Schubert Ogden, Wayne Banks, J. B. Holt, Bill Farmer, and Fred Carney. John Deschner, who retired in 1991, and Schubert Ogden, in 1993, had for many years team-taught the required two-semester course in systematic theology. Six appointed by Dean Joe Quillian retired: Dick Murray, David Switzer, Claus Rohlfs, Martha Gilmore, Jane Marshall, and Ruth Barnhouse. Three retirees had been Kirby appointments: Bill McElvaney, bishop-in-residence W. MacFerrin Stowe, and Mary Lou Santillán Baert.

Of the other departures, most had been appointed by Quillian, but three had been named by Kirby. Seven classroom faculty went to other academic positions; in the order of their departures they were James White, Harold Attridge, Phyllis Bird, Charles Thomas, Fred Streng, Millicent Feske, and Richard Heitzenrater. One, David Watson, took a Methodist church board position. Between 1982 and 1987 the intern faculty saw considerable turnover, with Dale Hensarling, Richard Stewart, James Gwaltney, Craig Emerick, and Lynn Mims leaving in that order. Three library administrators departed: Jerry Campbell in 1985 and in 1992 Roger Loyd and then Robert Maloy.

The many retirements and other departures from the Cuninggim and Quillian years marked the passing of the "second Perkins." For the most part their departures were scattered across Kirby's years as dean, but in 1993 seven left: Carney, McElvaney, Murray, Ogden, and Switzer retired, and Feske and Heitzenrater went to positions elsewhere.

The Perkins Senate had been the school's governing body since 1969. By 1981 it included the faculty, fifteen students, two alumni/ae, and the chair of the Trustees Committee for the School of Theology. From early in his tenure as dean, Kirby found the senate frustrating. He was perplexed about how to exercise his leadership with it, as one could not both participate in and preside over a deliberative group. Though the "senate is dominated by faculty," he said, it is "not faculty."[25] Under the existing system of governance the faculty had no opportunity to deliberate as faculty and decide about school policy.

In Kirby's first year as dean the members of the Community Life Committee decided, and the dean and others agreed, that all noncurricular aspects of Perkins life should undergo a major review. Responding to that judgment, the Advisory Council (the chairs of the standing committees of the senate) recommended, and the senate authorized, appointment of a community life study committee to conduct that review during the 1982–83 academic year. It was composed of four faculty, one staff member, five students, and a student spouse, with faculty member Edwin Sylvest as chair.[26]

In March 1983 this study committee, in one section of a lengthy report to the senate, observed that there were "complex issues related to our conformity to the 'By-Laws of Southern Methodist University' especially as they pertain to operation of our faculty in a system of shared governance." It proposed that the dean establish another special committee to propose a revision of the senate's organization, noting that this revision should "observe the principle of shared governance" and "honor the principles of a revitalized faculty and a strengthened student government." It further proposed that Perkins governance be the primary topic of discussion at the Senate Conference in the fall of 1983 and that the proposed revision of governance be presented for adoption by the end of the fall semester, so that it could take effect in the fall of 1984. The senate adopted the report after amending it to add the words, "Such revision shall conform to the requirements of the By-Laws of Southern Methodist University."[27]

The dean then appointed the Governance Study Committee, composed of two faculty members (Sylvest and me) and two students (Earl Bledsoe, co-convenor of the Perkins Student Council, and Barbara Johnson, a member of the Community Life Study Committee), with James Ward, associate dean, as chair. In its preliminary report for discussion at the Senate Conference on October 1, 1983, the committee observed that its proposals were not new but had already been widely discussed both in the Community Life Study Committee and between its members and others in the Perkins community. It pointed out that the SMU by-laws stipulated that decisions about several matters currently decided by the Perkins Senate were the responsibility of the faculty. Thus, the report continued, the senate could not have responsibility for the those areas. Furthermore, the committee judged that the senate, given its size and membership, did not constitute an adequate forum for faculty deliberation, which was most likely to occur when the faculty itself was the deliberative body. Yet the committee affirmed the appropriateness and importance of students' formal participation in the process of academic decision making.[28]

The inclination of the Governance Study Committee in this preliminary report was to propose two separate organizations: the faculty and a new, reconfigured senate. After discussing the report at length and making numerous suggestions, the Senate Conference voted 35 to 2, with some uncounted abstentions, that it was "in agreement with the general direction of the proposal."[29] The one-sidedness of the vote suggests that dissatisfaction with the senate was widespread, not only among faculty and administrators but also among students. In 1969 student leaders had pressed for participation in Perkins governance, but their successors in later years found this participation and its time demands less and less attractive. A further problem was the lack of continuity of student membership from year to year. Most student members were middlers, because most third-year students were on internship at least part of that year, and those returning to campus for a fourth year were rarely elected to the senate. Students made no serious effort to retain the old senate.

The Governance Study Committee then brought a fully developed proposal to the senate at its December 1983 meeting.[30] It defined the faculty as consisting of all full-time Perkins faculty and intern staff, the director of academic procedures, the associate dean of community life, and the director of admissions. It would be responsible for policy in all the areas stipulated by the SMU by-laws: admission requirements, courses of study, conditions for graduation, nature of the degrees to be conferred, rules and methods for conduct of the school's educational work, and recipients of degrees, awards, and prizes. Also included as areas of faculty responsibility would be continuing education and "faculty work and well-being." The report proposed a set of faculty committees, including the number of members for each (most including two or three students), and described the mandates of each committee, as well as two joint faculty-senate committees—nominations and long-range planning.

In this proposal the new senate would consist of ten students, six faculty, and five administrators and would be chaired by the dean. Its responsibilities, assisted by several committees, would include worship, convocations and special events, counseling and student services, alumni relations, and the arts. The student council would continue as before.

The old senate amended the report at a few places and then unanimously adopted its recommendations. The new governance plan took effect at the beginning of the 1984–85 academic year. In his address to the faculty conference in the fall of 1984 Kirby rejoiced in the faculty's reconstitution:

We, for the first time in more than a decade, will function without the Senate. . . . [The faculty has] a rich history of working together in a creative and harmonious manner and this new arrangement will offer us some distinct advantages over the former arrangement under the umbrella of the Senate. It will enable me, as your Dean, to bring before you in an open and forthright fashion matters of substance and policy, and to seek your advice as a faculty on a course of action. It will, I believe, enable me to be more responsive to you by being more aware of your concerns for Perkins.[31]

The new senate lasted only four years and then succumbed to the same difficulty students had with the old senate. Even a reduced level of participation in governance demanded more time and work than students were willing to sustain. It was dissolved in 1988, and its responsibilities reverted to the faculty, assisted by the student council and student members of various faculty committees.[32]

Another change related to Perkins governance occurred in 1984 with the establishment of the Perkins Executive Board. At its meeting that November the SMU Board of Trustees established executive boards for the university library and the individual schools, including Perkins. Their purpose was to advise the deans; serve as a link for the trustees, faculty, students, and the public; and support development programs. The Perkins Executive Board, answerable to the board of trustees, replaced the Committee on the School of Theology, established in 1917. It met for the first time January 22–23, 1986, and was chaired by Leighton K. Farrell, senior pastor of Highland Park United Methodist Church. Its initial twenty-one members included Elizabeth Perkins Prothro, two Methodist bishops, and the deans of three other seminaries—Candler, Duke, and Yale Divinity School. In his first report to the trustees, Farrell expressed appreciation to Kirby for the orientation provided to the members and for the opportunity the executive board gave for many more people to be involved in Perkins's affairs.[33]

During the 1970s the Perkins faculty had begun to become diverse in gender and ethnicity and had developed policies to guide its efforts toward diversity—in 1975 creating the Task Force on Minority Concerns, and in 1977 adopting "Guidelines for Enlarging Minority and Woman Membership in the Perkins Faculty and Intern Staff." Of the forty-five Perkins faculty and intern staff members when Jim Kirby arrived as dean in the fall of 1981, thirty-seven were non-Hispanic white men. Four were women: two full-time tenured members of the faculty (Phyllis Bird and Ruth Barnhouse), an associate director of the intern staff (Martha Gilmore), and a continuing adjunct professor in the church music program (Jane Marshall). Three were African Americans: two faculty members (Zan Holmes and Charles Thomas) and an associate director of the intern staff (Richard Stewart). One was Hispanic: Roy Barton, director of the Mexican American Program with the nontenure-track rank of associate professor. One administrator without faculty rank was a woman—Barbara Ruth, director of community life.

Kirby moved quickly to make both the faculty and administration more diverse. In four years—by the fall of 1985—he made twelve faculty and administrative staff appointments. Of these, five were women—two faculty members (Susanne Johnson and Marjorie Procter-Smith) and three administrators without faculty rank (Caraway, Ronck, and Sawyer). One was an African American member of the intern staff (Mims), and one classroom professor was Hispanic (Maldonado). In the same period five women and members of racial or ethnic minority groups left, for a net increase of two.[34]

From the fall of 1985 through the spring of 1994, of the many appointments Kirby made of faculty and administrative staff from outside Perkins, fourteen were women. Of these six were classroom faculty (in order of their appointments, Bassler, Fewell, Feske, Davis, Charry, and Palmer), two were intern faculty (Baert and Spurrell), and six were administrators (Hulse-Bowles, Alexander, Neaves, Virtue, Hervey, and Hotchkiss). Four of Kirby's appointees were African American: one classroom faculty (Walker), one intern faculty (Spann), and two administrators (Hervey and Wright). Baert was Hispanic, as was Pedraja. One was Asian—Habito. Nine women and minorities retired or departed during this period. By the end of Kirby's deanship, the net increase of minorities and women since 1981 was twelve. These figures do not include the three distinguished visiting professors who were Asian and African American.

During Kirby's deanship the number of non-Hispanic white male faculty members and administrators decreased from thirty-seven to twenty-three, even though he made twelve appointments in this category. With sixteen white men retiring in those years, a decrease was to be expected. Twelve other white male faculty members and administrators took positions elsewhere, and one died before retirement. In the fall of

Schubert M. Ogden, c. 1980s.

Zan W. Holmes, Jr., c. 1980s.

Phyllis Bird in class, c. 1980.

Claus H. Rohlfs.

David Maldonado, Roy Barton, Rosa Marina Barton, 2006.

From left: Albert Outler, Klaus Penzel, John Deschner, Leroy Howe, c. 1975.

Dean James E. Kirby, 1990.

The Perkins faculty, fall 1982. Seated, left to right: John Deschner, W. Richey Hogg, Charles M. Wood, Schubert M. Ogden, Dean James E. Kirby, Joseph L. Allen, Zan W. Holmes, Jr., H. Neill McFarland, Roy Barton. Standing: Roger Deschner, Susanne Johnson, Charles B. Thomas, David Lowes Watson, Guy D. Garrett, Klaus Penzel, Virgil Howard, William Matthews, David Switzer, William J. A. Power, Richard P. Heitzenrater, Dick Murray, James M. Ward, Edwin E. Sylvest, Claus H. Rohlfs, Lynn Mims, Frederick S. Carney, Victor P. Furnish, Phyllis Bird, John Holbert, William R. Farmer, Ruth Tiffany Barnhouse, Harold W. Attridge.

Dean Robin Lovin, 2001.
(©SMU 2001, photo by Jake Dean)

The Intern Faculty Reunion, November 16–17, 2000. Front row, from left: Richard Stewart, Emma Justes, Marilyn Spurrell, Lynn Mims. Middle row: Claus H. Rohlfs, Thomas W. Spann, James Gwaltney. Back row: Virgil Howard, William J. Bryan III, Bert Affleck, Craig Emerick.
(©SMU 2000, photo by Hillsman S. Jackson)

Dean Robin Lovin, Elizabeth Perkins Prothro, Decherd Turner, 1996.
(©SMU 1996, photo by Jean Cassen)

Vin and Caren Prothro in front of the renovated Perkins Chapel, September 1999.
(©SMU 1999, photo by Hillsman S. Jackson)

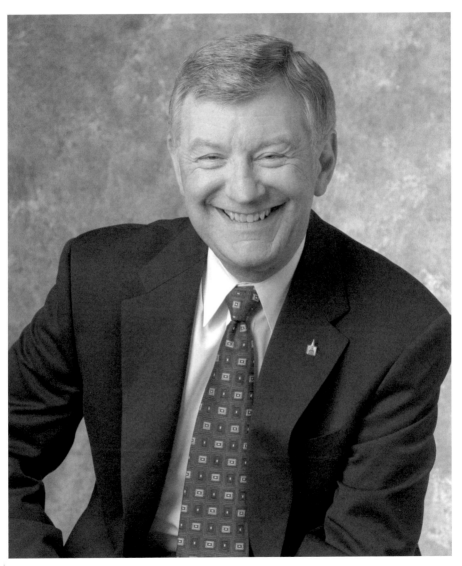

Dean William B. Lawrence, 2006.
(©SMU 2006, photo by Hillsman S. Jackson)

Victor Furnish, Dean Bill Lawrence, and Richard Heitzenrater, 2003.
(©SMU 2003, photo by Hillsman S. Jackson)

The Perkins quadrangle, 2009.

Perkins faculty and administrators, September 2010. First row, left to right: Timothy McLemore, Rebekah Miles, Ruben Habito, Jeanne Stevenson-Moessner, Richard Nelson, Dean Bill Lawrence, Paula Dobbs-Wiggins, Ted Campbell, Marjorie Procter-Smith. Second row: Joerg Rieger, Alyce McKenzie, Thomas Spann, Robert Hunt, Gary MacDonald, Susanne Johnson, Karen Baker-Fletcher, Tracy Anne Allred. Third row: Theo Walker, Roberta Schaafsma, Susanne Scholz, John Holbert, Evelyn Parker, Mark Stamm, Michael Hawn, Jaime Clark-Soles. Fourth row: Carlos Cardoza-Orlandi, Harold Recinos, Abraham Smith, Todd Rasberry, Roy Heller, Barry Hughes, William J. Bryan III, Valerie Karras, Duane Harbin.

(©SMU 2010, photo by Jake Dean)

1994, along with the twenty-three non-Hispanic white men, the faculty and administrators with faculty rank included sixteen women and minorities.

Kirby strongly encouraged the increased diversity and took pride in it, reviewing in his reports and addresses to the faculty the results of "our mutual determination to be responsive" to women and members of minority groups.[35] On occasion he would also identify issues that this process implied, as in his 1985 address at the fall faculty conference:

> We must establish clear guidelines to inform the choices we make with respect to new colleagues. What is the practical meaning of our commitment to have a faculty which is pluralistic? If necessary are we prepared to modify our expectations to accommodate minority persons to achieve the goal of representation? . . . How will we choose among groups for the faculty? . . . Will we give priority to certain groups, or will we try to balance the claims of all of them? The latter course, I fear, is destined to fail if we try it. . . . Progress toward any measure of inclusiveness will not happen if we do not make it happen.[36]

At the following year's faculty conference he told the gathering, "Last year I asked us to consider when we would have reached our goal of a pluralistic faculty. . . . I am not willing to accept the unspoken, 'As many as we can,' as either adequate or responsible. Before we begin again to recruit new persons for our faculty, I want to lay the question squarely on the table and urge us collectively to establish appropriate guidelines to follow in the future."[37]

In the fall of 1987 Kirby told the faculty he was "concerned about our ability to recruit and retain a faculty which is inclusive, United Methodist in its majority, and composed of persons who represent the highest potential for critical theological reflection and skills in teaching."[38]

The desire for clear guidelines was an understandable but elusive goal. In the fall of 1988, with the prospect of establishing five faculty search committees that fall, Fred Carney as chair of the Committee on Faculty distributed a memo to the faculty before a guild meeting to discuss the subject.[39] (Guild meetings are devoted to discussing topics of importance to the faculty, rather than conducting faculty business.) Carney offered some considerations he thought should guide faculty members' actions as they participated in the appointment process. The first and only absolutely necessary consideration, he said, was the prospective faculty member's academic quality; thus short lists of prospects should be made up only of those of "exceptional ability and achievement (adjusted to age and experience) in teaching and research." Second was the self-evident need to increase the number of women and ethnic minority members of the faculty. He judged that the criterion of quality had to be met before moving to the requirements of the second consideration. A third consideration was the desirability of having a better age balance among faculty members.

Carney's memo served as a stimulus for the faculty guild discussion. If that meeting was like most other guild meetings, the members expressed conflicting opinions, some agreeing and some disagreeing with Carney's ordering of the criteria. Perkins faculty searches continued without widely accepted clear criteria for the process.

More than three years later the Committee on Faculty, with W. J. A. Power as chair, presented a report to the faculty proposing procedures for increasing faculty "pluralism." As amended by the faculty, the report stated the "desire to obtain, as rapidly as responsibly possible, increased ethnic and gender diversity of the Perkins faculty which will enhance its quality and reflect a proper representation of women and of the racial and ethnic population of our region." It recommended that search committees follow these procedures for ranking those who appeared to be qualified for a position: "Place the names in groupings of rough similarity in level of qualifications . . . [such as] (a) excellent, (b) considerably more than qualified, (c) qualified"; consider all names in the highest grouping containing names." If this grouping does not contain such names, "two considerations would weigh strongly against moving to a lower grouping." For one, "this would involve a questionable compromise in quality," possibly "a form of reverse discrimination that might be legally challengeable." Also, within a grouping preference should go to "persons whose background, interests, perspectives, and abilities complement those of other members of the Perkins faculty."[40]

The report offered no judgment about what would constitute "a proper representation," except the implied judgment that it would be an larger one; it set no quotas. Likewise, it provided no guidance about how to judge the qualifications of prospects, perhaps assuming (questionably) that faculty members would have similar perspectives from which to make those judgments.

At the October 1983 meeting of the Perkins Senate, Susanne Johnson presented a document, drawn up by the Perkins Women Administrators and Faculty, entitled, "Proposal to Establish a Task Force on the Community of Women and Men." The purpose of the task force would be to investigate a wide range of issues in Perkins life as they pertain to women: course offerings, inclusiveness of programs, inclusive language, and affirmative action policies and procedures. The proposal was amended and adopted, and the task force was asked to report its recommendations to the senate the following April.[41]

In April, Marjorie Procter-Smith reported to the old senate for the task force, which proposed creation of a committee on women and ethnic minority concerns as a standing committee of the faculty and of the senate. The senate approved this proposal unanimously. The first year the committee gave special attention to the need for more inclusive worship at Perkins, better communication among women and men about ministry, and the need for a process to deal with sexual harassment at Perkins.[42] In the next few years it focused on two topics: sexual harassment—responding to it and sensitizing the community about it—and developing and conducting workshops on sexism and racism. The two workshops were created in 1988–89. Students were required to attend both each year, and the committee recommended that faculty attend at least one each year.

In this context of increasing faculty diversity, John Deschner, in an address to the faculty on March 21, 1991, spoke of the three periods of Perkins history: from 1915 to 1951, from 1951 to sometime in the 1980s, and, since the 1980s, the school's moving in a way that he could not predict—a "third Perkins."[43]

Deschner had a knack for perceiving significant developments and characterizing them in illuminating ways. When he spoke in the spring of 1991, the Perkins faculty was undergoing four kinds of changes. One was the departure of most of the remaining faculty members who arrived in the 1950s through the 1970s. Another was the faculty's increasing diversity by gender, race, and ethnicity, as well as the decrease in the proportion of those who were ordained and who were Methodists. Still another was an increasing diversity of its theological and social outlooks. The fourth was growing tensions in the members' work with one another.

New eras seldom emerge suddenly. The second Perkins was foreshadowed by

President Umphrey Lee's taking office in 1939, Joe and Lois Perkins's gifts beginning in 1944, and the appointment before 1951 of a few faculty who came to feel thoroughly at home with the post-1951 changes. Several faculty from the first Perkins continued through much of the decade of the 1950s, and a few remained much longer. Even so, only after Merrimon Cuninggim's arrival as dean in 1951 were there major changes in the curriculum, the racial composition of the student body, and in the size and theological orientations of the faculty.

Identifying the starting point for the third Perkins is more difficult. It emerged gradually. Diversification of the faculty began in the early 1970s and developed more rapidly in the 1980s. Significant diversity of faculty outlooks was always present, though it was increasing. It was present in the 1920s, for example, in the differences between Seneker and his colleagues. In the second Perkins it was evident in numerous ways: for example, from 1956, when John Deschner and Schubert Ogden joined the faculty with markedly different theological views, and in 1959, when both William Farmer and Victor Furnish arrived, bringing sharply different conceptions of the appropriate direction for New Testament scholarship. The years of Kirby's deanship, though, saw a greater degree of diversity of outlook, as well as of new faculty members' social locations (their places in society). Faculty tensions increased in the latter part of the 1980s, coming sharply to the forefront in the fall of 1992, threatening the collegiality of earlier years.

In these years and afterward, the Perkins faculty continued its extensive work of research and publication. Rather than attempt to survey this large and diverse body of scholarship, I have provided a list of books written by Perkins faculty and staff and published while they were at Perkins (see appendix C).

Several expressions of Perkins scholarship, some not listed in appendix C, call for mention here. The publication, beginning in 1984, of Albert Outler's four-volume edition of John Wesley's *Sermons*, was the first of the Wesley Works Editorial Project.[44] Richard Heitzenrater was likewise a major participant in the Wesley Works, serving as associate editor-in-chief and later as general editor. In addition, he edited Wesley's diaries after discovering the key to the code in which Wesley wrote them.[45] Five of the seven volumes of journal and diaries had appeared by the time Heitzenrater moved from Perkins to Duke in 1993.

John Deschner's scholarship during the 1970s and 1980s was expressed largely in the work of the Commission on Faith and Order of the World Council of Churches, of which he was a member for many years and the moderator from 1983 to 1991. Of the many studies issued by the commission, one of special significance on which Deschner and many others worked was *Baptism, Eucharist and Ministry,* issued in 1982 as a quest for agreement on those crucial matters of doctrinal division among the churches.[46] During the next seven years the commission received 186 responses from the churches, necessitating its continuing work on the subject.[47]

Fred Carney had initiated the Faculty Symposium in 1972, and he was the primary mover behind the organization of the Ethics Colloquy in 1983. As he explained, it was "intended for those students and faculty who want to engage in serious analysis of ethical issues, both theoretical and applied." Faculty attending these sessions over the years have included several from Perkins and others from the School of Law, the Cox School of Business, the Department of Philosophy of Dedman College, and occasionally from the University of Texas Southwestern Medical Center at Dallas. Ph.D. students in religious studies have regularly been participants, as have been a few seminary students with a special interest in ethics. The procedure of the colloquy has ordinarily been to circulate a scholarly paper or selection from a book or journal to be read in advance—often a work by an Ethics Colloquy member but sometimes by a visiting scholar. A session might begin with comments by the author and then a response by another member, followed by questions and discussion. Until 1993 Carney and I alternated years as Ethics Colloquy chairs; since 1995 the chair has been Charles Curran.[48]

In 1990 Perkins faculty members lost a longtime vehicle for their scholarly work. Since 1947 faculty members and others had frequently published articles in the *Perkins Journal.* The *Journal* was circulated to a few subscribers, including libraries, and free of charge to ministers in the South Central Jurisdiction. In 1990 it was discontinued, for several reasons: the many other scholarly journals in various theological fields, uncertainty in its readers' minds about its role, and soaring costs of publication and mailing. For forty-three years it provided a valuable service to Perkins and the church.[49]

Before the 1980s Perkins had three processes for evaluating faculty members' work: formal reviews regarding promotion and tenure; faculty members' annual reports to the dean, together with his responses; and student course evaluations. In the 1980s the faculty added to these a program of teaching enhancement groups, in which faculty members would observe and afterward discuss one another's teaching; after a few years they replaced it with a peer evaluation program.

Rank and tenure reviews of Perkins faculty, which had become more demanding in the 1970s, became increasingly so in the 1980s. During the five years when Hans Hillerbrand was provost (1981–86), the university raised its promotion and tenure standards. Tenure and promotion recommendations went from the various schools to the Council of Deans, which functioned as the University Rank and Tenure Committee. In 1986 Dean Kirby observed that recommendations "are not being brought which I believe would have come before us some years ago." In light of this new strictness, Perkins, he said, would need to look carefully at its procedures regarding promotion and tenure and, in particular, "the relative weight we assign to teaching and scholarly productivity."[50]

The formal procedure at Perkins was that the dean, in consultation with the faculty member subject to review, would prepare a dossier of evidence relevant to the assessment of the faculty member's teaching, scholarship, and other criteria. The Rank and Tenure Committee, with the dean and the academic associate dean present, would then in executive session review the appropriate evidence and advise the dean by individual comments without a vote or sense of the meeting. Thereafter the dean would decide whether to recommend renewal of a contract or to grant promotion and/or tenure, depending on the question being considered, and would convey this recommendation to the provost. After the review the dean was the only person authorized to discuss it with the faculty member.[51]

During the 1980s Kirby acted on several rank and tenure cases, in most instances recommending tenure and/or promotion or renewal of contract. In some instances, however, the outcome was otherwise. Like Quillian before him, when Kirby thought it likely that he would be recommending against granting tenure, he advised the faculty member to consider another position at Perkins or elsewhere and not go through a formal review. Some faculty in the 1980s took that option. In some cases, however, the faculty member moved after a negative recommendation by the dean. Those denied tenure responded in different ways. When one highly popular teacher received a negative decision, students went to his office to say that they were going to protest the action to the dean. The professor is reported to have replied to them, "No, he made the right judgment!" In another instance a faculty member appealed the dean's negative judgment to the provost, who upheld the dean's recommendation.

As is the case generally in the academy, untenured faculty members were nervous about their prospects, especially given the makeup of the Rank and Tenure Committee—six full professors elected by the tenure-track faculty. Perhaps with that anxiety in mind, the dean told the 1984 Faculty Conference that he thought the Rank and Tenure Committee could "serve us even better if it is not limited entirely to persons of full professorial rank." The next winter the faculty, following his suggestion, amended its by-laws to provide for the first time that as many as two of the six members of the committee could hold a rank lower than full professor, though such members were not to participate in committee deliberations about their own promotion or tenure.[52] At its next opportunity the faculty elected an assistant professor to the committee, and in most years since then at least one person of less than full professor rank has been a member.

Faculty members were first required to submit annual reports in 1970. At first they were due by June 1, and Quillian would reply to each one with a lengthy letter. In the spring of Kirby's first year as dean, he reported that with each member of the faculty and administrative staff he had "begun a regular formative review which will be conducted in the spring of each year."[53] Thereafter he would read each annual report, study the course evaluations, have a conference with the faculty member, and then write a long letter in response. With more than forty faculty members and administrators in residence, this was immensely time consuming but deeply appreciated by the faculty.[54]

Perkins students first began to develop questionnaires for student course evaluations in 1967 and 1968, in consultation with faculty members and the associate academic dean.[55] Since then the faculty, with students' suggestions, has periodically revised the forms. Both Quillian and Kirby made a practice of reviewing the evaluations and meeting each year with a committee of students to solicit their judgments about individual faculty members' teaching.

In 1981–82 the faculty developed a program of "teaching enhancement groups." This was an effort to meet one of the quality criteria used in apportioning the Ministerial Education Fund (the monies provided by the denomination for seminary education)—whether teaching was formally evaluated by faculty peers. The underlying principle of the groups was "that the best way to improve teaching is to facilitate reflection by each faculty member on her or his own teaching." To that end the Committee on Faculty, with faculty authorization, set up eight groups of four or five members each, randomly assigned, and made detailed suggestions about their procedure.[56] Each group, which was to work together for two academic years, proceeded in its own way. In some groups the members shared syllabi, audited one another's courses, and met periodically to discuss their teaching. There was general appreciation for the program, especially in its first year. However, because the groups were not part of a formal faculty evaluation process, this program did not meet the Ministerial Education Fund criterion. In the spring of 1985 the process was reconstituted on a voluntary basis in the form of pairs of faculty to be reassigned annually.

In the spring of 1985 the Task Force on Faculty Evaluation, chaired by Harold Attridge, proposed a new program—Faculty Peer Evaluation of Teaching and Scholarship—which the faculty adopted. It had two purposes: to meet the Ministerial Education Fund criterion by providing information for the dean's and the Rank and Tenure Committee's assessments of individual faculty members, and to strengthen teaching and scholarship. This new program required that each faculty member be reviewed on a regular basis in a process supervised by the Committee on Faculty. Instructors and assistant professors would be reviewed in the second year of each three-year appointment, and associate and full professors and intern staff at least every six years. Two faculty reviewers and the person being reviewed constituted each review committee. Their work included meetings to discuss the report of the reviewee's teaching and scholarship and visits to the reviewee's classes. Once this program began in the fall of 1985, the teaching enhancement groups ceased to function, and in 1987 the faculty formally discontinued them.[57]

In the first two years of peer evaluation, twenty-eight faculty members participated, either as reviewees (twelve) or reviewers or both. Responses from the faculty after the first year ranged from enthusiastic to affirmative to lukewarm. Some participants appreciated the collegiality it required, the seriousness of those doing the evaluations, and the benefits to both reviewers and reviewees. It took considerable time, with each faculty member participating in a peer evaluation committee an average of at least three times in a six-year period. For that reason the faculty amended the program in 1987 to reduce the frequency of reviews, especially for assistant professors. Now the average participation on a peer evaluation committee became three times each seven years—still a large demand of time.[58] Another problem was that untenured faculty women were uneasy when they were being reviewed by two older faculty members, usually men. In the fall of 1992, during a time of serious faculty conflict, the program was made optional for untenured faculty pending a review of the program.[59] Afterward it was continued at a reduced rate through the spring of 1996, when it was replaced by a less demanding "peer teaching groups" program.[60]

CURRICULUM CHANGES

In March 1981, in the last semester of Joe Quillian's deanship, the Perkins Senate commissioned a special committee to review the master of divinity (M.Div.) curriculum and to report to the senate in the spring of 1982. The last review of the basic degree curriculum had taken place in 1968–69. Even though Perkins had modified the M.Div. program a few times during the intervening years, problems had accumulated. On March 30 Quillian appointed the thirteen-member Committee to Study the Curriculum; the thirteen members were drawn from the intern staff (one), student body (two), alumni/ae (two), faculty (seven—I was the chair), and administration (James Ward, associate dean) Upon his arrival Kirby also became a committee member.

During the next twelve months the committee as a whole met thirty-one times; it held at least twenty other meetings with groups of students, alumni/ae, the divisions, and segments of the faculty and senate, and countless informal discussions occurred among individual members and with others—a highly consultative process. In the spring of 1982, in two long sessions, the senate amended and then adopted the committee's report, with the changes to go into effect in the fall of 1983.[61]

One result of the committee's work was a new divisional structure. Since 1953 the Perkins faculty had been structured in four divisions: I—The Church and Its Ministry; II—Christianity and Culture; III—The Christian Heritage (including the history of Christianity and systematic and moral theology); and IV—The Bible. The new structure eliminated Division II. Its stated purpose had been to introduce students to the relations between Christianity and culture, but that dialog had never been limited to members of Division II. Beyond that purpose the various cultural areas represented by the several Division II fields (philosophy, other religions, psychology, society, the arts, world Christianity, the black heritage) had little in common. The new divisional structure retained work in all these fields but located them in the other divisions. A second result of restructuring was the renumbering of the divisions, which had varied from ordinary practice in the theological world and failed to recognize the way some fields of theological study build on others.

The new structure, as refined during the following year, was this:

Division I: The Biblical Witness.

Division II: The Heritage of the Christian Witness in Its Religious and Cultural Context. (This division now included the history of religions, the history of Christianity, and world Christianity.)

Division III: The Interpretation of the Christian Witness. (Division III now included systematic theology, moral theology, and theology and culture.)

Division IV: The Witness of the Church and Its Ministry. (This division included several subfields.)[62]

This divisional structure persisted to 2010 with little change.

Several features of the M.Div. curriculum were left unchanged: Two-thirds of the hours required for graduation continued to be in required courses; the rest were in electives and, for United Methodist students, in six semester hours of studies in Methodism, required by the denomination. The required courses were distributed across the four divisions, varying from nine to fifteen semester hours in each (with additional required hours in Bible for those opting to take one or both biblical languages). Special examinations were still available as alternatives to several of the required courses, but now only fifteen semester hours could be earned that way. A full-time supervised internship of at least one semester continued to be required, to be taken after successful completion of at least thirty-six semester hours of coursework.

The main changes were these:

• The number of semester hours required for graduation was increased from seventy-eight (sixty-six in coursework plus twelve in the internship) to eighty-four (seventy-two in courses plus twelve in the internship).

- Students now had to take at least eighteen semester hours of coursework after the internship, as contrasted with nine previously.
- Instead of assigning all courses to two categories, introductory (general requirements) and advanced (electives), this curriculum included a third category of intermediate courses, some required, some elective.
- Instead of requiring twelve semester hours in an array of introductory ministry courses, the requirement was now five semester hours in a new two-semester introduction to ministry; one semester hour in spiritual formation (concurrent with introduction to ministry); three semester hours in preaching, now taught in the context of Christian worship; and six semester hours in intermediate courses in at least two "functions of ministry" other than preaching—for a total of fifteen required semester hours in ministry courses.
- After internship, students were required to take a three-semester-hour advanced seminar in theology and ministry in which the chief objective was to reflect theologically on the practice of ministry. Faculty for this course would be drawn from all the divisions.
- The required three-semester-hour course, "Introduction to Theology," was now eliminated. In its place students were to take one of several designated advanced courses focusing mainly on theological reflection.
- An interethnic experience would now be required of each student—approximately three to four clock hours a week—during the first two semesters at Perkins.
- The curriculum now designated specific courses totaling six semester hours that would meet the denomination's Methodism requirement.[63]

The study committee also proposed, and the senate adopted, a new program, leading to the degree of master of theological studies (M.T.S.), designed mainly for people wishing to do theological study but not seeking to be ordained. Admission requirements were to be the same as for the M.Div. degree, and financial aid was to be available on the same basis as for other basic degree programs. The program was to require forty-eight semester hours of coursework for graduation, with at least six semester hours of work in each of the four divisions.[64] The M.T.S. quickly attracted dozens of students each year.

• • •

When the doctor of ministry program was announced in 1973, it consisted of two tracks. The in-ministry track, requiring twenty-four semester hours, was open to students who had already completed the master of theology degree and had at least two years of full-time ministerial experience. The in-sequence track was for students who had not completed the master of theology; they had to have previously completed sixty semester hours of seminary, including the general requirements and the internship, and had to demonstrate ability to work exegetically in either Hebrew or Greek. They then would do forty-two additional hours, including a specialization in an area of ministerial practice and another specialization in Bible, history of Christianity, systematics, or moral theology.

Although the program attracted numerous students (enrollment of fourteen to forty each year through 1981), Perkins faculty and administrators came to be dissatisfied with the in-sequence track. One reason was that students on that track lacked the experience in ministry to benefit adequately from doctor of ministry study. Another was the inflexibility of the course schedule, so that many potential students—especially those living at a distance—could not take advantage of the program. With the approaching retirement of Howard Grimes, John Holbert became the director of the program in January 1982. After discussions with Grimes and the program's steering committee, Holbert soon proposed a major revision, eliminating the in-sequence track, requiring at least three years of ministerial practice before entrance, scheduling courses in the summer and in the January interterm, and offering more courses specifically for D.Min. students in order to provide them with better classroom peer relationships.[65] Eventually, the faculty adopted a revision much like this, though it went into effect only after the arrival of Stanley Menking as director in January 1985. Thereafter the program was in-ministry only and required the exercise of ministerial leadership under supervision, peer assessment as part of a practicum, and (as before) completion of a written project followed by an oral examination based on the project. A further revision in 1991 identified two tracks, either the pursuit of an area of special interest in ministry or a concentration in evangelism.[66]

Schubert Ogden continued as director of the Graduate Program in Religious Studies until 1990. That spring Dean Kirby appointed a committee of six, including four

Perkins professors and chaired by Professor Joseph Tyson of the Department of Religious Studies in SMU's Dedman College, to review the program. As the review got under way, Kirby appointed William Babcock to succeed Ogden as director.

In its report in the spring of 1991, the review committee found that despite a long-standing commitment to prepare teacher-scholars for academic leadership in colleges and universities, not only in schools of theology, the program's studies had concentrated in the history and theology of the Christian tradition, largely to take advantage of the strengths of the Perkins faculty. Its report reaffirmed that the program should be in religious studies broadly and should be located, as it had been, in the university's Dedman College, rather than Perkins. The committee saw no reason to think that the two forms of study, religious studies and theological studies, were incompatible.[67]

Still another review of the master of divinity curriculum occurred in fall 1989. In the preceding spring the standing Committee on Curriculum proposed, and the faculty approved, that a committee be established to review the program (in place since 1982) and report to the faculty by January 1, 1990.[68] This Curriculum Review Committee was chaired by Charles Wood and had a membership of eight, including Bishop Bruce Blake of the Dallas Area.

Several changes resulted: A new required course was devised—"Introduction to Theological Studies," described as "a consideration of the vocation of Christian theology" as related to church leadership, "and an orientation to the situation and problems of theological studies today." This was an introduction, not simply to Division III studies, but to the whole curriculum, and students were to take it in their first year. The requirement of an advanced course in theological reflection was dropped.

Another new requirement was for students to take twelve semester hours of mainly elective coursework in a "concentration"—"a group of courses related to each other in subject-matter, theme, or approach," which together would give students the chance to develop some depth in a limited subject. Students were to work with their faculty advisers to develop their proposals for the concentration.

At least nine semester hours of a student's thirty semester hours of elective work had to be taken in Divisions I, II, and III, and at least six semester hours of electives had to be taken in Division IV.

Changes were made in the required work in Division IV. Now each student was to take three semester hours in introductory preaching and six semester hours in designated courses in two areas of ministry other than preaching. The two-semester requirement in introduction to ministry had been dropped earlier.

Several changes were made in the internship requirement. To shorten the total time in the M.Div. program, students in a two-semester or one-year internship were permitted to take a three-semester-hour course during each regular semester of the internship. In certain cases students in a one-semester internship could simultaneously take a three-semester-hour course meeting once a week. Another change was to permit students to intern in either the third or fourth seminary year (rather than only in the third), given satisfactory completion of thirty-nine semester hours of required courses. Still another was introduction of the "concurrent internship," in which student pastors and some students in church staff positions could take two-year internships along with as many as nine semester hours of coursework each semester.

The required "Theology and Ministry Seminar," to be taken after the internship, was dropped after 1988–89.[69]

On the recommendation of the review committee, a small ad hoc committee reviewed the requirements in spiritual formation (spiritual disciplines appropriate to Christian faith), interethnic experience, and the workshops on racism and sexism. The faculty approved the committee's recommendation to continue all three requirements, with the workshops to be planned and implemented by the Committee on Women and Ethnic Minority Concerns.[70]

At the March 2, 1990, faculty meeting, Richard Heitzenrater, chair of the standing Committee on Curriculum, reported that the dean had asked the committee "to consider measures that would facilitate completion of the new curriculum in six terms." Pursuing that request, the committee recommended, and the faculty agreed, that the total semester-hours required for graduation be reduced from eighty-four to eighty-one.[71]

Another change to encourage recruitment of students came in the spring of 1991. Charles Wood, reporting for the Academic Council (made up of the chairs of standing committees), proposed instituting regular evening classes. The faculty approved the proposal unanimously, promising that in the next several years all required master of divinity courses would be available to evening students. This led to a class schedule that enabled enrollment by people working in full-time day positions. In the spring of 1994, however, the faculty modified its commitment to the evening program for M.Div. students. A study found that the evening program's financial contribution to Perkins was slight, that attrition among evening-only students was about 50 percent, and that the program created difficult staffing problems for the faculty. The faculty then voted to continue the evening program but to discontinue its commitment to new students entering after the fall of 1993 to offer all the required M.Div. courses in the evening. In the fall of 1995 the faculty reaffirmed its decision to continue the evening program so long as it did not create serious staffing difficulties, scheduling problems for other students, or unwise curriculum changes.[72]

PERKINS STUDENTS, 1981–1994

Various new or enlarged Perkins programs had enabled total enrollment from the mid- to late-1970s to remain relatively stable—between 414 and 461 (see appendix B, table 3). Enrollment in the basic degree program (master of theology, later named master of divinity), however, saw a reduction of roughly 10 percent from 1976 to 1980. This decline continued after Jim Kirby became dean in 1981, falling by another 26 percent between 1981 and 1994. Even so, because of enrollments in the masters programs in theological studies and sacred music and the doctor of ministry program, total Perkins enrollment increased from 1981 to 1984 to its largest point in at least thirty years, after which it too declined by 22 percent in the next ten years. Some other Methodist seminaries also reported declining enrollments between 1981 and 1994, including Claremont, Drew, Iliff, and Methodist in Ohio, though several others reported significant gains.[73]

Kirby was greatly concerned about the decline in enrollment and made strenuous efforts to overcome it. "Everything possible," he said, "must be done to reverse this trend."[74] During the next few years Perkins took several steps to try to increase the numbers. Kirby and the director of admissions, Linn Caraway, planned and implemented an aggressive recruitment program. After 1982 the new master of theological studies degree added twenty-five to fifty students to the total, including some from denominations not requiring the master of divinity for ordination.

As the decline continued through the 1980s, Kirby worked to reduce costs and increase scholarships, to make Perkins competitive with other seminaries, especially those in the Southwest. In 1987 he wrote that all theological schools were becoming regional, largely because of financial pressures on the students. In Kirby's opinion many students thought one seminary as good as another, since they all granted the degree that qualified them to be ordained. If so, it would be unrealistic to expect those students to pay more. He knew of no solution to this difficulty: "Students who elect to come to Perkins know they will invest more time and money because of their choice. It is a strong affirmation of our program that we are as competitive as we are. At the same time, we must give serious consideration to ways by which we can repackage our intern requirement to allow more flexibility for completion."[75]

From 1989 to 1991 the faculty agreed to several curriculum changes (described earlier) that were calculated to encourage enrollment. In addition, beginning in 1989–90 required courses were scheduled so that first-year part-time students could attend only on Tuesdays and Thursdays and second-year students only on Wednesdays and Fridays. Taken together, these changes apparently helped to slow the declining enrollment, though it remained a problem.

During these years women in the Perkins master of divinity program continued to increase both in numbers and in percentage of the total. In the fall of 1970, ten women enrolled (3.9 percent) and in 1980, seventy-nine (23.9 percent); in 1986 the program had ninety women (30.2 percent) and in 1993, ninety-seven (39.1 percent). The number of men, which had decreased sharply, to 251 in 1980, continued downward to 208 in 1986 and 151 in 1993. From 1980 to 1993 the increase of women prevented the overall decline from being far greater than it was.[76]

The total African American student enrollment had undergone a significant increase in the late 1970s, from twelve in the fall of 1974 to twenty-seven in 1980. Between 1981 and 1993 the numbers ranged between twenty-nine and forty-eight each year, in contrast to the small numbers before 1974. Hispanics, who had numbered seven to nine each year in the late 1970s, by the early 1990s had increased to fourteen to sixteen—a significant though modest increase. One native American was enrolled in the late 1980s and another in the early 1990s. By the late 1980s Perkins consistently enrolled at least twenty to thirty international students each year, and the quality of those admitted was improving. In the spring of 1987 Kirby reported that the following fall Perkins would add six new international students, chosen from among fifty-five applications. If more adequate financial aid had been available, many more of this group would have been eligible to be admitted.[77] In the late 1980s and early 1990s a majority of the international students were from Asia, most frequently from South Korea.

The average age of students in the master of divinity program at Perkins (and the master of theology program before it) had been rising. Although figures are not available before 1970, in the 1950s most Perkins students entered seminary either in the fall after graduation from college or within two or three years thereafter. But since about 1970 Perkins has seen an increasingly longer time elapse between college graduation and the matriculation of many of its students. This trend has been accentuated by the increase in the number of women students, many of whom have decided to seek ordination after some years either in another occupation or after their children have entered school. Eventually, Perkins began compiling data on students' ages. In 1970 the mean average age at seminary graduation was 27.7; in 1975 it was 29.8; in 1980, 31.1; and in 1989, 31.6. To look at it another way, in the fall of 1986, 56 percent of entering students were in their twenties, 34 percent in their thirties, and 10 percent were forty or older; by 1990, 37.9 percent were in their twenties, 44.7 percent in their thirties, and 17.4 percent were forty or older. In 1993, the mean average age of entering M.Div. women students was thirty-nine; that of men was thirty-one, and the average for both was thirty-four.[78]

THE FOOTBALL SCANDAL OF 1986–1987

In October and November 1986, Dallas television station WFAA aired charges by a former SMU linebacker that payments had been made to him when he played football at SMU, in violation of the rules of the National Collegiate Athletic Association (NCAA). As the scandal unfolded, investigators learned that off-campus boosters had been making payments to a number of players for several years, that this was widely known in the Athletic Department, and that the payments had been distributed by a member of the coaching staff. Furthermore, William Clements, chair of the board of governors; Edwin Cox, chair of the board of trustees; and Donald Shields, SMU's president, had all known about the payments. Eventually, it came out that Clements had ordered the athletic director to continue the payments, fearing that if payments were stopped, star players would leave and reveal why they were leaving.[79]

On November 21 the university announced the retirement of Shields for medical reasons, chief among them, Type 2 diabetes, seriously aggravated by the scandal. The board of governors then appointed William B. Stallcup, professor of biology, who at that time was provost ad interim, to be president ad interim, and Ruth Morgan, professor of political science and a former associate provost, to be provost ad interim. On December 5 the athletic director, head football coach, and assistant athletic director resigned. On February 25, 1987, the NCAA Committee on Infractions invoked the "death penalty," suspending the football program of SMU for the 1987 season and imposing other sanctions.[80] Subsequently, SMU canceled the 1988 football season as well.

The University Senate, the accrediting body of the Division of Higher Education of The United Methodist Church, conducted an inquiry, on the basis of which it issued a report in January 1987. It placed SMU on probation and recommended that the trustees conduct a self-study for the purpose of reorganizing the board and reforming many of its policies and practices. In response the trustees, meeting on February 5, established the Governance Committee of ten trustees, chaired by Leighton K. Farrell of Highland Park United Methodist Church. Its purpose would be to review SMU governance and to propose a new governance plan for the university.[81]

At a press conference on March 3, Clements, who the preceding November had been elected governor of Texas, acknowledged publicly for the first time that he and some other members of the board of governors had known about and taken part in the decision to continue payments to SMU student athletes after August 1985. At a meeting the next day the board of governors, from which Clements had previously resigned, passed a resolution calling for a committee of United Methodist bishops to investigate the charges about the athletic program, and the committee was established.[82] On March 20 the trustees abolished the board of governors, which had been seriously implicated in the scandal. In its place they established an interim executive committee that could act for the trustees, with Dallas oilman Ray L. Hunt as its chair.[83]

SMU faculty and students protested in a number of ways against the scandal and the university leaders' role in it. Prominent among the protests, on November 18 the SMU Faculty Senate, with Leroy Howe of Perkins as president, endorsed a petition signed by more than two hundred SMU faculty members, calling for "the immediate, unconditional and permanent abolition of quasi-professional athletics" at SMU.[84] Clements's March 3 statement had evoked widespread indignation within the university. One statement, adopted unanimously by the Perkins faculty on March 6, called for the governor to disclose the names of members and former members of the board of governors who had known about the decision, for such members to resign from the board of governors and board of trustees, and for an early reorganization of the board of trustees.[85]

At its May 8 meeting the board of trustees received the report of the Governance Committee. Among its recommendations adopted by the board were several designed to make the board an effective governing body of the university: a reduction in the number of trustees from more than seventy to a maximum of forty, including ex officio members; limits on how long members could serve on the board and how long officers could serve in any one office; and an increase from two to four in the number of regular board meetings per year. There were also several proposals to strengthen the office of the president.[86]

In early January 1987 the board of governors had named Ray Hunt to chair the nineteen-member Presidential Search Committee, of which Schubert Ogden of the Perkins faculty would be vice chair.[87] Ogden later said of Hunt, "In that role he was as effective as I can imagine anybody being," his "vision of the need for the highest quality" and his determination were unfailing, and he was a model of what it means to work as a trustee. Ogden played a major role in the search. Hunt, Ogden said, "wanted a strong faculty vice chair. He gave me absolute freedom to do that, and I exercised it."[88] Between January and April the committee compiled a list of 225 candidates and narrowed it to eleven. At that point a seven-person visitation committee interviewed the eleven at their home campuses. The search committee recommended three of the eleven to the Special Trustee Committee of eight trustees plus two ex officio members, including Ogden. On May 28 the special committee recommended A. Kenneth Pye to the board, which the following day elected him the ninth president of SMU.[89]

Pye, fifty-five, had served from 1955 to 1966 as professor of law and for five of those years as associate dean of the Georgetown Law Center. In 1966 he became professor of law at Duke University, where he remained until his move to SMU in 1987. While at Duke he was twice dean of Duke Law School, twice chancellor of the university (its second-highest administrative position), university counsel from 1971 to 1974, and acting president in 1979–80. He was a Roman Catholic, leading some

Methodists to wonder why the search committee had not recommended a Methodist. Ray Hunt's reply was that Pye "not only met but exceeded the stringent criteria the search committee required of any candidate. He is, indeed, the right man at the right time for SMU." Upon his election Pye told the trustees, "I am deeply honored by my selection as president of SMU. The university faces challenges, but even greater opportunities. The football scandal is behind it. The future is before it."[90]

On June 19 the bishops' committee brought its report to the trustees, now chaired by Ray Hunt. It provided an extended and detailed account of the scandal, placing these events in the context of the recent history of SMU governance. It noted that in 1967 the size of the board of trustees had been increased and steps had been taken that in effect made the board self-perpetuating; that the board of governors, meeting monthly, carried on much of the business of the university and in practice did not inform the trustees of many details of its actions; and that only three men—William Clements, Edwin Cox, and Robert Stewart—had chaired the board of governors since 1967. The bishops' committee reviewed events surrounding Paul Hardin's departure as president in 1974, including his report to the NCAA that the football coaching staff was making payments to players as reward for outstanding play. The bishops observed that SMU had a history of athletics rules violations going back to 1922, and observed, "Prior to 1983, the NCAA had investigated allegations and imposed sanctions against SMU's football program five times, in 1958, 1964, 1974, 1975, and 1981."[91]

The football scandal of 1986–87 was traumatic for all concerned at SMU. It brought the university and many of its leaders into disrepute. Yet out of the trauma came changes the university had needed for years: an end to a dysfunctional system of governance and reestablishment of the administrative power of the SMU president. After Kenneth Pye's arrival, an athletic director and a head football coach were appointed who were committed to abiding by the rules; and a special task force studied "what church-relatedness means to SMU and what should be SMU's relationship to the South Central Jurisdiction of The United Methodist Church."[92] Perkins School of Theology went about its work within the context of the scandal, the reorganization, and the subsequent recovery. Repairing and strengthening that context provided a situation in which Pye could, he said, pursue one of his goals—seeking to make Perkins School of Theology "among the finest in the nation.[93]

ACCUMULATING PRESSURES ON THE DEAN

During several years beginning in the mid-1980s, Jim Kirby experienced a series of events that increased the pressures on him as dean of Perkins. In 1984, after three years as dean of Perkins, he had expressed a sense of confidence about his work and about the future of the school, saying that now more than before he could sense the school's needs and make proposals that would address them.[94]

In the spring of 1985 Kirby suggested that the Committee on Faculty ask an outside evaluator, such as the dean of another seminary, to conduct a review of his work as dean in his fifth year in that office. Following up on the suggestion, the committee arranged for Leander Keck, dean of Yale Divinity School, to conduct a review. It was intended, not to cope with a problem, but to analyze the dean's work and offer suggestions about how it could become even more effective.[95]

During his visit to Perkins on October 10–11, 1985, Keck talked with forty-three people, including President Shields, Provost Hillerbrand, and many of the Perkins faculty and staff members. In his written report Keck took special note of the dean's strengths: good management, a stable temperament, keeping his own frustrations under control while he attended to the issues, following established procedures, and yet having his own style, one that was markedly different from that of his predecessor. Keck observed that Kirby "devotes an amazing amount of time to the annual review of individual faculty" and that "he enjoys the virtual unanimous respect and trust of faculty and staff, and he is confident and comfortable in his job."[96]

Keck did not find any major problems in Kirby's deanship, but he offered some suggestions. Although Perkins, along with the law school, enjoyed the reputation of being a pacesetter, "it would be foolish for Perkins to rely on its acknowledged achievement and standing and not attend carefully to the muscle-tone of its intellectual life. . . . In this connection, the quality of future faculty appointments will be decisive." Given its rapidly changing urban location with an "aggressive Christian 'conservatism,'" this was the time for Perkins "to re-envision its future in a compelling way." The dean would need to take the lead in this process, not alone but in a manner that would stimulate the faculty's imagination.[97]

Despite his sense of confidence, Kirby felt that the pressures of the deanship were increasing. In the spring of 1985 he observed that this had been his busiest year so far. In process were searches to fill five faculty positions and the directorship of

Bridwell Library, with the trips and conferences these entailed, in addition to his role as president of the Wesley Works Board of Directors. All this, he said, took a physical and emotional toll. "My greatest frustration," he explained, "results from being constantly distracted from the responsibilities which belong exclusively to me, such as long range planning, faculty development and cultivation."[98]

In his report Keck had suggested that a dean "needs time and 'space' in which to think long thoughts" and that it might be a good investment for Kirby to have a brief leave of absence.[99] In Kirby's annual report in the spring of 1986 he indicated that he would like a leave, to have time to rest and reflect. The SMU Board of Trustees had recently limited the time senior administrators could be away to three months, and Kirby wanted to move quickly to seize that opportunity. While the upheaval over the football scandal was settling down, he was able to take a leave in the summer of 1987. He reported that the summer was "refreshing and renewing" and that he returned "with a genuine sense of anticipation and satisfaction." He gave special thanks to Ward, the associate dean, who assumed the work of dean and who at no time called Kirby but "simply did the job well."[100]

While the university was moving to reform its governance and recover from the football scandal, Kirby was making plans in 1987 for a major new addition to the Perkins facilities. As part of a comprehensive report to the faculty, "A Vision of the Future: Looking into the 90's," he declared that Perkins needed a new building. Kirby Hall and Selecman Hall could not house the whole Perkins faculty when all were present, and there was no room for expansion; the two structures inadequately accommodated the Master of Sacred Music Program and the Christian Education Resource Center; large classes had to be held in the Lois Perkins Auditorium, a makeshift arrangement at best; and neither of the two halls was fully accessible to the disabled. Kirby presented initial diagrams of a three-story classroom and office building with twenty thousand square feet of floor space, and he invited the faculty to make suggestions. His estimate was that constructing the new building would cost $3.5 to $4 million and that endowment needed to support its operations would come to an additional $1.26 million.[101] Eventually plans were developed for what became known as the Link—between Selecman and Kirby halls.

At the same time Kirby identified several other major financial needs. At this time the renovation of Bridwell Library was yet to come, and Kirby projected that it would cost $1 to $1.5 million, plus $1.35 million for operations and automation. Still other needs—for scholarship endowment, endowed faculty chairs, and continuing education—would call for an additional $10 million. He saw the prospects for raising the money as bright.[102]

Although development efforts progressed well, with major capital gifts and commitments of $7 million in 1987–88, other needs, especially the renovation of Bridwell, were more pressing than a new academic building, for which no major donor emerged during Kirby's deanship. His was then the first of three plans over two decades and under three deans for a new academic building, a goal that was met only with the completion of Elizabeth Perkins Prothro Hall in 2009.

In the spring of 1988 Perkins President Pye commissioned special committees to review the current programs of each school and to offer advice and recommendations. The Blue Ribbon Committee he appointed for Perkins was chaired by Dennis Campbell, dean of Duke Divinity School, and included two other deans of university divinity schools, three local laity who were long-time supporters of Perkins, and Johnnie Marie Grimes, who had for many years been an assistant to President Willis Tate. The committee's report in the summer of 1989 offered several recommendations about Perkins and its relation to the church, the community, and the rest of the university.[103]

Kirby's lengthy written response to the report reveals how seriously he perceived the challenges in 1989. Among the difficulties he listed were these: conveying to the churches an accurate image of Perkins's dual mission of theological reflection and practical instruction for pastoral ministry; identifying the role of the seminary in the renewal of church life, which was in decline; devising a curriculum for students older and more diverse than previously; and recruiting a diverse faculty in a highly competitive hiring market, especially professors who are committed to educating people for ministry in local congregations. Perhaps the greatest difficulty of all was financial. He calculated that to fund the program Perkins needed to provide would require $56.3 million in new endowment, but even that sum would only cover costs at current levels.[104]

Kirby sent his response to several Perkins faculty and administrative staff members for their comments. Charles Wood's reply, agreeing with much that Kirby had said, nevertheless emphasized an aspect he thought the dean had neglected: "The overall effect is to give the impression of a beleaguered, problem-ridden school. . . . What I think I most missed in your comments was something on the order of an overall, synoptic response to the picture of the school, its mission, strengths, difficulties, and future, which the committee report projects."[105] Kirby's response reflected his frame of mind at the time.

Other matters during the next three years added to Kirby's sense of the burdens of his office. One was that Women's Week in February 1990 included a visit to Perkins by a witch. Kirby reported this brought far more fallout than he would have ever imagined, and that for the next several months he had to do damage control. A year later he was still receiving media inquiries about it. "One lesson . . . is to be sensitive to how our actions may be viewed by those outside our community. We should not allow ourselves to believe that we have complete freedom to do as we please." Another difficulty was that he sensed a widening gap between the school and the church. At the same time recruiting new faculty continued to be difficult, with several searches in this period continuing longer than anticipated. This was also a time of visits by several outside accrediting agencies: the Association of Theological Schools, Southern Association of Colleges and Schools, and Commission on Theological Education of the University Senate of The United Methodist Church.[106]

In the spring of 1991 Kirby reported to the Committee on Faculty, "This will mark the end of my tenth year as Dean of the Perkins School of Theology. When I accepted the job, I told the search committee I expected to serve ten years." He made clear that whatever was in the best interest of Perkins was what he wanted to do, whether that was to continue as dean or for the school to bring in new leadership. He again felt the need for some time off for rest and renewal, and he planned to speak with Provost Ruth Morgan about it.[107] He was on leave in the summer of 1991 and began work as coauthor of a new history of American Methodism.[108]

In his spring 1991 report Kirby suggested that the Committee on Faculty again invite an outside person to review his work as dean, as it had done in 1985.[109] The committee, with W. J. A. Power as chair, invited James L. Waits, former dean of Candler School of Theology and newly appointed director of the Association of Theological Schools, to conduct an on-campus review during 1991–92. As in 1985, this review was intended not to deal with a problem but to assess what decanal leadership of Perkins required at the time.[110]

Waits spent two days at Perkins in February 1992 and interviewed President Pye, Provost Morgan, and thirty-four members of the Perkins faculty and administrative staff. Later Waits held telephone interviews with Bishop Bruce Blake of the Dallas Area and Bishop William Oden of the Baton Rouge Area. In his report the following month, Waits observed, "The Dean enjoys widespread support and confidence among faculty, students, and university administrators. After eleven years in office there is a remarkable lack of criticism of the Dean and his administrative style or achievement. Indeed, respect is often expressed for his collegial approach and for his accessibility to faculty and students alike. The principal traits for which he is known are his proven gifts as a facilitator, his collegial style, and his capacities as a manager."[111]

Waits also noted the faculty's appreciation of Kirby's ability to evaluate faculty members and to treat them fairly, the support by the president and the provost, and the faculty's "unanimous appreciation" for the dean's risking himself in the face of recent church and public criticism of Perkins.

The report identified several "general concerns." The primary one was replacing faculty who would soon retire: "Considerable ambivalence is expressed concerning whether recent faculty appointments reflect the quality and potential for which these retiring faculty are widely known. Some disquiet is also reflected in the repeated observation that recent appointments seem to follow a kind of 'political correctness' rather than traditional respect for quality and scholarly rigor." Another concern was about conflicts with some of the leadership of The United Methodist Church in the region. "It appears," Waits wrote, "that the church in this region is harder on Perkins and its Dean than is the case between other United Methodist seminaries and their principal church constituencies." A third was about the morale of the dean in the face of external conflicts.[112]

The report concluded with several recommendations, the last of which had to do with the dean's tenure. Waits reported some disquiet by faculty members at Kirby's references to how long he should continue as dean. It was critical, Waits concluded, "that the Dean, whatever his decision, make his intentions known before any ambiguity about the long-term leadership of the school occurs."[113]

After further reflection during the summer of 1992, Kirby decided he would retire as dean of Perkins as soon as his successor could be chosen. When in August he informed Provost Morgan of his decision, she asked him to delay the announcement.

She was planning to leave the office of provost and thought it best that he wait until the search for a new provost got under way. He concurred, with the result that the Perkins community did not learn of his decision until March 1993.[114]

THE PERKINS FACULTY CONFLICT OF 1992

When Millicent "Millie" Feske joined the Perkins faculty in systematic theology in 1990, she became the first and, at the time, only faculty woman member of Division III (theology and ethics), a matter that other faculty women, all of whom were members of either Division I (Bible) or Division IV (the life and work of the church), considered to be important. A second woman, Ellen Charry, joined Division III in the fall of 1992. Because Feske had not finished her dissertation, she held the rank of instructor and so was not on tenure track. In September 1992, after she had completed her dissertation, she asked the dean to bring her name before the Rank and Tenure Committee for its advisory on whether he should offer her a contract as assistant professor. Standard Perkins procedure in rank and tenure deliberations at the time was that sessions were confidential, with no committee vote and no "sense of the meeting" but faculty members voicing their individual judgments on the basis of the extensive information provided them in advance. The advisory was given on September 23. Thereafter the dean decided not to offer her a contract, which meant that her faculty appointment would be terminated at the end of the spring semester of 1993.

At the regular faculty meeting of Friday, October 9, faculty members Bill McElvaney and Ed Poitras presented a statement that read in full, "We, the undersigned, express no confidence in the recent decision of the Dean to terminate Professor Millicent C. Feske." To it were affixed twenty-two names of Perkins faculty and administrative staff members. A few minutes before the faculty meeting, McElvaney and Poitras had gone to the dean's office and had for the first time informed him that they were going to present their statement. At the faculty meeting an unsigned paper was also distributed entitled "Process and Policy in the Review of Instructors at Perkins School of Theology," which listed what were identified as "serious problems with our current procedures and policies concerning employment and promotion," including that instructors, unlike faculty at other ranks, had no right to appeal the dean's decision.[115] Later in the meeting Marjorie Procter-Smith, chair of the Women and Ethnic Minority Concerns Committee (consisting of three faculty, one staff member, and four students), presented the committee's "Statement on Diversity and Collegiality," which declared the decision about Millicent Feske "is ill-advised," expressed doubt about the community's commitment to hear nontraditional theological voices, spoke of a "loss of trust in the Rank and Tenure Committee," and urged "that those responsible reverse this decision."[116]

Thus erupted the most serious internal conflict in the history of the Perkins faculty. Anger was widespread, both in the faculty meeting and for many months thereafter, both among those who had signed and those who had not, for sharply different reasons.

Kirby quickly formed a small ad hoc committee to which he named himself; Janice Virtue, director of academic procedures; Tom Spann, an intern faculty member (both Virtue and Spann had signed the "no confidence" statement), and me (I did not sign it), to consider ways of responding to the conflict. At the dean's request we began gathering names of people with special skills who might facilitate the faculty's handling of the conflict.

On Sunday, October 11, Dick Murray, who had agreed in a telephone conversation to have his name placed on the "no confidence" statement, sent an open letter to the dean in which he said that while he thought that the decision about Millie Feske ought to be reconsidered, he did not agree with the statement to which he had put his name. He observed that most signers "have come to Perkins under your deanship and are your appointments." (That was correct. Sixteen of the twenty-two signers had been appointed under Kirby's deanship, seven of them in the previous three years.) "I, for one," he concluded, "*do* have confidence in your leadership and I count you a good friend and colleague."[117] Of the twenty-two whose names were on the statement, Kirby later reported that fourteen eventually went to see him and in one way or another said they should not have signed it.[118]

On Monday, October 12, a group of six faculty members who had not signed the "no confidence" statement and who were aware of the search for a facilitator, sent a letter to the dean in which they declared that the "Statement on Diversity and Collegiality" and the "Process and Policy" statement "touch on issues that cut deeply into the heart of the Perkins community. It is also clear that both documents represent only one delineation of the issues and that they are deliberately framed in such a way as to disqualify and to exclude in advance all alternate views of what the issues are and how they should be approached." The six went on to say that because those statements were framed as they were, they should not "influence any agenda for any mediatorial process that the Perkins faculty may undertake." Furthermore, they wrote, "We want to make it clear that we will not ourselves participate in any mediatorial process for which the agenda has been influenced by these documents. If they do influence the agenda, we will regard that influence as tantamount to an attempt to determine the results of the mediation before it has even begun—an attempt, in short, to prevent any true mediation from taking place at all."[119]

By October 21 the committee of four had chosen two people—Dr. Paula Dobbs-Wiggins, a psychiatrist, and Marty Lumpkin, a psychologist—who together would try to help the faculty identify issues and communicate with one another about them. Dobbs-Wiggins and Lumpkin were invited to a previously scheduled faculty luncheon on November 4 at which they introduced themselves. The plan was for the faculty to meet as guild, rather than in a formal business meeting.[120]

The first such faculty guild meeting, lasting two and a half hours on Friday, November 6, at Highland Park United Methodist Church, was well attended—by thirty-eight of the forty-eight Perkins faculty and administrative staff members. The facilitators asked each person to write down two main concerns, which the facilitators collected and then read to the group without the writers' names.[121] Of the many concerns that emerged, each of the following was expressed by several people:

Lack of trust among members of the community
Freedom to disagree openly without intimidation
Unequal distribution of power
Seeming lack of respect for those with whose views one differs
Lack of unity to hold diverse people together
The need to recover a more collegial way of working together
How to have a more inclusive faculty without sacrifice of quality

Although there is no way to know who expressed what concern, people on both sides and in the middle of the conflict could have voiced most, if not all, of them. They show that the difficulties were about more than the termination of Millie Feske, though that was the precipitating event. The problems had been building for several years. On a few occasions the dean or others had referred to them openly in faculty meetings, but the faculty had not openly explored them together.[122] Acknowledging the presence of conflict was different from conducting processes of conflict resolution.

The faculty held a second guild meeting, lasting more than two hours, on November 16, again at Highland Park Church. The same two people acted as facilitators, and thirty-five faculty and staff members attended. When the facilitators invited those assembled to identify an agenda, this became an occasion for many to voice their own chief concerns.[123] Some of the signers of the "no confidence" statement spoke of being intimidated. Then an older and nonsigning faculty member said, "I'm intimidated. I fear not being heard. I would love dialog, but I don't know how to get it. I have been read out of the dialog." A few minutes later one of the signers expressed appreciation for that comment. Another time a signer declared, "We aren't naming the issues," and he specifically mentioned the "no confidence" statement and the letters a nonsigning administrator had sent to some of the signers that were interpreted as implicitly threatening. The atmosphere throughout the meeting was intense, and members expressed sharply opposing views.

Later in the meeting, after some had referred to the role of the Rank and Tenure Committee, the dean said it was important to know how the process works. "The Rank and Tenure Committee doesn't decide," he said; he was the one who had decided. Some members then raised questions about the criteria for the Rank and Tenure Committee's advisory, to which the dean replied that the criteria were explicitly stated and clear. "The question is were they considered. They were carefully considered."

In reflecting on the process, facilitator Lumpkin said he was "impressed by how directly you've talked with each other. There's a lot of pain." Some members on both sides spoke of the value of the process and wanted it to continue. Others said they felt too intimidated to speak out. Facilitator Dobbs-Wiggins encouraged the group to meet again before changing the process, and a date was set for a third session.

At the third faculty guild session, held for two hours on Monday, November 30, attendance dropped to thirty.[124] Lumpkin asked the members to express what they felt about the previous session and what they hoped for in this one. Several on both sides expressed pain and frustration at polarization and lack of progress. As one said,

"It's like the Book of Job—much is said, but little dialog." Another spoke of sadness at the "great change" in just the past three years: "It's like something has died. We're a sick school." Yet another thought it encouraging that so many had spoken, and several identified valuable comments people had made. Much anger remained: among the signers, anger toward the dean and the Rank and Tenure Committee; and among the nonsigners, anger toward those who brought the "no confidence" statement to the faculty meeting as they did and at not knowing who wrote it or the "Process and Policy" statement. A fourth guild meeting was set for the following Monday, December 7. A few days later the committee of four, having noted the frustration of many with the process, decided that there was a need for one more meeting before the holiday break and that this one would be without the facilitators. The other three committee members asked the dean to be the moderator, and he agreed to do so.

At the December 4 regular business meeting of the faculty, David Maldonado reported for the Committee on Faculty the appointment of an ad hoc committee of five faculty members "to assess our policies and procedures related to faculty promotion and tenure." He also announced that the Committee on Faculty would soon review peer review policy. In the meanwhile the committee proposed making peer review optional for nontenured faculty, and the faculty approved the proposal.[125]

At the December 7 guild meeting, attended by twenty-six, several signers gave reasons why they had signed, and there were some sharp exchanges. At the end of two hours the dean suggested forming "several self-selecting groups that cut across the lines" as a attempt to bridge the differences.[126] I know of one such small-group meeting (seven faculty, including the dean) in January 1993. There may have been others, and there were discussions between some individual signers and nonsigners.

At the end of the 1992–93 academic year, Feske, after her contract was not extended, went to a faculty position at an academic institution in the northeast.

In the spring of 1994, after the report of the ad hoc committee on promotion and tenure policies, the faculty made several changes in rank and tenure policy. Two of the more important were these: Whereas previously a member of the Rank and Tenure Committee could serve successive terms indefinitely, now after two successive terms the member had to take one year off before once again becoming eligible for election. A section was added about the normal pattern of review of an instructor, and it was specified that instructors could appeal a dean's negative decision.[127]

DEAN KIRBY'S RESIGNATION

On Wednesday, March 10, 1993, Kirby sent a notice to faculty members that he was calling a brief meeting for that Friday afternoon. They arrived to find present not only the dean but also President Pye and Provost Morgan. The dean read a statement in which he explained that in the summer of 1992 he had decided to retire as dean but at Morgan's request had not made his decision public Then, with the events of that fall, it did not seem to him to be the right time. Now, however, he was announcing that "as soon as a successor can be named, I will leave the office of dean." He planned to spend a year on leave and then return to teaching church history.

A faculty member asked Morgan whether the dean was pushed to retire. She answered, "Unequivocally, no." Was the retirement related to any series of events? "No." Pye expressed appreciation for Kirby's continuing until the provost search was under way. He then spoke of ruptures in collegiality during that academic year and the work that needed to be done to restore it. "Inclusivity is by no means in conflict with excellence. It is not the same as excellence."[128]

The search committee appointed to seek a new dean was chaired by James F. Jones Jr., dean of Dedman College. Its other members included five faculty: William Babcock, Jouette Bassler, Victor Furnish, Zan W. Holmes Jr., and Charles Wood; two pastors (in addition to Holmes, who was also pastor of St. Luke "Community" United Methodist Church): Noé Gonzales, pastor of Emanu-El United Methodist Church, and John Thornburg, pastor of Northaven United Methodist Church; Sarah Lancaster, a Perkins alumna and doctoral student in religious studies; Bishop J. Woodrow Hearn of the Texas Conference; and Bishop Joe A. Wilson of the Central Texas Conference.[129] In the spring of 1994 Pye announced the appointment of Robin W. Lovin, dean of the Theological School at Drew University, as dean of Perkins, effective July 1, 1994.

In the meantime Kirby continued his work as dean. In the spring of 1993 he witnessed the retirement of five professors with the cumulative total of 129 years on the Perkins faculty and the departure of two others after a total of nineteen years at Perkins. That spring saw the appointment of Valerie Hotchkiss to succeed Robert Maloy as director of Bridwell Library. The following year Perkins conducted searches in the fields of Christian education and systematic theology, leading to appointments of three people who would join the faculty in the fall of 1994: Deidre Palmer in

Christian education, and Luis Pedraja and Joerg Rieger in systematic theology. Kirby deferred filling other faculty vacancies, explaining that among the many things he wanted to do to assist his successor was "to hold open as many faculty and staff vacancies as possible."[130]

In his address to the faculty at its fall 1993 conference, Dean Kirby first reflected on his years as dean. He regretted the continuing decline in enrollment for the master of divinity program, not getting the Link built between Selecman and Kirby Buildings, and not being able to establish continuity in the development program because of the turnover in directors of development. On the other hand, he said, the school's endowment was nearly three times what it had been when he arrived, and the annual Loyalty Fund was now raising four times as much as when it began in 1981.

Then he spoke of the atmosphere in the faculty in the aftermath of the conflict: "We are walking carefully around each other, like persons in a marriage gone sour when the dangers of honest dialogue make the risks too high to take, unwilling to say what we really think or feel except to those who share our views. Some feel separated, others silenced. There is some fear and considerable lack of respect. It is not a healthy climate to nourish or support intellectual exchange and growth." It was not clear to him, he said, "whether we want to be reconciled or just to determine clearly who has power." In his years as dean, he continued, he had "seen our sincere determination to create race and gender inclusiveness at Perkins divide us on the quality of scholarship and the value of ideological commitments." John Deschner, he added, "reminded us that the only sure way to affirm a commitment to diversity is through unity. That was at risk last year, and I believe it remains at risk today."[131]

In the spring of 1994 Kirby reported to the Committee on Faculty that the past year "has been a quiet and, I hope, healing time." He rejoiced at Valerie Hotchkiss's work in the library, noted that three new young scholars were joining the faculty in the fall, and said, "I am both pleased and relieved by the appointment of Robin Lovin as dean." He looked forward to Lovin's arrival and to his own research leave in 1994–95 and return to the classroom in the fall of 1995.[132]

But 1994–95 did not work out as Kirby had planned. In August 1993 university president Pye had a mild heart attack and that November he was diagnosed with cancer of the esophagus. After treatment he was thought to be free of the cancer, but in June 1994 doctors found that it had spread throughout his body and was inoperable. After considering several names, Pye determined that Jim Kirby "would do an outstanding job as President *ad interim*." After Pye had obtained Kirby's consent to the appointment, Robert Dedman, chair of the board of trustees, held a press conference on June 22, with Pye, Kirby, and Ray Hunt present, and announced Kirby's appointment, which the board unanimously confirmed. Kenneth Pye died on July 11, 1994. For the next year Kirby presided over SMU, and the trustees conducted a search for a new president.[133]

1. James Edmund Kirby Jr., curriculum vitae, June 1979, James Edmund Kirby Jr. Papers, Bridwell Library; *Perkins Perspective* 20, no. 2 (winter 1980): 1, 2.
2. Joseph D. Quillian Jr., "Report of the Dean to the Faculty, Lakeview, September 23, 1960," 4; Quillian to Willis Tate, December 1, 1966, both in Quillian Papers, Bridwell Library.
3. Roger Loyd, "Epilogue I," in Lewis Howard Grimes, *History of the Perkins School of Theology*, edited by Roger Loyd (Dallas: Southern Methodist University Press, 1993), 203.
4. "Report of the Dean to the Committee on Faculty," April 27, 1982, Kirby Papers.
5. *Perkins Perspective* 21, no. 3 (summer 1982).
6. Ibid.
7. *Perkins Perspective* 23, no. 1 (fall 1983).
8. "Report of the Dean to the Committee on Faculty," April 27, 1982.
9. James Kirby, interview by author, June 18, 2008, Dallas.
10. *Perspective*, fall 1993, 21.
11. Joseph D. Quillian Jr., "Greatest Needs for the New Dean as I See It," comments to the Trustee Committee of the School of Theology, May 7, 1981, Kirby Papers; Kirby's address to the faculty, August 30, 1985, Kirby Papers.
12. "Report of the Dean to the Committee on Faculty," April 27, 1982.
13. "Report of the Dean to the Provost," May 13, 1983, Kirby Papers.
14. Kirby's address to the faculty conference, August 30, 1985, Kirby Papers.
15. Dean's report to the Committee on Faculty, spring 1985 and spring 1986; James E. Kirby, "A Vision of the Future: Looking into the 90's," August 31, 1987, 15, Kirby Papers.
16. "Annual Report of the Dean to the Committee on Faculty," April 4, 1988, Kirby Papers.
17. *Perspective*, fall 1991, 17.
18. James E. Kirby to Provost Hans Hillerbrand, May 13, 1983; "Reviewing the Decade," James E. Kirby, dean, for the Perkins Faculty Conference, September 15–16, 1989; "Annual Report of the Dean to the Committee on Faculty," April 1994, all in Kirby Papers; Linda Hervey to Joe Allen, October 13, 2009, in my personal files.
19. "Report of the Dean to the Committee on Faculty," April 27, 1982.
20. Faculty minutes, November 4, 1988.
21. James S. Thomas, *Methodism's Racial Dilemma: The Story of the Central Jurisdiction* (Nashville, Tenn.: Abingdon, 1992).
22. Board of trustees minutes, May 13, 1983.
23. Board of governors minutes, February 2, 1984.
24. The senate minutes for May 4, 1984, record that "Hogg moved to change the words 'intern staff' to 'intern faculty' throughout the By-laws of the Senate and Faculty. The motion was seconded and unanimously approved."

25. James Kirby, "Report to the Provost," May 13, 1983, Kirby Papers.

26. "Annual Report of the Community Life Committee," May 7, 1982; senate minutes, April 16 and May 7, 1982.

27. Senate minutes, March 25 and March 30, 1983.

28. "Governance at Perkins: A Preliminary Report," September 29, 1983 (attached to the senate minutes, September 30–October 1, 1983).

29. Senate minutes, October 1, 1983.

30. "Proposed Structure of Governance, 30 November 1983" (attached to senate minutes, December 9, 1983).

31. "Dean's Address to the Perkins Faculty Workshop," August 31, 1984, Kirby Papers.

32. Faculty minutes, April 8, 1988, and March 1, 1989 (with attached report from Associate Dean Ward).

33. Board of trustees minutes, November 2, 1984, and May 9, 1986; *Perkins Perspective* 25, no. 2 (winter 1985–86).

34. The totals in this section do not include appointments of Perkins faculty to be Perkins administrators and vice versa, of classroom faculty appointed to the intern staff, or of full-time faculty to be adjunct faculty.

35. Report of the Dean to the Committee on Faculty, 1985–86, 2, Kirby Papers.

36. "Dean's Address to the Faculty Conference," August 30, 1985, 11–12, Kirby Papers.

37. Ibid., September 12–13, 1986, 3, Kirby Papers.

38. James Kirby, notes for faculty workshop, fall 1987, Kirby Papers.

39. Memo to the Perkins Faculty on new faculty appointments, Fred Carney, chair, Committee on Faculty (no date, but before the October 14, 1988, meeting of the faculty as guild), Kirby Papers.

40. Committee on Faculty to the Perkins Faculty, "Procedures Leading to Appointment of New Faculty Members with Guidelines for Enlarging Minority and Women Membership on the Perkins Faculty," April 1, 1992, Kirby Papers.

41. Senate minutes, October 28, 1983; Perkins Women Administrators and Faculty to the Perkins Senate, October 28, 1983 (attachment to senate minutes of that date).

42. Senate minutes, April 13, 1984; Committee on Women and Ethnic Minority Concerns, "Annual Report to Perkins Faculty and Senate," April 29, 1985 (attachment to faculty minutes, May 3, 1985).

43. James Kirby, "Mission in the Nineties," Faculty Conference, September 20–21, 1991, Kirby Papers; Daniel Cattau, *Dallas Morning News*, May 24, 1993. See the preface, note 1.

44. John Wesley, *Sermons*, four volumes, edited by Albert C. Outler (Nashville, Tenn.: Abingdon, 1984–87).

45. John Wesley, *The Works of John Wesley: Journal and Diaries*, vols. 18–24, edited by W. Reginald Ward (journal) and Richard P. Heitzenrater (diaries) (Nashville, Tenn.: Abingdon, 1988–2003); see also Benjamin Ingham, *Diary of an Oxford Methodist: Benjamin Ingham, 1733–1734*, edited by Richard P. Heitzenrater (Durham, N.C.: Duke University Press, 1985), ix.

46. *Baptism, Eucharist and Ministry*, Faith and Order Paper No. 111 (Geneva: World Council of Churches, 1982).

47. John Deschner, "A Brief Overview of the Faith and Order Movement (ca. 1910–1989) and a Brief Selection from Faith and Order Documents," photocopy, 1989, 8–9; *Baptism, Eucharist & Ministry 1982-1990: Report on the Process and Responses* (Faith and Order Paper No. 149; Geneva: WCC Publications, 1990).

48. Ethics Colloquy file, in my personal files.

49. James E. Kirby, "A Farewell," *Perkins Journal*, July–October, 1990, 1.

50. "Dean's Address to the Faculty Conference," September 12–13, 1986, 9, Kirby Papers.

51. The report, "Rank and Tenure Policy and Procedures," adopted by the Perkins faculty February 22, 1985, for the most part retained the policies and procedures adopted earlier, most recently on May 8, 1970. One addition in 1985 provided for evaluations by outside referees; another was that a negative recommendation of the dean regarding promotion and/or tenure could be appealed to the provost and then to the president of the university.

52. "Dean's Address to the Faculty Workshop," August 31, 1984, 4; Committee on Faculty to the Perkins Faculty, February 15, 1985; faculty minutes, February 22, 1985, all in Kirby Papers.

53. "Report of the Dean to the Committee on Faculty," April 27, 1982, 4.
54. From the Committee on Faculty's synopsis, April 23, 1992, of the "Review of James E. Kirby, Dean, Perkins School of Theology, Southern Methodist University," by Dr. James L. Waits, Executive Director of the Association of Theological Schools. Waits wrote, "Strongest words of appreciation are reserved for [Kirby's] capacity to evaluate faculty," referring especially to the dean's annual evaluation sessions with faculty members.
55. Faculty minutes, December 8, 1967, and October 11, 1968.
56. Memo from the Senate Committee on Faculty to the Perkins School of Theology Faculty, February 11, 1982, Kirby Papers; faculty minutes, February 12 and March 26, 1982.
57. "Guidelines and Procedures for Faculty Evaluation of Teaching and Scholarship," attached to the faculty minutes of April 12, 1985; Committee on Faculty to the Perkins Faculty, "Proposed Revisions in the Peer Evaluation Program," March 3, 1987, attached to the faculty minutes of March 6, 1987.
58. Committee on Faculty to the Perkins Faculty, "Proposed Revisions"; faculty minutes, March 6, 1987.
59. Faculty minutes, December 4, 1992.
60. Committee on Faculty report, "Peer Teaching Groups: Description and Process," attached to faculty minutes, May 3, 1996.
61. Senate minutes, March 26 and April 16, 1982.
62. Perkins School of Theology catalog, 1983–84, 45, 53, 61, 68.
63. Curriculum Study Committee to the Perkins Senate, "Proposal for Revision of the Master of Divinity Curriculum, and Related Proposals," March 22, 1982, Kirby Papers; senate minutes, April 16, 1982; Catalog, 1983–84, 21–25.
64. Senate minutes, April 16, 1982; catalog, 1983–84, 25–26.
65. John Holbert to the D.Min. Steering Committee, April 5, 1982, Kirby Papers.
66. Catalog, 1985–86, 23–25, and 1991–92, 26–27.
67. Graduate Program in Religious Studies, Review Committee, "Final Report," May 20, 1991, files of the Graduate Program in Religious Studies, Office of the Graduate Program in Religious Studies.
68. Committee on Curriculum to the Perkins Faculty, April 6, 1989; faculty minutes, April 7, 1989.
69. Catalog, 1991–92, 17–20, 44.
70. J. Ward, for the Ad Hoc Committee on Formation, Interethnic Experience, and Workshops, to the Perkins Faculty, February 27, 1990; faculty minutes, March 2, 1990.
71. Curriculum Committee to the Perkins Faculty, April 4, 1990; faculty minutes, March 2 and April 6, 1990.
72. Faculty minutes, April 5, 1991, March 4, 1994, and December 1, 1995; Committee on Curriculum, evening program report, February 1994 (attached to faculty minutes of March 4, 1994); Long Range Planning Committee, proposals related to the evening program, November 28, 1995 (attached to faculty minutes of December 1, 1995).
73. William L. Baumgartner, ed., *Fact Book on Theological Education, 1987-1988* (Vandalia, Ohio: Association of Theological Schools, n.d.), 54–60; Gary Gilbert, ed., *Fact Book on Theological Education, 1993–1994* (Pittsburgh, Pa.: Association of Theological Schools, n.d.), 60–88.
74. Kirby to Hillerbrand, "Report to the Provost," May 13, 1983, Kirby Papers.
75. Kirby, "A Vision of the Future."
76. From records in the Perkins registrar's office.
77. *Black Seminarians at Perkins: Then and Now* (Dallas: Bridwell Library, 1994), n.p.; records in the Perkins registrar's office; Report of the Dean to the Committee on Faculty, April 1987.
78. From records in the Perkins registrar's office.
79. A documented record of the scandal, how it developed, and the university's response is to be found in "Report to the Board of Trustees of Southern Methodist University from the Special Committee of Bishops of the South Central Jurisdiction of the United Methodist Church," June 19, 1987, board of trustees minutes. For a later account that supplements the findings of the bishops' committee, see David Whitford, *A Payroll to Meet: A Story of Greed, Corruption, and Football at SMU* (New York: Macmillan, 1989).
80. Report of the Special Committee of Bishops, 30–33, 38.

81. *Daily Campus*, February 5 and 10, 1987; minutes of the executive committee of the board of trustees, June 26, 1987; "Report of the Governance Committee," Southern Methodist University Board of Trustees, April 30, 1987, 1, Kirby Papers.
82. Report of the Special Committee of Bishops, 4, 39.
83. James Kirby, "Confidential Draft—to the University Community," March 25, 1987, Kirby Papers; Southern Methodist University Board of Trustees, Workbook, May 8, 1987, VI–8.
84. *Daily Campus*, November 20, 1986.
85. "Statement by the Faculty of the Perkins School of Theology of Southern Methodist University," March 6, 1987 (faculty minutes).
86. "Report of the Governance Committee," 2–5, 8.
87. *Daily Campus*, January 13, 1987.
88. Schubert M. Ogden, interview by James Brooks, April 28, 2004 SMU Archive Series; *Dallas Morning News*, June 7, 1987.
89. *Dallas Morning News*, May 30 and June 7, 1987; *Daily Campus*, June 9, 1987.
90. *Dallas Morning News*, June 7, 1987; *Daily Campus*, June 9, 1987.
91. Report of the Special Committee of Bishops, 12–14.
92. "Report of the Task Force on Church-Relatedness," Southern Methodist University, January 25, 1989, in the personal files of Charles Wood.
93. *Dallas Morning News*, June 25, 1987.
94. "Report of the Dean to the Committee on Faculty," April 24, 1984; "Address to Perkins Faculty Workshop," August 31, 1984, both in Kirby Papers.
95. "Report of the Dean to the Committee on Faculty, 1984–85," no date, 4; Joseph L. Allen to Leander E. Keck, May 7, 1985, both in Kirby Papers.
96. Leander E. Keck, "Reflections on the Deanship of James E. Kirby," October 30, 1985, Kirby Papers.
97. Ibid.
98. "Report of the Dean to the Committee on Faculty, 1984–85."
99. Keck, "Reflections on the Deanship of James E. Kirby."
100. "Report of the Dean to the Committee on Faculty, 1985–86"; "Annual Report of the Dean," Perkins School of Theology, April 4, 1988, Kirby Papers.
101. Kirby, "A Vision of the Future," 14–15, 17.
102. Ibid., 15–17.
103. "Perkins in the Year 2000: A Report to the President of Southern Methodist University," July 5, 1989, Kirby Papers.
104. James E. Kirby, "A Response to the Report of the Blue Ribbon Committee," August 23, 1989, Kirby Papers.
105. Charles M. Wood to Kirby, August 28, 1989, Kirby Papers.
106. James E. Kirby, "Report to the Faculty Conference, September 14–15, 1990" (attachment to faculty minutes); "Annual Report of the Dean, Perkins School of Theology," March 1991, Kirby Papers.
107. "Annual Report of the Dean, Perkins School of Theology," March 1991.
108. "Annual Report of the Dean, Perkins School of Theology," April 1992, Kirby Papers.
109. "Annual Report of the Dean, Perkins School of Theology," March 1991.
110. W. J. A. Power to. Jim L. Waits, June 28, 1991, Kirby Papers.
111. James L. Waits, "Review of James E. Kirby, Dean, Perkins School of Theology, Southern Methodist University," March 20, 1992, 1, Kirby Papers.
112. Ibid., 2–3.
113. Ibid., 5.
114. From notes in my personal files that I took at the Perkins faculty meeting of March 12, 1993, with the announcement by Kirby and remarks by Morgan and Pye.
115. "Process and Policy in the Review of Instructors at Perkins School of Theology," no date, in my personal files.
116. Faculty minutes, October 9, 1992.
117. Dick Murray to Kirby, October 11, 1992, in my personal files.

118. James Kirby, personal communication with author, October 27, 2008.
119. William S. Babcock et al. to Kirby, October 12, 1992, in my personal files.
120. Kirby to the Perkins Faculty, October 21, 1992; Wood to the Perkins faculty, November 2, 1992; Kirby to the Perkins Faculty, November 4, 1992, in my personal files.
121. From notes I took at the November 6 faculty guild meeting, in my personal files.
122. A recent instance of reference to the problems was the dean's address to the faculty conference on September 18, 1992, in which he spoke at length of faculty conflict at Perkins. After some treatment of the subject he observed, "I do not believe the appropriate question before us is as much how to avoid any conflict we may be facing, as how to use it in a creative and positive manner in order to become a new community." He added, "We have created an atmosphere in which we expect to learn from one another. Nothing I know is more basic to respect. . . . Recently my fellow deans at SMU were astonished when I reported that we had been working on an understanding covering the sensitive issue of retirement. They have come to expect it of us" (Kirby Papers).
123. From notes I took at the November 16 faculty guild meeting, in my personal files.
124. From notes I took at the November 30 faculty guild meeting, in my personal files.
125. Faculty minutes, December 4, 1992.
126. From notes I took at the December 7 faculty guild meeting, in my personal files.
127. Committee on Faculty to the Faculty, "Rank and Tenure Policy Revisions," March 30, 1994 (attachment to faculty minutes of April 8, 1994); faculty minutes, April 8, 1994.
128. From notes I took at the March 12 meeting of the faculty, in my personal files.
129. *Perspective*, fall 1993, 20.
130. "Annual Report of the Dean to the Committee on Faculty, March, 1993," Kirby Papers.
131. "On Being Dean," Faculty Workshop, September 17, 1993, Kirby Papers.
132. "Annual Report, Dean James E. Kirby," April 1994, Kirby Papers.
133. Board of trustees minutes, September 23, 1994.

Reshaping Policy and Personnel, 1994–2002

R obin Warren Lovin, born in 1946 in Peoria, Illinois, received his under-graduate degree from Northwestern University in 1968 and his B.D. from Harvard in 1971. For the next three years he was an associate pastor and then a pastor in the Northern Illinois Conference of The United Methodist Church. In 1974 he returned to Harvard to do doctoral work in religious ethics, which he completed in 1978 with a dissertation entitled "The Constitution as Covenant: The Moral Foundations of Democracy and the Practice of Desegregation." In 1977–78 he was instructor in ethics at Candler School of Theology at Emory University. For the next thirteen years, as a member of the faculty at the Divinity School of the University of Chicago, he became known as one of the leading Christian ethicists in the country, publishing *Christian Faith and Public Choices: The Social Ethics of Barth, Brunner, and Bonhoeffer*, along with numerous major articles, and in 1987 he received a John Simon Guggenheim Fellowship.[1] In those years he continued to be active in The United Methodist Church and maintained a strong interest in the education of its clergy. This led him in 1991 to accept the position of dean and professor of ethics and society at the Theological School of Drew University. From that post he came to Perkins in 1994 as dean and professor of ethics.[2]

As dean, Jim Kirby had reorganized his administrators, increased the diversity of the faculty, enlarged the endowment, and initiated plans for a new classroom and office building. Those years had also seen a decline in enrollment, and the faculty conflict of 1992 had brought significant tensions to the surface.

Upon his arrival Robin Lovin took note of opportunities Perkins had before it, one of which, provided by the approaching retirement of older professors, was to bring to Perkins "the younger scholars who will set directions for theological studies" on into the twenty-first century. Another was created that summer by the Bridwell Foundation's $10 million endowment gift for Bridwell Library. Yet Perkins, Lovin said, also faced problems that were challenging all theological education: providing the church with large numbers of new leaders who would be diverse in race and gender, and preparing them to minister to congregations that ask increasingly probing questions, seek spiritual growth, and desire new avenues for service. The Perkins faculty, he said, was hoping "to link their tradition of scholarship and their commitment to ministry in new ways." He aimed to look to both sides of the seminary-church relationship.[3]

MOVING IN NEW DIRECTIONS

In his report at the 1994 fall faculty retreat, Lovin declared that this faculty was ready "to take a new look at ourselves and to move in new directions. Our first year together will be largely devoted to planning and setting those directions."[4] This called for developing a strategic plan for Perkins.

In the spring of 1991 the associate dean for academic affairs, Charles Wood, had proposed reestablishing a long-range planning committee as a regular committee of the faculty. During the 1980s, when such a committee had existed, it had usually been inactive. The faculty approved Wood's proposal and a new statement, "The Mission of Perkins School of Theology," which emphasized the interrelation of two aspects of this mission: preparing "effective leadership in the church" and "engaging in theological reflection on the church's faith, life, and mission in the world." It spoke of the Perkins's relationships to The United Methodist Church, to SMU, to its "unique geographical and cultural region," and to the worldwide Christian community.[5]

These actions proved to be important for Robin Lovin, given his emphasis on strategic planning. The most basic part of that planning, he said, would be clarity about what was distinctive in Perkins's institutional identity. In the face of outside pressures and criticisms, "our institutional self-presentation has become somewhat bland." He judged that Perkins needed to reflect on its present circumstances and set forth a vision of ministry inclusive of both evangelical and social ministry.[6]

Lovin suggested several ingredients of a plan that would express Perkins's identity: the shape of the faculty by the end of the decade, Bridwell Library, the Mexican American Program, continuing education, and recruitment and admissions in the face of a serious decline in recent inquiries to the admissions office. The school also would need a development plan to raise the money to support the proposals. Most of these plans were to be completed by May 1995—a strenuous agenda for the school in his first year as dean.[7]

In the fall of 1994 the faculty held several informal meetings in which Lovin provided his thinking about the process of planning, followed by small-group faculty discussions. In one meeting he declared that Perkins's chief long-range goal was to be "a center for theological leadership," and strategic planning should focus on what this would require in the next six months to a year.[8] The Long Range Planning Committee, chaired by Wood, shepherded the process through the faculty, which at its regular May meeting adopted the 1995 Strategic Plan.[9]

In its assessment of the current situation, the Strategic Plan concluded that the church neither assumed Perkins's role of leadership in United Methodist theological education nor left it unchallenged. Yet Perkins had more opportunities than it was using. To compete in its present environment, Perkins would need an efficient administration, increased financial resources, a strong faculty in "a period of generational transition," improved facilities, and an educational program available in other locations.[10]

The Strategic Plan then identified strategic initiatives in various aspects of Perkins life. One was to maintain the tenure-track and intern faculty at its present size while adding "at least one faculty appointment in a discipline devoted to study of the social context of ministry." Another was to increase enrollment by about fifty students, so that the total student body would be 435 to 450. A further initiative was to develop a plan for upgrading the existing buildings and adding new buildings where needed. An initiative for the internship was to study the process of pastoral formation, especially spiritual formation. For Perkins's outreach in the region, the plan proposed to begin offering courses in the Houston-Galveston area to be taught by Perkins faculty and applicable toward degree programs and to look into the possibility of additional extension programs in other locations. The report concluded that Perkins needed "a plan for securing the $16–20 million required for full implementation" of all these initiatives.[11]

To carry out the school's plans, Lovin made several changes in administrative personnel in the next few years and in the process reorganized some administrative offices. When he arrived in 1994, Perkins had three associate deans: academic affairs (David

Maldonado), external affairs (Stanley Menking), and students (Linn Caraway). When Lovin left in 2002, there was one associate dean—for academic affairs. The first of these offices remained as before, though with gradually increasing responsibilities. Three Perkins professors served in turn as associate academic dean: Maldonado until 1997, Jouette Bassler from 1997 to 2000, followed by Marjorie Procter-Smith.

The Office of External Affairs underwent a number of changes during Lovin's tenure. In 1996 Marilyn Alexander, who had been director of alumni relations since 1990, left Perkins for another position. Janice Virtue, who since 1992 had headed the Perkins registrar's office as director of academic procedures, then became director of Perkins relations, and Janelle Hampton, who had worked in academic procedures since 1989, succeeded Virtue as registrar. With Stanley Menking's retirement in December 1997 as associate dean for external affairs and Virtue's departure for a position at Duke in the summer of 1998, Lovin reorganized the office. In the fall of 1998 he brought in Gary MacDonald, who had been a pastor in the New England Conference of The United Methodist Church since receiving his M.Div. degree from Perkins in 1994. During Lovin's deanship MacDonald initially held the title of director of continuing education and public programs and handled much of what had been Menking's area of responsibility. Working with MacDonald in public relations was Roberta Cox, who moved to that office from the Bridwell Library staff in 1995.

As associate dean of students, Linn Caraway oversaw the work of recruitment, admissions, financial aid, and student services. Several changes occurred among the other staff members in that office. DeForrest Wiksten, a 1962 Perkins graduate, retired in 1995 from the North Texas Conference and succeeded Harry Wright as director of admissions. The next year Matthew Wehrly, who had since 1991 been assistant to the director of admissions, became director of financial aid, recruitment, and student services, the position he held until he left in 1998 for a post at Iliff. After Wiksten's retirement in 2000, Shonda Jones, who had come to Perkins in 1999 as director of student services, was in charge of recruitment and admissions. Upon Caraway's departure in 2001 Jones assumed her responsibilities as well until Jones left in 2003 for a position at Candler School of Theology. In 2001 Tracy Anne Allred arrived to serve as director of recruitment and admissions from a similar position at Duke Divinity School.

SMU's Office of Development and External Affairs appoints those who are to have special responsibility for Perkins development. In the spring of 1995 Todd Harris, a 1990 Perkins M.Div. graduate, assumed that responsibility but remained only one year. He was followed in the fall of 1996 by Scott Somers, a 1979 Perkins M.Div. graduate and a former pastor in the Southwest Texas Conference. At the same time Kirby, in addition to resuming his teaching and research, began to work part time in Perkins development, as director of principal gifts. These two appointments foreshadowed Perkins's participation in an SMU capital campaign beginning in 1997, a campaign that secured several significant large gifts for Perkins. Another addition to the development staff for Perkins was Mary Brouillette, who in 1999 became director of donor relations. Throughout the Lovin years Linda Hervey continued in the post of financial officer, which she had held since 1993.

Bishop John Wesley Hardt, who had been bishop-in-residence since 1988, retired in 2000 after holding that position at Perkins the longest of anyone. He was succeeded by Bishop David Lawson, who had served in episcopal areas in the North Central Jurisdiction.

To make seminary education more broadly available in the region, as well as to reverse declining enrollment at Perkins, Robin Lovin began work in the fall of 1994 to establish an extension program in the Houston area. After an exploratory meeting with leaders of the Texas Annual Conference in Houston in January 1995, Lovin was able to announce at the Texas Annual Conference on May 29 that "Perkins South" would offer its first classes in the fall of 1995. The program would enable students to take the initial portions of their work toward Perkins degrees—the master of divinity, master of theological studies, and master of religious education—in Houston-Galveston, after which they would complete their degree work at the Dallas campus. Lovin expressed his special thanks to James Moore, pastor of St. Luke's United Methodist Church in Houston, and Charles Millikan, pastor of Moody Memorial United Methodist Church in Galveston, for making their churches' facilities available and providing financial support for the program. As Millikan observed, "Houston is one of the few major metropolitan areas in the country without a permanent, fully accredited seminary."[12]

On June 17 a half-day orientation, "Inside Perkins Houston," took place at St. Luke's so prospective students could learn about the new program, meet Perkins faculty, and explore the possibility of vocations in ministry. Lovin told those attending that this was "a milestone in the life of Perkins School of Theology." "We will," he said, "find ways to make the residency requirements feasible for someone who continues to live and work here in Houston-Galveston." Fall semester classes began in Galveston on Saturday, August 26, with two courses: Lovin's "Philosophy and Theological Inquiry," especially designed for master of divinity students without previous work in philosophy; and Deidre Palmer's "The Church's Educational Ministry," which would enable students to meet requirements in either the master of religious education or the M.Div. program. Lovin and Palmer were accompanied to Houston by Caraway, associate dean of students, who provided Perkins South with leadership in spiritual formation, helping to establish the group's sense of community. In addition to two Saturday sessions in Galveston, the Perkins faculty members flew to Houston every other Tuesday afternoon, taught their classes from 6:30 to 9:00 p.m., and at 10:00 caught the last Southwest Airlines flight back to Dallas.[13]

The planners had not known how many students to expect; James Moore said they had initially hoped for twenty to twenty-five. In the fall of 1995 Perkins enrolled forty-nine, including thirty-nine beginning M.Div. students. In the spring 1996 semester, Ed Sylvest flew to Houston to teach "The History of Christianity," and Michael Hawn, "Word and Worship." Enrollment in the fall of 1996 increased to seventy-nine, more than three-fourths of whom were in the M.Div. program.[14]

Lovin continued to build the foundations for Perkins South. In the spring of 1996 he announced the appointment of a full-time director of the program, George M. Atkinson, previously pastor of Westbury United Methodist Church in Houston. Atkinson, with a B.D. from Perkins and a Ph.D. from SMU in theology, assumed the office on July 1. That summer Moody Memorial in Galveston, led by Millikan, decided to provide a grant of $100,000 to support the program.[15]

In the fall of 1996 the Long Range Planning Committee, after an extensive study and evaluation of the Houston-Galveston program's beginning, judged that it met the four conditions necessary for its continuation: the prospect of continuing adequate enrollment, the comparable academic quality of courses in Houston-Galveston and in Dallas, the prospect of adequate resources—faculty, financial, administrative, and physical—and a high level of support from churches in the Houston-Galveston area. The committee proposed that the program "be continued on an ongoing basis," the faculty approved, and Perkins South became a continuing part of Perkins's education work for the foreseeable future. Thereafter, fall enrollment while Lovin was dean ranged from a low of sixty-three to a high of ninety-four—encouraging in view of the resources the program required (see appendix B, table 4).[16]

Early in 1997 Lovin entered into conversations with Bishop Bruce Blake and other representatives of the Oklahoma Conference, representatives of St. Paul Theological Seminary in Kansas City, and officials at Oklahoma City University (OCU) about the possibility that Perkins and St. Paul could establish a joint extension program in Oklahoma. With this program Perkins expressed its commitment to make seminary education more easily available to Oklahomans and to encourage Methodists in Oklahoma to study at Perkins.

In December the faculty approved a proposal for twenty-four semester hours of courses (The United Methodist Church's "basic theological studies program")—two courses a semester—to be offered in a two-year period at OCU. Perkins faculty members would teach three of the eight courses, faculty from St. Paul (350 miles away) would teach three, and a professor from the Wimberly School of Religion at OCU would teach two. The goal was to have the equivalent of twenty-five students taking two courses each in a given semester and for half the M.Div. students to complete the degree at Perkins's Dallas campus.[17]

The program began in the fall of 1998, with Lovin offering "Introduction to Theological Studies" and Amy Oden, a professor at OCU, teaching "United Methodist Doctrine and Polity." Twenty-six students registered for a total of forty-five course enrollments. Then, in spring 1999, with courses taught by Oden and Lovett Weems, the president of St. Paul, the program had 29 students with forty-eight course enrollments. After an evaluation by the Long Range Planning Committee, the Perkins faculty in May 1999 voted to extend the program to a third year and the next December approved its continuation beyond the third year, provided St. Paul and OCU maintained their present level of support. Enrollment through the fall of 2002 ranged between twenty-five and thirty-four. In fall 2003, however, enrollment fell to eighteen, there were indications that St. Paul might not be able to provide faculty for its Oklahoma City courses, and the leaders of all three institutions when the program began had either departed or soon would. That fall the three schools agreed to close the program as of the end of the spring semester of 2004. Perkins's Tracy Anne Allred and Marjorie Procter-Smith flew to OCU and counseled with the students about how they might proceed.[18]

In fall 2001, three years after the Oklahoma City program began, Lovin and others, with the enthusiastic approval of several ministers in the Southwest Texas Conference, developed a preliminary plan "on an experimental basis" for an extension program, "Perkins Southwest," at University United Methodist Church in San Antonio, to begin in the fall of 2002. Its goal was to enable students there who could not move to Dallas for three years to enroll for a seminary degree. As the plan unfolded in the next year, students would be able to study toward a master's in divinity or a master's in church ministries (which replaced the master's in religious education in 2001). Students would be able to complete twenty-four semester hours in San Antonio but then would need to complete their degree requirements at the Dallas campus. Classes began in the fall of 2002, with Bassler and Wood each offering a basic course, and nineteen students enrolled. In the next four years, however, fall enrollment never rose higher than twenty-nine, and after church leaders in San Antonio in 2006 proposed terminating the program, Bill Lawrence, who succeeded Lovin as dean, and the Perkins faculty agreed to do so as of May 2007. The number of potential students in the area was smaller than had been expected (the San Antonio metropolitan area is much less Protestant than the Houston area), Perkins Southwest and Austin Presbyterian Seminary had been in stiff competition for students, and some felt that Perkins and the Southwest Texas Conference could have worked more closely together.[19]

In fall 1997, not long before the Perkins faculty approved the Oklahoma City program, the Doctor of Ministry Committee explored the possibility of offering a D.Min. course at Simpson College in Iowa, but those arrangements were discontinued after only three students enrolled. Then, in spring 1998, a Perkins survey of United Methodist pastors in Arkansas found that thirty-nine were interested in enrolling in the D.Min. program if they could take the courses at Hendrix College in Conway, Arkansas. That April the faculty approved a plan to offer one D.Min. course each semester at Hendrix and one each semester in Dallas. The Conway program was soon discontinued, while the Dallas program went on as before.[20]

The extension programs increased Perkins's enrollment and provided seminary education more widely in the region. The most significant and enduring increase came from the Houston-Galveston program; the others were smaller and were eventually terminated.

Roy Barton's retirement in 1995 as director of the Mexican American Program was an occasion for appreciating his contributions to the program and considering in what directions it should move. One of his major achievements since he assumed that post in 1974 was organizing the Hispanic Instructors—a group of Methodist Hispanic leaders from seminaries, universities, church agencies, and the pastorate who were willing to teach Hispanic students in clergy continuing education, in lay training seminars, and in the Perkins summer Course of Study School for pastors not seeking a seminary degree. With funding from The United Methodist Church's Division of Ordained Ministry beginning in 1976, the Hispanic Instructors became an advisory body to the church and the academy by reflecting on theology and Hispanic ministry. The Hispanic Instructors helped shape the national plan for Hispanic ministry adopted by the 1992 General Conference of The United Methodist Church. That plan led to the Lay Missioner–Pastor Mentor Program to equip teams of laity and pastors with the skills needed to do theology, reflect critically on scripture, and establish faith communities and community ministries.[21]

Barton also spearheaded the publication of a quarterly journal, *Apuntes*, intended "as a medium for theological exchange among Hispanics and other persons in the United States."[22] Under the editorship of Justo González, visiting professor of theology at the Interdenominational Theological Center in Atlanta and a member of the Rio Grande Conference, *Apuntes* first appeared in the spring of 1981 and continues to be published by the Mexican American Program at Perkins as an expression of a Hispanic perspective in Christian theology. As González explained in the first issue, the name of the journal was chosen for its ambiguity. It can be translated as "marginal notes," or it can refer to Hispanics' recognition that they are not at the power centers of society—thus the original subtitle of the journal, *Reflections from the Hispanic Margin*.[23] Because the Hispanic community in the United States is bilingual, *Apuntes* has been bilingual from its beginning—some articles in Spanish and some in English, with a brief summary in the other language following many of the articles.

Ed Sylvest has described Barton as "a master of the consultative process." For years he worked with many others to bring about a Hispanic studies track in the

Perkins master of divinity program, helped shape and staff the summer Course of Study School for its Spanish-speaking students, enhanced Rio Grande Conference Continuing Education, encouraged jurisdictional convocations on Hispanic ministry, and much else, bringing the program to the point where The United Methodist Church named Perkins as its center for Hispanic ministries.[24]

Upon Barton's retirement Robin Lovin invited twenty-one Hispanic leaders to meet with him on July 26, 1995, to discuss the future of the program. A Perkins committee, he said, would be making recommendations to the faculty about program and staffing, and he wanted to hear their ideas while planning was in its early stages. Then, and in another meeting on August 2, he assured them the program would continue and, he hoped, be expanded: "Nothing will be jettisoned." They offered their counsel about the program's leadership and expressed their appreciation for the sessions.[25]

In the spring of 1996 Lovin appointed Minerva Carcaño as the new director of the Mexican American Program, effective July 1. Since her graduation from Perkins in 1979, Carcaño had served as a pastor and then a district superintendent in the Rio Grande Conference, and, since 1992, minister-in-charge of the South Albuquerque Cooperative Ministry.

In the fall of 1995 a group of Mexican American church leaders had suggested that Lovin form an advisory committee for the Mexican American Program. After Carcaño arrived, she and Lovin implemented that suggestion and established an advisory committee of fifteen members. Although the group met only twice (in December 1996 and July 1998), it provided valuable dialog between Perkins and Mexican American leaders in the period of transition.[26]

With Carcaño as director of the program, Perkins arranged three joint occasions with the two Methodist seminaries in Mexico—Seminario Báez Camargo in Mexico City and Seminario Juan Wesley in Monterrey. The first was Seminario Báez Carmargo's anniversary celebration on October 9–12, 1997. Lovin led the Perkins delegation, which included professors Carcaño, Docampo, Hawn, Maldonado, Pedraja, and Sylvest. Ahead of the visit Lovin was asked to say words of greeting in Spanish at an appropriate time, which led him to send an SOS to David Maldonado: "I wonder if you could render the following into some acceptable (and easily pronounceable!) version of Spanish for me?" Maldonado apparently chose the right words, as the Seminario dean later wrote, "So far, we have received only good reports on the encounter. People feel there should be follow-up sessions."[27]

The second joint conference took place in Monterrey on October 9–10, 1998, with the celebration of the twenty-fifth anniversary of Seminario Juan Wesley. The theme was "The Pastorate of the New Millennium," with presentations by faculty members from Seminario Báez Camargo and from Perkins. On November 10–13, 1999, came a third joint conference, a celebration at Perkins of the twenty-fifth anniversary of its Mexican American Program, with representatives from all three seminaries. Several papers from that occasion were published in the summer 2000 edition of *Apuntes*.[28]

In June 2001 Minerva Carcaño accepted an appointment as district superintendent of the Metropolitan (Portland) District of the Oregon/Idaho Conference. While the directorship of the Mexican American Program was vacant in 2001–02, Ed Sylvest chaired a committee that gave it oversight. Lovin identified candidates for the position, which would be filled after appropriate inquiry and feedback but, because it was administrative, without a search committee or faculty advisory.

In the spring of 2002 Lovin appointed as director of the program, effective July 1, the Reverend G. Jean Treviño-Teddlie. With seminary study at Garrett Evangelical, Brite Divinity School at Texas Christian University, and United Theological Seminary in Dayton, Ohio, and a master's degree in social work, she had since 1994 worked for Hispanic ministries in the Central Texas Conference under assignment from the General Board of Global Ministries.[29] She had participated for years in activities of the Mexican American Program and was well acquainted with its work.

THE STUDENTS AND THEIR STUDIES

Between fall 1976 and fall 1994 enrollment in Perkins's master of divinity program declined from 365 to 231. Increased enrollment in the master of theological studies and the doctor of ministry program partially offset this decline; total enrollment increased from 461 in 1976 to 524 in 1984 but then declined to 408 in the fall of 1994. This was one reason Dean Lovin urged the faculty to initiate the Houston-Galveston and other extension programs. Aided by these programs, enrollment in the master of divinity program recovered to 300 in the fall of 2002, after a temporary decline in the fall of 2000 (see tables 3 and 4 in appendix B). With increases in M.T.S. and nondegree students, total enrollment in 2002 was the highest it had been since 1984.

But head count does not tell the whole story. Over the years, primarily because of outside employment, many students have taken less than a full load of courses. This phenomenon affects The United Methodist Church's calculation of how much a seminary is to receive each year from the Ministerial Education Fund, and it affects the size of classes and the workload of faculty members. A full load for a student is twelve semester-hours; anyone taking nine would be counted as having a "full-time-equivalent" (FTE) of 0.75. The FTE for all Perkins master's programs together decreased from 0.82 in 1991 to 0.66 in 2000.

While Lovin was dean, the percentage of women in all Perkins programs (including the Graduate Program in Religious Studies) continued the increase that had begun around 1970. Women accounted for 37.7 percent of total enrollment in the fall of 1994; by the fall of 2002 they were 49.6 percent of the total. Their numbers in all programs in those years rose from 154 in 1994 to 258 in 2002, an increase of more than 67 percent, whereas the number of men rose only 3 percent, from 254 to 262.

The number of African American students had begun to rise significantly after 1974. They increased from 10 percent of the total Perkins student body in 1994 (forty-one students) to 15.6 percent in 2002 (eighty-one students). The number of Hispanics continued at the modest level reached in the early 1990s—between nine and eighteen each year, or between 1.9 percent and 3.6 percent of the total student body. More Asian American students enrolled in these years, increasing from eight in 1994 to twenty in 2002. International students were a steady presence of 3 to 5 percent, and at least one Native American and sometimes three were enrolled each year.

As to denomination, United Methodists throughout this period constituted from 70 to 77 percent of the total each year, supplemented by about 5 percent who were members of other Methodist bodies. Another 5 percent were Episcopalians, 3 to 3.5 percent Baptists, 3 percent Presbyterians, and 9 to 14 percent members of other denominations.

The mean average age of Perkins master of divinity students had risen significantly since 1970 and continued to rise: from thirty-six for all Perkins M.Div. students in the fall of 1994 to forty in 2002. Each year from 1995 to 2002 women students were on average three to four years older than the men. The increase was accentuated by the extension programs: between 1996 and 1999 the median age of Houston and Oklahoma City students was three to seven years older than that of students at the Perkins Dallas campus. Many candidates for ordained ministry in recent years, in other Methodist seminaries as well as at Perkins, are training for their second career and thus are older than in earlier decades. This affects recruitment, as older students often seek the seminary that is least expensive and nearest to home. When older students enroll in seminary, they are likely to carry outside employment along with their studies. Thus with the increasing age of Perkins students has come a decline in the FTE figures noted earlier, with the result that students take longer to complete their studies. This in turn leaves fewer years in church positions for older students than for those who come to seminary straight from college. These difficulties are widespread in The United Methodist Church's recruitment for ministry.[30]

In 1997–98 the master of divinity program was subjected to its first major curriculum review since 1989–90. Jouette Bassler chaired the Curriculum Review Committee. Among the more prominent changes that emerged from that review were these:

- A new three-term-hour requirement, "The Church in Its Social Context," was to be taken before or along with the first courses in ministry. (Beginning with the 1999–2001 catalog, "term hours" replaced "semester hours.") This course, a response to comments from the dean and others that the curriculum needed to give more attention to the social context of ministry, was grouped with an already existing three-term-hour requirement, "World Religions and Christianity: A Global Perspective," in a category named "Contextual Studies."
- A two-semester introduction to the Christian heritage from its beginnings to the present replaced the six-term-hour requirement in the history of Christianity that had been split between a three-term-hour survey and three term hours in any intermediate course in Christian history.
- "Introduction to Theology," a three-term-hour course, became a first-year Division III requirement. It replaced "Introduction to Theological Studies," which was added in 1990 as a required introduction to the whole curriculum.

- A three-term-hour course, Word and Worship, became a Division IV requirement.

- The total number of term hours of courses required for graduation was increased from sixty-nine to seventy-two, plus the twelve-term-hour internship, for a total of eighty-four term hours. Space remained for only twenty-four term hours devoted to electives, instead of thirty.

- The minimum length of an approved internship was increased from eighteen weeks to six months. Full-time interns could no longer take academic coursework during the internship, no matter its length (six months, nine months, or a year).

- Concurrent internships were reduced from four semesters to twelve months, and students could take academic coursework during these internships.[31]

The review committee made plans to explore how to implement more effectively the already existing requirement of participation in a formation group concerning spiritual disciplines appropriate to Christian faith, as well as how the existing requirements about racism and sexism workshops and the interethnic experience should be fulfilled. Several of these changes—the required courses in worship and in the church and its social context, the revised history of Christianity requirement, and the increased attention to spiritual formation—had a bearing on faculty and administrative staff appointments in the next four years.

After the M.Div. program was revised, in 1998–99 the Curriculum Review Committee turned its attention to the other Perkins master's degree programs, with a dual concern: to make sure that Perkins was in compliance with the standards of the Association of Theological Schools and to take appropriate account of The United Methodist Church's provisions for a deacon's ordination.[32]

The Curriculum Review Committee's review of the master of theological studies program brought about a clearer catalog statement of its purposes: "As a foundation for further graduate study, for enhancement of lay leadership roles, or for personal enrichment" but, by implication, not for those intending ordination. As this degree was no longer seen as a route to ordination (some members of denominations other than The United Methodist Church had viewed it as such), courses in Division IV were no longer required.[33]

The faculty adopted the Curriculum Review Committee proposal that the master of religious education be replaced by a master of church ministries degree (C.M.M.) that would include different tracks appropriate to various types of specialized ministry. Each track would provide the educational requirements for ordination as deacon in The United Methodist Church. The initial track was in Christian education, and in 2000 the faculty added a second track, in urban ministry. The first students to enroll in the C.M.M. program, in fall 2001, had to complete fifty-four term hours for their degree; eighteen term hours were in required courses, thirty were in either the Christian education or the urban ministry track, and six were in a supervised internship.[34]

In 1998–99 a joint committee of faculty from Perkins and SMU's Meadows School of the Arts reviewed the master of sacred music degree program, restated its goals and objectives, and made changes in its required courses. One result was to strengthen the working relationship between the two schools; another was improvement in the program's student retention rate.[35]

In fall 2001 the faculty approved a proposal for Perkins and SMU's Dedman College Graduate Program to offer jointly a graduate certificate in women's studies. Its purpose would be to enhance students' lives—both female and male—through integrating theories about gender with knowledge of women's roles and achievements. The certificate required fifteen term hours in specified courses across a range of disciplines in the two schools.[36]

During the 1996–97 academic year several Perkins faculty members with a shared interest in the church's ministry to urban areas and a special interest in West Dallas, an economically depressed section of Dallas, formed a group they named the Urban Ministry Task Force. The task force decided to focus its attention on West Dallas in three ways: relating to groups already at work there, doing menial jobs there, and relating West Dallas to the wider Dallas community. In October 1997 the task force conducted a faculty consultation at Perkins and at the Wesley Rankin Community Center, attended by twenty Perkins faculty, administrators, and students and four community leaders. The consultation's purpose was to reflect theologically on urban ministry in relation to West Dallas and to explore the implications of an urbanizing society for the work of Perkins. Then, on April 16–18, 1998, the Convocation on Urban Ministry took place, attended by 150 people and planned under the leadership of the Reverend Henry Masters, pastor of St. Paul United Methodist Church in Dallas, who had joined the Perkins administrative staff as coordinator of urban ministries. Chaired by Minerva Carcaño, the task force focused on building relationships with the Hispanic and African American communities in Dallas. Over time it broadened its interests beyond West Dallas.[37]

In May 1999, responding to a proposal from the task force, the faculty created the Urban Ministry Steering Committee, a volunteer group accountable to the dean and the faculty that any faculty member or administrator could join. In April 2000 two further faculty decisions reflected the interest in urban ministry: the creation of the urban ministry track in the C.M.M. degree (discussed earlier), and the creation of a certificate in urban ministry within the M.Div. degree. To earn the certificate, students were to complete at least fifteen term hours in an approved list of urban ministry courses, participate in an approved urban ministry project, and complete an internship in an urban setting.[38]

One requirement emerging from the 1998 curriculum revision was that each student "participate in a Formation Group for two terms, normally the first year of study." Since 1990 the formation program (in which first-year M.Div. students were required to participate) had been overseen by the office of the associate dean for community life (later renamed associate dean of students). The group leaders—volunteering faculty and staff members—were not, however, given any special training in spiritual formation, and there was no generally shared understanding of its goals or how to achieve them.[39]

In 1999 Lovin began looking for a specialist in spiritual formation. The next year he appointed Frederick W. Schmidt, from the staff of the National Episcopal Cathedral in Washington, D.C., to be director of spiritual life and formation. At the fall faculty conference his first year, Schmidt led a discussion about the governing principles of spiritual formation. Afterward he gave two orientation sessions, one for several faculty members and others who volunteered to be group facilitators, and the other an all-day program, required of all students in the master's of divinity, sacred music, and church ministries programs, to help develop a theological vocabulary focusing on discernment and formation.[40]

Previously, students' participation in formation groups, though required, had been on a noncredit basis. Because Schmidt wanted the spiritual formation program to be part of students' academic program, he proposed, and the faculty concurred, that beginning in 2002, students studying for masters of divinity and of church ministries would receive one term hour (pass/fail) for the required two semesters' participation. The Spiritual Formation Program has continued in that way.[41]

Since 1991 the doctor of ministry program had allowed two options, either the pursuit of an area of special interest in ministry or a concentration in evangelism. In the spring of 2000 the faculty approved a revision that eliminated the first option and provided for three concentrations: evangelism (as before), parish leadership, and urban ministry. The degree required twenty-four term hours of coursework and three term hours for a written project.[42]

THE FACULTY AND ITS WORK

The Perkins faculty experienced turnover at a more rapid rate while Robin Lovin was dean than during any of the three previous decades. He knew when he came to Perkins that numerous retirements would occur, and he used the opportunity to shape the faculty for years to come. In his eight years as dean, Lovin brought in twenty-four new faculty members and administrators (see appendix A)—sixteen classroom faculty members, two intern faculty members, and six administrators. Most arrived in 1997 and after, when the pace became so rapid that by the fall of 2002 more than half the faculty had come to Perkins in the previous five years.

Lovin's appointments of classroom faculty included five in Division I (Bible): Roy Heller, Alejandro Botta, and Richard Nelson in Old Testament, and Jaime Clark-Soles and Abraham Smith in New Testament. Two were in Division II (the Christian heritage in its religious and cultural context): Bruce Marshall and David Price. In Division III one new appointment was in systematic theology, Karen Baker-Fletcher, and one in ethics, Rebekah Miles. Seven were in Division IV (the church and its ministry): Evelyn Parker (Christian education), Edwin Aponte and Harold Recinos (church and society), Scott Jones (evangelism), Alyce McKenzie (homiletics), Paula Dobbs-Wiggins (adjunct in pastoral care), and Mark Stamm (worship).

SMU's appointment in June 1995 of its tenth president, R. Gerald Turner, freed former dean Jim Kirby, who had served as interim president in 1994–95, to take a year of leave in 1995–96 and then return to his tenured position in church history at Perkins. Turner, a member of the Church of Christ, came to SMU after eleven years as chancellor of the University of Mississippi.

Several new Perkins appointments reflected changes in 1998 and afterward in the master of divinity curriculum and in areas of growing faculty interest. The decision to require the course "The Church in Its Social Context" was followed by the appointment of Aponte in 1998. Requiring "Word and Worship" led to the appointment in 2000 of Stamm to a new second faculty position in the field of worship. As noted earlier, Frederick W. Schmidt was appointed, also in 2000, to the new administrative post of director of spiritual life and formation. Reshaping the history of Christianity requirement led to the appointment in 2001 of Marshall as professor of historical theology. With the strong interest in urban ministry, Recinos, a specialist in that field, arrived in January 2002 to replace David Maldonado in that church and society position; Maldonado had left two years earlier to become president of Iliff School of Theology.

Lovin made two appointments to the intern faculty. After Marilyn Spurrell's departure, Isabel Docampo arrived in 1997 as assistant professor of supervised ministry. In January 1998 William Jennings Bryan III, previously pastor of Grace United Methodist Church and then of Lovers Lane United Methodist Church in Dallas, joined the intern staff and thereafter became its director. Bert Affleck, who had been the director since 1983, became director of supervisory studies until his retirement in 2002. After 1998 the intern faculty had five members—these three, Virgil Howard, and Tom Spann.

During Lovin's years as dean thirteen faculty (including administrators with courtesy faculty rank) retired, and eight went to positions elsewhere. The retirements included the last four of Merrimon Cuninggim's appointments (Victor Furnish, W. J. A. Power, James Ward, and me) and three of Joe Quillian's (Roy Barton, Leroy Howe, and Klaus Penzel). Others retiring during Lovin's deanship were Bert Affleck, Bishop John Wesley Hardt, Zan W. Holmes Jr., Stanley Menking, Edward Poitras, and James Wharton.

Of the eight faculty members who went to positions elsewhere during these years, six went to other academic positions (Clifton Black, Ellen Charry, Danna Nolan Fewell, David Maldonado, Deidre Palmer, and Luis Pedraja), and two took other annual conference appointments in The United Methodist Church (Minerva Carcaño and Marilyn Spurrell).

With all these departures, the only faculty members remaining in 2002 who had been at Perkins before 1981 were William Babcock, John Holbert, Virgil Howard, Edwin Sylvest, and Charles Wood.

When Lovin arrived, the faculty had sixteen members (in a faculty of thirty-nine) who were women and members of racial and ethnic minorities. By the end of his deanship in 2002 women and minorities accounted for nearly half (twenty of forty-one). These included three African American men, one Asian man, three Latino men, and thirteen women, including three African Americans and two Latinas. In addition, by 2002 several Perkins nonfaculty administrators were women, two of whom were African American. In the spring of 1970 Perkins faculty had consisted only of non-Latino white men, but by the fall of 2002 that group accounted for only slightly more than half the faculty.

Lovin also made several appointments to endowed chairs while he was dean. In 1993 the Albert Cook Outler Chair of Wesley Studies had become vacant with the departure of Richard Heitzenrater. That position was filled in 1995 with the appointment of William J. Abraham, who had previously been the McCreless Professor of Evangelism. This was the latest of several instances in which members of the Perkins faculty moved from one field to another (others had been John Holbert, Virgil Howard, and Leroy Howe). In 1997 Scott J. Jones was appointed to the McCreless chair vacated by Abraham. Marjorie Procter-Smith became LeVan Professor of Preaching and Worship in 1996; and in 1997 John Holbert was designated Lois Craddock Perkins Professor of Homiletics. In 2001 Richard D. Nelson came to the faculty as the W. J. A. Power Professor of Biblical Hebrew and Old Testament Interpretation.

One of Dean Lovin's goals in his faculty appointments, as he later described it, "was to see that Perkins students had an education that exposed them to the major theological options available today."[43] This was particularly evident in the membership of Division III. By 2002 that division included faculty working with several theological approaches: process theology (Karen Baker-Fletcher and Theodore Walker), Niebuhrian realism (Robin Lovin and Rebekah Miles), engagement with Thomas Aquinas (Bruce Marshall), dialog with other periods of the Christian tradition (William Abraham, Joerg Rieger, Charles Wood), engagement with evangelical theology (Abraham and, in Division IV, Scott Jones), postmodernism (Joerg Rieger), liberation theology (Baker-Fletcher, Rieger, Walker, and some members of other divisions), and use of the work of analytic philosophy (Abraham, Lovin, Marshall, Wood). Some of these faculty members came to Perkins before Lovin, of course, but Baker-Fletcher, Jones, Marshall, Miles, and Recinos were his appointments. A number of Perkins faculty members have expressed their appreciation for the theological diversity of the school. One judged that Lovin had consolidated theological diversity at Perkins for years to come and in doing so had weakened any tendency toward one dominant theological approach.

By the conclusion of his deanship, Robin Lovin had appointed twenty-four of the forty-one members of the faculty and had increased its gender, racial and ethnic, and theological diversity. This was the time of greatest change in the makeup of the faculty since the 1950s. In these years the third Perkins came fully into view.

Robin Lovin came to the Perkins deanship almost two years after the intense intrafaculty conflict of fall 1992. Although that conflict had caught many by surprise, Lovin thought that in an increasingly diverse faculty, conflict (though not necessarily that kind of conflict) was to be expected. He saw this as a faculty learning to live with conflict.[44] Yet the members went about their work together with sufficient common concerns and commitments to advance the goals of the school.

In that situation Lovin saw it as especially important to be supportive of the faculty women, whom he perceived as feeling marginalized after the 1992 conflict. One way he did this was to consult with them about important school policies. Another was to see that their promotions came in a timely manner. Thus Marjorie Procter-Smith became full professor in 1996, the second Perkins woman (after Jouette Bassler) to be promoted to that rank and the first to hold an endowed chair, and Danna Nolan Fewell became full professor in 1999. In 1997 Patricia Davis was promoted to associate professor and given tenure. Lovin also provided women with major opportunities for leadership. In 1997 he appointed Bassler as successor to David Maldonado as academic associate dean for a term of three years, and in her first year in that post she chaired the Curriculum Review Committee. In 2000 Procter-Smith followed Bassler as associate dean.

Unease continued in some faculty relationships. Some feared that the Perkins rank and tenure process would not be fair. Some suspicion of colleagues lingered because of their supposed stances or roles in the 1992 conflict. Friends of one of the faculty women reported that other faculty women would not speak to her.

At least twice late in Lovin's years as dean the unease became open discord. During one faculty advisory to the dean about a prospective appointment, those opposing it argued heatedly that the person would not be desirable as a colleague, whereas those supporting the appointment maintained with equal conviction that the prospect had strong scholarly credentials and would indeed be a good colleague. The vote was close, and afterward Dean Lovin chose not to go forward with the appointment, as was his prerogative. So bitter had been the discussion that one faculty member ceased attending faculty meetings thereafter. In another faculty advisory opponents of a prospect became convinced afterward that relevant information that might have led to a negative judgment had been suppressed.

One difficulty was that faculty members did not agree on the criteria for faculty appointments, some giving priority to diversity and others to academic quality, though the issue was seldom openly discussed. Some diversity proponents viewed the advocates of quality as stubbornly traditionalist and reluctant to give up power, while some of the proponents of quality viewed those pressing for diversity as supporting particular ideologies and politicizing the academic enterprise.

The new faculty arrived, however, without experience of past Perkins faculty tensions. The more newcomers, the more possibility for a fresh start in faculty relations. In his 1999 report to the Committee on Faculty, Lovin voiced the opinion that "as a faculty, we're listening to each other more than we did when I came. We're not so suspicious of each other, and if we sometimes get into conflicts with each other, at least the lines of demarcation are not always so predictable as they once were."[45] At the end of Lovin's deanship in 2002 the faculty was carrying on the school's work regardless of the members' disagreements, attempting to contain the conflicts within a collegial framework.

For years Perkins faculty members had carried heavy committee responsibilities. The review of 1968–69 had tried to reduce the problem but with little success. The situation was seen as sufficiently serious that the September 1998 faculty conference devoted two hours to discussing Perkins's "governance structure." In the process someone invited those interested to join a working group to consider whether some committees could simply be eliminated. The result was an ad hoc group known as the Governance Task Force. Its members prevailed upon Bill Babcock to write up its reports for presentation to the faculty.

After a November faculty guild discussion, and after several revised task force reports, the faculty at its May 1999 meeting adopted the following plan: It created three new committees. The Committee on Academic Programs would oversee all degree and academic programs of Perkins, including the intern program, the Mexican American Program, and continuing education. A new Committee on Community Life would oversee all Perkins programs concerning community life, worship, and the direction of spiritual life. The Committee on Student Development would oversee all programs, policies, and procedures regarding "student recruitment and admissions, financial aid, and the academic progress and standing of students in its degree programs."

It eliminated the curriculum, doctor of ministry, library, book store advisory, Houston/Galveston, academic procedures, admissions, and worship committees, as well as the old Community Life Committee. The functions of these committees would be turned over to one or another of the three new committees.

It left in place these committees: Faculty; Gender, Ethnic, and Racial Concerns (previously the Committee on Women and Ethnic Concerns); Long Range Planning; Scholarly Outreach; Rank and Tenure; and Nominations.

These changes reduced by more than a dozen the faculty members' committee memberships.

The goal was to maintain long-standing faculty oversight of school policies and practices while reducing the burdens thereof. Someone asked, "Can we reduce some actual *work*, not just the number of committees?" The skepticism was understandable; committees tend to beget subcommittees, and new task forces are easily added. Even so, faculty members had fewer standing committee memberships, and in a given year some had none at all. Some committee responsibilities of faculty members now fell to administrators, though with provision for faculty advice in difficult cases. That relief had a liability, however; it reduced faculty participation in matters such as applicants' qualifications for admission and students' readiness to be admitted to degree candidacy.[46]

• • •

In 1997 Ross Murfin, the SMU provost, initiated a change in rank and tenure proce-dure that was applied throughout the university. Previously, the university committee that advised the provost about cases for promotion and for tenure was the Council of Deans—a heavy burden on the deans, especially during each spring semester. In 1997 and 1998 Murfin formed the Provost's Faculty Advisory Committee on Promotion and Tenure, consisting of faculty representatives of the several schools.

In 1998 the new provost's advisory committee requested that the various schools of the university change their procedures so that each member of the school's rank and tenure committee would "vote" by means of a signed letter explaining her or his judgment.[47] Previously, members of the Perkins Rank and Tenure Committee had not voted on individual cases; instead, the members had expressed their indi-vidual judgments orally, after which the dean, having considered their advice, made a recommendation to the provost. The intention now was to increase the material available to the provost's advisory committee, strengthen each dossier, and make explicit the responsibility of each Rank and Tenure Committee member for her or his judgment.

After the 1992 faculty conflict, the faculty made optional the peer evaluation pro-gram then in effect for untenured tenure-track faculty, and the program continued at a reduced pace pending a review. In 1995–96, after review by an ad hoc committee chaired by Danna Fewell, the faculty changed the program to one of "peer teaching groups," with the aim of helping faculty members assess and improve their teaching abilities. Each tenured and intern faculty member was to participate in a group of three or four faculty members for one academic year in every six, thus reducing the time demands on individual faculty. Because some untenured tenure-track faculty had viewed the earlier peer evaluation groups as threatening, their participation in the new groups was made optional, and it was specified that "no materials from these groups may be used in Rank and Tenure considerations."[48]

In the spring of 2001, the fifth year of these groups' existence, the Committee on Faculty reviewed the program and proposed a thorough revision, which the fac-ulty approved. Participation in the peer teaching groups now became voluntary for all faculty, and the reporting procedure was simplified. After twenty years of experi-ments with various kinds of groups for faculty evaluation and improvement, the faculty now acknowledged these were supplementary to "the primary mechanism for regular annual review of faculty performance, . . . the annual faculty report to the Dean, including the review meeting with the Dean."[49]

RENOVATING PERKINS CHAPEL

Along with the opportunities Robin Lovin noted upon his arrival at Perkins, he also spoke of challenges, including "serious shortcomings in our physical environment." In the late 1980s Jim Kirby had overseen the development of a plan for the "Link" to connect Kirby and Selecman halls, but the money to make this possible had not been forthcoming. In his first report to the faculty in 1994, Lovin pointed out that Perkins needed the Link for several reasons: to provide accessibility, new kinds of space for classes and community gatherings, and a new, more welcoming main entrance to the school. Furthermore, "both of the academic buildings and Perkins Chapel need a thorough renovation to provide environments for work and worship that match today's needs and look toward the future, rather than back to the 1950's."[50]

The likely cost of these changes was daunting; Lovin later estimated that renovating, modestly expanding, and linking Kirby and Selecman Halls would cost $8 to $10 million. Since that money was not forthcoming in his first few years, and at the strong urging of university officials responsible for operating the buildings, he instead undertook the more limited project of redoing the heating, ventilation, and air-conditioning systems of Kirby Hall during the summer of 1998. This necessitated the relocation of its occupants, after which Lovin concluded "that piecemeal renovation of major building systems does not work very well."[51]

Renovation of Perkins Chapel was another matter; funds became available through the generosity of the Prothro family. Charles and Elizabeth Perkins Prothro were strongly interested in renovating the chapel, as were their son, Vincent (Vin), and his wife, Caren. In June 1996 President R. Gerald Turner and Dean Lovin visited Charles and Elizabeth and put before them several projects they hoped to accomplish for Perkins in the SMU capital campaign that was to begin in 1997. In February 1997, during Ministers' Week, SMU announced that the Prothros had given new gifts to Perkins of more than $7 million: $4 million to endow nine scholarship awards of $15,000 each for highly qualified students, $1 million to renovate Perkins Chapel, Elizabeth Perkins Prothro's collection of rare Bibles valued at more than $1.5 million, and $500,000 pledged earlier by the Joe and Lois Perkins Foundation. Half the scholarship fund would serve as a challenge grant to encourage friends of the school to match that amount with further scholarship gifts. As of 1997 the university estimated that the Perkins and Prothro families and their foundations had contributed more than $17.7 million to SMU, most of it designated for Perkins and Bridwell Library. In the next two years Vin and Caren Prothro contributed a substantial additional amount toward the chapel renovation, and Vin took an active part in planning and implementing the renovation and in encouraging matching scholarship gifts from the churches.[52]

As soon as the new Prothro gifts were announced, Lovin appointed the Committee on Chapel Renovations, chaired by Marjorie Procter-Smith, with representatives from various SMU groups that used the chapel. By early April 1997 this committee reported what it judged to be most needed in the renovations. In June, Perkins chose Good Fulton & Farrell of Dallas, based in Dallas and founded in 1982, to be the architects and Haws & Tingle of Fort Worth as general contractors. The architects and the committee, together with the university's Project Oversight Committee, worked hard to plan a renovation that would fit within the $1 million initial Prothro gift, but with urging from Vin Prothro they added renovation of the steeple, landscaping the grounds around the chapel, and several interior changes. Vin made sure the additional costs were covered. SMU trustee Bobby Lyle gave the Steinway piano for the chapel in honor of his wife, Perkins graduate and United Methodist pastor Katherine Glaze Lyle. The final cost of all aspects of the renovation, including the restoration of the organ, came close to $2 million.[53]

During the work on the interior of the chapel, Perkins held most of its community worship services in Kirby Parlor and the remainder in Selecman Hall: "worship in exile," as it was called. The hope had been that the renovation would be completed and the chapel ready for use in September 1998, but it took a year longer and several more months to complete restoration of the Aeolian-Skinner pipe organ, installed in 1950.[54] The organ's condition had so deteriorated that its breakdown in the midst of an important event was an ever-present danger. The Committee on Chapel Renovations readily approved the restoration. Then began a long process of planning and negotiating by the director of the Master of Sacred Music Program, Kenneth W. Hart, and the renowned organist George C. Baker III, consultants, with Marvin G.

Judy, president of the Schudi Organ Company of Dallas, which then designed, built, and installed the renovated organ. (Both Judy and Baker were sons of Perkins professors.) Perkins engaged Jean François Dupont, tonal finisher, to come from France three times to do the voicing (tone regulation). The organ renovation was made possible by generous gifts from the Horace C. Cabe Foundation, Mrs. George C. Baker Jr., George C. Baker III, and others.[55]

Several interior changes reflected major developments in Christian worship since the original construction of the chapel in 1950. The dais was enlarged and extended into the congregation, so that worship leaders were in the midst of the people. Lyle Novinski, a liturgical artist, designed a new altar table, baptistery, and pulpit that were movable, so they could be placed variously on the dais or simply removed. The first two rows of pews included short sections next to the center aisle that could be removed for further flexibility. The cross, also by Novinski, is the chapel's central symbol and is part of the center wall rather than free-standing; its gold leaf glows even in the dimmest light. Other interior changes included a new floor that enhances the acoustics; two curved ramps, one on each side leading up to the dais, which add accessibility as well as beauty; two built-in video cameras for classroom use; a subtle use of many shades of paint in off-whites, cool grays, and neutrals; new lighting; and improved heating and cooling systems.[56]

On September 7 (Elizabeth Perkins Prothro's birthday) and September 8, 1999, Perkins rededicated Perkins Chapel, celebrating the occasion with four services, including three sermons—by Dean Lovin; John Holbert, the Lois Craddock Perkins Professor of Homiletics; and Barbara Kelton, chaplain of SMU's Canterbury House, the Episcopal student organization.[57]

The restoration of the organ was not complete at the time of the rededication of the chapel; it continued into the spring of 2000. The organ dedication was held on March 31, 2000, followed by an inaugural recital on April 9 by Stephen Cleobury, director of the King's College Choir, Cambridge, England.[58]

The March 31 service included dedication of the organ in the chapel gallery. Since 1962 this small pipe organ had been a practice instrument in the music school. Eventually, it fell into disrepair, and in 1996 it was given to Perkins School of Theology. At the request of Hart, Robert Sipe of Dallas, one of the original builders, renovated and upgraded it. This was the organ used in the September 1999 celebration of the chapel renovation, and it has been used in many weddings and services since that time.[59]

Other developments in 1999 and after, along with the renovation of Perkins Chapel, had a positive effect on Perkins worship life: changing the weekly schedule to provide more satisfactory times for community worship, making the basic course in worship a requirement for the M.Div. degree, and the appointment of Mark Stamm as director of chapel worship (along with his faculty position in worship). The result has been what Michael Hawn has described as a healthy worship environment at Perkins.[60]

FURTHER PLANNING FOR THE FUTURE

A major part of the Prothro gifts announced in 1997 was the $4 million Scholarship Endowment Fund, half of which would be a Matching Gifts Program. Initially, the strategy was to seek individual donors whose gifts to Perkins scholarship funds would be matched by the Prothro Endowment Gift Fund. As the capital campaign continued, Perkins expanded that strategy to encourage each of the annual conferences in the South Central Jurisdiction to establish an endowment fund for scholarships primarily for students from that annual conference. The Prothro fund would then match those funds either 1-to-1 or 1-to-2 basis.

This annual conference plan proved to be highly successful. It soon gathered enough pledges to exceed the $4 million envisioned in the original Prothro Scholarship Endowment Plan, whereupon the Perkins Foundation agreed to continue the matching fund program beyond the amount of its initial pledge. In November 1999 Scott Somers, development officer, reported that the Annual Conference Matching Gifts Program totaled $5.4 million. It was anticipated that by the end of the SMU capital campaign in 2002, Perkins School of Theology's part would reach $9 million. By then the Perkins Prothro Foundation Matching Fund would provide an additional $5.6 million, which would produce a total of $14 million to $15 million in new Perkins scholarship endowment funds.[61]

Perkins had adopted a strategic plan in 1995, in the first year of Lovin's deanship, and by the fall of 2000 it was time to develop a new one. The first step in the process was to adopt a new mission statement. At the faculty's December meeting, the Long

Range Planning Committee, chaired by John Holbert, offered a draft statement that began, "The mission of Perkins School of Theology . . . is to equip students with wisdom and skills needed to assume leadership, both spiritual and practical, in the church and society." It identified several characteristics of Perkins as a community and listed four strategic goals. The faculty gave this draft "considerable discussion."[62]

Two days later Charles Wood sent a memo to the committee highlighting one problem he saw in this draft. It "portrays our mission almost exclusively as that of preparing persons for ministry. While this remains our primary educational mission to a greater extent than is true for many theological schools these days, I think it is a mistake to give the impression, as this draft does, that it is our *sole* mission." Wood contrasted this draft with the 1991 mission statement, which began, "The mission of Perkins School of Theology is to prepare women and men for effective leadership in the church, and to engage in theological reflection on the church's faith, life, and mission in the world," a twofold understanding of its mission. He then offered a revised first sentence that began, "The *primary* mission of Perkins . . . is to prepare men and women for Christian ministerial leadership" (emphasis added).[63]

The question of the "onefoldness" of Perkins's mission continued to be a central issue as the Long Range Planning Committee reworked the statement throughout that academic year, and Wood continued to offer ideas to the committee. In March, for example, after a draft statement from the committee did not include the word *primary*, he sent an e-mail to John Holbert that included this paragraph:

> If we say flatly that our mission is to prepare people for ministerial leadership, one might well ask why we are doing things that don't serve that mission: why support a GPRS [Graduate Program in Religious Studies]? Why an MTS degree? Why encourage faculty research and scholarly publication? Why do lay theological education as part of our continuing education program? If we say our primary mission is to prepare people for ministerial leadership, that qualification makes it somewhat easier to justify doing these other things, while still making it important to relate them in various ways to the primary mission. But without the "primary," the legitimacy of these other enterprises seems to me to be in doubt. Is that the intention?[64]

Holbert replied with appreciation, explained that the committee had no intention to downplay those other aspects of Perkins's work, and said he would suggest reinstating the word *primary*.[65]

At its April meeting the faculty adopted a mission statement that began: "The primary mission of Perkins School of Theology, as a community devoted to theological study and teaching in the service of the church of Jesus Christ, is to prepare women and men for faithful leadership in Christian ministry." It went on to identify Perkins's relationships to SMU, the universal church, The United Methodist Church specifically, and "its particular geographical and cultural setting in the southwestern United States" as "sources of strength and avenues of service for the school as it pursues its twin tasks of theological reflection and theological education to the glory of God."[66] Although this statement recognized that Perkins had two different kinds of mission, the 2001 statement differed significantly from that of 1991, which did not assert a priority of one aspect of its mission over the other.

Along with its work on the mission statement, the Long Range Planning Committee developed a strategic plan to express that mission. Intended to shape Perkins policies for the next five years, the plan took the form of a set of goals, along with several objectives that would point the way toward each goal. It evolved from a fifteen-month process of consultation, beginning with the 2000 fall faculty conference, between the Long Range Planning Committee and various other groups: Perkins senior administrators, two faculty conferences, the Committee on Faculty, the Academic Programs Committee, the Alumni Council, and the Perkins Executive Board. The Long Range Planning Committee itself held twenty meetings along the way.[67]

The strategic plan adopted by the faculty on December 3, 2001, consisted of six goals for Perkins:

Goal 1: Strengthen a faculty community that supports our curricular needs and the faculty's ongoing contribution to knowledge.

Goal 2: Strengthen courses and programs that deal with the church, its social context, and its global mission and ministry.

Goal 3: Strengthen courses and programs that equip church leaders with administrative and organizational skills.

Goal 4:   Strengthen courses and programs in the related areas of preaching, worship, and spiritual formation.

Goal 5:   Strengthen our efforts to make theological education more readily available to degree students and others.

Goal 6:   Strengthen recruitment and admissions for all degree programs.[68]

At that meeting the faculty directed most of its attention, not to these goals, which by then it had had sufficient time to consider and refine, but to amending several of the objectives that would help implement each goal. Along the way, Scott Jones asked why the plan made no mention of a much-needed new building. John Holbert's reply, that "it is so much a part of our corpuscles that mentioning it here is not necessary," did not appear to satisfy. After other faculty members suggested further needs that were not in the plan, the dean and others suggested adding a preamble to say that "these are not the only goals we have." The faculty approved that idea and thereafter unanimously approved the whole plan "with gratitude."[69]

DEAN LOVIN'S DEPARTURE AND THE APPOINTMENT OF A NEW DEAN

On May 7, 2001, in the midst of the Perkins faculty's work on its new mission statement and strategic plan, SMU announced the appointment of Robin Lovin as the new Cary M. Maguire University Professor of Ethics. William F. May, who had occupied the Maguire Chair since it was established in 1985, would be retiring that spring. Lovin would assume his new position in the fall of 2001 but would continue as Perkins dean while SMU conducted its search for his successor. The holder of the Maguire Chair, one of two university-wide chairs in ethics that report directly to the provost, is available to teach in all the schools of the university. May had taught in the college and Perkins, as well as in other schools, and Lovin would be available to do likewise. In addition, he would have wide freedom for research and writing, as well as to represent the university in the Dallas community and beyond. The holder of the other university chair in ethics, the Scurlock Professor in Human Values, had since 1991 been Charles E. Curran, who led the search committee for the Maguire Chair. Ross Murfin, the provost, observed that other schools had tried to lure Lovin away "with offers of at least one deanship and a presidency," and that he, Murfin, was delighted that SMU was "retaining [Lovin] as an outstanding scholar and researcher."[70]

In June, Murfin announced the membership of the Perkins Dean Search Committee, chaired by Jasper Neel, dean of Dedman College. The other twelve members of the committee included six Perkins faculty: William Abraham, Edwin Aponte, Paula Dobbs-Wiggins, John Holbert, Rebekah Miles, and Marjorie Procter-Smith. Two members were Perkins administrators: Shonda Jones, director of student services, and Gary MacDonald, director of continuing education and public programs. Other members were Mark Craig, senior pastor of Highland Park United Methodist Church; Bishop William B. Oden of the North Texas Area of The United Methodist Church; Caren Prothro, SMU board member and chair of its Committee on Academic Policy, Planning, and Management; and Mary Spradlin, Perkins student.[71] Its membership was diverse: seven men and six women, two African Americans, and one Hispanic. The faculty members varied widely in years of service at Perkins: three had arrived between 1979 and 1985 and the other three in 1998 and 1999. They also represented a variety of stances within the Perkins faculty.

The search committee members differed strongly as to their preferences for the appointment, as well as about what they considered to be appropriate actions in the face of their differences. In the spring of 2002 the provost issued an invitation to William B. Lawrence, associate dean for development and church relations at Candler School of Theology, Emory University, to become the next Perkins dean. At the May meeting of the trustees, Caren Prothro announced Lawrence's appointment, to take effect August 1, 2002.[72]

1. Robin W. Lovin, *Christian Faith and Public Choices: The Social Ethics of Barth, Brunner, and Bonhoeffer* (Philadelphia: Fortress, 1984).
2. Board of trustees minutes, May 20, 1994; Robin Warren Lovin, resumé, Robin W. Lovin Papers, Bridwell Library.
3. Robin W. Lovin, "A Word from the Dean," *Perspective*, fall 1994, 3.
4. Robin W. Lovin, "Dean's Report to Faculty Conference, Perkins School of Theology," September 16, 1994, 1, Lovin Papers.
5. Charles M. Wood to the Perkins Faculty, "Proposed Amendments to Articles of Operation and Bylaws," March 11, 1991, Joseph L. Allen Papers, Bridwell Library; faculty minutes, April 5, 1991; catalog, 1991–92, 8–10.
6. Lovin, "Dean's Report," 1994, 1–2.
7. Ibid., 6–10.

8. Robin W. Lovin, "Presentation to Faculty Long-Range Planning Discussion," December 9, 1994, Lovin Papers.
9. Faculty minutes, May 5, 1995.
10. "Report on Strategic Planning for Perkins School of Theology, Southern Methodist University, May 5, 1995" (attachment to the faculty minutes of that date), 4, 6, 7.
11. Ibid., 8–14.
12. Robin W. Lovin to the Rev. Charles R. Millikan, December 21, 1994; Lovin to the Rev. James W. Moore, December 21, 1994; Lovin appointment book, 1994–95, Lovin Papers; *Journal of the Texas Annual Conference,* 1995, p. 171; *Perspective,* Fall, 1995, 18.
13. Robin W. Lovin, "Introduction to Houston-Galveston Inside Perkins, June 17, 1995," Lovin Papers; Robin W. Lovin appointment books, 1994–95, 1995–96, Lovin Papers.
14. "Perkins South Completes First Successful Semester," *Perspective,* winter 1996, 23; "Minister and Author Leads Perkins Executive Board," *Perspective,* spring 1997, 13, 27; enrollment records in the Perkins registrar's office.
15. *Perspective,* summer 1996, 22.
16. Long Range Planning Committee to the Perkins Faculty, "The Houston-Galveston Program," December 3, 1996 (attachment to faculty minutes); faculty minutes, December 6, 1996.
17. Long Range Planning Committee, "A Proposal for Classes in Oklahoma: Preliminary Draft," November 5, 1997; faculty minutes, December 5, 1997.
18. Charles M. Wood, for the Long Range Planning Committee, "Oklahoma City Program Recommendation, May 3, 1999" (attachment to faculty minutes); Charles M. Wood, for the Long Range Planning Committee, "Oklahoma City program recommendation, November 30, 1999" (attachment to faculty minutes); faculty minutes, May 7 and December 3, 1999, and October 6, November 3, and December 1, 2003; Marjorie Procter-Smith to Joe Allen, November 3, 2009, in the author's personal files.
19. Lovin to faculty and administrators, "The San Antonio Program, PST: 'Perkins Southwest,'" September 10, 2001, Lovin Papers; catalog, 2003–2005, 13; faculty minutes, October 6, 2003, and October 30, 2006; Ed Sylvest, interview by author, May 28, 2009, Dallas.
20. Faculty minutes, April 3, 1998; "Doctor of Ministry Studies at Hendrix College, A Proposal," April 1, 1998 (attachment to faculty minutes, April 3, 1998); "Doctor of Ministry Annual Report," May 1, 1998, Allen Papers.
21. "Roy Barton: Ready for the Hand Off," *Perspective,* winter 1995, 14–15; Minerva Carcaño, "Lay Missioner—Pastor/Mentor Program: Teaming Up to Establish Faith Communities," *Perspective,* fall 1997, 7.
22. *Apuntes* 1, no. 1 (spring 1981): 2.
23. Justo L. González, "Prophets in the King's Sanctuary," *Apuntes* 1, no. 1 (spring 1981): 3. Beginning with the spring 2005 issue, the journal's subtitle became *Theological Reflection for the Hispano-Latino Context.*
24. Edwin Sylvest, "The Mexican American Program: Twenty-five Years of History," *Apuntes,* no. 3 (summer 2000): 53–54.
25. Lovin to twenty-one Methodist Hispanic leaders, July 17, 1995; Ignacio Castuera, Lydia Lebrón Rivera, Victor Pérez, and Paul Barton to Lovin (no date, but before August 18, 1995); Lovin to Castuera, Rivera, Pérez, and Barton, August 18, 1995, all in Lovin Papers.
26. David Maldonado to Lovin, December 19, 1995; Lovin to Jeannie Treviño-Teddlie, November 1, 1996, Lovin Papers.
27. Lovin to David Maldonado et al., September 9, 1997; Lovin to Maldonado, October 7, 1997; Cherie White to Lovin, November 11, 1997, Lovin Papers.
28. Maldonado to Lovin, April 8, 1997; Rev. Pedro Garcia to Lovin (no date); Minerva Carcaño to Lovin et al., August 21, 1998; "El Programa México Americano de la Escuela de Teología Perkins," November 10–13, 1999, Lovin Papers.
29. *Perspective,* fall 2002, 21.
30. The significance of the increase in the ages of seminary students was described as part of the evaluation of the Houston-Galveston Program in a paper, "The Program of Theological Studies in Houston

and Galveston and the Mission of Perkins School of Theology," November 20, 1996 (attachment to faculty minutes), December 6, 1996.

31. "Proposal for the M.Div. Curriculum," attachment to the faculty minutes, April 3, 1998; Perkins catalog, 1999–2001, 20–23; Robin Lovin, "Curriculum Review: A View from the Dean's Office. Report to the Annual Faculty Retreat," September 12, 1997, 5; Joe Allen, "Some Disjointed Thoughts about the Curriculum Review," September 13, 1997, 5, Allen Papers.

32. Curriculum Review Committee to Perkins Faculty, "Final Proposals," February 3, 1999, in the personal files of Charles Wood (hereafter, Wood's files); faculty minutes, February 5, 1999; Perkins catalog, 1999–2001, 23–30.

33. Curriculum Review Committee, "Final Proposals," 1–2.

34. Ibid., 3–5; faculty minutes, February 5, 1999 and April 7, 2000; catalog, 2001–2003, 21–24.

35. Michael Hawn to Joe Allen, December 3, 2009, in the author's personal files.

36. "Proposal for a Graduate Certificate in Women's Studies," attachment to faculty minutes, October 1, 2001; faculty minutes, October 1, 2001; catalog, 2003–2005, 35–37.

37. Faculty minutes, April 4, 1997; "Report of the Urban Ministry Task Force, 1997–1999," May 6, 1999 (attachment to the faculty minutes, May 7, 1999); *Perspective*, fall 1997, 18.

38. Faculty minutes, April 7, 2000; Urban Ministry Steering Committee, "Proposal for a Certificate in Urban Ministry," April 4, 2000, Wood's files; catalog, 2001–2003, 64–66.

39. Catalog, 1999–2001, 20, and 1990, 14; Frederick W. Schmidt, interview by author, May 13, 2009, Dallas.

40. Robin Lovin, interview by author, June 24, 2009, University Park, Texas; Schmidt interview. Schmidt's *What God Wants for Your Life: Finding Answers to the Deepest Questions* (New York: Harper San Francisco, 2005) expresses the perspective from which he was working in the spiritual formation program.

41. Jouette Bassler, for the Committee on Academic Programs, to the Perkins Faculty, "Spiritual Formation Requirement," May 2, 2001, Wood's files; faculty minutes, May 8, 2001; Schmidt interview. See catalog, 2001–2003, 66–67.

42. D.Min. Review and Proposal, May 5, 2000, Wood's files; faculty minutes, May 5, 2000.

43. Lovin interview.

44. Lovin interview, April 23, 2009. This section draws upon interviews with thirty-nine members of the Perkins faculty and administration who were active while Robin Lovin was dean.

45. Robin Lovin, "Dean's Annual Report to the Faculty, Perkins School of Theology, 1999," no date, Lovin Papers.

46. Governance Task Force to the Perkins Faculty, March 3, April 19, and April 22, 1999; minutes of the faculty as guild, November 13, 1998; faculty minutes, March 5, April 9, and May 7, 1999; William Babcock, telephone interview by author, April 16, 2009.

47. Faculty minutes, February 7, 1997, and November 6, 1998; "Improving the Promotion and Tenure Evaluation/Decision Process—Recommendations and Requests from the Provost's Advisory Committee on Promotion and Tenure," no date, but before October 31, 1998 (attachment to the faculty minutes of November 6, 1998).

48. Committee on Faculty to the Perkins Faculty, April 30, 1996; faculty minutes, May 3, 1996.

49. Charles M. Wood, for the Committee on Faculty, to the Perkins Faculty, "Revision of policy on Peer Teaching Groups," March 26, 2001 (attachment to faculty minutes of April 2, 2001); faculty minutes, April 2, 2001.

50. Robin Lovin, "Dean's Report to Faculty Conference, Perkins School of Theology, September 16, 1994," 4, Lovin Papers.

51. Robin W. Lovin, "Future Problems and Possibilities, or the Next Strategic Plan," Dean's Report to the Faculty Retreat, September 8, 1998, 4, Lovin Papers.

52. Robin Lovin to Joseph L. Allen, June 10, 2009, in the author's personal files; Lovin to Mr. and Mrs. Charles Prothro, August 5, 1996, Lovin Papers; Stephanie Allmon, "$7 Million Donated to Perkins," *Daily Campus*, February 5, 1997.

53. Lovin to Allen, June 10, 2009 in the author's personal files; faculty minutes, March 7 and April 4, 1997; *Perspective*, fall–winter 1999–2000, 1.

54. *Perspective*, fall 1998, 8–9; Lovin to Mr. and Mrs. Charles Prothro, June 6, 1997.

55. Kenneth W. Hart, "History of the Perkins Chapel Organs," unpublished and undated typescript in the author's personal files.

56. "Perkins Chapel through the Generations," 8–9; Marjorie Procter-Smith, "The Process of Change," 11, 26, 30; Lyle Novinski, "Designing for Tension," 12–13, all in *Perspective*, fall–winter 1999–2000.

57. *Perspective*, fall–winter 1999–2000, 1–7.

58. Hart, "History of the Perkins Chapel Organs"; Lovin to Allen, June 10, 2009; "Art & Soul: Ritual Arts: Sacred Time & Eternity, March 25–April 9, 2000," brochure for inaugural recital, Perkins Office of Public Affairs.

59. Hart, "History of the Perkins Chapel Organs."

60. Hawn to Allen.

61. Faculty minutes, November 5, 1999.

62. Long Range Planning Committee, "A Mission Statement for Perkins School of Theology," December 4, 2000 (attachment to the faculty minutes of that date); faculty minutes, December 4, 2000.

63. Wood to John Holbert, chair, Long Range Planning Committee, December 6, 2000, Wood's files; see catalog, 1991, 8.

64. Wood to Holbert, March 29, 2001, Wood's files.

65. Holbert to Wood, March 29, 2001, Wood's files.

66. Faculty minutes, April 2, 2001; catalog, 2001–2003, 9.

67. The Long Range Planning Committee to the Perkins Faculty, re the Strategic Plan, December 3, 2001, Wood's files.

68. "The Strategic Plan for Perkins School of Theology," December 3, 2001, Wood's files.

69. Faculty minutes, December 3, 2001. Perkins faculty minutes vary considerably in how much of the content of discussions is included. The minutes for all of 2001–2002 record much of the discussion in addition to the decisions.

70. SMU Office of News and Information, press release, May 7, 2001; faculty minutes, May 8, 2001.

71. Ross Murfin, vice president and provost, to the Perkins School of Theology Faculty and Staff, June 15, 2001, Wood's files.

72. Faculty minutes, April 1, 2002; board of trustees minutes, May 10, 2002.

CHAPTER 12

Approaching the Centennial, 2002–2010

W illiam Benjamin Lawrence received his bachelor's degree from Duke University in 1968 and his master's of divinity from Union Theological Seminary in New York in 1971. In May 1969, the same month he and Naomi Williams were married, he joined The United Methodist Church's Wyoming Conference, which was then located in northeastern Pennsylvania and southern New York. For more than two decades he served as a pastor there and then a district superintendent. In 1977 he entered doctoral study in homiletics and historical theology at Drew University, continuing as a pastor except for one year of leave at the beginning of his studies, and received his Ph.D. degree in 1984 with a dissertation later published as *Sundays in New York: Pulpit Theology at the Crest of the Protestant Mainstream, 1930–1955*.[1] In 1993 he joined the faculty of Duke University Divinity School as professor of the practice of Christian ministry and associate director of the J. M. Ormond Center for Research, Planning and Development. From 1998 to 2001 he was senior minister of Metropolitan Memorial United Methodist Church in Washington, D.C., and in 2000 he was also designated a Wesley Distinguished Faculty in the Theology and Practice of Ministry at nearby Wesley Theological Seminary. In 2001 he moved to Candler School of Theology at Emory University as associate dean for development and church relations, then to Perkins as dean in 2002.[2] In the 1990s Lawrence directed a five-year study of United Methodism and American culture, undertaken with a grant from the Lilly Foundation, and afterward coedited four volumes of essays and participated in writing a fifth, all of which grew out of that study.[3]

In his first fall report to the Perkins faculty, Lawrence—his colleagues ordinarily call him Bill—observed, "Deans are expected to lead and, in my own way with

367

my own style, I will strive to fulfill that responsibility. . . . It is my hope that you will find me to be collegial in manner, that you will find me committed to community in spirit, that you will find me celebrative of diversity, and that you will find me pastoral in temperament."[4]

Lawrence's faculty and administrators, in conversations with me, identified what they saw as prominent traits of his leadership.[5] Various people spoke of his impressive administrative ability; love for the United Methodist system and sophistication in working with it (reflected in his election at the General Conference of 2008 as one of nine members of The United Methodist Church's Judicial Council); attentiveness to pastoral concerns, both in private conversations and in faculty meetings; combination of formality and friendly affirmation; insistence on following the rules of parliamentary procedure and of established faculty procedures; and desire to avoid conflict and find consensus in faculty deliberations.

When Lawrence came to Perkins in 2002, eighteen administrators were responsible for various aspects of Perkins organizational life. Fifteen were not on tenure track, though some had courtesy faculty rank. They were

> Tracy Anne Allred, director of recruitment and admissions
>
> George Atkinson, director of the Houston-Galveston Program
>
> Mary Brouillette, director of donor relations
>
> William J. Bryan, director of the intern program and professional formation
>
> Roberta Cox, associate director of public affairs
>
> Janelle B. Hampton, registrar and director of academic procedures
>
> Duane Harbin, assistant dean for information technology and institutional research
>
> Linda Hervey, financial officer
>
> Valerie Hotchkiss, director of Bridwell Library
>
> Shonda Jones, director of student services
>
> David J. Lawson, bishop in residence
>
> Gary MacDonald, director of continuing education and public affairs
>
> Fred Schmidt, director of spiritual life and formation

Scott Somers, assistant dean for development and external relations

Jeannie Treviño-Teddlie, director of the Mexican American Program and codirector of the Course of Study School

Three others were tenure-track members of the faculty carrying out administrative tasks part time:

William S. Babcock, director of the Graduate Program in Religious Studies

Kenneth W. Hart, director of the Master of Sacred Music Program

Marjorie Procter-Smith, associate dean for academic affairs

Bill Lawrence has been described as a "hands-on" dean with his administrative staff, keeping in close touch with more than a dozen Perkins administrators and less directly with the others. Once a month he holds a mandatory Monday meeting with a group of about fourteen administrators for an hour and a half. The dean chairs and provides an agenda; the others have an opportunity to suggest items in advance. Different administrators report on what their office is doing, so that they learn about one another's work. This practice generates interaction among them; they are not "in silos," as one administrator expressed it. Lawrence works at keeping their morale high; he is generous with his praise for their achievements, in faculty meetings, formal reports, and comments outside Perkins.

Lawrence has made several changes in personnel and a few changes in the administrative structure. When he arrived, Marjorie Procter-Smith had for two years been academic associate dean, a position to which faculty members had since 1969 been appointed for three-year renewable terms. At the fall 2002 faculty conference Lawrence announced that he intended to review the structure of the position. Afterward he invited Procter-Smith to continue for an additional two years beyond her three-year appointment—to 2005—and she agreed to do so. She later said that when she first took on the post in 2000, "I expected I would hate it," but "I really enjoyed it." As Lawrence has explained it, appointing academic associate deans is never easy. The associate dean needs to be a full professor who is willing to take this office for a period without a leave, has administrative aptitude, and can get along with the dean. Of course the person must also be willing to accept the appointment. In 2000, when Robin Lovin asked John Holbert if he would consider being associate dean, Holbert "vigorously declined!"[6] In 2005 Ruben Habito succeeded Procter-Smith as associate dean, serving until 2008, when he was followed by Richard Nelson.

Since Gary MacDonald arrived in 1998, he had been director of continuing education and public programs, and Roberta Cox had been associate director for public affairs. In 2004 Lawrence divided this office. Cox became director of public affairs, while for a time MacDonald was director of continuing education and codirector of the Course of Study School, and still later served as director of advanced ministerial studies—with responsibility for the doctor of ministry program and continuing education. In 2006 Jeannie Treviño-Teddlie, who had until then worked with MacDonald on the Course of Study School, took over full responsibility for that program while continuing to direct the Mexican American Program. In 2008 Paul Escamilla came to Perkins as associate director of public affairs; he remained in that position until 2010, when he took a local church appointment in the Southwest Texas Conference. Replacing him at Perkins was Timothy McLemore, previously the pastor of Kessler Park United Methodist Church in Dallas.

Allred had arrived in 2001 as director of recruitment and admissions in the office headed by Shonda Jones. When Jones left in 2003, Allred became director of student services. Jason Pangiarella, who had a master of arts in religion from Yale Divinity School and had later been community life coordinator there, served as Perkins's director of recruitment and admissions from 2003 to 2007. He was followed by Herbert Coleman, who had experience in recruitment at Wesley Theological Seminary and had worked as a community organizer in Washington, D.C.

In the early years of Lawrence's deanship, Scott Somers, Mary Brouillette, and others with responsibility for Perkins development were working to raise money for the Perkins matching grant for student scholarships, with the goal of adding $10 million to Perkins's scholarship endowments. When Somers left SMU in 2005, SMU appointed Brouillette director of development for Perkins as it was developing its strategies for the university's upcoming Centennial Campaign, which would mark the hundredth anniversary of SMU's charter in 1911. Until her departure from Perkins in 2007, Brouillette was involved in raising money for Perkins's building project. Her successor was Todd Rasberry, who had received his M.Div. from Perkins in 1990, then had been a pastor in the Northwest Texas Conference and for ten years a development officer at Texas Tech University.[7]

Other Lawrence administrative appointments include Tonya Burton in 2003 to create and direct the Perkins Youth School of Theology, to help high school students reflect as Christians about their lives; Robert Hunt in 2004 as director of global theological education, a program that immerses Perkins students in another culture; Charles Wood in 2005 to follow William Babcock as director of the Graduate Program in Religious Studies; Bruce Marshall in 2010 to succeed Wood in the same post; Michael Hawn in 2005 to succeed Kenneth Hart as director of the Master of Sacred Music Program; Roberta Schaafsma in April 2007 as director of Bridwell Library, after Valerie Hotchkiss's departure in 2005 and James McMillin's service as interim director; Susan Buchanan in December 2007 as director of the Houston-Galveston Program, the post held by George Atkinson up to 2004; and Patricia Davis in 2008 to a new position as director of pastoral leadership.

During those years Lawrence developed a strong administrative staff with good morale, ready to work on the challenges facing Perkins.

THE BUILDING PROGRAM

Deans Jim Kirby and Robin Lovin had both drawn up plans for a major addition to the Perkins quadrangle. Kirby had overseen the renovation of Bridwell Library and Lovin that of Perkins Chapel as well as the heating, cooling, and ventilation systems of Selecman Hall and Kirby Hall. But the buildings still needed many improvements.

Lawrence focused on a building program from the time he arrived. At the 2002 faculty conference he spoke of the inadequacy of the facilities: inaccessible spaces, mechanical systems under strain, and an exterior that did not convey a ready welcome (a blank wall facing Highland Park United Methodist Church). He reported he had begun planning with Linda Hervey for the budgetary steps preparatory to a building program, and he was beginning to imagine a plan for facilities that would meet current needs and express what Perkins should be twenty-five years later.[8]

Before he could move ahead, however, preparatory work was necessary. R. Gerald Turner, SMU's president, had to agree that the program of raising scholarship endowments from the annual conferences was complete and to give permission for a major new renovation and construction project, both of which happened at

the end of 2004.⁹ The Long Range Planning Committee, then chaired by Charles
Wood, needed to gather information about space and facilities needs. The committee
completed that process in the spring of 2005.¹⁰

A greater hurdle was finding the money for the project, the cost of which would
be much more than $10 million. In September 2005 Lawrence announced that the
Perkins Prothro Foundation had made a commitment of $1 million so that the archi-
tects and engineers could plan for the changes. He explained that although money to
cover the building project had still to be raised, this step "allows us to proceed officially
within the University's guidelines to let a building committee begin its work."¹¹

Next, Lawrence formed a building committee, which, in keeping with university
terminology, was called the User Committee. The dean chaired it, with members
chosen from the faculty, staff, students, alumni/ae, and Perkins's executive board.
In cooperation with the university's Oversight Committee (the dean, as chair of
the User Committee, was a member), the User Committee began work on fund-
raising, determining the types of buildings Perkins needed, and planning the transition from the old to the new. In the spring of 2006, after receiving proposals from five
companies, the Oversight Committee chose the architectural firm of Good, Fulton,
and Farrell, which had also been the architects for the renovation of Perkins Chapel.
Then in October the Oversight Committee approved the architects' report and
recommendation.¹²

The concept for the project, as the dean presented it at the fall 2006 faculty
conference, called for demolition of the Selecman Hall auditorium and annex, construction of a large new building south of and in alignment with Selecman and Kirby
halls, and renovation of Selecman and Kirby, with elevators in all three buildings
and cloisters to connect the three. The new building and renovations would provide
public spaces for assemblies and meals, two large classrooms for as many as sixty
people each, rooms for seminars and conferences, and generously sized faculty offices.
The classrooms would include advanced technological capabilities. All three buildings
would be fully accessible, comply with safety requirements, have improved heating
and air-conditioning systems, and be environmentally sensitive.¹³

The estimated cost of the project was $12 million, although, as Lawrence
explained, "I suspect it will slide a little higher than that—but I know that the
President will not accept anything that rises to $13 million." In keeping with uni-

versity policy, commitments for 80 percent of the cost had to be in hand before construction could begin.[14]

For several months, while Good, Fulton, and Farrell drew up schematic designs for the new building and the renovation of Selecman and Kirby halls, Lawrence and Brouillette, the director of development, pursued donations. In January 2007 the *Dallas Morning News* announced a gift of $6 million from the Perkins Prothro Foundation. This brought the total gifts to SMU since 1913 from the Perkins and Prothro families and foundations to more than $36.3 million, most of it designated for Perkins School of Theology and Bridwell Library. An anonymous donor then gave $1 million through the Texas Methodist Foundation, Highland Park United Methodist Church gave $500,000 (and in 2008 pledged another $500,000), and other gifts, large and small, arrived, sufficient to begin construction.[15]

In March 2007 the dean announced that the groundbreaking would take place on Friday, September 7, Elizabeth Perkins Prothro's birthday, and that the new building would be named for her. The ceremonies that sunny day, coordinated by Roberta Cox, began with a prayer service in the chapel, followed by the ground-breaking ceremony and then a luncheon, both at the site of the future Elizabeth Perkins Prothro Hall. More than four hundred people heard words of celebration from Turner, Lawrence, and others. The new and renovated buildings were expected to be ready for use by fall 2009.[16]

February 2008 saw the demolition of Selecman auditorium and annex, and construction of Prothro Hall began. As the time approached for renovation of Selecman and Kirby halls, a subcommittee of the User Committee chaired by Ruben Habito worked out the logistics for the dislocations this would necessitate. Selecman Hall was to be vacated by June 1, 2008, and to be ready for reoccupancy by mid-December. Kirby Hall would be vacated in mid-December and repopulated by June 2009. Some faculty, administrators, and staff would move to offices in Moody Coliseum and some to the university's Perkins Administration Building; other faculty would work at home and come to campus for classes and meetings.[17] Classes would be held at Highland Park United Methodist Church.

In the fall of 2007 the User Committee asked faculty members to provide information about needs and desires for their offices. In December 2008 Jim McMillin, who chaired the construction subcommittee of the User Committee, had floor plans of Selecman offices drawn up for faculty members to view. The work stayed fairly close to schedule. Selecman Hall renovation was completed in January 2009, allowing administrators and faculty from Kirby Hall to move to Selecman and some faculty to move back in from home. Kirby Hall's renovation began that January and was completed in late June. There were difficulties: smaller offices than before, delays in installing bookshelves, insufficient shelf space, and, for a while, lack of access to offices after hours. A major sacrifice was the reduction of a sense of community—among faculty, administrators, and students. Lawrence kept everyone posted on how the work was going and followed up on people's concerns, and they in turn recognized the difficulties and were accommodating during the process. Construction of Prothro Hall was sufficiently far along in April 2009 that the City of University Park scheduled May 27 as the day when it would issue a certificate of occupancy.[18] As renovation of Kirby and Selecman halls neared completion, work followed on the cloisters connecting the buildings, the funds for which were given in memory of former chaplain J. Claude Evans by an anonymous donor. An outdoor labyrinth for prayer and meditation in honor of Ruben Habito was constructed between Prothro and Selecman halls. Then came new walkways and landscaping, and by early September the campus had returned almost to normal.

On September 11, 2009, Perkins dedicated the new and renovated buildings, beginning with a service of praise and thanksgiving in Perkins Chapel, which was full to overflowing with students, faculty, staff, alumni/ae, and friends. For the occasion Perkins had commissioned a hymn from John Thornburg, who had received his master of theology degree from Perkins in 1981. He set "Abram Never Wavered" to music composed by Carlton R. Young, director of the Master of Sacred Music Program from 1964 to 1975. There followed a dedication ceremony on the lawn south of the new Elizabeth Perkins Prothro Hall and lunch inside and outside the new building. That afternoon the community returned to Perkins Chapel to celebrate the life of Elizabeth Perkins Prothro, who had died only months earlier, on May 23, 2009, at age eighty-nine. In recalling her gifts of service, funds, Bible collections, and counsel to Perkins and to SMU, those gathered also remembered the gifts of her parents, Joe and Lois Perkins; her husband, Charles; and the many members of the family who continued to share in her commitment. On November 4 the Williams Preaching Lab in Prothro Hall was named in honor of Cecil Williams, bachelor of divinity graduate in 1955 and longtime pastor of Glide Memorial United Methodist Church in San Francisco.

The building project was a major achievement. One faculty member said it was "the big thing for this decade." The daily work of many people made it possible, but appreciation was especially widespread for Bill Lawrence's leadership, both its style and its substance. He received a standing ovation from the faculty at the 2009 fall conference. As a Perkins administrator said, "It took real motivation on the part of the dean to make this happen," as well as "his ability to navigate the academic and the United Methodist world." At the May 2010 faculty meeting Lawrence announced that by the end of that month Perkins would have received pledges and cash fully covering the $14.38 million cost of the building project; he expressed special thanks to Todd Rasberry and Linda Hervey for their work toward that goal.[19]

The building program was still a year from completion in 2008 when SMU began to suffer the effects of the worst recession since the Great Depression of the 1930s. Some large Wall Street investment firms failed; the Federal Reserve System and the federal government provided huge financial packages to enable banks to continue operations, and to General Motors and Chrysler to continue in business. The Dow Industrial Average fell to a low of 6,547 (from a peak of more than 14,000), and the nation's unemployment rate grew to more than 10 percent. Many private universities across the country saw the market value of their endowments reduced by a third or more.

By March 2009 the value of SMU's endowment portfolio had fallen by 27 percent. This and the uncertain economic situation led SMU administrators to consider reducing the budget by 2 percent overall for the next fiscal year. The smallest budget cuts were for academic programs, with larger reductions for athletics and administration. For the Perkins budget, as for those of the other schools of the university, the reduction was 1.75 percent. Although for Perkins that came to $89,000, Lawrence reported that with Linda Hervey's help, this decrease "will not materially affect the regular activities and programs at Perkins, nor will it eliminate any current positions." Neither would there be a need to impose a freeze on faculty or staff hiring or salaries. Regular activities and programs at Perkins would go on much as before.[20] The building program continued.

The Perkins endowment, most of which is restricted in how its income can be used, suffered along with that of the rest of SMU. Its market value, which was $147.2 million at the end of fiscal 2002, grew to $231.2 million in 2008 but then fell to $166.2 in 2009—a decrease of 28 percent. (Its book value grew from $69.6 million in May 2002 to $79.9 million in May 2009.) Because SMU distributes income from endowment in a way that takes account of fluctuations in the market, Perkins did not suffer a decline in income from endowment in fiscal 2009 but was expected to do so in subsequent years.[21]

Serious losses in Perkins's income occurred in the areas of gifts and tuition. As Lawrence explained to the faculty, donors were not ready to make financial commitments until the U.S. financial situation stabilized, and Perkins was considering extending the time period for donors to fulfill their existing commitments, perhaps to as late as 2013 or 2015. As for income from tuition, Perkins, like SMU, expected a reduction in enrollment. Lawrence praised Tracy Anne Allred and Herbert Coleman for their work in recruiting students, and he urged faculty members to assist in that work wherever possible. In the spring of 2010 Lawrence reported that Perkins would need to make further budget reductions for the next three fiscal years, the cumulative impact of which would reduce the school's budget by almost 7 percent.[22]

NEW PROGRAMS

Global Theological Education is one of several new Perkins programs that have enriched the school's educational work in the first decade of the twenty-first century. Before it became a formal program, Michael Hawn taught "Worship in a Global Perspective" as a "travel course" in South Texas and Mexico with five students in the January 1996 interterm. It was described in the Perkins catalog as an "on-site study of a particular tradition off campus." Perkins offered few travel courses in the 1990s.

This changed after the arrival in 2000 of David Lawson, who as bishop in residence vigorously pursued his personal commitment to global theological education. In the summer of 2001 he and Joerg Rieger took three students to Zimbabwe for what they called an "immersion course," one in which the students experienced a culture different from their own, encountered churches in the midst of a society in crisis, and reflected on the relevance of theology to that context. Thereafter Lawson, with several other faculty—John Holbert (chair), Hawn, Harold Recinos, and Rieger—

formed the Steering Committee on Globalization. Their goal, as Holbert explained it, was to have an international experience become a curricular requirement, though they knew Perkins would need to offer some immersion courses within the United States for students who for various reasons could not travel internationally.[23]

From this committee's discussions came a course description, adopted by the faculty in March 2002, that could cover various immersion courses: "Christian Mission in Cultural Context. A study of the mission, development, and influence of Christianity in various cultures, with special attention to the role of the church amid societal tensions, nationalism, and social change. The course may be taught as an overview course on campus, or off-campus as a focused, on-site study of a particular region of the world. Specific topic will vary with each offering. May be repeated for additional academic credit. One and one-half or three term hours. Prerequisite: Permission of the instructor for off-campus offerings."[24]

Encouraged by Lawson and by experience of the Zimbabwe course, faculty members offered several immersion courses in the next three years, including courses led by Recinos in El Salvador, Abraham Smith and Rieger in Brazil, Rieger in Germany, Hawn at Taizé in France, and Susanne Johnson in Honduras and Mexico. On-site courses were expensive, but by the time Lawson retired in 2004, he had raised about $100,000 to support the program.[25]

In 2004 Dean Lawrence appointed Robert Hunt to a one-year position as visiting professor of world religions and director of Global Theological Education Program. Hunt, who had received his master of theology degree from Perkins in 1982, and his wife, Lilian Wong, had in 1984 served in Malaysia on assignment from the UMC General Board of Global Ministries; until 1992 both were lecturers in a Malaysian seminary. In 1994 Hunt received his Ph.D. degree from the University of Malaya, and from 1993 to 1997 he was a lecturer at Trinity Theological College in Singapore. In those years he gave special attention to Islam and Muslim-Christian relations. From 1997 to 2004 he was pastor of an English-speaking congregation in Vienna, Austria. His experience overseas was directly pertinent to his new position.[26]

Up to this time no general plan had guided Perkins immersion courses; faculty members simply devised each course anew. Under Hunt's leadership that changed. In August 2004, soon after his arrival, he convened a meeting of the Steering Committee on Globalization and proposed a plan whereby Perkins would offer not one or two immersion course trips a year (as in the previous three years) but six, with fifty to sixty students participating. Though the steering committee members thought this ambitious, they encouraged him to continue with his planning.[27]

Hunt's responsibility as director was to manage the nonacademic aspects of the immersion courses. In a progress report in January 2005, he said that he planned to formulate policy guidelines, seek funds for travel expenses for students and faculty involved in the courses, contact potential sites (both within and outside the United States), initiate a series of annual newsletters about the program, hold seminars both before and after the courses, make travel arrangements, and work with the North Texas and Texas annual conferences to develop a program for Perkins faculty to engage UMC members in theological reflection on missions. The faculty responded positively to the report, and Hunt proceeded with his plans. In March 2005 Lawrence appointed him to a continuing administrative position as director of global theological education.[28]

With careful advance planning by Hunt and individual faculty members, three immersion courses were offered early in 2005: in Germany (led by Rieger), at Taizé (Hawn), and in Mexico (offered by the Mexican American Program and led by David Maldonado), with a total of forty-five students enrolled—far more than in previous immersions. In 2005–06 three immersions were added; in 2006–07 another three; in 2007–08 five; in 2008–09 six, with more than sixty students participating; in 2009–10 still another six.[29] Under Hunt's leadership the program became well established.

Faculty members have responded enthusiastically to the global theological education program, as have students in the master's degree programs. Tracy Anne Allred reported that it is a magnet for recruiting students. She said that at "Inside Perkins" sessions for prospective Perkins students, "their jaws drop" when Hunt tells where the next year's immersion courses will be held. As of 2010 an immersion course was not a curricular requirement, since this would intensify the problem of too few students in many elective courses; even so, a large percentage of Perkins master's students participate. By 2009 the program had significant financial support. It received two endowments in 2007, one from Perkins alumna Patria Smith and her husband, Paul, and the other from the family of former professor Richey Hogg. In February

2009 Hunt reported to the faculty that the SMU Board of Trustees had approved Perkins's providing full travel stipends for each M.Div. student to have one immersion course and partial stipends for students in the other master's programs. In the spring of 2009 Hunt announced "a generous three year grant" from the Woodworth Foundation in Oklahoma, supplementing the earlier endowments.[30]

Hunt has described global theological education as a program that prepares students to lead congregations, both within and outside the United States, in a culturally sensitive way. It helps them learn to build intercultural relationships and to learn from others with different outlooks and experiences.[31]

In the fall of 1991 William J. Abraham, who was then the McCreless Professor of Evangelism, proposed the establishment of the Perkins Center (initially it was called an institute) for the Advanced Study and Practice of Evangelism, and the faculty adopted the proposal.[32] The center's activities included sponsoring continuing education events that contribute to the study and practice of evangelism and enabling Perkins to provide resource people for conferences on evangelism. It also funded "the Polycarp Project," whereby students can study and do research at Perkins for degrees offered through Cliff College, a Methodist school in England affiliated with the University of Sheffield and the University of Manchester in England and the University of South Africa. The center continued while Scott Jones held the McCreless Chair (from 1997), but it became inactive after his departure in 2004.

After Elaine Heath came to the McCreless Chair in 2005, she reactivated the center but in a different form. In the spring of 2009 the center's board, which she chaired, decided to change the name to the Center for Missional Wisdom. This reflects its current priorities, which expanded the original goals of the center to include perspectives on holistic evangelism coming from "missional," "emerging," and "new monastic" communities. "New monastic" (a phrase coined by Dietrich Bonhoeffer) refers to a grassroots, ecumenical movement that today finds expression in many small Christian communities with a rule of practice, the practice of prayer, and action for justice in the wider community, including a concern for the environment. Heath herself started a new monastic community, and in the fall of 2009 she and some Perkins students organized Students of Missional Wisdom. She looks forward to a time when the center can raise funds and hire a director.[33]

• • •

In the late 1990s the Lilly Endowment began giving grants to seminaries to provide theological education for high school students who might sense a call to ministry or want to explore their faith, and by 2005 about fifty such programs were in operation around the country. In the fall of 2001 Perkins, at the initiative of faculty members Evelyn Parker and Joerg Rieger, and Shonda Jones, the director of student services, applied to the Lilly Endowment, and Perkins received a grant of $30,000 to begin planning for such a program, which was to be called the Perkins Youth School of Theology. In August 2002 the Lilly Endowment awarded Perkins $1.4 million to fund the youth school until July 2006.

In the summer of 2003 the Reverend Tonya Y. Burton became director of the program. Her master of divinity degree was from Vanderbilt University, and she had been a staff member at Metropolitan Baptist Church, Washington, D.C., as minister of discipleship, and at the D.C. Baptist Convention, coordinating volunteers for service opportunities. By January 2004 she had organized the Perkins youth program and had enrolled twenty-six students in the first year's class. The second class numbered thirty-one; classes since have been limited to fifteen to twenty.

The Perkins Youth School of Theology seeks to equip young people with skills for discerning their vocation and for critical theological reflection about their faith and their society. The Perkins program is unique in that it targets youth under pressure because of racial minority status, socioeconomic background, or other challenging circumstances. Those from other backgrounds are also welcome, and funds from the Lilly grant initially paid all the costs, whether the students were able to pay or not. The youth school holds an open house in the fall, after which students apply to the program. High school juniors and seniors may participate. To do so, the students must commit to a year of community service and have a mentor, who might be their youth director or other adult member of their church. The youth school also hosts the Spring Youth Forum, a one-day conference for high school youth in grades 10 to 12; a Perkins faculty member discusses with them a theme related to youth culture, faith, and society. The students then attend the three-week Summer Academy, a residential experience away from the campus, during which in addition to other activities they engage in theological study, with classes on theology, Bible, and the church in its social context.

The students represent several denominations and diverse cultures within the Dallas–Fort Worth and surrounding areas. The youth school provides them with information about how to apply to college and about financial aid options, and it tracks them through their junior year of college to learn about the youth school's influence on their vocational and educational choices. It also invites them to youth school alumni/ae gatherings to reconnect with one another and with Perkins faculty and staff. After the first year, which the Lilly Endowment fully funded, Lilly asked Perkins to contribute matching funds. Lilly renewed the grant in 2006, funding the program partially for four more years.[34]

In 2002–03 the Committee on Academic Programs, seeking to implement an objective in the 2001 Strategic Plan, created a task force "to develop a plan to establish Perkins School of Theology as a center for the study of the Hispanic Church." When the task force reported to the faculty in May 2004, a lengthy discussion ensued, the result of which was that the report was tabled but that work on the project continued.[35]

In November 2004 Dean Lawrence constituted a steering committee of nine, with Michael Hawn as its chair, and charged it with developing a plan for a Hispanic center. Its members included faculty, staff, students, and Latino/a church leaders, drawing upon the expertise of Edwin Aponte, David Maldonado, Harold Recinos, and others. The steering committee's report, presented to the faculty in March 2006, proposed establishment of "The Perkins School of Theology Center for the Study of Latino/a Christianity and Religions." The change of wording from *Hispanic* to *Latino/a* reflected the diversity of the social group under consideration. When the question arose whether the center and the Mexican American Program would compete for funds, Jeannie Treviño-Teddlie replied that the two should be seen as complementary, with funds for research going to the center and funds for ministry to the program. The faculty unanimously adopted the report, and later that spring Robert Blocker, the provost, authorized the creation of the center. Maldonado, who had been a Perkins faculty member for sixteen years and was president emeritus of Iliff School of Theology, was named its director.[36]

The mission of the center "is to promote a deeper understanding of the varieties of religious life and expression within the Latino communities in the United States and in Latin America," and thereby to strengthen and enrich the work of Perkins School of Theology. It conducts activities in three areas: educational programs, generation and promotion of research, and dissemination of information. After its authorization Maldonado helped establish an executive board (required by university procedures), set up an advisory board, and applied for a grant from the Luce Foundation. In the fall of 2007 Lawrence announced that the Luce Foundation had given the center a grant of $300,000 for program support. Among its activities in the first three years were establishing a fellowship for a doctoral student doing study and research on Hispanic theology and religion; bringing a visiting scholar to the Perkins campus each year; offering a seminar annually on a topic in Latino/a theology, religious life, and/or ministry; providing grants to Perkins faculty doing research on this subject; holding public workshops on issues of interest to the church and the community; offering campuswide "Interdisciplinary Dialogues" on topics related to Latino Christianity and religion; and fostering interfaith conversation with traditions beyond a Christian perspective.[37]

In 2008 Lawrence appointed Patricia Howery Davis to a new administrative position as director of leadership development. After a year and a half of conversations with the Perkins faculty and others, in February 2010 she presented a proposal to the faculty to create the Center for Leadership Development. The faculty discussed, amended, and adopted the proposal for submission to the dean and the provost for their approval, after which Perkins sought funding for the center from the Lilly Foundation.

The mission of the center is "to prepare graduate and undergraduate students, clergy, and laity to lead congregations, communities, and organizations toward more vigorous and effective participation in the practice of the Christian life—proclaiming and participating in the Reign of God on earth." In pursuit of this mission the center is to draw upon the resources of faculty from Perkins, the Cox School of Business, and the Dedman School of Law, as well as church and business leaders from the Dallas–Fort Worth area and beyond. Its goals are to help Perkins students and clergy to form "pastoral imagination" for leadership, train them to facilitate the practical work of the gospel in both the church and the world, help them develop management and leadership principles and the skills to implement them, deepen their understanding of the church's relation to other societal systems, support research about leadership of congregational and nonprofit organizations, and challenge undergraduates and others to consider church vocations.

Davis is to be the center's director; as stipulated in the *University Policy Manual* it will have an executive board (including at least three members of the faculty) and an advisory board of people from the wider community, with the Perkins dean as its ex officio chair.[38]

THE FACULTY AND ITS WORK

Robin Lovin had made twenty-four faculty and senior administrative appointments, twenty-two of them in the last five years of his deanship. Through the spring of 2010 Bill Lawrence had made twelve faculty appointments (see appendix A). Two were in Division I (Bible): Susanne Scholz and Sze-kar Wan; three in Division II (the Christian heritage and its religious and cultural context): Jessica Boon, Ted Campbell, and Valerie Karras; and six in Division IV (the church and its ministry): Christopher Anderson, Carlos Cardoza-Orlandi, Elaine Heath, Hugo Magallanes, Jeanne Stevenson-Moessner, and Bishop William B. Oden, who had just concluded eight years as presiding bishop in the Dallas area. As of 2010 Lawrence had had no occasion to make an appointment in Division III (theology and ethics). In 2006 he appointed Barry Hughes as an associate director of the intern program.

Continuing the attention to diversity, the appointments since 2002 included five women (one from Germany), two Latinos, and one Asian. Among the departures were three women and two Latinos. The promotions to full professor of Karen Baker-Fletcher and Jeanne Stevenson-Moessner in 2008 and Alyce McKenzie in 2009 brought the number of women who were full professors to four, which was encouraging to the morale of the women faculty and the faculty as a whole.

One goal in the 2006 Strategic Plan was to have four new endowed chairs. In 2008 Lawrence announced that Erroll and Barbara Wendland, laity from Temple, Texas, and long-time Perkins supporters, and their family had funded the Wendland-Cook Endowed Professorship in Constructive Theology. On January 1, 2009, Paul Ludden, the provost, announced Joerg Rieger as the first occupant of that chair. In the spring of 2009 the dean reported that an anonymous donor had made plans for a gift to endow a chair in New Testament studies. Also in May 2010 he reported that Michael Hawn had been named a University Distinguished Professor.[39]

While Lovin was dean, twenty-one faculty members, including administrators with courtesy faculty rank, had left Perkins. During Lawrence's first eight years as dean, from 2002 to 2010, the number was fifteen. The difference is attributable largely to fewer faculty retirements—eight under Lawrence, compared with thirteen under Lovin.

The retirements of William Babcock in 2005 and Edwin Sylvest in 2008 and the unexpected death of Virgil Howard left only two faculty who had joined the faculty before 1981—Charles Wood and John Holbert. Howard died on November 19, 2005, while he was attending the annual meeting of the American Academy of Religion and Society of Biblical Literature in Philadelphia. He had joined the Perkins faculty in 1975 and had become one of its most popular teachers, public lecturers, and leaders.

George Atkinson retired in 2004 from the post he had held for eight years as director of the Houston-Galveston Program. In 2005 Jim Kirby retired after twenty-four years as dean, acting president of SMU, and professor of church history; and Kenneth Hart concluded eighteen years as professor of sacred music and director of the Master of Sacred Music Program. Two years later Jouette Bassler, a member of the faculty in New Testament since 1986, retired; she had also served as academic associate dean from 1997 to 2000. David Lawson, who had become bishop in residence in 2000, retired in 2004, and his successor, William Oden, retired in 2008.

Of the six who went to positions elsewhere, four (Edwin Aponte, Alejandro Botta, Valerie Hotchkiss, and David Price) took academic posts. One went to a church position—Scott Jones, who was elected bishop in 2004 and assigned to the Kansas Area. Patricia Davis, who had previously completed a law degree and for a year had been a clerk for U.S. District Judge Harold Barefoot Sanders, resigned her faculty position in 2004 to join a law firm, although she continued to teach at Perkins as an adjunct professor and returned to Perkins in 2008 as director of pastoral leadership.

The faculty of 2010 included eight who arrived before 1990. Of a total of thirty-nine, twenty-nine had joined the faculty since the summer of 1997. Several of these twenty-nine had years of service elsewhere, so that the median age of the faculty was near what it was in the early 1990s, the midfifties. Three faculty members announced that they would soon retire: Charles Wood and Marjorie Proctor-Smith in 2011, and John Holbert in 2012.[40]

• • •

Because most of the faculty had arrived after 1997 and a new dean took the helm in 2002, the pattern of faculty relations changed, although it has continued to be characterized by the mixture of collegiality and tensions evident since the 1992 faculty conflict.[41]

In recent years faculty members have held differing opinions about various issues of school policy. The relation of diversity and quality is a continuing issue, with some faculty giving priority to gender and ethnic diversity while maintaining that doing so does not sacrifice quality, and others emphasizing the importance of academic quality while continuing to value diversity.

Disagreements about the future direction of Perkins have become more prominent. Some faculty hold that the only significant theological work is on behalf of the disadvantaged—a long-standing concern of liberation theology. Others maintain that it is important to continue the Perkins tradition, represented earlier in the work of Schubert Ogden and others, of pursuing the question of theological truth or credibility while continuing to seek social justice. Some view Perkins as a place of continuing theological diversity, with mutual acceptance and exchanges of ideas among the different positions.

One occasion for disagreement has been the election of new members of the Committee on Rank and Tenure at the May faculty meeting each year. Members and chairs of most faculty committees are nominated each spring by the Nominating Committee, and the faculty usually accepts its slate without change. The Rank and Tenure Committee is an exception to that procedure. Its membership is six faculty members who are elected for three-year terms, plus the dean and associate dean, ex officio. Two members (plus any replacements necessitated by faculty leaves or departures) are elected each year without nomination by the tenure-track members of the faculty, voting by secret ballot until there is a majority for each vacancy. Rank and tenure is an especially important committee because of what is at stake. In recent years a few faculty members have received a substantial vote on the first ballot, which reflects advance planning by groups of faculty.

Two faculty members are also elected each spring to the Nominating Committee by the faculty by secret ballot. (It also has two student members, and it is chaired by the associate dean.) Because some committee posts for which it makes nominations have considerable influence on faculty decisions, it too can be subject to competition among groups of faculty.

Disagreements have surfaced in recent years about the process of appointing new faculty members. According to Perkins procedures, many of which have been in place since 2006 (and some much longer), when an appointment is to be made, a task force appointed by the Committee on Faculty draws up a job description that goes to the faculty for adoption. Much of the content of job descriptions has been standard for years, but some matters can be contentious. One recent job description came to the faculty with the phrase "such as feminist and post-colonial studies," describing the desired methodology of the person to be appointed. During discussion one faculty member moved to delete that phrase, and the faculty approved the deletion by a one-vote margin. Then another member moved to add the phrase "such as feminist, postcolonial studies, and other contemporary approaches," and that motion was adopted.[42]

Once a job description is adopted and a search is authorized, the dean appoints a search committee. Since 2006 the practice has ordinarily been to invite two or three prospects to the campus for public visits. Afterward the dean confers with members of the Perkins community and, if it seems indicated, calls a meeting of the faculty in executive session to advise him and then to vote by secret ballot on one candidate.[43]

One recent faculty advisory was more than ordinarily intense, the members disagreeing heatedly about whether the search committee had followed the prescribed procedures. Many were dismayed, both by the action of the search committee and by feelings expressed during the advisory meeting. The official outcome was a negative vote on the one name the committee presented. The dean decided to restart the search the following fall.

Several kinds of fallout resulted from that incident. Because some faculty members were uncomfortable about that advisory meeting, they took steps to ensure that those they thought had caused the problem were not elected to the Rank and Tenure Committee that spring.

Another result of that advisory was that the Committee on Faculty set out to revise the search procedures. After much work, in March 2010 the committee, chaired by Jeanne Stevenson-Moessner, brought a proposal to the faculty that, while it retained much of the existing procedure, included several changes. In its report to the dean before a faculty advisory meeting, a search committee was no longer to rank the candidates who had made campus visits. The proposal also stipulated, "At the faculty advisory, all candidates who have made public visits will be discussed," and "the procedures will be in accordance with those established by the University." One aim underlying the proposal was to emphasize the participatory nature of the process—the faculty's participation as well as that of the dean, Committee on Faculty, search committee, student community, and, when appropriate, the chair of the SMU Department of Religious Studies. After much discussion and several amendments, all of which left the intent of the Committee on Faculty proposal intact, the faculty adopted it unanimously.[44]

In another type of fallout, several faculty women spoke against what they saw as bullying by some colleagues in recent years and called attention to a recent book on bullying in the academy.[45] One person spoke of the need for Perkins to be a theological community "where people can disagree and fight, but with forgiveness. We should model to students what a Christian community is. We are engaged in Christian formation. . . . There ought to be communication and hospitality."[46] In his report to the fall 2008 faculty conference, Lawrence commented on the phenomenon of bullying and spoke of the need to attend "to our own internal context," "to nurture our sense of community."[47] Since the spring of 2009 matters have appeared to be calmer. Although some members describe the faculty as deeply divided, one observed that "we're becoming more used to conflict," that this is probably wise, and that the conflict is less bipolar than it was.

Alongside the tensions, various Perkins activities in recent years have enhanced the faculty's sense of collegiality. A special concern has been untenured tenure-track new faculty—eight had arrived between 1997 and 2001. In 1995 the Committee on Faculty had begun a program of assigning to each assistant professor a pair of tenured faculty members to serve in an informal advisory role as mentors.[48] One who arrived after 1997 later explained that his mentors encouraged him to plan what he needed to do to attain tenure, and that he spent two years developing a research and publication plan to assist him in the process. For others the mentor program was less satisfactory, and after a few years it was discontinued. In their untenured years this group of assistant professors met several times to encourage one another toward tenure and to ask, "How are you progressing?" In time seven were promoted to the rank of associate professor with tenure, and the eighth left Perkins for another position before a tenure review. In its 2010 annual report the Committee on Faculty expressed its ongoing commitment to mentoring and supporting pretenure faculty.[49]

As associate dean, Marjorie Procter-Smith took several steps to assist younger faculty and enhance collegiality. In March 2003 she initiated an annual reception in Bridwell Library to celebrate faculty books published during the preceding year, a practice that has continued. She also included sessions during the fall faculty conferences to discuss the faculty's sense of vocation and to orient new faculty, and she invited new faculty to make presentations at faculty lunches.

For years Perkins faculty members have met several times a year to consider matters other than faculty business. These occasions include lunches at which a member presents a scholarly paper, guild meetings to discuss matters of common concern, and the symposium, which usually meets four times annually for discussion of some academic topic. A new kind of faculty gathering has been added during Bill Lawrence's deanship. He and his wife, Naomi, have on several occasions hosted large groups of Perkins faculty and spouses at a dinner in their home, with a presentation by someone from the wider community, followed by discussion.

A number of faculty readily express appreciation for their work together. One said he has found a strong sense of collegiality at Perkins that he had not seen at other places. Another declared, "There is no one on the faculty with whom I do not have a pleasant relationship, some stronger than others." Still another thought that, given faculty differences, "we work together remarkably well." One spoke of a growing sense of community among the women faculty. Several newer Perkins faculty members have said they appreciate the theological diversity at Perkins, and one spoke of having a vocation "to bridge gaps between people who have been at odds." Perkins faculty relations are most accurately interpreted, then, not as simply in tension nor simply collegial but as a mixture of the two.

The Graduate Program in Religious Studies (GPRS) is formally a program of Dedman College and not of Perkins School of Theology. Yet since its beginning in 1965 it has always been largely dependent on Perkins for its administrative leadership, faculty, and funding. Furthermore, Perkins faculty members who have been active in the program have viewed it as a major component of their own scholarly work. The GPRS is thus an important aspect of Perkins life.

With the appointment of many new Perkins faculty members after 1997, dissatisfactions with the GPRS became more evident. Some of the newer faculty saw it as exclusive, with decisions made by the director and Steering Committee without participation by other faculty. Some wanted to have "religion and culture" accepted as a field of specialization, and the Steering Committee accepted that idea. Several have been concerned about the lack of a Ph.D. program in practical theology. Faculty already active in the program have had their own worries about it, especially the need to maintain high academic standards and the lack of adequate stipends to attract many of the ablest students applying to graduate programs in religion.

With William Babcock, the program's director, planning to retire in 2005, the provost's office, Dean Lawrence, and Jasper Neel, dean of Dedman College, set up procedures for a review of the program. In the winter of 2004 Lawrence invited three scholars from other universities to visit the campus and conduct an external review. At the same time Ellen Jackofsky, associate provost of SMU, arranged for an internal SMU review to be conducted by a subcommittee of the Academic Programs Evaluation Committee, with Beth Thornburg, a law school professor, as its chair. The report of the internal committee, informed by its members' observations as well as by those of the external reviewers, was completed in January 2005.[50]

The report began by recognizing the considerable strengths and achievements of the Graduate Program in Religious Studies, its contributions to the university, its widely respected faculty, the superb resources available to it through Bridwell Library, and "the self-less and academically rigorous leadership that Professor Babcock has brought to the doctoral-level study of religion at SMU." The report then identified several challenges facing the program: stipends for students were "horrifyingly low"; the roles of the director and Steering Committee needed rethinking; who was a member of the program's faculty was ambiguous; the faculty had significant disagreements about the curriculum; and the program suffered "from being the responsibility of no one Dean," as "it belongs fully to neither Perkins nor Dedman." The report made several recommendations to deal with the difficulties. Ross Murfin, the SMU provost, in a response commending the review committee's work, reported that Lawrence had received a gift that for several years would allow for four $10,000 fellowships to be awarded annually to four students in the graduate program. To this Murfin committed an additional $10,000 award each year to a fifth student.[51] These actions relieved the stipend difficulty for the near future. More permanent assistance arrived later in 2005 when Robert Blocker, the newly appointed provost (replacing Murfin), responded to a proposal by a group that included deans Lawrence of Perkins, Neel of Dedman College, and Hal Williams of Graduate Studies, as well as other faculty, and approved a grant of $264,000 to increase stipends for students in the program. The plan was implemented with the graduate class entering in the fall of 2007.[52]

In the spring of 2005 Lawrence appointed Charles Wood the next director of the GPRS. That fall, following a recommendation from the review committee, Wood appointed a task force, consisting of three faculty from the Department of Religious Studies, six from Perkins, and Robin Lovin, then the Maguire University Professor of Ethics, to study and make recommendations about the program's governance and curriculum. During 2005–06 the task force developed a proposal on governance that the faculty for the GPRS then amended and approved. This action clarified the membership and responsibilities of the program's faculty and of the Steering Committee in ways that rendered them appropriately inclusive and responsive to faculty members' ideas.[53]

During 2006–07 the task force turned to curricular issues. Its proposals, adopted by the GPRS faculty in May 2007, replaced the earlier core seminar, which had occupied nearly the entire first year of doctoral study, with four individual one-semester courses to be taken during the first two years; this enabled students to pursue studies in their chosen fields from the time they entered the program. This and other curriculum changes were designed to allow for more classroom interaction among the students and more participation in regular courses as distinguished from independent study courses.[54]

These changes, together with the process Wood followed for their consideration, eased dissatisfactions about the Graduate Program in Religious Studies. Differences of opinion on substantive issues remained, but now there were open and agreed procedures for dealing with them. The faculty had worked through these differences in a way that fostered collegiality. This was the situation when in 2010 Wood concluded his time as director and Lawrence appointed Bruce Marshall to succeed Wood in that post.

THE STUDENTS AND THEIR STUDIES

Largely because of the addition of the Houston-Galveston extension program in 1995, the Oklahoma City program in 1998, and the San Antonio program in 2002, enrollment in Perkins's master of divinity program rose from 231 in 1994 to 300 in 2002. During the same period total enrollment for all Perkins programs rose from 408 to 520 (see appendix B, table 3). Since 2003, though, when total enrollment hit an all-time high of 544, Perkins has not been able to sustain the increase. From 2004 to 2009 M.Div. enrollment declined by nearly 37 percent, from 349 to 220, in part because of fewer students in the extension programs (see appendix B, table 4). In 2004 the three schools participating in the Oklahoma City program terminated it by mutual agreement, and Perkins ended the San Antonio program in 2007 after church leaders there proposed doing so. Houston-Galveston enrollment has continued at a level judged sufficient for the program to continue, though it declined from eighty-six in 2002 to fifty-eight in 2009.

Lawrence has identified several reasons that could account for the decrease in enrollments: more students completing their degrees more quickly, fewer people going into ministry as a second career, continuing difficulties in recruiting younger students, a decreased sense of responsibility on the part of pastors for calling others into ministry, and the notion held by some church leaders that the church can train its ministers less expensively, easily, and conveniently through various nondegree pro-grams rather than through seminaries. Fewer students are seeking master of divinity degrees today, reflecting widespread cultural changes, and the long-term enrollment problem is affecting many seminaries.[55]

As one response to the problem, in 2005–06 Lawrence initiated a market analysis of Perkins by an advertising company, with the goal of revising the school's recruitment practices. As a part of that revision, in 2009 Perkins's Office of Public Affairs launched a new Perkins web site to present the school to a wider and younger community in a readily accessible way. Lawrence has suggested that Perkins also consider fine-tuning the financial aid program, being more attentive to the church, offering more lay theological education, and seeking out the unchurched and the formerly churched who have been frustrated by lack of attention from religious institutions to their spiritual questions.[56]

The bright spot in the enrollment picture has been women. In the fall of 2003 the number of women in all programs exceeded 50 percent for the first time—275 women in a total enrollment of 544 (50.55 percent). In the next few years the percentage of women in all programs ranged from 48 to 54 percent, while in master's degree programs it was higher—50 to 61 percent. However, as total enrollment declined between 2003 and 2009, the number of women declined at about the same rate as that of men (30.5 and 30.1 percent, respectively).

The number of African American students ranged from eighty-three to seventy-eight between 2002 and 2007 but fell to sixty-two in 2008 and sixty-three in 2009. In those years they constituted 15 to 17.8 percent of the Perkins student body. At the May 2005 commencement SMU and Perkins celebrated the fiftieth anniversary of the graduation of its first African American students. Two of the five who had graduated in 1955 were present for the occasion—the Reverend James V. Lyles of Culver City, California, and the Reverend A. Cecil Williams of San Francisco. The number of Latino/a students dropped to a recent low of eight in 2004 but since has increased significantly, with twenty to twenty-two enrolled each year since 2006. Asian American students, after reaching a high point of twenty-three in 2003, fell to twelve in 2009. The number of international students has declined similarly, from a high of thirty-four in 2003 to eight in 2008, because of Homeland Security regulations since 9/11 that have had the effect of severely curtailing international students' access to the doctor of ministry program. In this period native Americans have maintained a steady presence of two to five each year. The percentage of whites each year has remained between 73 and 75 percent.

The percentage of the student body who are United Methodists has declined slightly from the previous decade. Between 1994 and 2002 it ranged from 70 to 77 percent; since 2003 it has been between 66 and 70.7 percent. In 2002 eighty-five Perkins students were either Episcopalian, Baptist, Presbyterian, or members of other Methodist bodies. That number increased to 119 in 2004 but since then, especially with a precipitous decline in the number of Episcopalian students, fell to forty-nine in 2009. In the same period members of other denominations have increased from fifty-four to sixty-two.

Between 2000 and 2006 the average age of Perkins students was forty, with women on average three to five years older than men. The average dropped to thirty-nine in 2009, in part reflecting the decline in enrollment in the Houston-Galveston program, where students are on average older than at the Dallas campus. In all programs the average age of the men declined from thirty-eight in 2002 to thirty-six in 2008; that of the women continued to be forty-two in those years.

In recent years the Perkins faculty has created a series of certificates to be awarded to students achieving different kinds of competence. Since 1988 Perkins has granted a certificate in Hispanic studies to students who complete fifteen term hours in designated courses in that field; are able to converse, read, and conduct worship services in Spanish; have substantial experience in a Hispanic context; and, where possible, have completed an internship in a Hispanic setting.[57]

The latter years of Lovin's deanship saw the creation of two additional certificates: in the spring of 2000, a certificate in urban ministry, recognizing special competence in that area of ministry by master of divinity students; ; and in the fall of 2001 a graduate certificate in women's studies for students completing special study of that subject.

The faculty has added three more types of certificates since 2002. In May 2005 it approved the Certificate in African American Church Studies, intended to broaden students' "understanding of African American religious experiences" and to "prepare for leadership in the black church or related social agencies." Requirements include completion of fifteen term hours in designated courses on the African American church and an internship in an African American church or related setting. A year later an amendment made clear that this certificate is also available to master of theological studies students (though that degree does not require an internship), provided they complete a major research project on the subject.[58]

In January 2006 the faculty approved the Certificate in Anglican Studies, with the purpose of "preparing students for ordination in the Episcopal Church USA and the larger Anglican tradition." Its requirements include completion of designated coursework in worship; the history of Christian doctrine; Anglican/Episcopal history, theology, and canon law; and either Hebrew or Greek.[59]

In March 2006 came approval of the Certificate in Pastoral Care, which recognizes students' preparation for various specialized pastoral care ministries and their introduction to the field of professional counseling. Requirements include fifteen term hours in designated or elective courses in pastoral care, an internship appropriate to this certificate, an interdisciplinary paper, and an oral defense of the paper.[60]

As each of these certificate programs had come about ad hoc, the faculty in the spring of 2008 approved a report that structured and limited future certificate proposals. The report recognized that in some cases certificates would require study beyond the usual ideas of a major or concentration.[61]

One objective stated in the 2006 Strategic Plan was to review the curriculum for all Perkins degree programs. Toward that end the Committee on Academic Programs in the fall of 2006 appointed the eleven-person Task Force on Curriculum Review, chaired by Evelyn Parker.

One proposal, in May 2008, was to hire a full-time professional student adviser–vocational adviser for the master of divinity (M.Div.), master of church ministries (C.M.M.), and master of theological studies (M.T.S.) degree programs. This person would assist new students in their vocational understandings and train the faculty members who would advise students throughout their studies. After much discussion the faculty tabled the proposal.[62]

The task force also proposed making the six-term-hour course "Interpretation of the Christian Message" mandatory for students on the Christian education track in the master of church ministries program, to conform to United Methodist require-ments for deacons. This requirement replaced the course "Moral Theology" and one course in Christian education. The faculty accepted this proposal.[63]

In October 2008 the faculty approved a third proposal revising the requirements for the master's in theological studies. The program thereafter required twelve term hours in four specific foundational courses, a concentration of twelve term hours beyond the foundational courses in one of six specified broad areas, twenty-four term hours of electives, and a thesis or other summative project that would integrate mate-rial from several courses. The latter requirement reflected a strong recommendation of the Association of Theological Schools. Earlier, in the spring of 2006, the faculty had approved a concentration in church music and worship within the master of theological studies program; this would serve people who had already completed graduate work in music and now were looking toward a position in church music and possible ordination as a deacon.[64]

The summer Bill Lawrence became dean of Perkins, Jeannie Treviño-Teddlie arrived as director of the Mexican American Program. Under her leadership the program has had eight program areas:

- Preparing Perkins students for ministries with Latinos. It advises Latino/a students, oversees the Certificate in Hispanic Studies, and supports L@s Seminaristas, an ecumenical student organization seeking to strengthen all aspects of Latino/a ministry.
- Providing short-term programs at Perkins to train local pastors and laity, through the Spanish Language Licensing School, the Course of Study School for pastors without seminary degrees (of which Treviño-Teddlie is director), and for laity and pastors through various training programs.
- Continuing to convene and support the Hispanic Instructors Program, organized by Roy Barton in the 1970s. This is a leadership group of clergy and scholars cultivating Hispanic Protestant theology.
- Providing continuing education events, lectures, symposia, and consultations on topics pertinent to ministry with Hispanics. One of these is the Barton Lecture each year during Ministers' Week, which the Mexican American Program coordinates with the Office of Continuing Education on a topic of special interest to Latinas/os.
- Publishing its journal of theology from a Hispano-Latino perspective, *Apuntes*, four times a year. Recently its circulation was more than nineteen hundred.
- Providing continuing education and consulting services for local congregations, groups of clergy, and others working to develop ministries with Latinas/os.
- Advocating in The United Methodist Church on behalf of Latina/o congregations and ministries, and cooperating with general denominational agencies, especially in implementing the National Plan for Hispanic-Latino Ministries and working with Methodists Associated to Represent the Cause of Hispanic Americans (MARCHA—the UMC's Hispanic caucus).
- Conducting the Hispanic Youth Leadership Academy, a program to encourage and mentor Hispanic young people who might consider a call to ordained ministry. Since its initial year, 2004, participation in this summer program has increased from sixteen to between twenty-five and forty-eight, with young

people attending from all five United Methodist jurisdictions. The academy helps the young people to enter college and, if they choose, seminary, and it recruits and trains mentors for each participant. In 2008 the Mexican American Program instituted an additional academy for college-age students, held at Drew University, with twenty participants the first time and twenty-five in 2009. The increase in Hispanic/Latino enrollment at Perkins—eight to eighteen each fall through 2005, but at least twenty each fall since 2006—may be attributable in part to the academy.[65]

These many activities reflect how much the Mexican American Program has recently developed in its work both within Perkins and in the wider community.

PERKINS IN 2010

Perkins has witnessed several achievements under Dean Bill Lawrence's leadership: constructing Prothro Hall and renovating Kirby and Selecman halls, creating several new programs, restructuring the Graduate Program in Religious Studies, making several new faculty appointments, and strengthening the administrative staff. These and other strengths will help it face what will likely be difficult years ahead.

1. William B. Lawrence, *Sundays in New York: Pulpit Theology at the Crest of the Protestant Mainstream, 1930–1955* (Lanham, Md.: American Theological Library Association and Scarecrow Press, 1996).
2. *Perspective*, fall 2002, 3; *General Minutes*, United Methodist Church, 2002.
3. Russell E. Richey, Dennis M. Campbell, and William B. Lawrence, eds., *Connectionalism: Ecclesiology, Mission, and Identity* (Nashville, Tenn.: Abingdon, 1997); William B. Lawrence, Dennis M. Campbell, and Russell E. Richey, ed., *The People(s) Called Methodist: Forms and Reforms of Their Life* (Nashville, Tenn.: Abingdon, 1998); Dennis M. Campbell, William B. Lawrence, and Russell E. Richey, eds., *Doctrines and Discipline* (Nashville, Tenn.: Abingdon, 1999); Russell E. Richey, William B. Lawrence, and Dennis M. Campbell, eds., *Questions for the Twenty-first Century Church* (Nashville, Tenn.: Abingdon, 1999); and Russell E. Richey, with Dennis M. Campbell and William B. Lawrence, *Marks of Methodism: Theology in Ecclesial Practice* (Nashville, Tenn.: Abingdon, 2005).
4. William B. Lawrence, "Report of the Dean, Faculty Conference, September 13, 2002," 2, 7, in the files of the Dean's Office, Perkins School of Theology (hereafter, dean's files).
5. Observations on this topic are drawn from interviews with fifty-five members of the Perkins faculty and administration active during Lawrence's deanship.
6. Lawrence, "Report of the Dean . . . , September 13, 2002"; Marjorie Procter-Smith, interview by author, May 5, 2009, Dallas; William B. Lawrence, interview by author, May 27, 2009, Dallas; John Holbert, interview by author, May 6, 2009, Dallas.
7. Faculty minutes, January 24, 2005; William B. Lawrence, "State of the School: Report of the Dean to the Faculty Conference, September 9, 2005"; William B. Lawrence, "Report of the Dean to the

Committee on Faculty, April 13, 2006"; Lawrence, "Report of the Dean to the Faculty Conference, September 14, 2007," all in dean's files; *Perspective,* spring 2008, 26.

8. Lawrence, "Report of the Dean . . ., September 13, 2002."
9. Lawrence, "Report of the Dean . . ., April 13, 2006."
10. Committee on Long Range Planning, "Annual Report to the Faculty, April 22, 2005," in the personal files of Charles M. Wood (hereafter, Wood's files).
11. Lawrence, "State of the School . . ., September 9, 2005" faculty minutes, October 3, 2005.
12. Lawrence, "Report of the Dean . . ., April 13, 2006"; William B. Lawrence, "The State of the School: Report of the Dean to the Faculty Conference, September 8, 2006," dean's files; faculty minutes, April 3 and October 30, 2006.
13. Lawrence, "State of the School . . ., September 8, 2006."
14. Ibid.
15. *Dallas Morning News,* January 28, 2007; *Perspective,* fall 2007, 4, 7; faculty minutes, January 29 and March 5, 2007, and October 27, 2008.
16. Faculty minutes, March 5, 2007; *Perspective,* fall 2007, 4, 5, 8.
17. Faculty minutes, February 4, 2008.
18. Ibid., September 12, 2008, October 1, 2007, December 1, 2008, March 2, 2009, April 6, 2009.
19. Ibid., May 3, 2010.
20. Ibid., March 2 and April 6, 2009.
21. Information provided by Linda Hervey, Perkins financial officer.
22. Faculty minutes, February 2 and April 6, 2009; William B. Lawrence, "Report to the Committee on Faculty, April 13, 2010" (attachment to the faculty minutes, May 3, 2010).
23. Catalog, 1995–96, 50; course schedules from registrar's office; Joerg Rieger, interview by author, May 5, 2009, Dallas; Lawrence interview; faculty minutes, March 5, 2001, and March 4, 2002; catalog, 2001–2003, 46, and 2003–2005, 54; Joerg Rieger to Joe Allen, August 11, 2009; John Holbert to Allen, August 11, 2009, both in author's personal files.
24. Faculty minutes, March 4, 2002.
25. Robert Hunt, interview by author, April 21, 2009, Dallas; Rieger interview; Susanne Johnson, interview by author, May 6, 2009, Dallas; Lawrence interview.
26. Robert Hunt, *Muslim Faith and Values: What Every Christian Should Know* (New York: General Board of Global Ministries, 2003), 197; Hunt interview.
27. Hunt interview.
28. Robert Hunt, "Progress Report on Global Theological Education at Perkins School of Theology, January 24, 2005," in the personal files of Charles M. Wood; faculty minutes, January 24 and March 7, 2005.
29. *Global Theological Education,* newsletter issued each spring and available at www.smu.edu/Perkins/FacultyAcademics/Global/Global_News.aspx.
30. Tracy Anne Allred, interview by author, May 8, 2009, Dallas; faculty minutes, February 2, 2009; *Global Theological Education* 5, no. 1 (spring 2008) and 6, no. 1 (spring 2009).
31. *Global Theological Education,* 6, no. 1 (spring 2009).
32. Faculty minutes, November 1, 1991.
33. Elaine Heath, interview by author, November 12, 2009, Dallas; William J. Abraham to Joe Allen, and Elaine Heath to Allen, both dated November 19, 2009, in the author's personal files; "The Center for Missional Wisdom: Cultivating Wisdom in Practices of Holistic Evangelism," 2010, in the author's personal files.
34. "Perkins Youth School of Theology: Leading with a Mission," December 1, 2003, in the personal files of Charles M. Wood; catalog, 2005–2007, 72–73; Tonya Burton, interview by author, September 1, 2009, Dallas; Rieger interview; faculty minutes, January 24, 2005, and November 17, 2006; Dorothy Botnick, "Perkins Youth School Continues in Guiding Young Theologians," *North Texas United Methodist Reporter,* January 21, 2005; William Lawrence, "High School Age Youth and Intellectual and Spiritual Challenge at Perkins," *North Texas United Methodist Reporter,* September 29, 2006; Tonya Burton to Joe Allen, November 21, 2009.

35. Committee on Academic Programs, "2002–2003 Annual Report," Wood's files; faculty minutes, May 3, 2004.

36. "A Report from the Steering Committee on Developing Perkins School of Theology as a Center for the Study of the Hispanic Church, December 8, 2005"; Michael Hawn, memo to faculty and administrators, February 1, 2006, Wood's files; faculty minutes, March 6, 2006; Lawrence, "State of the School . . ., September 8, 2006"; Perkins Office of Public Affairs, press release, September 14, 2006.

37. David Maldonado to Joe Allen, September 25, 2009, in the author's personal files.

38. Faculty minutes, February 1, 2010; "Center for Leadership Development, Perkins School of Theology, Southern Methodist University, Approved by Perkins Faculty, February 1, 2010," in the author's personal files.

39. Lawrence, "State of the School," September 8, 2006; William Lawrence, "Report of the Dean to the Committee on Faculty, April 10, 2008"; William Lawrence, "Report from the Dean to the Committee on Faculty, April 13, 2009," all in dean's files; faculty minutes, May 3, 2010.

40. Faculty minutes, February 1, 2010, and May 3, 2010.

41. This section draws upon interviews with fifty-five members of the Perkins faculty and administration who have been active while Lawrence has been dean.

42. Faculty minutes, May 7, 2007.

43. Committee on Faculty, "Procedures Leading to Appointment of New Faculty Members with Guidelines for Increasing the Ethnic and Gender Diversity of the Perkins Faculty," revised April 20, 2006, Wood's files.

44. Ibid., draft, February 28, 2010 (attachment to faculty minutes); faculty minutes, March 1, 2010.

45. Darla J. Twale and Barbara M. De Luca, *Faculty Incivility: The Rise of the Academic Bully Culture and What to Do about It* (San Francisco: Jossey-Bass, 2008).

46. Confidential interview by author of a member of the Perkins faculty, May 7, 2009, Dallas.

47. William Lawrence, "The State of the School: Report of the Dean to the Faculty Conference, September 12, 2008," dean's files.

48. Committee on Faculty, "New Faculty Mentor Program" (attachment to the faculty minutes of March 3, 1995).

49. Committee on Faculty, "Annual Report of the Committee on Faculty, 2009–2010" (attachment to the faculty minutes, May 4, 2010).

50. Faculty minutes, October 6, 2003; William Lawrence to Ross Murfin and Ellen Jackofsky, February 3, 2004; Jackofsky to Lawrence, February 4, 2004; Academic Programs Evaluation Committee Internal Review, Graduate Program in Religious Studies, January, 2005, all in the files of the Graduate Program in Religious Studies, Dedman College (hereafter, GPRS files).

51. Academic Programs Evaluation Committee Internal Review, 2–12; Ross C. Murfin to the Academic Program Evaluation Committee, April 5, 2005, GPRS files.

52. Charles Curran to Joe Allen, May 21, 2010; Charles Wood to Joe Allen, May 24, 2010, in the author's personal files.

53. GPRS Task Force on Governance and Curriculum, "Principles of Governance for the Graduate Program in Religious Studies," as proposed, March 2006, GPRS files.

54. Charles M. Wood, for the Task Force on Governance and Curriculum, to the GPRS faculty, April 19, 2007, GPRS files.

55. William B. Lawrence, reports to the faculty conferences of September 9, 2005, and September 12, 2008; Lawrence, "Report to the Committee on Faculty, April 13, 2010," dean's files.

56. William B. Lawrence to the Committee on Faculty, "Report from the Dean," April 13, 2009; Lawrence, "State of the School," report to the faculty conference of October 2, 2009, dean's files.

57. Catalog, 1988–89, 71–72.

58. Committee on Academic Programs, "A Proposal from the Committee on Academic Programs: Certificate in African American Church Studies," no date, Wood's files; faculty minutes, May 2, 2005; catalog, 2005–2007, 38–40; "A Proposal to Amend the Certificate in African American Church Studies," May 1, 2006, Wood's files; faculty minutes, May 1, 2006; catalog, 2007–2009, 35.

59. Committee on Academic Programs, "Proposal for the Certificate in Anglican Studies," no date, Wood's files; faculty minutes, January 30, 2006; catalog, 2007–2009, 35–36.
60. Committee on Academic Programs, "Proposal for a Certificate in Pastoral Care," no date, Wood's files; faculty minutes, March 6, 2006; catalog, 2007–2009, 36–38.
61. Committee on Academic Programs, "Report and Recommendations on Certificate Programs to the Curriculum Review Task Force," no date, Wood's files; faculty minutes, May 5, 2008.
62. Committee on Academic Programs, "Student Advising at Perkins: A Proposal," no date, Wood's files; faculty minutes, May 5, 2008.
63. Committee on Academic Programs, "Proposal for Changes in Requirements for the CMM Christian Education Track, Curriculum Review Task Force," April 24, 2008, Wood's files; faculty minutes, May 5, 2008.
64. Committee on Academic Programs, "Report and Recommendations of the Subcommittee on the M.T.S. Program of the Curriculum Review Task Force," October 27, 2008, Wood's files; faculty minutes, October 27, 2008; "Proposal for a Master of Theological Studies with Concentration in Church Music and Worship," no date, Wood's files; faculty minutes, April 3, 2006.
65. Jeannie Treviño-Teddlie, interview by author, May 18, 2009, Dallas; annual reports of the Mexican American Program to the General Board of Higher Education and Ministry, The United Methodist Church; Jeannie Treviño-Teddlie to Joe Allen, October 28, 2009, Joseph L. Allen Papers, Bridwell Library.

Afterword

During the past hundred years Perkins has moved through three stages. The first Perkins, with modest academic resources, aspired to provide a liberal Methodist theological education in its region. When the university opened in 1915, its school of theology, with four faculty members and thirteen graduate students, conducted its work in the east wing of the third floor of Dallas Hall. By 1924 it had a faculty of ten, a student body of forty-seven, and, for the first time, its own building—the original Kirby Hall—with a small theological library. After the economic hardships of the 1930s, in 1944 the School of Theology faculty numbered eight and a half and the student body 174, most of whom were from the Southwest, preparing to be pastors in the region. A notable strength throughout these years was the dedication of its deans and its faculty to the cause of theological education.

Events of the next few years transformed this first Perkins into something markedly different. In 1944 Joe and Lois Perkins decided to make a major donation to what in 1945 was named Perkins School of Theology in their honor. By 1951 their continued gifts and those of their friend J. S. Bridwell made possible construction of a new theology quadrangle of seven buildings, including a new library, at the southwest corner of the SMU campus. That year saw the appointment of a new dean, Merrimon Cuninggim, who brought a vision of a nationally and internationally renowned school that would be on the cutting edge of theological inquiry and education: a second Perkins. For the next four decades he and deans Joe Quillian and Jim Kirby presided over a faculty eventually numbering more than forty who pursued this vision. The second Perkins differed from the first in size, resources, global outlook, and its spirit of intellectual excitement after 1951.

Cuninggim's idea of a faculty was a group of colleagues working together on two projects: dialog in pursuit of theological insight, and mutual consultation in shaping the policies of the school. For him the chief method for both projects was uncoerced reasoning together. He set the example for this: in his faculty meetings, where he led but also allowed the faculty to override his own preferences; in his consultations with the group of five black students, in which he refused to tell them what they could and could not do; in his work with university officials, with whom he persistently and successfully reasoned in support of the racial desegregation of Perkins students; and in his *Dallas Morning News* replies to Lynn Landrum, where he appealed to readers to think clearly about Landrum's innuendos. Cuninggim's vision provided a model to which the other deans, the faculty, and the students of the second Perkins aspired.

The second Perkins was initially a fairly homogeneous community. The student body became desegregated in 1952, but the faculty remained entirely male and white for eighteen years longer. The faculty included people of different theological views, yet they were mostly differences within the liberal, mainstream Euro-American Protestant theological culture of the time. The deans and faculty of the second Perkins were in principle committed to social diversity because of their commitment to social justice, and they were committed to theological diversity, believing in the existence of a common humanity on the basis of which even those with the most diverse views could enter into dialog. These convictions led them to act in ways that significantly changed Perkins.

The third Perkins came about more gradually than the second. In the 1970s African Americans, Mexican Americans, and women began to join the faculty, a process that accelerated in the 1980s and 1990s, leading to a socially diverse faculty. The academic culture of the 1980s and afterward also encouraged greater theological diversity on the part of newcomers to the Perkins faculty. The third Perkins differs from the second in the increase in faculty tensions, although they exist amid a strong element of faculty collegiality.

The collegiality of the third Perkins finds expression in widely shared faculty commitments to educating students for church leadership, to maintaining the faculty's diversity, and to encouraging each member's scholarly development. One recurring source of tension is disagreement about whether diversity or academic quality should take priority in faculty appointments. Another is the lack of a common vision for theological education and for what constitutes worthwhile theological work. The difficulty of identifying a common vision may be inherent in diversity itself, which makes it difficult to articulate a common vision as self-confidently as in the days of Merrimon Cuninggim.

In the present situation Perkins faces challenges especially in three areas: the faculty, recruitment of students, and finances.

The Perkins faculty may choose to maintain its theological diversity, or it may encourage one kind of theological outlook and method to become dominant. Maintaining theological diversity may require special effort. For many years job descriptions for Perkins faculty appointments have included as a desirable qualification that the person have "interests, perspectives, and abilities that complement those of other members of the Perkins faculty." Continued theological diversity will depend on the attention given to that qualification.

The faculty also faces challenges concerning how its members work together as a faculty. The faculty's diversity assures that it will experience disagreements and conflicts, but conflict is not incompatible with a significant degree of collegiality, as has been demonstrated in recent years. The current faculty has the resources to continue to strengthen its collegial ethos as the context for its disagreements.

Perkins has experienced declines in enrollment repeatedly since the early 1960s, and each time it has temporarily remedied the problem with a combination of new programs and redoubled recruitment efforts, including improved financial packages for its students. The current decline may be more challenging than those of the past. Several circumstances will be difficult to overcome: the tendency of prospective students to seek seminaries that are nearby, preferably within driving distance of home; the economic downturn and the many seminary students who have families to support; the inclination of some in The United Methodist Church to question the importance of seminary education; the wider culture's lower esteem for church vocations than it once had; and, for prospective international students, the necessity to deal with Homeland Security restrictions.

Dean Lawrence and his administration are developing creative responses to the decline in enrollment, and the national and global economic situation will slowly improve. Homeland Security restrictions might be modified to take into account the special circumstances of ministerial students, though bringing this about would be difficult. As for the stance of The United Methodist Church toward ministerial education, its seminaries have many allies—their graduates—among the leaders of the church, and extended dialog about seminary education continues to be in order. The increasing secularization of the culture points to the importance of continuing engagement with the wider society in regard to cultural beliefs and values. The current enrollment decline tests the school's capacity to thrive in the environment of the early twenty-first century.

Financially, Perkins is fortunate, with a relatively large endowment and strong support from good friends in the wider community. Even so, questions are raised about the Ministerial Education Fund every quadrennium, several Perkins programs need greater long-term support, the cost of recruiting and retaining a strong faculty continually increases, and maintaining the superior quality of Bridwell Library will call for even greater resources. The need to increase endowment is constant.

Perkins faces these challenges from a position of strength in many regards: in its administration, faculty, student body, educational programs, library, endowment, physical plant, university environment, and church and community support. With these resources Perkins can capably continue to pursue its mission of theological reflection and preparing women and men for faithful leadership in Christian ministry.

Appendix A

MEMBERS OF THE PERKINS FACULTY BY YEAR OF APPOINTMENT

NAME	DATE OF APPOINTMENT	INITIAL SCHOOL OF THEOLOGY APPOINTMENT	DEPARTURE YEAR
Edwin D. Mouzon	1914	dean	1916
Ivan Lee Holt	1915	professor of Hebrew and Old Testament interpretation and chair of faculty	1918
Paul B. Kern	1915	professor of homiletics and religious efficiency	
	1920	dean	1926
James Kilgore	1915	professor of philosophy and psychology of religion	1935 retired
Frank Reedy	1915	instructor in Sunday school organization	1917
Frank Seay	1915	professor of New Testament Greek & interpretation	1920 died
Horace M. Whaling Jr.	1916	professor of church history and missions	1922
Hoyt M. Dobbs	1916	dean and professor of Christian doctrine	1920
Jesse L. Cuninggim	Jan. 1918	professor of religious education	1921
Comer M. Woodward	1918	professor of sociology	1924
B. Harvie Branscomb	1920	associate professor of New Testament	1925
John A. Rice	1920	professor of Old Testament	1921
Jesse Marvin Ormond	1921	Haynie Professor of Pastoral Administration	1923
Mims Thornburgh Workman	1921	instructor in Hebrew and Greek	1925
James Seehorn Seneker	1922	professor of religious education	1956 retired
Robert Wesley Goodloe	1922	associate professor of church history	1956 retired
John Harden Hicks	1922	associate professor of Old Testament	1957 retired

NAME	DATE OF APPOINTMENT	INITIAL SCHOOL OF THEOLOGY APPOINTMENT	DEPARTURE YEAR
William Daniel Bradfield	1922	professor of Christian doctrine	1936 retired
George F. Thomas	1923	assistant professor of New Testament	1925
Ora Miner	1924	professor of town and country church	1933
John Richard Spann	1924	professor of city church	1927
Charles McTyeire Bishop	1925	professor of New Testament	1935 retired
Alfred W. Wasson	1926	professor of missions	1934
Umphrey Lee	1927	professor of homiletics	1932
Harold G. Cooke	1928	professor of city church	1930
Eugene Blake Hawk	1933	dean and professor of homiletics	1951 retired
Nenien C. McPherson Jr.	1934	associate professor of systematic theology and philosophy of religion	1936
Wesley C. Davis	Jan. 1935	associate professor of New Testament	1959 retired
Paul A. Root	1935	professor of sociology of religion and ethics	1947 died
James T. Carlyon	1936	professor of Christian doctrine	1954 retired
Fred D. Gealy	Jan. 1939	professor of Greek, missions, and church music (visiting professor the 1st year)	1959 retired
Russell L. Dicks	1941	assistant professor of pastoral theology	1943
Albert William Martin	1945	professor of the local church	1957 retired
Earl Bowman Marlatt	Jan. 1946	professor of philosophy of religion and homiletics	1957 retired
Thomas Hodgin Marsh	1946	associate professor of speech	1963 died
Benjamin Ogilvie Hill	1946	visiting professor of missions	1952
William Warren Sweet	1948	professor of church history; chair of faculty	1952 retired
Lewis Howard Grimes	1949	assistant professor of religious education and sociology of religion	1982 retired
William A. Irwin	1950	professor of Old Testament	1955 retired
George C. Baker Jr.	1950	professor of homiletics	1970 retired
Decherd H. Turner	1950	librarian; assistant professor of bibliography	1980
Merrimon Cuninggim	1951	dean; professor of religion in higher education	1960
Albert Cook Outler	1951	professor of theology	1979 retired
Edward Hobbs	1952	assistant professor of New Testament	1958

NAME	DATE OF APPOINTMENT	INITIAL SCHOOL OF THEOLOGY APPOINTMENT	DEPARTURE YEAR
Marvin Judy	1952	associate professor of church administration and rural sociology	1977 retired
Joseph W. Mathews	1952	assistant professor of Christian ethics	1956
Levi A. Olan	1952	visiting faculty	1978 retired
Allen Lamar Cooper	1953	assistant professor of social ethics and counselor to students	1976 retired
Douglas E. Jackson	1954	assistant professor of sociology of religion	1984 retired
Charles H. "Joe" Johnson	1954	assistant professor of religious education	1957
	1958	associate professor of religious education	1964
H. Neill McFarland	1954	instructor in history of religions	1988 retired
Joseph D. Quillian Jr.	1954	professor of homiletics	
	1960	dean	1981
C. Herndon Wagers	1954	professor of philosophy of religion	1975 retired
Robert E. Elliott	Jan. 1955	assistant professor of pastoral theology	1980
James "Barney" McGrath	1955	instructor in speech (visiting 1st year)	1957
W. Richey Hogg	1955	assistant professor of missions	1987 retired
Kermit Schoonover	1955	professor of Old Testament	1975 retired
David C. Shipley	1955	professor of historical theology	1960
Sterling Wheeler	1955	vice president, SMU; professor of homiletics	1962
Richard C. Bush	1956	assistant professor of history of religions; director, school-church relations	Dec. 1959
John W. Deschner	1956	assistant professor of theology	1991 retired
Schubert M. Ogden	1956	instructor in theology	1969
	1972	professor of theology	1993 retired
Joseph L. Allen	1957	instructor in social ethics	Dec. 1998 retired
C. Wayne Banks	1957	assistant professor of Christian education; associate director, field work	1982 retired
Robert Floyd Curl	1957	professor of church administration; director, field work and school for approved supply pastors	1962
Emmanuel M. Gitlin	1957	assistant professor of Old Testament	1960

NAME	DATE OF APPOINTMENT	INITIAL SCHOOL OF THEOLOGY APPOINTMENT	DEPARTURE YEAR
H. Grady Hardin	1957	professor of homiletics	1981 retired
Roger E. Ortmayer	Feb. 1958	professor of Christianity and the arts	1966
Van A. Harvey	1958	assistant professor of contemporary theology	1968
Lloyd Pfautsch	1958	associate professor of sacred music	1964
John B. Holt	1958	associate professor of missions (visiting 1st year)	1982 retired
William R. Farmer	1959	associate professor of New Testament	1991 retired
Victor Paul Furnish	1959	instructor in New Testament	Dec. 2000 retired
W. J. A. Power	1959	instructor in Old Testament (visiting 1st year)	1999 retired
Frederick S. Carney	1960	assistant professor of Christian ethics	1993 retired
Franklin H. Littell	1960	professor of church history	1962
William C. Robinson Jr.	1960	assistant professor of New Testament	1970
James M. Ward	1960	assistant professor of Old Testament	2001 retired
Thompson L. Shannon	1961	professor of pastoral theology	1967
James F. White	1961	assistant professor of worship and preaching	1982
Klaus Penzel	1962	assistant professor of church history	Dec. 1995 retired
Alsie H. Carleton	1964	director, field education; professor of church administration	1968
William C. Martin	1964	lecturer in church administration	1968 retired
Ronald E. Sleeth	1964	professor of preaching	1976
Carlton R. Young	1964	associate professor of church music	1975
Joe R. Jones	1965	instructor in philosophical theology	1975
Richard T. Murray	1965	assistant professor of Christian education	1993 retired
David A. Robertson	1966	assistant professor of Old Testament	1969
Frederick J. Streng	1966	associate professor of history of religions	1989
William S. Babcock	1967	assistant professor of church history	2005 retired
David K. Switzer	1967	associate dean; assistant professor of pastoral theology	1993 retired
Paul E. Martin	1968	professor of practical theology; adviser on conference relations	1972 retired
Claus H. Rohlfs	Jan. 1969	director, field education; professor of church administration	1983

NAME	DATE OF APPOINTMENT	INITIAL SCHOOL OF THEOLOGY APPOINTMENT	DEPARTURE YEAR
Harville Hendrix	1969	instructor in pastoral theology	1978
Leroy T. Howe	1969	associate professor of philosophical theology	1998 retired
William M. Longsworth	1969	instructor in Christian ethics	1977
Nathaniel L. Lacy Jr.	1970	assistant professor of practical theology	1974
William W. Mount Jr.	1970	assistant professor of New Testament	1975
Alfredo Nañez	1970	professor of practical theology; lecturer in Mexican-American studies	1973 retired
Edwin E. Sylvest	1970	assistant professor of history of Christianity	2008 retired
James A. Gwaltney	1971	associate director, intern program	1974
	1975	administrative director, intern staff	1984
Phyllis A. Bird	1972	assistant professor of Old Testament	1985
Craig L. Emerick	1972	assistant director, intern staff	1986
George G. Hunter III	1972	McCreless Assistant Professor of Evangelism	Dec. 1976
W. Kenneth Pope	1972	bishop in residence	1976 retired
Roy D. Barton	Jan. 1974	director, Mexican American program; associate professor of practical theology	1995 retired
Zan W. Holmes Jr.	1974	associate professor of practical theology; associate director, intern program	2002 retired
Roger Neil Deschner	1975	director, master of sacred music program; associate professor of church music	1991 died
Virgil P. Howard	1975	visiting assistant professor of New Testament	2005 died
Emma Justes	1975	associate director, intern program	1979
O. Eugene Slater	1976	bishop in residence	1980 retired
Charles M. Wood	1976	assistant professor of theology	
Harold W. Attridge	1977	assistant professor of New Testament	1985
Martha Gilmore	1977	assistant director, intern program	1987 retired
Richard P. Heitzenrater	1977	associate professor of church history and Methodist studies	1993
Marvest Lawson	1977	associate director, intern program	1978
Rosalie Lawson	1977	associate director, intern program	1979

NAME	DATE OF APPOINTMENT	INITIAL SCHOOL OF THEOLOGY APPOINTMENT	DEPARTURE YEAR
David Lowes Watson	1978	McCreless Assistant Professor of Evangelism	1984
John C. Holbert	1979	visiting assistant professor of Old Testament	
Jane Marshall	1979	adjunct professor of choral conducting	1986 retired
Richard E. Stewart	1979	associate director, intern program	1982
Charles B. Thomas, Jr.	1979	assistant professor of sociology of religion	1985
W. McFerrin Stowe	1980	bishop in residence	1988 retired
Ruth Tiffany Barnhouse	1980	professor of psychiatry and pastoral care	1989 retired
Jerry Dean Campbell	1980	director, Bridwell Library	1985
Dale Hensarling	1980	assistant director, intern program	1982
Roger L. Loyd	1980	associate director, Bridwell Library; assistant professor of bibliography	1992
James E. Kirby Jr.	1981	dean; professor of church history	1994
	1994	President ad interim, SMU	1995
	1995	professor of church history	2005 retired
Lynn Mims	1982	associate director, intern program	1987
Susanne Johnson	1982	assistant professor of Christian education	
Bert Affleck	1983	director, internship program; professor of church administration	2002 retired
Marjorie Procter-Smith	1983	assistant professor of worship (visiting 1st year)	
David Maldonado Jr.	1984	associate professor of church and society (visiting 1st year)	2000
Stanley J. Menking	Jan. 1985	director, continuing education; director, D.Min. program; professor of practical theology	Dec. 1997 retired
William J. Abraham	1985	McCreless Associate Professor of Evangelism	
William F. May	1985	Cary Maguire University Professor of Ethics	2001 retired
William K. McElvaney	1985	LeVan Professor of Preaching and Worship	1993 retired
James A. Wharton	1985	Lois Craddock Perkins Professor of Homiletics	1996 retired
Mary Lou Santillán Baert	1986	associate director, intern program	1990 retired

NAME	DATE OF APPOINTMENT	INITIAL SCHOOL OF THEOLOGY APPOINTMENT	DEPARTURE YEAR
Jouette M. Bassler	1986	associate professor of New Testament	2007 retired
David Alfred Martin	1986	Elizabeth Scurlock University Professor of Human Values	1989
Theodore D. Walker Jr.	1986	assistant professor of ethics and society	
Danna Nolan Fewell	1987	assistant professor of Old Testament	2000
Kenneth W. Hart	1987	director, master of sacred music program; professor of sacred music	2005 retired
Robert Maloy	1987	director, Bridwell Library; professor of church history	1992
John Wesley Hardt	1988	bishop in residence	2000 retired
Marilyn Spurrell	1988	assistant professor of supervised ministry	1995
Thomas William Spann	1988	assistant professor of supervised ministry	
C. Clifton Black	1989	assistant professor of New Testament	1999
Ruben L. F. Habito	1989	associate professor of history of religions (visiting 1st year)	
Edward W. Poitras	Jan. 1990	professor of world Christianity	1997 retired
Millicent C. Feske	1990	instructor in systematic theology	1993
Charles E. Curran	1991	Elizabeth Scurlock University Professor of Human Values	
Patricia Howery Davis	1991	assistant professor of pastoral care	2004
	2008	director, pastoral leadership	
Ellen T. Charry	1992	assistant professor of systematic theology	1997
C. Michael Hawn	1992	associate professor of church music	
Valerie Hotchkiss	1993	director, Bridwell Library; associate professor of medieval studies	2005
Deidre Palmer	1994	assistant professor of Christian education	1998
Luis G. Pedraja	1994	assistant professor of systematic theology	2000
Joerg Rieger	1994	assistant professor of systematic theology	
Robin W. Lovin	1994	dean; professor of ethics	2002
	2001	Cary Maguire University Professor of Ethics	
George M. Atkinson	1996	director, Houston-Galveston Program	2004 retired

NAME	DATE OF APPOINTMENT	INITIAL SCHOOL OF THEOLOGY APPOINTMENT	DEPARTURE YEAR
Minerva Carcaño	1996	director, Mexican American Program	2001
Isabel Docampo	1997	assistant professor of supervised ministry	
Scott J. Jones	1997	McCreless Assistant Professor of Evangelism	2004
William J. Bryan III	Jan. 1998	director, intern program	
Edwin D. Aponte	1998	assistant professor of Hispanic Christianity and culture	2006
Evelyn L. Parker	1998	assistant professor of Christian education	
Alyce M. McKenzie	Jan. 1999	assistant professor of homiletics	
Paula Dobbs-Wiggins	1999	adjunct associate professor of pastoral care	
Roy L. Heller	1999	assistant professor of Old Testament (visiting 1st year)	
Rebekah Miles	1999	associate professor of ethics	
David Price	1999	associate professor of church history	2005
Frederick W. Schmidt	2000	director, spiritual life and formation	
Mark W. Stamm	2000	assistant professor of worship	
David J. Lawson	2000	bishop in residence	2004 retired
Jaime Clark-Soles	Jan. 2001	instructor in New Testament	
Karen Baker-Fletcher	2001	associate professor of systematic theology	
Alejandro F. Botta	2001	assistant professor of Hebrew Bible	2007
Bruce D. Marshall	2001	professor of historical theology	
Richard D. Nelson	2001	W. J. A. Power Professor of Biblical Hebrew and Old Testament Interpretation	
James A. McMillin	Jan. 2002	associate director, Bridwell Library; associate professor of American religions	
Harold J. Recinos	Jan. 2002	professor of church and society	
Abraham Smith	Jan. 2002	associate professor of New Testament	
Jeannie Treviño-Teddlie	2002	director, Mexican American Program	
William B. Lawrence	2002	dean; professor of American church history	
William B. Oden	2004	bishop in residence	2008 retired

NAME	DATE OF APPOINTMENT	INITIAL SCHOOL OF THEOLOGY APPOINTMENT	DEPARTURE YEAR
Elaine Heath	2005	McCreless Assistant Professor of Evangelism	
Valerie A. Karras	2005	assistant professor of church history	
Jeanne Stevenson-Moessner	2005	associate professor of pastoral care	
Christopher S. Anderson	2006	associate professor of sacred music	
Ted Campbell	2006	associate professor of church history	
Jessica A. Boon	Jan. 2007	assistant professor of church history	
Barry Hughes	Feb. 2007	associate professor of supervised ministry	
Hugo Magallanes	2007	associate professor of Christianity and cultures	
Sze-kar Wan	2007	professor of New Testament	
Susanne Scholz	2008	assistant professor of Old Testament	
Carlos Cardoza-Orlandi	2010	professor of global Christianities and mission studies	

Note: In addition to faculty in regular appointments, the list includes members of the professional intern staff, although they were not called faculty until 1984; administrators with courtesy faculty rank; and directors of Bridwell Library. Visiting and adjunct faculty are not included, except a few who taught for several years, nor are faculty whose primary appointment was in another school of Southern Methodist University. William F. May (1985), David Alfred Martin (1986), Charles E. Curran (1991), and Robin W. Lovin (2001) were appointed, in the years listed, to endowed chairs of the university that entail frequent teaching at Perkins School of Theology.

Table 1

PERKINS ENROLLMENT FOR THE REGULAR TERMS, 1945–1960

1945–46	182	1953–54	399
1946–47	195	1954–55	410
1947–48	224	1955–56	383
1948–49	237	1956–57	383
1949–50	309	1957–58	414
1950–51	394	1958–59	421
1951–52	440	1959–60	364
1952–53	416		

Note: Figures for 1945–57 are taken from "Summary of Enrollment" in issues of the Perkins catalog. They exclude auditors, the summer session, those taking correspondence courses, and students from other schools of the university who were taking Perkins courses. Figures for 1957–60 are from an enrollment study in the files of the Perkins registrar and are for the fall semester. Figures for the two periods are not fully comparable.

Table 2

PERKINS SCHOOL OF THEOLOGY BUDGETED INCOME, 1949–1960

Budgetary Year	Budgeted Income	Budgetary Year	Budgeted Income
1949–50	$120,000	1955–56	NA
1950–51	146,000	1956–57	$283,000
1951–52	154,000	1957–58	501,900
1952–53	223,550	1958–59	525,750
1953–54	NA	1959–60	523,750
1954–55	280,105		

Note: Figures are taken from board of trustees minutes for these years.

Appendix B

Table 3
FALL ENROLLMENT BY DEGREE PROGRAM, 1960–2009

Year	M.Div.	New M.Div.	S.T.M.	M.R.E./ C.M.M.	M.S.M.	M.T.S.	D.Min.	Ph.D./ M.A.	Nondeg.	Aud.	Total
1960	313	104	23	14	4				25	4	383
1961	302	100	18	15	15				18	3	371
1962	285	94	17	20	18				13	2	355
1963	279	94	25	16	9				18	5	353
1964	269	84	24	10	7				17	2	329
1965	253	79	17	21	12				19	7	329
1966	236	77	22	21	12			8	22	7	328
1967	255	95	27	26	11			14	16	4	353
1968	279	79	16	23	15			17	40	2	392
1969	273	80	17	15	15			17	44	1	382
1970	256	76	19	9	7			16	25	6	338
1971	270	72	12	4	13			19	26	0	344
1972	267	81	11	0	13			18	42	0	351
1973	274	94	4		20		25	20	52	0	395
1974	324	127	5		27		40	19	30	0	445
1975	347	106	2		31		35	22	11	0	448
1976	365	111			28		30	17	21	0	461
1977	348	77			23		14	16	10	3	414
1978	344	95			29		24	18	18	5	438
1979	331	93			37		27	22	15	2	434
1980	330	*		6	38		26	24	14	1	439
1981	315	*		11	39		35	23/0	13	1	437
1982	297	93		11	30	14	52	24/1	8	1	438
1983	314	91		12	27	27	75	27/0	8	2	492
1984	286	76		10	43	54	89	25/1	15	1	524
1985	279	76		19	38	52	72	29/1	15	2	507
1986	298	98		14	30	44	46	29/3	15	2	481
1987	270	74		17	27	42	53	22/4	9	0	444
1988	271	85		10	27	42	51	17/0	7	2	427
1989	250	76		17	24	29	54	17/2	6	2	401
1990	239	75		16	20	23	43	19/0	4	1	365
1991	252	93		12	25	30	29	25/0	3	3	379
1992	252	90		8	18	40	20	25/0	8	2	373

Year	M.Div.	New M.Div.	S.T.M.	M.R.E./ C.M.M.	M.S.M.	M.T.S.	D.Min.	Ph.D./ M.A.	Nondeg.	Aud.	Total
1993	248	72		13	18	43	35	28/0	6	5	396
1994	231	66		14	17	46	64	27	3	6	408
1995	265	103		14	15	45	52	25	5	7	428
1996	311	116		9	12	52	58	27	2	8	479
1997	291	82		14	11	50	60	28	5	6	465
1998	299	89		10	18	51	64	27	31	6	506
1999	288	89		10	17	58	66	26	37	1	503
2000	272	*		12	14	54	63	24	35	5	479
2001	292	*		13	12	63	66	29	29	3	507
2002	300	*		19	9	61	60	32	31	8	520
2003	340	*		21	9	53	66	26	25	4	544
2004	349	*		22	8	47	52	28	9	2	517
2005	317	*		24	8	48	51	30	15	1	494
2006	313	*		23	12	50	43	29	20	3	492
2007	280	*		20	14	47	33	30	13	7	444
2008	249	*		16	12	45	29	31/1	12	5	400
2009	220	*		18	15	46	32	32	14	2	379

Note: These figures are taken from summaries distributed to the faculty each fall by the Perkins registrar. They are not strictly comparable to the figures given in the Perkins catalogs in the 1950s and earlier years and used in table 1. The program here designated M.Div. was called bachelor of divinity until fall 1970, master of theology from fall 1970 through summer 1981, and master of divinity beginning in fall 1981. In 1999 the faculty created the master of church ministries degree (C.M.M.), and the existing master of religious education degree (M.R.E.) became one track within the C.M.M. In 2000 the faculty added a second C.M.M. track in urban ministry. *Nondeg.* = nondegree students; in the early years they were called special students. *Aud.* = auditors. A zero indicates a program that was offered but had no students that year. A blank space indicates a program that was not offered in that year. Thus the M.R.E. was not offered in 1973–79 and was reinstated in the fall of 1980. A slash between two figures in the Ph.D./M.A. column distinguishes between the Ph.D. and the M.A. students. Where no slash appears, all the students were enrolled in the Ph.D. program. An asterisk indicates figures were not available.

Table 4

FALL ENROLLMENT IN EXTENSION PROGRAMS, 1995-2009

	Houston-Galveston			Oklahoma City			San Antonio	
Year	M.Div.	(New M.Div.)	Total	M.Div.	(New M.Div.)	Total	M.Div.	Total, all ext. progams
1995	39	(39)	49					49
1996	61	(33)	79					79
1997	*	(20)	65					65
1998	64	(24)	77	3	(3)	26		103
1999	*	(29)	63	2	(1)	34		97
2000	*	*	94	1	*	30		124
2001	75	*	94	*	*	30		124
2002	*	*	86	*	*	25	19	130
2003	*	*	77	*	*	18	18	113
2004	*	*	68				28	96
2005	*	*	52				24	76
2006	*	*	41				29	70
2007	*	*	54					54
2008	*	*	66					66
2009	*	*	58					58

Note: Figures in parentheses represent new extension M.Div. students; those figures are included in the M.Div. and total figures. An asterisk indicates that the figure was not available. A blank space means the program was not offered in that year. Totals may include some students in other programs besides the M.Div.

Appendix C

SELECTED WORKS BY PERKINS FACULTY AND STAFF

Works listed are books published shortly before, while, or soon after their author and/or editor was a member of the Perkins School of Theology faculty or staff. Later editions are listed only when extensively revised. Articles and book chapters are listed only if their subject pertains to Perkins's history. Edited volumes are listed only if they consist of works by a major figure in church history and the editor provides an introduction.

Abraham, William J. *Aldersgate and Athens: John Wesley and the Foundations of Christian Belief.* Waco, Texas: Baylor University Press, 2010.

———. *An Introduction to the Philosophy of Religion.* Englewood Cliffs, N.J.: Prentice-Hall, 1985.

———. *The Art of Evangelism: Evangelism Carefully Crafted into the Life of the Local Church.* Calver, Sheffield [England]: Cliff College, 1993.

———. *Canon and Criterion in Christian Theology: From the Fathers to Feminism.* New York: Oxford University Press, 1998.

———. *Crossing the Threshold of Divine Revelation.* Grand Rapids, Mich.: William B. Eerdmans, 2006.

———. *The Logic of Evangelism.* Grand Rapids, Mich.: William B. Eerdmans, 1989.

———. *The Logic of Renewal.* Grand Rapids, Mich.: William B. Eerdmans, 2003.

———. *Waking from Doctrinal Amnesia: The Healing of Doctrine in the United Methodist Church.* Nashville, Tenn.: Abingdon, 1995.

———. *Wesley for Armchair Theologians.* Louisville, Ky.: Westminster John Knox Press, 2005.

Abraham, William J., and James E. Kirby, eds. *The Oxford Handbook of Methodist Studies.* New York: Oxford University Press, 2009.

Alexander, Marilyn Bennett, and James Preston. *We Were Baptized Too: Claiming God's Grace for Lesbians and Gays.* Louisville, Ky.: Westminster John Knox Press, 1996.

Allen, Joseph L. *Love and Conflict: A Covenantal Model of Christian Ethics*. Nashville, Tenn.: Abingdon, 1984.

———. "The Policy Process at Perkins in the Quillian Years." *Perkins Journal* 34 (spring 1981): 15–23.

———. *War: A Primer for Christians*. Nashville, Tenn.: Abingdon, 1991.

Allen, Ronald J., and John C. Holbert. *Holy Root, Holy Branches: Christian Preaching from the Old Testament*. Nashville, Tenn.: Abingdon, 1995.

Anderson, Christopher S. *Max Reger and Karl Straube: Perspectives on an Organ Performing Tradition*. Aldershot, U.K.: Ashgate, 2003.

Attridge, Harold W. *The Epistle to the Hebrews: A Commentary on the Epistle to the Hebrews*. Edited by Helmut Koester. Philadelphia: Fortress, 1989.

———. *The Interpretation of Biblical History in the* Antiquitates Judaicae *of Flavius Josephus*. Missoula, Mont.: Scholars Press for Harvard Theological Review, 1976.

———. Introduction to *First-Century Cynicism in the Epistles of Heraclitus*. Translated by Harold W. Attridge. Missoula, Mont.: Scholars Press, 1976.

———, ed. *Nag Hammadi Codex I (the Jung codex)*. 2 vols. Leiden: Brill, 1985.

Attridge, Harold W., and Robert A. Oden Jr. Introduction, critical text, translation, and notes for *Philo of Byblos, The Phoenician History*. Washington, D.C.: Catholic Biblical Association of America, 1981.

Babcock, William S. Introduction and notes for *Tyconius: The Book of Rules*. Translated by William S. Babcock. Atlanta: Scholars Press, 1989.

Baker-Fletcher, Karen. *Dancing with God: The Trinity from a Womanist Perspective*. St. Louis, Mo.: Chalice, 2006.

Barnhouse, Ruth Tiffany. *Clergy and the Sexual Revolution*. Washington, D.C.: Alban Institute, 1987.

———. *Homosexuality: A Symbolic Confusion*. New York: Seabury, 1977.

———. *Identity*. Philadelphia: Westminster, 1984.

Bassler, Jouette. *God and Mammon: Asking for Money in the New Testament*. Nashville, Tenn.: Abingdon, 1991.

———. *Navigating Paul: An Introduction to Key Theological Concepts*. Louisville, Ky.: Westminster John Knox Press, 2007.

———. *I Timothy, II Timothy, Titus*. Nashville, Tenn.: Abingdon, 1996.

Bird, Phyllis. *The Bible as the Church's Book*. Philadelphia: Westminster, 1982.

Bishop, Charles McTyeire. *Characteristics of the Christian Life: A Special Course for Young People's and Adult Classes in Church Schools, and for the Epworth League Reading Course*. Nashville, Tenn.: Cokesbury, 1925.

Black, C. Clifton. *The Disciples According to Mark: Markan Redaction in Current Debate*. Sheffield, U.K.: JSOT, 1989.

————. *Mark: Images of an Apostolic Interpreter*. Columbia: University of South Carolina Press, 1994.

Botta, Alejandro F. *Los Doce Profetas Menores*. Minneapolis, Minn.: Augsburg Fortress, 2006.

Branscomb, Bennett Harvie. *The Message of Jesus: A Survey of the Teaching of Jesus Contained in the Synoptic Gospels*. Nashville, Tenn.: Cokesbury, 1926.

Campbell, Ted A. *The Gospel in Christian Traditions*. New York: Oxford University Press, 2009.

Carlyon, James T. *Getting Acquainted with the New Testament*. Nashville, Tenn.: Cokesbury, 1938.

————. *Interpreting the Bible to Youth*. New York: Abingdon, 1954.

Carney, Frederick S., Introduction to *The Politics of Johannes Althusius*. Translated by Frederick S. Carney. Boston: Beacon, 1964.

Charry, Ellen T. *By the Renewing of Your Minds: The Pastoral Function of Christian Doctrine*. New York: Oxford University Press, 1997.

Clark, Linda J., Joanne Swenson, and Mark W. Stamm. *How We Seek God Together: Exploring Worship Style*. Bethesda, Md.: Alban Institute, 2001.

Clark-Soles, Jaime. *Death and the Afterlife in the New Testament*. New York: T and T Clark, 2006.

————. *Scripture Cannot Be Broken: The Social Function of the Use of Scripture in the Fourth Gospel*. Boston: Brill Academic, 2003.

Cuninggim, Jesse L., and Eric M. North. *The Organization and Administration of the Sunday School*. Nashville, Tenn.: Smith and Lamar, 1919.

Cuninggim, Merrimon. *Freedom's Holy Light*. New York: Harper and Brothers, 1955.

————. "Integration in Professional Education: The Story of Perkins, Southern Methodist University." *Annals of the American Academy of Political and Social Science*, March 1956, 109–15.

————. "The New Curriculum at Perkins." *Christian Century* 71 (April 28, 1954): 514–15.

————. *Perkins Led the Way: The Story of Desegregation at Southern Methodist University*. Dallas: Perkins School of Theology, Southern Methodist University, 1994.

Curran, Charles E. *Catholic Higher Education, Theology, and Academic Freedom*. Notre Dame, Ind.: University of Notre Dame Press, 1990.

————. *Catholic Moral Theology in the United States: A History*. Washington, D.C.: Georgetown University Press, 2008.

————. *The Catholic Moral Tradition Today: A Synthesis*. Washington, D.C.: Georgetown University Press, 1999.

————. *Catholic Social Teaching, 1891–Present: A Historical, Theological, and Ethical Analysis*. Washington, D.C.: Georgetown University Press, 2002.

————. *The Church and Morality: An Ecumenical and Catholic Approach*. Minneapolis, Minn.: Fortress, 1993.

———. *History and Contemporary Issues: Studies in Moral Theology*. New York: Continuum, 1996.

———. *The Living Tradition of Catholic Moral Theology*. Notre Dame, Ind.: University of Notre Dame Press, 1992.

———. *Loyal Dissent: Memoir of a Catholic Theologian*. Washington, D.C.: Georgetown University Press, 2006.

———. *Moral Theology at the End of the Century*. Milwaukee: Marquette University Press, 1999.

———. *The Moral Theology of Pope John Paul II*. Washington, D.C.: Georgetown University Press, 2005.

———. *The Origins of Moral Theology in the United States: Three Different Approaches*. Washington, D.C.: Georgetown University Press, 1997.

Davis, Patricia Howery. *Siding with the Judges: A Psychohistorical Analysis of Cotton Mather's Role in the Salem Witchcraft Trials*. Ann Arbor, Mich.: University Microfilms International, 1992.

Davis, Wesley. "The New Curriculum," *Perkins Journal* 6 (Spring 1953): 10-16.

De La Torre, Miguel, and Edwin David Aponte. *Introducing Latino/a Theologies*. Maryknoll, N.Y.: Orbis, 2001.

Deschner, John. "Albert Cook Outler, A Biographical Memoir." In John Deschner, Leroy T. Howe, and Klaus Penzel, eds., *Our Common History as Christians: Essays in Honor of Albert C. Outler*. New York: Oxford University Press, 1975, ix–xxi.

———. *Wesley's Christology: An Interpretation*. Dallas: Southern Methodist University Press, 1960.

Deschner, Roger. *Singing in the Church Choir*. Nashville, Tenn.: Discipleship Resources, 1990.

Dicks, Russell L. *Who Is My Patient? A Religious Manual for Nurses*. New York: Macmillan, 1941.

Escamilla, Paul. *Longing for Enough in a Culture of More*. Nashville, Tenn. Abingdon, 2007.

———. *True When Whispered: Hearing God's Voice in a Noisy World*. Nashville, Tenn.: Abingdon, 2010.

Farmer, William R. *The Gospel of Jesus: The Pastoral Relevance of the Synoptic Problem*. Louisville, Ky.: Westminster John Knox Press, 1994.

———. *Jesus and the Gospel: Tradition, Scripture, and Canon*. Philadelphia: Fortress, 1982.

———. *The Last Twelve Verses of Mark*. New York: Cambridge University Press, 1974.

———. *The Synoptic Problem: A Critical Analysis*. New York: Macmillan, 1964.

Farmer, William R., and Denis M. Farkasfalvy. *The Formation of the New Testament Canon: An Ecumenical Approach*. New York: Paulist, 1983.

Farmer, William R. and Roch Kereszty. *Peter and Paul in the Church of Rome: The Ecumenical Potential of a Forgotten Perspective.* New York: Paulist, 1990.

Feske, Millicent C. *A Reading of Sacrificial Elements in Modern Christology.* Ann Arbor, Mich.: University Microfilms International, 1995.

Fewell, Danna Nolan. *Circle of Sovereignty: Plotting Politics in the Book of Daniel.* Sheffield, U.K.: Almond, 1988. In 1991 the *Journal for the Study of the Old Testament* printed in its pages a revised and extended edition of this work.

Fewell, Danna Nolan, and David Miller Gunn. *Compromising Redemption: Relating Characters in the Book of Ruth.* Louisville, Ky.: Westminster John Knox Press, 1990.

———. *Gender, Power, and Promise: The Subject of the Bible's First Story.* Nashville, Tenn.: Abingdon, 1993.

Furnish, Victor Paul. Introduction, notes, and commentary for *II Corinthians.* Translated by Victor Paul Furnish. New York: Doubleday, 1984.

———. *Jesus According to Paul.* Cambridge: Cambridge University Press, 1993.

———. *Lent.* Philadelphia: Fortress, 1986.

———. *The Love Command in the New Testament.* Nashville, Tenn.: Abingdon, 1972.

———. *The Moral Teaching of Paul.* Nashville, Tenn.: Abingdon, 1979.

———. *The Moral Teaching of Paul: Selected Issues.* 2d and 3d rev. eds. Nashville, Tenn.: Abingdon, 1985, 2009.

———. *1 Thessalonians, 2 Thessalonians.* Nashville, Tenn.: Abingdon, 2007.

———. *Paul's Exhortations in the Context of His Letters and Thought.* Madison, Wisc.: Microcard Theological Studies no. 36, 1960.

———. *Theology and Ethics in Paul.* Nashville, Tenn.: Abingdon, 1968.

———. *The Theology of the First Letter to the Corinthians.* New York: Cambridge University Press, 1999.

Furnish, Victor Paul, and Richard L. Thulin. *Pentecost 3.* Philadelphia: Fortress, 1981.

Gealy, Fred D. *Celebration: A Reference and Study Guide.* Nashville, Tenn.: Graded Press, 1969.

———. *Let Us Break Bread Together: Communion Meditations for the Church Year.* New York: Abingdon, 1960.

Goodloe, Robert W. *The Principles and Development of Church Government, with Particular Application to Methodism.* Nashville, Tenn.: Cokesbury, 1932.

———. *The Sacraments in Methodism.* Nashville, Tenn.: Methodist Publishing House, 1953.

Grimes, Lewis Howard. *A History of the Perkins School of Theology.* Edited by Roger Loyd. Dallas: Southern Methodist University Press, 1993.

———. *The Christian Views History.* Nashville, Tenn.: Abingdon, 1969.

———. *The Church Redemptive.* Nashville, Tenn.: Abingdon, 1958.

———. *Cloud of Witnesses: A History of First Methodist Church, Houston, Texas.* Houston: First Methodist Church, 1951.

———. *Realms of Our Calling.* New York: Friendship, 1965.

———. *The Rebirth of the Laity.* Nashville, Tenn.: Abingdon, 1962.

Gunn, David M., and Danna Nolan Fewell. *Narrative in the Hebrew Bible.* New York: Oxford University Press, 1993.

Habito, Ruben. *Experiencing Buddhism: Ways of Wisdom and Compassion.* Maryknoll, N.Y.: Orbis, 2005.

———. *Healing Breath: Zen for Christians and Buddhists in a Wounded World.* Boston: Wisdom Publications, 2006.

———. *Healing Breath: Zen Spirituality for a Wounded Earth.* Maryknoll, N.Y.: Orbis, 1993.

———. *Living Zen, Loving God.* Boston: Wisdom, 2004.

———. *Originary Enlightenment: Tendai Hongaku Doctrine and Japanese Buddhism.* Tokyo: International Institute for Buddhist Studies of the International College for Advanced Buddhist Studies, 1996.

———. *Total Liberation: Zen Spirituality and the Social Dimension.* Rev. and expanded ed. Maryknoll, N.Y.: Orbis, 1989.

Hardin, H. Grady. *The Leadership of Worship.* Nashville, Tenn.: Abingdon, 1980.

Hardin, H. Grady, Joseph D. Quillian Jr., and James F. White. *The Celebration of the Gospel.* Nashville, Tenn.: Abingdon, 1964.

Hardt, John Wesley. *Forward in Faith: The Ministry and Mission of Marvin United Methodist Church, 1848–1998.* Austin, Texas: Nortex, 1999.

———. *Lakeview: A Story of Inspiring Unity.* Edited by Mary Lou Krause. Palestine, Texas: Board of Directors of the Lakeview Methodist Conference Center of The United Methodist Church, 1993.

Hardt, William C., and John Wesley Hardt. *Historical Atlas of Texas Methodism.* Garland, Texas: Crosshouse, 2008.

Harkness, Georgia. *Georgia Harkness: The Remaking of a Liberal Theologian.* Edited by Rebekah L. Miles. Louisville, Ky.: Westminster John Knox Press, 2010.

Harvey, Van A. *A Handbook of Theological Terms.* New York: Macmillan, 1964.

———. *The Historian and the Believer: The Morality of Historical Knowledge and Christian Belief.* New York: Macmillan, 1966.

Hawn, C. Michael. *Gather into One: Praying and Singing Globally.* Grand Rapids, Mich.: William B. Eerdmans, 2003.

———. *Halle, Halle: We Sing the World Round: Songs from the World Church for Children, Youth, and Congregation.* Garland, Texas: Choristers Guild, 1999.

———. *One Bread, One Body: Exploring Cultural Diversity in Worship.* Bethesda, Md.: Alban Institute, 2003.

Heath, Elaine A. *The Mystic Way of Evangelism: A Contemplative Vision for Christian Outreach.* Grand Rapids, Mich.: Baker Academic, 2008.

———. *Naked Faith: The Mystical Theology of Phoebe Palmer.* Eugene, Ore.: Pickwick, 2009.

Heath, Elaine A., and Scott Kisker. *Longing for Spring: A New Vision for Wesleyan Community.* Eugene, Ore.: New Monastic Library, 2009.

Heitzenrater, Richard P., *The Elusive Mr. Wesley: John Wesley His Own Biographer.* 2 vols. Nashville, Tenn.: Abingdon, 1984.

———. *"Faithful unto Death": Last Years and Legacy of John Wesley.* Catalogue for exhibition commemorating the bicentenary of John Wesley's death, Elizabeth Perkins Prothro Galleries. Dallas: Bridwell Library, 1991.

———. *Mirror and Memory: Reflections on Early Methodism.* Nashville, Tenn.: Kingswood, 1989.

Heller, Roy L. *Narrative Structure and Discourse Constellations: An Analysis of Clause Function in Biblical Hebrew Prose.* Harvard Semitic Studies no. 55. Winona Lake, Ind.: Eisenbrauns, 2004.

———. *Power, Politics, and Prophecy: The Character of Samuel and the Deuteronomistic Evaluation of Prophecy.* New York: T and T Clark, 2006.

Herzog, Frederick. *Theology from the Belly of the Whale: A Frederick Herzog Reader.* Edited by Joerg Rieger. Harrisburg, Pa.: Trinity, 1999.

Hicks, John H. *The Books of History.* Nashville, Tenn.: Abingdon-Cokesbury, 1947.

———. *The Scholia of Barhebraeus on the Book of Isaiah.* Chicago: University of Chicago Libraries, 1935.

Hobbs, Edward C., ed. *A Stubborn Faith: Papers on Old Testament and Related Subjects Presented to Honor William Andrew Irwin.* Dallas: Southern Methodist University Press, 1956.

Hogg, W. Richey. *New Day Dawning.* New York: World Horizons, 1957.

———. *One World, One Mission.* New York: Friendship, 1960.

Holbert, John C. *Preaching Job.* St. Louis, Mo.: Chalice, 1999.

———. *Preaching Old Testament: Proclamation and Narrative in the Hebrew Bible.* Nashville, Tenn.: Abingdon, 1991.

———. *The Ten Commandments: A Preaching Commentary.* Nashville, Tenn.: Abingdon, 2002.

Hotchkiss, Valerie. *Bridwell at Fifty: Books, Benefactors, and Bibliophiles: An Exhibition at Bridwell Library, Perkins School of Theology, Southern Methodist University, 8 February–2 June 2001.* Exhibition catalog. Dallas: Bridwell Library, 2001.

———. *Clothes Make the Man: Female Cross Dressing in Medieval Europe.* New York: Garland, 1996.

———. *Puer Natus Est: Images of the Nativity from the Thirteenth to the Twentieth Century.* Dallas: Bridwell Library, 1995.

Howard, Virgil P. *Das Ego Jesu in den Synoptischen Evangelien: Untersuchungen z. Sprachgebrauch Jesu*. Marburg, Germany: Elwert, 1975.

———. *Pentecost 1*. Philadelphia: Fortress, 1987.

Howe, Leroy T. *Angry People in the Pews: Managing Anger in the Church*. Valley Forge, Pa.: Judson, 2001.

———. *A Pastor in Every Pew: Equipping Laity for Pastoral Care*: Valley Forge, Pa.: Judson, 2000.

———. *Comforting the Fearful: Listening Skills for Caregivers*. New York: Paulist, 2003.

———. *Guilt: Helping God's People Find Healing and Forgiveness*. Nashville, Tenn.: Abingdon, 2003.

———. *The Image of God: A Theology for Pastoral Care and Counseling*. Nashville, Tenn.: Abingdon, 1995.

———. *Prayer in a Secular World*. Philadelphia: United Church Press, 1973.

Hunt, Robert. *Muslim Faith and Values: What Every Christian Should Know*. New York: GBGM, 2003.

Ingham, Benjamin. *Diary of an Oxford Methodist: Benjamin Ingham, 1733–1734*. Edited by Richard P. Heitzenrater. Durham, N.C.: Duke University Press, 1985.

Irwin, William A. *The Old Testament: Keystone of Human Culture*. New York: H. Schumann, 1952.

Irwin, William A., and Allen P. Wikgren. *The Ancestry of Our English Bible: An Account of Manuscripts, Texts, and Versions of the Bible*. 3d rev. ed. New York: Harper and Row, 1956.

Jackson, Douglas E. *The Downtown Church*. Philadelphia: Division of National Missions of the Board of Missions of The Methodist Church, 1958.

———. *Factors Differentiating between Effective and Ineffective Methodist Ministers*. Microfilm. Dallas: Bridwell Library, 1955.

———. *Stumbling Block: A Study of Alcohol and Christian Responsibility*. New York: Editorial Department, Joint Section of Education and Cultivation, Board of Missions of The Methodist Church, 1960.

Johnson, Charles H. *Implications of the Method of Correlation for the Use of the Bible in Christian Education*. Microform. Dallas: Bridwell Library, 1962.

Johnson, Susanne. *Christian Spiritual Formation in the Church and Classroom*. Nashville, Tenn.: Abingdon, 1989.

Jones, Scott J. *The Evangelistic Love of God and Neighbor: A Theology of Witness and Discipleship*. Nashville, Tenn.: Abingdon, 2003.

———. *United Methodist Doctrine: The Extreme Center*. Nashville, Tenn.: Abingdon, 2002.

Judy, Marvin T. *A Survey of Methodism in the Little Rock Conference*. Philadelphia: Department of Research and Surveys, Board of Missions, Division of National Missions, The Methodist Church, 1956.

———. *The Cooperative Parish in Nonmetropolitan Areas*. Nashville, Tenn.: Abingdon, 1967.

———. *From Ivy Tower to Village Spire: A History and Contemporary Appraisal of the Role of the Theological Seminary in Training for Ministry in the Small Membership Church in Town and Rural Areas*. Dallas: Southern Methodist University Print Office, 1984.

———. *The Larger Parish and Group Ministry*. New York: Abingdon, 1959.

———. *The Multiple Staff Ministry*. Nashville, Tenn.: Abingdon, 1969.

———. *The North Texas Conference, The Methodist Church: A Systematic Analysis*. Philadelphia: Department of Research and Surveys, Board of Missions, Division of National Missions, The Methodist Church, 1954.

———. *The Organization and Administration of a Methodist Church District: A Sociological Analysis*. Microform. Dallas: Bridwell Library: 1952–62.

———. *The Parish Development Process*. Nashville, Tenn.: Abingdon, 1973.

———. *You and Your Pastor: What You Can Expect*. Nashville, Tenn.: Abingdon, 1992.

Keck, Leander E., and Victor Paul Furnish. *The Pauline Letters*. Nashville, Tenn.: Abingdon, 1984.

Kirby, James E. *Brother Will: A Biography of William C. Martin*. Nashville, Tenn.: Abingdon, 2000.

———. *The Episcopacy in American Methodism*. Nashville, Tenn.: Kingswood, 2000.

Kirby, James E., Russell E. Richey, and Kenneth E. Rowe. *The Methodists*. Westport, Conn.: Greenwood, 1996.

Lawrence, William B. *Methodism in Recovery: Renewing Mission, Reclaiming History, Restoring Health*. Nashville, Tenn.: Abingdon, 2008.

Lee, Umphrey. *The Bible and Business*. New York: R. R. Smith, 1930.

———. *The Historical Backgrounds of Early Methodist Enthusiasm*. New York: Columbia University Press, 1931.

———. *Jesus, the Pioneer, and Other Sermons*. Nashville, Tenn.: Cokesbury, 1925.

———. *The Life of Christ: A Brief Outline for Students*. Nashville, Tenn.: Cokesbury, 1930.

———. *The Lord's Horseman*. New York: Century, 1928. Republished as *The Lord's Horseman: John Wesley the Man*. New York: Abingdon, 1954.

Lovin, Robin W. *Christian Ethics: An Essential Guide*. Nashville, Tenn.: Abingdon, 2000.

———. *Christian Realism and the New Realities*. New York: Cambridge University Press, 2008.

———. *Reinhold Niebuhr*. Nashville, Tenn.: Abingdon, 2007.

———. *Reinhold Niebuhr and Christian Realism*. New York: Cambridge University Press, 1995.

Magallanes, Hugo. *Introducción a la Vida y Teología de Juan Wesley.* Nashville, Tenn.: Abingdon, 2005.

Maldonado, David. *Crossing Guadalupe Street: Growing Up Hispanic and Protestant.* Albuquerque: University of New Mexico Press, 2001.

Maloy, Robert. *The Bible: 100 Landmarks from the Elizabeth Perkins Prothro Collection: A Guide to the Inaugural Exhibition in the Elizabeth Perkins Prothro Galleries Prepared by the J. S. Bridwell Foundation Librarian.* Dallas: Bridwell Library, 1990.

Marsh, Thomas H. *Preaching That Packs the Pews: A Study of William A. Quayle as a Preacher.* Dallas: Southern Methodist University Press, 1950.

Marshall, Bruce D. *Trinity and Truth.* Cambridge: Cambridge University Press, 2000.

Marshall, Jane M. *Grace, Noted.* Compiled and edited by Rosemary Heffley. Carol Stream, Ill.: Hope, 1992.

Martin, Paul E. *The Humanness of the Ministry: Some Informal Reflections.* Dallas: Perkins School of Theology, Southern Methodist University, 1973.

May, William F. *Beleaguered Rulers: The Public Obligation of the Professional.* Louisville, Ky.: Westminster John Knox Press, 2001.

———. *The Patient's Ordeal.* Bloomington, Ind.: Indiana University Press, 1991.

———. *The Physician's Covenant: Images of the Healer in Medical Ethics.* 2d rev. ed. Louisville, Ky.: Westminster John Knox Press, 2000.

———. *Testing the Medical Covenant: Active Euthanasia and Health Care Reform.* Grand Rapids, Mich.: William B. Eerdmans, 1996.

McElvaney, William K. *Becoming a Justice Seeking Congregation: Responding to God's Justice Initiative.* Bloomington, Ind.: iUniverse, 2009.

———. *Eating and Drinking at the Welcome Table: The Holy Supper for All People.* St. Louis, Mo.: Chalice, 1998.

———. *Preaching from Camelot to Covenant: Announcing God's Action in the World.* Nashville, Tenn.: Abingdon, 1989.

———. *Winds of Grace, Ways of Faith: Expanding the Horizons of Christian Spirituality.* Louisville, Ky.: Westminster John Knox Press, 1991.

McFarland, H. Neill. *Daruma: The Founder of Zen in Japanese Art and Popular Culture.* New York: Kodansha International/Harper and Row, 1987.

———. *The Rush Hour of the Gods: A Study of New Religious Movements in Japan.* New York: Macmillan, 1967.

McKenzie, Alyce M. *Hear and Be Wise: Becoming a Preacher and Teacher of Wisdom.* Nashville, Tenn.: Abingdon, 2004.

———. *Matthew.* Louisville, Ky.: Geneva, 1998.

———. *Novel Preaching: Tips from Top Writers on Crafting Creative Sermons.* Louisville, Ky.: Westminster John Knox Press, 2010.

———. *The Parables for Today.* Louisville, Ky.: Westminster John Knox Press, 2007.

———. *Preaching Biblical Wisdom in a Self-Help Society.* Nashville, Tenn.: Abingdon, 2002.

McMillin, James A. *Final Victims: Foreign Slave Trade to North America, 1783–1810.* Columbia: University of South Carolina Press, 2004.

Menking, Stanley J. *Helping Laity Help Others.* Philadelphia: Westminster, 1984.

Menking, Stanley J., and Barbara Wendland. *God's Partners: Lay Christians at Work.* Valley Forge, Pa.: Judson, 1993.

Miles, Rebekah L. *The Bonds of Freedom: Feminist Theology and Christian Realism.* New York: Oxford University Press, 2001.

———. *The Pastor as Moral Guide.* Minneapolis, Minn.: Fortress, 1999.

Murray, Dick. *Strengthening the Adult Sunday School Class.* Nashville, Tenn.: Abingdon, 1981.

———. *Teaching the Bible to Adults and Youth.* Nashville, Tenn.: Abingdon, 1987.

Murray, Dick, assisted by Ruth Murray Alexander and Ellen Shepard. *Teaching the Bible to Elementary Children.* Nashville, Ky.: Discipleship Resources, 1990.

Nañez, Alfredo, ed. *Himnario Metodista: Preparado y Editado Bajo la Direcció'n del Comite' del Himnario de la Conferencia Ri'o Grande de la Iglesia Metodista Unida.* Nashville, Ky.: Casa de publicaciones de la Iglesia Metodista Unida, 1973.

———. *History of the Rio Grande Conference of the United Methodist Church.* Dallas: Bridwell Library, Southern Methodist University, 1980.

Nelson, Richard D. *Deuteronomy: A Commentary.* Louisville, Ky.: Westminster John Knox Press, 2002.

———. *From Eden to Babel: An Adventure in Bible Study.* St. Louis, MO.: Chalice Press, 2006.

Ogden, Schubert M. *Christ without Myth: A Study Based on the Theology of Rudolf Bultmann.* New York: Harper and Brothers, 1961.

———. *Faith and Freedom: Toward a Theology of Liberation.* 1979. Revised and enlarged edition, Nashville, Tenn.: Abingdon, 1989.

———. Introduction to *Existence and Faith: Shorter Writings of Rudolf Bultmann.* Edited and translated by Schubert M. Ogden. New York: Meridian, 1960.

———. *Is There Only One True Religion or Are There Many?* Dallas: Southern Methodist University Press, 1992.

———. *On Theology.* San Francisco: Harper and Row, 1986.

———. *The Point of Christology.* San Francisco: Harper and Row, 1982.

———. *The Reality of God and Other Essays.* New York: Harper and Row, 1966.

———. *The Understanding of Christian Faith.* Eugene, Ore.: Cascade, 2010.

Olan, Levi A. *Judaism and Immortality.* New York: Union of American Hebrew Congregations, 1971.

————. *Maturity in an Immature World*. New York: Ktav, 1984.

————. *New Resources for a Liberal Faith*. Philadelphia: Maurice Jacobs, 1962.

————. *Prophetic Faith and the Secular Age*. New York: Ktav, 1982.

Outler, Albert C. *The Christian Tradition and the Unity We Seek*. New York: Oxford University Press, 1957.

————. *Evangelism in the Wesleyan Spirit*. Nashville, Tenn.: Tidings, 1971.

————. Introduction to *Augustine: Confessions and Enchiridion*. Edited by Albert C. Outler. Philadelphia: Westminster, 1955.

————. Introduction to *John Wesley*. Edited by Albert C. Outler. New York: Oxford University Press, 1964.

————. Introduction to John Wesley, *Sermons*. 4 vols. Edited by Albert C. Outler. Nashville, Tenn.: Abingdon, 1984–87.

————. *Methodist Observer at Vatican II*. Westminster, Md.: Newman, 1967.

————. *Psychotherapy and the Christian Message*. New York: Harper and Row, 1954.

————. *Theology in the Wesleyan Spirit*. Nashville, Tenn.: Tidings, 1975.

Parker, Evelyn L. *Trouble Don't Last Always: Emancipatory Hope among African American Adolescents*. Cleveland, Ohio: Pilgrim, 2003.

Pedraja, Luis G. *Jesus Is My Uncle: Christology from a Hispanic Perspective*. Nashville, Tenn.: Abingdon, 1999.

Pelikan, Jaroslav. *The Reformation of the Bible, the Bible of the Reformation*. Catalog of the Exhibition by Valerie Hotchkiss and David Price. Dallas: Bridwell Library, 1996.

Penzel, Klaus. Introduction to *Philip Schaff, Historian and Ambassador of the Universal Church: Selected Writings*. Edited by Klaus Penzel. Macon, Ga.: Mercer University Press, 1991.

Pope, W. Kenneth. *A Pope at Roam: The Confessions of a Bishop*. Nashville, Tenn.: Parthenon, 1976.

Power, W. J. A. *Once Upon a Time: A Humorous Re-Telling of the Genesis Stories*. Nashville, Tenn.: Abingdon, 1992.

Price, David Hotchkiss. *Albrecht Dürer's Renaissance: Humanism, Reformation, and the Art of Faith*. Ann Arbor: University of Michigan Press, 2003.

Price, David, and Charles C. Ryrie. *Let It Go Among Our People: An Illustrated History of the English Bible from John Wyclif to the King James Version*. Cambridge, U.K.: Lutterworth, 2004.

Procter-Smith, Marjorie. *The Church in Her House: A Feminist Emancipatory Prayer Book for Christian Communities*. Cleveland, Ohio: Pilgrim, 2008.

————. *In Her Own Rite: Constructing Feminist Liturgical Tradition*. Nashville, Tenn.: Abingdon, 1990.

———. *Prayer with Our Eyes Open: Engendering Feminist Liturgical Prayer.* Nashville, Tenn.: Abingdon, 1995.

———. *Shakerism and Feminism: Reflections on Women's Religion and the Early Shakers.* Old Chatham, N.Y.: Shaker Museum and Library, 1991.

———. *Women in Shaker Community and Worship: A Feminist Analysis of the Uses of Religious Symbolism.* Lewiston, N.Y.: E. Mellen, 1985.

Recinos, Harold J. *Good News from the Barrio: Prophetic Witness for the Church.* Louisville, Ky.: Westminster John Knox Press, 2006.

Rice, John A. *The Old Testament in the Life of Today.* New York: Macmillan, 1920.

Richey, Russell E., with Dennis M. Campbell and William B. Lawrence. *Marks of Methodism: Theology in Ecclesial Practice.* Nashville, Tenn.: Abingdon, 2005.

Rieger, Joerg. *Approaches to the Real: Liberation Theology and Spirituality in Latin America and North America: A Comparison of the Works of Gustavo Gutierrez and Frederick Herzog.* Microfilm. Ann Arbor, Mich.: UMI, 1998.

———. *Christ and Empire: From Paul to Postcolonial Times.* Minneapolis, Minn.: Fortress, 2007.

———. *God and the Excluded: Visions and Blind Spots in Contemporary Theology.* Minneapolis, Minn.: Fortress, 2001.

———. *No Rising Tide: Theology, Economics, and the Future.* Minneapolis, Minn.: Fortress, 2009.

———. *Remember the Poor: The Challenge to Theology in the Twenty-first Century.* Harrisburg, Pa.: Trinity, 1998.

Robinson, William Childs Jr. *Der Weg des Herrn: Studien zur Geschichte und Eschatologie im Lukas-Evangelium. Ein Gespräch mit Hans Conzelmann.* Übersetzt von Gisela und Georg Strecker. Hamburg: H. Reich, 1964.

Rohlfs, Claus H. Sr. "A History of the Development of the Perkins Intern Program." *Perkins Journal,* winter 1978, 1–12.

Root, Paul A. *The Nature and Social Significance of Tradition.* Dallas: Mathis, Van Nort, 1938.

Sawyer, Beverly. *Singer of Seasons: The Prayers of Beverly Sawyer.* Little Rock, Ark.: August House, 1982.

Schmidt, Frederick W. *Conversations with Scripture: The Gospel of Luke.* Harrisburg, Pa.: Morehouse, 2009.

———. *Conversations with Scripture: Revelation.* Harrisburg, Pa.: Morehouse, 2005.

———. *What God Wants for Your Life: Finding Answers to the Deepest Questions.* New York: HarperSanFrancisco, 2005.

———. *When Suffering Persists: A Theology of Candor.* Harrisburg, Pa.: Morehouse, 2001.

Scholz, Susanne. *Introducing the Women's Hebrew Bible.* London: T and T Clark, 2007.

———. *Sacred Witness: Rape in the Hebrew Bible.* Minneapolis, Minn.: Fortress, 2010.

Seay, Frank. *An Outline for the Study of Old Testament History.* Nashville, Tenn.: M. E. Church, South, 1917.

———. *An Outline for the Study of Old Testament Prophecy, Wisdom, and Worship.* Nashville, Tenn.: Publishing House of the M. E. Church, South, 1919.

Slater, Oliver Eugene. *Oliver's Travels: One Bishop's Journey: A Chronological Account of the Comings and Goings of Oliver Eugene Slater.* Nashville, Tenn.: Parthenon Press, 1988.

Sleeth, Ronald E. *Look Who's Talking: A Guide for Lay Speakers in the Church.* Nashville, Tenn.: Abingdon, 1977.

———. *Splinters in the Quick.* Waco, Texas: Word Books, 1971.

Snow, John, and Victor Paul Furnish. *Easter.* Philadephia: Fortress, 1975.

Stamm, Mark W. *Extending the Table: A Guide for a Ministry of Home Communion Serving.* Nashville, Tenn.: Discipleship Resources, 2009.

———. *Let Every Soul Be Jesus' Guest: A Theology of the Open Table.* Nashville, Tenn.: Abingdon, 2006.

———. *Our Membership Vows in the United Methodist Church.* Nashville, Tenn.: Discipleship Resources, 2002.

———. *Sacraments and Discipleship: Understanding Baptism and the Lord's Supper in a United Methodist Context.* Nashville, Tenn.: Discipleship Resources, 2001.

Stevenson-Moessner, Jeanne. *A Primer in Pastoral Care.* Minneapolis, Minn.: Fortress, 2005.

———. *Prelude to Practical Theology: Variations on Theory and Practice.* Nashville, Tenn.: Abingdon, 2008.

Stowe, W. McFerrin. *If I Were a Pastor.* Nashville, Tenn.: Abingdon, 1983.

Streng, Frederick. *Emptiness: A Study in Religious Meaning.* Nashville, Tenn.: Abingdon, 1967.

———. *Understanding Religious Life.* 2d ed. Belmont, Calif.: Wadsworth, 1976.

———. *Understanding Religious Man.* Belmont, Calif.: Dickenson, 1969.

Switzer, David K. "A Psychodynamic Analysis of Grief in the Context of an Interpersonal Theory of the Self." Ph.D. diss., School of Theology at Claremont, Calif., June 1966.

———. *The Dynamics of Grief.* Nashville, Tenn.: Abingdon, 1970.

———. *The Minister as Crisis Counselor.* Nashville, Tenn.: Abingdon, 1974.

———. *Pastor, Preacher, Person: Developing a Pastoral Ministry in Depth.* Nashville, Tenn.: Abingdon, 1979.

———. *Pastoral Care Emergencies: Ministering to People in Crisis.* New York: Paulist, 1989.

Switzer, David K., and Shirley Switzer. *Parents of the Homosexual.* Philadelphia, Pa.: Westminster, 1980.

Sylvest, Edwin E. Jr. *Motifs of Franciscan Mission Theory in Sixteenth-Century New Spain Province of the Holy Gospel.* Washington, D.C.: Academy of American Franciscan History, 1975.

Thomas, James S. *Methodism's Racial Dilemma: The Story of the Central Jurisdiction.* Nashville, Tenn.: Abingdon, 1992.

Tippy, Worth M., and Paul B. Kern. *A Methodist Church and Its Work.* Nashville, Tenn.: Lamar and Barton, 1919.

Walker, Theodore Jr. *Empower the People: Social Ethics for the African-American Church.* Maryknoll, N.Y.: Orbis, 1991.

———. *Mothership Connections: A Black Atlantic Synthesis of Neoclassical Metaphysics and Black Theology.* Albany: State University of New York Press, 2004.

Ward, James M. *Amos and Isaiah: Prophets of the Word of God.* Nashville, Tenn.: Abingdon, 1969.

———. *Amos, Hosea.* Atlanta: John Knox Press, 1981.

———. "Dean Quillian as Dean of the Perkins Faculty." *Perkins Journal* 34 (spring 1981): 8–14.

———. *Hosea: A Theological Commentary.* New York: Harper and Row, 1966.

———. *The Prophets.* Nashville, Tenn.: Abingdon, 1982.

———. *Thus Says the Lord: The Message of the Prophets.* Nashville, Tenn.: Abingdon, 1991.

Ward, James, and Christine Ward. *Preaching from the Prophets.* Nashville, Tenn.: Abingdon, 1995.

Wasson, Alfred Washington. *Church Growth in Korea.* International Missionary Council Occasional Papers, vol. 1. Chicago: University of Chicago Libraries, 1934.

Watson, David Lowes. "The Origins and Significance of the Early Methodist Class Meeting." Ph.D. diss., Duke University, 1978.

Wesley, John. *John Wesley's Sermons: An Anthology.* Edited by Albert C. Outler and Richard P. Heitzenrater. Nashville, Tenn.: Abingdon, 1991.

———. *The Works of John Wesley: Journal and Diaries.* Vols. 18–24. Edited by W. Reginald Ward (journal) and Richard P. Heitzenrater (diaries). Nashville, Tenn.: Abingdon, 1988–2003.

Wharton, James A. *Easter.* Philadelphia: Fortress, 1987.

White, James F. *Architecture at SMU: 50 Years and Buildings.* Dallas: Southern Methodist University Press, 1966.

———. *The Cambridge Movement: The Ecclesiologists and the Gothic Revival.* Cambridge: Cambridge University Press, 1962.

———. *Christian Worship in Transition.* Nashville, Tenn.: Abingdon, 1976.

———. *Introduction to Christian Worship.* Nashville, Tenn.: Abingdon, 1980.

———. *New Forms of Worship.* Nashville, Tenn.: Abingdon, 1971.

———. *Protestant Worship and Church Architecture: Theological and Historical Considerations.* New York: Oxford University Press, 1964.

———. *The Worldliness of Worship.* New York: Oxford University Press, 1967.

Wood, Charles M. *An Invitation to Theological Study.* Valley Forge, Pa.: Trinity, 1994.

———. *The Formation of Christian Understanding: An Essay in Theological Hermeneutics.* Philadelphia: Westminster, 1981.

———. *Love That Rejoices in the Truth: Theological Explorations.* Eugene, Ore.: Cascade, 2009.

_____. *The Question of Providence.* Louisville, Ky.: Westminster John Knox Press, 2008.

———. *Theory and Religious Understanding: A Critique of the Hermeneutics of Joachim Wach.* Missoula, Mont.: American Academy of Religion, 1975.

———. *Vision and Discernment: an Orientation in Theological Study.* Atlanta: Scholars Press, 1985.

Wood, Charles M., and Ellen Blue. *Attentive to God: Thinking Theologically in Ministry.* Nashville, Tenn.: Abingdon, 2008.

Index

world Christianity studies. *See* missions/missionary
    studies
World Methodist Council, 173
World Service funds, 83, 136, 228, 230
World War I period, 14–15
Worrell, Keith, 189
worship services, 146–47, 358–59
worship studies. *See* homiletics studies
Wright, C. S., 11
Wright, Harold S., Jr., 283, 294

Yale Divinity School, 107
Yap Kim Hao, 287
yearbook controversy, 60–61

Young, Carlton, R.
    with colleagues, photo section 1
    composition for dedication, 374
    hymnal revision, 175
    in list of faculty members, 408
    resignation, 212
    teaching assignments, 171, 206
Young Bin Im, 73
youth programs, during the 2000s, 371, 380–81,
    395–96

Zeppa, Joe, 246
Zimbabwe, immersion course, 376
Zumberge, James H., 235

JOSEPH L. ALLEN was for forty-one years a member of the Perkins faculty and is presently professor emeritus of ethics. He is a former president of the Society of Christian Ethics in the United States and Canada and the author of *Love and Conflict: A Covenantal Model of Christian Ethics* and *War: A Primer for Christians.*